MODERN POETRY

Essays in

EDITED BY

JOHN HOLLANDER

OXFORD UNIVERSITY PRESS
London Oxford New York

OXFORD UNIVERSITY PRESS
Oxford London New York
Glasgow Toronto Melbourne Wellington
Cape Town Salisbury Ibadan Nairobi Lusaka Addis Ababa
Bombay Calcutta Madras Karachi Lahore Dacca
Kuala Lumpur Hong Kong Tokyo

Library of Congress Catalogue Card Number: 68-17605
First published by Oxford University Press, New York, 1968
First published as an Oxford University Press paperback, 1968
This reprint, 1968

Printed in the United States of America

Preface

The aim of this collection is not so much to outline the history of modern poetry as to chronicle the ways in which it has been read. During the past half-century, critical journalists, academic scholars, and the poets themselves have played varying roles in interpreting texts and defining a canon. For much of the period covered by these essays, the literature which we now regard with what is already a historical interest was contemporary and even new; during the course of it, some of the poetry was becoming part of academic curricula which were, themselves, adopting some of the critical approaches demanded by the esthetic theories of modern literature. Certain problems result for the compiler of a volume like this one. In the case of some other epoch or convention (seventeenth-century poetry, Shakespeare, the novel, etc.) he might select a history of interpretative viewpoints from within the field of literary scholarship, perhaps observing how, at certain points, academic responses to the pressures of modern and even avant-garde literary ideas begin to appear.

In the case of modern poetry, however, it is only well into the period under scrutiny that academic literary scholarship becomes fully involved with contemporary texts. But it is not merely a question of a decent time interval between the new and the historic: twentieth-century cultural history traces the decrease of that interval. It was one of the principles of the modernist movement in poetry that, if academic literary studies were to be worth anything at all, the interval should vanish. At this moment, choking off exponentially, it appears almost to have done so.

Thus, while the most recent essays in this collection are by academic scholar-critics, the earliest ones are by some of the very poets with whose work a formal literary history of the period might start. It seemed, at the beginning, as if only poets had access to the sophisticated methods of interpretation that the new poetry, itself, required. Moving past this phase of manifesto and historical polemic, one finds a second group of critics, some of them, again, poets themselves, mediating between the generation of Eliot, Yeats, and Pound and their academic colleagues — what might be called the "generation" of Allen Tate, R. P. Blackmur, and Kenneth Burke. Then, after World War II, the so-called new criticism, whose origins were so closely linked to the development of modern poetry, gradually became part of academic literary study and even assimilated some of its methods of textual analysis to the historical study of literature. Finally, as some of the later essays in this volume (those by Professors Frye, Kermode, Whitaker, and Bloom, for example) will show, recent criticism has worked at a revaluation of the very revaluations of modern criticism that appear in the earlier essays, and at a revision of the polemical version of literary history that modernism propounded. The rejection of the attack on romanticism with which twentieth-century poetry launched its campaign, and the reinterpretation of its history in the light of romantic tradition, mark the most recent readings of modern poetry. Even a recent piece of close reading like Professor Vendler's reveals an attention to syntax and over-all dialectic which is a very different matter from the notation of tone and the unpacking of allusion of critics of thirty years earlier.

The editor has chosen in his selection of essays to fill out the history of critical approaches rather than to "cover" every poet of note. In some cases (Yeats and Eliot, for example) several sorts of reading are represented. There is some irony, perhaps, in the shift of interpretive role from the poet to the professional critic, whose distance from the polemical origins of his material enables him to gloss the contemporaneous more successfully than poets themselves can, writing as reviewers of each other's work. The later poetry of Wallace Stevens is an almost shocking case in point.

In its own way, this collection may comprise, for twentieth-century poetry in English, a kind of historical anatomy of modernism. As such, it concludes with the moment at which "modern" has begun to sound to both scholars and poets rather like the way "Edwardian" may have resonated in the 'twenties.

New York City J. H.
January 1968

Contents

EZRA POUND

A Retrospect [1]

(1913 and 1918)

There has been so much scribbling about a new fashion in poetry, that I may perhaps be pardoned this brief recapitulation and retrospect.

In the spring or early summer of 1912, 'H. D.,' Richard Aldington and myself decided that we were agreed upon the three principles following:

1. Direct treatment of the 'thing' whether subjective or objective.
2. To use absolutely no word that does not contribute to the presentation.
3. As regarding rhythm: to compose in the sequence of the musical phrase, not in sequence of a metronome.

Upon many points of taste and of predilection we differed, but agreeing upon these three positions we thought we had as much right to a group name, at least as much right, as a number of French 'schools' proclaimed by Mr. Flint in the August number of Harold Monro's magazine for 1911.

This school has since been 'joined' or 'followed' by numerous people who, whatever their merits, do not show any signs of agreeing with the second specification. Indeed *vers libre* has become as prolix and as verbose as any of the flaccid varieties that preceded it. It has brought faults of its own. The actual language and phrasing is often as bad as that of our elders without even the excuse that the words are shovelled in to fill a metric pattern or to complete the noise of a rhyme-sound. Whether or no the phrases followed by the followers are musical must

From *Literary Essays of Ezra Pound*. Reprinted by permission of New Directions Publishing Corporation and Faber and Faber, Ltd.

be left to the reader's decision. At times I can find a marked metre in 'vers libres,' as stale and hackneyed as any pseudo-Swinburnian, at times the writers seem to follow no musical structure whatever. But it is, on the whole, good that the field should be ploughed. Perhaps a few good poems have come from the new method, and if so it is justified.

Criticism is not a circumscription or a set of prohibitions. It provides fixed points of departure. It may startle a dull reader into alertness. That little of it which is good is mostly in stray phrases; or if it be an older artist helping a younger it is in great measure but rules of thumb, cautions gained by experience.

I set together a few phrases on practical working about the time the first remarks on imagisme were published. The first use of the word 'Imagiste' was in my note to T. E. Hulme's five poems, printed at the end of my 'Ripostes' in the autumn of 1912. I reprint my cautions from *Poetry* for March, 1913.

A FEW DON'TS

An 'Image' is that which presents an intellectual and emotional complex in an instant of time. I use the term 'complex' rather in the technical sense employed by the newer psychologists, such as Hart, though we might not agree absolutely in our application.

It is the presentation of such a 'complex' instantaneously which gives that sense of sudden liberation; that sense of freedom from time limits and space limits; that sense of sudden growth, which we experience in the presence of the greatest works of art.

It is better to present one Image in a lifetime than to produce voluminous works.

All this, however, some may consider open to debate. The immediate necessity is to tabulate A LIST OF DON'TS for those beginning to write verses. I can not put all of them into Mosaic negative.

To begin with, consider the three propositions (demanding direct treatment, economy of words, and the sequence of the musical phrase), not as dogma—never consider anything as dogma—but as the result of long contemplation, which, even if it is some one else's contemplation, may be worth consideration.

Pay no attention to the criticism of men who have never themselves written a notable work. Consider the discrepancies between the actual writing of the Greek poets and dramatists, and the theories of the Graeco-Roman grammarians, concocted to explain their metres.

LANGUAGE

Use no superfluous word, no adjective which does not reveal something.

Don't use such an expression as 'dim lands *of peace*.' It dulls the image. It mixes an abstraction with the concrete. It comes from the writer's not realizing that the natural object is always the *adequate* symbol.

Go in fear of abstractions. Do not retail in mediocre verse what has already been done in good prose. Don't think any intelligent person is going to be deceived when you try to shirk all the difficulties of the unspeakably difficult art of good prose by chopping your composition into line lengths.

What the expert is tired of today the public will be tired of tomorrow.

Don't imagine that the art of poetry is any simpler than the art of music, or that you can please the expert before you have spent at least as much effort on the art of verse as the average piano teacher spends on the art of music.

Be influenced by as many great artists as you can, but have the decency either to acknowledge the debt outright, or to try to conceal it.

Don't allow 'influence' to mean merely that you mop up the particular decorative vocabulary of some one or two poets whom you happen to admire. A Turkish war correspondent was recently caught red-handed babbling in his despatches of 'dove-grey' hills, or else it was 'pearl-pale,' I can not remember.

Use either no ornament or good ornament.

RHYTHM AND RHYME

Let the candidate fill his mind with the finest cadences he can discover, preferably in a foreign language,[2] so that the meaning of the words may be less likely to divert his attention from the movement; e.g. Saxon charms, Hebridean Folk Songs, the verse of Dante, and the lyrics of Shakespeare—if he can dissociate the vocabulary from the cadence. Let him dissect the lyrics of Goethe coldly into their component sound values, syllables long and short, stressed and unstressed, into vowels and consonants.

It is not necessary that a poem should rely on its music, but if it does rely on its music that music must be such as will delight the expert.

Let the neophyte know assonance and alliteration, rhyme immediate and delayed, simple and polyphonic, as a musician would expect to know harmony and counterpoint and all the minutiae of his craft. No time is too great to give to these matters or to any one of them, even if the artist seldom have need of them.

Don't imagine that a thing will 'go' in verse just because it's too dull to go in prose.

Don't be 'viewy'—leave that to the writers of pretty little philosophic essays. Don't be descriptive; remember that the painter can describe a landscape much better than you can, and that he has to know a deal more about it.

When Shakespeare talks of the 'Dawn in russet mantle clad' he presents something which the painter does not present. There is in this line of his nothing that one can call description; he presents.

Consider the way of the scientists rather than the way of an advertising agent for a new soap.

The scientist does not expect to be acclaimed as a great scientist until he has *discovered* something. He begins by learning what has been discovered already. He goes from that point onward. He does not bank on being a charming fellow personally. He does not expect his friends to applaud the results of his freshman class work. Freshmen in poetry are unfortunately not confined to a definite and recognizable class room. They are 'all over the shop.' Is it any wonder 'the public is indifferent to poetry?'

Don't chop your stuff into separate *iambs*. Don't make each line stop dead at the end, and then begin every next line with a heave. Let the beginning of the next line catch the rise of the rhythm wave, unless you want a definite longish pause.

In short, behave as a musician, a good musician, when dealing with that phase of your art which has exact parallels in music. The same laws govern, and you are bound by no others.

Naturally, your rhythmic structure should not destroy the shape of your words, or their natural sound, or their meaning. It is improbable that, at the start, you will be able to get a rhythm-structure strong enough to affect them very much, though you may fall a victim to all sorts of false stopping due to line ends and cæsurae.

The Musician can rely on pitch and the volume of the orchestra. You can not. The term harmony is misapplied in poetry; it refers to simultaneous sounds of different pitch. There is, however, in the best verse a sort of residue of sound which remains in the ear of the hearer and acts more or less as an organ-base.

A rhyme must have in it some slight element of surprise if it is to give pleasure; it need not be bizarre or curious, but it must be well used if used at all.

Vide further Vildrac and Duhamel's notes on rhyme in *'Technique Poétique.'*

That part of your poetry which strikes upon the imaginative *eye* of the reader will lose nothing by translation into a foreign tongue; that which appeals to the ear can reach only those who take it in the original.

Consider the definiteness of Dante's presentation, as compared with Milton's rhetoric. Read as much of Wordsworth as does not seem too unutterably dull.[3]

If you want the gist of the matter go to Sappho, Catullus, Villon, Heine when he is in the vein, Gautier when he is not too frigid; or, if you have not the tongues, seek out the leisurely Chaucer. Good prose will do you no harm, and there is good discipline to be had by trying to write it.

Translation is likewise good training, if you find that your original matter 'wobbles' when you try to rewrite it. The meaning of the poem to be translated can not 'wobble.'

If you are using a symmetrical form, don't put in what you want to say and then fill up the remaining vacuums with slush.

Don't mess up the perception of one sense by trying to define it in terms of another. This is usually only the result of being too lazy to find the exact word. To this clause there are possibly exceptions.

The first three simple prescriptions will throw out nine-tenths of all the bad poetry now accepted as standard and classic; and will prevent you from many a crime of production.

'. . . *Mais d'abord il faut être un poète,'* as MM. Duhamel and Vildrac have said at the end of their little book, *'Notes sur la Technique Poétique.'*

Since March 1913, Ford Madox Hueffer has pointed out that Wordsworth was so intent on the ordinary or plain word that he never thought of hunting for *le mot juste*.

John Butler Yeats has handled or man-handled Wordsworth and the Victorians, and his criticism, contained in letters to his son, is now printed and available.

I do not like writing *about* art, my first, at least I think it was my first essay on the subject, was a protest against it.

PROLEGOMENA [4]

Time was when the poet lay in a green field with his head against a tree and played his diversion on a ha'penny whistle, and Caesar's predecessors conquered the earth, and the predecessors of golden Crassus embezzled, and fashions had their say, and let him alone. And presumably he was fairly content in this circumstance, for I have small doubt that the occasional passerby, being attracted by curiosity to know why any one should lie under a tree and blow diversion on a ha'penny whistle, came and conversed with him, and that among these passers-by there was on occasion a person of charm or a young lady who had not read *Man and Superman;* and looking back upon this naïve state of affairs we call it the age of gold.

Metastasio, and he should know if any one, assures us that this age endures—even though the modern poet is expected to holloa his verses down a speaking tube to the editors of cheap magazines—S. S. McClure, or some one of that sort—even though hordes of authors meet in dreariness and drink healths to the 'Copyright Bill'; even though these things be, the age of gold pertains. Imperceivably, if you like, but pertains. You meet unkempt Amyclas in a Soho restaurant and chant together of dead and forgotten things—it is a manner of speech among poets to chant of dead, half-forgotten things, there seems no special harm in it; it has always been done—and it's rather better to be a clerk in the Post Office than to look after a lot of stinking, verminous sheep—and at another hour of the day one substitutes the drawing-room for the restaurant and tea is probably more palatable than mead and mare's milk, and little cakes than honey. And in this fashion one survives the resignation of Mr. Balfour, and the iniquities of the American customs-house, *e quel bufera infernal,* the periodical press. And then in the middle of it, there being apparently no other person at once capable and available one is stopped and asked to explain oneself.

I begin on the chord thus querulous, for I would much rather lie on what is left of Catullus' parlour floor and speculate the azure beneath it and the hills off to Salo and Riva with their forgotten gods moving unhindered amongst them, than discuss any processes and theories of art whatsoever. I would rather play tennis. I shall not argue.

CREDO

Rhythm.—I believe in an 'absolute rhythm,' a rhythm, that is, in poetry which corresponds exactly to the emotion or shade of emotion to be expressed. A man's rhythm must be interpretative, it will be, therefore, in the end, his own, uncounterfeiting, uncounterfeitable.

Symbols.—I believe that the proper and perfect symbol is the natural object, that if a man use 'symbols' he must so use them that their symbolic function does not obtrude; so that *a* sense, and the poetic quality of the passage, is not lost to those who do not understand the symbol as such, to whom, for instance, a hawk is a hawk.

Technique.—I believe in technique as the test of a man's sincerity; in law when it is ascertainable; in the trampling down of every convention that impedes or obscures the determination of the law, or the precise rendering of the impulse.

Form.—I think there is a 'fluid' as well as a 'solid' content, that some poems may have form as a tree has form, some as water poured into a vase. That most symmetrical forms have certain uses. That a vast number of subjects cannot be precisely, and therefore not properly rendered in symmetrical forms.

'Thinking that alone worthy wherein the whole art is employed.' [5] I think the artist should master all known forms and systems of metric, and I have with some persistence set about doing this, searching particularly into those periods wherein the systems came to birth or attained their maturity. It has been complained, with some justice, that I dump my note-books on the public. I think that only after a long struggle will poetry attain such a degree of development, or, if you will, modernity, that it will vitally concern people who are accustomed, in prose, to Henry James and Anatole France, in music to Debussy. I am constantly contending that it took two centuries of Provence and one of Tuscany to develop the media of Dante's masterwork, that it took the latinists of the Renaissance, and the Pleiade, and his own age of painted speech to prepare Shakespeare his tools. It is tremendously important that great poetry be written, it makes no jot of difference who writes it. The experimental demonstrations of one man may save the time of many—hence my furore over Arnaut Daniel—if a man's experiments try out one new rime, or dispense conclusively with one iota of currently accepted nonsense, he is merely playing fair with his colleagues when he chalks up his result.

No man ever writes very much poetry that 'matters.' In bulk, that is, no one produces much that is final, and when a man is not doing this highest thing, this saying the thing once for all and perfectly; when he is not matching Ποικιλόθρον', ἀθάνατ' 'Αφρόδιτα, or 'Hist—said Kate the Queen,' he had much better be making the sorts of experiment which may be of use to him in his later work, or to his successors.

'The lyf so short, the craft so long to lerne.' It is a foolish thing for a man to begin his work on a too narrow foundation, it is a disgraceful thing for a man's work not to show steady growth and increasing fineness from first to last.

As for 'adaptations'; one finds that all the old masters of painting recommend to their pupils that they begin by copying masterwork, and proceed to their own composition.

As for 'Every man his own poet,' the more every man knows about poetry the better. I believe in every one writing poetry who wants to; most do. I believe in every man knowing enough of music to play 'God bless our home' on the harmonium, but I do not believe in every man giving concerts and printing his sin.

The mastery of any art is the work of a lifetime. I should not discriminate between the 'amateur' and the 'professional.' Or rather I should discriminate quite often in favour of the amateur, but I should discriminate between the amateur and the expert. It is certain that the present chaos will endure until the Art of poetry has been preached down the amateur gullet, until there is such a general understanding of the fact that poetry is an art and not a pastime; such a knowledge of technique; of technique of surface and technique of content, that the amateurs will cease to try to drown out the masters.

If a certain thing was said once for all in Atlantis or Arcadia, in 450 Before Christ or in 1290 after, it is not for us moderns to go saying it over, or to go obscuring the memory of the dead by saying the same thing with less skill and less conviction.

My pawing over the ancients and semi-ancients has been one struggle to find out what has been done, once for all, better than it can ever be done again, and to find out what remains for us to do, and plenty does remain, for if we still feel the same emotions as those which launched the thousand ships, it is quite certain that we come on these feelings differently, through different nuances, by different intellectual gradations. Each age has its own abounding gifts yet only some ages transmute them into matter of duration. No good poetry is ever written in a manner twenty years old, for to write in such a manner shows conclusively that the writer thinks from books, convention and *cliché*, and not from life, yet a man feeling the divorce of life and his art may naturally try to resurrect a forgotten mode if he finds in that mode some leaven, or if he think he sees in it some element lacking in contemporary art which might unite that art again to its sustenance, life.

In the art of Daniel and Cavalcanti, I have seen that precision which I miss in the Victorians, that explicit rendering, be it of external nature, or of emotion. Their testimony is of the eyewitness, their symptoms are first hand.

As for the nineteenth century, with all respect to its achievements, I think we shall look back upon it as a rather blurry, messy sort of a period, a rather sentimentalistic, mannerish sort of a period. I say this without any self-righteousness, with no self-satisfaction.

As for there being a 'movement' or my being of it, the conception of poetry as a 'pure art' in the sense in which I use the term, revived with Swinburne. From the puritanical revolt to Swinburne, poetry had been merely the vehicle—yes, definitely, Arthur Symon's scruples and feelings about the word not withholding—the ox-cart and post-chaise for transmitting thoughts poetic or otherwise. And perhaps the 'great Victorians,' though it is doubtful, and assuredly the 'nineties' continued the development of the art, confining their improvements, however, chiefly to sound and to refinements of manner.

Mr. Yeats has once and for all stripped English poetry of its perdamnable rhetoric. He has boiled away all that is not poetic—and a good deal that is. He has become a classic in his own lifetime and *nel mezzo del cammin*. He has made our poetic idiom a thing pliable, a speech without inversions.

Robert Bridges, Maurice Hewlett and Frederic Manning are [6] in their different ways seriously concerned with overhauling the metric, in testing the language and its adaptability to certain modes. Ford Hueffer is making some sort of experiments in modernity. The Provost of Oriel continues his translation of the *Divina Commedia*.

As to Twentieth century poetry, and the poetry which I expect to see written during the next decade or so, it will, I think, move against poppy-cock, it will be harder and saner, it will be what Mr. Hewlett calls 'nearer the bone.' It will be as much like granite as it can be, its force will lie in its truth, its interpretative power (of course, poetic force does always rest there); I mean it will not try to seem forcible by rhetorical din, and luxurious riot. We will have fewer painted adjectives impeding the shock and stroke of it. At least for myself, I want it so, austere, direct, free from emotional slither.

What is there now, in 1917, to be added?

RE VERS LIBRE

I think the desire for vers libre is due to the sense of quantity reasserting itself after years of starvation. But I doubt if we can take over, for English, the rules of quantity laid down for Greek and Latin, mostly by Latin grammarians.

I think one should write vers libre only when one 'must,' that is to say, only when the 'thing' builds up a rhythm more beautiful than that of set metres, or more real, more a part of the emotion of the 'thing,' more germane, intimate, interpretative than the measure of regular accentual verse; a rhythm which discontents one with set iambic or set anapaestic.

Eliot has said the thing very well when he said, 'No *vers* is *libre* for the man who wants to do a good job.'

As a matter of detail, there is vers libre with accent heavily marked as a drum-beat (as par example my 'Dance Figure'), and on the other hand I think I have gone as far as can profitably be gone in the other direction (and perhaps too far). I mean I do not think one can use to any advantage rhythms much more tenuous and imperceptible than some I have used. I think progress lies rather in an attempt to approximate classical quantitative metres (NOT to copy them) than in a carelessness regarding such things.[7]

I agree with John Yeats on the relation of beauty to certitude. I prefer satire, which is due to emotion, to any sham of emotion.

I have had to write, or at least I have written a good deal about art, sculpture, painting and poetry. I have seen what seemed to me the best of contemporary work reviled and obstructed. Can any one write prose of permanent or durable interest when he is merely saying for one year what nearly every one will say at the end of three or four years? I have been battistrada for a sculptor, a painter, a novelist, several poets. I wrote also of certain French writers in *The New Age* in nineteen twelve or eleven.

I would much rather that people would look at Brzeska's sculpture and Lewis's drawings, and that they would read Joyce, Jules Romains,

Eliot, than that they should read what I have said of these men, or that I should be asked to republish argumentative essays and reviews.

All that the critic can do for the reader or audience or spectator is to focus his gaze or audition. Rightly or wrongly I think my blasts and essays have done their work, and that more people are now likely to go to the sources than are likely to read this book.

Jammes's 'Existences' in *'La Triomphe de la Vie'* is available. So are his early poems. I think we need a convenient anthology rather than descriptive criticism. Carl Sandburg wrote me from Chicago, 'It's hell when poets can't afford to buy each other's books.' Half the people who care, only borrow. In America so few people know each other that the difficulty lies more than half in distribution. Perhaps one should make an anthology: Romains's 'Un Etre en Marche' and 'Prières,' Vildrac's 'Visite.' Retrospectively the fine wrought work of Laforgue, the flashes of Rimbaud, the hard-bit lines of Tristan Corbière, Tailhade's sketches in 'Poèmes Aristophanesques,' the 'Litanies' of De Gourmont.

It is difficult at all times to write of the fine arts, it is almost impossible unless one can accompany one's prose with many reproductions. Still I would seize this chance or any chance to reaffirm my belief in Wyndham Lewis's genius, both in his drawings and his writings. And I would name an out of the way prose book, the *'Scenes and Portraits'* of Frederic Manning, as well as James Joyce's short stories and novel, 'Dubliners' and the now well known 'Portrait of the Artist' as well as Lewis's 'Tarr,' if, that is, I may treat my strange reader as if he were a new friend come into the room, intent on ransacking my bookshelf.

ONLY EMOTION ENDURES

'Only emotion endures.' Surely it is better for me to name over the few beautiful poems that still ring in my head than for me to search my flat for back numbers of periodicals and rearrange all that I have said about friendly and hostile writers.

The first twelve lines of Padraic Colum's 'Drover'; his 'O Woman shapely as a swan, on your account I shall not die'; Joyce's 'I hear an army'; the lines of Yeats that ring in my head and in the heads of all young men of my time who care for poetry: Braseal and the Fisherman, 'The fire that stirs about her when she stirs'; the later lines of 'The Scholars,' the faces of the Magi; William Carlos Williams's 'Postlude,' Aldington's version of 'Atthis,' and 'H. D.'s' waves like pine tops, and her verse in 'Des Imagistes' the first anthology; Hueffer's 'How red your lips are' in his translation from Von der Vogelweide, his 'Three Ten,' the general effect of his 'On Heaven'; his sense of the prose values or prose qualities in poetry; his ability to write poems that half-chant and are spoiled by a musician's additions; beyond these a poem by Alice Corbin, 'One City Only,' and another ending 'But sliding water over a stone.' These things have worn smooth in my head and I am not through with them, nor with Aldington's 'In Via Sestina' nor his other poems in 'Des Imagistes,' though people have told me their flaws. It may be that their content is too much embedded in me for me to look back at the words.

I am almost a different person when I come to take up the argument for Eliot's poems.

NOTES

1. A group of early essays and notes which appeared under this title in *Pavannes and Divisions* (1918). 'A Few Don'ts' was first printed in *Poetry,* I, 6 (March, 1913).
2. This is for rhythm, his vocabulary must of course be found in his native tongue.
3. Vide infra.
4. *Poetry and Drama* (then the *Poetry Review,* edited by Harold Monro), Feb. 1912.
5. Dante, *De Volgari Eloquio.*
6. (Dec. 1911).
7. Let me date this statement 20 Aug. 1917.

WILLIAM CARLOS WILLIAMS

Prologue to *Kora in Hell*

1918

The sole precedent I can find for the broken style of my prologue is *Longinus on the Sublime* and that one far-fetched.

When my mother was in Rome on that rare journey forever to be remembered, she lived in a small pension near the Pincio Gardens. The place had been chosen by my brother as one notably easy of access, being in a quarter free from confusion of traffic, on a street close to the park, and furthermore, the tram to the American Academy passed at the corner. Yet never did my mother go out but she was in fear of being lost. By turning to the left when she should have turned right, actually she did once manage to go so far astray that it was nearly an hour before she extricated herself from the strangeness of every new vista and found a landmark.

There has always been a disreputable man of picturesque personality associated with this lady. Their relations have been marked by the most rollicking spirit of comradeship. Now it has been William, former sailor in Admiral Dewey's fleet at Manila, then Tom O'Rourck who has come to her to do odd jobs and to be cared for more or less when drunk or ill, their Penelope. William would fall from the grape arbor much to my mother's amusement and delight and to his blustering discomfiture or he would stagger to the back door nearly unconscious from bad whiskey. There she would serve him with very hot and very strong coffee, then put him to scrubbing the kitchen floor, into his suddy pail pouring half a bottle of ammonia which would make the man gasp and water at the eyes as he worked and became sober.

Reprinted by permission of City Lights, Booksellers and Publishers, San Francisco.

She has always been incapable of learning from benefit or disaster. If a man cheat her she will remember that man with a violence that I have seldom seen equaled, but so far as that could have an influence on her judgment of the next man or woman, she might be living in Eden. And indeed she is, an impoverished, ravished Eden but one indestructible as the imagination itself. Whatever is before her is sufficient to itself and so to be valued. Her meat though more delicate in fiber is of a kind with that of Villon and La Grosse Margot:

Vente, gresle, gelle, j'ai mon pain cuit!

Carl Sandburg sings a Negro cotton picker's song of the boll weevil. Verse after verse tells what they would do to the insect. They propose to place it in the sand, in hot ashes, in the river, and other unlikely places but the boll weevil's refrain is always: 'That'll be ma HOME! That'll be ma HOOME!'

My mother is given over to frequent periods of great depression being as I believe by nature the most light-hearted thing in the world. But there comes a grotesque turn to her talk, a macabre anecdote concerning some dream, a passionate statement about death, which elevates her mood without marring it, sometimes in a most startling way.

Looking out at our parlor window one day I said to her: 'We see all the shows from here, don't we, all the weddings and funerals?' (They had been preparing a funeral across the street, the undertaker was just putting on his overcoat.) She replied: 'Funny profession that, burying the dead people. I should think they wouldn't have any delusions of life left.' W.—Oh yes, it's merely a profession. M.—Hm. And how they study it! They say sometimes people look terrible and they come and make them look fine. They push things into their mouths! (Realistic gesture) W.—Mama! M.—Yes, when they haven't any teeth.

By some such dark turn at the end she raises her story out of the commonplace: 'Look at that chair, look at it! [The plasterers had just left.] If Mrs. J. or Mrs. D. saw that they would have a fit.' W.—Call them in, maybe it will kill them. M.—But they're not near as bad as that woman, you know, her husband was in the chorus—has a little daughter Helen. Mrs. B., yes. She once wanted to take rooms here. I didn't want her. They told me: 'Mrs. Williams, I heard you're going to have Mrs. B. *She* is particular.' She said so herself. Oh no! Once she burnt all her face painting under the sink.

Thus, seeing the thing itself without forethought or afterthought but with great intensity of perception, my mother loses her bearings or associates with some disreputable person or translates a dark mood. She is a creature of great imagination. I might say this is her sole remaining quality. She is a despoiled, molted castaway but by this power she still breaks life between her fingers.

Once when I was taking lunch with Walter Arensberg at a small place on 63rd Street I asked him if he could state what the more modern painters were about, those roughly classed at that time as 'cubists': Gleizes, Man Ray, Demuth, Duchamp—all of whom were then in the city. He replied by saying that the only way man differed from every other creature was in his ability to improvise novelty and, since the pictorial artist was under discussion, anything in paint that is truly new, truly a fresh creation, is good art. Thus, according to Duchamp, who was Arensberg's champion at the time, a stained-glass window that had fallen out and lay more or less together on the ground was of far greater interest than the thing conventionally composed *in situ*.

We returned to Arensberg's sumptuous studio where he gave further point to his remarks by showing me what appeared to be the original of Duchamp's famous 'Nude Descending a Staircase.' But this, he went on to say, is a full-sized photographic print of the first picture with many new touches by Duchamp himself and so by the technique of its manufacture as by other means it is a novelty!

Led on by these enthusiasms Arensberg has been an indefatigable worker for the yearly salon of the Society of Independent Artists, Inc. I remember the warmth of his description of a pilgrimage to the home of that old Boston hermit who, watched over by a forbidding landlady (evidently in his pay), paints the cigar-box-cover-like nudes upon whose fingers he presses actual rings with glass jewels from the five-and-ten-cent store.

I wish Arensberg had my opportunity for prying into jaded households where the paintings of Mama's and Papa's flowertime still hang on the walls. I propose that Arensberg be commissioned by the Independent Artists to scour the country for the abortive paintings of those men and women who without master or method have evolved perhaps two or three unusual creations in their early years. I would start the collection with a painting I have by a little Englishwoman, A. E. Kerr, 1906, that in its unearthly gaiety of flowers and sobriety of design possesses exactly that strange freshness a spring day approaches without attaining, an expansion of April, a thing this poor woman found too costly for her possession—she could not swallow it as the Negroes do diamonds in the mines. Carefully selected, these queer products might be housed to good effect in some unpretentious exhibition chamber across the city from the Metropolitan Museum of Art. In the anteroom could be hung perhaps photographs of prehistoric rock-paintings and etchings on horn: galloping bisons and stags, the hind feet of which have been caught by the artist in such a position that from that time until the invention of the camera obscura, a matter of six thousand years or more, no one on earth had again depicted that most delicate and expressive posture of running.

The amusing controversy between Arensberg and Duchamp on one side, and the rest of the hanging committee on the other as to whether the porcelain urinal was to be admitted to the Palace Exhibition of 1917 as a representative piece of American sculpture, should not be allowed to slide into oblivion.

One day Duchamp decided that his composition for that day would be the first thing that struck his eye in the first hardware store he should enter. It turned out to be a pickax which he bought and set up in his studio. This was his composition. Together with Mina Loy and a few others Duchamp and Arensberg brought out the paper, *The Blind Man,* to which Robert Carlton Brown, with his vision of suicide by diving from a high window of the Singer Building, contributed a few poems.

In contradistinction to their South, Marianne Moore's statement to me at the Chatham parsonage one afternoon—my wife and I were just on the point of leaving—sets up a North: My work has come to have just one quality of value in it: I will not touch or have to do with those things which I detest. In this austerity of mood she finds sufficient freedom for the play she chooses.

Of all those writing poetry in America at the time she was here Marianne Moore was the only one Mina Loy feared. By divergent virtues these two women have achieved freshness of presentation, novelty, freedom, break with banality.

When Margaret Anderson published my first improvisations Ezra Pound wrote me one of his hurried letters in which he urged me to give some hint by which the reader of good will might come at my intention.

Before Ezra's permanent residence in London, on one of his trips to America—brought on I think by an attack of jaundice—he was glancing through some book of my father's. 'It is not necessary,' he said, 'to read everything in a book in order to speak intelligently of it. Don't tell everybody I said so,' he added.

During this same visit my father and he had been reading and discussing poetry together. Pound has always liked my father. 'I of course like your old man and I have drunk his Goldwasser.' They were hot for an argument that day. My parent had been holding forth in downright sentences upon my own 'idle nonsense' when he turned and became equally vehement concerning something Ezra had written: what in heaven's name Ezra meant by 'jewels' in a verse that had come between them. These jewels,—rubies, sapphires, amethysts and whatnot, Pound went on to explain with great determination and care, were the backs of books as they stood on a man's shelf. 'But why in heaven's name don't you say so then?' was my father's triumphant and crushing rejoinder.

The letter:

> . . . God knows I have to work hard enough to escape, not *propagande,* but getting entered in *propagande*. And America? What the h—l do you a blooming foreigner know about the place. Your *père* only penetrated the edge, and you've never been west of Upper Darby, or the Maunchunk switchback.
>
> Would H., with the swirl of the prairie wind in her underwear, or the Virile Sandburg recognize you, an effete easterner as a REAL American? INCONCEIVABLE!!!!!
>
> My dear boy you have never felt the whoop of the PEEraries. You have never seen the projecting and protuberant Mts. of the SIerra Nevada. WOT can you know of the country?
>
> You have the naive credulity of a Co.Claire emigrant. But I (*der grosse Ich*) have the virus, the bacillus of the land in my blood, for nearly three bleating centuries.
>
> (Bloody snob. 'eave a brick at 'im!!!) . . .
>
> I was very glad to see your wholly incoherent unamerican poems in the L.R.
>
> Of course Sandburg will tell you that you miss the 'big drifts,' and Bodenheim will object to your not being sufficiently decadent.
>
> You thank your blookin gawd you've got enough Spanish blood to muddy up your mind, and prevent the current American ideation from going through it like a blighted colander.
>
> The thing that saves your work is opacity, and don't forget it. Opacity is NOT an American quality. Fizz, swish, gabble, and verbiage, these are *echt americanisch*.

And alas, alas, poor old Masters. Look at Oct. Poetry.

Let me indulge the American habit of quotation:

'Si le cosmopolitisme littéraire gagnait encore et qu'il réussit à éteindre ce que les différences de race ont allumé de haine de sang parmi les hommes, j'y verrais un gain pour la civilisation et pour l'humanité tout entière. . . .

'L'amour excessif d'une patrie a pour immédiat corollaire l'horreur des patries étrangères. Non seulement on craint de quitter la jupe de sa maman, d'aller voir comment vivent les autres hommes, de se mêler à leur luttes, de partager leurs travaux, non seulement on reste chez soi, mais on finit par fermer sa porte.

'Cette folie gagne certains littérateurs et le même professeur, en sortant d'expliquer le Cid ou Don Juan, rédige de gracieuses injures contre Ibsen et l'influence, hélas, trop illusoire, de son oeuvre, pourtant toute de lumière et de beauté.' et cetera. Lie down and compose yourself.

I like to think of the Greeks as setting out for the colonies in Sicily and the Italian peninsula. The Greek temperament lent itself to a certain symmetrical sculptural phase and to a fat poetical balance of line that produced important work but I like better the Greeks setting their backs to Athens. The ferment was always richer in Rome, the dispersive explosion was always nearer, the influence carried further and remained hot longer. Hellenism, especially the modern sort, is too staid, too chilly, too little fecundative to impregnate my world.

Hilda Doolittle before she began to write poetry or at least before she began to show it to anyone would say: 'You're not satisfied with me, are you Billy? There's something lacking, isn't there?' When I was with her my feet always seemed to be sticking to the ground while she would be walking on the tips of the grass stems.

Ten years later as assistant editor of the *Egoist* she refers to my long poem, 'March,' which thanks to her own and her husband's friendly attentions finally appeared there in a purified form:

14 *Aug*. 1916

Dear Bill:—

I trust you will not hate me for wanting to delete from your poem all the flippancies. The reason I want to do this is that the beautiful lines are so very beautiful—so in the tone and spirit of your *Postlude*—(which to me stands, a Nike, supreme among your poems). I think there is *real* beauty—and real beauty is a rare and sacred thing in this generation—in all the pyramid, Ashur-ban-i-pal bits and in the Fiesole and in the wind at the very last.

I don't know what you think but I consider this business of writing a very sacred thing!—I think you have the 'spark'—am sure of it, and when you speak *direct* are a poet. I feel in the hey-ding-ding touch running through your poem a derivative tendency which, to me, is not *you*—not your very self. It is as if you were *ashamed* of your Spirit, ashamed of your inspiration!—as if you mocked at your own song. It's very well to *mock* at yourself—it is a spiritual sin to mock at your inspiration—

Hilda

Oh well, all this might be very disquieting were it not that 'sacred' has lately been discovered to apply to a point of arrest where stabilization has gone on past the time. There is nothing sacred about literature, it is damned from one end to the other. There is nothing in literature but change and change is mockery. I'll write whatever I damn please, whenever I damn please and as I damn please and it'll be good if the authentic spirit of change is on it.

But in any case H. D. misses the entire intent of what I am doing no matter how just her remarks concerning that particular poem happen to have been. The hey-ding-ding touch *was* derivative, but it filled a gap that I did not know how better to fill at the time. It might be said that that touch is the prototype of the improvisations.

It is to the inventive imagination we look for deliverance from every other misfortune as from the desolation of a flat Hellenic perfection of style. What good then to turn to art from the atavistic religionists, from a science doing slavery service upon gas engines, from a philosophy tangled in a miserable sort of dialect that means nothing if the full power of initiative be denied at the beginning by a lot of baying and snapping scholiasts? If the inventive imagination must look, as I think, to the field of art for its richest discoveries today it will best make its way by compass and follow no path.

But before any material progress can be accomplished there must be someone to draw a discriminating line between true and false values.

The true value is that peculiarity which gives an object a character by itself. The associational or sentimental value is the false. Its imposition is due to lack of imagination, to an easy lateral sliding. The attention has been held too rigid on the one plane instead of following a more flexible, jagged resort. It is to loosen the attention, my attention since I occupy part of the field, that I write these improvisations. Here I clash with Wallace Stevens.

The imagination goes from one thing to another. Given many things of nearly totally divergent natures but possessing one-thousandth part of a quality in common, provided that be new, distinguished, these things belong in an imaginative category and not in a gross natural array. To me this is the gist of the whole matter. It is easy to fall under the spell of a certain mode, especially if it be remote of origin, leaving thus certain of its members essential to a reconstruction of its significance permanently lost in an impenetrable mist of time. But the thing that stands eternally in the way of really good writing is always one: the virtual impossibility of lifting to the imagination those things which lie under the direct scrutiny of the senses, close to the nose. It is this difficulty that sets a value upon all works of art and makes them a necessity. The senses witnessing what is immediately before them in detail see a finality which they cling to in despair, not knowing which way to turn. Thus the so-called natural or scientific array becomes fixed, the walking devil of modern life. He who even nicks the solidity of this apparition does a piece of work superior to that of Hercules when he cleaned the Augean stables.

Stevens' letter applies really to my book of poems, *Al Que Quiere* (which means, by the way, 'To Him Who Wants It') but the criticism he makes of that holds good for each of the improvisations if not for the *œuvre* as a whole.

It begins with a postscript in the upper left hand corner: 'I think, after all, I should rather send this than not, although it is quarrelsomely full of my own ideas of discipline.'

April 9

My dear Williams:

. . . .

What strikes me most about the poems themselves is their casual character. . . . Personally I have a distaste for miscellany. It is one of the reasons I do not bother about a book myself.

[*Wallace Stevens is a fine gentleman whom Cannell likened*

to a Pennsylvania Dutchman who has suddenly become aware of his habits and taken to 'society' in self-defense. He is always immaculately dressed. I don't know why I should always associate him in my mind with an imaginary image I have of Ford Madox Hueffer.]

. . . My idea is that in order to carry a thing to the extreme necessity to convey it one has to stick to it; . . . Given a fixed point of view, realistic, imagistic or what you will, everything adjusts itself to that point of view; the process of adjustment is a world in flux, as it should be for a poet. But to fidget with points of view leads always to new beginnings and incessant new beginnings lead to sterility.

(This sounds like Sir Roger de Coverly)

A single manner or mood thoroughly matured and exploited is that fresh thing . . . etc.

One has to keep looking for poetry as Renoir looked for colors in old walls, woodwork and so on.

Your place is

—among children

Leaping around a dead dog.

A book of that would feed the hungry . . .

Well a book of poems is a damned serious affair. I am only objecting that a book that contains your particular quality should contain anything else and suggesting that if the quality were carried to a communicable extreme, in intensity and volume, etc. . . . I see it all over the book, in your landscapes and portraits, but dissipated and obscured. Bouquets for brides and Spencerian compliments for poets . . . There are a very few men who have anything native in them or for whose work I'd give a Bolshevik ruble. . . . But I think your tantrums not half mad enough.

[*I am not quite clear about the last sentence but I presume he means that I do not push my advantage through to an overwhelming decision. What would you have me do with my Circe, Stevens, now that I have double-crossed her game, marry her? It is not what Odysseus did.*]

I return Pound's letter . . . observe how in everything he does he proceeds with the greatest positiveness, etc.

Wallace Stevens

I wish that I might here set down my 'Vortex' after the fashion of London, 1913, stating how little it means to me whether I live here, there or elsewhere or succeed in this, that or the other so long as I can keep my mind free from the trammels of literature, beating down every attack of its *retiarii* with my *mirmillones*. But the time is past.

I thought at first to adjoin to each improvisation a more or less opaque commentary. But the mechanical interference that would result makes this inadvisable. Instead I have placed some of them in the preface where without losing their original intention (see reference numerals at the beginning of each) they relieve the later text and also add their weight to my present fragmentary argument.

V. No. 2. By the brokenness of his composition the poet makes himself master of a certain weapon which he could possess himself of in no other way. The speed of the emotions is sometimes such that thrashing about in a thin exaltation or despair many matters are touched but not held, more often broken by the contact.

II. No. 3. The instability of these improvisations would seem such that they must inevitably crumble under the attention and become particles of a wind that falters. It would appear to the unready that the fiber of the thing is a thin jelly. It would be these same fools who would deny touch cords to the wind because they cannot split a storm endwise and wrap it upon spools. The virtue of strength lies not in the grossness of the fiber but in the fiber itself. Thus a poem is tough by no quality it borrows from a logical recital of events nor from the events themselves but solely from that attenuated power which draws perhaps many broken things into a dance giving them thus a full being.

It is seldom that anything but the most elementary communications can be exchanged one with another. There are in reality only two or three reasons generally accepted as the causes of action. No matter what the motive it will seldom happen that true knowledge of it will be anything more than vaguely divined by some one person, some half a person whose intimacy has perhaps been cultivated over the whole of a lifetime. We live in bags. This is due to the gross fiber of all action. By action itself almost nothing can be imparted. The world of action is a world of stones.

XV. No. 1. Bla! Bla! Bla! Heavy talk is talk that waits upon a deed. Talk is servile that is set to inform. Words with the bloom on them run before the imagination like the saeter girls before Peer Gynt. It is talk with the patina of whim upon it makes action a bootlicker. So nowadays poets spit upon rhyme and rhetoric.

The stream of things having composed itself into wiry strands that move in one fixed direction, the poet in desperation turns at right angles and cuts across current with startling results to his hangdog mood.

XI. No. 2. In France, the country of Rabelais, they know that the world is not made up entirely of virgins. They do not deny virtue to the rest because of that. Each age has its perfections but the praise differs. It is only stupid when the praise of the gross and the transformed would be minted in unfit terms such as suit nothing but youth's sweetness and frailty. It is necessary to know that laughter is the reverse of aspiration. So they laugh well in France, at Coquelin and the *Petoman*. Their girls, also, thrive upon the love-making they get, so much so that the world runs to Paris for that reason.

XII. No. 2B. It is chuckleheaded to desire a way through every difficulty. Surely one might even communicate with the dead—and lose his taste for truffles. Because snails are slimy when alive and because slime is associated (erroneously) with filth, the fool is convinced that snails are detestable when, as it is proven every day, fried in butter with chopped parsley upon them, they are delicious. This is both sides of the question: the slave and the despoiled of his senses are one. But to weigh a difficulty and to turn it aside without being wrecked upon a destructive solution bespeaks an imagination of force sufficient to transcend action. The difficulty has thus been solved by ascent to a higher plane. It is energy of the imagination alone that cannot be laid aside.

Rich as are the gifts of the imagination bitterness of world's loss is not replaced thereby. On the contrary it is intensified, resembling thus possession itself. But he who has no power of the imagination cannot even know the full of his injury.

VIII. No. 3. Those who permit their senses to be despoiled of the things under their noses by stories of all manner of things removed and unattainable are of frail imagination. Idiots, it is true nothing is possessed save by dint of that vigorous conception of its perfections which is the imagination's special province but neither is anything possessed which is not extant. A frail imagination, unequal to the tasks before it, is easily led astray.

IV. No. 2. Although it is a quality of the imagination that it seeks to place together those things which have a common relationship, yet the coining of similes is a pastime of very low order, depending as it does upon a nearly vegetable coincidence. Much more keen is that power which discovers in things those inimitable particles of dissimilarity to all other things which are the peculiar perfections of the thing in question.

But this loose linking of one thing with another has effects of a destructive power little to be guessed at: all manner of things are thrown out of key so that it approaches the impossible to arrive at an understanding of anything. All is confusion, yet it comes from a hidden desire for the dance, a lust of the imagination, a will to accord two instruments in a duet.

But one does not attempt by the ingenuity of the joiner to blend the tones of the oboe with the violin. On the contrary the perfections of the two instruments are emphasized by the joiner; no means is neglected to give to each the full color of its perfections. It is only the music of the instruments which is joined and that not by the woodworker but by the composer, by virtue of the imagination.

On this level of the imagination all things and ages meet in fellowship. Thus only can they, peculiar and perfect, find their release. This is the beneficent power of the imagination.

Age and youth are great flatterers. Brooding on each other's obvious psychology neither dares tell the other outright what manifestly is the truth: your world is poison. Each is secure in his own perfections. Monsieur Eichorn used to have a most atrocious body odor while the odor of some girls is a pleasure to the nostril. Each quality in each person or age, rightly valued, would mean the freeing of that age to its own delights of action or repose. Now an evil odor can be pursued with praiseworthy ardor leading to great natural activity whereas a flowery skinned virgin may and no doubt often does allow herself to fall into destructive habits of neglect.

XIII. No. 3. A poet witnessing the chicory flower and realizing its virtues of form and color so constructs his praise of it as to borrow no particles from right or left. He gives his poem over to the flower and its plant themselves, that they may benefit by those cooling winds of the imagination which thus returned upon them will refresh them at their task of saving the world. But what does it mean, remarked his friends?

VII. *Coda.* It would be better than depriving birds of their song to call them all nightingales. So it would be better than to have a world stript of poetry to provide men with some sort of eyeglasses by which they should be unable to read any verse but sonnets. But fortunately although there are many sorts of fools, just as there are many birds which sing and many sorts of poems, there is no need to please them.

All schoolmasters are fools. Thinking to build in the young the foundations of knowledge they let slip their minds that the blocks are of gray mist bedded upon the wind. Those who will taste of the wind himself have a mark in their eyes by virtue of which they bring their masters to nothing.

All things brought under the hand of the possessor crumble to nothingness. Not only that: He who possesses a child if he cling to it inordinately becomes childlike, whereas, with a twist of the imagination, himself may rise into comradeship with the grave and beautiful presences of antiquity. But some have the power to free, say a young matron pursuing her infant, from her own possessions, making her kin to Yang Kuei-fei because of a haunting loveliness that clings about her knees, impeding her progress as she takes up her matronly pursuit.

As to the sun what is he, save for his light, more than the earth is: the same mass of metals, a mere shadow? But the winged dawn is the very essence of the sun's self, a thing cold, vitreous, a virtue that precedes the body which it drags after it.

The features of a landscape take their position in the imagination and are related more to their own kind there than to the country and season which has held them hitherto as a basket holds vegetables mixed with fruit.

VI. No. 1. A fish swimming in a pond, were his back white and his belly green, would be easily perceived from above by hawks against the dark depths of water and from below by larger fish against the penetrant light of the sky. But since his belly is white and his back green he swims about in safety. Observing this barren truth and discerning at once its slavish application to the exercises of the mind, a young man, who has been sitting for some time in contemplation at the edge of a lake, rejects with scorn the parochial deductions of history and as scornfully asserts his defiance.

XIV. No. 3. The barriers which keep the feet from the dance are the same which in a dream paralyze the effort to escape and hold us powerless in the track of some murderous pursuer. Pant and struggle but you cannot move. The birth of the imagination is like waking from a nightmare. Never does the night seem so beneficent.

The raw beauty of ignorance that lies like an opal mist over the west coast of the Atlantic, beginning at the Grand Banks and extending into the recesses of our brains—the children, the married, the unmarried—clings especially about the eyes and the throats of our girls and boys. Of a Sunday afternoon a girl sits before a mechanical piano and, working it with her hands and feet, opens her mouth and sings to the music

—a popular tune, ragtime. It is a serenade. I have seen a young Frenchman lean above the piano and looking down speak gently and wonderingly to one of our girls singing such a serenade. She did not seem aware of what she was singing and he smiled an occult but thoroughly bewildered smile—as of a man waiting for a fog to lift, meanwhile lost in admiration of its enveloping beauty—fragments of architecture, a street opening and closing, a mysterious glow of sunshine.

VIII. No. 1. A man of note upon examining the poems of his friend and finding there nothing related to his immediate understanding laughingly remarked: After all, literature is communication while you, my friend, I am afraid, in attempting to do something striking, are in danger of achieving mere preciosity.——But inasmuch as the fields of the mind are vast and little explored, the poet was inclined only to smile and to take note of that hardening infirmity of the imagination which seems to endow its victim with great solidity and rapidity of judgement. But he thought to himself: And yet of what other thing is greatness composed than a power to annihilate half-truths for a thousandth part of accurate understanding.

I have discovered that the thrill of first love passes! It even becomes the backbone of a sordid sort of religion if not assisted in passing. I knew a man who kept a candle burning before a girl's portrait day and night for a year—then jilted her, pawned her off on a friend. I have been reasonably frank about my erotics with my wife. I have never or seldom said, my dear I love you, when I would rather say: My dear, I wish you were in Tierra del Fuego. I have discovered by scrupulous attention to this detail and by certain allied experiments that we can continue from time to time to elaborate relationships quite equal in quality, if not greatly superior, to that surrounding our wedding. In fact, the best we have enjoyed of love together has come after the most thorough destruction or harvesting of that which has gone before. Periods of barrenness have intervened, periods comparable to the prison music in *Fidelio* or to any of Beethoven's pianissimo transition passages. It is at these times our formal relations have teetered on the edge of a debacle to be followed, as our imaginations have permitted, by a new growth of passionate attachment dissimilar in every member to that which has gone before.

It is in the continual and violent refreshing of the idea that love and good writing have their security.

Alfred Kreymborg is primarily a musician, at best an innovator of musical phrase:

We have no dishes
to eat our meals from.
We have no dishes
to eat our meals from
because we have no dishes
to eat our meals from

. . .

We need no dishes
to eat our meals from,
we have fingers
to eat our meals from.

Kreymborg's idea of poetry is a transforming music that has much to do with tawdry things.

Few people know how to read Kreymborg. There is no modern poet who suffers more from a bastard sentimental appreciation. It is hard to get his things from the page. I have heard him say he has often thought in despair of marking his verse into measures as music is marked. Oh, well—

The man has a bare irony, the gift of rhythm and *Others*. I smile to think of Alfred stealing the stamps from the envelopes sent for return of mss., to the *Others* office! The best thing that could happen for the good of poetry in the United States today would be for someone to give Alfred Kreymborg a hundred thousand dollars. In his mind there is the determination for freedom brought into relief by a crabbedness of temper that makes him peculiarly able to value what is being done here. Whether he is bull enough for the work I am not certain, but that he can find his way that I know.

A somewhat petulant English college friend of my brother's once remarked that Britons make the best policemen the world has ever witnessed. I agree with him. It is silly to go into a puckersnatch because some brass-button-minded nincompoop in Kensington flies off the handle and speaks openly about our United States prize poems. This Mr. Jepson—'Anyone who has heard Mr. J. read Homer and discourse on Catullus would recognize his fitness as a judge and respecter of poetry' —this is Ezra!—this champion of the right is not half a fool. His epithets and phrases—slipshod, rank bad workmanship of a man who has shirked his job, lumbering fakement, cumbrous artificiality, maundering dribble, rancid as *Ben Hur*—are in the main well-merited. And besides, he comes out with one fairly lipped cornet blast: the only distinctive U. S. contributions to the arts have been ragtime and buck-dancing.

Nothing is good save the new. If a thing have novelty it stands intrinsically beside every other work of artistic excellence. If it have not that, no loveliness or heroic proportion or grand manner will save it. It will not be saved above all by an attenuated intellectuality.

But all U. S. verse is not bad according to Mr. J., there is T. S. Eliot and his 'Love Song of J. Alfred Prufrock.'

But our prize poems are especially to be damned not because of superficial bad workmanship, but because they are rehash, repetition—just as Eliot's more exquisite work is rehash, repetition in another way of Verlaine, Baudelaire, Maeterlinck—conscious or unconscious—just as there were Pound's early paraphrases from Yeats and his constant later cribbing from the Renaissance, Provence and the modern French: Men content with the connotations of their masters.

It is convenient to have fixed standards of comparison: All antiquity! And there is always some everlasting Polonius of Kensington forever to rate highly his eternal Eliot. It is because Eliot is a subtle conformist. It tickles the palate of this archbishop of procurers to a lecherous antiquity to hold up Prufrock as a New World type. Prufrock, the nibbler at sophistication, endemic in every capital, the not quite (because he refuses to turn his back), is 'the soul of that modern land,' the United States!

Blue undershirts,
Upon a line,
It is not necessary to say to you
Anything about it—

I cannot question Eliot's observation. Prufrock is a masterly portrait of the man just below the summit, but the type is universal; the model in his case might be Mr. J.

No. The New World is Montezuma or, since he was stoned to death in a parley, Guatemozin who had the city of Mexico leveled over him before he was taken.

For the rest, there is no man even though he dare who can make beauty his own and 'so at last live,' at least there is no man better situated for that achievement than another. As Prufrock longed for his silly lady, so Kensington longs for its Hardanger dairymaid. By a mere twist of the imagination, if Prufrock only knew it, the whole world can be inverted (why else are there wars?) and the mermaids be set warbling to whoever will listen to them. Seesaw and blindman's buff converted into a sort of football.

But the summit of United States achievement, according to Mr. J.—who can discourse on Catullus—is that very beautiful poem of Eliot's, 'La Figlia Que Piange': just the right amount of everything drained through, etc., etc., etc., etc., the rhythm delicately studied and—IT CONFORMS! *ergo,* here we have 'the very fine flower of the finest spirit of the United States.'

Examined closely this poem reveals a highly refined distillation. Added to the already 'faithless' formula of yesterday we have a conscious simplicity:

> Simple and faithless as a smile and shake of the hand.

The perfection of that line is beyond cavil. Yet, in the last stanza, this paradigm, this very fine flower of U. S. art is warped out of alignment, obscured in meaning even to the point of an absolute unintelligibility by the inevitable straining after a rhyme, the very cleverness with which this straining is covered being a sinister token in itself.

> And I wonder how they should have been together!

So we have no choice but to accept the work of this fumbling conjurer.

Upon the Jepson filet Eliot balances his mushroom. It is the latest touch from the literary cuisine, it adds to the pleasant outlook from the club window. If to do this, if to be a Whistler at best, in the art of poetry, is to reach the height of poetic expression then Ezra and Eliot have approached it and *tant pis* for the rest of us.

The Adobe Indian hag sings her lullaby:

> The beetle is blind
> The beetle is blind
> The beetle is blind
> The beetle is blind, etc., etc.

and Kandinsky in his, *Ueber das Geistige in der Kunst,* sets down the following axioms for the artist:

> Every artist has to express himself.
> Every artist has to express his epoch.
> Every artist has to express the pure and eternal
> qualities of the art of all men.

So we have the fish and the bait, but the last rule holds three hooks at once—not for the fish, however.

I do not overlook De Gourmont's plea for a meeting of the nations, but I do believe that when they meet Paris will be more than slightly abashed to find parodies of the middle ages, Dante and *langue d'oc* foisted upon it as the best in United States poetry. Even Eliot, who is too fine an artist to allow himself to be exploited by a blockheaded grammaticaster, turns recently toward 'one definite false note' in his quatrains, which more nearly approach America than ever 'La Figlia Que Piange' did. Ezra Pound is a Boscan who has met his Navagiero.

One day Ezra and I were walking down a back lane in Wyncote. I contended for bread, he for caviar. I became hot. He, with fine discretion, exclaimed: 'Let us drop it. We will never agree, or come to an agreement.' He spoke then like a Frenchman, which is one who discerns.

Imagine an international congress of poets at Paris or Versailles, Remy de Gourmont (now dead) presiding, poets all speaking five languages fluently. Ezra stands up to represent U. S. verse and De Gourmont sits down smiling. Ezra begins by reading 'La Figlia Que Piange.' It would be a pretty pastime to gather into a mental basket the fruits of that reading from the minds of the ten Frenchmen present; their impressions of the sort of United States that very fine flower was picked from. After this Kreymborg might push his way to the front and read 'Jack's House.'

E. P. is the best enemy United States verse has. He is interested, passionately interested—even if he doesn't know what he is talking about. But of course he does know what he is talking about. He does not, however, know everything, not by more than half. The accordances of which Americans have the parts and the colors but not the completions before them pass beyond the attempts of his thought. It is a middle-aging blight of the imagination.

I praise those who have the wit and courage, and the conventionality, to go direct toward their vision of perfection in an objective world where the signposts are clearly marked, viz., to London. But confine them in hell for their paretic assumption that there is no alternative but their own groove.

Dear fat Stevens, thawing out so beautifully at forty! I was one day irately damning those who run to London when Stevens caught me up with his mild: 'But where in the world will you have them run to?'

Nothing that I should write touching poetry would be complete without Maxwell Bodenheim in it, even had he not said that the *Im-*

provisations were 'perfect,' the best things I had ever done; for that I place him, Janus, first and last.

Bodenheim pretends to hate most people, including Pound and Kreymborg, but that he really goes to this trouble I cannot imagine. He seems rather to me to have the virtue of self-absorption so fully developed that hate is made impossible. Due to this, also, he is an unbelievable physical stoic. I know of no one who lives so completely in his pretenses as Bogie does. Having formulated his world neither toothache nor the misery to which his indolence reduces him can make head against the force of his imagination. Because of this he remains for me a heroic figure, which, after all, is quite apart from the stuff he writes and which only concerns him. He is an Isaiah of the butterflies.

Bogie was the young and fairly well acclaimed genius when he came to New York four years ago. He pretended to have fallen in Chicago and to have sprained his shoulder. The joint was done up in a proper Sayre's dressing and there really looked to be a bona-fide injury. Of course he couldn't find any work to do with one hand so we all chipped in. It lasted a month! During that time Bogie spent a week at my house at no small inconvenience to Florence, who had two babies on her hands just then. When he left I expressed my pleasure at having had his company. 'Yes,' he replied, 'I think you have profited by my visit.' The statement impressed me by its simple accuracy as well as by the evidence it bore of that fullness of the imagination which had held the man in its tide while we had been together.

Charley Demuth once told me that he did not like the taste of liquor, for which he was thankful, but that he found the effect it had on his mind to be delightful. Of course Li Po is reported to have written his best verse supported in the arms of the Emperor's attendants and with a dancing girl to hold his tablet. He was also a great poet. Wine is merely the latchstring.

The virtue of it all is in an opening of the doors, though some rooms of course will be empty, a break with banality, the continual hardening which habit enforces. There is nothing left in me but the virtue of curiosity. Demuth puts in. The poet should be forever at the ship's prow.

An acrobat seldom learns really a new trick, but he must exercise continually to keep his joints free. When I made this discovery it started rings in my memory that keep following one after the other to this day.

I have placed the following *Improvisations* in groups, somewhat after the A.B.A. formula, that one may support the other, clarifying or enforcing perhaps the other's intention.

The arrangement of the notes, each following its poem and separated from it by a ruled line, is borrowed from a small volume of Metastasio, *Varie Poesie Dell' Abate Pietro Metastasio,* Venice, 1795.

September 1, 1918

T. S. ELIOT

Ezra Pound: His Metric and Poetry[1]

(1917)

I

'All talk on modern poetry, by people who know,' wrote Mr. Carl Sandburg in *Poetry,* 'ends with dragging in Ezra Pound somewhere. He may be named only to be cursed as wanton and mocker, poseur, trifler and vagrant. Or he may be classed as filling a niche today like that of Keats in a preceding epoch. The point is, he will be mentioned.'

This is a simple statement of fact. But though Mr. Pound is well known, even having been the victim of interviews for Sunday papers, it does not follow that his work is thoroughly known. There are twenty people who have their opinion of him for every one who has read his writings with any care. Of those twenty, there will be some who are shocked, some who are ruffled, some who are irritated, and one or two whose sense of dignity is outraged. The twenty-first critic will probably be one who knows and admires some of the poems, but who either says: 'Pound is primarily a scholar, a translator,' or 'Pound's early verse was beautiful; his later work shows nothing better than the itch for advertisement, a mischievous desire to be annoying, or a childish desire to be original.' There is a third type of reader, rare enough, who has perceived Mr. Pound for some years, who has followed his career intelligently, and who recognizes its consistency.

This essay is not written for the first twenty critics of literature, nor for that rare twenty-second who has just been mentioned, but for the admirer of a poem here or there, whose appreciation is capable of yielding him a larger return. If the reader is already at the stage where he can maintain at once the two propositions, 'Pound is merely a scholar' and 'Pound is merely a yellow journalist,' or the other two propositions, 'Pound is merely a technician' and 'Pound is merely a prophet of chaos,' then there is very little hope. But there are readers of poetry who have not yet reached this hypertrophy of the logical faculty; their attention might yet be arrested, not by an outburst of praise, but by a simple statement. The present essay aims merely at such a statement. It is not intended to be either a biographical or a critical study. It will not dilate upon 'beauties'; it is a summary account of ten years' work in poetry. The citations from reviews will perhaps stimulate the reader to form his own opinion. We do not wish to form it for him. Nor shall we enter into other phases of Mr. Pound's activity during this ten years; his writings and view on art and music; though these would take an important place in any comprehensive biography.

II

Pound's first book was published in Venice. Venice was a halting point after he had left America and before he had settled in England, and here, in 1908, *A Lume Spento* appeared. The volume is now a rarity of literature; it was published by the author and made at a Venetian press where the author was able personally to supervise the printing; on paper which was a remainder of a supply which has been used for a History of the Church. Pound left Venice in the same year, and took *A Lume Spento* with him to London. It was not to be expected that a first book of verse, published by an unknown American in Venice, should attract much attention. *The Evening Standard* has the distinction of having noticed the volume, in a review summing it up as:

> wild and haunting stuff, absolutely poetic, original, imaginative, passionate, and spiritual. Those who do not consider it crazy may well consider it inspired. Coming after the trite and decorous verse of most of our decorous poets, this poet seems like a minstrel of Provence at a suburban musical evening . . . The unseizable magic of poetry is in the queer paper volume, and words are no good in describing it.

As the chief poems in *A Lume Spento* were afterwards incorporated in *Personae,* the book demands mention only as a date in the author's history. *Personae,* the first book published in London, followed early in 1909. Few poets have undertaken the siege of London with so little backing; few books of verse have ever owed their success so purely to their own merits. Pound came to London a complete stranger, without either literary patronage or financial means. He took *Personae* to Mr. Elkin Mathews, who has the glory of having published Yeats' *Wind Among the Reeds,* and the *Book of the Rhymers' Club,* in which many of the poets of the '90s, now famous, found a place. Mr. Mathews first suggested, as was natural to an unknown author, that the author should bear part of the cost of printing. 'I have a shilling in my pocket, if that is any use to you,' said the latter. 'Well,' said Mr. Mathews, 'I want to publish it anyway.' His acumen was justified. The book was, it is true, received with opposition, but it was received. There were a few appreciative critics, notably Mr. Edward Thomas, the poet (known also as 'Edward Eastaway'; he has since been killed in France). Thomas, writing in the *English Review* (then in its brightest days under the editorship of Ford Madox Hueffer), recognized the first-hand intensity of feeling in *Personae:*

> He has . . . hardly any of the superficial good qualities of modern versifiers . . . He has not the current melancholy or resignation or unwillingness to live; nor the kind of feeling for nature which runs to minute description and decorative metaphor. He cannot be usefully compared with any living writers; . . . full of personality and with such power to express it, that from the first to the last lines of most of his poems he holds us steadily in his own pure grave, passionate world . . . The beauty of it 'In Praise of Ysolt' is the beauty of passion, sincerity and intensity, not of beautiful words and images and suggestions . . . the thought dominates the words and is greater than they are. Here 'Idyll for Glaucus' the effect is full of human passion and natural magic, without any of the phrases which a reader of modern verse would expect in the treatment of such a subject.

Mr. Scott James, in the *Daily News,* speaks in praise of his metres:

> At first the whole thing may seem to be mere madness and rhetoric, a vain exhibition of force and passion without beauty. But, as we read on, these curious metres of his seem to have a law and order of their own; the brute force of Mr.

Pound's imagination seems to impart some quality of infectious beauty to his words. Sometimes there is a strange beating of anapaests when he quickens to his subject; again and again he unexpectedly ends a line with the second half of a reverberant hexameter:

> Flesh shrouded, bearing the secret.

. . . and a few lines later comes an example of his favourite use of spondee, followed by dactyl and spondee, which comes in strangely and, as we first read it, with the appearance of discord, but afterwards seems to gain a curious and distinctive vigour:

> Eyes, dreams, lips, and the night goes.

Another line like the end of a hexameter is:

> But if e'er I come to my love's land.

But even so favourable a critic pauses to remark that:

> He baffles us by archaic words and unfamiliar metres; he often seems to be scorning the limitations of form and metre, breaking out into any sort of expression which suits itself to his mood.

and counsels the poet to 'have a little more respect for his art.'

It is, in fact, just this adaptability of metre to mood, an adaptability due to an intensive study of metre, that constitutes an important element in Pound's technique. Few readers were prepared to accept or follow the amount of erudition which entered into *Personae* and its close successor, *Exultations,* or to devote the care to reading them which they demand. It is here that many have been led astray. Pound is not one of those poets who make no demands of the reader; and the casual reader of verse, disconcerted by the difference between Pound's poetry and that on which his taste has been trained, attributes his own difficulties to excessive scholarship on the part of the author. 'This,' he will say of some of the poems in Provençal form or on Provençal subjects, 'is archaeology; it requires knowledge on the part of its reader, and true poetry does not require such knowledge.' But to display knowledge is not the same thing as to expect it on the part of the reader; and of this sort of pedantry Pound is quite free. He is, it is true, one of the most learned of poets. In America he had taken up the study of Romance Languages with the intention of teaching. After work in Spain and Italy, after pursuing the Provençal verb from Milan to Freiburg, he deserted the thesis on Lope de Vega and the Ph.D. and the professorial chair, and elected to remain in Europe. Mr. Pound has spoken out his mind from time to time on the subject of scholarship in American universities, its deadness, its isolation from genuine appreciation, and the active creative life of literature. He has always been ready to battle against pedantry. As for his own learning, he has studied poetry carefully, and has made use of his study in his own verse. *Personae* and *Exultations* show his talent for turning his studies to account. He was supersaturated in Provence; he had tramped over most of the country; and the life of the courts where the Troubadours thronged was part of his own life to him. Yet, though *Personae* and *Exultations* do exact something from the reader, they do not require a knowledge of Provençal or of Spanish or Italian. Very few people know the Arthurian legends well, or even Malory (if they did they might realize that the *Idylls of the King* are hardly more important than a parody, or a 'Chaucer retold for Children'); but no one accuses Tennyson of needing footnotes, or of superciliousness toward the uninstructed. The difference is merely in what people are prepared for; most readers could no more relate the myth of Atys correctly than they could give a biography of Bertrand de Born. It is hardly too much to say that there is no poem in these volumes of Mr. Pound which needs fuller explanation than he gives himself. What the poems do require is a trained ear, or at least the willingness to be trained.

The metres and the use of language are unfamiliar. There are certain traces of modern influence. We cannot agree with Mr. Scott James that among these are 'W. E. Henley, Kipling, Chatterton, and especially Walt Whitman'—least of all Walt Whitman. Probably there are only two: Yeats and Browning. Yeats in 'La Fraisne,' in *Personae,* for instance, in the attitude and somewhat in the vocabulary:

> I wrapped my tears in an ellum leaf
> And left them under a stone,
> And now men call me mad because I have thrown
> All folly from me, putting it aside
> To leave the old barren ways of men . . .

For Browning, Mr. Pound has always professed strong admiration (see 'Mesmerism' in *Personae*); there are traces of him in 'Cino' and 'Famam Librosque Cano,' in the same volume. But it is more profitable to comment upon the variety of metres and the original use of language.

Ezra Pound has been fathered with vers libre in English, with all its vices and virtues. The term is a loose one—any verse is called 'free' by people whose ears are not accustomed to it—in the second place, Pound's use of this medium has shown the temperance of the artist, and his belief in it as a vehicle is not that of the fanatic. He has said himself that when one has the proper material for a sonnet, one should use the sonnet form; but that it happens very rarely to any poet to find himself in possession of just the block of stuff which can perfectly be modelled into the sonnet. It is true that up to very recently it was impossible to get free verse printed in any periodical except those in which Pound had influence; and that now it is possible to print free verse (second, third or tenth-rate) in almost any American magazine. Who is responsible for the bad free verse is a question of no importance, inasmuch as its authors would have written bad verse in any form; Pound has at least the right to be judged by the success or failure of his own. Pound's vers libre is such as is only possible for a poet who has worked tirelessly with rigid forms and different systems of metric. His *Canzoni* are in a way aside from his direct line of progress; they are much more nearly studies in mediaeval appreciation than any of his other verse; but they are interesting, apart from their merit, as showing the poet at work with the most intricate Provençal forms—so intricate that the pattern cannot be exhibited without quoting an entire poem. (M. Jean de Bosschère, whose French is translated in the *Egoist,* has already called attention to the fact that Pound was the first writer in English to use five Provençal forms.) Quotation will show, however, the great variety of rhythm which Pound manages to introduce into the ordinary iambic pentameter:

> Thy gracious ways,
> O lady of my heart, have
> O'er all my thought their golden glamour cast;
> As amber torch-flames, where strange men-at-arms
> Tread softly 'neath the damask shield of night,
> Rise from the flowing steel in part reflected,
> So on my mailed thought that with thee goeth,
> Though dark the way, a golden glamour falleth.

Within the iambic limits, there are no two lines in the whole poem that have an identical rhythm.

We turn from this to a poem in *Exultations,* the 'Night Litany':

O God, what great kindness
have we done in times past
and forgotten it,
That thou givest this wonder unto us,
O God of waters?

O God of the night
What great sorrow
Cometh unto us,
That thou thus repayest us
Before the time of its coming?

There is evident, and more strongly in certain later poems, a tendency toward quantitative measure. Such a 'freedom' as this lays so heavy a burden upon every word in a line that it becomes impossible to write like Shelley, leaving blanks for the adjectives, or like Swinburne, whose adjectives are practically blanks. Other poets have manipulated a great variety of metres and forms; but few have studied the forms and metres which they use so carefully as has Pound. His ballad of the 'Goodly Fere' shows great knowledge of the ballad form:

I ha' seen him cow a thousand men
On the hills o' Galilee,
They whined as he walked out calm between
Wi' his eyes like the grey o' the sea.

Like the sea that brooks no voyaging
With the winds unleashed and free,
Like the sea that he cowed at Genseret
Wi' twey words spoke suddently.

A master of men was the Goodly Fere
A mate of the wind and sea,
If they think they ha' slain our Goodly Fere
They are fools eternally.

I ha' seen him eat o' the honey-comb,
Sin' they nailed him to the tree.

And from this we turn to a very different form in the 'Altaforte,' which is perhaps the best sestina that has been written in English:

Damn it all! all this our South stinks peace.
You whoreson dog, Papiols, come! let's to music!

I have no life save when the swords clash.
But ah! when I see the standards gold, vair, purple, opposing,
And the broad fields beneath them turn crimson,
Then howl I my heart nigh mad with rejoicing.

In hot summer have I great rejoicing
When the tempests kill the earth's foul peace,
And the lightnings from black heaven flash crimson,
And the fierce thunders roar me their music
And the winds shriek through the clouds mad, opposing,
And through all the riven skies God's swords clash.

I have quoted two verses to show the intricacy of the pattern.

The Provençal canzon, like the Elizabethan lyric, was written for music. Mr. Pound has more recently insisted, in a series of articles on the work of Arnold Dolmetsch, in the *Egoist,* on the importance of a study of music for the poet.

Such a relation between poetry and music is very different from what is called the 'music' of Shelley or Swinburne, a music often nearer to rhetoric (or the art of the orator) than to the instrument. For poetry to approach the condition of music (Pound quotes approvingly the dictum of Pater) it is not necessary that poetry should be destitute of meaning. Instead of slightly veiled and resonant abstractions, like:

Time with a gift of tears,
Grief with a glass that ran—

of Swinburne, or the mossiness of Mallarmé, Pound's verse is always definite and concrete, because he has always a definite emotion behind it.

Though I've roamed through many places,
None there is that my heart troweth
Fair as that wherein fair groweth
One whose laud here interlaces
Tuneful words, that I've essayed.
Let this tune be gently played
Which my voice herward upraises.

At the end of this poem the author appends the note:

'The form and measure are those of Piere Vidal's "*Ab l'alen tir vas me l'aire*." The song is only to be sung, and is not to be spoken.'

There are, here and there, deliberate archaisms or oddities (e.g., 'herward'); there are deliberately arbitrary images, having their place in the total effect of the poem:

> Red leaf that art blown upward and out and over
> The green sheaf of the world . . .
>
> The lotos that pours
> Her fragrance into the purple cup . . .
>
> Black lightning . . . [in a more recent poem]

but no word is ever chosen merely for the tinkle; each has always its part in producing an impression which is produced always through language. Words are perhaps the hardest of all material of art: for they must be used to express both visual beauty and beauty of sound, as well as communicating a grammatical statement. It would be interesting to compare Pound's use of images with Mallarmé's; I think it will be found that the former's, by the contrast, will appear always sharp in outline, even if arbitrary and not photographic. Such images as those quoted above are as precise in their way as:

> Sur le Noel, morte saison,
> Lorsque les loups vivent de vent . . .

and the rest of that memorable Testament.

So much for the imagery. As to the 'freedom' of his verse, Pound has made several statements in his articles on Dolmetsch which are to the point:

> Any work of art is a compound of freedom and order. It is perfectly obvious that art hangs between chaos on the one side and mechanics on the other. A pedantic insistence upon detail tends to drive out 'major form.' A firm hold on major form makes for a freedom of detail. In painting men intent on minutiae gradually lost the sense of form and form-combination. An attempt to restore this sense is branded as 'revolution.' It is revolution in the philological sense of the term . . .
>
> Art is a departure from fixed positions; felicitous departure from a norm . . .

The freedom of Pound's verse is rather a state of tension due to constant opposition between free and strict. There are not, as a matter of fact, two kinds of verse, the strict and the free; there is only a mastery which comes of being so well trained that form is an instinct and can be adapted to the particular purpose in hand.

After *Exultations* came the translation of the 'Sonnets and Ballate of Guido Cavalcanti.' It is worth noting that the writer of a long review in the *Quest*—speaking in praise of the translation, yet found fault with the author not on the ground of excessive mediaevalism, but because:

> he is concerned rather with the future than with a somewhat remote past, so that in spite of his love for the mediaeval poets, his very accomplishment as a distinctly modern poet makes against his success as a wholly acceptable translator of Cavalcanti, the heir of the Troubadours, the scholastic.

Yet the *Daily News,* in criticizing *Canzoni,* had remarked that Mr. Pound:

> seems to us rather a scholar than a poet, and we should like to see him giving his unusual talent more to direct translation from the Provençal.

and Mr. J. C. Squire (now the literary editor of the *New Statesman*), in an appreciative review in the *New Age,* had counselled the poet that he would:

> gain and not lose if he could forget all about the poets of Dante's day, their roses and their flames, their gold and their falcons, and their literary amorousness, and walk out of the library into the fresh air.

In *Ripostes* there are traces of a different idiom. Superficially, the work may appear less important. The diction is more restrained, the flights shorter, the dexterity of technique is less arresting. By romantic readers the book would be considered less 'passionate.' But there is a much more solid substratum to this book; there is more thought; greater depth, if less agitation on the surface. The effect of London is apparent; the author has become a critic of men, surveying them from a consistent and developed point of view; he is more formidable and disconcerting; in short, much more mature. That he abandons nothing of his technical skill is evident from the translation from the Anglo-Saxon, the 'Seafarer.' It is not a slight achievement to have brought to life alliterative verse: perhaps the 'Seafarer' is the only successful piece of alliterative verse ever written in modern English; alliterative verse which is not merely a clever tour de force, but which suggests the possibility of a new development of this form. Mr. Richard Aldington (whose own accomplishments as a writer of vers libre qualify him to speak) called the poem 'unsurpassed and unsurpassable,' and a writer in the *New Age* (a literary organ which has always been strongly opposed to metrical innovations) called it 'one of the finest literary works of art produced in England during the last ten years.' And the rough, stern beauty of the Anglo-Saxon, we may remark, is at the opposite pole from that of the Provençal and Italian poets to whom Pound had previously devoted his attention.

> May I for my own self song's truth reckon,
> Journey's jargon, how I in harsh days
> Hardship endured oft.

But we can notice in *Ripostes* other evidences than of versatility only; certain poems show Mr. Pound turning to more modern subjects, as in the 'Portrait d'une femme,' or the mordant epigram, 'An Object.' Many readers are apt to confuse the maturing of personality with desiccation of the emotions. There is no desiccation in *Ripostes*. This should be evident to anyone who reads carefully such a poem as 'A Girl.' We quote it entire without comment:

> The tree has entered my hands,
> The sap has ascended my arms,
> The tree has grown in my breast—
> Downward,
> The branches grow out of me, like arms.
>
> Tree you are,
> Moss you are,
> You are violets with wind above them.
> A child—so high—you are,
> And all this is folly to the world.

'The Return' is an important study in verse which is really quantitative. We quote only a few lines:

> See, they return; ah, see the tentative
> Movements, and the slow feet,
> The trouble in the pace and the uncertain
> Wavering!

Ripostes belongs to the period when Mr. Pound was being attacked because of his propaganda. He became known as the inventor of 'Imagism,' and later, as the 'High Priest of Vorticism.' As a matter of fact, the actual 'propaganda' of Mr. Pound has been very small in quantity. The impression which his personality made, however, is suggested by the following note in *Punch,* which is always a pretty reliable barometer of the English middle-class Grin:

> Mr. Welkin Mark (exactly opposite Long Jane's) begs to announce that he has secured for the English market the palpitating works of the new Montana (U.S.A.) poet, Mr. Ezekiel Ton, who is the most remarkable thing in poetry since Robert Browning. Mr. Ton, who has left America to reside for a while in London and impress his personality on English editors, publishers and readers, is by far the newest poet going, whatever other advertisements may say. He has succeeded, where all others have failed, in evolving a blend of the imagery of the unfettered West, the vocabulary of Wardour Street, and the sinister abandon of Borgiac Italy.

In 1913, someone writing to the New York *Nation* from the University of Illinois, illustrates the American, more serious, disapproval. This writer begins by expressing his objections to the 'principle of Futurism.' (Pound has perhaps done more than anyone to keep Futurism out of England. His antagonism to this movement was the first which was not due merely to unintelligent dislike for anything new, and was due to his perception that Futurism was incompatible with any principles of form. In his own words, Futurism is 'accelerated impressionism.') The writer in the *Nation* then goes on to analyse the modern 'hypertrophy of romanticism' into:

> The exaggeration of the importance of a personal emotion
> The abandonment of all standards of form
> The suppression of all evidence that a particular composition is animated by any directing intelligence.

As for the first point, here are Mr. Pound's words in answer to the question, 'Do you agree that the great poet is never emotional?'

> Yes, absolutely; if by emotion is meant that he is at the mercy of every passing mood . . . The only kind of emotion worthy of a poet is the inspirational emotion which energizes

and strengthens, and which is very remote from the everyday emotion of sloppiness and sentiment . . .

And as for the platform of Imagism, here are a few of Pound's 'Don'ts for Imagists':

> Pay no attention to the criticisms of men who have never themselves written a notable work.
>
> Use no superfluous word and no adjective which does not reveal something.
>
> Go in fear of abstractions. Don't retail in mediocre verse what has already been done in good prose.
>
> Don't imagine that the art of poetry is any simpler than the art of music or that you can please the expert before you have spent at least as much effort on the art of verse as the average piano teacher spends on the art of music.
>
> Be influenced by as many great artists as you can, but have the decency either to acknowledge the debt outright or try to conceal it.
>
> Consider the definiteness of Dante's presentation as compared with Milton's. Read as much of Wordsworth as does not seem to be unutterably dull.
>
> If you want the gist of the matter go to Sappho, Catullus, Villon when he is in the vein, Gautier when he is not too frigid, or if you have not the tongues seek out the leisurely Chaucer.
>
> Good prose will do you no harm. There is good discipline to be had by trying to write it. Translation is also good training.

The emphasis here is certainly on discipline and form. The Chicago *Tribune* recognized this as 'sound sense,' adding:

> If this is Imagism . . . we are for establishing Imagism by constitutional amendment and imprisoning without recourse to ink or paper all 'literary' ladies or gents who break any of these canons.

But other reviewers were less approving. While the writer in the *Nation,* quoted above, dreads the anarchy impending, Mr. William Archer was terrified at the prospect of hieratic formalization. Mr. Archer believes in the simple untaught muse:

> Mr. Pound's commandments tend too much to make of poetry a learned, self-conscious craft, to be cultivated by a guild of adepts, from whose austere laboratories spontaneity and simplicity are excluded . . . A great deal of the best poetry in the world has very little technical study behind it . . . There are scores and hundreds of people in England who could write this simple metre (i.e. of 'A Shropshire Lad') successfully.

To be hanged for a cat and drowned for a rat is, perhaps, sufficient exculpation.

Probably Mr. Pound has won odium not so much by his theories as by his unstinted praise of certain contemporary authors whose work he has liked. Such expressions of approval are usually taken as a grievance —much more so than any personal abuse, which is comparatively a compliment—by the writers who escape his mention. He does not say 'A., B., and C. are bad poets or novelists,' but when he says 'The work of X., Y., and Z. is in such and such respects the most important work in verse (or prose) since so and so,' then A., B., and C. are aggrieved. Also, Pound has frequently expressed disapproval of Milton and Wordsworth.

After *Ripostes* Mr. Pound's idiom has advanced still farther. Inasmuch as *Cathay*, the volume of translations from the Chinese, appeared prior to *Lustra*, it is sometimes thought that this newer idiom is due to the Chinese influence. This is almost the reverse of the truth. The late Ernest Fenollosa left a quantity of manuscripts, including a great number of rough translations (literally exact) from the Chinese. After certain poems subsequently incorporated in *Lustra* had appeared in *Poetry*, Mrs. Fenollosa recognized that in Pound the Chinese manuscripts would find the interpreter whom her husband would have wished; she accordingly forwarded the papers for him to do as he liked with. It is thus due to Mrs. Fenollosa's acumen that we have *Cathay;* it is not as a consequence of *Cathay* that we have *Lustra*. This fact must be borne in mind.

Poems afterwards embodied in *Lustra* appeared in *Poetry*, in April 1913, under the title of *Contemporanea*. They included among others 'Tenzone,' 'The Condolence,' 'The Garret,' 'Salutation the Second,' and 'Dance Figure.'

There are influences, but deviously. It is rather a gradual development of experience into which literary experiences have entered. These have not brought the bondage of temporary enthusiasms, but have liberated the poet from his former restricted sphere. There is Catullus and Martial, Gautier, Laforgue and Tristan Corbière. Whitman is certainly not an influence; there is not a trace of him anywhere; Whitman and Mr. Pound are antipodean to each other. Of *Contemporanea* the *Chicago Evening Post* discriminately observed:

> Your poems in the April *Poetry* are so mockingly, so delicately, so unblushingly beautiful that you seem to have brought back into the world a grace which (probably) never existed, but which we discover by an imaginative process in Horace and Catullus.

It was a true insight to ally Pound to the Latin, not to the Greek poets.

Certain of the poems in *Lustra* have offended admirers of the verse of the *Personae* period. When a poet alters or develops, many of his admirers are sure to drop off. Any poet, if he is to survive as a writer beyond his twenty-fifth year, must alter; he must seek new literary influences; he will have different emotions to express. This is disconcerting to that public which likes a poct to spin his whole work out of the feelings of his youth; which likes to be able to open a new volume of his poems with the assurance that they will be able to approach it exactly as they approached the preceding. They do not like that constant readjustment which the following of Mr. Pound's work demands. Thus has *Lustra* been a disappointment to some; though it manifests no falling off in technique, and no impoverishment of feeling. Some of the poems (including several of the *Contemporanea*) are a more direct statement of views than Pound's verse had ever given before. Of these poems, M. Jean de Bosschère writes:

> Everywhere his poems incite man to exist, to profess a becoming egotism, without which there can be no real altruism.
>
> I beseech you enter your life.
> I beseech you learn to say 'I'
> When I question you.
> For you are no part, but a whole;
> No portion, but a being.
>
> . . . One must be capable of reacting to stimuli for a moment, as a real, live person, even in face of as much of one's own powers as are arrayed against one; . . . The virile com-

plaint, the revolt of the poet, all which shows his emotion,—that is poetry.

> Speak against unconscious oppression,
> Speak against the tyranny of the unimaginative,
> Speak against bonds.
> Be against all forms of oppression,
> Go out and defy opinion.

This is the old cry of the poet, but more precise, as an expression of frank disgust:

> Go to the adolescent who are smothered in family.
> O, how hideous it is
> To see three generations of one house gathered together!
> It is like an old tree without shoots,
> And with some branches rotted and falling.

Each poem holds out these cries of revolt or disgust, but they are the result of his still hoping and feeling.

Let us take arms against this sea of stupidities. Pound . . . has experience of the folly of the Philistines who read his verse. Real pain is born of this stupid interpretation, and one does not realize how deep it is unless one can feel, through the ejaculations and the laughter, what has caused these wounds, which are made deeper by what he knows, and what he has lost . . .

The tone, which is at once jocund and keen, is one of Pound's qualities. Ovid, Catullus—he does not disown them. He only uses these accents for his familiars; with the others he is on the edge of paradox, pamphleteering, indeed of abuse . . .

This is the proper approach to the poems at the beginning of *Lustra*, and to the short epigrams, which some readers find 'pointless,' or certainly 'not poetry.' They should read, then, the 'Dance Figure,' or 'Near Perigord,' and remember that all these poems come out of the same man.

> Thine arms are as a young sapling under the bark;
> Thy face as a river with lights.
>
> White as an almond are thy shoulders;
> As new almonds stripped from the husk.

Or the ending of 'Near Perigord':

> Bewildering spring, and by the Auvezere
> Poppies and day's-eyes in the green email
> Rose over us; and we knew all that stream,
> And our two horses had traced out the valleys;
> Knew the low flooded lands squared out with poplars,
> In the young days when the deep sky befriended.
> And great wheels in heaven
> Bore us together . . . surging . . . and apart . . .
> Believing we should meet with lips and hands . . .
>
> There shut up in his castle, Tairiran's,
> She who had nor ears nor tongue save in her hands,
> Gone, ah, gone—untouched, unreachable!
> She who could never live save through one person,
> She who could never speak save to one person,
> And all the rest of her a shifting change,
> A broken bundle of mirrors . . . !

Then turn at once to 'To a Friend Writing on Cabaret Dancers.'

It is easy to say that the language of *Cathay* is due to the Chinese. If one looks carefully at (1) Pound's other verse, (2) other people's translations from the Chinese (e.g. Giles's), it is evident that this is not the case. The language was ready for the Chinese poetry. Compare, for instance, a passage from 'Provincia Deserta':

> I have walked
> into Perigord
> I have seen the torch-flames, high-leaping,
> Painting the front of that church,—
> And, under the dark, whirling laughter,
> I have looked back over the stream
> and seen the high building,
> Seen the long minarets, the white shafts.
> I have gone in Ribeyrac,
> and in Sarlat.
> I have climbed rickety stairs, heard talk of Croy,
> Walked over En Bertrans' old layout,
> Have seen Narbonne, and Cahors and Chalus,
> Have seen Excideuil, carefully fashioned.

with a passage from 'The River Song':

He goes out to Hori, to look at the wing-flapping storks,
He returns by way of Sei rock, to hear the new nightingales,
For the gardens at Jo-run are full of new nightingales,
Their sound is mixed in this flute,
Their voice is in the twelve pipes here.

It matters very little how much is due to Rihaku and how much to Pound. Mr. Ford Madox Hueffer has observed: 'If these are original verses, then Mr. Pound is the greatest poet of this day.' He goes on to say:

> The poems in *Cathay* are things of a supreme beauty. What poetry should be, that they are. And if a new breath of imagery and handling can do anything for our poetry, that new breath these poems bring . . .
>
> Poetry consists in so rendering concrete objects that the emotions produced by the objects shall arise in the reader . . .
>
> Where have you better rendered, or more permanently beautiful a rendering of, the feelings of one of those lonely watchers in the outposts of progress, whether it be Ovid in Hyrcania, a Roman sentinel upon the great wall of this country, or merely ourselves, in the lonely recesses of our minds, than the 'Lament of the Frontier Guard'? . . .
>
> Beauty is a very valuable thing; perhaps it is the most valuable thing in life; but the power to express emotion so that it shall communicate itself intact and exactly is almost more valuable. Of both these qualities Mr. Pound's book is very full. Therefore, I think we may say that this is much the best work he has done, for, however closely he may have followed his originals—and of that most of us have no means of judging—there is certainly a good deal of Mr. Pound in this little volume.

Cathay and *Lustra* were followed by the translations of Noh plays. The Noh are not so important as the Chinese poems (certainly not so important for English); the attitude is less unusual to us; the work is not so solid, so firm. *Cathay* will, I believe, rank with the 'Seafarer' in the future among Mr. Pound's original work; the Noh will rank among his translations. It is rather a desert after *Cathay*. There are, however, passages which, as Pound has handled them, are different both from the Chinese and from anything existent in English. There is, for example, the fine speech of the old Kagekiyo, as he thinks of his youthful valour:

> He thought, how easy this killing. He rushed with his spear-shaft gripped under his arm. He cried out, 'I am Kagekiyo of the Heike.' He rushed on to take them. He pierced through the helmet vizards of Miyanoya. Miyanoya fled twice, and again; and Kagekiyo cried: 'You shall not escape me!' He leaped and wrenched off his helmet. 'Eya!' The vizard broke and remained in his hand, and Miyanoya still fled afar, and afar, and he looked back crying in terror, 'How terrible, how heavy your arm!' And Kagekiyo called at him, 'How tough the shaft of your neck is!' And they both laughed out over the battle, and went off each his own way.

The Times Literary Supplement spoke of Mr. Pound's 'mastery of beautiful diction' and his 'cunningly rhythmical prose,' in its review of the Noh.

Even since *Lustra* Mr. Pound has moved again. This move is to the epic, of which three cantos appear in the American 'Lustra' (they have already appeared in *Poetry*—Miss Monroe deserves great honour for her courage in printing an epic poem in this twentieth century—but the version in *Lustra* is revised and is improved by revision). We will leave it as a test: when anyone has studied Mr. Pound's poems in *chronological* order, and has mastered *Lustra* and *Cathay,* he is prepared for the *Cantos*—but not till then. If the reader then fails to like them, he has probably omitted some step in his progress, and had better go back and retrace the journey.

NOTE

1. This little book was issued anonymously on November 12th, 1917 (New York, Alfred A. Knopf).

F. R. LEAVIS

The Situation at the End of World War I

(1932)

There were writing at the end of the war three poets in general acceptance who really were considerable poets: Hardy, Yeats and De la Mare. The last two were read and enjoyed by a comparatively large public; but Hardy's acceptance has, I shall offer reason for supposing, always been mainly formal (indeed, it was perhaps not yet general); so I shall leave him till last.

An account of Mr. Yeats's beginnings is an account of the poetical situation in the 'eighties and 'nineties. 'I had learned to think,' he tells us in *Essays,*[1] 'in the midst of the last phase of Pre-Raphaelitism.' And he describes his hostility to the later fashions in painting that his father favoured: 'I had seen the change coming bit by bit and its defence elaborated by young men fresh from the Paris art schools. "We must paint what is in front of us," or "A man must be of his own time," they would say, and if I spoke of Blake or Rossetti they would point out his bad drawing and tell me to admire Carolus Duran and Bastien-Lepage.' [2] But Mr. Yeats knew differently: 'In my heart I thought that only beautiful things should be painted, and that only ancient things and the stuff of dreams were beautiful.' [3]

He had made *Prometheus Unbound* his 'sacred book,' and had begun to write poetry in imitation of Shelley and Spenser, whose styles he had 'tried to mix together' in a pastoral play. His father introduced him to *The Earthly Paradise* and he came to know William Morris personally, and found him a congenial spirit. When he became one of the

From *New Bearings in English Poetry* by F. R. Leavis. Reprinted by permission of the University of Michigan Press and Chatto and Windus, Ltd.

Rhymers' Club along with Johnson, Dowson and the rest he readily adopted the current accent and idiom: 'Johnson's phrase that life is ritual expressed something that was in all our thoughts.'[4] They had their high-priest—'If Rossetti was a subconscious influence, and perhaps the most powerful of all, we looked consciously to Pater for our philosophy'—and no one exceeded Mr. Yeats in devotion. His early prose is sometimes comic in its earnestness of discipleship, in its unctuously cadenced concern for 'the transmutation of art into life':

> . . . tapestry, full of the blue and bronze of peacocks, fell over the doors, and shut out all history and activity untouched with beauty and peace; and now when I looked at my Crevelli and pondered on the rose in the hand of the Virgin, wherein the form was so delicate and precise that it seemed more like a thought than a flower, or my Francesca, so full of ghostly astonishment, I knew a Christian's ecstasy without his slavery to rule and custom. . . . I had gathered about me all gods because I believed in none, and experienced every pleasure because I gave myself to none, but held myself apart, individual, indissoluble, a mirror of polished steel.[5]

Yet if, dutifully, he 'noted also many poets and prose-writers of every age, but only those who were a little weary of life, as indeed the greatest have been everywhere,'[6] there is a recurrent theme, a recurrent tone, as, for instance, in his reference to 'simpler days before men's minds, subtilised and complicated by the romantic movement in art and literature, began to tremble on the verge of some unimagined revelation,'[7] that betrays later influences than Pater's. Pater modulates into the pronounced esotericism indicated by the title, *Rosa Alchemica;* an esotericism that was among the things brought back by Arthur Symons from Paris. The title Yeats gives to his autobiography over these years, *The Trembling of the Veil,* comes from Mallarmé, 'while,' he tells us,[8] 'Villiers de L'Isle Adam had shaped whatever in my *Rosa Alchemica* Pater had not shaped.' It is difficult for us to-day to regard *The Symbolist Movement in Art and Literature* as a work of great importance, but it was such to Yeats and his contemporaries, and this fact, together with the Continental developments that the book offers to reflect, may serve to remind us that the Victorian poetic tradition was not merely a poetic tradition, but a response to the general characteristics of the age.

'I am very religious,' says Mr. Yeats in his *Autobiographies,* 'and deprived by Huxley and Tyndall, whom I detested, of the simple-minded religion of my childhood, I had made a new religion, almost an infallible church of poetic tradition, of a fardel of stories, and of personages, and of emotions, inseparable from their first expression, passed on from generation to generation by poets and painters with some help from philosophers and theologians. I wished for a world where I could discover this tradition perpetually . . . I had even created a dogma: "Because those imaginary people are created out of the deepest instinct of man, to be his measure and his norm, whatever I can imagine those mouths speaking may be the nearest I can go to truth." ' [9] He hated Victorian science, he tells us,[10] with a 'monkish hate,' and with it he associated the Victorian world. Of *A Doll's House* he says characteristically: 'I hated the play; what was it but Carolus Duran, Bastien-Lepage, Huxley and Tyndall all over again; I resented being invited to admire dialogue so close to modern educated speech that music and style were impossible.' [11] Modern thought and the modern world, being inimical to the hopes of the heart and the delight of the senses and the imagination, are repudiated in the name of poetry—and of life.

This last clause, or the emphasis due to it, distinguishes him from the other Victorian romantics, distinguishes him too from his fellow esoterics. He may quote as epigraph to *The Secret Rose* Villiers de L'Isle Adam's 'As for living, our servants will do that for us'; but there is about his contemplated withdrawal a naïvely romantic, wholehearted practical energy that reminds us more of Shelley than of Rossetti or Pater. 'I planned a mystical Order,' he tells us in *Autobiographies,*[12] 'which should buy or hire the castle, and keep it as a place where its members could retire for a while from the world, and where we might establish mysteries like those of Eleusis and Samothrace; and for ten years to come my most impassioned thought was a vain attempt to find philosophy and create ritual for that Order. I had an unshakable conviction, arising how or whence I cannot tell, that invisible gates would open as they opened for Blake, as they opened for Swedenborg, as they opened for Boehme, and that this philosophy would find its manuals of devotion in all imaginative literature, and set before Irishmen for special manual an Irish literature which, though made by many minds, would seem the work of a single mind, and turn our places of beauty or legendary association into holy symbols.' It is not for nothing that the *Prometheus Unbound* had been his sacred book. And the latter part of this passage has another significance: Mr. Yeats was an Irishman.

But I anticipate: it is at his poetry that we should be looking by now; it is only as they arise directly out of his poetry that the considerations I have touched on in the last paragraph matter. His early verse bears out what he tells us of his beginnings. William Morris could say with truth, 'You write my sort of poetry.' [13] This (but for the last two lines, which suggest Tom Moore) Morris himself might have written:

> Autumn is over the long leaves that love us,
> And over the mice in the barley sheaves;
> Yellow the leaves of the rowan above us,
> And yellow the wet wild-strawberry leaves.
>
> The hour of the waning of love has beset us,
> And weary and worn are our sad souls now;
> Let us part, ere the season of passion forget us,
> With a kiss and a tear on thy drooping brow.

And Tennyson is behind this (though it could hardly be mistaken for Tennyson):

> 'Your eyes that once were never weary of mine
> Are bowed in sorrow under pendulous lids,
> Because our love is waning.'
>   And then she:
> 'Although our love is waning, let us stand
> By the lone border of the lake once more,
> Together in that hour of gentleness
> When the poor tired child, Passion, falls asleep:
> How far away the stars seem, and how far
> Is our first kiss, and ah, how old my heart!'

And this, with its characteristic burden, modulates into Keats and out again:

> The woods of Arcady are dead,
> And over is their antique joy;
> Of old the world on dreaming fed;
> Grey Truth is now her painted toy;
> Yet still she turns her restless head:
> But O, sick children of the world,
> Of all the many changing things
> In dreary dancing past us whirled,
> To the cracked tune that Chronos sings,

Words alone are certain good.
Where are now the warring kings,
Word be-mockers?—By the Rood
Where are now the warring kings?
An idle word is now their glory,
By the stammering schoolboy said,
Reading some entangled story:
The wandering earth herself may be,
Only a sudden flaming word,
In clanging space a moment heard,
Troubling the endless reverie.

. . .

The long poem which gave its name to the collection of 1889 (his first) might be described as Mr. Yeats's *Alastor* and *Endymion*. Its importance is what is indicated by this note: '. . . from the moment when I began the *Wanderings of Usheen* . . . my subject matter became Irish.' Mr. Yeats starts in the English tradition, but he is from the outset an Irish poet. The impulse behind the poem is the familiar one. A poet's day-dream could not easily be more cloudy and tenuous than the wistful Elysium of his Irish theme, with its 'dim, pale waters' and its realms

Where Aengus dreams from sun to sun
A Druid dream of the end of days;

and yet there is a paradoxical energy about the poem that distinguishes it from any of Morris's day-dreams: its pallor and weariness are not the exquisite aesthetic etiolation familiar to the

Poets with whom I learned my trade,
Companions of the Cheshire Cheese . . .

For Mr. Yeats's Irishness is more than a matter of using Irish themes and an Irish atmosphere. It means that his dream-world is something more than private, personal and literary; that it has, as it were, an external validation. It gives him the kind of advantage that he has in mind here:

> I filled my mind with the popular beliefs of Ireland. . . . I sought some symbolic language reaching far into the past and associated with familiar names and conspicuous hills that I might not be alone amid the obscure impressions of the senses,

> . . . or mourned the richness or reality lost to Shelley's *Prometheus Unbound* because he had not discovered in England or in Ireland his Caucasus.[14]

The advantage is put even more significantly here:

> I did not believe with my intellect that you could be carried away body and soul, but I believed with my emotions and the belief of the country people made that easy.[15]

In the world created with this kind of sanction he could preserve the 'higher reality' that his imagination and emotions craved, and without which life seemed worthless. His second collection of poems, *The Rose* (1893), frankly brings the cult of 'Eternal beauty wandering on her way,' with its Red Rose of 'an unimagined revelation,' into the world of Irish lore. But there is still a certain esoteric languor about this phase:

> Beauty grown sad with its eternity
> Made you of us, and of the dim grey sea;

and we are again reminded that we are in the 'nineties. ('With a rhythm that still echoed Morris I prayed to the Red Rose.') Here, too, belongs the unfortunate *Innisfree;* unfortunate, because it is Mr. Yeats's most anthologized poem and recalls to us his own note: 'I tried after the publication of *The Wanderings of Oisin* to write of nothing but emotion, and in the simplest language, and now I have had to go through it all, cutting out or altering passages that are sentimental from lack of thought.'[16]

But with *The Wind Among the Reeds* (1899) the dream-reality takes on a new life, and the poet inhabits it surely. And although the imagery of the Celtic Twilight is heavily worked—'pale,' 'dim,' 'shadowy,' 'desolate,' 'cloud-pale,' 'dream-heavy'—there is no languor or preciosity here. Indeed, 'passion-dimmed' and 'pale fire' are equally important in the vocabulary. For a new force has entered Mr. Yeats's poetry—love. It is mainly despairing love, and the poetry is extremely poignant. But for us the essential thing to note is how Mr. Yeats turns both exaltation and despair to the heightening of his dream-world, his substitute for the drab quotidian actuality of Huxley, Ibsen and Bastien-Lepage:

> When my arms wrap you round I press
> My heart upon the loveliness
> That long has faded from the world.

It is a perfectly sincere application of the platonic habit, but a very odd one:

> For that pale breast and lingering hand
> Come from a more dream-heavy land,
> A more dream-heavy hour than this;
> And when you sigh from kiss to kiss
> I hear white Beauty sighing, too,
> For hours when all must fade like dew,
> But flame on flame, and deep on deep,
> Throne over throne where in half sleep,
> Their swords upon their iron knees,
> Brood her high lonely mysteries.

—Transcendental Beauty, the mystical reality, belongs to a more dream-heavy hour even than that of the poetry, which is thus the dream of a dream. The syntax of the passage, curiously elusive as it is, suggests the equivocal status of Yeats's 'reality.' It is more than a literary fiction; love and the Irish background ('I believed with my emotions and the belief of the country people made that easy') enabled him to make it so. The resulting poetry has a fresh unliterary spontaneity comparable to that of Shelley's, but a spontaneity that has behind it Victorian literary sophistication instead of Wordsworth and the French Revolution, and so is the more remarkable an achievement. Yet everywhere there is a recognition, implicit in the shifting, cloudy unseizableness of the imagery, that this 'reality' must be illusory, and that even if it could be reached it would leave human longing unslaked. And this recognition is subtly turned into a strength: it validates, as it were, the idealizing fanaticism of the poetry and counterpoises the obsession with the transcendental, just as the exaltations and despairs of love are counterpoised by the sense that

> . . . time and the world are ever in flight;
> And love is less kind than the grey twilight,
> And hope is less dear than the dew of the morn.

The poetry of *The Wind Among the Reeds,* then, is a very remarkable achievement: it is, though a poetry of withdrawal, both more subtle and more vital than any pure product of Victorian romanticism. We might, as bearing on the strength it was to Mr. Yeats to be Irish, note further that with the Irish element in the poetry was associated a public and practical aim. Early and long service in the cause of a national renaissance, and, above all, of a national theatre, might be expected to turn even a poet of the Victorian dream-world into something else; and Mr. Yeats devoted to the Irish cause rare qualities of character and intelligence. Yet his resolute attempt upon the drama serves mainly to bring out the prepotence of the tradition he started in. His plays repudiate the actual world as essentially as his incantatory lyrics and his esoteric prose repudiate it. 'As for living, our servants will do that for us' —the epigraph might cover all three. A drama thus devoted to a 'higher reality' of this kind could hardly exhibit the dramatic virtues.

How insidious was the atmosphere that poets of his time breathed comes out in his critical writings. 'Tragic art,' he will tell us in a discussion of poetic drama,[17] 'passionate art, the drowner of dykes, moves us by setting us to reverie, by alluring us almost to the intensity of trance.' And so obviously acute is the critical intelligence at work that we try to find much virtue in that 'intensity.' Yet 'reverie' and 'trance' are dangerous words, and in the critic who announces that 'All art is dream,' [18] we fear the worst. 'Drama,' he will tell us again, [19] 'is a means of expression . . . and the dramatist is as free to choose where he has a mind to, as the poet of *Endymion,* or as the painter of Mary Magdalene at the door of Simon the Pharisee. So far from the discussion of our interests and the immediate circumstances of our life being the most moving to the imagination, it is what is old and far-off that stirs us the most deeply.' Reading this, we may applaud the challenge to Shaw and Ibsen, but we more than suspect the kind of dream he has in mind. Indeed, we know, for the bent is inveterate. 'Every writer,' he says,[20] 'even every small writer, who has belonged to the great tradition, has had his dream of an impossibly noble life, and the greater he is, the more does it seem to plunge him into some beautiful or bitter reverie.' This comes from an essay on Synge, and of Synge's rhythm he says: [21] 'It is essential, for it perfectly fits the drifting emotion, the dreaminess, the vague yet measureless desire, for which he would create a dramatic form. It blurs definition, clear edges, everything that comes from the will, it turns imagination from all that is of the present, like a gold background in a religious picture, and it strengthens in every emotion whatever comes to it from far off, from brooding memory and dangerous hope.'

Mr. Yeats the dramatist, that is, remains the poet who had 'learned to think in the midst of the last phase of Pre-Raphaelitism.' He differs from the Victorian romantics in the intensity with which he seeks his 'higher reality.' This difference we have attributed to his being Irish;

but it will not do to let this explanation detract from his rare distinction of mind and spirit. 'I had an invincible conviction . . . that the gates would open as they opened for Blake . . .'—this is not the anaemic reverie of Victorian romanticism: to nurse a luxury of defeat was not in Mr. Yeats's character; he was too strong and alive. He fought, paradoxical as it may seem, for victory, and it was not through any lack of intelligence or contempt for it that he found such a Quixotry possible. 'The dream-world of Morris,' he writes,[22] 'was as much the antithesis of daily life as with other men of genius, but he was never conscious of the antithesis and so knew nothing of intellectual suffering.' Mr. Yeats knew much of intellectual suffering, for the antithesis was terribly present to him: he had a magnificent mind, and less than the ordinary man's capacity for self-deception. 'It is so many years before one can believe enough in what one feels even to know what the feeling is,' he notes,[23] exemplifying that rare critical self-awareness of which the signs abound in his *Autobiographies* and *Essays*. 'I ceased to read modern books that were not books of imagination,' he reports;[24] but he read these last, one might almost say, in a scientific spirit. Indeed, his dealings with spiritualism, magic, theosophy, dream and trance were essentially an attempt to create an alternative science. The science of Huxley and Tyndall he had rejected in the name of imagination and emotion, but he had an intelligence that would not be denied. He exhibits for us the inner struggle of the nineteenth-century mind in an heroic form—heroic, and, because of the inevitable frustration and waste, tragic. 'From the moment when these speculations grew vivid,' he tells us,[25] 'I had created for myself an intellectual solitude.'

We may relate to this lonely struggle a remarkable change that manifests itself in Mr. Yeats's poetry when we compare *The Wind Among the Reeds* (1899) with *The Green Helmet* (1912). It is hard to believe that the characteristic verse of the later volume comes from the same hand as that of the earlier. The new verse has no incantation, no dreamy, hypnotic rhythm; it belongs to the actual, waking world, and is in the idiom and movement of modern speech. It is spare, hard and sinewy and in tone sardonic, expressing the bitterness and disillusion of a man who has struggled and been frustrated:

> The fascination of what's difficult
> Has dried the sap out of my veins, and rent
> Spontaneous joy and natural content
> Out of my heart.

It is true that the struggles he specifies here belong to the practical world, to 'this blind, bitter land':

> My curse on plays
> That have to be set up in fifty ways,
> On the day's war with every knave and dolt,
> Theatre business, management of men.

But this is not the whole tale; and if it is time that has brought this maturity, there are reasons why this maturity should be so sour.

> Though leaves are many, the root is one;
> Through all the lying days of my youth
> I swayed my leaves and flowers in the sun;
> Now I may wither into the truth

runs a quatrain headed *The Coming of Wisdom with Time*. Actuality has conquered:

> The holy centaurs of the hill are vanished;
> I have nothing but the embittered sun;
> Banished heroic mother moon and vanished,
> And now that I have come to fifty years
> I must endure the timid sun.

It is like an awakening out of drugs, a disintoxication; the daylight seems thin and cruel. He recognizes the real world, but it is too late; his strength has been wasted, and habit forbids readjustment.

> But I grow old among dreams,
> A weather-worn, marble triton
> Among the streams.

The poem this last comes from has for title *Men Improve with the Years,* which suggests well enough Mr. Yeats's peculiar bitterness, a bitterness mingled with scorn for humanity.[26]

Nevertheless, the poetry of this later phase is a remarkable positive achievement: Mr. Yeats was strong enough to force a triumph out of defeat. He speaks of a beauty

> . . . won
> From bitterest hours,

and it is this he serves instead of the cloudy glamour of the *Celtic Twilight;* a

. . . beauty like a tightened bow, a kind
That is not natural in an age like this.

The verse, in its rhythm and diction, recognizes the actual world, but holds against it an ideal of aristocratic fineness. It is idiomatic, and has the run of free speech, being at the same time proud, bare and subtle. To pass from the earlier verse to this is something like passing from Campion to Donne. The parallel, indeed, is not so random as it might seem. At any rate, Donne's name in connection with a poet capable of passionate intellectual interests, who from such a start achieved such a manner, leads us to reflect that if the poetic tradition of the nineteenth century had been less completely unlike the Metaphysical tradition Mr. Yeats might have spent less of his power outside poetry. The speculation is perhaps idle, but it calls attention to the way in which his verse developed into something that has the equivalent of certain seventeenth-century qualities. His use of the idiom and rhythm of speech is not all:

Plato thought nature but a spume that plays
Upon a ghostly paradigm of things;
Solider Aristotle played the taws
Upon the bottom of a king of kings;
World-famous golden-thighed Pythagoras
Fingered upon a fiddle stick or strings
What a star sang and careless Muses heard:
Old clothes upon old sticks to scare a bird.

—This (and the context more than bears out the promise of flexibility and variety of tone) is surely rather like seventeenth-century 'wit'; more like it than anything we expect to find in modern verse outside the work of certain post-war poets—poets who exhibit no completer escape from the Victorian poetical. The volume it comes from, indeed, appeared after the war. But *The Tower* (1928) merely develops the manner of *The Green Helmet* (1912), *Responsibilities* (1914), and *The Wild Swans at Coole* (1919).

In *The Tower* Mr. Yeats achieves a kind of ripeness in disillusion. The scorn so pervasive before is gone: his tragic horror at the plight of Ireland (as, for instance, in *Meditations in Time of Civil War*) is something different and more generous. There is indeed bitterness, but it is not the sterile kind. His raging against

Decrepit age that has been tied to me
As to a dog's tail

goes with a sense of ardent vitality:

. . . Never had I more
Excited, passionate, fantastical
Imagination, nor an ear and eye
That more expected the impossible;

and the excitement is as apparent as the bitterness in this poetry of the last phase. Each gives value to the other. He is capable of excitement, for instance, about the 'abstract things' that he describes as a *pis aller*. He turns with a pang from the varied 'sensual music' of the world, but he is drawn positively towards the 'monuments of unaging intellect':

An aged man is but a paltry thing,
A tattered coat upon a stick, unless
Soul clap its hands and sing, and louder sing
For every tatter in its mortal dress.

This (though there is always an ironical overtone) is the voice of one who knows intellectual passion. He does not deceive himself about what he has lost, but the regret itself becomes in the poetry something positive. His implications, in short, are very complex; he has achieved a difficult and delicate sincerity, an extraordinarily subtle poise.

What, then, it might be asked after this account of Mr. Yeats's achievement, is there to complain of? Does it really show that the tradition in the nineteenth century might with advantage have been other than it was? If he had to struggle with uncongenial circumstances, has not every great artist had to do so; and did he not, by admission, make triumphs of them? Mr. Yeats himself gives the answer in the bitter sense of waste he expresses characteristically, in the latest work as elsewhere. His poetry is little more than a marginal comment on the main activities of his life. No one can read his *Autobiographies* and his *Essays* without being struck by the magnificent qualities of intelligence and character he exhibits. His insight shows itself in his analysis of his own case, an analysis that suggests at the same time the complete achievement he was fated to miss: 'In literature,' he wrote in 1906,[27] 'partly from the lack of that spoken word which knits us to the normal man, we have lost in personality, in our delight in the whole man—blood, imagination, intellect, running together—but have found a new delight in essences, in states of mind, in pure imagination, in all that comes to us most easily in elaborate music.' And we find him remarking in *Autobiographies* [28] 'how small a fragment of our own nature can be brought to perfect expression, nor that even but with great toil, in a much divided civilisation.' Again,[29] by quoting his own verse, he explicitly relates the general reflection to his own case: 'Nor did I understand as yet how little that Unity [of Being], however wisely sought, is possible without a Unity of Culture in class or people that is no longer possible at all.

> The fascination of what's difficult
> Has dried the sap out of my veins, and rent
> Spontaneous joy and natural content
> Out of my heart.'

At this point it might be commented that Mr. Yeats turns out an unfortunate witness to have called. What he testifies against is not the poetic tradition, but the general state of civilization and culture; a state which, he contends, makes waste inevitable for the sensitive. But he implies nothing against holding that if the poetic tradition had been different, as it might very well have been, he might have brought more of himself to expression. Writing of the early Synge he says [30] significantly: '. . . the only language that interested him was that conventional language of modern poetry which has begun to make us all weary. I was very weary of it, for I had finished *The Secret Rose*, and felt how it had separated my imagination from life, sending my Red Hanrahan, who should have trodden the same roads with myself, into some undiscoverable country.' It is true that he successfully dropped this 'conventional language of modern poetry'; but early habits of mind and sensibility are not so easily dropped. The incidental confession he makes in a later poem—

> I have no speech but symbol, the pagan speech I made
> Amid the dreams of youth—

has much significance. For 'symbol' in his technical sense—symbol drawn from his cult of magic and the Hermetic sciences—is commonly felt to be an unsatisfactory element in his later verse, and to come from an unfortunate habit of mind. And his magic and occultism, of course, are the persistent and intense expression of the bent that expressed itself first of all in the 'conventional language of modern poetry':

—. . . The abstract joy,
The half read wisdom of daemonic images,
Suffice the aging man as once the growing boy.

Disillusion and waste were indeed inevitable; but not in the form in which Mr. Yeats suffered them. They might have been more significant. For Victorian romanticism was not the only possible answer to those modern conditions that Mr. Yeats deplores. If it were, poetry would cease to matter. Adult minds could no longer take it seriously. Losing all touch with the finer consciousness of the age it would be, not only irresponsible, but anaemic, as, indeed, Victorian poetry so commonly is. Mr. Yeats's career, then, magnificent as the triumph was that he compelled out of defeat, is a warning. It illustrates the special disability of the poet in the last century, and impressively bears out my argument about the poetic tradition. And it cannot be repeated. No Englishman in any case could have profited by the sources of strength open to Mr. Yeats as an Irishman, and no such source is open to any one now. No serious poet could propose to begin again where Mr. Yeats began.

Both Mr. Yeats's genius and the advantages he enjoyed as an Irishman are brought out by comparison with Walter de la Mare. Mr. de la Mare says of children, 'Between their dream and their reality looms no impassable abyss'; and his poetry is peculiarly related to childhood. He has written poems from the child's consciousness; poems that recapture the child's mentality as he describes it. These are very remarkable; but still more interesting from our point of view are the poems (by far the greater in number) in which the adult is present.

Very old are the woods;
  And the buds that break
Out of the briar's boughs,
  When March winds wake,
So old with their beauty are—
  Oh, no man knows
Through what wild centuries
  Roves back the rose.

—The well-known poem this comes from is frankly a piece of enchantment; the rhythm is a potent spell, and the appropriate hush establishes itself in the first line. Any one faced with describing the effect would set down 'glamour,' 'mystery,' 'wonder' among the key-words. Perhaps only a reader familiar with Mr. de la Mare would note that in this first stanza he is playing in particular upon reminiscences of the Sleeping Beauty. The suggestion may seem unnecessary, but it is not random, and it serves to point the observation that in general, however serious his intention, he is exploiting the fairytale stratum of experience.

He is often more urgently concerned with Time than in *All That's Past,* but he always uses, with varying degrees of subtlety, the same means of enchantment. 'Time dreams' [31] in his poetry:

> Our hearts stood still in the hush
> Of an age gone by.

He thus uses

> The skill of words to sweeten despair
> Of finding consolation where
> Life has but one dark end.

He is frank about the aim of his poetry and about his relations with childhood. He finds the modern world, with its science and its civilization, as uncongenial as Mr. Yeats found it. It is impossible either to conquer it or to become reconciled with it, so—

> What can the tired heart say
> Which the wise of the world have made dumb?
> Save to the lonely dreams of a child,
> Return again, come!

His poetry, then, is by admission a poetry of withdrawal, cultivating a special poetical 'reality': his world of dreams, nourished upon memories of childhood, is for him the intrinsically poetical.

But this is too simple an account of Mr. de la Mare. It suggests that he is always frank about what he is doing; or rather, it does not suggest the subtlety that attends upon the frankness. An adult can hardly, even in his poetry, always turn his back so directly and simply upon the world. Mr. de la Mare, as a matter of fact, is a great deal given to the contemplation of that human plight which desolates him. There is something odd about the manner of contemplation. He exhibits a characteristic subtlety that can fairly be called legerdemain: he produces, by the surreptitious suggestions of his verse, an effect contradictory to what he says. 'His utterance,' says Mr. I. A. Richards,[32] who acutely diagnoses the trick, 'in spite of his words, becomes not at all a recognition of this indifference [of the Universe to human desires], but voices instead an impulse to turn away, to forget it, to seek shelter in the warmth of his own familiar thicket of dream, not to stay out in the wind.' He has formed habits that make impossible such a frank recognition of the human plight as he seems to offer. The apparent recognition is not the frankness it pretends to be but an insidious enhancement of the spell, which is the more potent to soothe and lull when it seems to be doing the opposite. Mr. de la Mare's poetry cultivates subtler (and more dangerous) illusions than it professes.

The working of this surreptitious magic may be readily examined in *The Ghost,* a poem which contrasts conveniently with Hardy's *The Voice*. The explicit burden is the emptiness of utter loss:

> Nought but vast sorrow was there—
> The sweet cheat gone.

'Sweet cheat' fairly describes the poem. The sleight begins in the first stanza, and by the end of the second the spell is established. The reference to 'dreams' is not as negative as it pretends to be. The grave when described as 'the roots of the dark thorn' suggests dew, fragrance and fairies rather than death and decay. The fairy-tale atmosphere is fortified obviously by the second stanza, so that, though the third is glamourless enough, a strong habituation in the reader still survives to seize on any magic potentialities. They come in a most interesting way:

> Silence. Still faint on the porch
> Brake the flames of the stars.

The night-sky starlit (exemplifying the general tendency of his imagery to repeat itself far too much) recurs with notable frequency in Mr. de la Mare's verse: it lends itself peculiarly to his habitual legerdemain. Here its open function is to suggest the desolate, pygmy helplessness of man. But another set of associations also hangs about the starlit night; those avowed, for example, in *The Unchanging:* enchantment, mystery, elves, fragrance, dew; and these make their effect here. In such ways is produced the equivocal sweet poignancy characteristic of Mr. de la Mare.

To be able to work so insidious a spell as successfully as he does in his best poetry is to be in some measure a victim of it oneself. How unsatisfactory an addiction it is his own history as a poet suggests. His last serious volume of verse, *The Veil,* came out as long ago as 1921, and its contents seem to explain adequately why no later volume has followed. In *The Veil* the poignancy turns into a duller, heavier desolation; the dream takes on a nightmare quality; and the unwholesomeness of the fantasy-habit is, implicitly and explicitly, admitted. It is as if the disastrous consequences of drug-addiction were being recognized. Life seems now not tragic but flat and empty. 'I have come to the end of things,' says a character in one of his stories,[33] describing this state. 'For me, the spirit, the meaning—whatever you like to call it—has vanished, gone clean out of the world, out of what we call reality.' And this character plays with the idea of a pair of enchanted spectacles that should give meaning back to the world. But the magic has ceased to work for Mr. de la Mare. In such a poem as *The Familiar* he laments his estrangement from the spirit that wove the spell; and the spell in his poetry is visibly failing. When he essays a new kind of poetry that shall be solidly based in the actual world (see, for instance, *In the Dock*) he is capable of a gross badness shocking in so exquisite a poet. It seems, then, reasonable to suppose that he will not produce much more good poetry.

Since *The Veil* he has devoted himself to prose. His more successful stories derive from the same kind of impulse as his poetry. But the sharp critical awareness that guides him in his poetry does not function here: his main talent is not engaged. And success (or the absence of it) in prose is not the decisive local manifestation that it is in poetry. His continuing to seek the 'poetical' in prose has little bearing on our conclusion regarding the poet.

He has written a remarkable bulk of exquisite minor poetry (admirably appreciated by Mr. Middleton Murry in *Countries of the Mind*); but even this cloys, and the moral of his career can hardly be doubtful. He is the belated last poet of the Romantic tradition, and is already as remote as Poe from the present of poetry.

The Veil, where Mr. de la Mare recognizes the vanity of his poetic evasions, shows curious traces of Hardy's influence. It is as if, in his straits, he had gone for help to the poet most unlike himself, strong where he is weak. For Hardy may be so described: in their characteristic manners, the two poets offer an extreme contrast. The contrast comes out fairly in the two poems already suggested for comparison; for if *The Ghost* does not, as *The Voice* does, represent the very summit of its author's achievement, it is nevertheless characteristic. *The Voice* really does evoke the emptiness of utter loss, exhibiting that purity of recognition which is Hardy's strength. His verse has no incantation: it does what it says, and presents barely the fact recognized by a mind more than commonly responsible and awake.

The omission of Hardy from my summing-up of the nineteenth century has no doubt provoked some comment. Here, surely, is a Victorian poet who wrote great poetry evincing an intense concern, not with a world of day-dreams, but with the human situation as it appeared in the light of modern thought. And no one would accuse him of optimistic or sentimental evasions or insincerities. But Hardy did not begin to publish poetry until the very end of the last century, when some of his best still remained to write; so that, even if he had been a potential influence, he did not impinge until it was too late. By then the stresses incident to the most sensitive and aware had shifted and altered. Hardy is now seen to be truly a Victorian—a Victorian in his very pessimism, which implies positives and assurances that have vanished. He inhabits a solid world, with the earth firm under his feet. He knows what he wants, what he values and what he is. It is characteristic that he should end one of his best poems, *After a Journey*, a poem of retrospect in old age:

> . . . bring me here again!
> I am just the same as when
> Our days were a joy, and our paths through flowers.

Compare this poem, or any other of Hardy's best, with, say, one of Edward Thomas's (a representative modern sensibility), and Hardy's solidity appears archaic.

Hardy is a naïve poet of simple attitudes and outlook. The attitudes and outlook were the product of what Mr. I. A. Richards in *Science and Poetry* [34] calls 'the neutralization of nature.' Hardy's greatness lies in the integrity with which he accepted the conclusion, enforced, he believed, by science, that nature is indifferent to human values, in the completeness of his recognition, and in the purity and adequacy of his response. He was betrayed into no heroic postures. He felt deeply and consistently, he knew what he felt, and, in his best poems, communicated it perfectly. But there was little in his technique that could be taken up by younger poets, and developed in the solution of their own problems. His originality was not of the kind that goes with a high degree of critical awareness: it went, indeed, with a naïve conservatism. 'In his opinion,' reports Mr. Robert Graves in his superb autobiography, *Goodbye to All That*, '*vers libre* could come to nothing in England. "All we can do is to write on the old themes in the old styles, but try to do a little better than those who went before us."' And again: ' "Why!" he said, "I have never in my life taken more than three, or perhaps four drafts for a poem. I am afraid of it losing its freshness." '[35] It is all in keeping with this precritical innocence that his great poems should be only a very small proportion of his abundant output.

How small a proportion this is does not seem to be generally recognized: his rank as a major poet rests upon a dozen poems. These are lost among a vast bulk of verse interesting only by its oddity and idiosyncrasy, and as illustrating the habits that somehow become strength in his great poetry. The main impulse behind his verse is too commonly the mere impulse to write verse: 'Any little old song will do,'[36] as he says. And, often to the lilt of popular airs, with a gaucherie compounded of the literary, the colloquial, the baldly prosaic, the conventionally poetical, the pedantic and the rustic, he industriously turns out his despondent anecdotes, his 'life's little ironies,' and his meditations upon a deterministic universe and the cruel accident of sentience. The inveterate bent is significant, even if the verse has little intrinsic value: Hardy's great poetry is a triumph of character. Now and then, when he is deeply moved (the impulse is usually a poignant memory), this bent and these habits suddenly appear as strength, the oddity becomes an intensely personal virtue. *The Voice,* for instance, seems to start dangerously with a crude popular lilt, but this is turned into a subtle movement by the prosaic manner of the content, a manner that elsewhere would have been Hardy's characteristic gaucherie:

> Can it be you that I hear? Let me view you, then,
> Standing as when I drew near to the town
> Where you would wait for me: yes, as I knew you then,
> Even to the original air-blue gown!

By the end of this second stanza the bare matter-of-fact statement has already subdued the rhythm; the shift of stress on the rime ('viéw you then, 'knew you thén') has banished the jingle from it. In the next stanza we have an instance of his odd word-coinages:

> Or is it only the breeze, in its listlessness
> Travelling across the wet mead to me here,
> You being ever dissolved to existlessness,
> Heard no more again far or near?

—'Existlessness' (which he afterwards, and, I think, unfortunately, changed to 'wan wistlessness') is a questionable word, a characteristic eccentricity of invention; and yet here it sounds right. The touch that there may still be about the poem of what would normally have been rustic stiffness serves as a kind of guarantee of integrity. And then there is the exquisite modulation into the last stanza.[37]

Hardy needed a strong, immediately personal impulse before he could transform his innocent awkwardness in this way. The mere impulse to versify reflections and anecdotes in illustration of his 'philosophy' was not enough. His great poems, as a rule, start immediately out of his own remembered past, and are particular evocations of utter loss, the blindness of chance, the poignancy of love and its helplessness, and the cruelty of time. Such poems are *After a Journey, The Voice, The Self-Unseeing, A Broken Appointment, Neutral Tones, During Wind and Rain*. That the setting, explicit or implied, is generally rural is a point of critical significance. Hardy was a countryman, and his brooding mind stayed itself habitually upon the simple pieties, the quiet rhythms and the immemorial ritual of rustic life.

It is very largely in terms of the absence of these, or of any equivalent, that the environment of the modern poet must be described. Urban conditions, a sophisticated civilization, rapid change and the mingling of cultures have destroyed the old rhythms and habits, and nothing adequate has taken their place. The result is a sense, apparent in the serious literature of the day, that meaning and direction have vanished. These conditions, of course, partly account for the weakness of poetry in recent times: we should not expect them to favour a confident flow of creative power. But they are far from accounting wholly for the plight revealed by the Georgian anthologies and the latter part of *The Oxford Book of Victorian Verse*. Mr. Eliot's poetry is proof enough of this.

The almost unvarying way in which anthologists chose from his insignificant poems and leave out the great ones suggests that Hardy's repute is mainly conventional, and that he is little read, or, at any rate, little appreciated. It would no doubt be possible to point to his influence in contemporary verse, but a Hardy who can blend with the *Shropshire Lad* is not important.

Besides Hardy, Yeats and de la Mare there was supposed to be a galaxy of Georgian poets. The Georgian movement may fairly be considered as a 'movement,' since it can be considered as little else. 'There was,' writes [38] its promoter, E. M., 'a general feeling among the younger poets that modern English poetry was very good, and sadly neglected by readers.' There may very reasonably have been a general feeling that the Victorian Age was now well over, and that it was time we had a modern English poetry. At any rate, E. M. and his friends did their best, and were warmly supported by the public; *Georgian Poetry,* 1911–1912, the first of the series, came out, and 'its success outran our wildest hopes.' From then on, in general acceptance, the age was a poetical one. The 'corporate flavour' of the movement is admirably described by Mr. Middleton Murry in an article [39] that he wrote in 1919. There is no need to examine again the false simplicity that he diagnoses; but it may be worth remarking in this connection that a glance through *Poems of To-day* (two anthologies unfortunately much used in schools) suggests that R. L. Stevenson was a stronger influence as a poet than one would have thought possible. The *Shropshire Lad,* on the other hand, was a predestined victim.

But although Mr. Drinkwater may perhaps claim to be the representative Georgian poet the dominating figure is Rupert Brooke. Brooke had considerable personal force and became himself an influence. He energized the Garden-Suburb ethos with a certain original talent and the vigour of a prolonged adolescence. His verse exhibits a genuine sensuousness rather like Keats's (though more energetic) and something that is rather like Keats's vulgarity with a Public School accent. It is odd to be reminded that he was once thought 'complex'—almost a metaphysical poet:

> Mrs. Cornford tried to engage me in a controversy over the book—she and her school. They are known as the Heart-criers, because they believe all poetry ought to be short, simple, naïve, and a cry from the heart; the sort of thing an inspired only child might utter if it was in the habit of posing to its elders. They object to my poetry as unreal, affected, complex, 'literary,' and full of long words.[40]

The uneasiness betrayed here at the prevailing simplesse is not the same thing as complete awareness and immunity. And Brooke's 'complexity' amounts to little more than an inhibiting adolescent self-consciousness in an ironical disguise. In its extremer forms it is painfully embarrassing. The marks of his enthusiasm for Donne (who was then 'coming in') serve only to bring out how safe he was from such an influence. He borrows, for instance, 'scattering-bright' [41] and converts it to the vague uses of his adjectival glamour—'the inenarrable godhead of delight.' The adolescent zest with which he pursues this glamour (the intrinsically 'poetical') has, together with his adolescent yearning for a maternal bosom where

> Surely a shamed head may bow down at length,

ensured him a real popularity unknown to the other Georgians (except the present Poet Laureate).

He was in the first days of his fame notorious for his 'unpleasantness,' his 'realism.'

> I'm (of course) unrepentant about the 'unpleasant' poems. I don't claim great credit for the *Channel Passage:* but the point of it was (or should have been!) 'serious.' There are common and sordid things—situations or details—that may suddenly bring all tragedy, or at least the brutality of actual emotions, to you. I rather grasp relievedly at them, after I've beaten vain hands in the rosy mists of poets' experiences.[42]

—But he was always, as he reveals here, poetical at heart: the last sentence is especially betraying.

A grasping in a like spirit at common and sordid things was frequent among Georgian poets: there was a determination to modernize poetry, and bring it closer to life. The present Poet Laureate above all earned notoriety by his 'realism.' He crossed Yeats with Kipling, and managed to reconcile the sordid facts of life with the rosy mists of poets' experiences. If we bracket him with Flecker who, standing for Parnassian perfection, was supposed to stand apart, we make, from our point of view, the adequate comment on both: no serious effort of readjustment is involved in passing from one to the other. Later more subtle attempts to escape from the poetical were made by Mr. J. C. Squire, but they served only to call attention to the bankruptcy of tradition and the difficulty of a new start.

Opposed to these there is a group, including some respected names, that might be called academic. They are conscientious and persevering, and one of them at least has been admitted to immortality in the *Oxford* series; but it is hard to believe that they are read. Then there is the central group of Georgian poets who specialize in country sentiment and the pursuit of Beauty in her more chaste and subtle guises. Mr. Middleton Murry has dealt with them adequately in the article already mentioned, and there is no need to enumerate them here. But two poets commonly included deserve to be distinguished from the group: Mr. Edmund Blunden, because he has some genuine talent and is an interesting case, and Edward Thomas, an original poet of rare quality, who has been associated with the Georgians by mischance.

The Shepherd, Mr. Blunden's first mature book of verse, marked him out from the crowd as a poet who, though he wrote about the country, drew neither upon the *Shropshire Lad* nor upon the common stock of Georgian country sentiment. There was also in his poems, for all the rich rusticity, the homespun texture that is their warrant, a frank literary quality: Mr. Blunden was concerned with art; he was making something. And—what gives them their interest for us—corresponding to this quality in the form there appeared to be something in the intention behind: out of the traditional life of the English countryside, especially as relived in memories of childhood, Mr. Blunden was creating a world—a world in which to find refuge from adult distresses; above all, one guessed, from memories of the war.

The later volumes, *English Poems, Retreat* and *Near and Far,* confirm this conjecture. The peculiar poise that constituted Mr. Blunden's distinction has proved difficult to maintain. On the one hand, the stress behind the pastoral quiet becomes explicit in poems dealing with mental conflict, hallucination and war-experience; on the other, the literary quality becomes, in other poems, more pronounced, and takes the form of frank eighteenth-century echoes, imitations and reminiscences:

> From *Grongar Hill* the thrush and flute awoke,
> And Green's mild sibyl chanted from her oak,
> Along the vale sang Collins' hamlet bell.

Mr. Blunden's retreat is to an Arcadia that is rural England seen, not only through memories of childhood, but through poetry and art (see *A Favourite Scene recalled on looking at Birket Foster's Landscapes*).[43] Eighteenth-century meditative pastoral is especially congenial to him; he takes over even the nymphs and their attendant classicalities. On the other hand, he attempts psychological subtleties, and deals directly with his unease, his inner tensions, instead of implying them, as before, in the solidity of his created world. And it becomes plain that he is attempting something beyond him. The earlier method suited his powers and enabled him better to harmonize his various interests. There was something satisfying about the dense richness of his pastoral world, with its giant puff-balls and other evocations of animistic fancy instead of nymphs and naiads. But in the later volumes there is a serious instability in Mr. Blunden's art. The visionary gleam, the vanished glory, the transcendental suggestion remain too often vague, the rhythms stumble, and the characteristic packed effects are apt to degenerate into cluttered obscurity.

The development, however, it seems reasonable to suppose, was inevitable. A poet serious enough to impose his pastoral world on us at all could hardly rest in it. Indeed, it was interesting very largely for the same reasons that his tenure of it was precarious. The achievement in any case is a very limited one, but a limited achievement of that kind is notable to-day. Mr. Blunden's best poetry, with its simple movements, its conventional decorum, and its frank literary quality, is the poetry of simple pieties (even if the undertones that accompany the use-hallowed mannerisms and the weathered gravity are not so simple). He was able to be, to some purpose, conservative in technique, and to draw upon the eighteenth century, because the immemorial rural order that is doomed was real to him. It is not likely that a serious poet will be traditional in that way again. Mr. Blunden is at any rate significant enough to show up the crowd of Georgian pastoralists.

Only a very superficial classification could associate Edward Thomas with Mr. Blunden, or with the Georgians at all. He was a very original poet who devoted great technical subtlety to the expression of a distinctively modern sensibility. His art offers an extreme contrast with Mr. Blunden's. Mr. Blunden's poems are frankly 'composed,' but Edward Thomas's seem to happen. It is only when the complete effect has been registered in the reader's mind that the inevitability and the exquisite economy become apparent. A characteristic poem of his has the air of being a random jotting down of chance impressions and sensations, the record of a moment of relaxed and undirected consciousness. The diction and movement are those of quiet, ruminative speech. But the unobtrusive signs accumulate, and finally one is aware that the outward scene is accessory to an inner theatre. Edward Thomas is concerned with the finer texture of living, the here and now, the ordinary moments, in which for him the 'meaning' (if any) resides. It is as if he were trying to catch some shy intuition on the edge of consciousness that would disappear if looked at directly. Hence, too, the quietness of the movement, the absence of any strong accent or gesture.

October, for instance, opens with the Autumn scene:

> The green elm with the one great bough of gold
> Lets leaves into the grass slip, one by one,—
> The short hill grass, the mushrooms small milk-white,
> Harebell and scabious and tormentil,
> That blackberry and gorse, in dew and sun,
> Bow down to; and the wind travels too light

To shake the fallen birch leaves from the fern;
The gossamers wander at their own will.

The exquisite particularity of this distinguishes it from Georgian 'nature poetry.' But the end of the poem is not description; Edward Thomas's concern with the outer scene is akin to Mrs. Woolf's: unobtrusively the focus shifts [44] and we become aware of the inner life which the sensory impressions are notation for.

. . . and now I might
As happy be as earth is beautiful,
Were I some other or with earth could turn
In alternation of violet and rose,
Harebell and snowdrop, at their season due,
And gorse that has no time not to be gay.
But if this be not happiness,—who knows?
Some day I shall think this a happy day . . .

A whole habit of sensibility is revealed at a delicate touch.

October illustrates the method; but to see how subtly Thomas can use it (it is a method of exploration at the same time as one of expression) one must go to such a poem as *Old Man*. It starts with a quiet meditation upon 'Lad's-love or Old Man,' the 'hoar-green feathery herb almost a tree.' It passes to the child

Who plucks a feather from the door-side bush
Whenever she goes in or out of the house.

From the child there is an inevitable transition to the most poignant of realizations:

Not a word she says;
And I can only wonder how much hereafter
She will remember, with that bitter scent,
Of garden rows, and ancient damson trees
Topping a hedge, a bent path to a door,
A low thick bush beside the door, and me
Forbidding her to pick.
As for myself,
Where first I met the bitter scent is lost.
I, too, often shrivel the grey shreds,
Sniff them and think and sniff again and try
Once more to think what it is I am remembering,

Always in vain. I cannot like the scent,
Yet I would rather give up others more sweet,
With no meaning, than this bitter one.

I have mislaid the key. I sniff the spray
And think of nothing; I see and I hear nothing;
Yet seem, too, to be listening, lying in wait
For what I should, yet never can, remember:
No garden appears, no path, no hoar-green bush
Of Lad's-Love, or Old Man, no child beside,
Neither father nor mother, nor any playmate;
Only an avenue, dark, nameless, without end.

A phrase in the last passage—'listening, lying in wait for what I should, yet never can, remember'—describes admirably Thomas's characteristic manner. The intimations that come, as here, are not of immortality. And it would be difficult to set off Hardy's Victorian solidity better than by contrast with this poem. A far larger proportion of Thomas's work is good than of Hardy's (indeed, the greater part of the collected poems is good), but, on the other hand, one cannot say 'great' confidently of anything of Thomas's, as one can of Hardy's best. The very fidelity with which Thomas records the modern disintegration, the sense of directionlessness

—How dreary-swift, with naught to travel to,
Is Time— [45]

implies limitations. But Thomas's negativeness has nothing in common with the vacuity of the Georgians. He was exquisitely sincere and sensitive, and he succeeded in expressing in poetry a representative modern sensibility. It was an achievement of a very rare order, and he has not yet had the recognition he deserves.

Edward Thomas died in the war. The war, besides killing poets, was supposed at the time to have occasioned a great deal of poetry; but the names of very few 'war-poets' are still remembered. Among them the most current (if we exclude Brooke's) is Siegfried Sassoon's. But though his verse made a wholesome immediate impact it hardly calls for much attention here. Wilfrid Owen was really a remarkable poet, and his verse is technically interesting. His reputation is becoming well established. Isaac Rosenberg was equally remarkable, and even more interesting technically, and he is hardly known. But Edward Thomas, Owen and Rosenberg together, even if they had been properly recognized at once, could hardly have constituted a challenge to the ruling poetic fashions.

The opposition to the Georgians was already at the time in question (just after the war) Sitwellism. But the Sitwells belong to the history of publicity rather than of poetry. 'Imagism,' indeed, had been initiated before the war. One cannot say, of course, what part it may have played in the development of poets who are now important, but in itself it amounted to little more than a recognition that something was wrong with poetry.[46]

The debilitated nineteenth-century tradition, then, continued without serious challenge, and there had been nothing to suggest seriously a new start.

At this point it becomes necessary to mention a name that has been left out of the foregoing account—that of Bridges. It is not altogether an accident that no occasion should have presented itself of mentioning him before. If one does not care for him one may say that he is so academic that there is no reason why he should come anywhere in particular. If one feels respectful one may compare him to Landor and say that he is aloof. As for *The Testament of Beauty*, it had not come out at the time in question. That, however, is perhaps not excuse enough for shirking comment. I will say, then, that the description of it quoted from Mr. Squire in my introductory chapter seems to me fair. Bridges spent upon this crowning work of his life the profit of a life of technical experimenting, but his kind of interest in technique was not a kind that can concern us much in this study. In *The Testament of Beauty* the technique and the matter are, as it were, parallel interests, having no essential relation with each other. The book is a disquisition in verse that is scholarly and original, but dead. Whatever the commercial success of *The Testament of Beauty* may prove, it is not the existence of a keen and discriminating public for poetry.

NOTES

1. P. 430.
2. *Autobiographies,* pp. 141–2.
3. *Ibid.,* p. 101.
4. *Ibid.,* p. 372.
5. *Early Poems and Stories,* p. 466.
6. *Ibid.,* p. 485.
7. *Ibid.,* p. 471.
8. *Autobiographies,* p. 395.

9. *Autobiographies,* pp. 142–3.
10. *Ibid.*, p. 101.
11. *Ibid.*, p. 343.
12. *Ibid.*, p. 314.
13. *Autobiographies,* p. 181.
14. *Essays,* p. 434.
15. *Autobiographies,* p. 96.
16. *Early Poems and Stories,* p. v.
17. *Essays,* p. 303.
18. *Ibid.*, p. 354.
19. *Ibid.*, p. 352.
20. *Ibid.*, p. 376.
21. *Ibid.*, p. 371.
22. *Autobiographies,* p. 175.
23. *Ibid.*, p. 127.
24. *Ibid.*, p. 328.
25. *Ibid.*, p. 326.
26. Cf. We had fed the heart on fantasies.
    The heart's grown brutal from the fare,
    More substance in our enmities
    Than in our love;

    The Tower, p. 27.
27. *Essays,* p. 330. Cf. 'Donne could be as metaphysical as he pleased . . . because he could be as physical as he pleased.'—*Autobiographies,* p. 402.
28. p. 364.
29. *Autobiographies,* p. 436.
30. *Essays,* p. 370.
31. See *The Unchanging.*
32. *Science and Poetry,* p. 71.
33. *The Connoisseur,* p. 142.
34. See particularly sections v. and vii.
35. 'His taste in literature was certainly most unexpected. Once when Lawrence [T. E.] had ventured to say something disparaging against Homer's *Iliad* he protested: "Oh, but I admire the *Iliad* greatly. Why, it's in the *Marmion* class!" Lawrence could not at first believe that Hardy was not making a little joke.'—*Goodby to All That,* p. 378.
36. *'Any little old song'* (*Human Shows and Far Phantasies*).
37. I am assuming that every one interested enough to read this account will have opened the volume of Hardy at the poem.
38. *Memoir* (p. lxxvi) prefixed to *The Collected Poems of Rupert Brooke.* This *Memoir* tells one a great deal about the spirit of the movement.
39. *Present Condition of English Poetry* in *Aspects of Literature.*
40. *Memoir,* p. lxviii.
41. See *Beauty and Beauty* and Donne's *Aire and Angels.*

42. *Memoir,* p. lxvii.
43. *Retreat.*
44. I am assuming again that the interested reader will turn up the poem.
45 *The Glory.* (*Collected Poems.*)
46. 'I desired to see English become at once more colloquial and more exact, verse more fluid and more exacting of its practitioners, and above all, as I have said, that it should be realized that poetry, as it were dynamically, is a matter of rendering, not comment. You must not say: "I am so happy"; you must behave as if you were happy. . . .'—*Imagist Anthology,* 1930, Ford Madox Ford, pp. xiii–xiv. 'It legitimatized free verse, cleared the air of musty artifice and shallow sentiment, revived the clarity and conciseness of the Greeks, substituted classical objectivity for romantic cosmicism, demonstrated the effectiveness of the Oriental miniature, and accomplished a rewedding of the intellect and the emotions.'—*Ibid.*, Glenn Hughes, p. xvii.

W. B. YEATS

Introduction to *The Oxford Book of Modern Verse*

I

I have tried to include in this book all good poets who have lived or died from three years before the death of Tennyson to the present moment, except some two or three who belong through the character of their work to an earlicr period. Even a long-lived man has the right to call his own contemporaries modern. To the generation which began to think and read in the late eighties of the last century the four poets whose work begins this book were unknown, or, if known, of an earlier generation that did not stir its sympathy. Gerard Hopkins remained unpublished for thirty years. Fifty-odd years ago I met him in my father's studio on different occasions, but remember almost nothing. A boy of seventeen, Walt Whitman in his pocket, had little interest in a querulous, sensitive scholar. Thomas Hardy's poems were unwritten or unpublished. Robert Bridges seemed a small Victorian poet whose poetry, published in expensive hand-printed books, one could find behind glass doors in the houses of wealthy friends. I will consider the genius of these three when the development of schools gives them great influence. Wilfred Blunt one knew through the report of friends as a fashionable amateur who had sacrificed a capacity for literature and the visible arts to personal adventure. Some ten years had to pass before anybody understood that certain sonnets, lyrics, stanzas of his were permanent in our literature. A young man, London bred or just arrived there, would have felt himself repelled by the hard, cold energy of Henley's verse, called it rhetoric, or associated it in some way with

From *The Oxford Book of Modern Verse*. Reprinted by permission of The Clarendon Press, Oxford, Miss Anne Yeats and Mr. M. B. Yeats.

that propaganda whereby Henley, through the vehicle of a weekly review and a magazine that were financial failures, had turned the young men at Oxford and Cambridge into imperialists. 'Why should I respect Henley?' said to me Clement Shorter. 'I sell two hundred thousand copies a week of *The Sphere;* the circulation of *The National Observer* fell to two hundred at the end.' Henley lay upon the sofa, crippled by his incautious youth, dragged his body, crutch-supported, between two rooms, imagining imperial might. For a young man, struggling for expression, despairing of achievement, he remained hidden behind his too obvious effectiveness. Nor would that young man have felt anything but contempt for the poetry of Oscar Wilde, considering it an exaggeration of every Victorian fault, nor, except in the case of one poem not then written, has time corrected the verdict. Wilde, a man of action, a born dramatist, finding himself overshadowed by old famous men he could not attack, for he was of their time and shared its admirations, tricked and clowned to draw attention to himself. Even when disaster struck him down it could not wholly clear his soul. Now that I have plucked from the *Ballad of Reading Gaol* its foreign feathers it shows a stark realism akin to that of Thomas Hardy, the contrary to all its author deliberately sought. I plucked out even famous lines because, effective in themselves, put into the Ballad they become artificial, trivial, arbitrary; a work of art can have but one subject.

Yet each man kills the thing he loves,
   By each let this be heard,
Some do it with a bitter look,
   Some with a flattering word.
The coward does it with a kiss,
   The brave man with a sword!

Some kill their love when they are young,
   And some when they are old;
Some strangle with the hands of Lust,
   Some with the hands of Gold:
The kindest use a knife, because
   The dead so soon grow cold.

I have stood in judgement upon Wilde, bringing into the light a great, or almost great poem, as he himself had done had he lived; my work gave me that privilege.

II

All these writers were, in the eye of the new generation, in so far as they were known, Victorian, and the new generation was in revolt. But one writer, almost unknown to the general public—I remember somebody saying at his death 'no newspaper has given him an obituary notice'—had its entire uncritical admiration, Walter Pater. That is why I begin this book with the famous passage from his essay on Leonardo da Vinci. Only by printing it in *vers libre* can one show its revolutionary importance. Pater was accustomed to give each sentence a separate page of manuscript, isolating and analysing its rhythm; Henley wrote certain 'hospital poems,' not included in this book, in *vers libre*, thinking of his dramatic, everyday material, in that an innovator, but did not permit a poem to arise out of its own rhythm as do Turner and Pound at their best and as, I contend, Pater did. I shall presently discuss the meaning of this passage which dominated a generation, a domination so great that all over Europe from that day to this men shrink from Leonardo's masterpiece as from an over-flattered woman. For the moment I am content to recall one later writer:

> O wha's been here afore me, lass,
> And hoo did he get in?

The revolt against Victorianism meant to the young poet a revolt against irrelevant descriptions of nature, the scientific and moral discursiveness of *In Memoriam*—'When he should have been broken-hearted,' said Verlaine, 'he had many reminiscences'—the political eloquence of Swinburne, the psychological curiosity of Browning, and the poetical diction of everybody. Poets said to one another over their black coffee—a recently imported fashion—'We must purify poetry of all that is not poetry,' and by poetry they meant poetry as it had been written by Catullus, a great name at that time, by the Jacobean writers, by Verlaine, by Baudelaire. Poetry was a tradition like religion and liable to corruption, and it seemed that they could best restore it by writing lyrics technically perfect, their emotion pitched high, and as Pater offered instead of moral earnestness life lived as 'a pure gem-like flame' all accepted him for master.

But every light has its shadow, we tumble out of one pickle into another, the 'pure gem-like flame' was an insufficient motive; the sons of men who had admired Garibaldi or applauded the speeches of John Bright, picked Ophelias out of the gutter, who knew exactly what they wanted and had no intention of committing suicide. My father gave these young men their right name. When I had described a supper with Count Stenbock, scholar, connoisseur, drunkard, poet, pervert, most charming of men, he said 'they are the Hamlets of our age.' Some of these Hamlets went mad, some drank, drinking not as happy men drink but in solitude, all had courage, all suffered public opprobrium—generally for their virtues or for sins they did not commit—all had good manners. Good manners in written and spoken word were an essential part of their tradition—'Life,' said Lionel Johnson, 'must be a ritual'; all in the presence of women or even with one another put aside their perplexities; all had gaiety, some had wit:

Unto us they belong,
To us the bitter and gay,
Wine and woman and song.

Some turned Catholic—that too was a tradition. I read out at a meeting of The Rhymers' Club a letter describing Meynell's discovery of Francis Thompson, at that time still bedded under his railway arch, then his still unpublished *Ode to the Setting Sun*. But Francis Thompson had been born a Catholic; Lionel Johnson was the first convert; Dowson adopted a Catholic point of view without, I think, joining that church, an act requiring energy and decision.

Occasionally at some evening party some young woman asked a poet what he thought of strikes, or declared that to paint pictures or write poetry at such a moment was to resemble the fiddler Nero, for great meetings of revolutionary Socialists were disturbing Trafalgar Square on Sunday afternoons; a young man known to most of us told some such party that he had stood before a desk in an office not far from Southampton Row resolved to protect it with his life because it contained documents that would hang William Morris, and wound up by promising a revolution in six months. Shelley must have had some such immediate circle when he wrote to friends urging them to withdraw their money from the Funds. We poets continued to write verse and read it out at 'The Cheshire Cheese,' convinced that to take part in such movements would be only less disgraceful than to write for the newspapers.

III

Then in 1900 everybody got down off his stilts; henceforth nobody drank absinthe with his black coffee; nobody went mad; nobody committed suicide; nobody joined the Catholic church; or if they did I have forgotten.

Victorianism had been defeated, though two writers dominated the movement who had never heard of that defeat or did not believe in it; Rudyard Kipling and William Watson. Indian residence and associations had isolated the first, he was full of opinions, of politics, of impurities—to use our word—and the word must have been right, for he interests a critical audience to-day by the grotesque tragedy of 'Danny Deever,' the matter but not the form of old street ballads, and by songs traditional in matter and form like the *'St. Helena Lullaby.'* The second had reached maturity before the revolt began, his first book had been published in the early eighties. 'Wring the neck of rhetoric,' Verlaine had said, and the public soon turned against William Watson, forgetting that at his best he had not rhetoric but noble eloquence. As I turn his pages I find verse after verse read long ago and still unforgettable, this to some journalist who, intoxicated perhaps by William Archer's translations from Ibsen, had described, it may be, some lyric elaborating or deepening its own tradition as of 'no importance to the age':

> Great Heaven! When these with clamour shrill
>   Drift out to Lethe's harbour bar
> A verse of Lovelace shall be still
>   As vivid as a pulsing star:

this, received from some Miltonic cliff that had it from a Roman voice:

> The august, inhospitable, inhuman night
> Glittering magnificently unperturbed.

IV

Conflict bequeathed its bias. Folk-song, unknown to the Victorians as their attempts to imitate it show, must, because never declamatory or eloquent, fill the scene. If anybody will turn these pages attending to poets born in the 'fifties, 'sixties, and 'seventies, he will find how successful are their folk-songs and their imitations. In Ireland, where still lives almost undisturbed the last folk tradition of western Europe, the songs of Campbell and Colum draw from that tradition their themes, return to it, and are sung to Irish airs by boys and girls who have never heard the names of the authors; but the reaction from rhetoric, from all that was prepense and artificial, has forced upon these writers now and again, as upon my own early work, a facile charm, a too soft simplicity. In England came like temptations. The *Shropshire Lad* is worthy of its fame, but a mile further and all had been marsh. Thomas Hardy, though his work lacked technical accomplishment, made the necessary correction through his mastery of the impersonal objective scene. John Synge brought back masculinity to Irish verse with his harsh disillusionment, and later, when the folk movement seemed to support vague political mass excitement, certain poets began to create passionate masterful personality.

V

We remembered the Gaelic poets of the seventeenth and early eighteenth centuries wandering, after the flight of the Catholic nobility, among the boorish and the ignorant, singing their loneliness and their rage; James Stephens, Frank O'Connor made them symbols of our pride:

> The periwinkle, and the tough dog-fish
> At eventide have got into my dish!
> The great, where are they now! the great had said—
> This is not seemly, bring to him instead
> That which serves his and serves our dignity—
> And that was done.
>
> I am O'Rahilly:
> Here in a distant place I hold my tongue,
> Who once said all his say, when he was young!

I showed Lady Gregory a few weeks before her death a book by Day Lewis. 'I prefer,' she said, 'those poems translated by Frank O'Connor because they come out of original sin.' A distinguished Irish poet said a month back—I had read him a poem by Turner—'We cannot become philosophic like the English, our lives are too exciting.' He was not thinking of such passing episodes as civil war, his own imprisonment, but of an always inflamed public opinion that made sonnet or play almost equally perilous; yet civil war has had its effect. Twelve years ago Oliver Gogarty was captured by his enemies, imprisoned in a deserted house on the edge of the Liffey with every prospect of death. Pleading a natural necessity he got into the garden, plunged under a shower of revolver bullets and as he swam the ice-cold December stream promised it, should it land him in safety, two swans. I was present when he fulfilled that vow. His poetry fits the incident, a gay, stoical—no, I will not withhold the word—heroic song. Irish by tradition and many ancestors, I love, though I have nothing to offer but the philosophy they deride, swashbucklers, horsemen, swift indifferent men; yet I do not think that is the sole reason, good reason though it is, why I gave him considerable space, and think him one of the great lyric poets of our age.

VI

We have more affinity with Henley and Blunt than with other modern English poets, but have not felt their influence; we are what we are because almost without exception we have had some part in public life in a country where public life is simple and exciting. We are not many; Ireland has had few poets of any kind outside Gaelic. I think England has had more good poets from 1900 to the present day than during any period of the same length since the early seventeenth century. There are no predominant figures, no Browning, no Tennyson, no Swinburne, but more than I have found room for have written two, three, or half a dozen lyrics that may be permanent.

During the first years of the century the best known were celebrators of the country-side or of the life of ships; I think of Davies and of Masefield; some few wrote in the manner of the traditional country ballad. Others, descended not from Homer but from Virgil, wrote what the young communist scornfully calls 'Belles-lettres': Binyon when at his best, as I think, of Tristram and Isoult: Sturge Moore of centaurs, amazons, gazelles copied from a Persian picture: De la Mare short lyrics that carry us back through *Christabel* or *Kubla Khan*.

> Through what wild centuries
> Roves back the rose?

The younger of the two ladies who wrote under the name of 'Michael Field' made personal lyrics in the manner of Walter Savage Landor and the Greek anthology.

None of these were innovators; they preferred to keep all the past their rival; their fame will increase with time. They have been joined of late years by Sacheverell Sitwell with his *Canons of Giant Art,* written in the recently rediscovered 'sprung verse,' his main theme changes of colour, or historical phase, in Greece, Crete, India. *Agamemnon's*

Tomb, however, describes our horror at the presence and circumstance of death and rises to great intensity.

VII

Robert Bridges seemed for a time, through his influence on Laurence Binyon and others less known, the patron saint of the movement. His influence—practice, not theory—was never deadening; he gave to lyric poetry a new cadence, a distinction as deliberate as that of Whistler's painting, an impulse moulded and checked like that in certain poems of Landor, but different, more in the nerves, less in the blood, more birdlike, less human; words often commonplace made unforgettable by some trick of speeding and slowing,

> A glitter of pleasure
> And a dark tomb,

or by some trick of simplicity, not the impulsive simplicity of youth but that of age, much impulse examined and rejected:

> I heard a linnet courting
>   His lady in the spring!
> His mates were idly sporting,
>   Nor stayed to hear him sing
>   His song of love.—
> I fear my speech distorting
>   His tender love.

Every metaphor, every thought a commonplace, emptiness everywhere, the whole magnificent.

VIII

A modern writer is beset by what Rossetti called 'the soulless self-reflections of man's skill'; the more vivid his nature, the greater his boredom, a boredom no Greek, no Elizabethan, knew in like degree, if at all. He may escape to the classics with the writers I have just described, or with much loss of self-control and coherence force language against its will into a powerful, artificial vividness. Edith Sitwell has a temperament of a strangeness so high-pitched that only through this artifice could it find expression. One cannot think of her in any other age or country. She has transformed with her metrical virtuosity traditional metres reborn not to be read but spoken, exaggerated metaphors into mythology, carrying them from poem to poem, compelling us to go backward to some first usage for the birth of the myth; if the storm suggest the bellowing of elephants, some later poem will display 'The elephant trunks of the sea.' Nature appears before us in a hashish-eater's dream. This dream is double; in its first half, through separated metaphor, through mythology, she creates, amid crowds and scenery that suggest the Russian Ballet and Aubrey Beardsley's final phase, a perpetual metamorphosis that seems an elegant, artificial childhood; in the other half, driven by a necessity of contrast, a nightmare vision like that of Webster, of the emblems of mortality. A group of writers have often a persistent image. There are 'stars' in poem after poem of certain writers of the 'nineties as though to symbolize an aspiration towards what is inviolate and fixed; and now in poem after poem by Edith Sitwell or later writers are 'bones'—'the anguish of the skeleton,' 'the terrible Gehenna of the bone'; Eliot has:

> No contact possible to flesh
> Allayed the fever of the bone.

and Eleanor Wylie, an American whose exquisite work is slighter than that of her English contemporaries because she has not their full receptivity to the profound hereditary sadness of English genius:

> Live like the velvet mole:
> Go burrow underground,
>
> And there hold intercourse
> With roots of trees and stones,
> With rivers at their source
> And disembodied bones.

Laurence Binyon, Sturge Moore, knew nothing of this image; it seems most persistent among those who, throwing aside tradition, seek something somebody has called 'essential form' in the theme itself. A fairly well-known woman painter in September drew my house, at that season almost hidden in foliage; she reduced the trees to skeletons as though it were mid-winter, in pursuit of 'essential form.' Does not intellectual analysis in one of its moods identify man with that which is most persistent in his body? The poets are haunted once again by the Elizabethan image, but there is a difference. Since Poincaré said 'space is the creation of our ancestors,' we have found it more and more difficult to separate ourselves from the dead when we commit them to the grave; the bones are not dead but accursed, accursed because unchanging.

> The small bones built in the womb
> The womb that loathed the bones
> And cast out the soul.

Perhaps in this new, profound poetry, the symbol itself is contradictory, horror of life, horror of death.

IX

Eliot has produced his great effect upon his generation because he has described men and women that get out of bed or into it from mere habit; in describing this life that has lost heart his own art seems grey, cold, dry. He is an Alexander Pope, working without apparent imagination, producing his effects by a rejection of all rhythms and metaphors used by the more popular romantics rather than by the discovery of his own, this rejection giving his work an unexaggerated plainness that has the effect of novelty. He has the rhythmical flatness of The *Essay on Man*—despite Miss Sitwell's advocacy I see Pope as Blake and Keats saw him—later, in *The Waste Land,* amid much that is moving in symbol and imagery there is much monotony of accent:

> When lovely woman stoops to folly and
> Paces about her room again, alone,
> She smooths her hair with automatic hand,
> And puts a record on the gramophone.

I was affected, as I am by these lines, when I saw for the first time a painting by Manet. I longed for the vivid colour and light of Rousseau and Courbet, I could not endure the grey middle-tint—and even to-day Manet gives me an incomplete pleasure; he had left the procession. Nor can I put the Eliot of these poems among those that descend from Shakespeare and the translators of the Bible. I think of him as satirist rather than poet. Once only does that early work speak in the great manner:

> The host with someone indistinct
> Converses at the door apart,
> The nightingales are singing near
> The Convent of the Sacred Heart,

And sang within the bloody wood
When Agamemnon cried aloud,
And let their liquid siftings fall
To stain the stiff dishonoured shroud.

Not until *The Hollow Men* and *Ash-Wednesday,* where he is helped by the short lines, and in the dramatic poems where his remarkable sense of actor, chanter, scene, sweeps him away, is there rhythmical animation. Two or three of my friends attribute the change to an emotional enrichment from religion, but his religion compared to that of John Gray, Francis Thompson, Lionel Johnson in *The Dark Angel,* lacks all strong emotion; a New England Protestant by descent, there is little self-surrender in his personal relation to God and the soul. *Murder in the Cathedral* is a powerful stage play because the actor, the monkish habit, certain repeated words, symbolize what we know, not what the author knows. Nowhere has the author explained how Becket and the King differ in aim; Becket's people have been robbed and persecuted in his absence; like the King he demands strong government. Speaking through Becket's mouth Eliot confronts a world growing always more terrible with a religion like that of some great statesman, a pity not less poignant because it tempers the prayer book with the results of mathematical philosophy.

Peace. And let them be, in their exaltation.
They speak better than they know, and beyond your understanding,
They know and do not know, that acting is suffering
And suffering is action. Neither does the actor suffer
Nor the patient act. But both are fixed
In an eternal action, an eternal patience
To which all must consent that it may be willed
And which all must suffer that they may will it,
That the pattern may subsist, for the pattern is the action
And the suffering, that the wheel may turn and still
Be forever still.

X

Ezra Pound has made flux his theme; plot, characterization, logical discourse, seem to him abstractions unsuitable to a man of his generation. He is mid-way in an immense poem in *vers libre* called for the moment *The Cantos,* where the metamorphosis of Dionysus, the descent of Odysseus into Hades, repeat themselves in various disguises, alway in association with some third that is not repeated. Hades may become the hell where whatever modern men he most disapproves of suffer damnation, the metamorphosis petty frauds practised by Jews at Gibraltar. The relation of all the elements to one another, repeated or unrepeated, is to become apparent when the whole is finished. There is no transmission through time, we pass without comment from ancient Greece to modern England, from modern England to medieval China; the symphony, the pattern, is timeless, flux eternal and therefore without movement. Like other readers I discover at present merely exquisite or grotesque fragments. He hopes to give the impression that all is living, that there are no edges, no convexities, nothing to check the flow; but can such a poem have a mathematical structure? Can impressions that are in part visual, in part metrical, be related like the notes of a symphony; has the author been carried beyond reason by a theoretical conception? His belief in his own conception is so great that since the appearance of the first Canto I have tried to suspend judgement.

When I consider his work as a whole I find more style than form; at moments more style, more deliberate nobility and the means to convey it than in any contemporary poet known to me, but it is constantly interrupted, broken, twisted into nothing by its direct opposite, nervous obsession, nightmare, stammering confusion; he is an economist, poet, politician, raging at malignants with inexplicable characters and motives, grotesque figures out of a child's book of beasts. This loss of self-control, common among uneducated revolutionists, is rare—Shelley had it in some degree—among men of Ezra Pound's culture and erudition. Style and its opposite can alternate, but form must be full, sphere-like, single. Even where there is no interruption he is often content, if certain verses and lines have style, to leave unabridged transitions, unexplained ejaculations, that make his meaning unintelligible. He has great influence, more perhaps than any contemporary except Eliot, is probably the source of that lack of form and consequent obscurity which is the main defect of Auden, Day Lewis, and their school, a school which, as will presently be seen, I greatly admire. Even where the style is sustained throughout one gets an impression, especially when he is writing in *vers libre,* that he has not got all the wine into the bowl, that he is a brilliant improvisator translating at sight from an unknown Greek masterpiece:

See, they return; ah, see the tentative
Movements, and the slow feet,
The trouble in the pace and the uncertain
Wavering!

See, they return, one, and by one,
With fear, as half-awakened;
As if the snow should hesitate
And murmur in the wind,
        and half turn back;

These were the Wing'd-with-awe,
        Inviolable.
Gods of the winged shoe!
With them the silver hounds,
        sniffing the trace of air!

XI

When my generation denounced scientific humanitarian pre-occupation, psychological curiosity, rhetoric, we had not found what ailed Victorian literature. The Elizabethans had all these things, especially rhetoric. A friend writes 'all bravado went out of English literature when Falstaff turned into Oliver Cromwell, into England's bad conscience'; but he is wrong. Dryden's plays are full of it. The mischief began at the end of the seventeenth century when man became passive before a mechanized nature; that lasted to our own day with the exception of a brief period between Smart's *Song to David* and the death of Byron, wherein imprisoned man beat upon the door. Or I may dismiss all that ancient history and say it began when Stendhal described a masterpiece as a 'mirror dawdling down a lane.' There are only two long poems in Victorian literature that caught public attention; *The Ring and the Book* where great intellect analyses the suffering of one passive soul, weighs the persecutor's guilt, and *The Idylls of the King* where a poetry in itself an exquisite passivity is built about an allegory where a characterless king represents the soul. I read few modern novels, but I think I am right in saying that in every novel that has created an intellectual fashion from Huysmans's *La Cathédrale* to Ernest Hemingway's *Farewell to Arms,* the chief character is a mirror. It has sometimes seemed of late years, though not in the poems I have selected for this book, as if the poet could at any moment write a poem by re-cording the fortuitous scene or thought, perhaps it might be enough to put into some fashionable rhythm—'I am sitting in a chair, there are three dead flies on a corner of the ceiling.'

Change has come suddenly, the despair of my friends in the 'nineties part of its preparation. Nature, steel-bound or stone-built in the nineteenth century, became a flux where man drowned or swam; the moment had come for some poet to cry 'the flux is in my own mind.'

XII

It was Turner who raised that cry, to gain upon the instant a control of plastic material, a power of emotional construction, Pound has always lacked. At his rare best he competes with Eliot in precision, but Eliot's genius is human, mundane, impeccable, it seems to say 'this man will never disappoint, never be out of character. He moves among objects for which he accepts no responsibility, among the mapped and measured.' Generations must pass before man recovers control of event and circumstance; mind has recognized its responsibility, that is all; Turner himself seems the symbol of an incomplete discovery. After clearing up some metaphysical obscurity he leaves obscure what a moment's thought would have cleared; author of a suave, sophisticated comedy he can talk about 'snivelling majorities'; a rich-natured friendly man he has in his satirical platonic dialogue *The Aesthetes* shot upon forbidden ground. The first romantic poets, Blake, Coleridge, Shelley, dazed by new suddenly opening vistas, had equal though different inconsistencies. I think of him as the first poet to read a mathematical equation, a musical score, a book of verse, with an equal understanding; he seems to ride in an observation balloon, blue heaven above, earth beneath an abstract pattern.

We know nothing but abstract patterns, generalizations, mathematical equations, though such the havoc wrought by newspaper articles and government statistics, two abstractions may sit down to lunch. But what about the imagery we call nature, the sensual scene? Perhaps we are always awake and asleep at the same time; after all going to bed is but habit; is not sleep by the testimony of the poets our common mother? In *The Seven Days of the Sun,* where there is much exciting thought, I find:

> But to me the landscape is like a sea
> The waves of the hills

And the bubbles of bush and flower
And the springtide breaking into white foam!

It is a slow sea,
Mare tranquillum,
And a thousand years of wind
Cannot raise a dwarf billow to the moonlight.

But the bosom of the landscape lifts and falls
With its own leaden tide,
That tide whose sparkles are the lilliputian stars.

It is that slow sea
That sea of adamantine languor,
Sleep!

I recall Pater's description of the Mona Lisa; had the individual soul of da Vinci's sitter gone down with the pearl divers or trafficked for strange webs? or did Pater foreshadow a poetry, a philosophy, where the individual is nothing, the flux of *The Cantos* of Ezra Pound, objects without contour as in *Le Chef-d'œuvre Inconnu,* human experience no longer shut into brief lives, cut off into this place and that place, the flux of Turner's poetry that within our minds enriches itself, redreams itself, yet only in seeming—for time cannot be divided? Yet one theme perplexes Turner, whether in comedy, dialogue, poem. Somewhere in the middle of it all da Vinci's sitter had private reality like that of the Dark Lady among the women Shakespeare had imagined, but because that private soul is always behind our knowledge, though always hidden it must be the sole source of pain, stupefaction, evil. A musician, he imagines Heaven as a musical composition, a mathematician, as a relation of curves, a poet, as a dark, inhuman sea.

The sea carves innumerable shells
Rolling itself into crystalline curves
The cressets of its faintest sighs
Flickering into filagreed whorls,
Its lustre into mother-of-pearl
Its mystery into fishes' eyes
Its billowing abundance into whales
Around and under the Poles.

XIII

In *The Mutations of the Phoenix* Herbert Read discovers that the flux is in the mind, not of it perhaps, but in it. The Phoenix is finite mind rising in a nest of light from the sea or infinite; the discovery of Berkeley in 'Siris' where light is 'perception,' of Grosseteste, twelfth-century philosopher, who defines it as 'corporeality, or that of which corporeality is made.'

All existence
  past, present and to be
  is in this sea fringe.
There is no other temporal scene.
The Phoenix burns spiritually
  among the fierce stars
  and in the docile brain's recesses.
Its ultimate spark
you cannot trace . . .

Light burns the world in the focus of an eye.

XIV

To Dorothy Wellesley nature is a womb, a darkness; its surface is sleep, upon sleep we walk, into sleep drive the plough, and there lie the happy, the wise, the unconceived;

They lie in the loam
Laid backward by slice of the plough;
They sit in the rock;
In a matrix of amethyst crouches a man . . .

but unlike Turner or Read she need not prove or define, that was all done before she began to write and think. As though it were the tale of Mother Hubbard or the results of the last general election, she accepts what Turner and Read accept, sings her joy or sorrow in its presence, at times facile and clumsy, at times magnificent in her masculine rhythm, in the precision of her style. Eliot and Edith Sitwell have much of their intensity from a deliberate re-moulding or checking of past impulse, Turner much of his from a deliberate rejection of current belief, but here is no criticism at all. A new positive belief has given to her, as it gave to Shelley, an uncheckable impulse, and this belief is all the more positive because found, not sought; like certain characters in William Morris she has 'lucky eyes,' her sail is full.

I knew nothing of her until a few months ago I read the opening passage in *Horses,* delighted by its changes in pace, abrupt assertion, then a long sweeping line, by its vocabulary modern and precise;

> Who, in the garden-pony carrying skeps
> Of grass or fallen leaves, his knees gone slack,
> Round belly, hollow back,
> Sees the Mongolian Tarpan of the Steppes?
> Or, in the Shire with plaits and feathered feet,
> The war-horse like the wind the Tartar knew?
> Or, in the Suffolk Punch, spells out anew
> The wild grey asses fleet
> With stripe from head to tail, and moderate ears?

The swing away from Stendhal has passed Turner; the individual soul, the betrayal of the unconceived at birth, are among her principal themes, it must go further still; that soul must become its own betrayer, its own deliverer, the one activity, the mirror turn lamp. Not that the old conception is untrue, new literature better than old. In the greater nations every phase has characteristic beauty—has not Nicholas of Cusa said reality is expressed through contradiction? Yet for me, a man of my time, through my poetical faculty living its history, after much meat fish seems the only possible diet. I have indeed read certain poems by Turner, by Dorothy Wellesley, with more than all the excitement that came upon me when, a very young man, I heard somebody read out in a London tavern the poems of Ernest Dowson's despair—that too living history.

XV

I have a distaste for certain poems written in the midst of the great war; they are in all anthologies, but I have substituted Herbert Read's *End of a War* written long after. The writers of these poems were invariably officers of exceptional courage and capacity, one a man constantly selected for dangerous work, all, I think, had the Military Cross; their letters are vivid and humorous, they were not without joy—for all skill is joyful—but felt bound, in the words of the best known, to plead the suffering of their men. In poems that had for a time considerable fame, written in the first person, they made that suffering their own. I have rejected these poems for the same reason that made Arnold withdraw his *Empedocles on Etna* from circulation; passive suffering is not a theme for poetry. In all the great tragedies, tragedy is a joy to the man who dies; in Greece the tragic chorus danced. When man has withdrawn into the quicksilver at the back of the mirror no great event becomes luminous in his mind; it is no longer possible to write *The Persians, Agincourt, Chevy Chase:* some blunderer has driven his car on to the wrong side of the road—that is all.

If war is necessary, or necessary in our time and place, it is best to forget its suffering as we do the discomfort of fever, remembering our comfort at midnight when our temperature fell, or as we forget the worst moments of more painful disease. Florence Farr returning third class from Ireland found herself among Connaught Rangers just returned from the Boer War who described an incident over and over, and always with loud laughter: an unpopular sergeant struck by a shell turned round and round like a dancer wound in his own entrails. That too may be a right way of seeing war, if war is necessary; the way of the Cockney slums, of Patrick Street, of the *Kilmainham Minut,* of *Johnny I hardly knew ye,* of the medieval *Dance of Death*.

XVI

Ten years after the war certain poets combined the modern vocabulary, the accurate record of the relevant facts learnt from Eliot, with the sense of suffering of the war poets, that sense of suffering no longer passive, no longer an obsession of the nerves; philosophy had made it part of all the mind. Edith Sitwell with her Russian Ballet, Turner with his *Mare Tranquillum,* Dorothy Wellesley with her ancient names—'Heraclitus added fire'—her moths, horses and serpents, Pound with his descent into Hades, his Chinese classics, are too romantic to seem modern. Browning, that he might seem modern, created an ejaculating man-of-the-world good humour; but Day Lewis, Madge, MacNeice, are modern through the character of their intellectual passion. We have been gradually approaching this art through that cult of sincerity, that refusal to multiply personality which is characteristic of our time. They may seem obscure, confused, because of their concentrated passion, their interest in associations hitherto untravelled; it is as though their words and rhythms remained gummed to one another instead of separating and falling into order. I can seldom find more than half a dozen lyrics that I like, yet in this moment of sympathy I prefer them to Eliot, to myself—I too have tried to be modern. They have pulled off the mask, the manner writers hitherto assumed, Shelley in relation to his dream, Byron, Henley, to their adventure, their action. Here stands not this or that man but man's naked mind.

Although I have preferred, and shall again, constrained by a different nationality, a man so many years old, fixed to some one place, known to friends and enemies, full of mortal frailty, expressing all things not made mysterious by nature with impatient clarity, I have read with some excitement poets I had approached with distaste, delighted in their pure spiritual objectivity as in something long foretold.

Much of the war poetry was pacificist, revolutionary; it was easier to look at suffering if you had somebody to blame for it, or some remedy in mind. Many of these poets have called themselves communists, though I find in their work no trace of the recognized communist philosophy and the practising communist rejects them. The Russian government in 1930 silenced its Mechanists, put Spinoza on his head and claimed him for grandfather; but the men who created the communism of the masses had Stendhal's mirror for a contemporary, believed that religion, art, philosophy, expressed economic change, that the shell secreted the fish. Perhaps all that the masses accept is obsolete—the Orangeman beats his drum every Twelfth of July—perhaps fringes, wigs, furbelows, hoops, patches, stocks, Wellington boots, start up as armed men; but were a poet sensitive to the best thought of his time to accept that belief, when time is restoring the soul's autonomy, it would be as though he had swallowed a stone and kept it in his bowels. None of these men have accepted it, communism is their *Deus ex Machina,* their Santa Claus, their happy ending, but speaking as a poet I prefer tragedy to tragi-comedy. No matter how great a reformer's energy a still greater is required to face, all activities expended in vain, the unreformed. 'God,' said an old country-woman, 'smiles alike when regarding the good and condemning the lost.' MacNeice, the anti-communist, expecting some descent of barbarism next turn of the wheel, contemplates the modern world with even greater horror than the communist Day Lewis, although with less lyrical beauty. More often I cannot tell whether the poet is communist or anti-communist. On what side is Madge? Indeed I know of no school where the poets so closely resemble each other. Spender has said that the poetry of belief must supersede that of personality, and it is perhaps a belief shared that has created their intensity, their resemblance; but this belief is not political. If I understand aright this difficult art the contemplation of suffering has compelled them to seek beyond the flux something unchanging, inviolate, that country where no ghost haunts, no beloved lures because it has neither past nor future.

This lunar beauty
Has no history
Is complete and early;
If beauty later
Bear any feature
It had a lover
And is another.

XVII

I read Gerard Hopkins with great difficulty, I cannot keep my attention fixed for more than a few minutes; I suspect a bias born when I began to think. He is typical of his generation where most opposed to mine. His meaning is like some faint sound that strains the ear, comes out of words, passes to and fro between them, goes back into words, his manner a last development of poetical diction. My generation began that search for hard positive subject-matter, still a predominant purpose. Yet the publication of his work in 1918 made 'sprung verse' the fashion, and now his influence has replaced that of Hardy and Bridges. In sprung verse a foot may have one or many syllables without altering the metre, we count stress not syllable, it is the metre of the *Samson Agonistes* chorus and has given new vitality to much contemporary verse. It enables a poet to employ words taken over from science or the newspaper without stressing the more unmusical syllables, or to suggest hurried conversation where only one or two words in a sentence are important, to bring about a change in poetical writing like that in the modern speech of the stage where only those words which affect the situation are important. In syllabic verse, lyric, narrative, dramatic, all syllables are important. Hopkins would have disliked increase of realism; this stoppage and sudden onrush of syllables were to him a necessary expression of his slight constant excitement. The defect or limitation of 'sprung verse,' especially in five-stress lines, is that it may not be certain at a first glance where the stress falls. I have to read lines in *The End of a War* as in *Samson Agonistes* several times before I am certain.

XVIII

That I might follow a theme I have given but a bare mention or none at all to writers I greatly admire. There have, for instance, been notable translators. Ezra Pound's *Cathay* created the manner followed with more learning but with less subtlety of rhythm by Arthur Waley in many volumes; Tagore's translation from his own Bengali I have praised elsewhere. Æ (George Russell) found in Vedantic philosophy the emotional satisfaction found by Lionel Johnson, John Gray, Francis Thompson in Catholicism and seems despite this identity of aim, and the originality and beauty of his best work, to stand among the translators, so little has he in common with his time. He went to the *Upanishads,* both for imagery and belief. I have been able to say but little of translations and interpretations of modern and medieval Gaelic literature by Lady Gregory, James Stephens, Frank O'Connor. Then again there are certain poets I have left aside because they stand between two or more schools and might have confused the story—Richard Hughes, Robert Nichols, Hugh M'Diarmid. I would, if I could, have dealt at some length with George Barker, who like MacNeice, Auden, Day Lewis, handled the traditional metres with a new freedom —*vers libre* lost much of its vogue some five years ago—but has not their social passion, their sense of suffering. There are one or two writers who are not in my story because they seem to be born out of time. When I was young there were almost as many religious poets as love poets and no philosophers. After a search for religious poetry, among the new poets I have found a poem by Force Stead, until lately chaplain of Worcester, and half a dozen little poems, which remind me of Emily Brontë, by Margot Ruddock, a young actress well known on the provincial stage. I have said nothing of my own work, not from modesty, but because writing through fifty years I have been now of the same school with John Synge and James Stephens, now in that of Sturge Moore and the younger 'Michael Field': and though the concentration of philosophy and social passion of the school of Day Lewis and in MacNeice lay beyond my desire, I would, but for a failure of talent have been in that of Turner and Dorothy Wellesley.

A distinguished American poet urged me not to attempt a representative selection of American poetry; he pointed out that I could not hope to acquire the necessary knowledge: 'If your selection looks representative you will commit acts of injustice.' I have therefore, though with a sense of loss, confined my selections to those American poets who by subject, or by long residence in Europe, seem to English readers a part of their own literature.

Certain authors are absent from this selection through circumstances beyond my control. Robert Graves, Laura Riding, and the executors of Canon John Gray and Sir William Watson have refused permission. Two others, Rudyard Kipling and Ezra Pound, are inadequately represented because too expensive even for an anthologist with the ample means the Oxford University Press puts at his disposal.

September, 1936 W. B. YEATS

CLEANTH BROOKS

The Modern Poet and the Tradition

(1939)

Modern poetry is still regarded by the overwhelming majority as on principle antitraditional—not only by its adverse critics but by its proponents. The history of modern American poetry as written by the Untermeyers and Monroes tends to take something of the following form: The modern American poet has rid himself of clichés, worn-out literary materials, and the other stereotypes of Victorianism. Having sloughed off these dead conventions, he has proceeded (with the critic's hearty approval) to write of American scenes, American things, and the American people.

In so far as the tradition is to be understood as meaning 'Victorianism,' the approval given is just. There is obviously no value in adhering to lifeless conventions. But a healthy tradition is capable of continual modification, and the English tradition includes much more than the nineteenth century. The tendency to identify the tradition with Victorianism is in itself a vivid testimony to the thinness of the tradition in America. The new poets tended to make the simplest sort of readjustment, that of flat rejection. The net result of the revolt was probably healthy. At the same time, one must now see more and more clearly that much of the poetry of this revolt was negative in effect; and one must realize that a number of poets were then hailed as geniuses, not so much for what they wrote as for what they refused to write. Too often the American poet, after discarding the rags of Victorianism, was to be found walking in a barrel.

From *Modern Poetry and the Tradition* by Cleanth Brooks. Reprinted by permission of the publisher, The University of North Carolina Press.

One effect of the revolt was to set a higher premium on originality in itself. The insistence on originality, too, was healthy. But as Eliot has pointed out: 'The most individual parts of [the poet's] work may be those in which the dead poets, his ancestors, assert their immortality most vigorously.' This sort of originality the poets of the revolt did not possess: their most individual passages are those in which they are most strongly merely themselves; their most imitative, those in which they lean hardest, consciously or unconsciously, on the poets of the past.

This is strikingly true of Vachel Lindsay, for example. His Victorian passages represent him uniformly at his worst: see, for example, his 'Galahad, Knight Who Perished' or 'The Litany of the Heroes.' To be still more specific, his 'General Booth Enters Heaven' is good in proportion as the poet has violated Victorian conventionality—the conception of heaven as an American small town with the court house in the square, and the audacious introduction of the Salvation Army band and parade into heaven itself. The poem is weak in proportion as the lines are padded with 'literary' phrases—American bums described as

Lurching *bravos* from the ditches dank

or, after their regeneration, more startlingly 'literary' still, as

Sages and *sybils* now, and athletes clean,
Rulers of empires, and of forests green!

Edgar Lee Masters will also furnish some extreme examples. His *Spoon River Anthology,* clearly his best and healthiest work, shows Masters again and again, when he wishes to rise to a point of sublimity, returning as a matter of necessity to Victorian diction, rhythms, and sentiment. After a number of sordid, sociological epitaphs, Masters will give us this sort of thing, as in his 'Anne Rutledge':

Wedded to him, not through union,
But through separation.
Bloom forever, O Republic,
From the dust of my bosom!

One sympathizes with the intention of the poet here. Presumably, the poet wants his vision of a beautiful life to seem to arise out of a total view of society—a view which does not blink at the ugliness that is there. But the portrait of Lincoln's sweetheart stands on a different level of perception from those of her fellow-townsmen. The poet refuses to consider her in terms of the total view—as the diction, imagery, and rhythms of her epitaph indicate. We get an anomalous Victorian patch in the prevailingly frank and 'modern' examination.

This healthy animus against second-hand, 'literary' subject matter tended, moreover, in practice, to confine the poet to realistic, 'American' materials—on the surface at least. And the concomitant reaction against Victorian 'messages' and statements tended to make the poet content merely with the presentation of a surface. Sandburg, for example, often displays a crust of modern American materials thrown over statements which are as vague, and sometimes as sentimental, as those of Whitman.

In general, the revulsion from Victorianism manifested itself in a preoccupation with the materials of poetry as such. This preoccupation revealed itself in two forms. In the first place, it revealed itself in a tendency to rest in the mere objective description of things (the kind of poetry which John Crowe Ransom has defined as *physical* poetry, a poetry of things without ideas).

In the second place, the preoccupation with subject matter expressed itself in a tendency to substitute new and unworked material for old. Here is to be placed Whitman's appeal to the Muse to migrate from the European scene to the poetic exploitation of a virgin continent. The tendency merges with self-conscious nationalism, or more lately, with certain kinds of regionalism, to produce a poetry of local color. To take recent examples, Paul Engle's 'American Song' will illustrate the first case; Jesse Stuart's 'Man with a Bull-Tongue Plow,' the second.

But whether, as with the Imagists, the poet was primarily cosmopolitan, or whether he was the native local colorist like Sandburg, in neither case was he able to make much more than superficial changes in the organization of his poetry. The Imagist Manifesto is symptomatic; it proclaimed the legitimacy of experiment and innovation in subject matter and in versification. But it did not strike at the heart of the problem by redefining the structure of poetry. For example, the Manifesto attempted to liberalize the Victorian restrictions which hedged about the 'poetic.' Steam engines, said the Imagists, were also to be regarded as poetic—that is, as possible material for poetry. But the Manifesto did not indicate what use was to be made of them in the new poetry. Most of all, it did nothing to determine the relationship of these new materials to the older 'poetic' materials. And this relationship is a matter of basic importance.

The Manifesto was obviously sound, in so far as it went. But one can now point out (making use of a justified hindsight) how limited it was. Its function was fundamentally negative—its real importance, that of cutting away dead wood.

If we have been led to consider imagist poetry as essentially symbolist poetry *manqué,* we must consider the poetry which attempted to resolve violent discords as metaphysical poetry *manqué*. It is true that Sandburg in his 'Definitions of Poetry' proposes that poetry is a 'synthesis of hyacinths and biscuits'; but neither his own poetry nor that of the other poets of the revolt succeeds in making so daring or interesting a fusion. The synthesis is as thin and oversimple as are the Imagists' 'symbols.' If this statement seems ungracious, one need only remind the reader that credit for helping clear the ground of dead materials (here freely given) is another thing than credit for positive achievement. The positive achievement is there, but usually on thc simplest of levels. Sandburg's poem, 'Washington Monument by Night,' presents a sort of epitome of the characteristic strength and weakness of these poets—if not as a typical specimen, at least as a sort of fable. The poem begins auspiciously enough with a description of the physical object:

I

The stone goes straight.
A lean swimmer dives into night sky. . . .

But as the poet moves away from the monument as an object to the monument as a symbol, the poem weakens. The psychology of Washington, the man, is far less sharply realized. We get the most general and indefinite aspects—a sort of common denominator of all situations in which strong men battle with fate.

VI

Tongues wrangled dark at a man.
He buttoned his overcoat and stood alone.

And finally, with the attempt to concentrate the meaning, the poem peters out completely:

VIII

The name of an iron man goes over the world.
It takes a long time to forget an iron man.

IX

[The lines of this stanza are thus in the poem.]

. . . .

. . . .

The lack of psychological subtlety, the lack of complexity in the poet's attitude, the weak dramatic sense, the general crudity of 'form'—all these are aspects of a violent repudiation of the poetic tradition. The poets attempt to do in one generation what it requires generations of poets to do. The result is a retreat toward the elementary, undifferentiated 'stuff of poetry.' Indeed, there is a great deal of primitivism to be found in the poetry of the revolt. With the rejection of formal verse systems there is a reversion to loose chant lines and repetition (Sandburg's 'Chicago'); complex structure, logical or symbolical, gives way to the simple method of development by cumulative accretion—poems develop by the poet's piling up detail on detail (H. D.'s 'Sea Gods'); raw 'content' overrides and determines form (Masters' *Spoon River Anthology*).

Granting his circumstances, each of these poets is to be congratulated on having chosen as he did. If the traditional forms were stifling, then the poet did best to write without conscious form; if the poet's poetic ancestors were not an aid but a burden, he did best to dispense with their help, and start again from scratch. But the choice is a hard one: it certainly enforces tremendous limitations on the poet's flexibility and range.

One can see the importance of this effect by comparing the poets of the revolt with those of the Romantic period. When Wordsworth and Coleridge rejected Pope and Dr. Johnson, they did not expatriate themselves; they found in the tradition elements previously neglected which were apt to their purpose; among other things, the romantic Shakespeare and the folk ballad. Carl Sandburg, on the other hand, in rejecting Keats and Tennyson, cuts himself off from the English tradition altogether.

Victorian poetry was, as we have seen, a poetry of sharp exclusions. What was required in our own time was a poetry based upon a principle of inclusion. The rediscovery of the school of Donne becomes, thus, an event of capital importance. It is a discovery particularly associated with Eliot, but one which other poets, the Nashville group, for example, made for themselves. The poetry of Allen Tate, John Crowe Ransom, and Robert Penn Warren will furnish some very clear instances of the third revolution in poetry.

These poets make a good choice here to illustrate the point, not only because of the intrinsic goodness of their poetry and because their criticism helped accomplish the revolution, but also because their achievement is closely associated with the vexed questions of regionalism and traditionalism—questions raised in acute form by all American poetry. The two questions are, obviously, intimately bound up with the technique of inclusion. We have suggested that the problem posed for poets like Masters and Sandburg was this: a choice between the raw, unqualified present, and the dead past. The poets who have been able to avoid the dilemma have succeeded in avoiding it because they could weld past with present. Indeed, every past is dead which is unconnected with the present—the past of the literary vacuum. Conversely, a present which is nothing but the immediate present of sensation—the present unrelated to history—is not even the present. It is apt to be merely a collection of sensations, or at best, unrelated images.

The problem presented by an attempt to hold on to a tradition is, thus, ultimately a problem of sincerity or integrity. To take a specific case, and, since the poets chosen for discussion here are Southern poets, one relevant to Southern poets: the Old South cannot exist in the mind of the modern Southerner apart from its nonexistence in the present. The sentimentalist can, of course, dwell upon the Old South exclusively, giving a romantic construct which has no connection with the present and therefore no real connection with the actual South of the past. (It is not even a paradox to say that we cannot know the past without knowing the present.) Consequently, the Southern poet who is unwilling to sentimentalize the past or to limit himself to objective descriptions of the local color of the present, must of necessity mediate his account of the Old South through a consciousness of the present; that is, of its present nonexistence. (This general principle applies, of course, to whatever other subject matter he may use.) To sum up, his experience will include both positive and negative elements, and his real test as a poet will be his ability to bring the two sorts into unity.

In the same way the relation of the poet to his particular region is subsumed under the problem of integrity. Nineteenth-century poets like Stedman or Taylor felt that they could detach themselves from America and strike directly at the universal. But their poems seem too empty and thin—literary in the worst sense. The converse belief—that poetry should merely express the local color of a region—is false also.[1]

The depth of our confusion on the point is to be seen in the tendency—still active—to associate tradition with dead conventionality and regionalism with mere local color. With the poets whom we are to consider, the structure of inclusion is the basic structure. For example, in John Crowe Ransom's or Allen Tate's verse, for all their interest in regionalism, a description of the Southern scene never becomes the *raison d'être* of the poem. The following lines from Ransom are thoroughly Southern:

> Autumn days in our section
> Are the most used-up thing on earth . . .
> Having no more colour nor predilection
> Than cornstalks too wet for the fire

but the figure serves the poem—is not served by it. The distinction is most important.

In Robert Penn Warren's sequence of poems, 'Kentucky Mountain Farm' the reader might expect to find an exploitation of Southern rural life, and there is enough accurate description to validate the poet's localizing of his scene. Consider, for instance, the third poem of the sequence, 'History among the Rocks.' The poet recounts the various ways of dying in the country of the rocks—freezing, drowning, the bite of the copperhead in the wheat:

> By flat limestone, will coil the copperhead,
> Fanged as the sunlight, hearing the reaper's feet.

But the items of local color are absorbed in the poem as adjuncts of the larger theme. These ways of dying are all 'natural,' and the poet, by making them seem to inhere in the landscape, makes them seem easy, effortless, appropriate. 'But,' the poet goes on to say,

> there are other ways, the lean man said:
> In these autumn orchards once young men lay dead . . .
> Grey coats, blue coats. Young men on the mountainside
> Clambered, fought. Heels muddied the rocky spring.
> Their reason is hard to guess, remembering
> Blood on their black mustaches in moonlight.

This sort of death—death sought for—cuts in sharply and puzzlingly across the other kinds of death. The poet does not, however, allow his poem to fall into an easy resolution with a comment on the meaninglessness of war in general. The young men's death is 'unnatural' but that quality allows of more than one interpretation: it may signify that all war is meaningless, but it may also suggest that their choice was not an easy one and therefore meaningful and heroic for them. The poet himself abjures explicit commentary:

> Their reason is hard to guess and a long time past:
> The apple falls, falling in the quiet night.

The last figure not only recapitulates the earlier examples of 'natural' death, it comes with an ambiguity to accentuate the ironic contrast. Man is not merely natural; his capacity for defying nature is the typically *human* trait. But the poet does not elaborate on the young men's act, or try to justify it explicitly. Their reason is 'hard to guess,' and it happened a long time ago. The poet is willing to let the matter rest in calling attention to the contrast of the apple's effortless fall.

The poem is typical of the general structure of Warren's poems, a structure which may be described as follows: There is a rich and detailed examination of the particular experience with the conclusion, which may be drawn from the experience, coming as a quietly ironical statement or as modest and guarded understatement. It is as though the poet felt that only the minimum of commentary was allowable if he was not to do violence to the integrity of the experience. This general method is frequently used in order to state a theme closely related to that of the poem just discussed: the relation of the rational to the irrational, of the experience as experience to the interpretation or commentary on the experience.

This is the theme, for example, of 'Aged Man Surveys the Past Time.' The old man weeps, and perhaps

> Grief's smarting condiment may satisfy
> His heart to lard the wry and blasphemous theme.

The blasphemous theme is that regret is linked to the stuff of experience—whatever the commentary on experience and whatever the true account of experience may be.

> Truth, not truth. The heart, how regular
> And sure! How ambidextrous is rĕgret!
> Time has no mathematic.

Man's regret is a handle which will fit either tool—either a knowable universe or an unknowable.

By fruitful grove, unfruited now by winter,
The well-adapted and secular catbird
Whimpers its enmity and invitation.
Light fails beyond the barn and blasted oak.

Man is not 'secular.' He is cut off from nature, and consequently can take the bird's call as 'enmity' or 'invitation,' for it is both and neither. Nature is indifferent and goes on with its regular processes. Evening is falling; spring has come, and 'godless summer' will follow.

So much for the theme. But the poem 'works' in somewhat more intricate fashion. The inflections of tone are managed largely by the rhythm and imagery. For example, the man's grief springs from the fact that he is not 'well-adapted,' not 'natural' like the bird. But his sorrow—the imagery suggests ironically—is thoroughly 'natural':

And aged eyes, like twilit rain, their effort
Spill gentlier than herb-issue on a hill.

The bird 'whimpers' in company with the weeping man; but the 'whimper,' one realizes in a moment, is only ironically appropriate to the scene. The bird is not 'weeping' with the man, or indeed weeping at all. The word 'whimper' merely describes accurately the bird's song.

Ironical shifts of tone are used far more violently in 'The Return: an Elegy.' The poem has for its subject the experience of the son returning home at the death of his mother, and in the poem occur elements of memory and of grief, scenes from the landscape flashing through the train window on the homeward journey, memories of childhood, and the various associations—both serious and frivolous—that death and dying have. The discordant elements appear as the casual, irrelevant, and even bawdy associations which flicker through the consciousness when the mind is held in the grip of a deep grief. For example, after such a passage as

The wheels hum hum
The wheels: I come I come
Whirl out of space through time O wheels
Pursue down backward time the ghostly parallels
Pursue past culvert cut fill embankment semaphore
Pursue down gleaming hours that are no more.
The pines, black, snore

follows

turn backward turn backward o time in your flight
and make me a child again just for tonight
good lord he's wet the bed come bring a light

What grief hath the heart distilled?
The heart is unfulfilled
The hoarse pine stilled

The shock of these discordant associations could be justified on the basis of honesty. But one need not rest the case for them with this. Their general function is to accommodate the poem to reality, toughening it against the sentimental. They guarantee the intensity of the positive passages, and particularly, the climax of the poem. The poem ends as follows:

If I could pluck
Out of the dark that whirled
Over the hoarse pine over the rock
Out of the mist that furled
Could I stretch forth like God the hand and gather
For you my mother
If I could pluck
Against the dry essential of tomorrow
To lay upon the breast that gave me suck
Out of the dark the dark and swollen orchid of this sorrow.

The last image, when we reach it, is so heavily charged with the tension that it comes with sharp impact. But in another context the image might easily become soft and spurious. The poem, written in terms of conventional exclusions, would have had to forego intensity in order to avoid sentimentality.

The use of contrasts may be less violent, however, as in the fine 'Bearded Oaks,' where the surface of the poem is smooth, and even suave, though the internal structure is a pattern of contrasts and resolutions. The poem has for its subject the contemplation of a moment which, in its ideality, seems to lie out of time altogether and to partake of the nature of eternity. The quality of the experience is built up carefully; the atmosphere is one of almost preternatural relaxation and quiet. But the smoothness of the poem is not devised merely to harmonize with the quiet and perfection of the hour under the oaks. The unity which it represents is achieved by the resolution of complexities, and thus the structure of the poem reflects what the poem is saying:

And violence, forgot now, lent
The present stillness all its power.

In like manner, the tone of effortless intuition—direct and unclouded illumination—is played off against the rather intricate logical relations which it overlays. The effect is much like that which Marvell achieves in many of his poems.

The sharpness of the imagery and its ordination parallel Marvell again. The poet begins by comparing the scene under the oaks to the bed of the sea. And with the second stanza, far from abandoning the image, the poet continues to develop it:

The grasses, kelp-like, satisfy
The nameless motions of the air . . .

The qualities of the experience receive their development in terms of this dominant image. The lovers in their untroubled stillness at the bottom of the sea of time rest, as if made of coral. And, like coral, ages have gone into their making. Now they lie far below the storms of the troubled surface, and

Passion and slaughter, ruth, decay
Descended, whispered grain by grain,
Silted down swaying streams, to lay
Foundation for our voicelessness.

All our debate is voiceless here,
As all our rage is rage of stone;

The resolution of the experience and the exit from it is made in terms —not so much of irony as—of understatement.

So little time we live in Time,
And we learn all so painfully,
That we may spare this hour's term
To practice for Eternity.

The experience is rare and precious, but the emphasis on that fact is made obliquely. The poet does not exult in the sense of revelation which the hour has given, or proclaim that the meaning of life has been revealed to him in the experience. Rather, he makes what amounts to a covert apology for his indulgence in the experience. The hour may be 'spared'; and the reason given adds a new development to the thought. The hour seems out of time and like eternity, but since life 'in Time' is short, the lovers may well use it 'to practice for Eternity.' The development here is especially rich. If the hour under the oaks is associated with 'Eternity,' that eternity is also associated with death. If death—in its resemblance to the passive quiet of the hour—is made more acceptable, the process also works the other way; the hour is qualified by being associated with death. The effect is to make the tone of the last stanza seem modest and restrained. The poet has not in his experience of the hour lost his hold on reality.

The 'Letter from a Coward to a Hero' will illustrate another delicate handling of tone. The poem begins frankly enough as a letter. The hero's day (any man's day) with its confusion and disappointment, is suggested; and the poet, after reviewing it, says,

> I think you deserved better;
> Therefore I am writing you this letter.

The letter is personal, and deals with the springs of the hero's courage. The broken shards of the hero's day recall the confused, 'plural' experience of childhood:

> The scenes of childhood were splendid,
> And the light that there attended,
> But is rescinded:
> The cedar,
> The lichened rocks,
> The thicket where I saw the fox,
> And where I swam, the river.

The plurality of the child's world does not require 'heroism.' But the plurality of the world in which the 'coward' lives is not attended by a splendid light, nor is it a succession of fairy-tale wonders.

> Guns blaze in autumn and
> The quail falls and
> Empires collide with a bang
> That shakes the pictures where they hang . . .
> But a good pointer holds the point
> And is not gun-shy;
> But I
> Am gun-shy.

The violence, the abrupt transitions, are functional. They indicate the reasons for gun-shyness—'the sudden backfire,' which causes the coward to break his point. But the image of the pointer, one notices, is being used to qualify and define the coward's attitude toward the hero. The virtues of the pointer are solid virtues—but they are hardly the virtues of the imagination. The coward cannot propose to claim them, though he admires the good pointer.

The poem does not veer off into a mockery of the hero, however. The poet is sincere in his admiration and even tender.

> You have been strong in love and hate. . . .
> Rarely, you've been unmanned;
> I have not seen your courage put to pawn.

But disaster won't play according to the rules. There comes another image from the boyhood scene which opens the poem. Even if disaster is outstripped in the race,

> . . . he will cut across the back lot
> To lurk and lie in wait.

And then another image, also from the boyhood scene, which goes further to define the poet's attitude:

> Admired of children, gathered for their games,
> Disaster, like the dandelion, blooms,
> And the delicate film is fanned
> To seed the shaven lawn.

The ironic shock resides primarily in the comparison of disaster to the familiar, commonplace flower. But the irony goes on to inform the deeper relations: the figure implies that the hero, like a child, is playing with disaster; the quality of disaster, it is suggested, is its ability to propagate itself innocently in the most 'shaven lawn.' The coward is really standing in the role of Tiresias; but the tone of the utterance is that of a boyhood friend; and the example is one drawn from a childish game.

The last section of the poem states indirectly the reasons for the speaker's 'cowardice,' and, by implication, his criticism of the hero's 'heroism.' The criticism takes the form of a question:

> At the blind hour of unaimed grief,
> Of addition and subtraction,
> Of compromise,
> Of the smoky lecher, the thief,

Of regretted action,
At the hour to close the eyes,
At the hour when lights go out in the houses . . .
Then wind rouses
The kildees from their sodden ground:
Their commentary is part of the wind's sound.
What is that other sound,
Surf or distant cannonade?

But the hero at such hours is apparently not troubled by intimations of fear. He is beset by no such questions. And the speaker can finally resolve his mixture of admiration and criticism only by a piece of whimsy.

No doubt, when corridors are dumb
And the bed is made,
It is your custom to recline,
Clutching between the forefinger and thumb
Honor, for death shy valentine.

The note of real admiration is guaranteed by the tone of the banter. The admiration is genuine. But one observes that the whimsical compliment, *though* compliment, at the same time reduces the hero to a small boy, and, ironically, a shy young boy.

A number of Warren's poems, we have said, concern themselves with explorations of the problem of knowledge: What is the relation of actor to the act—of the thing done to the interpretations which are placed upon it, the 'meanings' that it bears. His most ambitious treatment of this occurs in the brilliant 'History.' Here the theme is dramatized by the poet's making the speaker of the poem a member of some band of invaders on the point of descending upon the land which they are to conquer. The imagery of the poem suggests that the invaders are the Israelites preparing to take the Promised Land, but they are any invaders, or more largely still, any men entering upon any decisive act.

The speaker recalls the hardships, the dangers, the hunger now past. He sees before him

The delicate landscape unfurled:
A world
Of ripeness blent, and green:
The fruited earth,

Fire on the good hearth,
The fireside scene.

This is the land which they are to seize and possess. But the speaker goes on to survey the future:

In the new land
Our seed shall prosper, and
In those unsifted times
Our sons shall cultivate
Peculiar crimes,
Having not love, nor hate,
Nor memory.

But some, in that distant future, world-weary and 'defective of desire,' will ponder on what their ancestors have done, will strive, vainly, to assess the motives of their ancestors' action, and will

In dim pools peer
To see, of some grandsire,
The long and toothéd jawbone greening there.

The situation is peculiarly the modern situation: we are obsessed with a consciousness of the past which drives us back upon history in a search for meanings. The absolutes are gone—are dissolved, indeed, by our consciousness of the past—by our consciousness of a plurality of histories and meanings. For us, the moderns, as for the descendants of the invaders of the poem, time is

. . . the aimless bitch
—Purblind, field-worn,
Slack dugs by the dry thorn torn—
Forever quartering the ground in which
The blank and fanged
Rough certainty lies hid.

The fall of night stirs him out of his reverie. It is time for the attack. And why are they to attack? He tries to frame an answer, and by the very act of searching for an answer, indicates what he is to say in the lines that follow:

We seek what end?
The slow dynastic ease,
Travail's cease?

Not pleasure, sure:
Alloy of fact?
The act
Alone is pure.

The act is the only absolute, the irreducible item which begets the explanations rather than that which is explained by them.

The poem levels out to an end with another glance at the time of the future:

We shall essay
The rugged ritual, but not of anger.
Let us go down before
Our thews are latched in the myth's languor,
Our hearts with fable grey.

The poem, for all its use of the Israelites, is a modern poem. Its focus lies in the 'unsifted times' where men have 'not love, nor hate,/Nor memory.' Its integrity rests in the fact that it does not flinch from the modern problem. The Israelites do not become merely decorative figures. All men are Jews—wanderers, rootless, seeking a promised land. America, in especial, is the latest promised land, and the Israelites constitute an especially apt symbol for ourselves.

The poem, thus, deals with the poet's own environment, with America, and, indeed, with the South. The problem raised in terms of the Israelites is a variation of that raised by the young men whose heels 'muddied the rocky spring.' In the poem, the items of past and present are unified by an act of the imagination which, if it transcends the region, remains rooted in it and derives its vitality from it.

These general points may all be illustrated from the poetry of John Crowe Ransom; but it may be valuable to take a more special approach to his work. Ransom's characteristic instrument is that of irony. But the irony remains always an instrument—it never becomes a mere attitude adopted by the poet for its own sake.

In its simplest form it is to be found in poems like 'Amphibious Crocodile,' where it lies very close to mere good-humored self-deprecation. Mr. Robert Crocodile undertakes the Grand Tour and tries successively the various expected careers before giving up and settling down in the family creek. But even here the attitude is not quite so simple nor so light as we have stated it. It is only a step further to the quality of self-irony to be found in 'Tom, Tom, the Piper's Son,' where the speaker's whimsy is playful in only the more serious senses of the word.

Certainly Ransom's more typical irony is to be found in his commentaries on the human predicament, commentaries which he usually finds occasion for by throwing aspects of that predicament into the form of a little fable. But the commentary is not stated as a conclusion to the fable—it is, rather, diffused throughout the fable as the qualifying tone with which the poet relates it. For this reason, it is difficult to isolate the commentary in each instance. Indeed, tone is so important in Ransom's poetry and so intimately related to the effect of each poem as a whole that quotation of fragments from his poetry does Ransom an especial injustice.

One cannot hope, therefore, to give a full sense of the power of his poems short of quoting them in their entirety, but it will be possible to indicate something of their structure and something of the basic attitude from which the poet's irony springs.

To an astonishing degree, the problems which engage Ransom's attention turn out to be aspects of one situation: that of man's divided sensibility.

There is the ironical commentary on Ralph ('Morning') whose vision of loveliness as he lies half-awake—

> . . . such a meadow
> Of wings and light and clover,
> He would propose to Jane then to go walking—

is dismissed by the return of his 'manliness':

> Suddenly he remembered about himself,
> His manliness returned entire to Ralph;
> The dutiful mills of the brain
> Began to whir with their smooth-grinding wheels—

so that he is left with

> Simply another morning, and simply Jane.

Or there is the case of the 'poor bookish hind' of the 'Miller's Daughter' with 'too much pudding' in his head 'of learned characters and scraps of love' and tongue-tied before the fabulous daughter of the mill, whose eyes 'are a blue stillwater,' and can only

> . . . stare—
> A learned eye of our most Christian nation

And foremost philosophical generation—
At primary chrome of hair. . . .

In the form most familiar to us, the division reveals itself in the contrast between the broken and confused life of the mature man and the innocent and total world of childhood which he has grown out of. The characters of 'Eclogue' comment on the change from the time when

. . . precious little innocents were we.
Said a boy, 'Now shall we let her be the fox?'
Or a girl, 'Now which of you will climb the tree?'
We were quick-foot the deer, strong-heart the ox,
Business-man the bee. . . .

We were spendthrifts of joy when we were young,
But we became usurious, and in fright
Conceived that such a waste of days was wrong
For marchers unto night . . .

. . . And every day since then
We are mortals teasing for immortal spoils,
Desperate women and men.

The poem has its focus in the plight of the lovers, but not romantically or exclusively. Even here the lovers are moderns, and their predicament, though universally human, is a symbol of the predicament of a scientific civilization.

The desperation of Ransom's characters springs finally from the fact that they cannot attain unity of being. Childhood—the childhood of a race or of a culture—gives a suggestion of what such unity can be, but development into maturity, and specialization, break up the harmony of faculties and leave intellect at war with emotion, the practical life with the life of sentiment, science with poetry.

In Ransom's poetry it is this conflict which receives most attention. It is the theme, for example, of 'Persistent Explorer,' whose fable is that of the poet himself thrown up upon the neutralized world of modern science. The explorer hears a waterfall, and then climbs to a height from which to look at it. It teases his ears and eyes with the suggestion that it is something more than mere water falling.

But listen as he might, look fast or slow,
It was water, only water, tons of it

Dropping into the gorge, and every bit
Was water—the insipid chemical H_2O.

The thunder of the cataract is appropriately loud enough to be the voice of a god; the mist that rises from it, beautiful enough to be that from which a goddess appears. But no god speaks to him, no goddess appears. Moreover, the poet has too much integrity to resolve his theme with an easy pathos. He must confess that he does not even know what he would have the cataract 'mean' to him.

What would he have it spell? He scarcely knew;
Only that water and nothing but water filled
His eyes and ears, nothing but water that spilled;
And if the smoke and rattle of water drew

From the deep thickets of his mind the train,
The fierce fauns and the timid tenants there,
That burst their bonds and rushed upon the air,
Why, he must turn and beat them down again.

But the poet also rejects the resolution of his dilemma afforded by 'romantic irony'—the self-pitying disillusionment with science:

So be it. And no unreasonable outcry
The pilgrim made; only a rueful grin
Spread over his lips until he drew them in;
He did not sit upon a rock and die.

There were many ways of dying. . . .

But there were many ways of living too,
And let his enemies gibe, but let them say
That he would throw this continent away
And seek another country,—as he would do.

The protagonist of the poem refuses anything less than the complete experience. He is not retreating before the advance of science. He is significantly an 'explorer,' not a refugee.

The relation of science to poetry has been treated by Ransom in his discussion of religion, *God Without Thunder*. Science gives always an abstract description, and because abstract, powerful; whereas poetry attempts a complete, a total description of the object, including not only those elements which make the knowledge 'useful,' but other 'useless' elements as well. And religion differs from philosophy, which abstracts at least to the level of principles, by clothing the principles in the garb of poetry, and thus prefers full-bodied gods to mere principles. A diet of straight science, because science is power-knowledge, may contribute to *hubris;* whereas poetry (as an element of religion or merely as poetry), because it forces on the attention elements which cannot be absorbed in a practical program, constantly reminds man that the thing described lies outside man's control, and thus rebukes *hubris.*

To revert to terms already developed, poetic description involves a technique of inclusion rather than of exclusion. A civilization which has narrowed its sensibility with a regimen of power-knowledge, like Ralph, wakes to find that the world has become in a special and serious sense, stale, flat, and unprofitable. Ransom's poetry resolutely sets about to include 'the other side.' But it represents this other side, not by preachments, but by attempting to restore the total view. And the index of that totality is the ironic tone of the poem.

In emphasizing the center to which Ransom's irony refers, we must not give the impression that the special difficulty of the modern poet is his only theme, or that the rueful grin is the only gesture allowed to him as ironist. Having defined the central impulse of his poetry and his basic method, we shall have no difficulty in finding examples of an abundant variety of themes and attitudes. But the variety is a variety of ironies.

It is this method of indirection which allows Ransom to treat, with absolute sureness, subjects which most modern poets tend to shrink from—a child's first acquaintance with death ('Janet Waking') or the homesickness of one lover for another ('Winter Remembered'). To illustrate from the former poem, the poet begins by giving the exposition perfectly casually. The setting is that of typical American domesticity —even suburban:

Beautifully Janet slept
Till it was deeply morning. She woke then
And thought about her dainty-feathered hen,
To see how it had kept.

One kiss she gave her mother,
Only a small one gave she to her daddy
Who would have kissed each curl of his shining baby;
No kiss at all for her brother.

But Chucky, the pet hen, is dead. The poet treats its death mock-heroically:

> And purply did the knot
> Swell with the venom and communicate
> Its rigour! Now the poor comb stood up straight
> But Chucky did not.

No special importance attaches to Janet or to Chucky. The whole incident is perfectly ordinary. The poet implies that we are free to be amused at it—he is not trying to surround it with any special sanctity. And it is for this reason, that the pathos of the last stanzas seems to emerge legitimately from the incident—is not forced into the incident by the poet.

> So there was Janet
> Kneeling on the wet grass, crying her brown hen
> (Translated far beyond the daughters of men)
> To rise and walk upon it.
>
> And weeping fast as she had breath
> Janet inplored us, 'Wake her from her sleep!'
> And would not be instructed in how deep
> Was the forgetful kingdom of death.

The poet, in effect, retains his tone of objectivity: he is willing to deal with the whole episode as an incident in Janet's education. Janet has difficulty with her lesson. She 'would not be instructed.' That Janet's difficulty is a universally human one does not need to be underscored by the poet. The effect is made indirectly.

The method of indirection renders successful the poems on the Old South, poems which one might think would surely offer this poet his most severe tests in maintaining firmness of tone. 'The Old Mansion,' for instance, suggests to the poet that

> Here age seemed newly imaged for the historian
> After his monstrous châteaux on the Loire,
> A beauty not for depicting by old vulgarian
> Reiterations which gentle readers abhor.

Consequently, the poet goes on to describe the old house in terms which avoid the 'old vulgarian/Reiterations' (though the hard-boiled modern reader is embraced by the irony too in being characterized as 'gentle'). The poet proceeds to develop the pathos in terms of an ironical commentary which keeps steadily in mind the fact that his reader has his mouth set for a succession of clichés.

It is an extreme indirection which contributes the obscurity to one of the most difficult of Ransom's poems, 'Painting: a Head.' The theme of this poem is roughly the same as that of 'Two Gentlemen in Bonds': the human predicament of being divided into head and body. But the poem actually begins as a whimsical meditation on the portrait head on the wall.

The poet plays with the accidental symbolism involved in the fact that the portrait shows the head and no body—the head removed from the body by 'dark severance.' It is characteristic of heads, the poet observes, to attempt to be 'absolute and to try decapitation.' The face revealed in the portrait in question, however, is 'too happy' and beautiful to have belonged to that class of heads. It is the head of a man of thirty and

> Discovers maybe thirty unwidowed years
> Of not dishonoring the faithful stem.

It is, moreover, the head of a nameless man, and thus has not been taken as a trophy by the 'historian headhunters.' For the artist to have painted it as removed from the body was, therefore, a piece of 'capital irony.'

But the poet, in the very process of pointing out that the portrait on which he meditates is not that of a man who was guilty of forcing abstraction, has made his case against abstraction, and is allowed to shift his tone from teasing whimsy into what amounts to the serious fantasy of fable:

> Beauty is of body.
> The flesh contouring shallowly on a head
> Is a rock-garden needing body's love
> And best bodiness to colorify
>
> The big blue birds sitting and sea-shell flats
> And caves and on the iron acropolis
> To spread the hyacinthine hair and rear
> The olive garden for the nightingales.

One may generalize by saying that Ransom's irony never becomes a stereotype. It is a function of the entire poem and consequently varies from poem to poem. At the one extreme, it does not flatten out into mere satire; at the other extreme, it does not fail to obtain altogether. It is always present, if only as a sense of aesthetic distance.

Indeed, Ransom's forte is the subtlety and firmness of tone which he achieves. His poems are as little amenable to paraphrase as are any poems that one can think of. It is probably because he is able to transmit so definitely shades of attitude which can be perceived and yet which defy exact description in prose commentary that critics are so often moved to metaphorical descriptions of his method—descriptions which sometimes convey little more than a recognition that something has been achieved in the poetry. Ransom's triumphs, like those of the poets of the early seventeenth century, are triumphs in the handling of tone. And his fundamental relation to those poets lies in the brilliance of his handling of tone—not in the use of a particular diction or 'conceits' or in his taking a particular attitude toward certain themes. It is rather in the attention which he has given to the definition and communication of delicate shadings of attitude as a problem in itself. His poems bear their own self-criticism. And this is why they are unsentimental, tough-minded, and penetrating, and why the serious ones are powerful in the responses which they evoke.

Allen Tate's poetry, too, illustrates what we have called a structure of synthesis, and furnishes even more violent illustrations than does Ransom's. Tate constantly throws his words and images into active contrast. Almost every adjective in his poetry challenges the reader's imagination to follow it off at a tangent. For instance, in the 'Ode to the Confederate Dead,' November becomes not 'drear' November, 'sober' November, but

> *Ambitious* November with the humors of the year
> [italics mine].

The 'curiosity of an angel's stare' is not 'idle' or 'quiet' or 'probing' or any other predictable adjective, but 'brute' curiosity. This is the primary difficulty that Tate's poetry presents to the reader who is unacquainted with his dominant themes: the surface of the poem, in its apparently violent disorder, may carry him off at tangents.

There is some justification, therefore, for approaching Tate's poetry through an account of his basic themes—all the more since these themes are closely related to the poetic method itself. We may conveniently begin by examining a very important passage in his essay on

'Humanism and Naturalism.' In discussing attitudes toward history, he describes two ways of viewing the past. The first is that which gives what may be called the scientist's past, in which events form a logical series; the second is that which gives what Tate himself calls the 'temporal past.'

'. . . the logical series is quantitative, the abstraction of space. The temporal series is, on the other hand, space concrete. Concrete, temporal experience implies the existence of a temporal past, and it is the foundation of the religious imagination; that is to say, the only way to think of the past independently of . . . naturalism is to think religiously; and conversely, the only way to think religiously is to think in time. Naturalistic science is timeless. A doctrine based upon it, whether explicitly or not, can have no past, no idea of tradition, no fixed center of life. The "typically human" is a term that cannot exist apart from some other term; it is not an absolute; it is fluid and unfixed.

'To de-temporize the past is to reduce it to an abstract lump. To take from the present its concrete fullness is to refuse to let standards work from the inside. It follows that "decorum" must be "imposed" from above. Thus there are never specific moral problems (the subject matter of the arts) but only fixed general doctrines without subject matter—that is to say, without "nature." '

In other words, the artist today finds that his specific subject matter tends to be dissolved in abstractions of various sorts. His proper subjects—specific moral problems—are not to be found in an abstract, logical series, for in such a series there are no standards of any sort—and nothing specific, nothing concrete.

Tate's preoccupation with history and time in his poetry is thus closely related to Ransom's characteristic problem: that of man living under the dispensation of science—modern man suffering from a dissociation of sensibility.

Tate goes on to say in the same essay: 'The "historical method" has always been the anti-historical method. Its aim is to contemporize the past. Its real effect is to detemporize it. The past becomes a causal series, and timeless . . .' Tate's concern here is with the neohumanists, but the generalization may be applied to the arts without distorting it too violently. Carl Sandburg, for example, will supply an example pat to our purpose. Consider his 'Four Preludes on Playthings of the Wind.'

After the first Prelude with its 'What of it? Let the dead be dead,' and after the second Prelude which describes an ancient city (Babylon?)

with its cedar doors and golden dancing girls and its ultimate destruction, Prelude Three begins:

> It has happened before.
> Strong men put up a city and got
>   a nation together,
> And paid singers to sing and women
>   to warble: We are the greatest city,
>   the greatest nation,
>   nothing like us ever was.

But, as the poem goes on to point out, the ultimate dancers are the rats, and the ultimate singers, the crows. The poet's intention, presumably, is to contemporize the past. The real effect is to detemporize it. Babylon or Nineveh becomes interchangeable with Chicago. Chicago receives a certain access of dignity from the association; Babylon, a certain humanity and reality; and the poet is allowed to imply, with a plausible finality, that human nature fundamentally doesn't change.

Sandburg's primary impulse seems to be a revulsion from the 'literary' past—the people of the past, too, hired singers, ran night-clubs, and joined booster societies. But Sandburg's contemporizing of the past springs also—probably unconsciously—from the fact that he is immersed in a scientific civilization.

Tate not only cannot accept Sandburg's detemporized past; he must strive actively to ascertain what meaning the past can have for modern man who has so many inducements to consider it merely as a logical series. This, I take it, is the primary theme of 'The Mediterranean,' 'Aeneas at Washington,' and even—in a varied form—of the 'Ode to the Confederate Dead.' Aeneas possessed a concrete past—moved from a particular Troy to found a particular Rome. We, on the other hand, who have 'cracked the hemispheres with careless hand,' in abolishing space have also abolished time. The poem is not a lament, nor is it a 'sighing for vanished glories.' It is a recognition and an exploration of our dilemma. Modern man, like the Aeneas of Tate's poem, is obsessed with the naturalistic view of history—history as an abstract series. He sees

> . . . all things apart, the towers that men
> Contrive I too contrived long, long ago.

But Aeneas has been acquainted with another conception of history.

Now I demand little. The singular passion
Abides its object and consumes desire
In the circling shadow of its appetite.

(We may gloss the last quoted lines as follows: In his 'Religion and the Old South,' Tate argues that the naturalistic view of history is intent on utility; but in the case of concrete history, the 'images are only to be contemplated, and perhaps the act of contemplation after long exercise initiates a habit of restraint, and the setting up of absolute standards which are less formulas for action than an interior discipline of the mind.')

Modern man with his tremendous historical consciousness is thus confronted with a dilemma when asked for the meaning of his actions:

. . . Stuck in the wet mire
Four thousand leagues from the ninth buried city
I thought of Troy, what we had built her for.

The problem of history receives a somewhat similar treatment in the fine 'Message from Abroad.' The form into which the problem is cast is peculiarly that of the American confronted with the lack of 'history' of his own land and thrown up against the immense 'history' of Europe. Stated in somewhat altered form, it is the problem of man, who requires a history in which he can participate personally, lost in the vast museum galleries of western civilization.

Provence,
The Renascence, the age of Pericles, each
A broad, rich-carpeted stair to pride
. . . they're easy to follow
For the ways taken are all notorious,
Lettered, sculptured and rhymed. . . .

But 'those others,' the ways taken by his ancestors, are

. . . incuriously complete, lost,
Not by poetry and statues timed,
Shattered by sunlight and the impartial sleet.

He can find, to mark those ways,

Now only
The bent eaves and the windows cracked,
The thin grass picked by the wind,
Heaved by the mole. . . .

The tall 'red-faced' man cannot survive the voyage back to Europe:

> With dawn came the gull to the crest,
> Stared at the spray, fell asleep
> Over the picked bones, the white face
> Of the leaning man drowned deep. . . .

And the poet is finally forced to admit that he cannot see the ancestors, and can merely conjecture

> What did you say mornings?
> Evenings, what?
> The bent eaves
> On the cracked house,
> That ghost of a hound . . .
> The man red-faced and tall
> Will cast no shadow
> From the province of the drowned.

Obviously Tate's poetry is not occupied exclusively with the meaning of history. But his criticism of merely statistical accounts of reality serves as an introduction to the special problems of his poetry in much the same way that Ransom's comments on the relation of science to the myth serve as an approach to his.

Attention to his criticism will illuminate, for example, the positive position from which he comments on our present disintegration:

> The essential wreckage of your age is different,
> The accident the same; the Annabella
> Of proper incest, no longer incestuous:
> In an age of abstract experience, fornication
> Is self-expression, adjunct to Christian euphoria. . . .
>
> 'Causerie'

Or, to make the application to the subject of poetry itself, one may quote from the same poem:

> We have learned to require
> In the infirm concessions of memory
> The privilege never to hear too much.
> What is this conversation, now secular,
> A speech not mine yet speaking for me in

The heaving jelly of my tribal air?
It rises in the throat, it climbs the tongue,
It perches there for secret tutelage
And gets it, of inscrutable instruction. . . .

The situation described is peculiarly that of the modern poet. His speech is a mass of clichés—of terms which with their past associations seem too grandiloquent and gaudy, or, with their past content emptied, now seem meaningless. 'Vocabulary/Becomes confusion,' and without vocabulary man is lost.

Heredity
Proposes love, love exacts language, and we lack
Language. When shall we speak again? When shall
The sparrow dusting the gutter sing? When shall
This drift with silence meet the sun? When shall
I wake?

We may state the situation in still other terms: Man's religion, his myths, are now merely private fictions. And as Tate has remarked in one of his essays, '. . . a myth should be in conviction immediate, direct, overwhelming, and I take it that the appreciation of this kind of imagery is an art lost to the modern mind.' The lover in Tate's 'Retroduction to American History,' has lost his appreciation of such imagery. He 'cannot hear. . . . His very eyeballs fixed in disarticulation. . . . his metaphors are dead.'

Tate's metaphors are very much alive; it is through the production of energetic metaphor, of live 'myths' that the poet attempts to break through the pattern of 'abstract experience' and give man a picture of himself as man. Hence his preoccupation with time and mortality and 'specific moral problems.' But as a matter of integrity, he cannot take the short cut which Tennyson tends to take to these subjects. One cannot find a living relation between the present and the past without being honest to the present—and that involves taking into account the anti-historical character of our present.

In his 'Retroduction to American History,' the poet asks why 'in such serenity of equal fates'—that is, why, if life is merely a causal sequence, merely abstract experience—has Narcissus 'urged the brook with questions?' In a naturalistic world, the brook, like Mr. Ransom's cataract, is only so much water; and we have the absurdity which the poet proceeds to point out:

Merged with the element
Speculation suffuses the meadow with drops to tickle
The cow's gullet; grasshoppers drink the rain.

Self-scrutiny, introspection, in a purely mechanistic universe, is merely a romantic gesture—'Narcissism.' In the 'Ode to the Confederate Dead,' Narcissism figures again, though without a specific symbol.

As Tate has said in a recent article: 'The poem is "about" solipsism or Narcissism, or any other *ism* that denotes the failure of the human personality to function properly in nature and society. Society (and "nature" as modern society constructs it) appears to offer limited fields for the exercise of the whole man, who wastes his energy piecemeal over separate functions that ought to come under a unity of being. . . . Without unity we get *the remarkable self-consciousness* of our age [italics mine].'

In the 'Ode,' the Narcissism of the present forms one term of the contrast; the 'total' world in which the dead soldiers fulfilled themselves, the other. But the poet refuses to take the easy romantic attitude toward the contrast. The world which the dead soldiers possessed is not available to the speaker of the poem, for that kind of world is the function of a society, not something which can be wrought out by the private will. Moreover, the poet is honest: the leaves, for him, *are* merely leaves.

The irony expressed in the poem, then, is not the romantic irony of the passage quoted from Tate's criticism in Chapter III. It is a more complex irony, and almost inevitably, a self-inclusive irony. Such an irony is found also in 'Last Days of Alice,' 'The Sonnets at Christmas,' 'The Meaning of Life,' and 'The Meaning of Death.'

Before considering these poems, however, it is well to note a further criticism of naturalism in Tate's prose. The naturalistic view of experience (history as an abstract series) suggests an 'omnipotent human rationality.' It can only predict success. The poet (who, by virtue of being a poet, is committed to the concrete and particular) is thus continually thrown into the role of Tiresias.

A number of Tate's poems are ironical treatments of rationality, 'The Eagle,' for example. It is not the heart which fears death, but the mind, 'the white eagle.' And in the 'Epistle to Edmund Wilson,'

The mind's a sick eagle taking flight. . . .

The theme is most powerfully stated in the last of the 'Sonnets of the Blood.' The brother is cautioned to

Be zealous that your numbers are all prime,
Lest false division with sly mathematic
Plunder the inner mansion of the blood. . . .
. . . the prime secret whose simplicity
Your towering engine hammers to reduce,
Though driven, holds that bulwark of the sea
Which breached will turn unspeaking fury loose
To drown out him who swears to rectify
Infinity. . . .

If the blood is a symbol of the nonrational, concrete stuff of man which resists abstract classification, by the same token it symbolizes man's capacity to be more than an abstract integer, and therefore signifies man's capacity for sin. In an age of abstract experience sin is meaningless.

In 'Last Days of Alice,' the logical, self-consistent but inhuman world of *Through the Looking-Glass* becomes an ironical symbol of the modern world. The poet maintains most precisely the analogy between Alice gazing 'learnedly down her airy nose' into the abstract world of the mirror, and modern man who has also turned his world into abstraction. The subsidiary metaphors—'Alice grown . . . mammoth but not fat,' symbolizing the megalomania of the modern; Alice 'turned absent-minded by infinity' who 'cannot move unless her double move,' symbolizing the hypostasis of the modern—grow naturally out of the major symbolism. The poem is witty in the seventeenth-century sense; the reference to the Cheshire cat with his abstract grin, a witty comparison. But the wit, the sense of precision and complexity, is functional. It contributes the special quality of irony necessary to allow the poet to end his poem with the positive outcry:

O God of our flesh, return us to Your Wrath,
Let us be evil could we enter in
Your grace, and falter on the stony path!

Man's capacity for error, his essential unpredictability, is referred to in a number of Tate's poems. It is the basis of the beautiful 'Ode to Fear.'

My eldest companion present in solitude,
Watch-dog of Thebes when the blind hero strove:
'Twas your omniscience at the cross-road stood
When Laius, the slain dotard, drenched the grove.

Now to the fading, harried eyes immune
Of prophecy, you stalk us in the street
From the recesses of the August noon,
Alert world over, crouched on the air's feet.

You are the surety to immortal life,
God's hatred of the universal stain. . . .

There is an especially rich development of this theme in the twin poems, 'The Meaning of Life,' and 'The Meaning of Death.' The first opens with a dry statement of the point as if in a sort of apologetic monotone:

Think about it at will; there is that
Which is the commentary; there's that other,
Which may be called the immaculate
Conception of its essence in itself.

But the essence must not be turned into mere abstraction by the commentary, even though the commentary is so necessary that the essence is speechless without it. The poet goes on to apologize for the tone of tedious explication:

I was saying this more briefly the other day
But one must be explicit as well as brief.
When I was a small boy I lived at home
For nine years in that part of old Kentucky
Where the mountains fringe the Blue Grass,
The old men shot at one another for luck;
It made me think I was like none of them.
At twelve I was determined to shoot only
For honor; at twenty not to shoot at all;
I know at thirty-three that one must shoot
As often as one gets the rare chance— *
In killing there is more than commentary.

Our predicament is that the opportunity for any meaningful action rarely offers itself at all.

* I shall expect some one to wrench this statement into a symptom of the poet's 'Fascism.' A prominent critic, in order to make such a point, has already twisted out of its context Tate's statement that the Southerner can only take hold of his tradition 'by violence.' In the context in which it occurs, it obviously means 'by politics' as opposed to 'by religion.'

With the last lines the poet shifts the tone again, modulating from the half-whimsical, personal illustration into a brilliant summarizing figure:

> But there's a kind of lust feeds on itself
> Unspoken to, unspeaking; subterranean
> As a black river full of eyeless fish
> Heavy with spawn; with a passion for time
> Longer than the arteries of a cave.

The symbol of the concrete, irrational essence of life, the blood, receives an amazing amplification by its association with the cave. The two symbols are united on the basis of their possession of 'arteries.' The blood is associated with 'lust,' is 'subterranean' (buried within the body), is the source of 'passion.' But the added metaphor of the cave extends the associations from those appropriate to an individual body to something general and eternal. The reference to the fish may be also a fertility symbol. But the fish are 'eyeless' though 'heavy with spawn.' The basic stuff of life lacks eyes—cannot see even itself; and filled with infinite potentialities, runs its dark, involved, subterranean course. The metaphor is powerful and rich, but it gives no sense of having been spatchcocked on to the poem. The blood symbol is worked out only in terms of the cave symbol; the two cannot be broken apart. Moreover, it has been prepared for in the casual personal allusion which precedes it. It too is a part of 'old Kentucky/Where the mountains fringe the Blue Grass.'

'The Meaning of Death' also begins quietly, as 'An After-Dinner Speech.' The speech is addressed to us, the moderns, who have committed ourselves to commentary—complete, lucid, and full. We have no passion for time—have abolished time.

> Time, fall no more.
> Let that be life—time falls no more. The threat
> Of time we in our own courage have foresworn.
> Let light fall, there shall be eternal light
> And all the light shall on our heads be worn
>
> Although at evening clouds infest the sky
> Broken at base from which the lemon sun
> Pours acid of winter on a useful view. . . .

The concession announced by 'although' is important in developing the tone. Incorrigible optimists that we are, we say hopefully that there shall be eternal light although one must admit that the evening light does not suggest the warmth of life but freezes the landscape with cold, pours acid upon it, turns it into something which is a vanity and meaningless. (The psychological basis for the symbolism here is interesting. The 'lemon sun' indicates primarily the color of the evening sun, but 'lemon' carries on over into a suggestion of something acid and astringent.)

But, the poet observes, our uneasiness is really groundless. Tomorrow surely will bring 'jocund day' and the colors of spring. If one in boyhood connected fear with the coming on of the dark at evening, that was merely because one was a small boy. We, at least, have given up that past with its irrationalities and superstitions:

> Gentlemen! let's
> Forget the past, its related errors, coarseness
> Of parents, laxities, unrealities of principle
>
> Think of tomorrow. Make a firm postulate
> Of simplicity in desire and act
> Founded on the best hypotheses;
> Desire to eat secretly, alone, lest
> Ritual corrupt our charity . . .

Ritual implies a respect for the thing as thing; it implies more than an abstract series—implies a breach in our strict naturalism. That naturalism must be maintained

> Lest darkness fall and time fall
> In a long night . . .

and thus spoil our plans for the conquest of time—spoil our plans for the reduction of everything to abstraction where, we hope,

> . . . learned arteries
> Mounting the ice and sum of barbarous time
> Shall yield, without essence, perfect accident.

The last phrase suggests the final metaphor of 'The Meaning of Life,' and with the final line of this poem, the speaker drops his ironical pretense of agreement with the 'gentlemen' and shifts into another quality of irony, a deeper irony, returning to the cave metaphor:

> We are the eyelids of defeated caves.

We are the generation that has broken with history, the generation that has closed the mouth of the cave. The word 'eyelids' indicates the manner of the closing: the suggestion is that the motion is one of languor and weariness as one might close his eyelids in sleep. The vitality is gone.

A similar theme is to be found in 'The Oath' though the setting and the treatment of the theme in this poem are very different. The two friends are sitting by the fire in the gathering twilight.

> It was near evening, the room was cold,
> Half-dark; Uncle Ben's brass bullet-mould
> And powder-horn and Major Bogan's face
> Above the fire in the half-light plainly said:
> There's naught to kill but the animated dead.
> Horn nor mould nor major follows the chase.

Then one of the friends proposes the question, 'Who are the dead?'

> And nothing more was said. . . .
> So I leaving Lytle to that dream
> Decided what it is in time that gnaws
> The aging fury of a mountain stream
> When suddenly, as an ignorant mind will do,
> I thought I heard the dark pounding its head
> On a rock, crying: *Who are the dead?*
> Then Lytle turned with an oath—By God it's true!

The thing that is true is obvious that *we* are the dead. The dead are those who have given in to abstraction, even though they may move about and carry on their business and be—to use the earlier phrase in the poem—the 'animated dead.' A mountain stream ceases to be a mountain stream when its bed has become worn level. It might even be termed a 'defeated' mountain stream when it has lost the activity which gave its career meaning.

NOTE

1. Whitman may be thought to have resolved the contradiction by finding a new unity; and certainly he struggled to achieve this. But the diverse elements in all but his best poetry tend to stay apart: there is, on the one hand, the particularity of the long 'catalogue' passages, and on the other, the too frequent, vague, and windy generality about democracy

and progress. Emily Dickinson, on the other hand, does achieve very often a unity which is thoroughly faithful to her New England environment and yet is not limited to local color. Her best poetry obviously manifests a structure of inclusion, and significantly enough, displays the vigorous, sometimes audacious metaphor, which we have seen to be a characteristic of the other types of poetry which we have examined.

RANDALL JARRELL

Texts from Housman

(1939)

The logic poetry has or pretends to have generally resembles induction more than deduction. Of four possible procedures (dealing entirely with particulars, dealing entirely with generalizations, inferring the relatively general from the relatively particular, and deducing the particular from the more general), the third is very much the most common, and the first and second are limits which 'pure' and didactic poetry timidly approach. The fourth is seldom seen. In this essay I am interested in that variety of the third procedure in which the generalizations are implicit. When such generalizations are simple ones, very plainly implied by the particulars of the poem, there will be little tendency to confuse this variety of the third procedure with the first procedure; when they are neither simple nor very plainly implied, the poem will be thought of as 'pure' (frequently, 'nature') poetry. This is all the more likely to occur since most 'pure' poetry is merely that in which the impurity, like the illegitimate child of the story, is 'such a little one' that we feel it ought to be disregarded. Of these poems of implicit generalization there is a wide range, extending from the simplest, in which the generalizations are made obvious enough to vex the average reader (some of the 'Satires of Circumstance,' for instance), to the most complicated, in which they entirely escape his observation ('To the Moon'). The two poems of Housman's which I am about to analyze are more nearly of the type of 'To the Moon.'

From *Kenyon Review* I (1939). Reprinted by permission of Mrs. Randall Jarrell and *Kenyon Review*.

2.

Crossing alone the nighted ferry
With the one coin for fee,
Whom, on the wharf of Lethe waiting,
Count you to find? Not me.

The brisk fond lackey to fetch and carry,
The true, sick-hearted slave,
Expect him not in the just city
And free land of the grave.

The first stanza is oddly constructed; it manages to carry over several more or less unexpressed statements, while the statement it makes on the surface, grammatically, is arranged so as to make the reader disregard it completely. Literally, the stanza says: *Whom do you expect to find waiting for you? Not me.* But the denying and elliptical *not me* is not an answer to the surface question; that question is almost rhetorical, and obviously gets a *me;* the *not me* denies *And I'll satisfy your expectations and be there?*—the implied corollary of the surface question; and the flippant and brutal finality of the *not me* implies that the expectations are foolish. (A belief that can be contradicted so carelessly and completely—by a person in a position to know—is a foolish one.) The stanza says: *You do expect to find me and ought not to* and *You're actually such a fool as to count on my being there?* and *So I'll be there, eh? Not me.*

Some paraphrases of the two stanzas will show how extraordinarily much they do mean; they illustrate the quality of poetry that is almost its most characteristic, compression. These paraphrases are not very imaginative—the reader can find justification for any statement in the actual words of the poem. (Though not in any part considered in isolation. The part as part has a misleading look of independence and reality, just as does the word as word; but it has only that relationship to the larger contexts of the poem that the words which compose it have to it, and its significance is similarly controlled and extended by those larger units of which it is a part. A poem is a sort of onion of contexts, and you can no more locate any of the important meanings exclusively in a part than you can locate a relation in one of its terms. The significance of a part may be greatly modified or even in extreme cases completely reversed by later and larger parts and by the whole. This will be illustrated in the following discussion: most of the important meanings attached to the first stanza do not exist when the stanza is considered in isolation.) And the paraphrases are not hypertrophied, they do not even begin to be exhaustive.

Stanza 1: Do you expect me to wait patiently for you there, just as I have done on earth? expect that, in Hell, after death, things will go on for you just as they do here on earth? that there, after crossing and drinking Lethe and oblivion, I'll still be thinking of human you, still be waiting faithfully there on the wharf for you to arrive, with you still my only interest, with me still your absolutely devoted slave,—just as we are here? Do you really? Do you actually suppose that you yourself, then, will be able to expect it? Even when dead, all alone, on that grim ferry, in the middle of the dark forgetful river, all that's left of your human life one coin, you'll be stupid or inflexible or faithful enough to *count* on (you're sure, are you, so sure that not even a doubt enters your mind?) finding me waiting there? How are we to understand an inflexibility that seems almost incredible? Is it because you're pathetically deluded about love's constancy, my great lasting love for you? (This version makes the *you* sympathetic; but it is unlikely, an unstressed possibility, and the others do not.) Or is it that you're so sure of my complete enslavement that you know death itself can't change it? Or are you so peculiarly stupid that you can't even conceive of any essential change away from your past life and knowledge, even after the death that has destroyed them both? Or is it the general inescapable stupidity of mankind, who can conceive of death only in human and vital terms? (Housman's not giving the reasons, when the reasons must be thought about if the poem is to be understood, forces the reader to make them for himself, and to see that there is a wide range that must be considered. This is one of the most important principles of compression in poetry; these implied foundations or justifications for a statement might be called *bases*.) Are you actually such a fool as to believe that? So I'll be there? Not me. You're wrong. There things are really different.

One of the most important elements in the poem is the tone of the *not me*. Its casualness, finality, and matter-of-fact bluntness give it almost the effect of slang. It is the crudest of denials. There is in it a laconic brutality, an imperturbable and almost complacent vigor; it has certainly a sort of contempt. Contempt for what? Contempt at himself for his faithlessness? contempt at himself for his obsessing weakness—for not being faithless now instead of then? Or contempt at her, for being bad enough to keep things as they are, for being stupid enough to imagine that they will be so always? The tone is both threatening and disgusted. It shivers between all these qualities like a just-thrown knife. And to what particular denial does this tone attach? how specific, how general a one? These are changes a reader can easily ring for himself; but I hope he will realize their importance. Variations of this formula of alternative possibilities make up one of the most valuable resources of the poet.

The second stanza is most thoroughly ambiguous; there are two entirely different levels of meaning for the whole, and most of the parts exhibit a comparable stratification. I give a word-for-word analysis:

Do not expect me to be after death what I was alive and human: the *fond* (1. *foolish;* 2. *loving*—you get the same two meanings in the synonym *doting*) *brisk* (the normal meanings are favorable: *full of life, keenly alive or alert, energetic;* but here the context forces it over into *officious, undignified, solicitous, leaping at your every word*—there is a pathetic ignoble sense to it here) *lackey* (the most contemptuous and degrading form of the word *servant:* a servile follower, a toady) *to fetch and carry* (you thought so poorly of me that you let me perform nothing but silly menial physical tasks; thus, our love was nothing but the degrading relationship of obsequious servant and contemptuous master), *the true* (1. *constant, loyal devoted, faithful;* 2. *properly so-called, ideally or typically such*—the perfectly slavish slave) *sick-hearted* (1. cowardly, disheartened in a weak discouraged ignoble way, as a Spartan would have said of helots, 'These sick-hearted slaves'; 2. sick at heart at the whole mess, his own helpless subjection. There was a man in one of the sagas who had a bad boil on his foot; when asked why he didn't limp and favor it, he replied: 'One walks straight while the leg is whole.' If the reader imagines this man as a slave he will see sharply the more elevated sense of the phrase *sick-hearted slave*) *slave* (1. the conventional hardly meant sense in which we use it of lovers, as an almost completely dead metaphor; this sense has very little force here; or 2. the literal *slave:* the relation of slave to master is not pleasant, not honorable, is between lovers indecent and horrible, but immensely comprehensive—their love is made even more compulsive and even less favorable). But here I leave the word-by-word analysis for more general comment. I think I hardly need remark on the shock in this treatment, which forces over the conventional unfelt terms into their literal degrading senses; and this shock is amplified by the paradoxical fall through *just city* and *free land* into *the grave.* (Also, the effect of the *lackey—carry* and versification of the first line of the stanza should be noted.)

Let me give first the favorable literal surface sense of *the just city and free land of the grave,* its sense on the level at which you take Housman's Greek underworld convention seriously. The house of Hades is the *just city* for a number of reasons: in it are the three just judges; in it are all the exemplary convicts, from Ixion to the Danaides, simply dripping with justice; here justice is meted equally to the anonymous and rankless dead; there is no corruption here. It is the *free land* because here the king and the slave are equal (though even on the level of death as the Greek underworld, the horrid irony has begun to intrude—Achilles knew, and Housman knows, that it is better to be the slave of a poor farmer than king among the hosts of the dead); because here we are free at last from life; and so on and so on.

But at the deeper level, the *just* fastened to *city,* the *city* fastened to *grave,* have an irony that is thorough. How are we to apply *just* to a place where corruption and nothingness are forced on good and bad, innocent and guilty alike? (From Housman's point of view it might be called mercy, but never justice.) And the *city* is as bad; the cemetery looks like a city of the graves, of the stone rectangular houses—but a city without occupations, citizens, without life: a shell, a blank check that can never be filled out. And can we call a land *free* whose inhabitants cannot move a finger, are compelled as completely as stones? And can we call the little cave, the patch of darkness and pressing earth, the *land* of the grave?

And why are we told to expect him not, the slave, the lackey, in the just city and free land of the grave? Because he is changed now, a citizen of the Greek underworld, engrossed in its games and occupations, the new interests that he has acquired? O no, the change is complete, not from the old interests to new ones, but from any interests to none; do not expect him because he has ceased to exist, he is really, finally different now. It is foolish to expect *anything* of the world after death. But we can expect nothingness; and that is better than this world, the poem is supposed to make us feel; there, even though we are overwhelmed impartially and completely, we shall be free of the evil of this world—a world whose best thing, love, is nothing but injustice and stupidity and slavery. This is why the poet resorts to the ambiguity that permits him to employ the adjectives *just* and *free:* they seem to apply truly on the surface level, and ironically at the other; but in a way they, and certainly the air of reward and luck and approbation that goes with them, apply truly at the second level as well. This is the accusation and condemnation of life that we read so often in Housman: that the grave seems better, we are glad to be in it.

We ought not to forget that this poem is a love-poem by the living 'me' of the poem to its equally living 'you': *when we are dead things will be different—and I'm glad of it*. It is, considerably sublimated, the formula familiar to such connections: *I wish I were dead;* and it has more than a suspicion of the child's *when I'm dead, then they'll be sorry*. It is an accusation that embodies a very strong statement of the underlying antagonism, the real ambivalence of most such relationships. The condemnation applied to the world for being bad is extended to the *you* for not being better. And these plaints are always pleas; so the poem has an additional force. Certainly this particular-seeming little poem turns out to be general enough: it carries implicit in it attitudes (aggregates of related generalizations) toward love, life, and death.

3.

It nods and curtseys and recovers
    When the wind blows above,
The nettle on the graves of lovers
    That hanged themselves for love.

The nettle nods, the wind blows over,
    The man, he does not move,
The lover of the grave, the lover
    That hanged himself for love.

This innocent-looking little nature poem is actually, I think, a general quasi-philosophical piece meant to infect the reader with Housman's own belief about the cause of any action. (I am afraid it is a judgment the reader is likely neither to resist nor recognize.) The nettle and the wind are Housman's specific and usual symbols. Housman's poetry itself is a sort of home-made nettle wine ('out of a stem that scored the hand/I wrung it in a weary land'); the nettle has one poem entirely to itself, XXXII in *New Poems*. No matter what you sow, only the nettle grows; no matter what happens, it flourishes and remains—'the numberless, the lonely, the thronger of the land.' It peoples cities, it waves above the courts of kings; 'and touch it and it strings.' Stating what symbols 'mean' is a job the poet has properly avoided; but, roughly, the nettle stands for the hurting and inescapable conditions of life, the prosperous (but sympathetically presented and almost admiringly accepted) evil of the universe—'great Necessity,' if you are not altogether charmed by it. What the wind is Housman states himself (in 'On Wenlock Edge the wind's in trouble'; but it is given the same value in several other poems, notably 'The weeping Pleiads wester'): the 'tree of man' is never quiet because the wind, 'the gale of life,' blows through it always.

What I said just before the analysis of the first stanza of 'Crossing alone the nighted ferry' is true here too; many of one's remarks about the first stanza of this poem will be plausible or intelligible only in the light of one's consideration of the whole poem. In the first line, *It nods and curtseys and recovers,* there is a shock which grows out of the contrast between this demure performance and its performer, the Housman nettle. The nettle is merely repeating above the grave, compelled by the wind, what the man in the grave did once, when the wind blew through him. So living is (we must take it as being) just a repetition of little meaningless nodding actions, actions that haven't even the virtue of being our own—since the wind forces them out of us; life as the wind makes man as the tree or nettle helpless and determined. This illustrates the general principle that in poetry you make judgments by your own preliminary choice of symbols, and force the reader who accepts the symbols to accept the judgments implicit in them. A symbol, like Bowne's 'concept,' is a nest of judgments; the reader may accept the symbols, and then be cautious about accepting judgments or generalizations, but the damage is done.

The images in the poem are quite general: 'the nettle on the graves of lovers that hanged themselves for love' is not any one nettle, not really any particular at all, but a moderately extensive class. (If Housman were writing a pure poem, a nature poem, he would go about it differently; here the generality is insisted on—any lover, any nettle will do well enough: if you prove something for *any* you prove it for *all,* and Housman is arranging all this as a plausible *any.*) There is of course irony, at several levels, in a nettle's dancing obliviously (*nod* and *curtsey* and *recover* add up to *dance*) on the grave of the dead lover. All flesh is grass; but worse here, because the grass which is the symbol for transitoriness outlasts us. (The reader may say, remembering *The stinging nettle only will still be found to stand:* 'But the nettle is a symbol of lasting things to Housman, not of transitory ones.' Actually it manages for both here, for the first when considered as a common symbol, for the second when considered as Housman's particular one.

But this ambiguity in symbols is frequent; without it they would be much less useful. Take a similar case, *grass:* this year's grass springs up and withers, and is shorter than man; but *grass,* all grass, lasts forever. With people we have different words for the two aspects, *men* and *man.* The whole business of thinking of the transitory grass as just the same more lasting than man—in one form or another, one of the stock poetic subjects—is a beautiful fallacy that goes like this: *Grass*—the year-after-year process—is more lasting than *men;* substituting *man* for *men* and this year's blade for the endless grass, you end by getting a proposition that everybody from Job on down or up has felt, at one time or another, thoroughly satisfactory.) Why a nettle to dance on the grave? Because in English poetry flowers grow on the graves of these lovers who have died for love, to show remembrance; Housman puts the nettle there, for forgetfulness. In the other poems the flower 'meant' their love—here the nettle means it. All the nettle's actions emphasize its indifference and removedness. The roses in the ballads were intimately related to the lovers, and entwined themselves above the graves —the nature that surrounded the lovers was thoroughly interested in their game, almost as human as they; the nettle above this grave is alone, inhuman and casual, the representative of a nature indifferent to man.

The fifth and sixth lines of the poem are there mainly to establish this shocking paradox: here is a sessile thing, a plant, that curtseys and nods, while the man, the most thoroughly animate of all beings, cannot even move. Looked at in the usual way this is gloomy and mortifying, and that is the surface force it has here; but looked at in another way, Housman's way, there is a sort of triumph in it: the most absolute that man can know. That is what it is for Housman. Once man was tossed about helplessly and incessantly by the wind that blew through him—now the toughest of all plants is more sensitive, more easily moved than he. In other words, death is better than life, nothing is better than anything. Nor is this a silly adolescent pessimism peculiar to Housman, as so many critics assure you. It is better to be dead than alive, best of all never to have been born—said a poet approvingly advertised as seeing life steadily and seeing it whole; and if I began an anthology of such quotations there it would take me a long time to finish. The attitude is obviously inadequate and just as obviously important.

The triumph here leads beautifully into the poem's final statement: the triumph at being in the grave, one with the grave, prepares us for the fact that it was the grave, not any living thing, that the lover loved, and hanged himself for love of. The statement has some plausibility: hanging yourself for love of someone is entirely silly, so far as any possession or any furthering of your love is concerned, but if you are in love with death, killing yourself is the logical and obvious and only way to consummate your love. For the lover to have killed himself for love of a living thing would have been senseless; but his love for her was only ostensible, concealing—from himself too—the 'common wish for death,' his real passion for the grave.

But if this holds for this one case; if in committing this most sincere and passionate, most living of all acts (that is, killing yourself for love; nothing else shows so complete a contempt for death and consequences, so absolute a value placed on another living creature), the lover was deceiving himself about his motives, and did it, not for love of anything living, but because of his real love for death; then everybody must do everything for the same reason. (This is a judgment too exaggerated for anyone to expect to get away with, the reader may think; but judgments of life tend to this form—'Vanity, vanity, all is vanity.') For the lover is the perfectly simplified, extreme case. This is what is called a crucial experiment. (It is one of Mill's regular types of induction.) The logic runs: If you can prove that in committing this act—an act about the motives of which the actor is so little likely to be deceived, an act so little likely to have the love of death as his motive —the actor was deceived, and had the love of death as his motive, then you can prove it for any other act the motive of which is more likely to be the love of death, and about the motives of which it is more likely that the actor might be deceived.

But for the conclusion to be true the initial premise must be true, the lover's one motive must have been the wish for death; and Housman has of course not put in even a word of argument for the truth of that premise, he has merely stated it, with the most engaging audacity and dogmatism—has stated it innocently, as a fact obvious as any other of these little natural facts about the wind and the nettle and the cemetery. He has produced it not as a judgment but as a datum, and the sympathetic reader has accepted it as such. He is really treating it as a percept, and percepts have no need for proof, they are neither true nor false, they are just there. If he had tried to prove the truth of the premise he would have convinced only those who already believed in the truth of the conclusion, and those people (i.e., himself) didn't need to be convinced. With the poem as it is, the reader is convinced; or if he objects, the poet can object disingenuously in return, 'But you've made the absurd error of taking hypothetical reasoning as categorical. My form is: *If* A, *then* B; I'm not interested in *proving* A. Though, of course, if you decide to remove the *if,* and assert A, then B is asserted also; and A is awfully plausible, isn't it?—just part of the data of the poem; you could hardly reject it, could you?'

Two of the generalizations carried over by this poem—that our actions are motivated by the wish for death, that our ostensible reasons for acts are merely rationalizations, veneers of apparent motive overlying the real levels of motivation—are, in a less sweeping form, psychological or psychoanalytical commonplaces today. But I am not going to hold up Housman's poem as a masterly anticipation of our own discoveries; so far as I can see, Housman was not only uninterested but incapable in such things, and pulled these truths out of his pie not because of wit, but because of the perverse and ingenious obstinacy that pulled just such gloomy judgments out of any pie at all. Here the shock and unlikeliness of what he said were what recommended it to him; and the discovery that these have been mitigated would merely have added to his gloom.

R. P. BLACKMUR

The Shorter Poems of Thomas Hardy

(1940)

Both for those who enjoy the bulk of Thomas Hardy's poems and for those whose genuine enjoyment of a few poems is almost overcome by a combination of depression and dismay at the bulk, the great need is some sort of canon—a criterion more for exclusion than for judgment. At the general enjoyers this essay is not directly aimed; nor is it meant to be as irritating as it will seem because it names what it discards more clearly than it specifies what it keeps. It is meant rather to be a help—a protection, a refuge—for those who see in Hardy's poetry a great art beaten down, much of it quite smothered to death, by the intellectual machinery by means of which Hardy expected it to run and breathe free.

However abnormal, the condition is far from unusual. If we may say that in Shelley we see a great sensibility the victim of the early stages of religious and philosophical decay in the nineteenth century, and that in Swinburne we see an even greater poetic sensibility vitiated by the substitution of emotion for subject matter, then it is only a natural step further to see in Hardy the consummate double ruin of an extraordinary sensibility that had been deprived of both emotional discipline and the structural support of a received imagination. Hardy was a free man in everything that concerns the poet; which is to say, helpless, without tradition; and he therefore rushed for support into the slavery of ideas whenever his freedom failed him. The astonishing thing is—as with Shelley and Swinburne to a lesser degree—that he was able to bring so much poetry with him into a pile of work that shows, like a brush heap, all the disadvantages of the nineteenth-century mind as it affected poetry, and yet shows almost none of the difficulties—whether overcome, come short of, or characteristic—belonging to the production or appreciation of poetry itself. The poetry is there—permanently; and it is our business to get at it. What obstructs us is man-made, impermanent, and need not have been there at all. It is a thicket of ideas, formulas, obsessions, undisciplined compulsions, nonce insights, and specious particularities. That is, it is accidental, not substantial, and can be cleared away; then we can come at the feeling, the conviction, the actuality, that are there, not underneath, but throughout the body of poetry.

Everybody who has read a volume of Thomas Hardy's verse retains a secure impression, like the smart of a blow, of what it was like. Everybody who has read the Apology prefixed to *Late Lyrics* knows that Hardy and many of his reviewers disagreed as to what made the blow smart. The reviewers referred to unrelieved pessimism; Hardy insisted he was no pessimist, was applying ideas to life, and that the smart came from 'exacting a full look at the worst.' That the reviewers were right on instinct, ignorantly and with the wrong slogan, and that Hardy was also right, with an equivalent ignorance and a misapprehension of *his* slogan, is a part of what these notes are meant to show as a basis for exclusion. We are committed then to a study of ignorance in poetry. Specifically, we are bound to segregate examples of those ideas which Hardy applied, like inspection stickers, to those stages of activity which most appealed to him as life, and then to see what happened to the poetry as a consequence.

What Hardy meant by his submission to Arnold's phrase about poetry's being a criticism of life—and that is what his own phrase amounts to—is neither always clear nor always consistent. But he did use ideas and did apply them, and we may provisionally say what the practice amounted to. Hardy seems to have used the word *idea* to represent a pattern of behavior, judgment, or significance. He wrote as if his ideas had an authority equal to their availability, and as if that authority were both exclusive and sufficient. If you had the pattern everything else followed and followed right. Pattern was the matrix of experience. If you could show experience as pattern, you showed all that could be shown; what would not fit, what could not be made to fit the pattern, did not count. Further, Hardy's idea-patterns were not heuristic, not designed to discover, spread, or multiply significance, but were held rather as rigid frames to limit experience so far as possible and to substitute for what they could not enclose. This is the absolutist, doctrinaire, as we now call it totalitarian, frame of mind: a mind of great but brittle rigidity, tenacious to the point of fanaticism, given when either hungry or endangered to emotion: a mind that seems to require, whether for object or outlet, eventual resort to violence. For only by violence, by violation, can experience be made to furnish it satisfaction.

We are familiar with the consequences of this frame of mind in religion, in politics, and in what passes for philosophy. We should also be familiar with it in the chores of daily life: the life we get over with as so much blind action, but which yet needs its excuse, its quick, quibbled justification. We are not familiar with it in the works of rational imagination—at least not as a dominant value or as a source of strength. When we see it, we see it as weakness, as substitution, precisely as work not done: as, at its best, melodrama, and at its worst, dead convention or the rehearsal of formula; and that is what we see in the great bulk of Hardy's verse. The very frame of mind that provided the pattern of his writing provided also, and at once, the terms of its general failure: leaving success, so far as his conscious devotions went, an accident of escape from the governing frame. Concern is in the end with the success, and will show it no accident; in the meantime with the considerations that make it seem so.

It is worth mentioning that the effect of the great liberating ideas of the nineteenth century upon Hardy's ideas was apparently restrictive and even imprisoning. The inductive ideas—the opening areas of experience—associated with the names of Huxley and Mill and Darwin and Arnold, Maxwell and Kelvin, Acton, Lecky, Bellamy, and Marx; all this affected Hardy if at all mostly as so much dead deductive limitation: a further measure for the cripplement of human sensibility. It is this effect that we have in mind I think when we refer to Hardy's stoicism, his pessimism, or to any of the forms of his addiction to a mechanically deduced fate. His gain from the impact of the new sciences and the new democracy, and from the destruction of dead parts of religion by the Higher Criticism, was all loss in his work: a loss represented by what we feel as the privation of his humanity. To push the emphasis an inch, it sometimes seems that his sensibility had lost, on the expressive level, all discrimination of human value, human dignity, and the inextricability in the trope of human life, of good and evil. It was a terrible privation for his work, and he bore it—that was his stoicism—without ever either the smile or the revulsion of recognition; he bore it, as a practical writer, by making various mechanical substitutions: keeping the violence without the value, the desperation without the dignity, the evil without the good—so far as these operations could be performed without mortality—as the basis of substitution.

It is in these substitutions that we find the obsessive ideas that governed the substance and procedure of the great bulk of the poems. Some of these obsessions—for they lost the pattern-character of ideas and became virtually the objects of sensibility rather than the skeleton of attention—have to do with love, time, memory, death, and nature, and have to do mainly with the disloyalty, implacability, or mechanical fatality of these. Some are embedded in single words and their variations; some in tones of response; some in mere violence of emotion; some in the rudimentary predictive pattern of plot; again many in complications of these. The embedded forms, in turn, largely control by limitation, by asserting themselves as principles of exclusion more than by their force as agents of selection, what is actually noted, observed, represented in the poem in question. Were one master of the counters Hardy uses, one could, so much does the production of his poems follow the rules, once the poem was begun, play the hand out for him to the end. Almost the only objective influence consistently exerted upon his verse is the influence of meter; from which indeed his happiest and some of his most awkward effects come. There remain, of course, besides, neither objective nor otherwise, but pervasive, the fermenting, synergical influence of words thrown together, and the primary influence of the rhythm of his sensibility; that double influence in language used, which a skillful poet knows how to invoke, and which *is* invoked in just the degree that he has the sense of the actuality wanted already within him, when it shows as the very measure of his imagination and the object of his craft, but which, in the poet who, like Hardy, has violated his sensibility with ideas, comes only adventitiously and in flashes, and shows chiefly as the measure of imagination missed.

Neither what is adventitious nor what is missed can be dealt with at length. Our waking concern must be with what is plotted, excreted, left as sediment—with what is used. In running over the thousand odd pages of Hardy's verse, feeling them as mass if not as unity, we wake at once, under the obsessive heads listed above, especially to the obsession of what will here be called crossed fidelities as of the commanding, determining order for the whole mass—though not of the poems we most value. By crossed fidelities I mean the significant subject matter of all those poems dealing with love, young, mature, or married, or with the conventional forms of illicit sexual passion, in which at least one and often all the represented characters commits, has committed, or longs to commit fraud upon the object of fidelity, or else loses the true object by mischance, mistake, or misunderstanding, or else discovers either in the self or the object through mere lapse of time or better acquaintance some privy devastating fault. Surely no serious writer ever heaped together so much *sordid* adultery, so much *haphazard* surrender of human value as Hardy did in these poems, and with never a pang or incentive but the pang of pattern and the incentive of inadequacy, and yet asked his readers to consider that haphazard sordor a full look at the worst—a tragic view of life—exacted with honesty and power.

How it came about is I suppose simple. Hardy had a genuine insight into the instability of irresponsible passion and the effect upon it of conventional and social authority. *Jude* was his clearest expression of that insight, and *Tess* the deepest, though neither touches for imaginative strength and conviction, for expensiveness of moral texture as opposed to cheapness, *Cousine Bette, Madame Bovary,* or *Anna Karenina.* But he had the insight, and saw it strike home; therefore he applied it. Unfortunately, he had to a great degree what can only be characterized as a scandalous sensibility. Seeing or guessing the vast number of disorderly, desperate marriages in the world he knew, he applied his combination of insight and observation almost solely to the scandalous pattern—precisely as Antony and Cleopatra, Solomon and Sheba, are heard of in smoking rooms and country stores, only without the dirt or the relish, just the pattern. The pattern as it is repeated more and more barely becomes at first cynical and then meretricious. Hardy mistook, in short, the imaginative function of insight just as he fell short of the imaginative value of convention. Insight is to heighten the significance *of* something; it reveals the pattern *in* the flesh, the trope or forward stress of life. Convention is to determine how the value of that forward stress, so embedded, so empatterned, is received. In works of imagination they make a dichotomy where if either branch is dead the vitality of the tree is impaired. You cannot express, you cannot dramatize human life unless your insight and your convention —your simplifications of substance—are somehow made to seem the very form of that life. Your handy formula will not do, unless you every time, by the persuasive force of your drama, carry it back to the actual instance of which, in your case of instruments, it is the cheap abstraction. That, again, is the skill of the artist; that he knows how to invest any formula, however barrenly presented—like that of *Lear,* say—with enough of the riches of direct sensibility to make it actual and complete for sense and interest; when insight and convention and formula become, as they properly ought to be, all afterthought.

Here is a handy juncture to introduce an image from the early Hardy, before he undertook to substitute his own formulas for those traditionally available, and leant naturally upon the strength of his predecessors to buttress his effects. One of the earliest dated poems is the series of four Shakespearean sonnets called "She to Him." They are facile in mood and mode: it is the jilted lover addressing the beloved after the fashion of Shakespeare or Sidney or Drayton in easy iambics stretched out for meter and rhyme and composed largely on the *when* and *then* scheme. We have the Sportsman Time, Life's sunless hill and fitful masquerade, and we have a good deal of desolated martyrdom supporting a deathless love—all properties so dear because so adequately ominous to the young sensibility, and all used well enough to make, for the reader, a good journeyman's exercise, and show, in the poet, positive promise. What we see in these sonnets is, with one exception, the traditional body of poetry absorbing, holding, expressing the individual apprentice until, if he does, he finds the skill and the scope to add to that body. The exception leaps out: one of the best tropes Hardy ever produced and perhaps the only one of similar excellence in its kind.

> Amid the happy people of my time
> Who work their love's fulfilment, I appear
> Numb as a vane that cankers on its point,
> True to the wind that kissed ere canker came: . . .

Grant its point, which is universally easy, and the metaphor is inexhaustible: it stretches, living, in every direction through its theme. The lines are well enough known and have been quoted before, for example in Symons' early essay on Hardy's verse, and too much ought not to be made of them here, yet they are so startling in Hardy's general context that it seems plausible to look for some other explanation of their appearance than the accidental.

The theory of accidents in poetry like that of idiopathy in medicine is only a cloak for inadequate observation and explains nothing. Language in the form of poetry is as objective as a lesion of the meninges; only we get at the objectivity by different jumps of the inspecting imagination. The appearance of Hardy's trope, if it was not accidental, was, let us say, due to the fertility of the form which he was practicing; the form dragged it out of him. Not the metrical form alone, not any aspect of it separately, but the whole form of the Elizabethan sonnet taken as a mode of feeling and the composition of feeling—that was the enacting agent. The generalized trope of the mind was matrix for the specific trope of sensibility. Precisely as we are able, as readers, to respond to the form—the energizing pattern of music and meaning—of this special type of sonnet as something felt, so Hardy in this figure was able to work from his own feelings into the form *as a poet:* he made something, however fragmentarily, *of* the form. The test of manufacture is that both speed and meaning are absolute, at once in terms of themselves and in terms of the form they exemplify. The tautology between form and significance is absolute within the limits of language and inexhaustible within the limits of apprehension. It might be put that Hardy was here almost only the transmitting agent of an imaginative event that occurred objectively in the words and the pattern of the words; when the true or ultimate agency might be thought of as lying in the invoked reality of the whole form. It is the tradition not only at work, but met, and used. Doubtless Hardy had read a good deal of Elizabethan and Jacobean poetry, and got from his reading the themes as well as the means of his early poems; certainly in this poem, for two lines, he got the full authority of the form at once as a cumulus and as a fresh instance. Authority, then, is the word of explanation that we wanted, and we may take it in two senses: as the principle of derived right and as the very quality of authorship which has as its perfection the peculiar objective virtue of anonymity. That is one's gain from tradition: anonymous authority. We shall come at it later in these notes otherwise and expensively derived.

Meanwhile it is a good deal of weight to heap on two lines; the pity is that it cannot be generally heaped over the whole body of Hardy's verse. That is the privative fact about most of Hardy's verse: he dispensed with tradition in most of his ambitious verse; it is willful where it should be authoritative, idiosyncratic where it should be anonymous; it is damaged—Mr. Eliot would say it is damned—by the vanity of

Hardy's adherence to his personal and crotchety obsessions. It is so by choice, but not exactly by discrimination; rather choice by a series of those chances to whose operation in the moral field Hardy was so warmly addicted. (We might risk it parenthetically that Hardy was incapable of the act of choice precisely as he was incapable of discerning the ideal which would have made choice necessary.) Hardy never rejected the tradition of English poetry; probably, indeed, if he thought about it at all, he thought he followed it and even improved it by his metrical experiments. What he did was more negative than rejection. He failed to recognize and failed to absorb those modes of representing felt reality persuasively and credibly and justly, which make up, far more than meters and rhymes and the general stock of versification, the creative habit of imagination, and which are the indefeasible substance of tradition. Put another way, it is the presence of that achieved tradition which makes great poems resemble each other as much as they differ and even 'sound' so much alike; and to its absence is due both the relative unreality and incompatibility of minor poetry—especially in its failures. But, to return to Hardy in relation to the major modes of tradition, no poet can compose the whole of his poetry himself, and if he does not go for help to poetic authority he will go elsewhere, substituting the extra-poetic for the poetic as much as may be necessary all along the line just to get the poem on paper. Hardy's elsewhere was not far off: it was in his own head: in his own ideas taken as absolute and conceived as persuasive by mere statement. The result was that he was relieved of the responsibilities of craft; and the worse result for the reader is that, lacking the persuasiveness of craft—lacking objective authority—the validity of the poems comes to depend on the validity of the ideas in that vacuum which is the medium of simple assertion. What we have is the substitution of the authoritarian for the authoritative, of violence for emotion, frenzy for passion, calamity by chance for tragedy by fate.

Hardy, of course, could not have accepted any such description of his intellectual behavior toward his verse. What he thought he did was, to repeat, to apply his ideas pretty directly to life; and it probably never occurred to him that his practice involved any substitution—or thereby any weakening, any diminution of either life or idea—of intellectual or emotional predilection for actual representation. Judging by his practice he did not know what substitution was, and evidently felt that he quickened the life and heightened the reality of his poems by making their action—what they were meant to show—so often hinge upon an unrepresented, a merely stated idea. In short, and this is what we have been leading up to, what Hardy really lacked was the craft of his profession—technique in the wide sense; that craft, which, as a constant, reliable possession, would have taught him the radical necessity as it furnished the means, of endowing every crucial statement with the virtual force of representation. The availing fount of that enabling craft springs from the whole tradition of poetry. Just as we say that his mastery of the particular, limited tradition of seventeenth-century metaphysical poetry enabled Henry King to compose his 'Exequy,' so we may say that every poet writes his poetry only as his poetry embodies what is necessary of the whole tradition. The same is true of reading poetry, but on a lesser level; where we often call the mastery of tradition the cultivation of taste, and ought sometimes to call it just getting used to what a poem or body of poetry is about. In Hardy's case, the interesting fact is that he sometimes possessed the tradition and sometimes did not; and the fertile possibility is that possession or lack may explain what otherwise seems the accident of success or failure.

To his ideas as such, then, there is no primary objection. The objection is to his failure to absorb them by craft into the representative effect of his verse. Indeed, from a literary point of view, all that is objectionable in Hardy's ideas would have been overcome, had they been absorbed; for they would have struck the reader as consequences instead of instigators of significance. It is the certification of craft, that what it handles it makes actual: objective, authoritative, anonymous. The final value of a poet's version of the actual is another matter, which literary criticism may take up but with which it ought not to be preoccupied. The standards engaged in the discernment of value cannot be exclusively literary standards. Here, at least for the moment, let us stick to those values which can be exemplified in terms of craft.

Some of Hardy's best effects—which should be kept in mind while looking at his worst—come when his triple obsession with death, memory, and time makes by mutual absorption something of a trinity. It is an absorption which excludes both that 'full look at the worst' which he wanted his poems to exact, and also the mechanical crux of what we have called crossed fidelities. Then the business of the poet proceeded free of the violation of ideas, and the ideas became themselves something seen or felt. Here is the nubbin of what is meant, from the poem 'One We Knew.'

She said she had often heard the gibbet creaking
  As it swayed in the lightning flash,
Had caught from the neighbouring town a small child's shrieking
  At the cart-tail under the lash . . .

With cap-framed face and long gaze into the embers—
  We seated around her knees—
She would dwell on such dead themes, not as one who remembers,
  But rather as one who sees.

There is a dignity of tone, and a sense of release in the language, in the poems of this order, which give them a stature elsewhere beaten down: the stature of true or fundamental poetic piety. Since the effect is produced as the series of details, it needs to be shown in the full length of such a poem as 'She Hears the Storm.'

There was a time in former years—
  While my roof-tree was his—
When I should have been distressed by fears
  At such a night as this!

I should have murmured anxiously,
  'The pricking rain strikes cold;
His road is bare of hedge or tree,
  And he is getting old.'

But now the fitful chimney-roar,
  The drone of Thorncombe trees,
The Froom in flood upon the moor,
  The mud of Mellstock Leaze,

The candle slanting sooty wick'd,
  The thuds upon the thatch,
The eaves-drops on the window flicked,
  The clacking garden-hatch,

And what they mean to wayfarers,
  I scarcely heed or mind;
He has won that storm-tight roof of hers
  Which Earth grants all her kind.

The true piety here exemplified consists in the celebration of the feeling of things for their own sake and not for the sake of the act of feeling;

and the celebration becomes poetic when the things are so put together as to declare their own significance, when they can be taken to mean just what they are—when the form, the meter, the various devices of poetry merely provide the motion of the meaning. In this poem and in others of its class, Hardy obtains objective and self-sufficient strength precisely by *reducing* his private operative means to a minimum, by getting rid of or ignoring most of the machinery he ordinarily used altogether. Instead of applying ideas to life—instead of turning the screws to exact meaning—he merely took what he found and let the words it came in, put it together. Doubtless, if asked, he would have said that the poem came on inspiration, and would have valued it less highly as craft for that reason. He evidently preferred to assault his material with an emotion, preferably violent, and an idea, preferably distraught, in either hand. At any rate, something such was his regular practice, so long continued—over sixty years—that it seems certain he could never have noticed that his poems produced more emotion and even developed more nearly into ideas, when he came to them, as it were, quite disarmed.

This is no argument for what is called inspired writing, as inspiration is commonly understood. It would be a better account of the matter to say that there was more work, far more attention to the complex task of uniting diverse and disparate detail, in the preparation of 'She Hears the Storm,' or in a single line like 'My clothing clams me, mire-bestarred,' than in a whole handful of those poems deliberately critical of life. It is simply that Hardy was unaware of the nature of poetic work, or of how much he did in spite of himself, or of how vastly much more was done for him in those remote, impressionable, germinal areas of the sensibility—that work which transpires, almost without invocation and often beyond control, to show as both fresh and permanent in what we choose to call *our* works of imagination. The final skill of a poet lies in his so conducting the work he does deliberately do, that the other work—the hidden work, the inspiration, the genius—becomes increasingly available not only in new poems but in old poems re-read.

The only consistent exhibition of such skill in the last century is in the second half of the career of W. B. Yeats. In prose there are others —Mann, James, Gide, possibly Proust, and perhaps Joyce. But these are not our concern and we need not think of them except to buttress the force with which we come back to the example of Yeats as it sits beside the example of Hardy. Yeats was addicted to magic, to a private symbolism, in much the same way, and for similar reasons, that

Hardy was addicted to his set of ideas. Each had been deprived by his education, or the lack of it, of an authoritative faith, and each hastened to set up a scaffold out of the nearest congenial materials strong enough and rigid enough to support the structure imagination meant to rear. It was, and remains, a desperate occupation for each; for the risk was that the scaffold might become so much more important than the poetry as to replace it, and the mere preliminary labor come to be the sum of the work done. Such is indeed the condition of most ambitious poetry seriously regarded, and not only in our own day with its invitation to privation but even in the ages of faith. The poetic imagination is seldom able either to overcome or to absorb the devices by which alone it undertakes its greater reaches. Shakespeare is perhaps the only poet in English whose work habitually overcame its conscious means; which is why we say it is so good a mirror looked at generally, and why, looked at specifically, we say it is all in the words. None of it, where it is good, transcends anything or is about anything: it is itself, its own intention as well as its own meaning. Hence the evident fact that it cannot be imitated except ruinously. You can use Shakespeare but you cannot imitate him; for the imitable elements in his work are either vestigial or unimportant. Yeats's poetry rarely overcame its means, but it usually absorbed them in his best work so that they became part of its effect. The devices of his private symbolism can be discriminated but they cannot be disengaged from the poems where he used them; the devices, that is, are partly what the poems are about, and to the degree that they are discriminated, whether for or against, they limit the vitality—the meaning—of the poems in which they occur. You need to know beforehand what Yeats meant to do, and that knowledge delimits the poem and makes it precarious. It is the key that may be lost. With the key, the poetry of Yeats may be both used and imitated; for the discriminated symbolism, once made objective in Yeats's poems, can be put to similar use elsewhere. Hardy's poetry, relatively, almost never either overcame or absorbed its means. On the contrary, the more ambitious the poem, the more the means tend to appear as the complete substitute for the poem; so that what should have been produced by the progression of the poem never appears except in the form—or formula—of intention. Thus Hardy's ambitious poetry may be imitated, and often is, but cannot be used, which is why the imitations are bad. For in the class of poems we speak of, the imitable elements—all that goes by rote, by declaration, by formula, all that can be re-duplicated—constitute almost all that is actually in the words. The rest—what

Hardy wanted to write about—is only imputedly present and never transpires except as the sympathetic reader, entertaining similar intentions and inviting identic emotions, finds himself accepting the imputed as actual. It may be observed that such readers are common and inhabit all of us to the great detriment of our taste but to the great benefit, too, of our general sensibility; which brings us to the problem of approach central to all our reading, not only the reading of poets like Hardy where it is necessary to show great good will, but also poets like Yeats where it is less necessary, and poets like the best of Shakespeare where it may impede reading in the proper sense.

If we were not initially ready to accept an author's formula we could never discover what he had done with or in spite of it. There is the benefit. The evil lies in that sloth of mind which finds acceptable only those formulas which are familiar, or violent, and which insists on recognizing just what was expected—or 'desired'—and nothing else. In this confusion of good and evil—of good will and sloth—lies one aspect of the problem of approach. As Hardy himself did not know, neither does the reader know how far in a given poem sloth or good will is responsible for the initial effect. We look at a poem that has all the airs and makes all the noises of setting considerable matters in motion. Does it so? or is it merely about the business of searching for a subject to use the airs and noises on? If the latter, does it after all succeed, by divine accident, in catching the subject by the throat or tail? or is it windmill fighting—a whirling, a whirring, and all gone? Certainly the fine lines and passages that vein bad poetry are come at —written and read—somewhat that way; and we need not value them less for that—though we need not thereby value more the slag in which they occur. The economical writ does not run in our experience of poetry, as any library or the best anthology will show. We put up with what we get, no matter what the expense and wastage, in order to use what little we can discover.

Discovery is judgment, and the best judgment is bound to falter, either allowing the poem too little through a deficiency of good will, or accepting as performance what was only expected through undiscriminated sloth, or on both sides at once by overlooking the poem's stretches of plain good writing—writing in the language that, as Marianne Moore says, 'cats and dogs can read.' Take Hardy at his face value and you may falter in the first or second fashion, depending on whether his machinery repels or fascinates you. Take him seriously, and you are liable to the third error; he gets in his own way so much of the time, you do not notice when his poems go straight, or if you do you think the instances not his but anonymous and ignore them when for that very reason you ought to value them most. Anonymity is the sign of the objective achieved at the blessed expense of the personal, whether in the poet or the reader, and is just what to look for when the bother is done. It is only in its imperfections, which distract us as revery or literary criticism, that good poetry fails to reach the condition of anonymity. Only then can there be anything like unanimity between the poem and its readers. For it is a curious thing that when the author pokes his head in so does the reader, and straightway there is no room for the poem. It is either cramped or excluded.

Fortunately for purposes of elucidation, Hardy gives us many versions of his favorite themes. Most of them appear on aesthetically impoverished levels, but occasionally there is a version, enriched both aesthetically and morally, that reaches into the anonymous and objective level. Let us take, for example, a group of poems occurring in *Satires of Circumstance,* all coming pretty much together in the book, and all on Hardy's principal obsessed theme of crossed fidelities. If we select the appropriate facts to emphasize about them, we should have some sort of standard, a canon of inclusion as well as exclusion, to apply roughly throughout the mass of Hardy's work. The poems chosen are called 'The Telegram,' 'The Moth-Signal,' 'Seen by the Waits,' 'In the Days of Crinoline,' and 'The Workbox.'

All these deal one way or another with conflicting loyalties—crossed fidelities—in the double field, as Hardy commonly takes it to be, of love and marriage. The skeleton in the closet of marriage is love, and is often articulated in the light of the honeymoon. Thus in 'The Telegram' the bride either deliberately or distractedly declares to the groom that her true love is not for him but for someone else who, she has just learned by telegram, lies ill and perhaps dying. The bride, stung by the roused apprehension of death, shows her falsity by proving an anterior allegiance to which, in turn, by the fact of marriage, she had already been false. To any wakened sensibility the situation cries out for treatment, promising from the riches of feeling involved, a tragic perspective brought to the focus of emotion. I will not say Hardy preferred, but at any rate he used the violence of ill-chosen circumstance as the sole agent of discovery and engine of emotion. The fatalized, which is to say mechanized, coincidence of the telegram and the honeymoon, seizes on precisely its capacity for riches and no more. It is one of those instances where everything depends on the joint operation of the reader's good will and sloth. If he accepts beforehand the first five stanzas of the poem as somehow both equivalent to Hardy's intention and a furnishing forth of his (the reader's) general store of emotion, then the sixth stanza—what Hardy *made* of the poem—will seem a sufficient delivery of riches. It is the groom who speaks:

What now I see before me is a long lane overhung
With lovelessness, and stretching from the present to the grave.
And I would I were away from this, with friends I knew when young,
    Ere a woman held me slave.

On the other hand, if he persuades his taste to operate—if he is interested in the creation or sedimentation of poetic emotion rather than the venting of his own—he will reject not Hardy's formula but what Hardy did with it, or more exactly he will reject what the formula did to the possibility of a poem. It let the poem down, up to the last stanza —let it down in all but a line or so to about as low a level of writing as a poem can touch and survive at all. The two passably good lines, it may be observed, have no intimate connection with the movement of the poem but merely serve to give a setting: representing a kind of objective circumstance as compared to the chosen circumstance of the telegram.

—The yachts ride mute at anchor and the fulling moon is fair,
And the giddy folk are strutting up and down the smooth parade, . . .

In short, it would seem that where Hardy felt his formula at work he apparently felt no need to employ more than the most conventional stock phraseology. Yet where the formula did not apply he was quick to write as a poet should. Coming now to the last stanza, quoted above, we see that it cheats the sensibility that it ought to have enriched. It is neither guaranteed by what went before, nor does it itself, working backward, pull the poem together. It is something added, not something made; something plainly a substitute for what, whatever it was, ought to have been there. There is no quarrel with the generalness of its statement; its rhythm is strong and invigorates the worn imagery; but it plainly misses with its lame last line any adequate relation to the emotion the poem was meant to construct. Because it would serve as well as an appendage to some other poem as it serves for this, it fails here. Without any intention of rewriting Hardy's intended poem, but just to tinker with the poem as it is, let us try altering the last line to read: 'Ere a man had made me slave'; which would give the words to the bride instead of the groom, and makes poetic sense if not a good verse. Better still would be the deletion of the last line and the substitution of plural for singular personal pronouns in the remaining three lines of the stanza. Either of these stanzas would compel the final stanza both to work back into and draw sustenance from the rest of the poem. Neither change, nor any similar change, could redeem the plain bad writing, but at least all six stanzas would then make an effect of unity for the written aspect of the poem. The unwritten poem—the undeclared possibility—must be left to those with so much superfluous sloth of good will as to *prefer* their poems unwritten.

'The Moth-Signal,' the next poem on our list, shows in its first half the immediate advantage of being relatively well-written as verse, and therefore, just in that well-writtenness, shows the parts of the poem yoked together in a proper poetic conspiracy up to the very end. Here a husband reads, a moth burns in the candle flame, a wife waits and watches. After a light word or two, the wife goes out to look at the moon while the husband goes on with his reading 'In the annals of ages gone,'—a phrase which prepares for what follows objectively, as the *idea* of the burned moth (not the image, which is imperfect) prepares for what follows symbolically and dramatically. At that point, as the quality of the thought begins to strain a little, the quality of the writing begins to slip.

> Outside the house a figure
> Came from the tumulus near,
> And speedily waxed bigger,
> And clasped and called her Dear.
>
> 'I saw the pale-winged token
> You sent through the crack,' sighed she.
> 'That moth is burnt and broken
> With which you lured out me.
>
> 'And were I as the moth is
> It might be better far
> For one whose marriage troth is
> Shattered as potsherds are!'

The metaphor, with straining, becomes inexact with relation to the emotion; both fall mutually out of focus, as that point of strain where inner tension snaps is reached; and the poem ends, like 'The Telegram,' inadequately to its promise—which is to say awkwardly.

Then grinned the Ancient Briton
  From the tumulus treed with pine:
'So, hearts are thwartly smitten
  In these days as in mine!'

It is a question, perhaps, whether 'The Moth-Signal' is one of those poems that 'exact a full look at the worst' or rather instances one of those humorous poems which Hardy said he put in to lighten the burden of that look. There is a tradition, however poor in itself yet honored because ancient, that allows the humorous poet to overlook what would have otherwise been the exigencies of his craft; so that if this is a humorous poem, then it is plain why the rhyme-sounds were allowed to knock both sense and motion out of kilter in the second half of the poem. Perhaps the second half decided to be humorous. Perhaps only the last stanza. If the poem is not to be taken as humorous but as serious with a quality of levity—or low-level poetic wit—meant to tie it together in the reader's response, then one or two suggestions may be made about the order in which the units of perception are arranged. The grinning Briton ought not to be where he is; if anywhere, he should appear after the first stanza quoted above. The reader may try the transposition and see. But then the poem would lack an ending, a rounding off? Not at all, the ending already exists, occupying a place where it does no good but merely kills time while the wife leaves the house. It is the stanza preceding the stanzas quoted above. If it is shifted to its natural terminal position, the poem will come to a proper end with the transposed Briton even deeper in mind. In its present situation the first line of the stanza reads, 'She rose,' that is, to go out. Now we want her back among her potsherds, so we will put it merely:

[When she returned, unheeding]
  Her life-mate then went on
With his mute and museful reading
  In the annals of ages gone.

The point is not that these tinkerings and transpositions actually improve the poems—they may, or may not—but that the poems so lack compositional strength, which is what is meant by inevitability, that they lay themselves open to the temptation of re-composition.

The next poem, 'Seen by the Waits,' carries the moral progress of this order of Hardy's poetry one step further backward—into the arms of deliberate, unvarnished anecdote. A wait, it should be said, is a band of musicians and singers who play and sing carols by night at Christmas and the New Year in the expectation of gratuities. There are many waits in Hardy's poems, put there partly because he loved them and their old music, and partly because they made excellent agents of observation and even better foils to what they observed. The observation was the gratuity. In this poem the waits play by moonlight outside the manor-lady's window, and looking up see her image in a mirror dancing 'thin-draped in her robe of night,' making 'a strange phantasmal sight.' The poem ends:

> She had learnt (we heard when homing)
> That her roving spouse was dead:
> Why she had danced in the gloaming
> We thought, but never said.

Here again the sloth of good will can accept the manufactured observation as genuine if it likes. There is indeed a kind of competence about the poem, as about so many of Hardy's poems based upon his obsessive formulas, that strikes as more astonishing the more you realize what it misses or overlooks: the competence, precisely, of the lyric exercise joined *mechanically* to a predetermined idea, without that attention to language—the working of words among themselves—that makes competence mastery and the mechanical juncture organic. It is not a quibble but a conviction that you cannot, without sublime inspiration, make out of bad writing—'glancing to where a mirror leaned . . . robe of night' or, in the context, the word 'gloaming'—out of such verbal detritus you cannot make a good poem.

'In the Days of Crinoline' is another case in point, but from a slightly different angle. If 'Seen by the Waits' remains an unactualized anecdote because carelessly written, 'In the Days of Crinoline' remains at its low poetic level because no amount of competence could have raised the conception as taken, the *donnée* from which it springs, to a higher level. It remains versification because there was nothing in it to make poetry of. The *donnée* is on the plain scandal level—almost the limerick level—of the cuckolded vicar, and should have appeared in a bawdier *Punch* or a less sophisticated *New Yorker*, where the pat competence of its rhyme scheme and final smacking gag might shine like mastery. Substance and form are for once indistinguishable (though *not* inextricable) because both are trick, and no more. The vicar complacently lets his wife go off to her lover because she wears a plain tilt-bonnet. Once out of sight she draws an ostrich-feathered hat from under her skirts where she then pins her dowdy hood, reversing the operation when she returns home.

> 'To-day,' he said, 'you have shown good sense,
> A dress so modest and so meek
> Should always deck your goings hence
> Alone.' And as a recompense
> He kissed her on the cheek.

What we have been showing is, to repeat, a variety of the ills brought upon Hardy's verse by the substitution of formula for form and of preconceived or ready-made emotion for builded emotion—emotion made out of the materials of the poem. The track through this exhibition has been downward, but it has nevertheless been leading up to the sight of a poem in which the formula is no longer a formula but a genuine habit of seeing, and in which the emotion, however ready-made it may have been for Hardy, yet appears to come out of and crown the poem. The formula discovers the form; the obsession makes the emotion; which are the preliminary conditions to good poetry where they affect the matter at all. For the whole emphasis of practical argument is this: that it is not formula or obsessed emotion that works evil but the fact of stopping short at them, so that they substitute for what they actually spring from. But here is the poem, called 'The Workbox,' which it would be unfair not to quote complete.

> 'See, here's the workbox, little wife,
> That I made of polished oak.'
> He was a joiner, of village life;
> She came of borough folk.
>
> He holds the present up to her
> As with a smile she nears
> And answers to the profferer,
> ' 'Twill last all my sewing years!'
>
> 'I warrant it will. And longer too.
> 'Tis a scantling that I got
> Off poor John Wayward's coffin, who
> Died of they knew not what.
>
> 'The shingled pattern that seems to cease
> Against your box's rim

Continues right on in the piece
  That's underground with him.

'And while I worked it made me think
  Of timber's varied doom;
One inch where people eat and drink,
  The next inch in a tomb.

'But why do you look so white, my dear,
  And turn aside your face?
You knew not that good lad, I fear,
  Though he came from your native place?'

'How could I know that good young man,
  Though he came from my native town,
When he must have left far earlier than
  I was a woman grown?'

'Ah, no. I should have understood!
  It shocked you that I gave
To you one end of a piece of wood
  Whose other is in a grave?'

'Don't, dear, despise my intellect,
  Mere accidental things
Of that sort never have effect
  On my imaginings.'

Yet still her lips were limp and wan,
  Her face still held aside,
As if she had known not only John,
  But known of what he died.

This is about the maximum value Hardy ever got by the application of this idea—this formula and this obsession—to life; and it amounts, really, in the strictest possible sense of a loose phrase, to a reversal of Hardy's conscious intent: here we have the application to the idea of as much life as could be brought to bear. To define the value is difficult. Like many aspects of poetry it can best be noted by stating a series of negative facts. The poem has no sore thumbs; since its emotion is self-created it maintains an even tone and speed. It is without violence of act and assertion; the details presented are deep and tentacular enough in their roots to supply strength without strain. The coincidence upon which the release of emotion depends seems neither incredible nor willful; because it is prepared for, it is part of the texture of the feelings in the poem, and therefore seems natural or probable. There are no forced rhymes, no wrenchings of sense or meter; there was enough initial provision of material, and enough possible material thereby opened up, to compel—or tempt—the poet to use the full relevant resources of his craft. Put positively, the formula fitted the job of work, and in the process of getting the job done was incorporated in the poem. It is still there; it still counts, and shapes, and limits; but it is not a substitute for any wanted value: it is just the idiosyncrasy of the finished product—the expression on the face—in much the same sense that the character of a wooden box is determined by the carpenter's tools as much as by his skill.

All this is to beg the pressing but craven question of stature, which requires dogmas that are not literary dogmas to answer, and is therefore not primarily within the province of these notes. In a secondary sense it is not hard to see—one cannot help feeling—that even at its maximum executed value, this formula of production limits the engaged sensibility more than the consequent release is worth; which may be a matter of accident not of principle; for other formulas, when they become habits of seeing and feeling, expand the sensibility in the very terms of the control that the formulas exert. The general formula of ballad-tragedy, for example, as in 'The Sacrilege,' allows and *demands* a greater scope in music and therefore, possibly, makes a wider range of material available for treatment. Certainly 'The Sacrilege,' 'The Trampwoman's Tragedy' and 'A Sunday Morning Tragedy' are poems of wider scope and excite deeper responses than even the best of the crossed-fidelity lyrics, despite the fact that they rest upon substantially similar ideas. The double agency—musical and compositional—of the refrain is perhaps responsible; for the refrain—any agency at once iterative and variable about a pattern of sound—is a wonderful device for stretching and intensifying the process of sensibility. Yeats and Hardy are the great modern masters of refrain; Hardy using it to keep the substance of his ballads—what they were actually about—continuously present, Yeats using it to develop and modify the substance otherwise made present. Returning to the crossed-fidelity formula, it is the difference between the concrete poetic formula—so concrete and so poetic that, like rhyme, it is almost part of the language, an objective habit of words in association—and the abstract intellectual formula, which is a reduction, a kind of statistical index, of the concrete and poetic, and which requires, for success, re-expansion in every instance. Hardy, lacking direct access to all that is meant by the tradition of craft, condemned himself, in a great part of his serious poetry—in over two hundred poems—to the labor of re-making the abstract as concrete, the intellectual as actual. That he had a naturally primitive intelligence, schematized beyond discrimination, only made the labor more difficult. Success—I do not mean greatness but just the possible limited achievement—came about once in ten times. About twenty of these lyrics reach more or less the level of 'The Workbox'; none of them reach the level achieved in certain poems which escape the formula altogether. Yet they make—not the twenty but the whole lump of two hundred—the caricature by which Hardy's shorter verse is known; which is why so much space has been here devoted to them. Caricature is the very art of formula.

The true character beneath the caricature and which made the caricature possible—the whole fate of Hardy's sensibility—appears not in these poems where he deliberately undertook the profession of poet, but rather either in those poems where he was overweeningly compelled to react to personal experience or in those poems where he wrote to celebrate an occasion. In neither case was there room for the intervention of formula. It is a satire of circumstance indeed, that for Hardy the wholly personal and the wholly objective could alone command his greatest powers; and it is in this sense that Eliot's remark that Hardy sometimes reached the sublime without ever having passed through the stage of good writing, is most accurate. The clear examples are such poems as those about the loss of the *Titanic,* with its extraordinary coiling imagery of the projected actual, by which the capacity for experience is stretched by the creation of experience: such poems as those on Leslie Stephen and Swinburne, each ending with a magnificently appropriate image, Stephen being joined to the Schreckhorn which he had scaled, and Swinburne joined with the waves—

> Him once their peer in sad improvisations,
> And deft as wind to cleave their frothy manes—

and again such poems as 'Channel Firing' and 'In Time of "The Breaking of Nations,"' which need no comment; and finally in such poems as 'An Ancient to Ancients' with its dignity and elegance making the strength of old age. But these poems are or ought to be too generally received to permit their being looked at as anything except isolated, like something in the Oxford Book of English Verse. Keeping their special merit in mind as a clue to what we do want, let us look at certain other poems, not yet isolated by familiarity, and perhaps not deserving to be because not as broadly useful, which achieve objectivity on the base of a deep personal reaction. If they can be made to show as part, and the essential, idiosyncratic part, of what Hardy's poetry has to give as value, then we can stop and have done, knowing what to exclude and what to keep close.

The poems chosen have all to do with death, and the first, 'Last Words to a Dumb Friend,' was occasioned by the death of a white cat and is one of two poems which may, or may not, refer to the same pet animal. The other poem, 'The Roman Gravemounds,' derives its effect from the collocation of Caesar's buried warriors and the cat about to be buried. Hardy had a perennial interest in Roman relics and used them frequently as furniture for his poems when some symbol of age, time passing, past, or come again, was wanted; and if in 'The Roman Gravemounds' he had a definite design it was surely at once to heighten and to stabilize the man's sense of loss.

> 'Here say you that Caesar's warriors lie?—
> But my little white cat was my only friend!
> Could she but live, might the record die
> Of Caesar, his legions, his aims, his end!'

But Hardy, oddly enough for him, apparently thought the effect strained or sentimental; for he adds, in the voice of the hypothetical observer of the burial, a superficial, common-sense moral which quite reduces and unclinches the dramatic value of the poem.

> Well, Rome's long rule here is oft and again
> A theme for the sages of history,
> And the small furred life was worth no one's pen;
> Yet its mourner's mood has a charm for me.

Granted the method—the hypothetical observer, the interposition of the stock intellectual consideration, and the consequent general indirectness of presentation—that was about all Hardy could do with the subject. By making it 'objective' in the easy sense he made almost nothing of it; which is another way of putting our whole argument about the effect of formula in the crossed-fidelity lyrics.

The true charm of the mourner's mood, only imputed in 'The Roman Gravemounds,' is made actual in 'Last Words to a Dumb Friend' through a quite different set of approaches, all direct, all personal, amounting to the creation or release of objective experience. Let us observe the stages of approach, not to explain the process but to expand our sense of participation in it. First there is the selectively detailed materialization of what it was that died: purrer of the spotless hue with the plumy tail, that would stand, arched, to meet the stroking hand. After the tenderness of immediate memory comes the first reaction: never to risk it again.

Better bid his memory fade,
Better blot each mark he made,
Selfishly escape distress
By contrived forgetfulness,
Than preserve his prints to make
Every morn and eve an ache.

Then come eight lines which envisage what must be done, and the impossibility of doing it, to blot the memory out. All this Hardy supplied, as it were, by a series of directly felt observations; and these, in their turn, released one of those deeply honest, creative visions of man in relation to death which summoned the full imagination in Hardy as nothing else could.

Strange it is this speechless thing, . . .
Should—by crossing at a breath
Into safe and shielded death,
By the merely taking hence
Of his insignificance—
Loom as largened to the sense,
Shape as part, above man's will,
Of the Imperturbable.

As a prisoner, flight debarred,
Exercising in a yard,
Still retain I, troubled, shaken,
Mean estate, by him forsaken;
And this home, which scarcely took
Impress from his little look,
By his faring to the Dim
Grows all eloquent of him.

Housemate, I can think you still
Bounding to the window-sill,

Over which I vaguely see
Your small mound beneath the tree,
Showing in the autumn shade
That you moulder where you played.

Andrew Marvell hardly did better; and the end rises like the whole of Yeats's 'A Deep-sworn Vow.' You can say, if you like, that all Hardy had to do was to put it down, which explains nothing and begs the question of poetic process which we want to get at. What should be emphasized is, that in putting it down, Hardy used no violence of intellect or predilection; the violence is inside, working out, like the violence of life or light. The burden of specific feeling in the first part of the poem set enough energy up to translate the thought in the second half to the condition of feeling; and the product of the two is the poetic emotion which we feel most strongly as the rhythm, not the pattern-rhythm of the lines, but the invoked rhythm, beating mutually in thought and feeling and syllable, of the whole poem.

Rhythm, in that sense, is the great enacting agent of actuality in poetry, and appears seldom, without regard to good will or application, and is fully operative only when certain other elements are present in combination, but by no means always materializes even then. Perhaps, for the poet, it is what comes when, in Eliot's language, he sees beneath both beauty and ugliness, 'the boredom, the horror, and the glory'; what Eliot had in mind, too, when he said that he who has once been visited by the Muses is ever afterwards haunted. However that may be, it involves the power of words to preserve—to create—a relation to experience, passionate quite beyond violence, intense beyond any tension. Hardy's poetry engaged that power now and again, but most purely when responding directly and personally to death or the dead. 'Last Words to a Dumb Friend' is only a single example, chosen for the unfamiliar dignity Hardy brought to the subject. The twenty-one poems, written after the death of his first wife, which appear under the motto: *Veteris vestigia flammae,* give, as a unit, Hardy's most sustained invocation of that rhythm, so strong that all that was personal—the private drive, the private grief—is cut away and the impersonal is left bare, an old monument, mutilated or weathered as you like to call it, of that face which the personal only hides. Here, for example, is one of the shorter, called 'The Walk.'

You did not walk with me
Of late to the hill-top tree

By the gated ways,
As in earlier days;
You were weak and lame,
So you never came,
And I went alone, and I did not mind,
Not thinking of you as left behind.

I walked up there to-day
Just in the former way;
Surveyed around
The familiar ground
By myself again:
What difference, then?
Only that underlying sense
Of the look of a room on returning thence.

Like the others in the series, it is a poem almost without style; it is style reduced to anonymity, reduced to riches: in the context of the other twenty, precisely the riches of rhythm.

As Theodore Spencer has remarked (in conversation, but no less cogently for that) Hardy's personal rhythm is the central problem in his poetry. Once it has been struck out in the open, it is felt as ever present, not alone in his thirty or forty finest poems but almost everywhere in his work, felt as disturbance, a pinioning, or a liberation; sometimes present as something just beyond vision, sometimes immanent, sometimes here; sometimes beaten down, mutilated, obliterated by ideas, formulas, obsessions, but occasionally lifting, delivering into actuality, the marks of life lived. If these notes have served any useful purpose it is double: that by naming and examining the obstacles set up by a lifetime of devoted bad or inadequate practice, we are better able both to value what we exclude and to acknowledge—which is harder than to value—the extraordinary poetry which was produced despite and aside from the practice. Hardy is the great example of a sensibility violated by ideas; and perhaps the unique example, since Swift, of a sensibility great enough—locked enough in life—to survive the violation.

F. O. MATTHIESSEN

Tradition and the Individual Talent

(1935)

> It is part of the business of the critic . . . to see literature steadily and to see it whole; and this is eminently to see it *not* as consecrated by time, but to see it beyond time; to see the best work of our time and the best work of twenty-five hundred years ago with the same eyes.
>
> —Introduction to *The Sacred Wood.*

In *After Strange Gods: A Primer of Modern Heresy,* T. S. Eliot stated that his aim was to develop further the theme of 'Tradition and the Individual Talent,' which is probably his best-known essay. Nearly thirty years have now elapsed since it was written—and over thirty since his first notable poem, 'The Love Song of J. Alfred Prufrock'—a detail which underscores the fact that it is no longer accurate to think of Eliot's work as new or experimental. Indeed, with younger readers 'Tradition and the Individual Talent' is now as much of a classic as Matthew Arnold's 'The Study of Poetry'; and putting those essays side by side one can observe that Eliot's is equally packed with trenchant remarks on the relation of present to past, as well as on the nature of poetry itself.

It is illuminating to go further and juxtapose the whole range of these writers' achievements. For, by so doing, one becomes aware of the extent to which Eliot's criticism has quietly accomplished a revolution: that in it we have the first full revaluation of poetry since *Essays in Criticism* appeared in 1865. Arnold's observations on the historical course of English poetry, his classification of the romantics of the age just before him, his dismissal of Dryden and Pope as authors of an age of prose, his exaltation of Milton, and his depreciation of Chaucer on the score of lacking 'high seriousness'—all of these views, sensitively elaborated, not only persuaded his generation but also, as

From *The Achievement of T. S. Eliot,* third edition, by F. O. Matthiessen.

Eliot has remarked, largely remain as the academic estimates of to-day. It is worth noting that A. E. Housman, who professed not to be a critic, also held most of them in his widely read lecture of 1933, 'The Name and Nature of Poetry.' Housman's enthusiasms remained those of the time when he was an undergraduate: he could see nothing in the seventeenth-century metaphysicals but perverse over-intellectualization, and he almost paraphrased Arnold's remarks on the school of Dryden. Moreover, when one goes through the names of the principal English critics since Arnold's death and since the brief plunge into the dead alley of aestheticism in the 'nineties, it is apparent that such representative work as that of Saintsbury, Whibley, or Bradley, or even that of W. P. Ker, was historical rather than critical, in the sense that it was engaged with description and categorization, filling in the outlines traced by Arnold, and only incidentally, if at all, raising any new questions. In America, Irving Babbitt, also indebted to Arnold (more, perhaps, than he recognized), was concerned with the relation of the artist's thought to society, but not at all with the nature of art.[1] In the years just before the First World War, the speculations of T. E. Hulme and Ezra Pound brought a new quickening of life which prepared the way for Eliot's own development; but there was no detailed intensive re-examination of the quality and function of poetry until the publication of *The Sacred Wood* in 1920.

It could not be wholly clear then, but it has become so now, that the ideas first arriving at their mature expression in that volume definitely placed their author in the main line of poet-critics that runs from Ben Jonson and Dryden through Samuel Johnson, Coleridge, and Arnold. In fact, what has given the note of authority to Eliot's views of poetry is exactly what has made the criticism of the other writers just named the most enduring in English. They have not been merely theorists, but all craftsmen talking of what they knew at first hand. When Dryden writes about Chaucer, or Coleridge about Wordsworth, or Eliot about Donne, we may not agree on all points, but we take them seriously since we can observe at once their intimate understanding of what they are saying. With the generation of readers since the First World War, Donne has assumed the stature of a centrally important figure for the first time since the seventeenth century; and his rise has been directly connected with the fact that Eliot has enabled us to see him with fresh closeness, not only by means of his analysis of the method of metaphysical poetry but also because he has renewed that method in the rhythms and imagery of his own verse.

When Eliot is thought of in connection with Arnold, probably the first thing that comes to mind is his reaction to the famous statement that the poetry of Dryden and Pope was 'conceived and composed in their wits, genuine poetry is conceived . . . in the soul'; his brief retort about poetry 'conceived and composed in the soul of a mid-century Oxford graduate.' In addition, one has the impression of deft, if inconspicuous sniping, kept up over quite a few years. What Eliot has attacked principally is not the conception of poetry as criticism of life; indeed, no one lately has taken that phrase very seriously except in so far as it throws light on Arnold's own poetry. The main offensive has been against certain jaunty inadequacies in Arnold's thought and, in particular, against his loose identification of poetry with religion. And yet, in his most recent remarks about Arnold, Eliot has recognized him as a friend, if not as a master; as one whose work at its best, both in verse and in criticism, has more to say to us than that of any other poet of his time.

Consequently, in any effort to gauge Eliot's achievement, to indicate just what traditions have entered into the shaping of his talent, it is important to remind oneself of the actual closeness of these two writers in the qualities of mind which they value. It might almost be either who remarks that 'Excellence dwells among rocks hardly accessible, and a man must almost wear his heart out before he can reach her.' For certainly there is in each a full understanding of the unremitting discipline for the critic in learning 'to see the object as it is'; an equal insistence on the current of fresh ideas in which a society must move as a primary condition for the emergence of mature art; an equal veneration for French intelligence; and, again and again, a similar scoring, not by logic, but by flexibility, resilience, and an intuitive precision. In addition, in more than one notable passage, such as those which reflect on the lonely relation of the thinker to society, there is almost an identical tone. When Arnold realizes that in a sense the critic's goal is never reached, that it is kept in sight only by unending vigilance, he says: 'That promised land it will not be ours to enter, and we shall die in the wilderness: but to have desired to enter it, to have saluted it from afar, is already, perhaps, the best distinction among contemporaries; it will certainly be the best title to esteem with posterity.' And Eliot takes up the echoing theme:

> It is not to say that Arnold's work was vain if we say that it is to be done again; for we must know in advance, if we are pre-

> pared for that conflict, that the combat may have truces but never a peace. If we take the widest and wisest view of a Cause, there is no such thing as a Lost Cause because there is no such thing as a Gained Cause. We fight for lost causes because we know that our defeat and dismay be the preface to our successors' victory, though that victory itself will be temporary; we fight rather to keep something alive than in the expectation that anything will triumph.

Although Eliot relates to the central values stressed by Arnold to a degree which has not heretofore been recognized, it would be misleading to slur over the equally marked divergences between them. The chief difference separating in quality both their criticism and verse is suggested in Eliot's remark that 'Arnold's poetry has little technical interest.' With Arnold, in so far as you can make such a division, the emphasis is on substance rather than on form. Such emphasis led him into his attempted definition of poetry as criticism of life, a phrase which would apply equally well to a novel as to a poem, and which wholly fails to suggest the created vision of life which constitutes the essence of all art. The same emphasis also runs through Arnold's essays, where he gives us estimates of the value to the human spirit of poetry and of individual poets, but, although he frequently refers to 'the laws of poetic beauty and poetic truth,' no detailed or even incidental examination of the precise nature of those laws emerges. With Eliot, the emphasis is on form. His essays on various Elizabethan dramatists, for example, are not concerned with the full-length rounded estimate, but with close technical annotation of detail. It is possible that he may sometimes regret his too sharp reversal: 'The spirit killeth, but the letter giveth life'; and yet it represents the intensity of his dissatisfaction with the copious expansiveness of Arnold's age, with Swinburne and Tennyson far more than with Arnold himself. In thoughtful reaction, Eliot's method is spare and economical. He watches with the trained eye of the hawk, and then swoops on the one point that will illustrate the quality of the whole. His brief essays present in clearest outline the segment of the curve from which the complete circle can be constructed.

It is this preoccupation with craftsmanship that has enabled him to relish so fully the virtues of Dryden. But Dryden's power has been, so to speak, simply one of Eliot's incidental discoveries. The principal elements entering into his revaluation of poetry can be most briefly described in terms of the poets who have left the deepest and most lasting mark on his own work: the seventeenth-century English metaphysicals, the nineteenth-century French symbolists, and Dante.[2] Such a combination of interests, which he possessed even before his earliest published work, might at first glance seem not only unlikely but exotic for a young man of New England stock, born in St. Louis and educated at Milton and Harvard. But actually they are not so. They relate organically to his background, though an adequate demonstration of that fact would require a still unwritten chapter of American intellectual history,[3] and might even surprise Eliot himself. Yet it is not to be forgotten that the symbolist movement has its roots in the work of the most thoroughly conscious artist in American poetry before Eliot, Edgar Poe; and that, therefore, in Eliot's taste for Baudelaire and Laforgue as well as for Poe, the wheel has simply come full circle. It is increasingly apparent that the renaissance of the New England mind, from Emerson and Thoreau to Emily Dickinson, felt a deep kinship with the long buried modes of thought and feeling of the seventeenth century; in fact, Emily Dickinson's poetry, especially, must be described as metaphysical. I do not suggest that Eliot is directly indebted to any of these writers; indeed, he once remarked to me both of his sustained distaste for Emerson, and of the fact that he had never read Miss Dickinson.

It must be noted, however, if only by way of parenthesis, that there is one author who grew out of the New England tradition to whom Eliot is greatly indebted. When he first began to write he could find among living artists of the older generation no poet who satisfied him, but, as Ezra Pound has remarked, it was Henry James, as well as Conrad, who taught them both 'that poetry ought to be as well written as prose.' In Eliot's case James taught him even more than that. In his tribute shortly after the novelist's death,[4] Eliot spoke of him as 'the most intelligent man of his generation,' by which he meant that, undistracted by 'ideas,' James had maintained a point of view and had given himself wholly to the perfection of his craft, and that he had reflected on the novel as an art 'as no previous English novelist had done.' In addition, Eliot was fascinated by the way in which James did not simply relate but made the reader co-operate; by the richness of his 'references'; by the way, for example, in *The Aspern Papers,* he managed to give the whole feeling of Venice by the most economical strokes. Indeed, Eliot has said that the method in this story—'to make a place real not descriptively but by something happening there'—was what stimulated him to try to compress so many memories of past moments of Venice into his dramatic poem, superficially so different from James, 'Burbank with a Baedeker: Bleistein with a Cigar.' [5] And what is even more significant, Eliot has perceived that James's 'real progenitor' was Hawthorne, that he cannot be understood without Hawthorne, that the essential strain common to them both was 'their indifference to religious dogma at the same time as their exceptional awareness of spiritual reality,' their 'profound sensitiveness to good and evil,' their extraordinary power to convey horror.[6]

This brings us back to the point that no more than Henry James can Eliot be understood without reckoning with the Puritan mind. Its special mixture of passion overweighed by thought (as well as the less attractive combination of high moral idealism restrained by practical prudence that was probed by Santayana in 'The Genteel Tradition'); its absorption in the problem of belief and its trust in moments of vision; its dry, unexpected wit; its dread of vulgarity, as perplexing to the creator of 'Sweeney Erect' as to Henry James; its consciousness of the nature of evil, as acute in 'The Turn of the Screw' as in 'Ethan Brand' or 'Gerontion'; its full understanding of the dark consequences of loneliness and repression which are expressed in 'The Love Song of J. Alfred Prufrock' as well as in *The Scarlet Letter;* its severe self-discipline and sudden, poignant tenderness, to be found alike in Jonathan Edwards and in the author of *Ash Wednesday*—such attributes and preoccupations are common to the whole strain to which Eliot inextricably belongs. The natural relation of Dante to many elements in that strain is at once apparent. It need only be added that from Longfellow through Charles Eliot Norton, Santayana, and Charles Grandgent there was an unbroken line of Dante scholarship at Harvard. It may be that in the end Eliot gained a more challenging insight into the technical excellences of *The Divine Comedy* through conversations with Ezra Pound, but, at all events, in the preface to his own introduction to Dante he lists as his principal aids all the names which I have just mentioned.

To arrive not only at Eliot's debt to tradition but at an understanding of what he has himself added to it, it is essential at least to suggest more specific reasons why he has been attracted to these particular poets, and the exact use he has made of them. The need is more real in Eliot's case than it would be in most, since his own verse bears everywhere evidence of how his reading has been carried alive into his mind, and thus of his conception of poetry 'as a living whole of all the poetry that has ever been written.' [7] Holding such a conception of the integral relation of the present to an alive past, believing that it is necessary for the poet to be conscious, 'not of what is dead, but of what is already living,' he naturally also believes that one of the marks of a mature poet is that he should be 'one who not merely restores a tradition which has been in abeyance, but one who in his poetry re-twines as many straying strands of tradition as possible.' Perhaps the process would have been more compellingly described as 'fusing together' rather than 're-twining'; for only by some such process can the poet's work gain richness and density.

It is hardest to suggest in brief compass the extent of Eliot's feeling for Dante, since he has himself devoted many careful pages to defining exactly what he means by calling him the most universal poet in a modern language. That he does so regard him is of considerable significance in throwing light on what qualities Eliot most values in poetry, especially since he dwells chiefly on the power of Dante's precision of diction, and of his clear, visual images. He does not hesitate to say that he believes Dante's simple style, his great economy of words, makes him the most valuable master for any one trying to write poetry himself. That he does not believe this style simple to attain is indicated by his laconic sentence: 'In twenty years I have written about a dozen lines in that style successfully; and compared to the dullest passage of the "Divine Comedy," they are "as straw." ' It is also apparent, in view both of 'The Hollow Men' and of the direction towards which he has been moving since *Ash Wednesday,* that although he carefully avoids saying that either Shakespeare or Dante is the 'greater,' he is himself drawn more closely to the latter, who, though he did not embrace so wide an 'extent and variety of human life,' yet understood 'deeper degrees of degradation and higher degrees of exaltation.' It would be glib to say that in *The Waste Land* and 'The Hollow Men' Eliot wrote his *Inferno,* and that since then his poems represent various stages of passing through a *Purgatorio;* still such a remark may possibly illuminate both his aims and achievement.

It is easier to illustrate the impact made upon Eliot by the more restricted qualities of seventeenth-century metaphysical poetry, particularly since they have also appealed to many other readers of to-day. For it is not accidental that the same people who respond to Proust and Joyce have also found something important in Donne. The remark that we have in the work of this poet 'the fullest record in our literature of the disintegrating collision in a sensitive mind of the old tradition and the new learning' might very well have been made about *The Waste Land*.[8] For, as has been frequently observed, Donne's poetry also was born in part out of an increase of self-consciousness. His probing, analytic mind was keenly aware of the actual complexity of his feelings, their rapid alterations and sharp antitheses; and our more complete awareness of the sudden juxtapositions of experience, of, in Eliot's phrase, 'the apparent irrelevance and unrelatedness of things,' has drawn us strongly to him. The jagged brokenness of Donne's thought has struck a responsive note in our age, for we have seen a reflection of our own problem in the manner in which his passionate mind, unable to find any final truth in which it could rest, became fascinated with the process of thought itself. Eliot's earlier enthusiasm for this element in Donne's mind is now considerably qualified in view of his own growing desire for order and coherence; as is also some of his first response to the realization that we have in Donne the expression of an age that 'objects to the heroic and sublime and objects to the simplification and separation of the mental faculties.' But that such qualities have been deeply felt by a whole generation of readers since 1918 is demonstrated by the fact that even a character in Hemingway's *Farewell to Arms* could quote from a metaphysical poem. It may be that in reaction against Donne's previous neglect our generation has gone to the extreme of exaggerating his importance; and yet it would be hard to overestimate the value of his discoveries as an artist. What he strove to devise was a medium of expression that would correspond to the felt intricacy of his existence, that would suggest by sudden contrasts, by harsh dissonances as well as by harmonies, the actual sensation of life as he had himself experienced it. In sharp revolt against the too superficial beauty of *The Faerie Queene* and the purely 'literary' conventions of the sonneteers, he knew that no part of life should be barred as 'unpoetic,' that nothing in mature experience was too subtly refined or too sordid, too remote or too commonplace to serve as material for poetry. His great achievement lay in his ability to convey 'his genuine whole of tangled feelings,' as in 'The Extasie,' the extraordinary range of feeling—from the lightest to the most serious, from the most spiritual to the most sensual—that can inhere in a single mood. This 'alliance of levity and seriousness' by which, as Eliot has observed, the seriousness is not weakened but intensified, 'implies a constant inspection and criticism of experience'; it involves 'a recognition, implicit in the expression of every experience, of other kinds of experience which are possible.' Such recognition demands a mind that is at once maturely seasoned, wise and discerning—and imaginative, a combination sufficiently rare to cause Eliot to maintain that 'it is hardly too much to say that Donne enlarged the possibilities of lyric verse as no other English poet has done.[9]

But Donne's technical discoveries did not belong to him alone. They were a product of a whole mode of thought and feeling which has seemed to Eliot the richest and most varied that has ever come to expression in English. He has described this mode as a development of sensibility, 'a direct sensuous apprehension of thought, or a recreation of thought into feeling,' which means that for all the most notable poets of Donne's time there was no separation between life and thought, and that their way of feeling 'was directly and freshly altered by their reading.' Such interweaving of emotions and thought exists in Chapman and Webster, and in the dense, masterful irregularity of the later plays of Shakespeare. It was as true for these poets as for Donne that 'a thought was an experience' which modified their capacity of feeling. As a result they could devour and assimilate any kind of experience, so that in their poetry passages of philosophical speculation stimulated by Montaigne or Seneca throb with as living a pulse as their own direct accounts of human passion. Indeed, one has only to turn to Montaigne and *Hamlet* and *Measure for Measure,* or to North's *Plutarch* and *Antony and Cleopatra* and *Coriolanus,* for complete examples of how reading as well as thought could be absorbed as vital experience.

How entirely Eliot believes such a capacity to be the only right state for the mature poet is emphasized by his extended comment that 'when a poet's mind is perfectly equipped for its work, it is constantly amalgamating disparate experience; the ordinary man's experience is chaotic, irregular, fragmentary. The latter falls in love, or reads Spinoza, and these two experiences have nothing to do with each other, or with the noise of the typewriter or the smell of cooking; in the mind of the poet these experiences are always forming new wholes.' That such a conviction concerning the creative process has sprung from one of Eliot's most recurrent discoveries about the nature of life is revealed when we find him writing, in a very different connection: 'It is probable that men ripen best through experiences which are at once sensuous and intellectual; certainly many men will admit that their keenest ideas have come to them with the quality of a sense perception; and that their keenest sensuous experience has been "as if the body thought." ' He was led to that reflection in contrasting the qualities of

Henry James and Henry Adams, a contrast that brings out once more the elements that Eliot is continually stressing as characteristic of the greatest art. It also reveals a certain similarity that he felt between James and metaphysical poetry, thus making more apparent why he has been attracted to both and indicating the relations between two strands in his tradition. Deeply impressed by the acuteness of Adams's intelligence, Eliot yet felt a lack of full ripeness in his writing when compared with that of James. He expressed his distinction between them thus: 'There is nothing to indicate that Adams's senses either flowered or fruited. . . Henry James was not, by Adams's standards, "educated," but particularly limited; it is the sensuous contributor to the intelligence that makes the difference.' [10]

In perhaps the most exciting phrase in all of his criticism, Eliot has called this rare fusion a way of feeling thought 'as immediately as the odour of a rose.' Such a capacity was possessed by later men in the seventeenth century, by Crashaw and Vaughan, and, in Eliot's account, found its last mature poetic voice in Andrew Marvell. The one thing common to the whole group, so diverse in their gifts and points of view, is, in Eliot's regard, 'that firm grasp of human experience, which is a formidable achievement of the Elizabethan and Jacobean poets.' He adds a further remark: 'This wisdom, cynical perhaps but untired (in Shakespeare, a terrifying clairvoyance), leads toward, and is only completed by, the religious comprehension'—a remark more heavily freighted with implications for his own development than would have been apparent at the time it was written, in 1921, the year before the publication of *The Waste Land*.

Similarities between Eliot's technical devices and those of Donne have been often observed: [11] the conversational tone, the vocabulary at once colloquial and surprisingly strange—both of these a product of Eliot's belief in the relation of poetry to actual speech, and paralleling his use of 'non-poetic' material; the rapid association of ideas which demands alert agility from the reader; the irregular verse and difficult sentence structure as a part of fidelity to thought and feeling; and, especially, the flash of wit which results from the shock of such unexpected contrasts. But actually the manner in which sudden transitions are made in Eliot's verse owes much more to the method of the French symbolists.[12] I. A. Richards has spoken of *The Waste Land* as 'a music of ideas,' a phrase which suggests Eliot's particular attraction to Laforgue. By both poets connecting links are left out, as they are not by Donne, in an effort to utilize our recent closer knowledge of the working of the brain, of its way of making associations. That is to say, Eliot wants to suggest in the rhythms of his verse the movement of thought in a living mind, and thus to communicate the exact pattern of his meaning not so much by logical structure as by emotional suggestion. He is aware that such a method is dangerous, that it can easily lead into the false identity, 'Poésie, musique, c'est même chose,' [13] which caused the vague obscureness of so much of Mallarmé's verse. But Eliot is equally sure that poetry can approach the condition of music without sacrificing its definite core of meaning so long as it has 'a definite emotion behind it.' [14] He has understood the many-sided problem of the poet. He knows that he must not sacrifice either sense to sound, or sound to sense: 'Words are perhaps the hardest of all material of art: for they must be used to express both visual beauty and beauty of sound, as well as communicating a grammatical statement.' [15]

In the preface to his translation of Perse's *Anabase* Eliot takes pains to point out that the French poet's suppression 'of explanatory and connecting matter' is not at all owing 'to incoherence, or to the love of cryptogram,' but to the deliberate belief that he can secure his most concentrated effect by the ordered compression of his sequence of images. Eliot is likewise convinced that 'there is a logic of the imagination as well as a logic of concepts,' and, as he states elsewhere, that the one test of whether the sudden contrasts and juxtapositions of modern poetry are successful or not 'is merely a question of whether the mind is *serré* or *delié,* whether the whole personality is involved.' For, in words that take on greater significance the more one examines Eliot's own work, 'it is the unity of a personality which gives an indissoluble unity to his variety of subject.'

The principal quality which drew Eliot to the symbolists is one they possess in common with the metaphysicals, 'the same essential quality of transmuting ideas into sensations, of transforming an observation into a state of mind.' This quality might be defined more technically as 'the presence of the idea in the image,' a definition with which I shall have more to do below. In both schools there is the demand for compression of statement, for centring on the revealing detail and eliminating all inessentials, and thus for an effect of comprehensiveness to be gained by the bringing to bear of a great deal of packed experience onto a single moment of expression. In the symbolists there is an increased allusiveness and indirection, a flexibility in their verse designed to catch every nuance of their feeling. Such technical agility fascinated

Eliot, especially in Laforgue, since it was coupled there with an unusual verbal adroitness—a combination of 'recondite words and simple phrasing,' which is also to be found everywhere in Eliot's own early work; and likewise with a mocking-serious, worldly-aesthetic attitude which spoke directly to his own youthful sophistication. As a result, 'Prufrock,' in the movement of its verse, its repetitions, and echoes, and even in its choice of theme, seems of all Eliot's poems to have been written most immediately under Laforgue's stimulus (though brought to a finished perfection of form which Laforgue's more impromptu verse scarcely attained); just as the verse of 'Gerontion' reveals the fullest impression of Eliot's mastery of the Jacobean dramatists.

The condensation of form that was demanded both by Donne and the symbolists logically builds its effects upon sharp contrasts, and makes full use of the element of surprise, which Eliot, as well as Poe, considers to have been 'one of the most important means of poetic effect since Homer.' It is always one of the prime functions of poetry to break through our conventional perceptions, to startle us into a new awareness of reality. As Hulme observed, 'poetry always endeavours to arrest you, and to make you continuously see a physical thing, to prevent you gliding through an abstract process.' In the poetry that Eliot most admires, poetry which has secured a union of thought and emotion, there will inevitably be an unexpected bringing together of material from seemingly disparate experiences. The reading of Spinoza and the smell of cooking will very possibly both enter into the full expression of a state of feeling, just as the most refined speculation from the Church fathers, a vivid detail from contemporary exploration, and the most coarsely sensual flash of wit unite in a single stanza of Donne's to make the expression of his love a concrete, living thing, very different from an abstract statement. Eliot's own kind of witty surprise is created in such a line as

> I have measured out my life with coffee spoons.

'I have measured out my life'—the general, platitudinous reflection is suddenly punctuated with an electric shock which flashes into the mind of the reader, in a single, concrete, ironic picture, Prufrock's whole futile way of existence.[16]

But if the details of Eliot's style show everywhere the mark of his responsive mastery of the later symbolists, as well as of the metaphysicals, the impression of Baudelaire upon his spirit has been even more profound. The reason why he seems to have been stirred more deeply by *Les Fleurs du Mal* than by any other poetry written in the nineteenth century is, I think, suggested by the words which he has italicized in the sentence that indicates the nature of this debt:

> It is not merely in the use of imagery of common life, not merely in the use of imagery of the sordid life of a great metropolis, but in the elevation of such imagery to the *first intensity*—presenting it as it is, and yet making it represent something much more than itself—that Baudelaire has created a mode of release and expression for other men.

For Baudelaire's intensity is the result of his having 'a sense of his own age,' a quality not easy to analyse, but one which, as Eliot stresses it again and again in the course of discussing very different poets, is revealed to be one of his fundamental tests for great poetry. Such a sense is at an opposite pole from a familiarity with the surface details of a time, or from a sense of fashion. When Eliot finds that Blake possessed this sense as well as Villon, it is seen to consist in a condensed, bare honesty that can strike beneath the appearances of life to reality, that can grasp so strongly the intrinsic elements of life in the poet's own day that it likewise penetrates beneath the apparent variations of man from one epoch to another to his essential sameness. Eliot is quite aware that the degree of consciousness on the artist's part of such a sense has varied greatly in different ages, that whereas the great French novelists from Stendhal and Flaubert through Proust were deliberately occupied with analysing conditions of society as well as the individual, with chronicling 'the rise, the régime, and the decay of the upper bourgeoisie,' on the other hand, it is in the very lack of such consciousness of social change and decay, 'of corruptions and abuses peculiar to their own time, that the Elizabethan and Jacobean dramatists are blessed. We feel that they believed in their own age, in a way in which no nineteenth- or twentieth-century writer of the greatest seriousness has been able to believe in his age. And accepting their age, they were in a position to concentrate their attention, to their respective abilities, upon the common characteristics of humanity in all ages, rather than upon the differences.'

But in any age the thing of highest importance for the poet is to 'express with individual differences the general state of mind, not as a *duty,* but simply because'—if he possesses that rare, unyielding honesty which alone will give his work depth—'he cannot help participating in it.' In such fashion Eliot dwells repeatedly on the integral relation of any poet's work to the society of which he is a part, to the climate of thought and feeling which give rise to his expression. In line with such reflections Eliot can say: 'The great poet, in writing himself, writes his time.[17] Thus Dante, hardly knowing it, became the voice of the thirteenth century; Shakespeare, hardly knowing it, became the representative of the end of the sixteenth century, of a turning point in history.'

In the case of Baudelaire, this ability to go beneath appearances to the most recurrently pervading elements of life was the result of the peculiar dogged strength with which he felt the torturing impact of the great modern city upon the lonely individual. For the very intensity of his suffering enabled him to see through the slogans of his age in a way that Victor Hugo, for example, could not; enabled him to cut beneath its 'bustle, programmes, platforms, scientific progress, humanitarianism, and revolutions which improved nothing' to a real perception of good and evil. Such a perception Eliot defines, in *After Strange Gods,* as 'the first requisite of spiritual life.' It is very close to Yeats's mature discovery that we begin to live only 'when we have conceived life as tragedy.' For both Yeats and Eliot recognize that there can be no significance to life, and hence no tragedy in the account of man's conflicts and his inevitable final defeat by death, unless it is fully realized that there is no such thing as good unless there is also evil, or evil unless there is good; that until this double nature of life is understood by a man, he is doomed to waver between a groundless, optimistic hopefulness and an equally chaotic, pointless despair. Eliot has learned from his own experience that the distinguishing feature of a human life consists in the occasions on which the individual most fully reveals his character, and that those are the moments of intense 'moral and spiritual struggle.' It is in such moments, rather than in the 'bewildering minutes' of passion 'in which we are all very much alike, that men and women come nearest to being real'—an affirmation which again underscores his inheritance of the central element in the Puritan tradition. And he has concluded that 'if you do away with this struggle, and maintain that by tolerance, benevolence, inoffensiveness, and a redistribution or increase of purchasing power, combined with a devotion, on the part of an élite, to Art, the world will be as good as anyone could require, then you must expect human beings to become more and more vaporous.'

It is their penetration to the heart of this struggle between the mixed good and evil in man's very being, and thus to the central factors in human nature, which forms a common element between the three strains of poetry that have affected Eliot most deeply, between such writers as Dante, Webster, and Baudelaire. And consequently, when at the end of the first section of *The Waste Land,* Eliot's lines contain allusions to all three of these poets, he is not making a pastiche of his reading, or arbitrarily associating unrelated fragments:

> Unreal City,
> Under the brown fog of a winter dawn,
> A crowd flowed over London bridge, so many,
> I had not thought death had undone so many.
> Sighs, short and infrequent, were exhaled,
> And each man fixed his eyes before his feet.
> Flowed up the hill and down King William Street,
> To where Saint Mary Woolnoth kept the hours
> With a dead sound on the final stroke of nine.
> There I saw one I knew, and stopped him, crying: 'Stetson!
> 'You who were with me in the ships at Mylae!
> 'That corpse you planted last year in your garden,
> 'Has it begun to sprout? Will it bloom this year?
> 'Or has the sudden frost disturbed its bed?
> 'Oh keep the Dog far hence, that's friend to men,
> 'Or with his nails he'll dig it up again!
> 'You! hypocrite lecteur!—mon semblable—mon frère!'

He wanted to present here the intolerable burden of his 'Unreal City,' the lack of purpose and direction, the inability to believe really in anything and the resulting 'heap of broken images' that formed the excruciating contents of the post-War state of mind. But his city is Baudelaire's city as well, 'où le spectre en plein jour raccroche le passant'; it is the modern megalopolis dwarfing the individual. And it is given an additional haunting dimension as a realm of death in life by being linked with Dante's Limbo, the region of those dead who while on earth 'lived without praise or blame,' who had not been strong enough in will or passion either to do good or evil, and so were condemned for ever to wander aimlessly, in feverish, useless motion. And as this throng moves through the murky streets of wintry London, as dark at nine as at dawn, on its way, presumably, to jobs in shops and offices, the poet encounters one with whom he has shared experiences and now shares memories of war. The sense of the agonizing, since futile, effort to escape those memories, to bury those dead for good, is increased by a reminiscence of the dirge in *The White Devil,* one of the most poignantly terrifying passages in Webster's tragedy. And thus the three principal strains of poetry which have spoken so intimately to Eliot merge in a moment of acutely heightened consciousness. Eliot is not making mere literary allusions. He is not 'imitating' these poets; nor has he mistaken literature for life. Each of these references brings with it the weight of its special context, its authentic accent of reality, and thus enables Eliot to condense into a single passage a concentrated expression of tragic horror. And lest the reader think that such an awareness of the Unreal City is something special to the reading and experience of the poet, he, as well as Stetson, is reminded that it belongs both to Eliot and Baudelaire, and to himself, as part of the modern world, as well.

NOTES

(In making citations from Eliot's essays I have given the detailed reference only in the case of those not included in his half dozen small volumes, which are mentioned in my Biographical Note, or in his one-volume collection of *Selected Essays,* 1917–1932.)

1. I have cited only the outstanding figure. Paul Elmer More expounded the same general doctrine as Babbitt, with greater distinction as a stylist, but with less challenging vigour. Also following the lead of Arnold, More learned much from French criticism, especially from Sainte-Beuve, who was his model in the long series of *Shelburne Essays.* But there is a significant distinction between them: Sainte-Beuve was a psychologist, More was primarily a moralist.

   Among other works of American criticism, Van Wyck Brooks's *America's Coming of Age,* 1915, holds a position of particular importance for having awakened a fresh interest in our own past for a whole decade of readers. But Brooks has always been a social critic, preoccupied with the conditions affecting the creative life rather than with analysis of the nature of literature itself; and my generalization concerning *The Sacred Wood* still holds.
2. A complete account of the traditions which have affected Eliot's poetry would have to consider his revulsions in addition to his enthusiasms, for the very fact of reacting against a thing inevitably leaves a mark of its impact upon you. Just as Coleridge and Wordsworth still display some traces of the eighteenth-century poetic diction they had so violently rejected, and Donne cannot be fully understood without the Elizabethan sonneteers who were his foil, so the course of Eliot's development can be charted only by reckoning with such figures as Shelley and Swinburne and the Pre-Raphaelites, poets by whom he did not escape being in-

fluenced during the formative years of his adolescence. Indeed, part of the reason for writing his essay on Swinburne's poetry seems to have been to give the rationale of his own reaction from it.

For a revealing description of the various stages in the growth of Eliot's interests in poetry, from boyhood through adolescence to maturity, see the 'Note on the Development of "Taste" in Poetry' appended to the first of his Norton Lectures.

3. I have attempted to sketch that chapter in *American Renaissance* (1941), particularly in 'The Metaphysical Strain.'
4. This was published in *The Egoist,* January 1918.
5. This brief indication of the essentially dramatic quality of Eliot's poetry (no less than in James's stories) will be developed in my third chapter.
6. Eliot's observations on the basic relation between James and Hawthorne were made in an unpublished lecture on the former, given at Harvard in the spring of 1933 in a course on Contemporary Literature. (The lectures on Pound, Joyce, and Lawrence to which I refer below were also part of this course. It was a great advantage for me to have access to Eliot's notes for these lectures, for which I am indebted not only to Eliot himself but also to Theodore Spencer, who collaborated in the course.)

Eliot's estimate of Hawthorne is further revealed in a review of the second volume of *The Cambridge History of American Literature* which he wrote for *The Athenaeum,* 25 April 1919:

> Neither Emerson nor any of the others was a real observer of the moral life. Hawthorne was, and was a realist. He had, also, what no one else in Boston had—the firmness, the true coldness, the hard coldness of the genuine artist. In consequence, the observation of moral life in *The Scarlet Letter,* in *The House of the Seven Gables,* and even in some of the tales and sketches, has solidity, has permanence, the permanence of art. It will always be of use; the essays of Emerson are already an encumbrance. The work of Hawthorne is truly a criticism—true because a fidelity of the artist and not a mere conviction of the man—of the Puritan morality, of the Transcendentalist morality, and of the world which Hawthorne knew. It is a criticism as Henry James's work is a criticism of the America of his times, and as the work of Turgenev and Flaubert is a criticism of the Russia and the France of theirs.

In speaking of James's effort to present evil in 'The Turn of the Screw,' Eliot remarked that among other novelists only Hawthorne, Dostoevsky, and the Conrad of 'Heart of Darkness' were comparable in their 'essential moral preoccupation. . . . Evil is rare, bad is common. Evil cannot even be perceived but by a very few.'

For further development of Eliot's relation to his American background, see *American Renaissance:* 'From Hawthorne to James to Eliot.'

7. As relevant first comment on the important question of what is living and what is dead, on what precisely is meant by 'experience,' I want simply to present the following passages from Eliot:

> There is a shallow test which holds that the original poet goes direct to life, and the derivative poet to 'literature.' When we look into the matter, we find that the poet who is really 'derivative' is the poet who *mistakes* literature for life, and very often the reason why he makes this mistake is that—he has not read enough. The ordinary life of ordinary cultivated people is a mush of literature and life. There is a right sense in which for the educated person literature *is* life, and life *is* literature; and there is also a vicious sense in which the same phrases may be true. We can at least try not to confuse the material and the use which the author makes of it. (Introduction to the Poems of Ezra Pound.)
>
> We dwell with satisfaction upon the poet's difference from his predecessors, especially his immediate predecessors; we endeavour to find something that can be isolated in order to be enjoyed. Whereas if we approach a poet without this prejudice we shall often find that not only the best, but the most individual parts of his work may be those in which the dead poets, his ancestors, assert their immortality most vigorously. And I do not mean the impressionable period of adolescence, but the period of full maturity. ('Tradition and the Individual Talent.')
>
> One of the surest of tests is the way in which a poet borrows. Immature poets imitate; mature poets steal; bad poets deface what they take, and good poets make it into something better, or at least something different. The good poet welds his theft into a whole of feeling which is unique, utterly different from that from which it was torn; the bad poet throws it into something which has no cohesion. A good poet will usually borrow from authors remote in time, or alien in language, or diverse in interest. ('Philip Massinger.')

I hope that the point of view outlined in these passages receives adequate justification in the course of my essay, since such a point of view is crucial to any understanding of the value of history, and of what is meant by 'tradition'—a word that has been so misused by academic worshippers of the past that it is necessary to demonstrate how it can have life. Eliot's first discovery of its vitality took the following expression (in 'Tradition and the Individual Talent'):

> Yet if the only form of tradition, of handing down, consisted in following the ways of the immediate generation before us in a blind or timid adherence to its successes, 'tradition' should positively be discouraged. We have seen many such simple currents soon lost in the sand; and novelty is better than repetition. Tradition is a matter of much wider significance. It cannot be inherited, and if you want it you must obtain it by great labour. It involves, in the first place, the historical sense, which we may call nearly indispensable to anyone who would continue to be a poet beyond his twenty-fifth year; and the historical sense involves a perception, not only of the pastness of the past, but of its presence; the historical sense compels a man to write not merely with his own generation in his bones, but with a feeling that the whole of the literature of Europe from Homer and within it the whole of the literature of his own country has a simultaneous existence and composes a simultaneous order. This historical sense, which is a sense of the timeless as well as of the temporal and of the timeless and of the temporal together, is what makes a writer traditional. And it is at the same time what makes a writer most acutely conscious of his place in time, of his contemporaneity.

The position outlined in this passage is carried to a more comprehensive maturity in *After Strange Gods.* Consequently I return to it in my sixth chapter.

8. It was made by Professor H. J. C. Grierson in connection with Donne's 'Second Anniversary,' in the Introduction to *Metaphysical Lyrics and Poems of the Seventeenth Century* (Oxford, 1921).
9. Eliot has written of Donne not only in his essay on 'The Metaphysical Poets' but also in a review in *The Nation and Athenaeum,* 9 June 1923. In addition he contributed an essay on 'Donne in Our Time' to *A Garland for John Donne,* ed. Theodore Spencer (Cambridge, Mass., 1931). His Clark Lectures, delivered at Cambridge, England, in 1926, on the metaphysical poetry of the seventeenth century in comparison and contrast with that of the Italian thirteenth century have not yet been published. Perhaps the most trenchant evaluation of the nature of metaphysical poetry that he has made is in his poem, 'Whispers of Immortality.' Certainly there has never been a more suggestive discernment of Donne's quality than in the two quatrains:

> Donne, I suppose, was such another
> Who found no substitute for sense;
> To seize and clutch and penetrate,
> Expert beyond experience,

He knew the anguish of the marrow
The ague of the skeleton;
No contact possible to flesh
Allayed the fever of the bone.

10. Eliot made this contrast in review of *The Education of Henry Adams,* in *The Athenaeum,* 23 May 1919.

In the light of the similar quality that Eliot detects in James and the seventeenth-century poets, it is not surprising to find that he refers to James elsewhere as 'un romancier métaphysique.' (See his 'Note sur Mallarmé et Poe,' *La Nouvelle Revue Française,* November 1926.)

11. Particularly by George Williamson, *The Talent of T. S. Eliot* (University of Washington Chapbooks, No. 32, Seattle, 1929). Williamson also furnishes an interesting example of the fructifying power of Eliot's criticism, since in the Preface to *The Donne Tradition, A Study in English Poetry from Donne to the Death of Cowley* (Cambridge, Mass., 1930) he tells how, having first been fascinated by Eliot's kinship to Donne, he thus 'became absorbed in the Donne tradition through a contemporary poet.' That the whole point of view for Williamson's valuable study of the seventeenth century grew organically from a few of Eliot's packed remarks indicates also the great further potential value that Eliot's criticism may have for literary scholarship. A much needed, detailed critical estimate of the whole group of Elizabethan dramatists could take its fresh line of departure from Eliot's brief essays.

12. The qualities by which Eliot was drawn especially to Laforgue and Corbière, as well as in some degree to such of their more recent followers as Jean de Bosschère and Guillaume Apollinaire, have been outlined by René Taupin, *L'Influence du symbolisme français sur la poésie américaine* (1910–20) (Paris, 1929), pp. 211–40. Although Eliot has since reacted strongly against the *fin de siècle* aestheticism with which Arthur Symons diluted his translation of Baudelaire, he nevertheless still recognizes his early indebtedness to Symons, *The Symbolist Movement in Literature* (1899):

> I myself owe Mr. Symons a great debt. But for having read his book I should not, in the year 1908, have heard of Laforgue and Rimbaud; I should probably not have begun to read Verlaine, and but for reading Verlaine, I should not have heard of Corbière. So the Symons book is one of those which have affected the course of my life.

Eliot's earliest published poems, those contributed to *The Harvard Advocate* in the years 1909–10, already begin to show the mark of Laforgue.

13. The phrase is actually that of the Abbé Brémond, *La Poésie pure* (Paris,

1926), p. 23; but it compresses Mallarmé's persistent belief in the possibility of developing 'un art d'achever la transposition, au Livre, de la symphonie.'

14. The whole passage, from Eliot's early essay on 'Ezra Pound, His Metric and Poetry,' 1917, is relevant to an understanding of Eliot's own position, then in process of formulation:

> Such a relation between poetry and music is very different from what is called the 'music' of Shelley or Swinburne, a music often nearer to rhetoric (or the art of the orator) than to the instrument. For poetry to approach the condition of music (Pound quotes approvingly the dictum of Pater) it is not necessary that poetry should be destitute of meaning. Instead of slightly veiled and resonant abstractions, like
>
> Time with a gift of tears,
> Grief with a glass that ran—
>
> of Swinburne, or the mossiness of Mallarmé, Pound's verse is always definite and concrete, because he has always a definite emotion behind it.

That Eliot has believed Mallarmé in danger of being overrated by the English reader while more expert poets among the symbolists were being ignored, did not prevent him from writing an extremely acute note on the common attributes of 'metaphysical' poetry shared by Donne, Poe, and Mallarmé. (See *La Nouvelle Revue Française,* November 1926.)

15. From the same essay on Pound.

16. This particular line is also an example of Eliot's use of the conceit, the distinguishing device by which the metaphysical poets made both their witty and imaginative connections between things apparently unlike. Eliot himself has pointed out, in his essay on 'The Metaphysical Poets,' how this kind of unexpected linking can score its effect 'by brief words and sudden contrasts'; or again by 'a development of rapid association of thought which requires considerable agility on the part of the reader.' Donne's most characteristic use of the conceit is perhaps not to be found in the condensed form of a single line—though many of these are as memorable as 'A bracelet of bright hair about the bone'; but rather in 'the elaboration . . . of a figure of speech to the farthest stage to which ingenuity can carry it.' Such is his famous comparison of two lovers to a pair of compasses—a comparison seemingly so grotesque, but actually, in the context of the poem, so effective. A comparable example of the elaborated conceit in Eliot is his description of the fog in terms of a cat:

The yellow fog that rubs its back upon the window-panes,
The yellow smoke that rubs its muzzle on the window-panes
Licked its tongue into the corners of the evening,
Lingered upon the pools that stand in drains,
Let fall upon its back the soot that falls from chimneys,
Slipped by the terrace, made a sudden leap,
And seeing that it was a soft October night,
Curled once about the house, and fell asleep.

There is no point in entering here into further technical analysis of the nature of the conceit—a task which has been well carried out by George Williamson on the lines adumbrated by Eliot. But it is essential to emphasize that by writing in this way neither Donne nor Eliot is engaging in intellectual stunts or decorating his verse with brilliant but pointless ingenuity. For the conceit exists not just to shock or startle, though that is one of its valuable attributes. It is an integral element of the metaphysical style since it is the most compelling means of making the desired union of emotion and thought by bringing together widely divergent material in a single image. Instead of being ornamental, it is wholly functional: only by its use does the poet feel that he can express the precise curve of his meaning. If the reader objects that the meaning would be much better conveyed in plain speech without resort to such tortuous comparisons, let him bear in mind Hulme's remark that 'Plain speech is essentially inaccurate. It is only by new metaphors . . . that it can be made precise.'

To a greater degree than the objective decorative comparison the conceit enables the reader to *feel* the mind of the poet actually working; it is an image wherein the imaginative act itself has become analytical. Consequently, as Williamson has concluded (and a good deal of what I have just written is a condensation of his account): the elaborated conceit is successful 'when the idea and the figure become one'; the condensed conceit is successful 'when the image is the very body of the thought.' In both cases the test is the very one which Hulme applies to the question of sincerity in poetry: 'If it is sincere in the accurate sense, when the whole of the analogy is necessary to get out the exact curve of the feeling or thing you want to express—there you seem to me to have the highest verse, even though the subject be trivial and the emotions of the infinite far away.' (For other passages from Hulme which closely parallel Eliot's own views of the nature of poetry, see Chap. III, note 1, below.)

Eliot's conceits sometimes have the look of being too studied; that is to say, of coming into existence not because the poet's mind has actually felt keenly an unexpected similarity between unlikes but as though he too consciously set out to shock the reader. Such an objection might be made against the opening lines of 'Prufrock':

> Let us go then, you and I,
> When the evening is spread out against the sky
> Like a patient etherised upon a table.

Even though the reader can perceive wherein the comparison holds, he may still have the sensation that it is too intellectually manipulated, not sufficiently felt. But in the general texture of his verse Eliot really depends very little upon elaborate conceits: the double description of the cat and the foggy evening, whereby both are present to the reader with a richly heightened acuteness, is by far his most conspicuous use of the device in its expanded form. His usual way of surprising the reader into a new perception of reality is by means of the nuance rather than the conceit, by the rapid associations of his shifting thought, and by the accompanying deft and subtle exactness of his verbal contrasts:

> At the violet hour, the evening hour that strives
> Homeward, and brings the sailor home from sea,
> The typist home at teatime, clears her breakfast, lights
> Her stove, and lays out food in tins.
> Out of the window perilously spread
> Her drying combinations touched by the sun's last rays,
> On the divan are piled (at night her bed)
> Stockings, slippers, camisoles, and stays.
> I Tiresias, old man with wrinkled dugs
> Perceived the scene, and foretold the rest—
> I too awaited the expected guest.
> He, the young man carbuncular, arrives,
> A small house agent's clerk, with one bold stare,
> One of the low on whom assurance sits
> As a silk hat on a Bradford millionaire.

The limpid description of the evening, with its romantic associations heightened by the echo of Stevenson's 'Requiem' as well as by the emulation of some lines of Sappho (of which Eliot tells us in a note), is suddenly startled into a new aspect by the introduction of the typist. It is worth observing that this effect of surprise is made partly by the equally sudden shift in syntax, whereby 'the typist,' at first the object of 'brings,' becomes in turn the subject of 'clears.' Such breaking through the rules of conventional grammar, as the irregular lines break through conventional versification, corresponds to Eliot's remark that 'the structure of the sentences [of the metaphysical poets] is sometimes far from simple, but this is not a vice; it is a fidelity to thought and feeling.'

Throughout the passage there is a similar weaving back and forth from phrases embodying traditional loveliness to phrases rising from sharp, realistic perceptions of the actual city. 'Out of the window perilously spread'—the adverb quickens anticipation, which is quickly disappointed by 'her drying combinations'; but at once another association of beauty is brought by the phrase 'touched by the sun's last rays.' So, too the word 'divan' raises all its glamorous connotations from the Orient, which are instantly broken into by the realization that this is the kind of perfected folding divan that can be bought at a bargain at Selfridge's or Macy's, and which is designed to do double work. So, too, with the expression 'expected guest': the classic connotations of the ceremonious relation between host and guest and the anticipation of the arrival are immediately jolted by the appearance of 'the young man carbuncular.' And here, possibly, should be noted another kind of contrast: the full, deep vowel-sounds of the adjective corresponding to the natural beauty of the thing, so unfortunately altered by its human analogy.

His 'one bold stare' is an example of how great a range of meaning can be packed into a phrase when it has a double relation in the syntax, when, in this case, it modifies both 'arrives' and 'clerk.' For it thereby not only describes him at the moment of his arrival but also suggests the whole contour of his character: that this stare is perhaps his one distinguishing trait. And thus we are prepared for the summation of him in one of Eliot's most brilliantly effective condensed conceits:

> One of the low on whom assurance sits
> As a silk hat on a Bradford millionaire.

His arrogance and cheapness, his brash vulgarity, his strutting show of confidence which gives itself away at every move and betrays an inner ignorance and insecurity—all these reflections are suggested to the reader by the unexpected comparison to the awkward angle at which the crass new-rich man wears his hat.

The final effect of the whole passage, it should be noted, is not to weaken the force of either half of the contrasting terms. The beauty of the evening is not destroyed by the city. The situation of the girl is not being caricatured or mocked: its pathos is underlined by the contrast between her surroundings and those of traditional 'romantic love.' The juxtaposition and union of opposites (according to Grierson the distinguishing feature of metaphysical poetry) produces likewise here the result of intensifying both. The whole scene is presented with an extraordinary fullness of actuality.

Such manner of minute analysis is not meant to imply that Eliot's verse is a kind of special art. Indeed, equally careful reading—as Richards has demonstrated in *Practical Criticism*—is demanded of any poem in which a mature author has utilized all the resources of language and feeling at his command. This would be true of the Odes of Keats as well as of the later plays of Shakespeare.

17. As Eliot notes, an expression very close to this was used by Rémy de Gourmont in speaking of Flaubert: 'Il n'y a de livres que ceux où un écrivain s'est raconté lui-même en racontant les mœurs de ses contemporains—leurs rêves, leurs vanités, leurs amours, et leurs folies.' In any full account of the development of Eliot's critical theory it would be essential to dwell on his early obligations to de Gourmont, of whom he remarked in his essay on 'The Perfect Critic': 'Of all modern critics, perhaps Rémy de Gourmont had most of the general intelligence of Aristotle. An amateur, though an excessively able amateur, in physiology, he combined to a remarkable degree sensitiveness, erudition, sense of fact and sense of history, and generalizing power.'

What Eliot gained from reading such books as *Le Problème du style* and *La Culture des idées* is best shown in his further remark that de Gourmont was 'the critical consciousness of a generation,' who could 'supply the conscious formulas of a sensibility in process of formation.' It is worth noting, however, that in recent years Eliot has referred to de Gourmont much less frequently; and certainly Eliot's matured critical ideas are more complex and resilient than de Gourmont's, precisely as his mind is of tougher fibre.

Eliot's more demonstrably enduring debts are to such thinkers as Irving Babbitt, Charles Maurras, and T. E. Hulme. Ants Oras has dealt with some of these relations of Eliot's thought in his informative if somewhat pedestrian study of *The Critical Ideas of T. S. Eliot* (Tartu, Esthonia, 1932).

But behind any tangible debts and obscured by their sharp divergence of approach, there is to be discovered everywhere in Eliot's work his kinship to Matthew Arnold, a kinship to be noted in their views of the relation of the individual to society, as well as on such matters as the importance of wholeness of structure in a work of art.

KENNETH BURKE

Motives and Motifs in the Poetry of Marianne Moore

(1945)

In this essay we would characterize the substance of Miss Moore's work as a specific poetic strategy. And we would watch it for insights which the contemplation of it may give us into the ways of poetic and linguistic action generally. For this purpose we shall use both her recently published book, *What Are Years,* and her *Selected Poems,* published in 1935 with an introduction by T. S. Eliot (and including some work reprinted from an earlier volume, *Observations*).

On page 8 of the new book, Miss Moore writes:

> The power of the visible
> is the invisible;

and in keeping with the pattern, when recalling her former title, *Observations,* we might even have been justified in reading it as a deceptively technical synonym for 'visions.' One observes the visibles—but of the corresponding invisibles, one must be visionary. And while dealing much in things that can be empirically here, the poet reminds us that they may

> dramatize a
> meaning always missed
> by the externalist.

It is, then, a relation between external and internal, or visible and invisible, or background and personality, that her poems characteristically establish. Though her names for things are representative of attitudes, we could not say that the method is Symbolist. The objects exist too fully in their own right for us to treat them merely as objective words for subjects. T. S. Eliot says that her poetry 'might be classified as "descriptive" rather than "lyrical" or "dramatic." ' He cites an early poem that 'suggests a slight influence of H. D., certainly of H. D. rather than of any other "Imagist." ' And though asserting that 'Miss Moore has no immediate poetic derivations,' he seems to locate her work in the general vicinity of imagism, as when he writes:

> The aim of 'imagism,' so far as I understand it, or so far as it had any, was to introduce a peculiar concentration upon something visual, and to set in motion an expanding succession of concentric feelings. Some of Miss Moore's poems—for instance with animal or bird subjects—have a very good spread of association.

I think of William Carlos Williams. For though Williams differs much from Miss Moore in temperament and method, there is an important quality common to their modes of perception. It is what Williams has chosen to call by the trade name of 'objectivist.'

Symbolism, imagism, and objectivism would obviously merge into one another, since they are recipes all having the same ingredients but in different proportions. In symbolism, the subject is much stronger than the object as an organizing motive. That is, it is *what the images are symbolic of* that shapes their treatment. In imagism, there would ideally be an equality of the two motives, the subjective and objective. But in objectivism, though an object may be chosen for treatment because of its symbolic or subjective reference, once it has been chosen it is to be studied in its own right.

A man might become an electrician, for instance, because of some deep response to electricity as a symbol of power. Yet, once he had become an electrician and thus had converted his response to this subject into an objective knowledge of its laws and properties, he would thereafter treat electricity as he did, not because each of his acts as an electrician would be symbolic like his original choice of occupation, but because such acts were required by the peculiar nature of electricity. Similarly, a poet writing in an 'objectivist' idiom might select his subject because of some secret reference or personal significance it has had for him; yet having selected it, he would find that its corresponding object had qualities to be featured and appraised for themselves. And he might pay so much attention to such appraisal that the treatment of the object would in effect 'transcend' the motive behind its original singling-out.

Thus, the poem 'Four Quartz Crystal Clocks' (in *What Are Years*) begins:

> There are four vibrators, the world's exactest clocks;
> and these quartz time-pieces that tell
> time intervals to other clocks,
> these worksless clocks work well;
> and all four, independently the
> same, are there in the cool Bell
> Laboratory time
>
> vault. Checked by a comparator with Arlington
> they punctualize . . . (Etc.)

I think there would be no use in looking for 'symbolist' or 'imagist' motives behind the reference to the fact that precisely *four* clocks are mentioned here. It is an 'objectivist' observation. We read of four, not because the number corresponds, for instance, to the Horsemen of the Apocalypse, but simply because there actually are four of them in the time vault. Similarly, 'cool Bell Laboratory time vault' might have outlying suggestions of something like the coolness of a tomb—but primarily one feels that the description is there for purposes of objective statement; and had the nature of the scene itself dictated it, we should be reading of a 'hot Bell Laboratory time tower.' Though not journalism, it is reporting.

Yet any reader of Miss Moore's verse will quickly acknowledge that this theme, which provides an 'objective' opportunity for the insertion of transitions between such words as 'exactest,' 'punctualize,' 'careful timing,' 'clear ice,' 'instruments of truth,' and 'accuracy,' is quite representative of her (and thus 'symbolic' in the proportions of imagism). And the secondary level of the theme (its quality as being not the theme of clocks that tell the time, but of clocks that tell the time to clocks that tell the time)—I should consider thoroughly symbolic, as signalizing a concern not merely for the withinness of motives, but for the withinness-of-withinness of motives, the motives behind motives.[1]

We can call Miss Moore 'objectivist,' then, only by taking away the epithet in part. For though many details in her work seem to get there purely out of her attempt to report and judge of a thing's intrinsic qualities, to make us feel its properties as accurately as possible, the fact remains that, after you have read several of her poems, you begin to discern a strict principle of selection motivating her appraisals.

In *Selected Poems,* for instance, consider the poem, 'People's Surroundings,' that gives us a catalogue of correspondence between various kinds of agents and the scenes related to their roles. The poet is concerned to feature, in a background, the details that are an objective portrait of the person to whose kind of action this background belongs. 'A setting must not have the air of being one'—a proscription one can observe if he makes the setting the extension of those in it. Here are relationships among act, scene, and agent (I use the three terms central to the philosophy of drama embodied in Henry James's prefaces). And among these people who move 'in their respective places,' we read of

. . . the acacia-like lady shivering at the touch of a hand,
lost in a small collision of orchids—
dyed quicksilver let fall
to disappear like an obedient chameleon in fifty shades of mauve and amethyst.

Here, with person and ground merged as indistinguishably as in a pontillist painting by Seurat, the items objectify a tentative mood we encounter throughout Miss Moore's verses. The lines are like a miniature impression of her work in its entirety. And when, contemplating a game of bowls, she writes, 'I learn that we are precisians, not citizens of Pompeii arrested in action/as a cross-section of one's correspondence would seem to imply,' she here 'learns' what she is forever learning, in her contemplation of animals and natural and fabricated things, as she seeks to islolate, for her appreciation and our own, the 'great amount of poetry in unconscious fastidiousness.'

I think appreciation is as strong a motive in her work as it was in the work of Henry James. 'The thing is to lodge somewhere at the heart of one's complexity an irrepressible *appreciation,*' he says in his preface to *The Spoils of Poynton.* And: 'To criticise is to appreciate, to appropriate, to take intellectual possession, to establish in fine a relation with the criticised thing and make it one's own.' It is a kind of private property available to everyone—and is perhaps the closest secular equivalent to the religious motive of glorification. It is a form of gratitude. And following out its possibilities, where one might otherwise be querulous he can instead choose to be precise. This redemption or transformation of complaint is, I think, essential to the quality of perception in Miss Moore's verse. (Rather, it is an anticipation of complaint: getting there first, it takes up all the room.)

In 'Spenser's Ireland' (*What Are Years*), we may glimpse somewhat how this redemption can take place. Beginning in a mood of appreciation almost studious, the poem ends

> The Irish say your trouble is their
> trouble and your
> joy their joy? I wish
> I could believe it;
> I am troubled, I'm dissat-
> isfied, I'm Irish.

Since it is towards this end that the poem is directed, we may assume that from this end it derives the logic of its progression.

Note the general tenor of the other observations: on family, on marriage, on independence and yielding, on the freedom of those 'made captive by supreme belief.' There is talk of enchantments, of transformations, of a coat 'like Venus' mantle lined with stars . . . the sleeves new from disuse,' of such discriminations as we get

> when large dainty
> fingers tremblingly divide the wings
> of the fly.

And there are lines naming birds, and having a verbal music most lovely in its flutter of internal rhymes:

> the guillemot
> so neat and the hen
> of the heath and the
> linnet spinet-sweet.

All these details could be thought of as contextual to the poem's ending (for, if you single out one moment of a poem, all the other moments automatically become its context). If, then, we think of the final assertion as the act, we may think of the preceding contextual material as the scene, or background, of this act (a background that somehow contains the same quality as the act, saying implicitly what the act of the final assertion says explicitly). Viewed thus we see, as the underlying structure of this 'description,' a poem that, if treated as a lyric, would have somewhat the following argument: 'Surrounded with details appropriate to my present mood, with a background of such items as go with matters to do with family, union, independence, I, an Irish girl (while the birds are about—and sweetly) am dissatisfied.'

I won't insist that I'm not wrong. But in any case, that's the way I read it. And I would discern, behind her 'objectivist' study and editorializing, what are essentially the lineaments of a lyric. But where the lyrist might set about to write, 'In the moonlight, by the river, on a night like this in Spain,' I can think of Miss Moore's distributing these items (discreetly and discretely) among conversational observations about the quality of light in general and moonlight in particular, about rivers mighty and tiny, in mountains, across plains, and emptying into the desert or the sea, about the various qualifications that apply to the transformation from twilight to darkness, in suburbs, or over bays, etc.; and from travel books of Spain we might get some bits that, pieced together, gave us all those elements into which, in her opinion, the given night in Spain should be 'broken down.'

We might try from another angle by suggesting that Miss Moore makes 'because' look like 'and.' That is, the orthodox lyrist might say, in effect, 'I am sad *because* the birds are singing thus.' A translation into Miss Moore's objectivist idiom would say in effect: 'There are such and such birds—*and* birds sing thus and so—*and* I am sad.' The scenic material would presumably be chosen because of its quality as objective replica of the subjective (as observed moments in the scene that correspond to observing moments in the agent). But even where they had been selected because of their bearing upon the plaint, her subsequent attention to them, with appreciation as a motive, would transform the result from a purely psychologistic rhetoric (the traditional romantic device of simply using scenic terms as a vocabulary for the sympathetic naming of personal moods). And the result would be, instead, an appraisal or judgment of many things in and for themselves. They would be encouraged to disclose their traits, not simply that they might exist through the vicarage of words, but that they might reveal their properties as workmanship (workmanship being a trait in which the ethical and the esthetic are one).

What are years? That is, if we were to assemble a thesaurus of all the important qualifications of the term 'years' as Miss Moore uses it, what would these qualifications be? I suppose a title is always an assertion because it is a thing—and every thing is positive. Years, we learn by her opening poem of that title, are at least a quality of observation (vision), involving the obligation of courage, of commands laid upon the self to be strong, to see deep and be glad. And years possess the quality of one

> . . . who
> accedes to mortality
> and in his imprisonment, rises
> upon himself as
> the sea in a chasm . . .

Who does this, we are told, 'sees deep and is glad.' Years are also, by the nature of the case, steps from something to something. And to indicate a curve of development from the earlier volume, we might recall this same theme (of the rising water) as it was treated previously. I refer to a poem, 'Sojourn in the Whale,' which, beginning on the theme, 'Trying to open locked doors with a sword,' had likewise talked of Ireland. It is addressed to 'you,' a 'you' who has heard men say: 'she will become wise and will be forced to give/in. Compelled by experience, she/will turn back; water seeks its own level.' Whereat

> . . . you
> have smiled. 'Water in motion is far
> from level.' You have seen it, when obstacles happened to bar
> the path, rise automatically.

In the earlier poem, the figure was used defensively, even oppositionally. It is a tactic not common in Miss Moore's verse; as against the dialectician's morality of eristic, she shows a more feminine preference for the sheer ostracizing of the enemy, refuting by silence—disagreement implying the respect of intimacy, as in her poem on 'Marriage,' wittily appraising the 'fight to be affectionate,' she quotes, 'No truth can be fully known until it has been tried by the tooth of disputation.'

(When Miss Moore was editor of *The Dial,* her ideal number, as regards the reviews and articles of criticism, would I think have been one in which all good books got long favorable reviews, all middling books got short favorable reviews, and all books deserving of attack were allowed to go without mention. One can imagine how such a norm could be reached either charitably, through stress upon appreciation as motive, or not so charitably, by way of punishment, as when Miss Moore observes in 'Spenser's Ireland': 'Denunciations do not affect the culprit: nor blows, but it/is torture to him not to be spoken to.' We need not decide between these motives in all cases, since they can comfortably work in unison.)

In contrast with the 'oppositional' context qualifying the figure of the rising water in the earlier poem, 'Sojourn in the Whale,' its later variant has a context almost exaltedly positive. And repeating the same pattern (of affirmation in imprisonment) in another figure, the later poem widens the connotations of the years thus:

> . . . The very bird
> grown taller as he sings, steels
> his form straight up. Though he is captive
> his mighty singing
> says satisfaction is a lowly
> thing, how pure a thing is joy.
> This is mortality,
> this is eternity.

The pattern appears more conversationally (*What Are Years,* p. 12) in the suggestion that it must have been a 'humorous' workman who made

> this greenish Waterford
> glass weight with the summit curled down toward
> itself as the
> grass grew,

and in 'The Monkey Puzzle' (*Selected Poems*) we read

> its tail superimposed upon itself in a complacent half spiral,
> incidentally so witty.

Still, then, trying to discover what are years (or rather, what all are years), we might also recall, in *Selected Poems,* the poem on 'The Fish,' where the one fish featured as representative of its tribe is observed 'opening and shutting itself like/an/injured fan'—in quality not unlike 'The Student' of *What Are Years* who

> . . . is too reclusive for
> some things to seem to touch
> him, not because he
> has no feeling but because he has so much.

As the poem of 'The Fish' develops, we might say that the theme is transferred 'from the organism to the environment'; for we next read of a chasm through which the water has driven a wedge—and injury is here too, since

> All
> external
> marks of abuse are present on this
> defiant edifice.—

And finally

> Repeated
> evidence has proved that it can live
> on what cannot revive
> its youth. The sea grows old in it.

A chasm in the sea, then, becomes rather the sea in a chasm. And this notable reversal, that takes place in the areas of the 'submerged,' would also seem to be an aspect of 'years.' Which would mean that 'years' subsume the synecdochic possibilities whereby those elements that cluster together can represent one another: here the active can become passive, the environed can become the environment, the container can be interchangeable with the contained. In possessing such attributes, 'years' are poetry.

We may at this point recall our beginning—the citation concerning visible and invisible. In 'The Plumet Basilisk' (*Selected Poems*) we read of this particular lizard that, 'king with king,'

> He leaps and meets his
> likeness in the stream.

He is (in the poem it is a quotation)

> 'the ruler of Rivers, Lakes, and Seas,
> invisible or visible'—

and as scene appropriate to the agent, this basilisk is said to live in a basilica. (Another lizard, in the same poem, is said to be 'conferring wings on what it grasps, as the airplant does'; and in 'The Jerboa,' we are told of 'this small desert rat' that it 'honours the sand by assuming its colour.') Likewise

> the plumet portrays
> mythology's wish
> to be interchangeably man and fish.

What I am trying to do, in reaching out for these various associations, is to get some comprehensive glimpse of the ways in which the one pervasive quality of motivation is modified and ramified. I am trying, in necessarily tenuous material, to indicate how the avowed relation between the visible and the invisible finds variants, or sophistications, in 'objectivist' appreciation; how this appreciation, in an age of much querulousness, serves rather to transcend the querulous (*Selected Poems,* p. 34: 'The staff, the bag, the feigned inconsequence/of manner, best bespeak that weapon, self-protectiveness'); and how this same pattern takes form in the theme of submergence, with its interchangeabilities, and so in the theme of water rising on itself. At another point the motive takes as its object the motif of the spinster ('You have been compelled by hags to spin/gold thread from straw,' with incidental suggestions of esthetic alchemy, lines that appear in 'Sojourn in the Whale,' and so link with submergence, Ireland, and the theme of spirited feminine independence, thus relating to kindred subjects in the later poem, 'Spenser's Ireland'). I have also suggested that a like quality of imagination is to be found in the intellectual ways of one who selects as his subject not clocks, but clocks for clocks. (To appreciate just what goes on here, one might contrast these contemplative clocks—serene in their role as the motives behind motives—with the ominous clock-faces of Verhaeren, or in the grotesque plays of Edmund Wilson, which no one seems to have read but me.) From these crystal clocks, I could then advance to another variant, as revealed in the treatment of ice and glass. These would, I think, be animated by the same spirit. See for instance (in *Selected Poems*) the study of the glacier as 'an octopus of ice':

> this fossil flower concise without a shiver,
> intact when it is cut,
> damned for its sacrosanct remoteness.

'Relentless accuracy is the nature of this octopus/with its capacity for fact'—which would make it a glacier with an objectivist esthetic. And two levels of motive are figured in the splendid concluding vista of

> . . . the hard mountain 'planed by ice and polished by the wind'—
> the white volcano with no weather side;
> the lightning flashing at its base,
> rain falling in the valleys, and snow falling on the peak—.[2]

We might have managed more easily by simply demarcating several themes, like naming the different ingredients that go to make up a dish. Or as with the planks that are brought together, to make a campaign platform, regardless of their fit with one another. But the relation among the themes of a genuine poetry is not of this sort. It is *substantial*—which is to say that all the branches spread from a single trunk.

I am trying to suggest that, without this initial substantiality, 'objectivism' would lead not to the 'feigned inconsequence of manner' that Miss Moore has mastered, but to inconsequence pure and simple. But because of this substantiality, the surfaces are derived from depth; indeed, the strict lawfulness in their choice of surfaces is depth. And the objects treated have the property not simply of things, but of volitions. They derive their poignancy as motifs from their relation to the sources of motive. And the relation between observer and observed is not that of news and reporter, but of 'conversities' (her word).

In the earlier volume there is a poem, 'Black Earth,' wherein surprisingly the poet establishes so close an identification with her theme as not merely to 'observe' it with sympathy and appreciation, but to speak for it. This is one of her rare 'I' poems—and in it the elephant sometimes speaks with the challenge and confidence of an Invictus. Beginning on the theme of emergence (coupled with delight in the thought of submergence at will), there is first a celebration of the sturdy skin; then talk of power ('my back is full of the history of power'); and then: 'My soul shall never be cut into/by a wooden spear.' Next comes mention of the trunk, and of poise. And interwoven with the vigor of assertion, the focal theme is there likewise:

> that tree-trunk without
> roots, accustomed to shout
> its own thoughts to itself . . .

and:

> . . . The I of each is to
> the I of each
> a kind of fretful speech
> which sets a limit on itself; the elephant is
> black earth preceded by a tendril?

I think we can make a point by recalling this earlier poem when, in 'Smooth Gnarled Crape Myrtle' (*What Are Years*), the theme of the elephant's trunk appears again, this time but in passing, contextual and 'tangential' to the themes of birds, union, loneliness:

. . . 'joined in
friendship, crowned by love.'
An aspect may deceive; as the
elephant's columbine-tubed trunk
held waveringly out—
an at will heavy thing—is
delicate.

Surely, 'an at will heavy thing' is a remarkable find. But one does not make such observation by merely looking at an elephant's trunk. There must have been much to discard. In this instance, we can know something about the omissions, quite as though we had inspected earlier drafts of the poem with their record of revisions. For though a usage in any given poem is a finished thing, and thus brilliant with surface, it becomes in effect but 'work in progress' when we align it with kindred usages (emergent, fully developed, or retrospectively condensed) in other poems. And here, by referring to 'Black Earth,' we can find what lies behind the reference to the elephant's trunk in 'Smooth Gnarled Crape Myrtle.' We can know it for a fact what kind of connotations must, for the poet, have been implicit in the second, condensed usage. Hence we can appreciate the motives that enabled this trunk to be seen not merely as a *thing,* but as an *act,* representative of the assertion in 'Black Earth.' And by reviewing the earlier usage we can know the kind of volitional material which, implicit in the later usage, led beyond the perception of the trunk as a thing to this perception of it as an act. At such moments, I should say, out of our idealistic trammels we get a glimpse of realism in its purity.

Or let us look at another instance. Sensitivity in the selection of words resides in the ability, or necessity, to feel behind the given word a history—not a past history, but a future one. Within the word, collapsed into its simultaneous oneness, there is implicit a sequence, a complexity of possible narratives that could be drawn from it. If you would remember what words are in this respect, and how in the simultaneity of a word histories are implicit, recall the old pleasantry of asking someone, 'What's an accordion,' whereat invariably as he explains he will start pumping a bellows.

Well, among Miss Moore's many poems enunciating aspects of her esthetic credo, or commenting on literary doctrines and methods, there is one, 'To a Snail,' beginning:

> If 'compression is the first grace of style,'
> you have it. Contractility is a virtue
> as modesty is a virtue.

And this equating of an esthetic value with a moral one is summed up by locating the principle of style 'in the curious phenomenon of your occipital horn.'

In her poem on the butterfly (*What Are Years,* p. 17), the mood of tentativeness that had been compressed within the term 'contractility' reveals its significant narrative equivalents. As befits the tentative, or contractile, it is a poem of jeopardy, tracing a tenuous relationship between a butterfly ('half deity half worm,' 'last of the elves') and a nymph ('dressed in Wedgewood blue'), with light winds (even a 'zephyr') to figure the motives of passion. Were not the course of a butterfly so intrinsically akin to the 'inconsequential ease' and 'drover-like tenacity' of Miss Moore's own versa-tilities, one might not have much hope for a poem built about this theme (reminiscent of many musical Papillons—perhaps more than a theme, perhaps a set idiom, almost a form). Here, with the minute accuracy of sheerly "objectivist" description, there is a subtle dialectic of giving and receiving, of fascinations and releases—an interchange of delicately shaded attitudes. In this realm, things reached for will evade, but will follow the hand as it recedes.

Through the tracery of flight, there are two striking moments of stasis, each the termination of a course: one when 'the butterfly's tobacco-brown unglazed/china eyes and furry countenance confront/the nymph's large eyes'—and the second when, having broken contact with the nymph's 'controlled agitated glance,' the 'fiery tiger-horse' (at rest, but poised against the wind, 'chest arching/bravely out') is motivated purely by relation to the zephyr alone. The poem concludes by observing that this 'talk' between the animal and the zephyr 'was as strange as my grandmother's muff.'

I have called it a poem of jeopardy. (When butterfly and nymph confront each other, 'It is Goya's scene of the tame magpie faced/by crouching cats.') It is also a poem of coquetry (perhaps our last poem of coquetry, quite as this butterfly was the last of the elves—coquetry now usually being understood as something that comes down like a ton of brick).[3]

The tentativeness, contractility, acquires more purely the theme of jeopardy in 'Bird-Witted' (*What Are Years*), reciting the incident of the 'three large fledgling mocking-birds,' awaiting 'their no longer larger mother,' while there approaches

the
intellectual cautious-
ly c r e e p ing cat.

If her animals are selected for their 'fastidiousness,' their fastidiousness itself is an aspect of contractility, of jeopardy. 'The Pangolin' (*What Are Years*), a poem which takes us through odd nocturnal journeys to the joyous saluting of the dawn, begins: 'Another armoured animal'—and of a sudden you realize that Miss Moore's recondite menagerie is almost a thesaurus of protectivenesses. Thus also, the poem in which occur the lines anent visible and invisible, has as its conclusion:

unsolicitude having swallowed up
all giant birds but an
alert gargantuan
little-winged, magnificently
speedy running-bird. This one
remaining rebel
is the sparrow-camel.

The tentativeness also manifests itself at times in a cult of rarity, a collector's or antiquarian interest in the present, a kind of stylistic tourism. And it may lead to a sheer word play, of graduated sort (a Laforguian delight in showing how the pedantries can be reclaimed for poetry):

The lemur-student can see
that the aye-aye is not

an angwan-tíbo, potto, or loris.

Yet mention of the 'aepyornis' may suggest the answer we might have given, were we up on such matters, to one who, pencil in hand and with the newspaper folded to make it firmer, had asked, 'What's a gigantic bird, found fossil in Madagascar in nine letters?' As for her invention, 'invis ible,' I can't see it.

Tonally, the 'contractility' reveals itself in the great agility, even restlessness, which Miss Moore imparts to her poetry by assonance, internal rhyme, and her many variants of the run-over line. We should also note those sudden nodules of sound which are scattered throughout her verses, such quick concentrations as 'rude root cudgel,' 'the raised device reversed,' 'trim trio on the tree-stem,' 'furled fringed frill,' or tonal episodes more sustained and complex, as the lines on the birds in Ireland (already quoted), or the title, 'Walking-Sticks and Paper-Weights and Water-Marks,' or

> . . . the redbird
> the red-coated musketeer,
> the trumpet-flower, the cavalier,
> the parson, and the
> wild parishioner. A deer-
> track in a church-floor
> brick . . .

One noticeable difference between the later selection and the earlier one is omission of poems on method. In *Selected Poems* there were a great many such. I think for instance of: 'Poetry,' containing her ingenious conceit, 'imaginary gardens with real toads in them'; 'Critics and Connoisseurs'; 'The Monkeys'; 'In the Days of Prismatic Colour'; 'Picking and Choosing'; 'When I Buy Pictures'; 'Novices' (on action in language, and developed in imagery of the sea); 'The Past is the Present' ('ecstasy affords/the occasion and expediency determines the form'); and one which propounds a doctrine as its title: 'In This Age of Hard Trying, Nonchalance is Good and.'

But though methodological pronouncements of this sort have dropped away, in the closing poem on 'The Paper Nautilus,' the theme does reappear. Yet in an almost startlingly deepened transformation. Here, proclaiming the poet's attachment to the poem, there are likenesses to the maternal attachment to the young. And the themes of bondage and freedom (as with one 'hindered to succeed') are fiercely and flashingly merged.

NOTES

1. In passing we might consider a whole series of literary ways from this point of view. Allegory would deal with correspondences on a purely dogmatic, or conceptual basis. In the article on 'Vestments,' for instance, in the *Encyclopædia Britannica,* we read of various 'symbolical interpretations': '(1) the *moralizing school,* the oldest, by which—as in the case of St. Jerome's treatment of the Jewish vestments—the vestments are

explained as typical of the virtues proper to those who wear them; (2) the *Christological school, i. e.* that which considered the minister as the representative of Christ and his garments as typical of some aspects of Christ's person or office—*e. g.* the stole is his obedience and servitude for our sakes; (3) the *allegorical school,* which treats the priest as a warrior or champion, who puts on the amice as a helmet, the alb as a breastplate, and so on.' A work constructed about the systematic use of any such theories of correspondence would, to our way of thinking, be allegorical. The symbolic would use an objective vocabulary for its suggestion of the subjective, with the subjective motive being organizationally more important than the objective one. The specific literary movement called Symbolism would exemplify this stress to a large extent, but would also gravitate towards Surrealism, which stresses the incongruous and contradictory nature of motives by the use of gargoyles as motifs. Imagism would be 'personalistic,' in the idealistic sense, in using scenic material as the reflection, or extension of human characters. The 'objectivist,' though rooted in symbolic and imagist concerns, would move into a plane where the object, originally selected by reason of its subjective reference, is studied in its own right. (The result will be 'descriptive' poetry. And it will be 'scientific' in the sense that, whereas poetry is a kind of act, the descriptiveness of science is rather the *preparation* for an act, the delayed action of a Hamletic reconnaissance in search of the accurate knowledge necessary for the act. And descriptive poetry falls across the two categories in that it acts by describing the scene preparatory to an act.) Naturalism has a greater stress upon the scenic from the polemic or depreciatory point of view (its quasi-scientific quality as delayed action, or preparation for action, often being revealed in that such literature generally either calls for action in the non-esthetic field or makes one very conscious of the fact that a 'solution' is needed but is not being offered). True realism is difficult for us to conceive of, after so long a stretch of monetary idealism (accentuated as surrealism) and its counterpart, technological materialism (accentuated as behaviorism and operationalism), while pragmatic philosophies stress *making* and *doing* and *getting* in a localized way that obscures the realistic stress upon the *act*. The German term, *Realpolitik,* for instance, exemplifies a crude brand of pragmatism that completely misrepresents the realistic motive. The communicative nature of art gives all art a realistic ingredient, but the esthetic philosophies which the modern artist consciously or unconsciously absorbs continually serve to obscure this ingredient rather than to cultivate it.

2. This is cited from the poem that follows the one on 'Marriage,' and is in turn followed by 'Sea Unicorns and Land Unicorns.' The three could be taken together as a triptych that superbly illustrates three stages in the development of one idea. First, we have the subtly averse poem on marriage (done in a spirit of high comedy that portrays marital quarrelings

as interrelated somewhat like the steps of a minuet). Then comes the precise yet exalted contemplation of the glacier. And finally a discussion of the unicorn, a legendary solitaire:

> Thus this strange animal with its miraculous elusiveness,
> has come to be unique,
> 'impossible to take alive,'
> tamed only by a lady inoffensive like itself—
> as curiously wild and gentle.

And typically, she cites of it that, since lions and unicorns are arch enemies, and 'where the one is the other cannot be missing.' Sir John Hawkins deduced an abundance of lions in Florida from the presence of unicorns there.

The theme of the lightning that flashes at the base of the glacier is varied in the unicorn poem (in a reference to 'the dogs/which are dismayed by the chain lightning/playing at them from its horn'). And it is varied also in a poem on the elephant (still to be discussed) that

> has looked at the electricity and at the earth-
> quake and is still
> here; . . .

3. In the earlier volume there is an epigram-like poem, 'To a Steam Roller,' that I have always thought very entertaining. It excoriates this sorry, ungainly mechanism as a bungling kind of fellow that, when confronting such discriminations as are the vital purpose of Miss Moore's lines, would 'crush all the particles down/into close conformity, and then walk back and forth/on them.' We also read there:

> As for butterflies, I can hardly conceive
> of one's attending upon you, but to question
> the congruence of the complement is vain, if it exists.

Heretofore I had been content to think of this reference to a butterfly simply as a device for suggesting weight by a contrasting image of lightness. But the role of butterfly as elf conversant to nymph might also suggest the presence of such overtones as contrasting types of masculinity. (This would give us a perfect instance of what Coleridge meant by fancy, which occurs when we discern behind the contrast an element that the contrasted images share in common.)

As for the later poem, where the theme of the butterfly is fully developed, I might now try to make more clearly the point I had in mind with reference to the two moments of stasis. In the opening words ('half deity half worm' and 'We all, infant and adult, have/stopped to watch the butterfly') the poem clearly suggests the possibility that it will figure two levels of motivation, a deity being in a different realm of motives than a worm, and the child's quality of perception being critically distinct from the adult's. Examining the two moments of stasis, we find here too the indications of an important difference between them. At the first stasis, elf and nymph confront each other, while 'all's a-quiver with significance.' But at the final stasis, the conversity is between butterfly and west wind, a director colloquy (its greater inwardness linking it, in my opinion, with the motive-behind-motive figuration in the theme of clocks-for-clocks). At this second stage, the butterfly is called 'historic metamorphoser/and saintly animal'; hence we may take it that the 'deity' level of motive prevails at this second stage. The quality of the image in the closing line ('their talk was as strange as my grandmother's muff') would suggest that the deified level is equated with the quality of perception as a child. (The grandmother theme also appears in 'Spenser's Ireland,' where we are told that 'Hindered characters . . . in Irish stories . . . all have grandmothers.' Another reason for believing that the second stage of the butterfly poem is also the 'motives-behind-motives' stage is offered tenuously by this tie-up with the word 'hindered,' since the final poem in the book, as we shall know when we come to it, does well by this word in proclaiming a morality of art.)

Another poem, 'Virginia Britannia' (*What Are Years*), that seems on the surface almost exclusively descriptive (though there is passing reference to a 'fritillary' that 'zig-zags') is found to be progressing through scenic details to a similar transcendence. At the last, against sunset, two levels are figured, while the intermediate trees 'become with lost identity, part of the ground.' The clouds, thus marked off, are then heralded in words suggestive of Wordsworth's ode as 'to the child an intimation of/what glory is.'

YVOR WINTERS

The Significance of *The Bridge,* by Hart Crane or What Are We To Think of Professor X?

(1947)

In speaking of the 'significance' of *The Bridge,* I am using the word 'significance' in both of its common meanings: I refer to the content which the author apparently wished to communicate and also to the 'moral,' so to speak, that we as observers and as members of his society may deduce from his effort and from the qualities of its success or failure. It is the second sense of the word that I should like to emphasize if I had time, but before I can begin on it I must deal somehow with the first: What is *The Bridge* about? What did Crane think he was getting at?

Most of Crane's thought, and this is especially true of *The Bridge,* was derived from Whitman. This fact is generally recognized. It is my personal impression likewise, and my personal impression is derived not only from a study of the works of Crane and of Whitman, but also from about four years of frequent and regular correspondence with Crane and from about four long evenings of uninterrupted conversation with him. Crane and I began publishing poems in the same magazines about 1919; I started quarreling with Harriet Monroe about 1925 or 1926 to get Crane's poems into *Poetry: A Magazine of Verse;* Crane and I started corresponding shortly thereafter; I spent a few evenings talking to Crane during the Christmas holidays of 1927; our correspondence ended as a result of my review of *The Bridge* in 1930; and about two or two and a half years later Crane committed suicide.

Most of Crane's thought was, as I say, derived from Whitman. In

From *In Defence of Reason* by Yvor Winters. Reprinted by permission of the estate of the publisher, Alan Swallow.

turn, nearly all of Whitman's thought was derived from Emerson, or could easily have been. Whitman professed himself Emerson's disciple, and Emerson offered Whitman his professional blessing. But Emerson in turn was in no wise original, at least as regards the bare formulae of his thought: his ideas are the commonplace ideas of the romantic movement, from the time of the third Earl of Shaftesbury to the present. In the restating of these ideas, however, Emerson did something which was important, at least in the American context. What were these ideas, and what did Emerson do to them?

The ideas were, briefly, these:

God and his creation are one. God is good. Man, as part of the creation, is part of God, and so is good. Man may therefore trust his impulses, which are the voice of God; through trusting them absolutely and acting upon them without reserve, he becomes one with God. Impulse is thus equated with the protestant concept of conscience, as a divine and supra-rational directive; and surrender to impulse, which unites one with God, becomes equivalent in a sense to the traditional and Catholic concept of the mystical experience. We are confronted here with an illogicality, for our first principles tell us that man is a part of God whether he trusts his impulses or not; but this is merely a part of the illogicality which denies the validity of Reason. For Emerson, as for other Romantics, Reason is the source of all evil, is the adversary of Impulse, and is that which has no part in God in a universe in which everything is a part of God and in which everything is good. In life and in art the automatic man, the unreflective creature of impulse, is the ideal; he is one with God and will achieve the good life and great art.

Let me quote from Emerson on these subjects:

As to the pantheistic doctrine, he writes, for example, in *Nature:*

> The knowledge that we traverse the whole scale of being from the center to the poles of nature, and have some stake in every possibility, lends that sublime luster to death, which philosophy and religion have too outwardly striven to express in the popular doctrine of the immortality of the soul. The reality is more excellent than the report. Here is no ruin, no discontinuity, no spent ball. The divine circulations never rest nor linger. Nature is the incarnation of a thought, and turns to a thought again, as ice becomes water and gas. The world is mind precipitated, and the volatile essence is forever es-

> caping again into the state of free thought. Hence the virtue and pungency of the influence on the mind of natural objects, whether inorganic or organized. Man imprisoned, man crystallized, man vegetative, speaks to man impersonated.

In the last sentence, 'man imprisoned' is in apposition with 'man crystallized' and with 'man vegetative,' terms which may be translated respectively as 'God in the form of a crystal' and as 'God in the form of a cabbage'; the expression 'man impersonated' may be translated as 'God in the form of man,' or more simply, as 'man.' The passage, like many others in Emerson, indicates that man in death remains immortal while losing his identity. The concept is doubtless comprehensible to those who understand it. I once argued this issue with Crane, and when he could not convert me by reason, he said: 'Well, if we can't believe it, we'll have to kid ourselves into believing it.' Something of the same attitude seems to be implied in a passage in his poem *The Dance* (that section of *The Bridge* which deals most explicitly with this notion) in which he begs his Indian medicine man to 'Lie to us! Dance us back the tribal morn!'

There are innumerable passages in Emerson on the divine origin of impulse and on its trustworthiness. In *The Poet* he writes as follows (here as elsewhere the italics are mine):

> It is a secret which every intellectual man quickly learns, that beyond the energy of his possessed and conscious intellect he is capable of a new energy (as of an intellect doubled on itself), *by abandonment to the nature of things;* that beside his privacy of power as an individual man, there is a great public power on which he can draw, *by unlocking at all risks his human doors* and suffering the ethereal tides to roll through him. . . .

In *Spiritual Laws* he writes:

> A little consideration of what takes place around us every day would show us that a higher law than that of our will regulates events; that our painful labors are very unnecessary and altogether fruitless; that *only in our easy, simple, spontaneous action we are strong, and by contenting ourselves with obedience we become divine.* . . . We need only obey. There is guidance for each of us, and by lowly listening we shall hear the right word. *Why need you choose* so painfully

> your place, and occupation, and associates, and modes of action, and of entertainment? Certainly there is a possible right for you *that precludes the need of balance and of willful election.* For you there is a fit place and congenial duties. Place yourself in the middle of the stream of power and wisdom which flows into you as life, place yourself in the full center of that flood, then you are *without effort* impelled to truth, to right, and to perfect contentment.

And in *The Oversoul:*

> Ineffable is the union of man and God in every act of the soul. The simplest person who in his integrity worships God becomes God. . . . He believes that he cannot escape from his good. The things that are really for thee gravitate to thee. You are running to meet your friend. *Let your feet run, but your mind need not.* If you do not find him, will you not acquiesce that it is best you should not find him? for there is a power, which, as it is in you, is in him also, and could therefore very well bring you together, if it were for the best.

The last three passages all point unmistakably to Emerson's concept of automatism as the equivalent of the mystical experience; and in the last passage quoted the concept is very dramatically expressed—one could hardly ask for anything more explicit. Closely related to this notion is the familiar romantic notion of the beatitude of ignorance and of mediocrity, to say nothing of the beatitude of infancy. We are familiar with Gray's mute inglorious Miltons and with Wordsworth's young child who was a mighty prophet, seer blest. Similarly Emerson writes in *Spiritual Laws:*

> The intellectual life may be kept clean and healthful, if man will live the life of nature, and not import into his mind difficulties which are none of his. *No man need be perplexed in his speculations.* Let him do and say what strictly belongs to him, and *though very ignorant of books,* his nature shall not yield him any intellectual obstructions and doubts.

A passage such as this one makes very short work of our universities. In *Self-Reliance* Emerson writes:

> What pretty oracles nature yields us on this text in the face and behavior of children, babes, and even brutes! That di-

> vided and rebel mind, that distrust of a sentiment because our arithmetic has computed the strength and means opposed to our purpose, these have not. Their mind being whole, their eye is as yet unconquered, and when we look in their faces we are disconcerted. Infancy conforms to nobody; all conform to it; so that one babe commonly makes four or five out of the adults who prattle and play to it.

This passage is offered as a kind of vision of social beatitude. Unfortunately for those of us whose curiosity is insatiable, Emerson does not take the next step in his argument: although he tells us what happens when we have one babe (conforming to nobody) and four or five adults (conforming to the babe), he does not say what happens when we have five or six babes (all conforming to nobody): therein lies the crux of the matter.

Emerson was not wholly unaware of the theoretical objections which could be made to his position, but unless we are to assume that he personally was a corrupt and vicious man, which I think we can scarcely do, we are forced to admit that he simply did not know what the objections meant. In *Self-Reliance* he wrote:

> I remember an answer which when quite young I was prompted to make to a valued adviser, who was wont to importune me with the dear old doctrines of the church. On my saying. 'What have I to do with the sacredness of traditions, if I live wholly from within?' my friend suggested,—'But these impulses may be from below, not from above.' I replied, 'They do not seem to me to be such; but if I am the Devil's child, I will live then from the Devil.' No law can be sacred to me but that of my nature. Good and bad are but names very readily transferable to that or this; the only right is what is after my constitution; the only wrong what is against it.

Emerson's friend, in this passage, offers the traditional objection of the Roman Church to the quietistic schismatic; and Emerson appears to be ignorant of the traditional functions of the Devil and of the viscera. But in the last few statements in this passage we see clearly another consequence of the Emersonian position: its thoroughgoing relativism. That is right for me which is after my constitution; that is right for you which is after yours; the Oversoul will guide us both in the ways which best befit us, if we will both only follow our impulses.

My impulse to commit incest may horrify you; your impulse to commit murder and arson may horrify me; but we should ignore each other and proceed.

In *Circles,* Emerson writes to the same purpose, at the same time suggesting a new difficulty, with which, however, he is not impressed. He says:

> And thus, O circular philosopher, I hear some reader exclaim, you have arrived at a fine Pyrrhonism, at an equivalence and indifferency of all actions, and would fain teach us that, if we are true, forsooth, our crimes may be lively stones out of which we shall construct the temple of the true God!
>
> I am not careful to justify myself. . . . But lest I should mislead any when I have my own head and obey my whims, let me remind the reader that I am only an experimenter. Do not set the least value on what I do, or the least discredit on what I do not, as if I pretended to settle anything as true or false. I unsettle all things. No facts are to me sacred; none are profane; I simply experiment, an endless seeker, with no Past at my back.

Here Emerson suggests the difficulty that he has eliminated values: in teaching that everything is good, he has merely arrived at the conclusion that everything is equal to everything else, for nothing is either good or bad unless there are grounds for distinction. Emerson has arrived at a doctrine of equivalence, a doctrine to the effect that there are no grounds for choice; and he hopes to save himself only through not having to make a choice, through leaving choice wholly to God and to performing, himself, as an automaton. And in the last expression, in which he describes himself as an 'endless seeker, with no Past at my back,' we see his glorification of change as change; we can find this elsewhere in Emerson; we can find it likewise in Whitman; it is one of the most important ideas of *The Bridge*. It should be observed that the glorification of change as change is a necessary part of a system in which every act is good, in which there is no way to choose between courses of action, in which there is no principle of consistency, and in which there is no conception of a goal other than to be automatically controlled from moment to moment.

It is not surprising that Emerson should regard that art as the best which is the most nearly extemporaneous. He wrote in *Art:*

> But true art is never fixed, but always flowing. The sweetest music is not in the oratorio, but in the human voice when it speaks from its instant life tones of tenderness, truth, or courage. The oratorio has already lost its relation to the morning, to the sun, and to the earth, but that persuading voice is in tune with these. All works of art should not be detached, but extempore performances. A great man is a new statue in every attitude and action. A beautiful woman is a picture which drives all beholders nobly mad. Life may be lyric or epic, as well as a poem or a romance.

This view of art rests on the assumption that man should express what he is at any given moment; not that he should try by all the means at his disposal to arrive at a true understanding of a given subject or to improve his powers of understanding in general. Related to this notion is the principle that if we will only express what we are at any given moment, if we will only record our casual impressions, we may be sure to equal Shakespeare. This is from *Self-Reliance:*

> In every work of genius we recognize our own rejected thoughts; they come back to us with a certain alienated majesty. Great works of art have no more affecting lesson for us than this. They teach us to *abide by our spontaneous impression* with good-humored inflexibility then most when the whole cry of voices is on the other side. Else tomorrow a stranger will say with masterly good sense precisely what we have thought and felt all the time, and we shall be forced to take with shame our own opinion from another.

And this is from *The Oversoul:*

> The great poet makes us feel our own wealth, and then we think less of his compositions. . . . Shakespeare carries us to such a lofty strain of intelligent activity, as to suggest a wealth which beggars his own. . . . The inspiration which uttered itself in *Hamlet* and *Lear* could utter things as good from day to day forever. Why, then, should I make account of *Hamlet* and *Lear,* as if we had not the soul from which they fell as syllables from the tongue?

The natural conclusion from these speculations would be that the most effective writing is automatic writing. In the poem entitled *Merlin,* in which *Merlin* is viewed as the bard, Emerson writes:

> Great is the art,
> Great be the manners, of the bard.
> He shall not his brain encumber
> With the coil of rhythm and number;
> But leaving rule and pale forethought,
> He shall aye climb
> For his rime.
> 'Pass in, pass in,' the angels say,
> 'In to the upper doors,
> Nor count compartments of the floors,
> But mount to Paradise
> By the stairway of surprise.'

In Whitman and his close followers there is occasionally a momentary approach to the kind of automatic writing here suggested; but this ideal was most nearly fulfilled by another line of Romantic writers, and probably reached Crane by way of them, in the main: the line starting with Poe, and proceeding through Verlaine, Mallarmé, Rimbaud, and the lesser Symbolists to such Americans as Pound, Eliot, and Stevens. The concept of automatic writing is an inevitable development from the initial Romantic ideas, and it is bound to appear whenever the ideas long govern literary practice. Crane had almost no French—I spent a couple of hours one evening taking him through various poems by Rimbaud—but his friends had doubtless translated the French poets for him and described them, and he knew the later Americans very thoroughly. He told me once that he often did not understand his poems till after they were written; and I am fairly confident that this kind of experimentation was common in Crane's generation and earlier, and in fact that it is still common in certain quarters. I know that I myself engaged in it with great fascination when I was young, and I know that certain other persons did so. The result is likely to be a poetry which frequently and sometimes wholly eludes paraphrase by at least a margin, but which appears constantly to be suggesting a precise meaning.

Many poets engage in the practice only semi-consciously; in general, one may say that wherever the poet's sensibility to the connotation of language overbalances his awareness of the importance of denotation, something of the kind is beginning: it is this unbalance which distinguishes the Shakespeare of the sonnets, for example, most sharply from his great contemporaries, such as Jonson, Greville, Donne, and even Sidney. But beginning with the notion of organic form, the notion that the subject, or the language, or the oversoul, or something else operates freely through the poet, who is merely a passive medium, the doctrine begins to be explicit. The beginnings, in theory, may be traced perhaps as far back as Edward Young, certainly as far as Coleridge; and *Kubla Khan* is perhaps the first ambitious experiment in actual practice. Emerson states the theory with an explicitness which verges on violence, but does not appear seriously to have practiced it. Poe's concept of poetry as something which deals with certain materials of this life only incidentally, in the hopes that meanings otherwise unattainable may be suggested, begins to describe the kind of poetry which will result when automatic writing is practiced by men of talent: a poetry which appears always to be escaping the comprehension, yet which is always perceptible; a poetry which deals with the fact of nature *dans sa presque disparition vibratoire,* to use a phrase from Mallarmé, 'in its vibratory almost-disappearance.'

Mallarmé employs this phrase in an essay called *Relativement au vers:* in English, *On the Subject of the Poetic Line*. In this essay he describes the kind of 'pure' poetry in which he is interested, the poetry in which feeling is as nearly as possible isolated from all denotation, and near the end he writes the following passage, which I shall render as nearly verbatim as possible, in spite of any awkwardness which may seem to result:

> The pure work implies the elocutory disappearance of the poet, who cedes the initiative to the words, mobilized through the shock of their inequality; they light each other with reciprocal reflections like a virtual train of fires upon jewels, replacing the respiration perceptible in the lyric inspiration of former times or the enthusiastic personal direction of the phrase.

And Rimbaud, in his poem *Bonheur,* states that the charm of which he has made a magic study has taken possession of him body and soul, with the result that his language is no longer to be understood, but takes wing and escapes. Verlaine offers a somewhat more cautious statement of the same doctrine in his poem entitled *Art Poétique,* in which he praises the 'drunken song,' the word exhibiting a content of 'error,' in which the indecisive is joined to the precise. Rimbaud's poem might easily have been written by Emerson: in fact Rimbaud's *Fêtes de la Faim* resembles Emerson's *Mithridates* very closely in imagery and in symbolism, though it resembles the stylistic quality of Emerson's best verse less closely than does *Bonheur*. And the passage from Mallarmé, if we make allowances for certain personal mannerisms, might well have been written by Emerson. But Rimbaud and Mallarmé put the doctrine into practice, not occasionally but systematically, and the result was a revolution in style, both in verse and in prose. One of the most eminent practitioners of the semi-automatic method in more recent times was the late W. B. Yeats, with his notions of demonic possession and dictation.

The ideas of Emerson were, as I have said, merely the commonplaces of the Romantic movement; but his language was that of the Calvinistic pulpit. He was able to present the anarchic and anti-moral doctrines of European Romanticism in a language which for two hundred years had been capable of arousing the most intense and the most obscure emotions of the American people. He could speak of matter as if it were God; of the flesh as if it were spirit; of emotion as if it were Divine Grace; of impulse as if it were conscience; and of automatism as if it were the mystical experience. And he was addressing an audience which, like himself, had been so conditioned by two hundred years of Calvinistic discipline, that the doctrines confused nothing, at the outset, except the mind: Emerson and his contemporaries, in surrendering to what they took for impulse, were governed by New England habit; they mistook second nature for nature. They were moral parasites upon a Christian doctrine which they were endeavoring to destroy. The same may be said of Whitman, Emerson's most influential disciple, except that Whitman came closer to putting the doctrine into practice in the matter of literary form: whereas Emerson, as a poet, imitated the poets of the early 17th century, whose style had been formed in congruence with the doctrines of Aristotle, Aquinas, and Hooker.

I cannot summarize the opinions of Whitman in this essay as fully as I have summarized those of Emerson. I must ask my readers to accept on faith, until they find it convenient to check the matter, the generally accepted view that the main ideas of Whitman are identical with those of Emerson. Whitman believed this; Emerson believed it; and scholarly specialists in both men believe it. I wish to quote a part—only a small part—of Professor Floyd Stovall's summary of Whitman's views.[1] Professor Stovall is a reputable scholar. Every detail which he gives is referred by a footnote to its source in Whitman. I believe that his summary, purely as a summary, is accurate. He writes:

> He saw that creation is a continuous organic growth, not a work that is begun or finished, and the creative force is the procreative impulse in nature. *Progress is the infallible consequence* of this creative force in nature, *and though the universe is perfect at any given moment, it is growing constantly toward higher orders of perfection.* If new forms are needed they are produced as surely as if designed from the beginning. 'When the materials are all prepared and ready, the architects shall appear.' Every moment is a consummation developed from endless past consummations and preparing for endless consummations in the future. . . .
>
> Nature is not only perfect but also divine. Indeed it is perfect because it is divine. There is no division in nature . . . no separate deity looking down from some detached heaven upon a temporal world that his hand created and may destroy at pleasure. That which is at all is of God. . . . *Whatever is is well, and whatever will be will be well.* . . . God is in every object, because every object has an eternal soul and passes eventually into spiritual results. . . .
>
> . . . The seed of perfection is in each person, but *no matter how far he advances, his desire for further advancement remains insatiable.*
>
> The final purpose of this restlessness of spirit in man and nature is the continuity of life. Nothing is real or valid, not even God, except in relation to this purpose. . . . Something, Whitman perceives, drives man forward along the way to perfection, which passes through birth, life, death, and burial; he does not fully understand what it is, but he knows that it is form, union, plan—that it is happiness and eternal life.
>
> Whitman calls it soul, this mysterious something, strangely linked with the procreative impulse, that gives form and continuity to the life of nature and impels man toward happiness and immortality. . . .

The ignorance both of philosophy and theology exhibited in such ideas as these is sufficient to strike one with terror. But I must limit myself to only a few comments at the present moment. I wish to call attention especially to the passages which I have italicized: (1) 'Progress is the infallible consequence,' or to put it more briefly, progress is infallible; (2) 'though the universe is perfect at any given moment, it is growing constantly toward higher orders of perfection'; (3) 'Whatever is is well, and whatever will be will be well'; and (4) 'No matter how far man advances, his desire for further advancement remains insatiable.'

I wish to insist on this: that it is impossible to speak of higher orders of perfection unless one can define what one means by the highest order and by the lowest order, and this Whitman does not venture to do. Higher and lower, better and worse, have no meaning except in relation to highest and lowest, best and worst. Since Whitman has identified God with the evolving (that is, with the changing) universe, he is unable to locate a concept of best or highest, toward which evolution is moving, for that concept would then be outside of God and would supersede God; it would be, in theological language, God's final cause; and such a concept would be nonsense. Whitman tells us that whatever happens to exist is perfect, but that any change is necessarily toward a 'higher' order of perfection. The practical effect of these notions is merely to deify change: change becomes good of necessity. We have no way of determining where we are going, but we should keep moving at all costs and as fast as possible; we have faith in progress. It seems to me unnecessary to dwell upon the dangers of such a concept.

Hart Crane was not born into the New England of Emerson, nor even into the New York of Whitman; he was born in 1899 in Cleveland, Ohio. The social restraints, the products of generations of religious discipline, which operated to minimize the influence of Romantic philosophy in the personal lives of Emerson and of Whitman, were at most only slightly operative in Crane's career. He was unfortunate in having a somewhat violent emotional constitution: his behavior on the whole would seem to indicate a more or less manic-depressive make-up, although this diagnosis is the post-mortem guess of an amateur, and is based on evidence which is largely hearsay. He was certainly homosexual, however, and he became a chronic and extreme alcoholic. I should judge that he cultivated these weaknesses on principle; in any event, it is well known that he cultivated them assiduously; and as an avowed Whitmanian, he would have been justified by his principles in cultivating all of his impulses. I saw Crane during the Christmas week of 1927, when he was approximately 29 years old; his hair was graying, his skin had the dull red color with reticulated grayish traceries which so often goes with advanced alcoholism, and his ears and knuckles were beginning to look a little like those of a pugilist. About a year later he was deported from France as a result of his starting an exceptionally violent commotion in a bar-room and perhaps as a result of other activities. In 1932 he committed suicide by leaping from a steamer into the Caribbean Sea.

The doctrine of Emerson and Whitman, if really put into practice, should naturally lead to suicide: in the first place, if the impulses are indulged systematically and passionately, they can lead only to madness; in the second place, death, according to the doctrine, is not only a release from suffering but is also and inevitably the way to beatitude. There is no question, according to the doctrine, of moral preparation for salvation; death leads automatically to salvation. During the last year and a half of Crane's life, to judge from the accounts of those who were with him in Mexico, he must have been insane or drunk or both almost without interruption; but before this time he must have contemplated the possibilities of suicide. When his friend Harry Crosby leapt from a high window in one of the eastern cities, I wrote Crane a note of condolence and asked him to express my sympathy to Mrs. Crosby. Crane replied somewhat casually that I need not feel disturbed about the affair, that he was fairly sure Crosby had regarded it as a great adventure.

In the course of my correspondence with Crane, I must somewhere have made a moralizing remark which I have now forgotten but of which Crane disapproved. I remember Crane's answer: he said that he had never in his life done anything of which he had been ashamed, and he said this not in anger but in simple philosophical seriousness. This would be a sufficiently surprising remark from any son of Adam, but as one thinks of it and of Crane in retrospect, one can understand it, I believe, only in one way, as an assertion of religious faith, neither more nor less.

Crane published two volumes of poetry during his life-time, *White Buildings* in 1926, and *The Bridge* in 1930. His collected poems appeared in 1933, including additional work from earlier and later periods. The element of obscurantism in the details of Crane's writing, some of it probably intentional, makes it difficult to paraphrase him as fully and precisely as one might paraphrase George Herbert or Ben Jonson. Nevertheless, the general drift of *The Bridge* is clear, and most of the detail is clear. I cannot allow myself at present to do more than discuss the skeletal plan of the work; but the skeletal plan will serve my present purpose. *The Bridge* endeavors to deal in some measure with the relationship of the individual American to his country and to God and with the religious significance of America itself. It reaches its first climax in the poem called *The Dance,* which deals with the apotheosis of the individual, and its second in *Atlantis,* which deals with the apotheosis of the nation. *The Bridge* is a loosely joined sequence of lyrics, and some of the individual pieces have only a tenuous connection with the principal themes.

The first poem is the dedicatory piece to the Brooklyn Bridge. Crane regarded the Brooklyn Bridge as the most beautiful artifact in North America, and largely for this reason he chose it as a symbol. The dedicatory poem is mainly descriptive of the literal bridge, but contains hints of the religious symbolism to follow; so far as the total symbolism is concerned, it has something of the nature of an unrestrained pun: Crane's poem is a bridge; it joins the past to the present, the present to the future, life to death, non-being to birth, the old world to the new; the United States is a bridge which joins the two oceans. The next poem, *Ave Maria,* is a monologue spoken by Columbus as he is approaching America; Columbus appears to be secondarily the unborn soul approaching birth and the man of the past approaching modernity.

The next five poems are grouped under the heading, *Powhatan's Daughter*. Pocahontas, in these poems, is the symbol of the American soil, and the five poems deal more or less clearly with the awakening love of the young protagonist for his country and for the deity with which his country is identified. We have here a characteristically Whitmanian variation on Emerson's pantheism: for Emerson God and the universe were one, but for Whitman the American soil was the part of the universe to be especially worshipped, so that the pantheistic mysticism tends to become a national mysticism; Sandburg carries this delimitation further by insisting on the Mississippi Valley as the region of chief emphasis and creates a kind of regional mysticism; and we get precisely this Sandburgian mysticism in the third poem in the group which I am now discussing, the poem called *The River:* when Crane was writing this poem, he informed me that he was rewriting Sandburg in the way in which he ought to be written. I wish to make myself clear on one point in this connection: I do not object to these poets' feeling a love for their country or for their region; but I believe that nothing save confusion can result from our mistaking the Mississippi Valley for God.

The first poem in this group of five is *The Harbor Dawn;* it deals with the awakening of the protagonist in a room in New York, a room overlooking the harbor; this protagonist had been previously the unborn soul of the *Ave Maria;* the modern man is now born and the woman with him is vaguely identified as Pocahontas. The second poem in the group, *Van Winkle,* is a flashback to the childhood of the protagonist: we see the schoolboy becoming acquainted with the figures of North American mythology, with Cortez and with Captain Smith and with others. The boy is loosely equated with Rip Van Winkle, as one who has awakened after a long time ('400 years and more'), and so is connected with the Columbus of *Ave Maria.* The third poem in the group is *The River.* This poem opens with a vision of the countryside as seen fragmentarily from the window of the Twentieth Century Limited, a symbolic railway train; then the train suddenly moves ahead and leaves the protagonist walking down the tracks in the company of various hoboes. The hoboes are the intercessors: they introduce the adolescent boy to the soil, to Pocahontas, since they are among the few people left who will take the time really to know the land and its old gods. We then see the train again, and the travelers within are separated from the soil and the folk by their wealth, luxury, and speed; they are advised to 'lean from the window if the train slows down,' and make the acquaintance of the folk; and we then have a vision of the folk flowing in a kind of symbolic river toward the gulf of eternity. This symbolic river is described in the last five stanzas simply as if it were the real Mississippi. Until we get to the last portion of the poem, the section beginning, 'And Pullman breakfasters glide glistening steel,' the writing is predominantly pretty bad; from there on it is predominantly very powerful and becomes steadily more powerful, with only a few slight lapses, to the end. This is the one deeply impressive passage of any length in *The Bridge,* and along with a few earlier poems is probably the best writing in Crane. The pantheism is subdued here; the emphasis is on the country and the folk and on the poet's love for them; and the rhetoric is magnificent. The following poem is called *The Dance.* In this piece the protagonist takes a canoe trip up the Hudson River, finally leaves his canoe and climbs into the mountains, and at the same time appears to proceed into the remote past. He finally comes to an Indian dance, where a captured warrior is being burned at the stake; the warrior in death is married to Pocahontas, or in other words is united with the American soil. The tone of the poem is nervous and violent; the poem contains some of the most brilliant lines in Crane and some of the most grotesque; and at the end it illustrates very dramatically the difficulty of the pantheistic doctrine. The warrior is united with the soil, which is God; his identity is presumably lost in this union; yet the language in which the union is described is in part the language of the traditional poetry of devotion, but is mainly the language of love poetry: that is, personal extinction is described for the most part as if it were the consummation of a marriage and in some part as if it were a form of personal immortality. There is a violent dislocation here between the motivating theme and the emotion resulting from it; the poem is not merely confused, but it is confused in a manner which is suicidal. As I have said elsewhere, one does not deal adequately with the subject of death and immortality by calling the soil Pocahontas, and by then writing a love poem to an imaginary maiden who bears the name of Pocahontas. The misuse of metaphor here, the excursion by way of metaphor into pure irrelevance, is irresponsible almost to madness. Yet this poem is one of the two major crises in the sequence: in this poem the relationship of the protagonist to the soil, to God, and to eternity, is presumably established. The last poem in the group is called *Indiana;* in this poem a frontier mother bids farewell to her son and begs him to return home eventually. The mother may have been related loosely in Crane's mind to Pocahontas conceived as a mother; it is hard to be sure about this, but if she is not so related, there is no very evident reason for her being here. The poem is weak and sentimental.

The poems thus far have dealt primarily with what one might call the private spiritual experience, or the fate of the individual; those to follow deal primarily with the public spiritual experience, or the fate of the nation. There are qualifications to this statement, of course: *The River,* for example, as we have seen, deals with a vision of the folk, but it deals primarily with the individual's awakening to the folk and his share in their life; there is an element of private experience in a later poem, *Cape Hatteras,* but it is a secondary element; the *Three Songs,* which follow *Cape Hatteras,* deal with private experience, but have no real place in the sequence. It is worth noting that the poems thus far described, with the exception perhaps of *Indiana,* have a certain structural relationship to each other; whereas those which follow, and which deal with the public experience, are thrown together very loosely, and the aspects of the public experience with which they deal are few and appear to be selected almost at haphazard. Although Crane had curious ideas about the individual, he yet had ideas; but he was simply at a loss in dealing with society either in the present or in the historical past, for his ideas of the individual really preclude the possibility of a society.

The first of the later poems is a piece called *Cutty Sark,* a very slight but perversely amusing meditation on the great days of the American clipper ships. The main reason for the inclusion of such a piece is Crane's enthusiasm for everything pertaining to the sea, but the ships represent a heroic portion of the American past and can be made a symbol of the type of adventurousness treated more explicitly in *Cape Hatteras.* Next comes *Cape Hatteras,* which is primarily an invocation to Walt Whitman and an explicit acceptance of his doctrines. The Whitmanian doctrine which Crane emphasizes in this poem is the doctrine of an endless procession of higher and higher states of perfection, or what I have called the doctrine of change for its own sake. Crane restates Whitman's symbol of the open road in terms of a vision of airplanes traveling farther and farther into remotest space, airplanes which are more or less the successors of the clipper ships of *Cutty Sark:*

> Years of the modern! Propulsions toward what capes!

And again:

> And now as launched in abysmal cupolas of space,
> Toward endless terminals, Easters of speeding light—
> Vast engines outward veering with seraphic grace
> On clarion cylinders pass out of sight
> To course that span of consciousness thou'st named
> The Open Road—thy vision is reclaimed.

Cape Hatteras is followed by *Three Songs* which are only loosely, if at all, connected with the central theme. When Crane was putting the sequence into final order, he wrote me that he wanted to include the songs because he liked them, but that he was not sure the inclusion would be justified. The first song is called *Southern Cross:* it is a kind of love poem addressed to the constellation of that name as if the constellation were a woman or a female divinity; the constellation is equated with Eve, Magdalen, Mary, and 'simian Venus,' as if all conceivable types of love, like all types of woman, were one and were in some way identified with the mystical experience. The next song, *National Winter Garden,* is a vision of love as lust; and the third, *Virginia,* is a very slight and casual vision of sentimental love in the city. The poems obviously have no place in this latter half of the sequence, and they would probably fit but little better into the first half. And the significance of the trilogy, simply in itself, and as a related group, is not clear, nor, I think, is the significance of any one of the three songs except the second, with its forthright and ugly portrayal of lust. The recognition of ugliness which we get here, in *Quaker Hill,* and in *The Tunnel,* is strictly speaking out of place in an optimistic system or at best can be justified only by Pope's formula:

> Whatever wrong we call,
> May, must be right, as relative to all,

which is poor consolation when one is in the predicament. Next comes *Quaker Hill,* a poem which compares the past with the present: Crane borrows his procedure from Eliot, and compares a sentimentalized past with a vulgar present; neither past nor present is understood, nor is there any apparent effort to understand either; both are presented impressionistically. The poem contributes nothing which is not better accomplished by *The Tunnel.*

Next come the two concluding poems, which may be regarded as companion pieces. Superficially regarded, *The Tunnel* is a fragmentary description of a ride in the subway, but it is offered as an account of a kind of inferno through which one must proceed to the final vision; into it Crane has crammed as many as possible of the ugliest details of modern urban life. No reason for the necessity of such an inferno, or purgatory, is offered; the account is given because the literal subway exists and perhaps because Crane had his periods of depression; there is obviously no intellectual grasp of the subject: *The Tunnel* is not well written, but this sudden outburst of ugliness has a curious pathos, nevertheless. It is as if the facts of Crane's life had suddenly and for the moment rebelled against his faith. We see the same Crane who in *The Dance* identifies himself with the warrior at the stake and cries out in one of the purest and most moving lines of our time, but with no understanding of his agony:

> I could not pick the arrows from my side.

But *The Tunnel* offers a kind of ugliness which is not justified by the Whitmanian theme and so cannot be treated in terms of the theme. It was an ugliness which Crane experienced, in part as a result of his acceptance of the theme and the fallacies of the theme, but to treat it in these terms he would have had to understand the fallacies and what had happened to him as a result of them. He did not understand, and the poem is an assortment of impressions without meaning. He abandons these particular impressions in the final poem, *Atlantis,* but a few years later they or others like them destroyed him.

In the last poem, *Atlantis,* the bridge is seen in apotheosis. The bridge is the United States of the future, reaching from ocean to ocean, from time to eternity; on it are spread cities and farmlands; from it skyscrapers rise to remoter and remoter distances, as the Whitmanian airplanes had risen earlier:

> Like hails, farewells—up planet-sequined heights
> Some trillion whispering hammers glimmer Tyre:
> Serenely, sharply up the long anvil cry
> Of inchling aëons silence rivets Troy.

The poem is unfortunately the most obscurely written in the sequence, if one examines it closely and from line to line; and I confess that I find it next to impossible to decipher except in what seem to me its most general intentions. As nearly as I can understand it, it offers a vision of physical splendor as a symbol for some kind of spiritual splendor; but the spiritual state in question remains undefined, and the final vision is without meaning: what we see ultimately is higher and higher skyscrapers, more and more marvelous in appearance, but ascending into heights of which the nature is uncertain. At the end Crane returns to the pantheism of the central poems:

> O Answer of all,—Anemone,—
> Now while thy petals spend the suns about us, hold—
> (O Thou whose radiance doth inherit me)
> Atlantis,—hold thy floating singer late!

A passage which is, I imagine, Crane's equivalent for Whitman's 'Look for me under your bootsoles.'

I have indicated the main diffculties in *The Bridge* as I have proceeded in my summary; and I have indicated also the main connections with Emerson and Whitman—in fact, the main difficulties and the main connections are identical with each other. The work as a whole is a failure. It builds up to two climaxes, one in *The Dance,* and one in *Atlantis,* both of which are incomprehensible. As a whole it is loosely constructed. The incomprehensibility and the looseness of construction are the natural result of the theme, which is inherited from Whitman and Emerson. The style is at worst careless and pretentious, at second-best skillfully obscure; and in these respects it is religiously of its school; and although it is both sound and powerful at its best, it is seldom at its best. Yet the last fifty-five lines of *The River,* and numerous short passages in *The Dance* and in *Atlantis* and a few short passages elsewhere, take rank, I am certain, among the most magnificent passages of Romantic poetry in our language; and at least two earlier poems, *Repose of Rivers* and the second of the *Voyages,* are quite as fine. The second of the *Voyages,* in fact, seems to me, as it has seemed to others, one of the most powerful and one of the most nearly perfect poems of the past two hundred years.

The difficulties inherent in the Whitmanian theme come out more clearly in Crane than in Whitman or in Emerson because of the more intense religious passion of the man. He is not content to write in a muddling manner about the Way; he is concerned primarily with the End. And in *The Dance* and in *Atlantis* respectively, he goes to the End. But his end is not an end in either case: it is a void. He does not discover this fact himself, but the passion and the linguistic precision with which he endeavors to render his delusion make it impossible, I think, that we should fail to recognize the delusion for what it is. And the same passion, functioning in his life, made him realize both the Way and the End completely, as Emerson and Whitman were incapable of doing. We have, it would seem, a poet of great genius, who ruined his life and his talent by living and writing as the two greatest religious teachers of our nation recommended.

Is it possible to shrug this off?

I would like at this point to consider the case and the arguments of Professor X. Professor X can be met four or five times on the faculty of nearly every university in the country: I have lost count of the avatars in which I have met him. He usually teaches American literature or American history, but he may teach something else. And he admires Emerson and Whitman.

He says that Emerson in any event did not go mad and kill himself; the implication is that Emerson's doctrines do not lead to madness and suicide. But in making this objection, he neglects to restate and defend Emerson's doctrines as such, and he neglects to consider the historical forces which restrained Emerson and which had lost most of their power of restraint in Crane's time and part of the country. He says that insanity is pathological and that a philosophy cannot be blamed for a pathological condition. Insanity, however, can be both induced and cured; any man can go mad under the proper pressure or influence; and although some cases of insanity, like some cases of tuberculosis, are incurable, many cases are dealt with successfully and many medical men are engaged professionally in dealing with them; and the technique of curing such cases is in a large measure a matter of explaining to the patient what is wrong with him and of securing his cooperation in the formation of desirable habits. And as a matter of curious but nevertheless historical fact, we have a rather large number of madmen and near madmen among literary men of established reputation from the middle of the eighteenth century onward and few or none before that time: once the romantic ideas have been generally accepted and the corresponding attitudes ingrained, we begin to observe such men as Smart, Chatterton, Collins, Clare, Blake, and the second James Thomson, to mention no others. The Emersonian doctrine, which is merely the romantic doctrine with a New England emotional coloration, should naturally result in madness if one really lived it; it should result in literary confusion if one really wrote it. Crane accepted it; he lived it; he wrote it; and we have seen what he was and wrote.

Professor X says, or since he is a gentleman and a scholar, he implies, that Crane was merely a fool, that he ought to have known better. But the fact of the matter is, that Crane was not a fool. I knew Crane, as I know Professor X, and I am reasonably certain that Crane was incomparably the more intelligent man. As to Crane's ideas, they were merely those of Professor X, neither better nor worse; and for the rest, he was able to write great poetry. In spite of popular and even academic prejudices to the contrary, it takes a very highly developed intelligence to write great poetry, even a little of it. So far as I am concerned, I would gladly emulate Odysseus, if I could, and go down to the shadows for another hour's conversation with Crane on the subject of poetry; whereas, politeness permitting, I seldom go out of my way to discuss poetry with Professor X.

Professor X, as a sentimentalist, is inclined to speak of the magic of poetry; he uses the term *magic* in a figurative sense which he has probably never endeavored to define. There is something supernatural about poetry, however, in a simple, literal, and theological sense, which Professor X in all likelihood has seldom considered. In poetry one mind acts directly upon another, without regard to 'natural' law, the law of chemistry or of physics. Furthermore, the action is not only an action by way of idea, but by way of emotion and moral attitude; it is both complex and elusive. Poetry is a medium by means of which one mind may to a greater or less extent take possession of another, almost in the sense in which the term *possession* is used in demonology. It is a well-known fact, to medieval and to modern psychologists alike, that our emotional prejudices may pervert our rational faculty. If we enter the mind of a Crane, a Whitman, or an Emerson with our emotional faculties activated and our reason in abeyance, these writers may possess us as surely as demons were once supposed to possess the unwary, as surely as Whitman possessed Crane, as surely as Whitman and Emerson were possessed by their predecessors. If we come to these writers with all our faculties intact, however; if we insist on understanding not only what they are but what they are not; we can profit by what they may have to offer and at the same time escape being bemused by their limitations. Crane and Emerson possessed, for example, the gift of style without the gift of thought. They occasionally happen upon subjects, or fringes of subjects, which permit their talents to function with relatively little hindrance from their deficiencies. This happens to Emerson in the *Concord Hymn,* in *Days,* and in various fragments, and to Crane in the poems and passages which I have mentioned. Every such poem or fragment offers a particular critical problem, and some such problems are very curious and difficult; I cannot settle all of them at present in general terms. If we can isolate that which is good, these writers offer us something positive, however little in actual bulk; they offer us limited regions in which they may actually aid us to grow, to come to life.

Aquinas tells us that a demon may be said to be good in so far as he may be said to exist; that he is a demon in so far as his existence is incomplete. This statement is a necessary part of the doctrine of evil as deprivation. But a demon, or a genius, may be almost wholly deprived of being in large areas in which theoretically he ought to exist, and at the same time may have achieved an extraordinary degree of actuality in the regions in which he does exist; and when this happens, his persuasive power, his possessive power, is enormous, and if we fail to understand his limitations he is one of the most dangerous forces in the universe. Our only protection against him is the critical faculty, of which, I fear, we have far too little. The difference here, between Crane and Professor X, is not that Professor X possesses a wider intelligence, for we have seen that he does not, but that he possesses a less intensely active intelligence. The difference, I believe, is this: that Crane was absolutely serious and Professor X is not serious. Professor X is not restrained by the cast-iron habits which held Emerson in position, but he does not need to be; he is a man who conforms easily. He conforms to established usages because he finds life pleasanter and easier for those who do so; and he is able to approve of Emerson because he has never for a moment realized that literature could be more than a charming amenity. He believes that we should not be too critical of literature; that we should try to appreciate as much literature as possible; and that such appreciation will cultivate us. Professor X once reproved me for what he considered my contentiousness by telling me that he himself had yet to see the book that he would be willing to quarrel over. Professor X, in so far as he may be said to have moral motion, moves in the direction indicated by Emerson, but only to the extent of indulging a kind of genteel sentimentality; he is restrained from going the limit by considerations that he cannot or will not formulate philosophically but by which he is willing to profit. His position is that of the dilettante: the nearest thing he has to a positive philosophy is something to which he would never dare commit himself; that which keeps him in order is a set of social proprieties which he neither understands nor approves. In a world of atomic bombs, power politics, and experts in international knavery, he has little to guide him and he offers extremely precarious guidance to others; yet by profession he is a searcher for truth and a guide to the young.

Professor X will defend democracy in Emersonian terms, never stopping to consider that a defense of democracy which derives ultimately from the doctrine of natural goodness, of the wisdom of the untrained and mediocre mind, and of the sanctity of impulse is the worst kind of betrayal. He tells us that Emerson was an 'idealist,' but he does not tell us what kind. He tells us that Emerson taught self-reliance, but not that Emerson meant reliance on irresponsible impulse. He will cite us a dozen fragments of what might be mistaken for wisdom, and cite Emerson as the source; but he will neither admit what these fragments mean in the Emersonian system nor go to the trouble of setting them in a new system which would give them an acceptable meaning—and which would no longer be Emersonian. If one insists on driving him back to the naked generative formulae, the only terms which give any of his ideas any precision, he is inclined to find one naive, bigoted, or ludicrous, but he will not say precisely why.

Crane, however, had the absolute seriousness which goes with genius and with sanctity; one might describe him as a saint of the wrong religion. He had not the critical intelligence to see what was wrong with his doctrine, but he had the courage of his convictions, the virtue of integrity, and he deserves our respect. He has the value of a thoroughgoing demonstration. He embodies perfectly the concepts which for nearly a century have been generating some of the most cherished principles of our literature, our education, or politics, and our personal morals. If Crane is too strong a dose for us, and we must yet retain the principles which he represents, we may still, of course, look to Professor X as a model. But we shall scarcely get anything better unless we change our principles.

NOTE

1. *Walt Whitman: Representative Selections, with Introduction, Bibliography, and Notes,* by Floyd Stovall; American Book Company; 1934. P. xxxvii.

WILLIAM EMPSON

How To Read a Modern Poem

(1947)

The critics agree with hardly a dissenting voice that Dylan Thomas is a splendid poet, but it is unusual for anyone to undertake to say what he means, as I am doing here.

He works by piling up many distant suggestions at once, and half the time is not 'saying anything' in the ordinary meaning of the term. You are not expected to take in the whole of this poem on a first reading as the eye goes down the page, which is what good prose ought to allow you to do; the thing is meant to grow in the mind, or at least echo about there. On the other hand, I think there is no reason to feel that 'modern' poetry is some obscure new trick. Poets have always worked by piling up suggestions. Dylan Thomas does it more than most; you may say too much, but there is no fundamental difference of technique from older poets, certainly not from Shakespeare.

The difficulty about trying to give the meaning in prose is that the critic seems to be reading an unreasonable amount 'into' the passage he has chosen, so that it comes to look harder to understand rather than easier. The extra meanings are in the detail all right, but they are being put in all the time, as part of the style, and a reader gets used to picking them up casually. The fundamental ideas which Dylan Thomas is expressing in his rich technique are, I think, rather few, and the same explanations would do again and again. So you can enjoy one of the poems and form an opinion about it without making up your mind on the meaning of all the details. Also, as a rule, there is not much development in his poems; what stick in your mind are single rich phrases rather than a connected argument—

From *The Strand* (March 1947). Reprinted by permission of the author.

While the worm builds with the red straws of venom
My nest of mercies in the rude, red tree—

and even these seem to point all ways rather than sum anything up. His last book, *Deaths and Entrances,* does contain a higher proportion of poems which you would remember as units, though it is still using the same concentrated technique.

In the poem printed here the title gives you the subject, and what Dylan Thomas feels about it is evidently like what many other people would feel. But even so, taking it line by line, there is a good deal which I feel I haven't got to the bottom of. Also, though this is a different matter, obscurity in a writer may be due, not to concentration, but to a refusal to speak out. This poem tells us that Dylan Thomas *isn't* going to say something. I take it that the child was killed in an air raid, and that Dylan Thomas won't say so because he is refusing to be distracted by thoughts about the war from thoughts about the child herself or about death in general.

It is perhaps worth saying that the form is a repeated rhyming verse with the rhymes in the order 'abcabc,' having three stresses (or emphasised syllables) in the 'b' lines and five in the others. Nearly all the poems in the book are in regular though sometimes complex stanzas. The bad rhymes, I think, satisfy the ear like ordinary rhymes, and are not meant, as in some poets' use of them, to suggest strain or horror.

The first two verses and the next line are one sentence, with the skeleton grammar 'Till doomsday (or my death) I will not mourn the child.' *Darkness* is described as *making* mankind, *fathering* birds, etc., and *humbling* all; the same form as 'bed-making.' This would be a less discouraging bit of grammar if hyphens were put in, but you would need six of them and it would look ugly. The poem starts with a great mouthful as for a cosmic occasion. I am not sure about the distinction between *making* and *fathering;* perhaps the construction of *mankind* is a special process, as in Genesis. The darkness, anyway, is the unknown, undeveloped Nature from which all life came and to which it returns, also the particular night before Doomsday or before the day of Thomas's death. At Doomsday the sea gives up its dead; we may be meant to think of the water *tumbling* off them, and the sea might be *harnessed* in that it is at last controlled. Waves are called white horses. But the phrase is much more beautiful than this explanation; it may have an idea of the sea invading the land to end the world, and yet it

THE POEM

BY DYLAN THOMAS

A Refusal to Mourn the Death, by Fire, of a Child in London

Never until the mankind making
Bird beast and flower
Fathering and all humbling darkness
Tells with silence the last light breaking
And the still hour
Is come of the sea tumbling in harness

And I must enter again the round
Zion of the water bead
And the synagogue of the ear of corn
Shall I let pray the shadow of a sound
Or sow my salt seed
In the least valley of sackcloth to mourn

The majesty and burning of the child's death.
I shall not murder
The mankind of her going with a grave truth
Nor blaspheme down the stations of the breath
With any further
Elegy of innocence and youth

Deep with the first dead lies London's daughter,
Robed in the long friends,
The grains beyond age, the dark veins of her mother,
Secret by the unmourning water
Of the riding Thames.
After the first death, there is no other.

could be just an affectionate description of a quiet morning sea. Shakespearean lovers tumble each other, but the word is more likely to suggest puppies.

The hour, at any rate, is an apocalyptic one, and the second verse gives it more positively mysterious or religious language. Dylan Thomas, like the dead girl, is to return to a state like that before birth, the heaven of the womb; the *bead* is I think simply a drop of water regarded as self-completing, making a round unit which does not spread into the outside world; but it could suggest the amœba as the undeveloped primitive cell of living jelly. A suggestion of beads as used for counting prayers would fit the general religious background and the word *pray* two lines later; the qualifying word *water* then dissolves this prayer, because Dylan Thomas's religion is pantheistic and absorbs the Godhead into the world.

Here I am evidently wandering from the direct impact of the line, but Dylan Thomas does not fit things into compartments and likes to throw extra suggestions into any possible phrase which merely belongs to the whole theme. *Corn,* which he must also re-enter, was said by St. Paul to die in the ground before it sprouts; and bread and water are, in any case, the fundamental life-givers. The *ear* is a group of grains, who may be seen as piously collected to pray in their *synagogue;* but I suppose all our group activities are thought of as first made possible by the development of the blind life of the single cell.

The general theme is that Dylan Thomas at death, no less than the burned girl, must be absorbed into the Nature from which further life may mysteriously be born. The terms perhaps seem Jewish rather than Christian, but I should think he is remembering the Welsh Nonconformist preachers he heard as a boy.

Not till then will he *let pray* (as it might be 'let drop') even the ghost of a sound, which might seem external to him and outside his control. Nor will he drop a tear, though it is described in terms that recall both the *water bead* and the *corn grain,* and these appeared separate from his conscious will. To wet the smallest fold of his clothes with tears is compared to sowing a valley, on the general rule that events in Dylan Thomas's body are related pantheistically to more massive ones outside. *Seed* implies that the tear would be fertile if he allowed it to fall, but perhaps *salt* denies this, or the idea is that to allow false sentiment would encourage the sprouting of large weeds.

The wave breaks at the beginning of the third verse as the poem turns from Dylan Thomas and the universe to the child. *Mankind* is now used again as the name of a quality of her death; she is not chiefly to be thought of as a girl child, because death and suffering are common to all, and because she deserves to be treated with dignity. *Grave* seems to be a pun on 'solemn' and 'burial-place'; the poet will not make her death seem trivial by uttering platitudes suited to funerals. But this seems an improbably weak interpretation for *murder mankind,* and I think one might take the whole line another way. The mankind of her going may be all the men who made the world situation in which she was killed; with an ironical reassurance the poet announces that he will not give these people their due. The Stations of the Cross are, of course, the series of incidents on the way to the Crucifixion often painted round the Roman Catholic churches; those of the *breath* are the normal sufferings, different for each age-group but common to all mankind.

Dylan Thomas will not blaspheme his way down these stations, as by making a speech wherever the train stops, nor will he break down the partitions between them by some blasphemy, for example by talking about the child as if she were a grown-up. *Further:* someone has already done it. *Innocence* indeed; the child had the life suited to her age; for instance, her sexlessness or undeveloped kind of sex ought not to be talked about as a model of adult chastity. The reality behind all this, I believe, is that Dylan Thomas had been tempted to write war propaganda, both by indignation and by the opportunities of his profession, and then felt that this would be disgusting; it would be making use of the child, and what was said would have nothing to do with her actual experiences. The final poem therefore does not even admit that there was a war.

Instead the last verse practically ignores her, and deals with death in general. However, she has now a *long* gown like an angel or like a shroud; these clothes are *friends* because all matter has become her friend; she has returned to it. Or indeed *long* (when we get to *age* in the next line) means that these friends last for ever. And then again the clothes, since she was burned to ashes, are now *grains* of dust, recalling the earlier grains of corn which promised further life (so that both parts of the conventional angel picture are denied). They are *beyond age* because death is clearly beyond *old* age (the age of the child ought not to be considered) and because being particles like atoms they are unchanged at all the stages of development of the things they build up. *Veins* in Dylan Thomas are nearly always puns connecting the part of the body and the ore hidden in the earth, because of the pervading pantheism of his ideas and the hint of a magical belief that one person's body can affect everything. The dust of the child has gone underground into mother earth, and can be mined out again for new uses; and yet the earth, like the *friends,* is still treated as alive. *Riding:* the Thames is cheerful and practical, both riding over the earth and being ridden by men; and if treated as alive no doubt Father Thames is riding the Thames.

The plain meaning of the last line is that the child has no more pain and is well rid of such a world; it suggests also that she lives for ever as part of Nature. But the overtone is a summing up of the real theme. We ought not to talk nonsense about her; we cannot make her repeat her agonies for our own purposes, though we would be likely to do so if we were able.

MARIUS BEWLEY

Some Aspects of Modern American Poetry

(1954)

I

It is easier to admit a difference between English and American poetry than to analyse what the exact nature of that difference is. Poets and critics frequently speak of vocabulary, metric, syntax, and punctuation as though such things explained the difference between the two poetries. Certainly one would not wish to underestimate their importance. But ultimately such considerations are the expression of a divergence in attitude which is ulterior to themselves. They are secondary rather than primary characteristics. But to get behind such characteristics, obtrusive as they are, to something essential and final is extremely difficult. I believe it may be possible to move a little way in the right direction by considering the different conceptions which now prevail in England and America of what the function of a poet in society is. I do not necessarily mean the consciously held idea, for that frequently seems identical in both countries; rather, I mean the function that is involuntarily served when the poet is actually practising his art: that is to say, the kind of relationship envisaged between his art and the community in which, and for which, he writes, and the range and efficacy of possibilities which he instinctively sees as inhering in the exercise of the creative faculty. Whatever his particular conception of function may be, it plainly cannot sustain itself in an exclusively literary atmosphere. In the nature of the case it is immediately dependent on the energy, direction, and general health of the society in which it occurs. For a poet is a man in whose creative talent the energy of a society becomes momentarily focused.

From *The Complex Fate* by Marius Bewley. Reprinted by permission of Chatto and Windus Ltd.

Before considering the present state of American poetry it will be well to recall, however briefly, the principal verse writers in America during the nineteenth century. The names that come first to mind are Poe, Whitman, and Emily Dickinson. In the case of Poe our indebtedness, such as it is, is indirect, by way of his influence on the French Symbolists. But it is difficult not to doubt that if Baudelaire had known English better he would have liked Poe less. Emily Dickinson established a line that emerged in the twentieth century in Edna St. Vincent Millay, and since her in a school of coyly baroque poets of whom Mr. Dunstan Thompson might be taken as the representative example.[1] In the case of Walt Whitman, whose impact has been so great, it may appear foolhardy to depart from the conventional estimate of him without offering a detailed discussion, but even such a glancing reference as this can afford to suggest that the effect of Whitman's poetry has not been entirely fortunate on the development of American writing. His poetic discoveries were real enough in their way, but they had an effect on American art somewhat similar to the effects of the New World on Spain. The sudden acquisition of all that gold to be had with so little effort undermined everybody's morale, and in the end the losses may well have exceeded the profit. What seems to be clear is that the best American intelligence during the nineteenth century went into the production of prose. It has only been with the twentieth century that the American achievement in poetry has begun to assume impressive characteristics. The energy which, under Whitman, dissipated itself in fusillades of patriotic and expansive metaphor, is now more surely co-ordinated with critical intelligence, and placed at the disposal of an American sensibility which, if not entirely at its ease in verse, is admirably intent on learning discipline and poise.

It is precisely at this point of 'energy' that one may begin to differentiate between English and American poetry today. The energy of poetry and the energy of society are ultimately embedded in each other, and the effects of the War on the general life of England, together with the comparative escape of America, are considerations that cannot be neglected. And they do point to a situation or state in English poetry that is undeniable—a state which Mr. Cyril Connolly described for an American audience as one of 'exhaustion.'

The tradition of poetry flows unevenly, and at times dwindles, not even to a tiny trickle, but to a series of little stagnant ponds in which all life appears on the point of expiring. The reason seems to be that at infrequently spaced intervals a generation of poets is born which mobilizes speech and energy in such quantities, and under such new aspects, that the poets who occur between two such periods depend largely on the idiom and modes of feeling developed by their predecessors to express their own ideas. This is not usually owing to the lack of original talent in the later poets, but to the fact that the sensibility of the age has not yet changed sufficiently to justify that modification which an original poet must impose on old forms. The time has not yet developed those new requirements and urgencies which would make any such modifications intelligible to any envisaged public, or even to the poet himself. For if poets create the speech of their time, they cannot create it out of improper materials. They have to await the moment at which creation becomes possible. The 'exhaustion' of English poetry today is obviously part of that more general exhaustion which inevitably followed the War, for the energy of literature and society is, to a large extent, one energy. The listlessness which settled down on art was not entirely the listlessness *of* art.

On the other hand, it would appear that American poets have come through the War with an emboldened sense of function and responsibility. If, in view of the quality of much of their work, the conviction seems a little naïve, I am trying to point here to an attitude, a psychological situation, rather than offer a critical examination of individual writers. This conviction of function, of important work to do, arises first of all from the material circumstances of American life, its overwhelming activity on every side, its mere physical appearance of abundance and directed energy. Since the War there has been an intensification of the desire to explore and define American experience, not in itself only, but in its relations with the world. And the fact that the American poet, unlike the English poet, is not inclined to resent his present government, permits him to feel functionally associated with that experience. What the vast horde of American poets mean by American experience is, of course, something that cannot safely be generalized about for more than one poet at a time, but all the poets have this—and perhaps only this—in common: each is aware that his own experience is American, and the sense of it gives him confidence and a feeling that what he has to say is important. The result may often be extremely bad poetry, but it is something very different from 'exhaustion.' For example, opening a recent anthology I find this poem by Mr. James Laughlin, the editor of *New Directions*. I am tempted to quote it entire because I cannot quite imagine the attitude expressed in it transposed over into the English scene under any circumstances whatever, and it illustrates in a disarmingly frank-faced manner the attitude I have been speaking of, even to its title, 'Go West Young Man':

> Yessir they're all named
> either Ken or Stan or Don
> every one of them and
>
> those aren't just nick-
> names either no they're
> really christened like
>
> that just Ken or Stan or
> Don and you shake hands
> with anybody you run into
>
> no matter who the hell
> it is and say 'glad to
> know you Ken glad to
>
> know you Don' and then
> two minutes later (you
> may not have said ten
>
> words to the guy) you
> shake hands again and
> say 'glad to have met
>
> you Stan glad to' and
> they haven't heard much
> about Marx and the class
>
> struggle because they
> haven't had to and by
> god it makes a country
>
> that is fit to live in
> and by god I'm glad to
> know you Don I'm glad!

Whatever one might say about a piece like that, it does rest amazingly secure in its sense of the goodness of its own experience. It shows no doubts. Like a great deal of American writing, it is pure and emphatic assertion. Whether it has logic or not, it has a good deal of will in its make-up, and one is really surprised at the strength of the conviction behind it. Now these elements that are so apparent here—security and faith in its own experience (whatever that experience may be), a reliance on will and assertion, and a feeling that it is pretty important, are the most reliable signs by which to identify an American poem today. They are not infallible, but they are better signs than syntax, vocabulary, and rhythm. They rarely exist as openly and simply as in 'Go West Young Man.' Sometimes the disguise is very deep indeed, but under whatever tropical growth of cynicism or tortuous self-questionings the poet may hide, if one listens carefully enough the voice of the American is heard at last expressing his satisfaction in his own being. To take a fairly obvious example of this disguised security, Mr. Delmore Schwartz ends a recent poem in which he carefully delineates the successive disillusionments of life in these three verses:

Illusion and madness mock the years
  (A Godforsaken farce at best),
And yet through all these mounting fears
  How glad I am that I exist!

How strange the truth appears at last!
  I feel as old as outworn shoes,
I know what I have lost or missed,
  Or certainly will some day lose,

And yet this knowledge, like the Jews,
Can make me glad that I exist!
      with a hey ho, the foolish past,
      and a ho ho and a ha ha at last.

Any English reader would probably have some difficulty in distinguishing this tone from the bravado of Henley, but nevertheless (and I am not thinking merely of the Elizabethan décor) it is something quite different. The attitude behind it is a reflection of an important part of American character—an ability to see-saw from cynicism into optimism and enthusiasm, and a moment later, rigorous conviction. Whatever disabilities may attend it, its chief virtue is quickness of recovery. Americans could hardly get on without it, and it is therefore not to be dismissed as a merely shallow or silly or insubstantial attitude. Mr. Schwartz's poem is trivial enough, but I say all this because it is not a bad poem in the way I am fairly certain most English readers will conclude. And this attitude which is behind it is an important part of that larger complex of qualities which I am trying to suggest is one of the chief distinctions between the quality of English and American poetry.

But perhaps I may make my point more clearly by glancing at an essay by Mr. Schwartz which he calls *The Grapes of Crisis.* Mr. Schwartz presents some evidence in this article to suggest that since the First World War, but gaining incredible momentum since the Second, a change has been occurring in American character—a change which is registered in American art, particularly in literature and films. New books have sorrowful titles: *Lord Weary's Castle, The Dispossessed, The Victim,* etc. New films have unhappy endings. And the Daisy Millers of American literature have given place to the nymphomaniac of *A Streetcar Named Desire.* All this Mr. Schwartz sees as evidence of a crushing disillusionment—an abandonment of traditional American optimism. But however persuasive the evidence may seem; Mr. Schwartz's own conclusions indicate that the change has so far been confined to the surface. Pointing to the cynicism which, in some respects, has overtaken the American literary scene, Mr. Schwartz accepts it as the basis of a real advance—the creation of

> the possibility of a genuinely tragic art. Nobility is quickened by tragedy and nurtured by necessity. Once the mind is capable of regarding the future with a sense of tragedy and a sense of comedy, instead of requiring the forced smiles (and the whistling in the dark) of dogmatic optimism, the awakened consciousness is prepared to respond to existence with courage and intelligence.

Thus the strategy of Mr. Schwartz's criticism follows the strategy of his poem, quoted above. At the last moment a joyful and unexpected reversal assures us that the American has come through. This is a deeper kind of optimism than the one which Mr. Schwartz has made the subject of his own paper. I doubt if it can ever lead on to genuinely tragic art, but it represents a valid resilience which may ward off tragedy outside the realm of art.

II

I wish in these remarks to examine rather closely the work of only one young American poet. There is good reason for such abstinence. The great number of American poets, all with established reputations, is itself discouraging for anyone attempting a 'survey.' Any attempt to deal with them comprehensively could hardly be anything but confusing in a brief essay. But one should not be misled by mere multitude into supposing that Americans are essentially more interested in literature than the English. Although the details of Tocqueville's analysis of American writing have changed since he wrote *Democracy in America* over a century ago, the greater number of American poets may still be explained as the product of peculiarly democratic processes of thought:

> Taken as a whole, literature in democratic ages can never present, as it does in the periods of aristocracy, an aspect of order, regularity, science, and art; its form will, on the contrary, ordinarily be slighted, sometimes despised. Style will frequently be fantastic, incorrect, overburdened, and loose—almost always vehement and bold. Authors will aim at rapidity of execution, more than at perfection of detail. Small productions will be more common than bulky books; there will be more wit than erudition, more imagination than profundity; and literary performances will bear marks of an untutored and rude vigour of thought—frequently of great variety and singular fecundity. The object of authors will be to astonish rather than to please, and to stir the passions more than to stir the taste. Here and there indeed, writers will doubtless occur who will choose a different track, and who will, if they are gifted with superior abilities, succeed in finding readers, in spite of their defects or their better qualities; but these exceptions will be rare, and even the authors who shall so depart from the received practice in the main subject of their works, will always relapse into it in some lesser details.

There are ways in which this description no longer applies. For example, there is a growing emphasis on technique among American poets, and a taste for complicated metrical forms, which is replacing the older hackneyed emphasis on experimentalism that predominated in the 'twenties and held on tenaciously through the 'thirties. But Tocqueville's passage is still true enough to suggest why being a poet comes more easily in America than in England. Many modern American poets have acquired great skill in writing in intricate metrical patterns, but the complications of form which they pursue frequently seem to be achieved with facility rather than sustained with conviction or an un-brittle poise. There is a disquieting tendency on the part of many American critics to refer to such poets as 'great technicians.' I say it is 'disquieting' because a highly ordered form in poetry ought to relate to patterns of living, to organizations of feeling and thinking, somewhat less technological than the favoured term implies. It is difficult to imagine an early critic reading 'Alexander's Feast' for the first time and exclaiming, 'What a great technician Dryden is!' 'Technician' in such a context means nothing more than 'verbal engineer,' which may be why the critics of a highly technological civilization have come to favour it so much.

The 'technicians' among modern American poets may be divided into several categories, but perhaps those who take religion as their theme, no doubt seeing in the order of their verse a correspondence to the order of their theology, are the most important. To this group the young American poet belongs whom I earlier mentioned as the one poet whose verse I should consider with some care in this paper: I mean Mr. Robert Lowell.[2] There are several reasons for selecting Lowell's verse in preference to that of other writers of his generation (Mr. Lowell was born in 1917). First of all, he has received a degree of recognition far beyond that accorded any other new writer during the 'forties, and the tributes have ranged from publicity in *Time* to accolades from T. S. Eliot and Santayana. From the first the most distinguished American critics appeared to enter a conspiracy for the purpose of establishing Lowell's literary reputation on as sound a base in as short a time as possible. The enthusiasm of his admirers has been equalled on this side of the Atlantic only by the boosters of Dylan Thomas. And undeniably Lowell's verse has a great deal of intrinsic interest. It is integrated with the American background and the New England tradition to a degree unique among contemporary poets; while traditional, it also represents something new, though not perhaps quite as new as critics have claimed; and it is intensely serious—sometimes over-reachingly so. In its own distinctive way it is alive with that sense of reponsibility and function I have predicated of American poets in general.

But since my own criticism of Lowell's poetry will be considerably less enthusiastic than the prevailing view, I should like to say at once what I believe its virtues are. In several of his poems there is an immediacy of relation between his sensibility and the old New England of shipping and the sea that comes off with great distinction. 'The Quaker Graveyard in Nantucket' which begins,

A brackish reach of shoal off Madaket,—
The sea was still breaking violently and night
Had steamed into our North Atlantic Fleet,

is as original and fine a poem as America has lately produced. There is a kind of enduring newness in the evocations of the poetry that assert themselves more solidly with time. Speaking of a burial at sea,

We weight the body, close
Its eyes and heave it seaward whence it came,
Where the heel-headed dogfish barks its nose
On Ahab's void and forehead . . .

But it is difficult to quote piecemeal from such a poem.

An important element in Mr. Lowell's poetry is his feeling for Puritan New England. At the time most, if not all, of these poems were written, Lowell was a convert to the Catholic Church, and the Church forms a large part of their subject matter; but Lowell is not, as Mr. John Berryman has called him, 'the master of the Catholic subject without peer since Hopkins.' The quality of Lowell's sensibility depends almost entirely on its intractable Protestant puritanism, and it is never at its ease in Catholic images. The very structure of his sensibility is centred in considerations that were of overwhelming importance to the early New Englanders, but which are alien to Catholic feeling—ideas of innate depravity, the utter corruption of human nature and creation, regeneration, damnation of the non-Elect, and a habit of tortuous introspection to test the validity of grace in the soul. All these doctrines have in Lowell's poetry professedly undergone conversion to Rome, but on the face of it they still look very much their old Protestant selves. One critic wrote of Lowell's poetry that it exposed 'the full force of the collision between a long heritage of New England Calvinism and the tenets of the Roman Catholic Church.' Although the critic did not use the description in an unfavourable sense, it remains a very good one of what happens in Lowell's verse. A head-on collision between the Catholic tradition and an Apocalyptic Protestant sensibility is exactly what occurs in a verse like the following from 'Where the Rainbow Ends':

In Boston serpents whistle at the cold.
The victim climbs the altar stair and sings:
'Hosannah to the lion, lamb, and beast
Who fans the furnace face of IS with wings:

I breathe the ether of my marriage feast.'
At the high altar, gold
And a fair cloth. I kneel and the wings beat
My cheek. What can the dove of Jesus give
You now but wisdom, exile? Stand and live,
The dove has brought an olive branch to eat.

The poem of which this is the third verse has a certain impressiveness, but it is characteristically reluctant to yield up its meaning. It contains some extremely awkward images which need not be examined here as this quality of awkwardness can be better studied in some other verses, and a good many of the lines are far from being inevitably precise in their meaning. For example, the first line above may mean that in Boston sin is non-sensuous and chillblained, being the result mainly of the more frigid spiritual vices. But I should hesitate to stake anything of value on such a reading being the correct one. As for the remainder of this verse, it appears likely that the poet has just received Holy Communion, but if so, he celebrates it in an Apocalyptic terminology that seems unsuitable for such a subject. In this poem the two traditions collide, but it is a collision only—the metaphorical impact of staunchly opposed opposites. Mr. Lowell himself seems not even to be aware of the polarity involved, and none of the struggle of the opposing traditions get through into the texture of his verse.

The Puritan saints, so far from resting on assurances of their election, gave themselves up to some of the most agonizing soul probing ever encouraged by any religion. They examined endlessly the nature of the grace they felt in their souls that they might be sure it was authentic and not a temptation from the Devil; they searched the Scriptures for confirmation, and analysed endlessly the movements of their hearts. All this developed a tone, an attitude—and despite the Catholic gesturing, it is an attitude one finds in Lowell's poetry. This attitude or tone sometimes becomes feverishly tortuous, and leads Lowell into attenuations so rarefied, and through logical transitions so slippery and concealed, that it is frequently impossible to follow him all the way. The poem 'Colloquy in Black Rock' is an example of one of these dialogues between Lowell and his own heart as a preparation for its fuller possession by Christ. It is a dull poem, but nevertheless it is worth considering as a way of approaching his most serious defect—the conviction that he is being, not only intelligible, but highly ordered and logical in the disposition of his images and the structure of his thought when, in reality, his experience is claustrophobically private and subjective. Despite the rigorous appearance of an objective framework of logic 'The Ferris Wheel' is such a poem, and it could be duplicated in this quality by many other of Lowell's verses.

A number of Lowell's poems can be interpreted in purely Protestant terms—for example, 'The Drunken Fisherman,' which is one of his best pieces. And no doubt it would be fairer to Lowell if one were to concentrate on these. But Lowell was specifically acclaimed as a Catholic poet, and to this fact he no doubt owes a good deal of his recognition. But whenever the subject is pointedly Catholic there is something disturbing in the tone. Turning to 'A Prayer for My Grandfather to Our Lady,' Lowell's uncertainty or awkwardness is unmistakable under the boldness of feeling in a passage like this one addressed to the Blessed Virgin:

> O Mother, I implore
> Your scorched blue thunderbreasts of love to pour
> Buckets of blessings on my burning head
> Until I rise like Lazarus from the dead:
> *Lavabis nos et super nivem delabor.*

This is a network of conflicting connotations that operates at cross-purposes. 'Thunderbreasts,' I presume, is meant to suggest the mythical Thunderbird of various Indian tribes, which was supposed to bring rain, and so the word may imply the life-giving qualities of Our Lady's love. But Our Lady and the Thunderbird (if it *is* intended, and I don't see what else could be meant here) belong to traditions too remote from each other to coalesce imaginatively at the low pressure to which they are submitted. Blue, of course, is Mary's colour. And perhaps 'blue thunderbreasts' is meant to emphasize the blue heavens from which rain and grace come. But the quality of Lowell's sensibility is such (and I am thinking of the poem in the full context of the volume) that the word seems likely to start a train of disease images. 'Buckets of blessings on my burning head' is breath-takingly infelicitous. Apart from the ugly sound of it, and the almost Gilbert and Sullivan visual image it presents, it suggests that Our Lady is dousing a halo, which can hardly be what is meant. I am not merely trying to be difficult, but I find this passage typical in the awkward qualities I have mentioned. It frequently happens that when Mr. Lowell is dealing with a religious subject something seems to go wrong with his verse—not inevitably so, for

'The Holy Innocents' is a very good poem. But a religious theme is usually a signal for intolerable strain.

This strain is not lessened when Mr. Lowell relates human action to religious significance. His sequence of four poems, 'Between the Porch and the Altar,' is a melodramatic narration of a man who deserts his wife and two children for another woman, gets killed in a motor accident, and goes to Hell. At any rate, that is the action as far as I can follow it, but the character of the seducer seems strangely uneven. In the first poem he is a son with a mother fixation. In the second he is a Concord farmer who, in the closing image, is identified with Adam in the act of committing Original Sin. In the fourth poem he turns up, rather sportily, in a night club shortly before his fatal mishap. Here is the opening of the fourth poem, and it illustrates the recurrence of that strain or awkwardness that I have just noted elsewhere:

> I sit at a gold table with my girl
> Whose eyelids burn with brandy. What a whirl
> Of Easter eggs is coloured by the lights,
> As the Norwegian dancer's crystalled tights
> Flash with her naked leg's high-booted skate,
> Like Northern Lights upon my watching plate.
> The twinkling steel above me is a star;
> I am a fallen Christmas tree. Our car
> Races through seven red lights—then the road
> Is unpatrolled and empty, and a load
> Of ply-wood with a tail-light makes us slow.
> I turn and whisper in her ear. You know
> I want to leave my mother and my wife,
> You wouldn't have me tied to them for life. . . .

Apparently at that moment the accident occurs which, in view of the sentiments he is expressing just then, sends him straight to the Devil.

The first thing one notices about this passage is a characteristic wooden ugliness that is related to the rhythm—particularly to Mr. Lowell's flattening habit of placing a cæsura just before the last foot of every line. It is a common practice with him, and can be better observed in a poem like 'After the Surprising Conversions':

> I preached one morning on a text from Kings;
> He showed concernment for his soul. Some things
> In his experience were hopeful. He
> Would sit and watch the wind knocking a tree. . . .

But to return to the earlier quotation—the rhythmical flatness is matched by an unsatisfactoriness in the images themselves. Anticipating the descent into Hell in the last part of the poem, the second line strains too hard to get as much sordidness as possible out of a few glasses of brandy, and the sense of strain is not reduced by the absurd image of the Easter eggs, which is obviously introduced for the purpose of recalling the Redemption, quite as if by accident. Again, I wonder why the nationality of the fancy skater is insisted on since the only purpose that particular exactness can serve is to start the American reader thinking of Sonja Henie. Nor can I understand in what relevant sense the speaker's plate may be said to be 'watching,' unless, indeed, he is speaking, not of the plate on the gold table, but of his retina which he compares to a photographic plate. In the next line it is extremely difficult to know what the twinkling steel is. It may possibly mean that a sword is hanging above the poet's head, and that the consequent feeling of uncertainty which it engenders is a warning which might, if heeded, save him, and which for that reason he compares to the star of Bethlehem. But it is asking more than reasonable co-operation from any reader to put any very precise sense in the lines at all. The same kind of muzziness attends the next image into which the figure of the twinkling star naturally moves, 'I am a fallen Christmas tree.' This could, no doubt, mean a number of things, but it hardly seems to mean anything with much certainty. The action which is recorded in the last lines is handled laboriously and jerkily, and the closing bit of 'wickedness' is blurted out in an extremely youthful way.

Most critics have referred to Mr. Eliot as among Lowell's chief influences, but he seems to be much nearer Edwin Arlington Robinson. Both poets are disconcertingly fond of classic allusions, and they both present little tin-types of unusual American characters and episodes. And both have a disastrously 'literary' taste for the more romantic and ancient themes. We find Mr. Lowell writing exotic little set pieces (but on the surface quite 'modern' and difficult to read): 'Napoleon Crosses the Berezina,' 'Charles the Fifth and the Peasant,' or 'The Fens' (after Cobbett). As for Mr. Lowell's rhythm, a passage like the following from Robinson is much nearer a good deal of Lowell's verse than anything in Eliot:

> Now I call that as curious a dream
> As ever Meleager's mother had—
> Æneas, Alcibiades, or Jacob.

I'll not except the scientist who dreamed
That he was Adam or that he was Eve
At the same time; or yet that other man
Who dreamed that he was Æschylus, reborn
To clutch, combine, compensate, and adjust
The plunging and unfathomable chorus
Wherein we catch, like a bacchanale through thunder,
The chanting of the new Eumenides,
Implacable, renacent, farcical,
Triumphant, and American.

I should find myself hard-pressed if I were asked to put a particular passage from Lowell against that to demonstrate my point, but with the exception of several poems that seem to me highly distinguished, the volume as a whole is alive with echoes of that kind of writing. Yet Lowell's two or three really successful poems are strikingly original; but original also is a peculiar kind of ugliness which runs through much of his verse. Some of his lines remain in the memory as classic examples of verbal and visual infelicity, for example:

Her Irish maids could never spoon out mush
Or orange juice enough . . .

In the most literal sense Lowell's world is astonishingly without colour. His images are nearly all grey or black or white, and they gravitate towards such unpleasant items as snow, ice, snakes choking ducklings, melted lard, dead cats, rats, coke barrels, iron tubs, fish, mud, Satan, rubble, stones, smoke, coke-fumes, hammers, the diseases of old age, and every possible variation on the most depressing aspects of winter. Except in a few poems I cannot see that Lowell transcends the dreary materials he builds them with. On the few occasions he achieves beauty in his poetry the sea is likely to be beating coldly and sombrely in the background.

And yet, under these disagreeable surfaces, Lowell's poetry does give evidence of an unusual integrity. It proves, I think, that the sense of function which I earlier predicated of the American poet, is not wholly, and in all cases, a product of America's material activity. Among its deeper historical roots one may point to the New England puritanism of the seventeenth century, which regarded logic and rhetoric as a means of knowing and communicating Divine Truth. It is under the banners of logic and rhetoric, although these are subsumed in the name of poet, that Mr. Lowell undertakes his work. And it makes little difference from the viewpoint of his intention that the logic is often elusive and the rhetoric unappealing. No poet could well conceive of a greater function than this religious onslaught on Truth, and it is, as I have tried to indicate, a function made wholly valid by the tradition from which Mr. Lowell emerges.

III

There is not much doubt that, historically, Robert Lowell is the most important figure in American poetry among those who came to prominence during the 'forties. But he must still be reckoned a comparatively young writer, with a very limited amount of work behind him, and one must not hesitate to ask who is the most intrinsically important poet now writing in America. There are only three possibilities: Robert Frost, Ezra Pound, and Wallace Stevens. The poetry of Frost, however sensitively related in its colloquial rhythms and its subject matter to its New England background, is hardly of a stature to give decisive orientation or a very considerable new impulse to American writing. Despite its rhythmical distinction and beauty it is yet more parochial than befits the work of a nation's first poet. Much of Frost's later writing gives the impression that a sensibility equipped to deal effectively with such subjects as Edward Thomas took as his province has tended to overload itself with material no longer intimately related to those central springs from which his earlier poetry issued.

Pound is the most difficult of all to assess. He is a monumental fragment of a city that may, or may not, have been there, and it is no part of the purpose of these present notes to consider the evidences. But it is probable that he will continue to preoccupy the Americans more than the other two. Pound's relative looseness of erudition, the apparent flow and volume of his writing, the easy American strut of his assurance, may merely duplicate, on a higher and tighter level, the effects of *Leaves of Grass* on American poetry. Of the three poets mentioned it is Pound, paradoxically, who seems closest to his countrymen. His Americanism is of an orthodox variety merely turned wrong side out. His dogmatic assertiveness, his sense of importance and function, his speedy acquisition of foreign cultures, are all of a kind that is characteristically American. With much less ability and a different orientation he might easily have stayed at home and become another William Carlos Williams.

Wallace Stevens is less understandable to the American literary scene, and his poetry will have less direct influence than Pound's. And yet it is probable that he is the greatest of the three—certainly, he seems the only American poet whose work might be able to counteract the spiritually loose-jointed, tragic influence of Whitman. The poetry of Stevens is frequently painfully difficult:

> The poem must resist the intelligence
> Almost successfully.

But this difficulty inheres in his profound recognition of the inexplicable quality of experience. He has created his poetry out of images and phrases the meaning of which has to be learned in the same painstaking way one might learn a foreign language. It is only after the reader has become thoroughly familiar with this vocabulary that Stevens' images and phrases assert their intimacy with the American language, and that he begins to discover how importantly and intensely Stevens' central meaning inheres in the heart of all his poetry. Imaginative insight, the intuition of art (by which Stevens means the creative, synthesizing insight of any human being at his moments of most intense awareness) become, in one way and another, the subject of all his poetry, and the essence of its form. Stevens' poetry has an appearance of highly coloured artificiality. It is filled with images of art, and the appearances in the world it offers correspond to the appearances of the real world only in the most esoteric of ways. But these appearances express that central meaning and take fire from it so that what in the beginning appeared to us as artificiality ends, by virtue of that very quality, in showing forth and emphasizing the life-giving power of the legend with which Stevens is concerned. But it is impossible to discuss Stevens' poetry within the limits prescribed by the present discussion. I have only wished to indicate here his relative position in the larger group of American poets. A fuller examination of his poetry must be postponed till the following essay.

IV

I have been concerned with pointing to the existence of an attitude to poetry which, if properly protected and developed, might become a satisfactory foundation for a highly productive period in American literature. It has been necessary to keep in mind some of the dangers that such an attitude runs; and they are numerous in a commercial society such as America's in which any enthusiasm or conviction is likely to be at the mercy of the exploiter. But, after all, such dangers are extraneous. Before bringing these notes to a close I should like to probe a little deeper into the nature of the American's sense of function and responsibility where poetry is concerned, and endeavour to see if it carries any specific principle of limitation inherent in itself, and, if so, how this affects the nature of the poetry produced.

It is possible to approach the problem by considering the American emphasis on the positive affirmation, on the exercise of will, and on the belief that the future can be engineered profitably if one only has the engineers and the materials—in short, by examining the largely activist modes of American feeling and thinking. It is doubtful if the greatest poetry is ever written in these modes, which are never wholly disinterested. If poetry is a fiat, it is never mere assertion, however brave; and if it is a source of truth, it is yet never praiseworthy for its dogma. Probably the greatest poetry of our time is Eliot's *Four Quartets*. Possibly the Quartets owe some of their popularity to the fact that dogma can be extricated from them, but that is by the way. If Mr. Eliot was once an American poet (and he may still not be an *English* poet), he never expressed the distance of his sensibility from American modes more fully than in these poems. A measure of that distance may be found in such lines as,

> I said to my soul, be still, and wait without hope
> For hope would be hope for the wrong thing; there is yet faith
> But the faith and the love and the hope are all in the waiting.
> Wait without thought, for you are not ready for thought:
> So the darkness shall be the light, and the stillness the dancing.

That great poetry and intense experience should come out of something undergone or suffered in this way is not the first lesson one learns from American poetry. It fails to understand that element of passivity which is part of the base of great art, and it frequently mistakes the turmoil for the reality. Americans are supposed to like—or to have liked in the past—classical art. But it is the rhetorical gesture and not the moment of repose that they are inclined to value most. Mr. Eliot's lines express their remoteness from the American sensibility in a number of ways. The American would not snub Hope (which in his heart at least he would surely capitalize) in the way that Mr. Eliot does. He knows that Hope literally cleared the wilderness, and confronted with the solid monuments she has erected across the continent, the most critical of poets would hesitate to question too radically whether or not it was, after all, hope of the wrong thing. I do not mean that the American poet might not be as critical on the surface as the English poet, but he is too much a part of the fabric to question too radically unless he should also be willing to remove himself from the scene for good. There is a profundity of questioning possible in these matters which is irreconcilable with the term 'American' being still applied to the questioner in any sense that is significant in such a discussion as the present one. Nor would the American sensibility, which is nervous and impatient, understand the goodness of waiting. To be up and doing, even in matters of spirituality—to say nothing of poetry—is its sweetness and joy. Nor could it suppose it was not ready for thought, for too many fragments of eighteenth-century rationalism still inhere in its composition. And it would have some difficulty in distinguishing thought from the process of technology, with which it has enjoyed great success. Above all it could not accept the resignation of the last line.

The sense of function in the American poet is deeply influenced and essentially modified by this activism. This activism is likely to discourage the greatest poetic achievement, but this, at least, can be said for it: it conceives poetry in a public capacity, and the poetry it produces frequently has something of the forum in it. It is not likely to enlarge experience by the insights of original genius operating at the highest level of the imagination, but it is able to explore and define experience deliberatively or imaginatively within certain set boundaries and propositions. Such poetry will tend to have a validity in the American scene that it will not always be able to carry over into other contexts. If we can say that this is a serious criticism, we should not lose sight of the more difficult point that the very limitation carries its intimate importance for the American tradition itself, which is still in a formative stage.

NOTES

1. Mr. Dunstan Thompson's *Poems* were published in England in 1946.
2. *Poems: 1938–1949*. Faber and Faber.

NORTHROP FRYE

The Realistic Oriole: A Study of Wallace Stevens

(1957)

Wallace Stevens was a poet for whom the theory and the practice of poetry were inseparable.* His poetic vision is informed by a metaphysic; his metaphysic is informed by a theory of knowledge; his theory of knowledge is informed by a poetic vision. He says of one of his long meditative poems that it displays the theory of poetry as the life of poetry (486), and in the introduction to his critical essays that by the theory of poetry he means 'poetry itself, the naked poem' (*N.A.* vii). He thus stands in contrast to the dualistic approach of Eliot, who so often speaks of poetry as though it were an emotional and sensational soul looking for a 'correlative' skeleton of thought to be provided by a philosopher, a Cartesian ghost trying to find a machine that will fit. No poet of any status—certainly not Eliot himself—has ever 'taken over' someone else's structure of thought, and the dualistic fallacy can only beget more fallacies. Stevens is of particular interest and value to the critical theorist because he sees so clearly that the only ideas the poet can deal with are those directly involved with, and implied by, his own writing: that, in short, 'Poetry is the subject of the poem' (176).

* All references to Stevens' poetry are accompanied by the page number in *The Collected Poems of Wallace Stevens,* 1954, and all references to his critical essays by the page number in *The Necessary Angel,* 1951, preceded by the letters *N.A.* I am sorry if this procedure makes the article typographically less attractive, but the proper place for such references, the margin, has disappeared from modern layout.

It has been established in criticism ever since Aristotle that histories are direct verbal imitations of action, and that anything in literature with a story in it is a secondary imitation of an action. This means, not that the story is at two removes from reality, but that its actions are representative and typical rather than specific. For some reason it has not been nearly so well understood that discursive writing is not thinking, but a direct verbal imitation of thought; that any poem with an idea in it is a secondary imitation of thought, and hence deals with representative or typical thought: that is, with forms of thought rather than specific propositions. Poetry is concerned with the ambiguities, the unconscious diagrams, the metaphors and the images out of which actual ideas grow. Poet and painter alike operate in 'the flux Between the thing as idea and the idea as thing' (295). Stevens is an admirable poet in whom to study the processes of poetic thought at work, and such processes are part of what he means by the phrase 'supreme fiction' which enters the title of his longest poem. The poet, he says, 'gives to life the supreme fictions without which we are unable to conceive of it' (*N.A.* 31), and fictions imitate ideas as well as events.

Any discussion of poetry has to begin with the field or area that it works in, the field described by Aristotle as nature. Stevens calls it 'reality,' by which he means, not simply the external physical world, but 'things as they are,' the existential process that includes ordinary human life on the level of absorption in routine activity. Human intelligence can resist routine by arresting it in an act of consciousness, but the normal tendency of routine is to work against consciousness. The revolution of consciousness against routine is the starting-point of all mental activity, and the centre of mental activity is imagination, the power of transforming 'reality' into awareness of reality. Man can have no freedom except what begins in his own awareness of his condition. Naturally historical periods differ greatly in the amount of pressure put on free consciousness by the compulsions of ordinary life. In our own day this pressure has reached an almost intolerable degree that threatens to destroy freedom altogether and reduce human life to a level of totally preoccupied compulsion, like the life of an animal. One symptom of this is the popular demand that the artist should express in his work a sense of social obligation. The artist's primary obedience however is not to reality but to the 'violence from within' (*N.A.* 36) of the imagination that resists and arrests it. The minimum basis of the imagination, so to speak, is ironic realism, the act of simply becoming aware of the surrounding pressures of 'things as they are.' This develops the sense of alienation which is the immediate result of the imposing of consciousness on reality:

From this the poem springs: that we live in a place
That is not our own and, much more, not ourselves. (383)

The 'act of the mind' (240) in which imagination begins, then, is an arresting of a flow of perceptions without and of impressions within. In that arrest there is born the principle of form or order: the inner violence of the imagination is a 'rage for order' (130). It produces the 'jar in Tennessee' (76), the object which not only is form in itself, but creates form out of all its surroundings. Stevens follows Coleridge in distinguishing the transforming of experience by the imagination from the re-arranging of it by the 'fancy,' and ranks the former higher (ignoring, if he knew it, T. E. Hulme's clever pseudo-critical reversal of the two). The imagination contains reason and emotion, but the imagination keeps form concrete and particular, whereas emotion and reason are more apt to seek the vague and the general respectively.

There are two forms of mental activity that Stevens regards as unpoetic. One is the breaking down of a world of discrete objects into an amorphous and invisible substratum, a search for a 'pediment of appearance' (361), a slate-colored world of substance (15, 96) which destroys all form and particularity, symbolized by the bodiless serpent introduced in 'The Auroras of Autumn' (411), 'form gulping after formlessness.' This error is typically an error of reason. The other error is the breaking down of the individual mind in an attempt to make it a medium for some kind of universal or pantheistic mind. This is typically an error of emotion, and one that Stevens in his essays calls 'romantic,' which is a little confusing when his own poetry is so centrally in the Romantic tradition. What he means by it is the preference of the invisible to the visible which impels a poet to develop a false rhetoric intended to be the voice, not of himself, but of some invisible superbard within him (*N.A.* 61). In 'Jumbo' (269), Stevens points out that such false rhetoric comes, not from the annihilation of the ego, but from the ego itself, from 'Narcissus, prince Of the secondary men.' Such an attitude produces the 'nigger mystic' (195, 265), a phrase which naturally has nothing to do with Negroes, but refers to the kind of intellectual absolute that has been compared to a night in which all cows are black, a world clearly no improvement on 'reality,' which is also one color (*N.A.* 26).

A third mode of mental activity, which is poetic but not Stevens' kind of poetry, is the attempt to suggest or evoke universals of mind or substance, to work at the threshold of consciousness and produce what Stevens calls 'marginal' poetry and associates with Valéry (*N.A.* 115). Whatever its merit, such poetry for him is in contrast with 'central' poetry based on the concrete and particular act of mental experience. Stevens speaks of the imagination as moving from the hieratic to the credible (*N.A.* 58), and marginal poetry, like the structures of reason and the surrenderings of emotion, seeks a 'hierophant Omega' (469) or ultimate mystery. There is a strong tendency, a kind of intellectual death-wish, to conceive of order in terms of finality, as something that keeps receding from experience until experience stops, when it becomes the mirage of an 'after-life' on which all hierophants, whether poets or priests, depend. But for the imagination 'Reality is the beginning not the end' (469), 'The imperfect is our paradise' (194), and the only order worth having is the 'violent order' produced by the explosion of imaginative energy, which is also a 'great disorder' (215).

This central view of poetry is for Stevens based on the straight Aristotelian principle that if art is not quite nature, at least it grows naturally out of nature. He dislikes the term 'imitation,' but only because he thinks it means the naïve copying of an external world: in its proper Aristotelian sense of creating a form of which nature is the content, Stevens' poetry is as imitative as Pope's. Art then is not so much nature methodized as nature realized, a unity of being and knowing, existence and consciousness, achieved out of the flow of time and the fixity of space. In content it is reality and we are 'Participants of its being' (463); in form it is an art which 'speaks the feeling' for 'things as they are' (424). All through Stevens' poetry we find the symbol of the alphabet or syllable, the imaginative key to reality which, by bringing reality into consciousness, heightens the sense of both, 'A nature that is created in what it says' (490).

However, the imagination does bring something to reality which is not there in the first place, hence the imagination contains an element of the 'unreal' which the imaginative form incorporates. This unreal is connected with the fact that conscious experience is liberated experience. The unreal, 'The fabulous and its intrinsic verse' (31), is the sense of exhilaration and splendor in art, the 'radiant and productive' atmosphere which it both creates and breathes, the sense of the virile and the heroic implied by the term 'creative' itself, 'the way of thinking by which we project the idea of God into the idea of man' (*N.A.* 150).

All art has this essential elegance or nobility, including ironic realism, but the nobility is an attribute of art, not its goal: one attains it by not trying for it, as though it were definable or extrinsic. Although art is in one sense an escape from reality (i.e., in the sense in which it is an escape *of* reality), and although art is a heightening of consciousness, it is not enough for art simply to give one a vision of a better world. Art is practical, not speculative; imaginative, not fantastic; it transforms experience, and does not merely interrupt it. The unreal in imaginative perception is most simply described as the sense that if something is not there it at least ought to be there. But this feeling in art is anything but wistful: it has created the tone of all the civilizations of history. Thus the 'central' poet, by working outwards from a beginning instead of onwards toward an end, helps to achieve the only genuine kind of progress. As Stevens says, in a passage which explains the ambivalence of the term 'mystic' in his work: 'The adherents of the central are also mystics to begin with. But all their desire and all their ambition is to press away from mysticism toward that ultimate good sense which we term civilization' (*N.A.* 116).

Such ultimate good sense depends on preserving a balance between objective reality and the subjective unreal element in the imagination. Exaggerating the latter gives us the false heroics that produce the aggressive symbols of warfare and the cult of 'men suited to public ferns' (276). Exaggerating the former gives us the weariness of mind that bores the 'fretful concubine' (211) in her splendid surroundings. Within art itself there has been a corresponding alternation of emphasis. In some ages, or with some poets, the emphasis is on the imaginative heightening of reality by visions of a Yeatsian 'noble rider'

> On his gold horse striding, like a conjured beast,
> Miraculous in its panache and swish. (426)

At other times the emphasis is ironic, thrown on the minimum role of the imagination as the simple and subjective observer of reality, not withdrawn from it, but detached enough to feel that the power of transforming it has passed by. These two emphases, the green and the red as Stevens calls them (340), appear in Stevens' own poetry as the summer vision and the autumn vision respectively.

The summer vision of life is the *gaya scienza* (248), the 'Lebensweisheitspielerei' (504), in which things are perceived in their essential radiance, when 'the world is larger' (514). This summer vision extends all over the *Harmonium* poems, with their glowing still lifes and gorgeous landscapes of Florida and the Caribbean coasts. Its dominating image is the sun, 'that brave man' (138), the hero of nature who lives in heaven but transforms the earth from his mountain-top (65), 'the strong man vaguely seen' (204). As 'we are men of sun' (137), our creative life is his, hence the feeling of alienation from nature in which consciousness begins is really inspired by exactly the opposite feeling. 'I am what is around me' (86), the poet says; the jar in Tennessee expresses the form in Tennessee as well as in itself, and one feels increasingly that 'The soul . . . is composed Of the external world' (51) in the sense that in the imagination we have 'The inhuman making choice of a human self' (*N.A.* 89), a subhuman world coming to a point of imaginative light in a focus of individuality and consciousness. Such a point of imaginative light is a human counterpart of the sun. The poet absorbs the reality he contemplates 'as the Angevine Absorbs Anjou' (224), just as the sun's light, by giving itself and taking nothing, absorbs the world in itself. The echo to the great trumpet-call of 'Let there be light' is 'All things in the sun are sun' (104).

The are two aspects of the summer vision, which might be called, in Marvellian language, the visions of the golden lamp and of the green night. The latter is the more contemplative vision of the student in the tradition of Milton's penseroso poet, Shelley's Athanase, and Yeats's old man in the tower. In this vision the sun is replaced by the moon (33 ff.), or, more frequently, the evening star (25), the human counterpart of which is the student's candle (51, 523). Its personified form, corresponding to the sun, is often female, an 'archaic' (223) or 'green queen' (339), the 'desired' (505) one who eventually becomes an 'interior paramour' (524) or Jungian anima (cf. 321), the motionless spinning Penelope (520) to whom every voyager returns, the eternal Eve (271) or naked bride (395) of the relaxed imagination. Here we are, of course, in danger of the death-wish vision, of reading a blank book. Some of the irony of this is in 'Phosphor Reading by his Own Light' (267), as well as in 'The Reader' (146). The bride of such a narcist vision is the sinister 'Madame La Fleurie' (507). But in its genuine form such contemplation is the source of major imagination (387–8), and hence Stevens, like Yeats, has his tower-mountain of vision or 'Palaz of Hoon' (65; cf. 121), where sun and poet come into alignment:

> It is the natural tower of all the world,
> The point of survey, green's green apogee,

But a tower more precious than the view beyond,
A point of survey squatting like a throne,
Axis of everything. (373)

From this point of survey we are lifted above the 'cat,' symbol of life absorbed in being without consciousness, and the 'rabbit' who is 'king of the ghosts' and is absorbed in consciousness without being (209, 223).

The autumnal vision begins in the poet's own situation. To perceive 'reality' as dingy or unattractive is itself an imaginative act ('The Plain Sense of Things,' 502), but an ironic act, an irony deepened by the fact that other modes of perception are equally possible, the oriole being as realistic as the crow (154), and there can be no question of accepting only one as true. It is a curious tendency in human nature to believe in disillusionment: that is, to think we are nearest the truth when we have established as much falsehood as possible. This is the vision of 'Mrs. Alfred Uruguay' (248), who approaches her mountain of contemplation the wrong way round, starting at the bottom instead of the top. (Her name is apparently based on an association with 'Montevideo.') The root of the reductive tendency, at least in poetry, is perhaps the transience of the emotional mood which is the framework of the lyric. In *Harmonium* the various elaborations of vision are seen as projected from a residual ego, a comedian (27 ff.) or clown (Peter Quince is the leader of a group of clowns), who by himself has only the vision of the '*esprit bâtard*' (102), the juggler in motley who is also a magician and whose efforts are 'conjurations.' When we add the clown's conjurations to the clown we get 'man the abstraction, the comic sun' (156): the term 'abstraction' will meet us again.

This *esprit bâtard* or dimmed vision of greater maturity, *un monocle d'un oncle*, so to speak, comes into the foreground after the 'Credences of Summer' (372) and the 'Things of August' (489) have passed by. In September the web of the imagination's pupa is woven (208); in November the moon lights up only the death of the god (107); at the onset of winter the auroras of a vanished heroism flicker over the sky, while in the foreground stand the scarecrows or hollow men of the present (293, 513).

To this vision belong the bitter 'Man on the Dump' (201), the ironic 'Esthetique du Mal' (313), with its urbane treatment of the religio-literary clichés, such as 'The death of Satan was a tragedy For the imagination,' which are the stock in trade of lesser poets, and the difficult and painfully written war poems. It is more typical of Stevens, of course, to emphasize the reality which is present in the imaginative heightening of misery, the drudge's dream of 'The Ordinary Women' (10) which none the less reminds us that 'Imagination is the will of things' (84). The true form of the autumnal vision is not the irony which robs man of his dignity, but the tragedy which confers it ('In a Bad Time,' 426).

At the end of autumn come the terrors of winter, the sense of a world disintegrating into chaos which we feel socially when we see the annihilating wars of our time, and individually when we face the fact of death in others or for ourselves. We have spoken of Stevens' dislike of projecting the religious imagination into a world remote in space and time. The woman in 'Sunday Morning' (66) stays home from church and meditates on religion surrounded by the brilliant oranges and greens of the summer vision, and in 'A High-Toned Old Christian Woman' (59) it is suggested that the poet, seeking an increase rather than a diminishing of life, gets closer to a genuinely religious sense than morality with its taboos and denials. For Stevens all real religion is concerned with a renewal of earth rather than with a surrender to heaven. He even says 'the great poems of heaven and hell have been written and the great poem of the earth remains to be written' (*N.A.* 142). It is part of his own ambition to compose hymns 'Happy rather than holy but happy-high' (185) which will 'take the place Of empty heavens' (167), and he looks forward to a world in which 'all men are priests' (254). As this last phrase shows, he has no interest in turning to some cellophane-wrapped version of neo-paganism. He sees, like Yeats, that the poet is a 'Connoisseur of Chaos' (215) aware that 'Poetry is a Destructive Force' (192), and Stevens' imagery, for all its luxuriance and good humor, is full of menace. From the 'firecat' of the opening page of the *Collected Poems,* through the screaming peacocks of 'Domination of Black' (8), the buzzard of 'The Jack-Rabbit' (50; cf. 318), the butcher of 'A Weak Mind in the Mountains' (212), the bodiless serpent of 'The Auroras of Autumn' (411) and the bloody lion of 'Puella Parvula' (456), we are aware that a simple song of *carpe diem* is not enough.

In the later poems there is a growing preoccupation with death, as, not the end of life or an introduction to something unconnected with life, but as itself a part of life and giving to life itself an extra dimension. This view is very close to Rilke, especially the Rilke of the Orpheus sonnets, which are, like Stevens' poetry in general, 'a constant sacrament of praise' (92). 'What a ghastly situation it would be,' Stevens remarks, 'if the world of the dead was actually different from the world of the living' (*N.A.* 76), and in several poems, especially the remarkable 'Owl in the Sarcophagus' (431), there are references to carrying on the memories or 'souvenirs' of the past into a world which is not so much future as timeless, a world of recognition or 'rendezvous' (524), and which lies in the opposite direction from the world of dreams:

> There is a monotonous babbling in our dreams
> That makes them our dependent heirs, the heirs
> Of dreamers buried in our sleep, and not
> The oncoming fantasies of better birth. (39)

In the poems of the winter vision the solar hero and the green queen become increasingly identified with the father and mother of a Freudian imago (439). The father and mother in turn expand into a continuous life throughout time of which we form our unitary realizations. The father, 'the bearded peer' (494), extends back to the primordial sea (501), the mother to the original maternity of nature, the 'Lady Lowzen' of 'Oak Leaves are Hands' (272). In 'The Owl in the Sarcophagus' these figures are personified as sleep and memory. The ambivalence of the female figure is expressed by the contrast between the 'regina of the clouds' in 'Le Monocle de Mon Oncle' (13) and the 'Sister and mother and diviner love' of 'To the One of Fictive Music' (87). The poet determined to show that 'being Includes death and the imagination' (444) must go through the same world as the 'nigger mystic,' for a 'nigger cemetery' (150) lies in front of him too, just as the sunrise of the early play, *Three Travellers Watch a Sunrise,* is heralded by a hanged man. The search for death through life which is a part of such recreation leads to a final confronting of the self and the rock (*N.A.* viii), the identification of consciousness and reality in which the living soul is identified with its tombstone which is equally its body (528). In this final triumph of vision over death the death-symbols are turned into symbols of life. The author of the Apocalypse prophesies to his 'back-ache' (which is partly the *Weltschmerz* of the past) that the venom of the bodiless serpent will be one with its wisdom (437). The 'black river' of death, Swatara (428), becomes 'The River of Rivers in Connecticut' (533), a river *this* side of the Styx which 'flows nowhere, like a sea' because it is in a world in which there is no more sea.

If we listen carefully to the voice of 'the auroral creature musing in the mind' (263), the auroras of autumn will become, not the after-images of remembrance, but the *Morgenrot* of a new recognition. As the cycle turns through death to a new life, we meet images of spring, the central one being some modification of Venus rising from the sea: the 'paltry nude' of the poem of that name (5); 'Infanta Marina' (7); Susanna lying in 'A wave, interminably flowing' (92); 'Celle qui fût Heaulmiette' (438) reborn from the mother and father of the winter vision, the mother having the 'vague severed arms' of the maternal Venus of Milo. This reborn girl is the Jungian anima or interior paramour spoken of before, the 'Golden Woman in a Silver Mirror' (460). She is also associated with the bird of Venus, 'The Dove in the Belly' (366; cf. 357 and 'Song of Fixed Accord,' 519). It is also a bird's cry, but one outside the poet, which heralds 'A new knowledge of reality' in the last line of the *Collected Poems*. The spring vision often has its origin in the commonplace, or in the kind of innocent gaudiness that marks exuberant life. Of the spring images in 'Celle qui fût Heaulmiette' the author remarks affectionately, 'Another American vulgarity'; the 'paltry nude' is a gilded ship's prow, and the 'emperor of ice-cream' presides over funeral obsequies in a shabby household (64). 'It is the invasion of humanity That counts,' remarks a character in *Three Travellers Watch a Sunrise*. 'Only the rich remember the past,' the poet says (225) and even in 'Final Soliloquy of the Interior Paramour' (524) there is still a parenthetical association of new vision with a poverty which has nothing to lose.

In 'Peter Quince at the Clavier' beauty is called 'The fitful tracing of a portal.' Portal to what? The word itself seems to mean something to Stevens (*N.A.* 60, 155), and in the obviously very personal conclusion of 'The Rock' it is replaced by 'gate' (528). Perhaps Stevens, like Blake, has so far only given us the end of a golden string, and after traversing the circle of natural images we have still to seek the centre.

The normal unit of poetic expression is the metaphor, and Stevens was well aware of the importance of metaphor, as is evident from the many poems which use the word in title or text. His conception of metaphor is regrettably unclear, though clearer in the poetry than in the essays. He speaks of the creative process as beginning in the perception of 'resemblance,' adding that metamorphosis might be a better word (*N.A.* 72). By resemblance he does not mean naïve or associative resemblance, of the type that calls a flower a bleeding heart, but the repetitions of color and pattern in nature which become the elements of formal design in art. He goes on to develop this conception of resemblance into a conception of 'analogy' which, beginning in straight allegory, ends in the perception that 'poetry becomes and is a transcendent analogue composed of the particulars of reality' (*N.A.* 130). But nowhere in his essays does he suggest that metaphor is anything more than likeness or parallelism. 'There is always an analogy between nature and the imagination, and possibly poetry is merely the strange rhetoric of that parallel' (*N.A.* 118).

Clearly, if poetry is 'merely' this, the use of metaphor could only accentuate what Stevens' poetry tries to annihilate, the sense of a contrast or great gulf fixed between subject and object, consciousness and existence. And in fact we often find metaphor used pejoratively in the poems as a form of avoiding direct contact with reality. The motive for metaphor, we are told, is the shrinking from immediate experience (288). Stevens appears to mean by such metaphor, however, simile or comparison, 'the intricate evasions of as' (486; cf. 'Add This to Rhetoric,' 198). And metaphor is actually nothing of the kind. In its literal grammatical form metaphor is a statement of identity: this is that, A is B. And Stevens has a very strong sense of the crucial importance of poetic identification, 'where as and is are one' (476), as it is only there that one finds 'The poem of pure reality, untouched By trope or deviation' (471). Occasionally it occurs to him that metaphor might be used in a less pejorative sense. He speaks of 'The metaphor that murders metaphor' (*N.A.* 84), implying that a better kind of metaphor can get murdered, and 'Metaphor as Degeneration' (444) ends in a query how metaphor can really be degeneration when it is part of the process of seeing death as a part of life.

When metaphor says that one thing 'is' another thing, or that a man, a woman and a blackbird are one (93), things are being identified *with* other things. In logical identity there is only identification *as*. If I say that the Queen of England 'is' Elizabeth II, I have not identified one person with another, but one person as herself. Poetry also has this type of identification, for in poetic metaphor things are identified with each other, yet each is identified as itself, and retains that identity. When a man, a woman and a blackbird are said to be one, each remains what it is, and the identification heightens the distinctive form of each. Such a metaphor is necessarily illogical (or anti-logical, as in 'A violent disorder is an order') and hence poetic metaphors are opposed to likeness or similarity. A perception that a man, a woman and a blackbird were in some respects alike would be logical, but would not make much of a poem. Unfortunately in prose speech we often use the word identical to mean very similar, as in the phrase 'identical twins,' and this use makes it difficult to express the idea of poetic identity in a prose essay. But if twins were really identical they would be the same person, and hence could be different in form, like a man and the same man as a boy of seven. A world of total simile, where everything was like everything else, would be a world of total monotony; a world of total metaphor, where everything is identified as itself and with everything else, would be a world where subject and object, reality and mental organization of reality, are one. Such a world of total metaphor is the formal cause of poetry. Stevens makes it clear that the poet seeks the particular and discrete image: many of the poems in *Parts of a World,* such as 'On the Road Home' (203), express what the title of the book expresses, the uniqueness of every act of vision. Yet it is through the particular and discrete that we reach the unity of the imagination, which respects individuality, in contrast to the logical unity of the generalizing reason, which destroys it. The false unity of the dominating mind is what Stevens condemns in 'The Bagatelles the Madrigals' (213), and in the third part of 'The Pure Good of Theory' (331–2), where we find again a pejorative use of the term metaphor.

When a thing is identified as itself, it becomes an individual of a class or total form: when we identify a brown and green mass as a tree we provide a class name for it. This is the relating of species to genera which Aristotle spoke of as one of the central aspects of metaphor. The distinctively poetic use of such metaphor is the identifying of an individual with its class, where a tree becomes Wordsworth's 'tree of many one,' or a man becomes mankind. Poets ordinarily do not, like some philosophers, replace individual objects with their total forms; they do not, like allegorists, represent total forms by individuals. They see individual and class as metaphorically identical: in other words they work with *myths,* many of whom are human figures in whom the individual has been identified with its universal or total form.

Such myths, 'archaic forms, giants Of sense, evoking one thing in many men' (494) play a large role in Stevens' imagery. For some reason he speaks of the myth as 'abstract.' 'The Ultimate Poem is Abstract' (429; cf. 270, 223 and elsewhere), and the first requirement of the 'supreme fiction' is that it must be abstract (380), though as far as dictionary meanings are concerned one would expect rather to hear that it must be concrete. By abstract Stevens apparently means artificial in its proper sense, something constructed rather than generalized. In such a passage as this we can see the myth forming out of 'repetitions' as the individual soldier becomes the unknown soldier, and the unknown soldier the Adonis or continuously martyred god:

> How red the rose that is the soldier's wound,
> The wounds of many soldiers, the wounds of all
> The soldiers that have fallen, red in blood,
> The soldier of time grown deathless in great size. (318)

Just as there is false metaphor, so there is false myth. There is in particular the perverted myth of the average or 'root-man' (262), described more expressively as 'the total man of glubbal glub' (301). Whenever we have the root-man we have, by compensation, 'The superman friseured, possessing and possessed' (262), which is the perversion of the idea of *Übermenschlichkeit* (98) into the Carlylean great man or military hero. Wars are in their imaginative aspect a 'gigantomachia' (289) of competing aggressive myths. The war-myth or hero of death is the great enemy of the imagination: he cannot be directly fought except by another war-myth; he can only be contained in a greater and more genuine form of the same myth (280, section xv). The genuine form of the war-hero is the 'major man' (334; 387–8) who, in 'The Owl in the Sarcophagus,' is personified as peace (434), the direct opposite of the war-hero, and the third of the figures in 'the mythology of modern death' which, along with sleep and memory, conquer death for life.

We thus arrive at the conception of a universal or 'central man' (250), who may be identified with any man, such as a fisherman listening to wood-doves:

> The fisherman might be the single man
> In whose breast, the dove, alighting, would grow still. (357)

This passage, which combines the myth of the central man with the anima myth of the 'dove in the belly' (366), is from a poem with the painfully exact title, 'Thinking of a Relation between the Images of Metaphors.' The central man is often symbolized by glass or transparency, as in 'Asides on the Oboe' (250) and in 'Prologues to What is Possible' (515). If there is a central man, there is also a central mind (298) of which the poet feels peculiarly a part. Similarly there is a 'central poem' (441) identical with the world, and finally a 'general being or human universe' (378), of which all imaginative work forms part:

> That's it. The lover writes, the believer hears,
> The poet mumbles and the painter sees,
> Each one, his fated eccentricity,
> As a part, but part, but tenacious particle,
> Of the skeleton of the ether, the total
> Of letters, prophecies, perceptions, clods
> Of color, the giant of nothingness, each one
> And the giant ever changing, living in change. (443)

In 'Sketch of the Ultimate Politician' (335) we get a glimpse of this human universe as an infinite City of Man.

To sum up: the imaginative act breaks down the separation between subject and object, the perceiver shut up in 'the enclosures of hypothesis' (516) like an embryo in a 'naked egg' (173) or glass shell (297), and a perceived world similarly imprisoned in the remoteness of its 'irreducible X' (*N.A.* 83), which is also an egg (490). Separation is then replaced by the direct, primitive identification which Stevens ought to have called metaphor and which, not having a word for it, he calls 'description' (339) in one of his definitive poems, a term to which he elsewhere adds 'apotheosis' (378) and 'transformation' (514; cf. *N.A.* 49), which come nearer to what he really means. The maxim that art should conceal art is based on the sense that in the greatest art we have no sense of manipulating, posing or dominating over nature, but rather of emancipating it. 'One confides in what has no Concealed creator' (296), the poet says, and again:

> There might be, too, a change immenser than
> A poet's metaphors in which being would
>
> Come true, a point in the fire of music where
> Dazzle yields to a clarity and we observe,
>
> And observing is completing and we are content,
> In a world that shrinks to an immediate whole,
>
> That we do not need to understand, complete
> Without secret arrangements of it in the mind. (341)

The theoretical postulate of Stevens' poetry is a world of total metaphor, where the poet's vision may be identified with anything it visualizes. For such poetry the most accurate word is apocalyptic, a poetry of 'revelation' (344) in which all objects and experiences are united with a total mind. Such poetry gives us:

. . . the book of reconciliation,
Book of a concept only possible
In description, canon central in itself,
The thesis of the plentifullest John. (345)

Apocalypse, however, is one of the two great narrative myths that expand 'reality,' with its categories of time and space, into an infinite and eternal world. A myth of a total man recovering a total world is hardly possible without a corresponding myth of a Fall, or some account of what is wrong with our present perspective. Stevens' version of the Fall is similar to that of the 'Orphic poet' at the end of Emerson's *Nature:*

Why, then, inquire
Who has divided the world, what entrepreneur?
No man. The self, the chrysalis of all men

Became divided in the leisure of blue day
And more, in branchings after day. One part
Held fast tenaciously in common earth

And one from central earth to central sky
And in moonlit extensions of them in the mind
Searched out such majesty as it could find. (468–9)

Such poetry sounds religious, and in fact does have the infinite perspective of religion, for the limits of the imagination are the conceivable, not the real, and it extends over death as well as life. In the imagination the categories of 'reality,' space and time, are reversed into form and creation respectively, for art is 'Description without Place' (339) standing at the centre of 'ideal time' (*N.A.* 88), and its poetry is 'even older than the ancient world' (*N.A.* 145). Religion seems to have a monopoly of talking about infinite and eternal worlds, and poetry that uses such conceptions seems to be inspired by a specifically religious interest. But the more we study poetry, the more we realize that the dogmatic limiting of the poet's imagination to human and subhuman nature that we find, for instance, in Hardy and Housman, is not normal to poetry but a technical *tour de force*. It is the normal language of poetic imagination itself that is heard when Yeats says that man has invented death; when Eliot reaches the still point of the turning world; when Rilke speaks of the poet's perspective as that of an angel containing all time and space, blind and looking into himself; when Stevens finds his home in 'The place of meta-men and para-things' (448). Such language may or may not go with a religious commitment: in itself it is simply poetry speaking as poetry must when it gets to a certain pitch of metaphorical concentration. Stevens says that his motive is neither 'to console Nor sanctify, but plainly to propound' (389).

In *Harmonium,* published in the Scott Fitzgerald decade, Stevens moves in a highly sensuous atmosphere of fine pictures, good food, exquisite taste and luxury cruises. In the later poems, though the writing is as studiously oblique as ever, the sensuousness has largely disappeared, and the reader accustomed only to *Harmonium* may feel that Stevens' inspiration has failed him, or that he is attracted by themes outside his capacity, or that the impact of war and other ironies of the autumnal vision has shut him up in an uncommunicative didacticism. Such a view of Stevens is of course superficial, but the critical issue it raises is a genuine one.

In the criticism of drama there is a phrase in which the term 'theatrical' becomes pejorative, when one tries to distinguish genuine dramatic imagination from the conventional clichés of dramatic rhetoric. Of course eventually this pejorative use has to disappear, because Shakespeare and Aeschylus are quite as theatrical as Cecil de Mille. Similarly, one also goes through a stage, though a shorter one, in which the term 'poetic' may acquire a slightly pejorative cast, as when one may decide, several hundred pages deep in Swinburne, that Swinburne can sometimes be a poetic bore. Eventually one realizes that the 'poetic' quality comes from allusiveness, the incorporating into the texture of echoes, cadences, names and thoughts derived from the author's previous literary experience. Swinburne is poetic in a poor sense when he is being a parasite on the literary tradition; Eliot is poetic in a better sense when, in his own phrase, he steals rather than imitates. The 'poetic' normally expresses itself as what one might loosely call word-magic or incantation, charm in its original sense of spell, as it reinforces the 'act of the mind' in poetry with the dream-like reverberations, echoes and enlarged significances of the memory and the unconscious. We suggested at the beginning that Eliot lacks what Stevens has, the sense of an autonomous poetic theory as an inseparable part of poetic practice. On the other hand Eliot has pre-eminently the sense of a creative tradition, and this sense is partly what makes his poetry so uniquely penetrating, so easy to memorize unconsciously.

In Stevens there is a good deal of incantation and imitative harmony; but the deliberately 'magical' poems, such as 'The Idea of Order at Key

West,' 'To the One of Fictive Music,' and the later 'Song of Fixed Accord' have the special function of expressing a stasis or harmony between imagination and reality, and hence have something of a conscious rhetorical exercise about them. In 'The Idea of Order at Key West' the sense of carefully controlled artifice enters the theme as well. In other poems where the texture is dryer and harder, the schemata on which 'word-magic' depends are reduced to a minimum. The rhymes, for instance, when they occur, are usually sharp barking assonances, parody-rhymes (e.g., 'The Swedish cart to be part of the heart,' 369), and the metres, like the curious blank *terza rima* used so often, are almost parody-metres. A quality that is not far from being anti-'poetic' seems to emerge.

Just as the 'poetic' is derived mainly from the reverberations of tradition, so it is clear that the anti-'poetic' quality in Stevens is the result of his determination to make it new, in Pound's phrase, to achieve in each poem a unique expression and force his reader to make a correspondingly unique act of apprehension. This is a part of what he means by 'abstract' as a quality of the 'supreme fiction.' It was Whitman who urged American writers to lay less emphasis on tradition, thereby starting another tradition of his own, and it is significant that Whitman is one of the very few traditional poets Stevens refers to, though he has little in common with him technically. It is partly his sense of a poem as belonging to experiment rather than tradition, separated from the stream of time with its conventional echoes, that gives Stevens' poetry its marked affinity with pictures, an affinity shown also in the curiously formalized symmetry of the longer poems. 'Notes Towards a Supreme Fiction,' for instance, has three parts of ten sections each, each section with seven tercets, and similarly rectangular distributions of material are found in other poems.

When we meet a poet who has so much rhetorical skill, and yet lays so much emphasis on novelty and freshness of approach, the skill acquires a quality of courage: a courage that is without compromise in a world full of cheap rhetoric, yet uses none of the ready-made mixes of rhetoric in a world full of compromise. Stevens was one of the most courageous poets of our time, and his conception of the poem as 'the heroic effort to live expressed As victory' (446) was unyielding from the beginning. Courage implies persistence, and persistence in a distinctive strain often develops its complementary opposite as well, as with Blake's fool who by persisting in his folly became wise. It was persistence that transformed the tropical lushness of *Harmonium* into the austere clairvoyance of *The Rock,* the luxurious demon into the necessary angel, and so rounded out a vision of major scope and intensity. As a result Stevens became, unlike many others who may have started off with equal abilities, not one of our expendable rhetoricians, but one of our small handful of essential poets.

A. ALVAREZ

D. H. Lawrence: The Single State of Man

(1957)

Art itself doesn't interest me, only the spiritual content.
D. H. Lawrence, Letter to Eunice Tietjens, 1917.

The only native English poet of any importance to survive the First World War was D. H. Lawrence.[1] Yet his verse is very little read. As a minor adjunct to the novels it has come in, on occasions, for a little off-hand comment. More often it is used as a go-between, joining the prose to the biography. Anthologists have printed a few poems grudgingly, out of piety, and even the critic who introduced the best English selection, in *The Penguin Poets,* seemed to feel that the poems succeed despite themselves, because they were written by Lawrence.

I had better state my position straight away: I think the poems very fine indeed, with a fineness of perception and development that was always Lawrence's, and an originality that makes them as important as any poetry of our time. For their excellence comes from something that is rare at best, and now, in the 1950s, well-nigh lost: a complete truth to feeling. Lawrence is the foremost emotional realist of the century. He wrote too much verse, like Hardy and Whitman, the two poets who influenced him most. But even his badness is the badness of genius; and there are quite enough good poems to make up for it. As for the influences and the styles he brushed with, Georgian and Imagist, I will have nothing to say of them here. They have no part in his best work.

Lawrence's poetry is usually hustled out of court by way of its 'carelessness.' I believe it was Eliot who first said that Lawrence wrote only sketches for poems, nothing ever quite finished. In one way there is some truth to this: he was not interested in surface polish; his verse is informal in the conventional sense. Indeed, the tighter the form the more the poet struggles:

> Many roses in the wind
> Are tapping at the window-sash.
> A hawk is in the sky; his wings
> Slowly begin to plash.
> ('Love Storm')

It is the last word that jars. I see what he means, but the need to rhyme is like a wedge driven between the object and the word. The thing is forced and uneasy, even a little journalistic. Again and again, when Lawrence uses strict metrical forms, the poetry fails because of them, or succeeds despite them. At times he can manage complicated stanzas, but only because they allow him to get away from close correspondence of rhyme; they give him space to move around. The fainter the chime, the more remote the echo, the more convinced the poetry seems; close and perfect rhyme is invariably a constriction to him. For an essential part of Lawrence's genius was his fluency; and I mean something more literal than the ease with which he wrote: rather, the sense of direction in all the flowing change and variation in his work. This fluency has its own forms without its own conventions. It is not plottable: ear-count, finger-count and what might be called the logic of received form have nothing to do with it. What matters is the disturbance. 'It doesn't depend on the ear, particularly,' he once wrote, 'but on the sensitive soul.' It is something that can never be laid out into a system, for it comes instead from the poet's rigorous but open alertness. And so there is care, even discipline, but no formal perfection and finish. In an introductory note to *Fire and Other Poems* Frieda Lawrence wrote: 'He just wrote down his verse as it came to him. But later, when he thought of putting them into a book to be printed, he would work them over with great care and infinite patience.' And she has remarked that in a way he worked harder at his poetry than at the novels. When the prose would not go right he threw it away and began afresh. But the poems he worked over again and again. As proof there are the early drafts of 'Bavarian Gentians' and 'The Ship of Death,' which are now printed as an appendix to the *Collected Poems*. Still, his diligence had nothing to do with mere technical efficiency. Lawrence's controlling standard was delicacy: a constant, fluid awareness, nearer the checks of intimate talk than those of regular prosody. His poetry is not the outcome of rules and formal craftsmanship, but of a purer, more native and immediate artistic sensibility. It is poetry because it could not be otherwise.

He was well aware of what he was about. He put his case in the introduction to *New Poems:*

> To break the lovely form of metrical verse, and dish up the fragments as a new substance, called *vers libre,* this is what most of the free-versifiers accomplish. They do not know that free verse has its own *nature,* that it is neither star nor pearl, but instantaneous like plasm. . . . It has no finish. It has no satisfying stability, satisfying for those who like the immutable. None of this. It is the instant; the quick.

If Lawrence is trying to get the weight of formalism off his back, it is not for laziness. 'The instant; the quick' is as difficult to catch, to fix in exact language, as the most measured and stable formulations of experience. For this sort of impulse is in opposition to poetic conventions. The writer can never rely on a code of poetic manners to do part of the work for him. At the same time, of course, Lawrence knew his own powers and limitations well enough to realize that 'art' in some way deflected him from the real poetry. 'Art for my sake,' he said. Perhaps this is what he meant in the introduction to the *Collected Poems:*

> The first poems I ever wrote, if poems they were, was when I was nineteen: now twenty-three years ago. I remember perfectly the Sunday afternoon when I perpetrated those first two pieces: 'To Guelder Roses' and 'To Campions'; in springtime, of course, and, as I say, in my twentieth year. Any young lady might have written them and been pleased with them; as I was pleased with them. But it was after that, when I was twenty, that my real demon would now and then get hold of me and shake more real poems out of me, making me uneasy. I never 'liked' my real poems as I liked 'To Guelder Roses.' . . . Some of the earliest poems are a good deal rewritten. They were struggling to say something which it takes a man twenty years to be able to say. . . . A young man is afraid of his demon and puts his hand over the demon's mouth some-

> times and speaks for him. And the things the young man says are very rarely poetry. So I have tried to let the demon say his say, and to remove the passages where the young man intruded. So that, in the first volume, many poems are changed, some entirely rewritten, recast. But usually this is only because the poem started out to be something which it didn't quite achieve, because the young man interfered with his demon.

This is at the opposite pole to Eliot's defence of Pound's hard work. For Eliot, the continued business of versifying was a way of keeping the bed aired until such time as the Muse should decide to visit. Lawrence's work was in coming to terms with his demon, so that the utterance would be unhindered. For it was the utterance, what he had to say, which was poetic; not the analysable form and technique. So for all his trouble, he never innovated in Pound's or Eliot's way. His discoveries were a matter of personal judgment and response. In the poems the speed and stress varies with the immediate, inward pressure. This is why the words 'loose' and 'careless' so clearly do not describe Lawrence's verse.

To have an example down on the page, there is 'End of Another Home Holiday.' To my mind, it is the best of the early *Rhyming Poems*. The demon has his say without awkwardness, but there is just enough of the earlier contrivance to show what Lawrence had left behind:

When shall I see the half-moon sink again
Behind the black sycamore at the end of the garden?
When will the scent of the dim white phlox
Creep up the wall to me, and in at my open window?

Why is it, the long, slow stroke of the midnight bell
    (Will it never finish the twelve?)
Falls again and again on my heart with a heavy reproach?

The moon-mist is over the village, out of the mist speaks the bell,
And all the little roofs of the village bow low, pitiful,
  beseeching, resigned.
—Speak, you my home! what is it I don't do well?

Ah home, suddenly I love you
As I hear the sharp clean trot of a pony down the road,

Succeeding sharp little sounds dropping into silence
Clear upon the long-drawn hoarseness of a train across the valley.

. . .

The light has gone out from under my mother's door.
  That she should love me so!—
  She, so lonely, greying now!
  And I leaving her,
  Bent on my pursuits!

    Love is the great Asker.
    The sun and the rain do not ask the secret
    Of the time when the grain struggles down in the dark.
    The moon walks her lonely way without anguish,
    Because no-one grieves over her departure.

Forever, ever by my shoulder pitiful love will linger,
Crouching as the little houses crouch under the mist when I turn.
Forever, out of the mist, the church lifts up a reproachful finger,
Pointing my eyes in wretched defiance where love hides her face to
    mourn.

    Oh! but the rain creeps down to wet the grain
    That struggles alone in the dark,
    And asking nothing, patiently steals back again!
    The moon sets forth o' nights
    To walk the lonely, dusky heights
    Serenely, with steps unswerving;
    Pursued by no sigh of bereavement,
    No tears of love unnerving
    Her constant tread:
    While ever at my side,
    Frail and sad, with grey, bowed head,
    The beggar-woman, the yearning-eyed
    Inexorable love goes lagging.

  The wild young heifer, glancing distraught,
  With a strange new knocking of life at her side
    Runs seeking a loneliness.
  The little grain draws down the earth, to hide.
  Nay, even the slumberous egg, as it labours under the shell
    Patiently to divide and self-divide,
  Asks to be hidden, and wishes nothing to tell.

But when I draw the scanty cloak of silence over my eyes
Piteous love comes peering under the hood;
Touches the clasp with trembling fingers, and tries
To put her ear to the painful sob of my blood;
While her tears soak through to my breast,
    Where they burn and cauterise.

. . .

The moon lies back and reddens.
In the valley a corncrake calls
    Monotonously,
With a plaintive, unalterable voice, that deadens
    My confident activity;
With a hoarse, insistent request that falls
    Unweariedly, unweariedly,
Asking something more of me,
    Yet more of me.

I have put the poem there in full because, like all of Lawrence's verse, it needs its whole length to express its complexity. It seems to me a difficult poem. Yet there is nothing immediately incomprehensible about it, none of those tought intellectual obstacles that stop you short in Eliot's work. There is a curious intermixing of people and scene and nature. But beyond that the difficulty is in the state of mind: the pull between love and guilt, the tension between man and child.

It is all in the first four lines. They have a kind of awakened rhythm which cuts below the expectations of formality to the 'sensitive soul.' As Lawrence said of a line by Whitman, 'It makes me prick my innermost ear.' Only in the first ten-syllabled line will finger-count pay. After that the poem moves off on its own way. There is more in question than nostalgia: the speed of the lines varies with the flexibility of the talking voice. Part troubled, part meditative, the nostalgia is quickened instead of being expanded into a mood. If my comments are vague and assertive, I can only add another assertion: they have to be. Everything depends on the reader's direct response to the rhythm. In that is all the disturbance which the rest of the poem defines.

Perhaps 'define' is the wrong word; 'draw out' might be closer. For what follows is done without a hint of abstraction. What is there to be defined is a complex of feelings, nothing that can be tidily separated out into formulae. All that is possible, and all the poet attempts, is to reach through intelligence some balance in the conflict.

Why is it, the long, slow stroke of the midnight bell
(Will it never finish the twelve?)
Falls again and again on my heart with a heavy reproach?

There are three forces: the young man, literary and fond of word-painting; then, undercutting him, uneasy impatience; and finally, guilt. Mercifully, there is no need to go through the poem line by line to show how these two feelings take over all the details of the scene, so that it becomes a sort of living presence for the poet to face. The result is that he can move from his village to his mother, from natural to artistic creation, without the least strain.

The poet is peculiarly unembarrassed and open about his feelings. He values his independence, but he doesn't assert it: the hint of self-absorption in 'Bent on my pursuits' has the same touch of irony about it as, for example,

But when I draw the scanty cloak of silence over my eyes
Piteous love comes peering under the hood;

And his central theme, 'Love is the great Asker,' is both acknowledgment *and* criticism: the demands of love touch the vital part of him, 'Where they burn and cauterise'; yet even while they expose what is shallow and selfish in him, they expose themselves by their own nagging insistence.

The theme is love, but there is nothing in the poem of a 'Definition of Love,' with all that implies of dapper logic and clear-cut distinctions. Lawrence's logic is more intimate. It is carried forward by a rigorous worrying, probing down to the quick of the feelings. Although the personal conflict is set off by the cycle of nature, no parallels are drawn. The forces work in harmony rather than in contradistinction. Despite all the talk of the sun and the moon, the grain and the heifer, and even that 'slumberous egg,' the focus stays personal. In phrases like

No tears of love *unnerving*
Her constant tread

you see how the same difficult, intimate preoccupation runs under the whole thing. So without any of Marvell's syllogizing there is still a completeness to the poem; in the end, something has been settled. It is done by what Eliot called a 'logic of sensibility' (though, in fact, he probably meant something quite different). The toughness, instead of being in the logic, is in the truth to feeling, the constant exertion of the poet's intelligence to get close to what he really feels, not to accept on the way any easy formulation or avoidance.

This is why a set metre would have been impossible—as it was impossible in Coleridge's 'Dejection.' Each line has its own force and rhythm, and they flow together, varying with the shifts in feeling. This is true of almost all Lawrence's poems; the inner pressure and disturbance gives to every one its own inherent form. Each starts afresh and appeals directly to the attention of 'the sensitive soul.' The controlling factor is in the intelligence. His poems are not effusions; they don't run off with him. Instead, the intelligence works away at the emotions, giving to each poem a finished quality, an economy in all the repetitions. It is a matter of the fullness with which the subject is presented.

This intelligent honesty and pertinacity of Lawrence's verse has had very little attention. The poems which have come in for most notice, the *Birds, Beasts and Flowers,* are usually thought of as little more than vivid little pieces of description, like the so-called 'lyric' passages in his novels. In fact, the nature poems are quite as personal as any of his others. In them he doesn't merely describe, nor does he go at his subjects with a preconceived idea and try to twist them into meanings they would not naturally take. They are neither all subject nor all poet. It is a matter of a vital and complex relationship between the two, difficult, fluent, inward and wholly unabstract. He even avoids the final abstraction of formal perfection. For that gives to experience a kind of ghostly Platonic idealness: in the end, everything is so perfectly accounted for that the poetic world is complete and isolated. In the relationship Lawrence tries to catch, everything is in flux; it is a flow between two creatures, with nothing fixed. The artist has constantly to improvise at the full pitch of his intelligence. And according to Lawrence, who judged intelligence by its delicacy and awareness, not by its command of rationalization, the greater the intelligence the nearer the result came to poetry:

> It has always seemed to me that a real thought, a single thought, not an argument, can only exist easily in verse, or in some poetic form. There is a didactic element about prose thoughts which makes them repellent, slightly bullying.
>
> (Foreword to *Pansies*).

The same sort of intelligence is at work in the novels, but the actual method is rather different. Again, the didactic sections hardly matter

—though in some of the later novels they take up more space than they are worth. The whole method is to set the characters in motion, so there is a curious fusion of feeling and action, each dependent on the other, deepening the other, and yet resisting any single interpretation. Hence the word 'symbolism' that is often tacked on to his method; I prefer Dr. Leavis's term, 'dramatic poem.' Of course, Lawrence himself is there in all his novels; but at the remove of fiction. There is no need to make an exact identification, for the author has given himself enough room to dramatize and judge with a free hand. The poems are more intimate, and their personal statements are outright. He said of the *Collected Poems:* 'I have tried to establish a chronological order, because many of the poems are so personal that, in their fragmentary fashion, they make up a biography of an emotional and inner life.' There precisely is the difference: the theme of both the novels and the poems is fulfilment, the spiritual maturity achieved between man and woman. But in the novels the fulfilment is acted out; the forces, like the morality, are 'passionate, implicit.' By contrast, the poems present nakedly the inner flow that runs below the actions, the forces before they are externalized in drama. It is as though they presented not the body that acts but the blood itself, the lifeline of experience and feeling that feeds and supports the novels.

Here, for example, is a passage from a novel which develops much the same theme as 'End of Another Home Holiday':

> No man was beyond woman. But in his one quality of ultimate maker and breaker, he was womanless. Harriet denied this, bitterly. She wanted to share, to join in, not to be left out lonely. He looked at her in distress, and did not answer. It is a knot that can never be untied; it can only, like a navel string, be broken or cut.
>
> For the moment, however, he said nothing. But Somers knew from his dreams what she was feeling: his dreams of a woman, a woman he loved, something like Harriet, something like his mother, and yet unlike either, a woman sullen and obstinate against him, repudiating him. Bitter the woman was grieved beyond words, grieved till her face was swollen and puffy and almost mad or imbecile, because she had loved him so much, and now she must see him betray her love. That was how the dream woman put it: he had betrayed her great love, and she must go down desolate into an everlasting hell, denied,

and denying him absolutely in return, a sullen, awful soul. The face reminded him of Harriet, and of his mother, and of his sister, and of girls he had known when he was younger—strange glimpses of all of them, each glimpse excluding the last. And at the same time in the terrible face some of the look of that bloated face of a madwoman which hung over Jane Eyre in the night in Mr. Rochester's house.

The Somers of the dream was terribly upset. He cried tears from his very bowels, and laid his hand on the woman's arm saying:

'But I love you. Don't you *believe* in me? Don't you *believe* in me?' But the woman, she seemed almost old now—only shed a few bitter tears, bitter as vitriol, from her distorted face, and bitterly, hideously turned away, dragging her arm from the touch of his fingers; turned, as it seemed to the dream-Somers, away to the sullen and dreary, everlasting hell of repudiation.

He woke at this, and listened to the thunder of the sea with horror. With horror. Two women in his life he had loved down to the quick of life and death: his mother and Harriet. And the woman in the dream was so awfully his mother, risen from the dead, and at the same time Harriet, as it were, departing from this life, that he stared at the night-paleness between the window-curtains in horror.

'They neither of them believed in me,' he said to himself. Still in the spell of the dream, he put it into the past tense, though Harriet lay sleeping in the next bed. He could not get over it.

This is from *Kangaroo,* where Somers is no less Lawrence than the much younger man who wrote the poem. And the same demon is at work in both, the same crucifixion between guilt and love, between independent male activity and unanswerable emotional ties; and, in the end, the same sense of inevitable betrayal. Yet although the dream allows Lawrence to use a kind of emotional shorthand and a bare directness of presentation, the novel and the poem only converge from opposite directions. In the verse the feelings *are happening* to the poet in all their conflict. In the novel they are embodied in action. They are given sides and the complexity is left to flower in the spaces between.

The whole of Lawrence's power and originality as a poet depends on the way he keeps close to his feelings. This is why he had to rid himself of conventional forms. The poems take even their shape from the feelings. And so it is a long way off the mark to think of them as jotted-down talk. The span of the lines is not that of the talking voice. The tone is: that is, it is direct and without self-consciousness. But the poems, for instance, use more repetitions than talk. Yet this is a matter of fullness, not of rhetorical elaboration. It is part of the purposefulness with which the poems explore the emotions in their entirety. And with the same sureness he can let them go; when he is writing from no more than an impulse or an irritation, short and transient, the poetry is equally brief and to the point—*Pansies,* for example; but when the feelings are profound and sustained, so is the verse-form: as in, say, 'Bavarian Gentians,' one of his masterpieces. The dependence of the form on the subject means that the poems find it very hard to rarify themselves into mere words and device.

The lines themselves help to the accuracy and delicacy of the expression. They are a means of emphasis rather than a pause for breath:

He drank enough
And lifted his head, dreamily, as one who has drunken,
And flickered his tongue like a forked night on the air, so black,
Seeming to lick his lips,
And looked around like a god, unseeing, into the air, . . .
('Snake')

Again, it is a question of movement, or rather of two movements, one playing against the other. There are actions, the ordinary, recognizable sanity of things happening in a human, or almost human way; these get the short matter-of-fact lines: 'He drank enough,' 'Seeming to lick his lips.' And then, in subtle contrast, is the running, disturbed movement of the longer lines in which the poet catches up the factual description into his own excitement. The known merges with the unknown: 'as one who has drunken' becomes 'like a forked night on the air,' and ends 'like a god.' And so, within the framework of a description, the interchange between these two creatures takes on the dignity of a strange visitation. He is unloosing, in fact, the reserves of power of two earlier lines in the poem:

Someone was before me at my water-trough,
And I, like a second comer, waiting.

For all the implications, there is nothing 'other-worldly' about this. The stuff of Lawrence's poetry, the 'lifeline,' are those essential experiences in which he registers his full humanity. His poems are the inner flow of a man in the act of becoming aware—aware not only of his feelings and their cause, but of their full implications. By the flexibility of his verse-forms he can catch this flow in all its immediacy, and with peculiarly little fuss. For fuss has no part in what he has to say. Lawrence is not a mystic; his poetry has to do with recognitions, not with revelations. It should be read not against the cant of 'dark gods' and the stridency of *The Plumed Serpent,* but against the sanity of the 'creed' with which he answered Benjamin Franklin:

That I am I.
That my soul is a dark forest.
That my known self will never be more than a little clearing in the forest.
That gods, strange gods, come forth from the forest into the clearing of my known self, and then go back.
That I must have the courage to let them come and go.
That I will never let mankind put anything over me, but that I will always try to recognize and submit to the gods in me and the gods

There is only reverence, attention, awareness and an unprejudiced independent intelligence at the bottom of this; no other-worldliness, nothing in the least of overblown pretension. It is the imaginative strength with which Lawrence voiced the fullness of his humanity that has got him the name of mystic and prophet, as it did for Blake. Lawrence does not have second sight, he has only a piercingly clear first sight. His genius is in rendering that, rather than waiting until his perceptions have gathered about them a decent abstraction, as the warm-blooded body of a whale is enclosed in protective blubber. Lawrence's mysticism is merely his first-handness, his distance from convention.

Earlier, I remarked that the controlling force in the verse is neither any formal metrical guide nor a set of preordained principles; it is the working intelligence. On this his most genuine and effective poetry relies. The intelligence is primarily in the honesty with which he acknowledges his feelings and recognizes his motives with neither shuffling nor abstraction. But it is there too in the wit, the endless liveliness of his verse:

How beastly the bourgeois is
especially the male of the species—

Presentable, eminently presentable—
shall I make you a present of him?

Or

It is a fearful thing to fall into the hands of the living God
But it is a much more fearful thing to fall out of them . . .

Or

You tell me I am wrong.
Who are you, who is anybody to tell me I am wrong?
I am not wrong.

The closeness of this last to 'For Godsake hold your tongue, and let me love' seems to me to be apparent enough. Yet Lawrence's verse, for all its wit and swing, has never been resurrected in the craze for Donne. The reason is simply that the twentieth-century Metaphysical style has been used as an excuse for obliqueness. The canons of irony invoked to display its excellence are merely ways of avoiding commitment, a technical sleight of mind by which the poet can seem to take many sides while settling, in fact, for none. Lawrence, clearly, does not suffer from this—neither, I believe, did Donne. The wit of both is not a sparkle on top of indifference; it is a manifestation of intelligence:

Imagine that any mind ever *thought* a red geranium!
As if the redness of a red geranium could be anything but a
sensual experience
and as if sensual experience could take place before there
were any senses.
We know that even God could not imagine the redness of a
red geranium
nor the smell of mignonette
when geraniums were not, and mignonette neither.
And even when they were, even God would have to have
a nose to smell at the mignonette.
You can't imagine the Holy Ghost sniffing at cherry-pie
heliotrope.
Or the Most High, during the coal age, cudgelling his mighty
brains
even if he had any brains: straining his mighty mind
to think, among the moss and mud of lizards and mastodons
to think out, in the abstract, when all was twilit green and
muddy:
'Now there shall be tum-tiddly-um, and tum-tiddly-um,
hey presto! scarlet geranium!'

We know it couldn't be done.
But imagine, among the mud and the mastodons
god sighing and yearning with tremendous creative yearning,
in that dark green mess
oh, for some other beauty, some other beauty
that blossomed at last, red geranium, and mignonette.

It is hard to know whether to emphasize more the ease and originality of the piece, or its tact. There is neither a jot of pretentiousness in the poem, nor of vulgarity, though the opportunity for both certainly offered. Lawrence uses his wit not in the modern fashion, to save his face, but to strengthen the seriousness of what he has to say. There is no disproportion between the colloquial liveliness of the opening and the equally alive tenderness of the close. The wit is not a flourish; it is one of the poetic means; it preserves the seriousness from sentimentality and overstatement, as the seriousness keeps the wit from flippancy.

Lawrence wrote too many poems. Their standard is not uniformly high; some of them are frankly bad. In this count I am leaving out *Pansies* and *Nettles*. Though some of these are good, they were intended primarily as squibs; and even if they have a serious enough edge to their satire, few are particularly memorable as poetry. Nor is he to be held responsible for the faults of his early verse; they are the faults of a poet who is still trying to find his own voice. The bad poems are those which have a complete originality, yet still fail. For example, the sequence 'Wedlock' in *Look! We Have Come Through!* the transitional volume. Like his best poems, they go down to the pith of the feelings and present that in its singleness. But they fail because they are too naked. It is as though the feelings were overwhelming beyond speech, yet still the poet insisted on nothing less than their full force, muffled by no sort of poetic device. In 'Burnt Norton' Eliot justifies a long series of images which suggest an intense experience without stating it, by the comment: 'Human kind Cannot bear very much reality.' In these poems, Lawrence is insisting on nothing short of the emotional reality, and the poetry cannot quite bear it. They are not private as the *Pisan Cantos* are private; they have no references which remain in the poet's keeping. They are private in the other sense: they make the reader feel he is listening in where he shouldn't be. It is for this reason that *Look!*, although it contains some excellent poems, is more successful as a series than in any one piece. Lawrence himself said, 'They are intended as an essential story, or history, or confession,' and Amy Lowell thought they made up 'a greater novel even than *Sons and Lovers.*' That is an overstatement which was worth making. The impact of the book seems to me as direct and painful as anything since Clare. Yet it would be hard to localize this power in any one poem. If some of the pieces fail because of their nakedness, it is because they are approaching the vanishing-point of poetry, where expression itself is some sort of intrusion. It took genius and great courage even to fail in that way. When Lawrence's poems are bad they are victims of that peculiar honesty which, at other times, made for their strength.

Lawrence was honest about the emotions without being absorbed in them for their own sakes. He is not taken up in himself. The life-line of his poems is something more active, harder and more delicate. 'But it's no good,' he wrote to Murry, 'Either you go on wheeling a wheelbarrow and lecturing at Cambridge and going softer and softer inside, or you make a hard fight with yourself, pull yourself up, harden yourself, throw your feelings down the drain and face the world as a fighter. —You won't though.' Lawrence's poems are about that 'hard fight.' He never relished his feelings, nor played with them in front of the mirror; hence he never simplified them. But he always kept extraordinarily close to them; and so he never fell into oversubtlety, the intellectual counterpart of emotional looseness. The language of the poems, lucid, witty, vivid, often a bit slangy, preserved the balance. It made any kind of overstatement or evasion very hard.

The question why Lawrence's poetry has had so little recognition, despite its originality, delicacy, wit and, above all, its honesty and intelligence, is answered in that word 'carelessness.' Our modern poetry began with a vigorous attack on outworn conventions of feeling and expression. But the emphasis has gradually gone so much on the craft and technicality of writing that the original wholeness and freshness is again lost. One sort of academic nullity has been replaced by another: the English 'gentleman-of-letters' conceit, which prevailed at least until the end of the Georgians, has gone under. In its place is a Germanic *ponderismuskeit,* a deadening technical thoroughness. Lawrence's demon is as out of place in that as it was in the old port-and-tweed tradition.

I used to think that one of the troubles with the poetry we have now was that, despite the stress Eliot has laid on the intelligence, no one seemed capable of thinking. I was wrong—not about the inability to think, but in expecting it at all; or at least in expecting thinking to be carried on with something of the precision of the seventeenth century.

Of course, no one is trained in the syllogism; nowadays that sort of logical clarity is impossible, or it is forced. In place of the old patterns the modern poet has to rely far more heavily on his own native intelligence, on his ability to feel accurately, without conceit or indulgence; to feel, that is, when he has 'thrown his feelings down the drain.' He is left then not with a vague blur of emotions or a precise, empty dialectic, but with the essential thread that runs beneath the confusion, with 'the instant; the quick.' This, I believe, is the real material of poetry, material which could not take any other form. This inner logic is quite as difficult as its older formal counterpart. It depends on getting close to the real feelings and presenting them without formulae and without avoidance, in all their newness, disturbance and ugliness. If a poet does that he will not find himself writing in Lawrence's style; but, like Lawrence, he may speak out in his own voice, single and undisguised.[2]

NOTES

1. Robert Graves, whose poetry I admire, does not seem to me to have survived the war. For all his debonairness he has remained essentially a war poet. That is, he has created a drawing-room art out of anything but drawing-room feelings. His moments of savagery and tenderness appear like crevasses in a snowfield, unexpected and disconcerting. Lawrence himself summed it up in *Aaron's Rod:* 'In this officer, of course, there was a lightness and an appearance of bright diffidence and humour. But underneath it was all the same as in the common men of all combatant nations: the hot, seared burn of unbearable experience, which did not heal nor cool, and whose irritation was not to be relieved. The experience gradually cooled on top: but only with a surface crust. The soul did not heal, did not recover.'
2. Since writing this chapter it has occurred to me that the clue to the technical originality of Lawrence's mature verse may be that it has a different metrical norm from most other English poetry. Its point of departure is not the iambic pentameter; instead, it is the terser movement of his narrative *prose*. I can see no other way of explaining the extraordinarily wide and subtle variation of rhythmical period within the span of the single line of free verse.

GROVER SMITH

Visions and Revisions: the 'Ariel Poems'

(1957)

Eliot himself bears witness (1932) to the suggestion 'that a dramatic poet cannot create characters of the greatest intensity of life unless his personages, in their reciprocal actions and behaviour in their story, are somehow dramatizing, but in no obvious form, an action or struggle for harmony in the soul of the poet.' [1] This formula, which Eliot complained that the dramatist John Ford had neglected, might be useful to a playwright, though the words 'in no obvious form,' very strictly construed, could vitiate any outside critical judgments it inspired. Regrettably the ideal animating the formula is merely chimerical if a writer packs all the important conflict into one personage, substitutes declamation for drama, and leaves to the supporting characters no task but nugatory comment and static personification. Eliot has impressive success in conceiving a protagonist and bitter difficulty in manipulating the other actors so that they, and not simply the protagonist's utterances, carry on the dramatic movement. This is one reason his poems are better than his first plays. The 'struggle for harmony in the soul of the poet' often traduces the other dramatic values by assuming objective form as a monologue more suitable for a poem.[2] That form dominates later works of his third period, from 1927 to 1932. None of the major poems except 'Triumphal March,' the worst of the lot, pretends to be anything technically but a meditation by a single voice; even 'Triumphal March' has a strong monologue at the core. For the sake of his art at the time, it is fortunate that Eliot was able to keep away from poetic drama and exercise the skill he best understood.

The internal conflict in 'Journey of the Magi' (1927) is typical for the period. This poem was Eliot's first contribution to Faber and Faber's 'Ariel Poems' by contemporary writers. The numbers of the series, he has remarked, 'were published during four or five successive years as a kind of Christmas card. Nobody else seemed to want the title afterward, so I kept it for myself simply to designate four of my poems which appeared in this way.' [3] These were 'Journey of the Magi,' 'A Song for Simeon,' 'Animula,' and 'Marina.' His fifth such poem, 'Triumphal March,' forms the opening of *Coriolan;* 'The Cultivation of Christmas Trees,' a companion piece to 'Animula,' dates from Faber's revival of the series in 1954.[4] 'Journey of the Magi,' though it seems a new version of 'Gerontion,' differs from it thematically in ignoring the panorama of history. Hence its drama of a bewildered, shaken man, despite remoteness from the contemporary scene, appears more pertinent than that of 'Gerontion' to Eliot's own spiritual quest. Examined along with external evidence of his beliefs, the poem seems to concern a more advanced stage of the religious struggle already manifested.

Eliot's confirmation as an Anglican churchman occurred in 1927, the year in which he became a British subject. His statement of his tenets, in the Preface to *For Lancelot Andrewes* (1928),[5] followed by two years the original publication of the title essay, itself a clue to his position. His occasional reviews had also revealed an intellectual attitude toward Christianity consistent with his later profession of belief. But the earliest hint of the direction in which he was set had presented itself in his poems. These, however, had affirmed the emotional hollowness of the soul distraught between the demands of flesh and spirit; they had implied nothing about the intellectual religious convictions of their author. Eliot has remarked that rational assent to Christianity may precede Christian sentiments; his conversion could have come only at the end of a long period of vacillation.[6]

'Journey of the Magi' is the monologue of a man who has made his own choice, who has achieved belief in the Incarnation, but who is still part of that life which the Redeemer came to sweep away.[7] Like Gerontion, he cannot break loose from the past. Oppressed by a sense of death-in-life (Tiresias' anguish 'between two lives'), he is content to submit to 'another death' for his final deliverance from the world of old desires and gods, the world of 'the silken girls.' It is not that the

Birth that is also Death has brought him hope of a new life, but that it has revealed to him the hopelessness of the previous life. He is resigned rather than joyous, absorbed in the negation of his former existence but not yet physically liberated from it. Whereas Gerontion is 'waiting for rain' in this life, and the hollow men desire the 'eyes' in the next life, the speaker here has put behind him both the life of the senses and the affirmative symbol of the Child; he has reached the state of desiring nothing. His negation is partly ignorant, for he does not understand in what way the Birth is a Death; he is not aware of the sacrifice. Instead, he himself has become the sacrifice; he has reached essentially, on a symbolic level true to his emotional, if not to his intellectual, life, the humble, negative stage that in a mystical progress would be prerequisite to union. Although in the literal circumstances his will cannot be fixed upon mystical experience, because of the time and condition of his existence, he corresponds symbolically to the seeker as described by St. John of the Cross in *The Ascent of Mount Carmel.* Having first approached the affirmative symbol, or rather, for him, the affirmative reality, he has experienced failure; negation is his secondary option.

The quest of the Magi for the Christ child, a long arduous journey against the discouragements of nature and the hostility of man, to find at last a mystery impenetrable to human wisdom, was described by Eliot in strongly colloquial phrases adapted from one of Lancelot Andrewes' sermons of the Nativity:

> A cold coming they had of it at this time of the year, just the worst time of the year to take a journey, and specially a long journey in. The ways deep, the weather sharp, the days short, the sun farthest off, *in solstitio brumali,* 'the very dead of winter.' [8]

Also in Eliot's thoughts were the vast oriental deserts and the camel caravans and marches described in *Anabase,* by St.-J. Perse. He himself had begun work in 1926 on an English translation of that poem, publishing it in 1930.[9] Other elements of his tone and imagery may have come from Kipling's 'The Explorer' and from Pound's 'Exile's Letter.' The water mill was recollected from his own past; for in *The Use of Poetry,* speaking of the way in which 'certain images recur, charged with emotion,' he was to mention 'six ruffians seen through an open window playing cards at night at a small French railway junction where there was a water-mill.' [10] In vivifying the same incident, the fine proleptic symbolism of 'three trees on the low sky,' a portent of Calvary, with the evocative image of 'an old white horse' introduces one of the simplest and most pregnant passages in all of his work:

> Then we came to a tavern with vine-leaves over the lintel,
> Six hands at an open door dicing for pieces of silver,
> And feet kicking the empty wine-skins.

Here are allusions to the Communion (through the tavern 'bush'), to the paschal lamb whose blood was smeared on the lintels of Israel, to the blood money of Judas, to the contumely suffered by Christ before the Crucifixion, to the soldiers casting lots at the foot of the Cross, and, perhaps, to the pilgrims at the open tomb in the garden.

The arrival of the Magi at the place of Nativity, whose symbolism has been anticipated by the fresh vegetation and the mill 'beating the darkness,' is only a 'satisfactory' experience. The narrator has seen and yet he does not fully understand; he accepts the fact of Birth but is perplexed by its similarity to a Death, and to death which he has seen before:

> All this was a long time ago, I remember,
> And I would do it again, but set down
> This set down
> This: were we led all that way for
> Birth or Death? [11]

Were they led there for Birth or for Death? or, perhaps, for neither? or to make a choice between Birth and Death? And whose Birth or Death was it? their own, or Another's? Uncertainty leaves him mystified and unaroused to the full splendor of the strange epiphany. So he and his fellows have come back to their own Kingdoms, where,

> . . . no longer at ease here, in the old dispensation,
> With an alien people clutching their gods

(which are now alien gods), they linger not yet free to receive 'the dispensation of the grace of God.' [12] The speaker has reached the end of one world, but despite his acceptance of the revelation as valid, he cannot gaze into a world beyond his own.

'A Song for Simeon' (1928) derived its title from the 'Nunc dimittis,' or 'Song of Simeon' in the Prayer Book. The prayer that follows the second lesson at Evensong is taken from chapter 2 of Luke, recounting the ritual presentation of the child Jesus at the temple. Eliot based his poem upon this passage. But in so doing he developed the character of Simeon into a parallel to that of the speaker in the previous monologue and, rather more conspicuously, to that of Gerontion. Simeon's spiritual crisis is not quite as in 'Journey of the Magi'; like Gerontion's it looks into the future. What Simeon sees is the harassment and persecution of those, ironically enough, who, like himself, shall credit the vision now appearing. Whereas Gerontion in his 'sleepy corner' sees destruction engulf the worldly or profane, Simeon, though awaiting a tranquil death for himself, sees the destruction, as the world accounts it, that must overtake the righteous. This is a necessary destruction if life is to come out of death, but Simeon himself is unprepared to face it. Here again is the renunciation of an old life without a concentrated search for 'the ultimate vision.' Simeon is not only a soul relinquishing the life of the senses, a Tiresias; he is a soul that through its greater prescience, as it were contagiously, bears the sufferings of men elected to encounter suffering through action. But in his own person he is not constrained to pass from the one realm into the other, from the old dispensation into the new. Thus like the Magi he is simply transient between two worlds; the difference is that like Tiresias he understands the movement from the one into the other. He has passed the stage of Gerontion, who has lost the Word, and that of the hollow men, who are not freed from the circuit of the prickly pear.

The monologue, a tired murmur of an old, old man, starts with a brief section displaying familiar symbols from 'Gerontion' and *The Waste Land* to create a new statement concerning death and rebirth. The stubborn approach of spring, with hyacinths symbolizing pagan life and fertility, is contrasted with the stubborn duration of winter. Snow and flowers, as in 'Gerontion' and 'The Burial of the Dead,' bring into opposition the two principles everlastingly alternating in the cycle, here again represented by an old man and a 'depraved May.' But the spring brings also the Child, and the hyacinths have a new meaning, in view of which the fertility cults of Rome belong with the 'winter sun' that 'creeps by the snow hills.' For in the spring a new Light shines, to turn pagan death into life, making an end of the old life, 'light . . . /Like a feather on the back of my hand'—recalling the final scene of *King Lear*. Meanwhile Simeon awaits 'the wind that chills towards the dead land,' partly the whirlwind of death in 'Gerontion,' partly the wind of the Spirit in Ezekiel, a breath restoring life to the dead through the death of Christ. The feather blown in the wind (contrast 'White feathers in the snow') will thus be blown into the hands of God.

But the change itself imposes a terrible trial upon the human soul. The surge of a new life, whether the sexual struggle of Gerontion and Tiresias or their spiritual struggle which is this narrator's as well, amounts to no placid awakening. Not for nothing is time's April 'the cruellest month'; it arouses the spirit of decision. The Women of Canterbury, in *Murder in the Cathedral,* beseech the Archbishop to return to France, that they may be spared the new suffering. Simeon, too, that he may not outlive this beginning, not participate in the vitalizing growth of the new faith, prays for peace through 'the still unspeaking and unspoken Word,' the eternal countertype of strife. He resembles Gerontion or the protagonist of 'Journey of the Magi'; for he too is unwilling to be caught up in a life inflicting violence and calamity. In a plea for a tranquil death, he offers testimony to his past righteousness:

> I have walked many years in this city,
> Kept faith and fast, provided for the poor,
> Have given and taken honour and ease.
> There went never any rejected from my door.

It is precisely 'honour and ease' that the future must withhold; his own 'faith and fast' will not avail in 'the time of sorrow.' Like Christ, 'despised and rejected of men; a man of sorrows, and acquainted with grief,' [13] his posterity will be driven, Christian and Jew, 'to the goat's path, and the fox's home,/Fleeing from the foreign faces and the foreign swords.' [14] Christ himself is to say, 'The foxes have holes, and the birds of the air have nests; but the Son of man hath not where to lay his head.' [15] The symbols here pertain to the Way of Sorrows and the Passion. Simeon is speaking of something which he cannot know about; what nevertheless assumes importance is not 'the mountain of Zion, which is desolate, the foxes walk upon it' (Lam. 5:18), but the scourging of Christ, the Stations of the Cross, the weeping of the Virgin on Calvary, and even the day of the last 'abomination of desolation' when the inhabitants of Judea shall flee to the mountains.[16] From such future vicissitudes, Simeon would be preserved through the peace of 'the still unspeaking and unspoken Word.'

This poem and 'Journey of the Magi' are in one way simpler and in another way more intricate than 'The Hollow Men.' First, they omit the harrowing struggle with sexual desire. They have, it is true, 'the silken girls' and the 'Roman hyacinths'; these, however, symbolize what the old men have already put away from them (the hyacinths, unlike those in *The Waste Land,* connoting little more than the pagan and sensual aspect of rebirth, like the lilacs bred 'out of the dead land') and no longer express the tension between lust and love that dismays Gerontion and Tiresias. Corresponding to the eyes of 'The Hollow Men' and the hyacinth girl of *The Waste Land* are the Birth in 'Journey of the Magi' and the Word in 'A Song for Simeon.' These poems, like the others, set up an affirmative, numinous symbol, uniting flesh and spirit, and show it to be inapprehensible. The sufferers in them, as much as the hollow men, must turn unfulfilled toward death. The difficulty here is that a new element has obtruded into Eliot's usual pattern: the soul vanquished not by sex or unbelief but by sheer spiritual incapacity. The fact that these men are old, Eliot having economically used the same symbol of age to suggest impotence and unbelief (Gerontion) and twisted desire (Tiresias), seems to point to the Pauline sense of 'old man,' the unregenerate. At any rate, the Magi and Simeon, like Gerontion, appear to symbolize the soul's enchainment to the past, and its inability to desert its bonds at the cost of a painful readjustment. These men are still in and of the world, still spiritually uncleansed of the human taint. It is this that makes them 'old' men: 'After such knowledge, what forgiveness?'

Though both of these poems depict the failure of affirmation, they do not explicitly praise the other way, of abnegation and martyrdom of spirit. But they draw up a pattern for *Murder in the Cathedral, The Family Reunion, Four Quartets,* and *The Cocktail Party*. The humility to which the Magi and Simeon descend is that of conscious ignorance and inadequacy. This humility, however, comes but a step before the deliberately chosen ignorance of the mystical Dark Night as Eliot has described it in 'East Coker':

> In order to arrive at what you do not know
> You must go by a way which is the way of ignorance.

And that is the martyrdom of the 'old' man in soul and mind; it, in turn, comes but a step before the full sacrifice of Thomas Becket at Canterbury. Thus 'Journey of the Magi' and 'A Song for Simeon' are not entirely poems of despair. They foreshadow the way in which purgation compensates for the debility of body and will and the scars of disappointment.

Except for 'The Hollow Men,' 'Animula' (1929) is Eliot's most pessimistic poem. The state described and its symbolic configuration are the same as in 'Journey of the Magi' and 'A Song for Simeon.'

> Wandering between two worlds, one dead,
> The other powerless to be born.

But those poems limit grief by pinpointing it in the dramatic contexts. They have a historical focus. Simeon and the Magi must endure an external necessity wherein they can know only the Incarnation, not the Atonement. It is not so much that their own potentialities are weak as that a superior order has confined them to a dispensation of law instead of love. The Atonement was retroactive without bestowing the consolation of perceived grace. These men have, but do not know, the benefits of Christ's still unrevealed sacrifice. They are joyless, and the more so because, Tantalus-like, they verge so close to what they cannot grasp. Curiously, in this one aspect, both poems are less, not more, intimate to the Eliot problem as such: detachment is mitigating. 'Animula,' on the other hand, makes so general a pronouncement, not about a single spiritual dilemma but about the helplessness of the whole human condition, that it contrives to be more dismal and more personal at the same time. In 'Animula' the soul, despite its natural appetite for good, can do nothing whatever. By resistance and inertia, it misses an 'offered good' and ignores the grace extended.

As a philosophic poem, 'Animula' is prosaic in tone and traditional in meter. The rhyming pentameter is monotonously regular; the diction flat. One is dismayed to see in Eliot so cheap a phrase as 'fragrant brilliance' and to be afflicted with the unintended overtones of so carelessly chosen a name as 'Boudin.' [17] But the technical disorders of the poem do not infect the treatment of its theme.

As usual the discovery of hollowness in the world of the natural man heralds no spiritual rebirth. In 'Animula' the soul is kept back by the confused meshes of its past, by time, and can only live 'first in the silence after the viaticum.' The poem does not emphasize the desirability of death and contains no hint of an overwhelming experience which astonishes and arrests the eager soul in its progress. It suggests, however, something of the immobile hopelessness depicted in Part V of 'The Hollow Men,' though, again, it lacks even the memory of any symbol such as the eyes with their connotation of eternity coinciding with the temporal world. The only analogue to the obsessive lost experience is a gentle 'whisper of immortality,'

> . . . pleasure
> In the brilliant fragrance of the Christmas tree,
> Pleasure in the wind, the sunlight and the sea.

In value this corresponds approximately to the pagan 'Roman hyacinths' of Simeon's past and to the 'regretted'

> . . . summer palaces on slopes, the terraces,
> And the silken girls bringing sherbet.

The new life toward which 'Animula' points is 'the warm reality, the offered good,/. . . the importunity of the blood,' just as in the preceding poems the ideal is the Word and the Child. The inability to reach it is identified both with the breaching of childhood naïveté and with the invasion of this by adult perplexities, as in Vaughan's 'The Retreat' or Wordsworth's 'Ode on Intimations of Immortality.'

> Full soon thy Soul shall have her earthly freight,
> And custom lie upon thee with a weight,
> Heavy as frost, and deep almost as life!

The title 'Animula' recalls Hadrian's compassionate address to his soul; [18] the lines are now probably best known in Byron's translation. Pater took from them a chapter heading for *Marius the Epicurean*. Eliot began with an adaptation from *Purgatorio,* XVI, 'Esce di mano a lui, che la vagheggia/prima che sia . . ./l'anima semplicetta' ('From the hand of Him who loves her before she is, there issues, in the manner of a little child that plays, now weeping, now laughing, the simple soul: who knows nothing save that, moved by a joyous creator, she turns willingly to that which gives her pleasure. First she tastes the flavor of a trifling good; by it she is beguiled, and after it she runs, if neither guide nor rein turn back her longing. Wherefore it was needful to put law as a curb, needful to have a sovereign who might descry at least the pinnacle of the true city'). Even though the soul takes its greatest pleasure in the search for God, toward whom its free will, stimulated by appetite, naturally moves it, it is easily deflected by frivolities and evils. 'Animula' assumes that such distraction is inevitable. Blame for the soul's travail rests with the 'pain of living and the drug of dreams,' from which ensue the cramping of will, the inhibition and misdirection of desire. Stifled by all that 'perplexes and offends,' the soul takes refuge in barren learning. It becomes 'irresolute and selfish, misshapen, lame,' no longer exuberant, incapable of living. It seems to have no choice but denial, passivity. It can yield to the behest neither of flesh nor of spirit.[19]

Thematic resemblances in 'Animula,' not so much to the other 'Ariel Poems' as to 'A Cooking Egg' and 'Dans le Restaurant,' form a connective with an earlier period in Eliot's development. The image of 'Floret, by the boarhound slain between the yew trees,' recreates in the closing strophe the situation of the old waiter alarmed in childhood by the 'gros chien.' But now the symbolism of the dog may imply a broader reference. Even though Floret, as Eliot has said in a letter quoted by Ethel Stephenson, 'is so entirely imaginary that there is really no identification to be made . . . perhaps [he] may suggest not wholly irrelevantly to some minds certain folklore memories.' [20] The figure is in some sort an avatar of the fertility god, here depicted between the yew trees of death and resurrection, slain and waiting for rebirth. Adonis, deprived of virility and life under the tusks of the boar, is as much his archetype as is the quester in *The Waste Land,* whose buried life is menaced by the nails of the dog. The fate of Actaeon, ruined by his vision of beauty too divine for mortal beholding, might best translate into mythological language the deliberately vague connotations of the image. And Dante's greyhound, the *Veltro,* would provide a helpful association: as a hound of heaven it embodies a paradox of destruction and restoration, like the tiger in 'Gerontion' and the leopards in *Ash Wednesday*. But Eliot cannot be above suspicion of having lifted the image from *The Hound of the Baskervilles.* The onomatopoeic Guiterriez and Boudin are those who, denying the blood and pursuing their ceaseless pattern in mockery of truth, 'represent,' according to Eliot, 'different types of career, the successful person of the machine age and someone who was killed in the last war [i.e., World War I].' [21] At any rate they are exasperating. Eliot, having changed the men's names, has no legitimate reason to allege that they are in the poem at all; if they are in the poem, it is unfinished until the reader can identify them. The finely shocking terminal line of 'Animula,' in substituting 'birth' for 'death,' compensates slightly for this brummagem device.

'Marina' (1930) departs radically from the tone established in the three poems grouped with it. Although its protagonist confronts a symbol of vital restoration, the meeting signifies no transcendent communion impossible to him but, on a dream level, the benign and even triumphant realization of joy in a human relationship. The context designated in the title is that of Pericles' reunion with his daughter Marina in Shakespeare's *Pericles*. The recognition scene there (Act V, scene 1) has more than once been extolled by Eliot for its dramatic and symbolic force.[22] The incredible, yet miraculously probable, reunion of the lost daughter with the old king in the drama is like a rebirth of the king himself, a recovery of hope despaired of. Marina's birth at sea—virtually, one might say, of the sea—is perfected by her deliverance from shame and death. To Pericles, finding her alive whom he has thought dead, she seems the incarnation of a vision.

Against this almost beatific discovery Eliot set for his epigraph line 1138 of Seneca's *Hercules Furens,* 'Quis hic locus, quae regio, quae mundi plaga?' ('What place is this, what land, what quarter of the globe?'). These words are the first clouded mutterings of Hercules as he awakes from the unconscious fit into which he has sunk overcome by madness. Having ascended from his labor in the underworld, where he secured the dog Cerberus, he has been driven to frenzy through Juno's jealousy of him as Alcmena's son. In his madness he has turned his envenomed arrows against his own children, and now, his senses gradually returning, he is about to recognize the enormity. The total situation, antithetical to that in *Pericles,* discloses, in contrast with the discovery of Marina in Eliot's poem, not only the horror of death but the horror of personal defeat suffered by Hercules. As the assassin of his children he has met disaster through a turn of Fortune's wheel, the reverse of that which has blessed Pericles; and whereas Pericles' daughter is alive, Hercules' children are lying slaughtered. The crime of Hercules succeeds a moment of overweening pride, the moment of his highest exultation; he has completed his twelfth and final labor and has killed the tyrant who abused his household, but he has incurred divine resentment. With such a career of arrogant boastfulness, leading to deprivation and ruin, Eliot contrasted the gracious experience of Pericles by a somewhat oversubtle mingling. In a letter written to Sir Michael Sadler in May, 1930, Eliot spoke of having used the scenes from the two plays so as to form a 'crisscross' between them. 'Marina' owes to Seneca the rhetoric of its opening line and the undercurrent of irony produced by the confluence of death and life.

The poem is a monologue, spoken precisely at the instant of recognition. Pericles is not sure whether he has crossed the boundaries of dream into reality. His experience belongs to a kind of halfway world, the atmosphere of which pervades his words. As in a dream, he is standing on the deck of a vessel approaching land, from whose granite shores are borne the scent of pine and the song of the woodthrush—images rising out of some buried recollection and made vivid as he becomes conscious of his daughter's presence. The images objectify the emotion stirring in him. They obliterate the memory of other images—those of men associated with the sins of envy, pride, sloth, and concupiscence, and with the state of death consequent upon habitual sin. These

> Are become insubstantial, reduced by a wind,
> A breath of pine, and the woodsong fog
> By this grace dissolved in place.

Marina's apparent restoration has conferred a grace, a life-giving and sin-purging benediction. His dream seems palpable; Marina seems a living creature in whom the idea, the figment, becomes objectively real and in achieving transformation both clearer and less clear, because different:

> What is this face, less clear and clearer
> The pulse in the arm, less strong and stronger—
> Given or lent? more distant than stars and nearer than the eye.[23]

She seems tangibly one who, as in *Ash Wednesday,* 'moves in the time between sleep and walking':

> Whispers and small laughter between leaves and hurrying feet
> Under sleep, where all the waters meet.[24]

As a fulfilment, she surpasses even his pathetic fatherly yearning for lost 'small daughter,' without, in any measure, having the inadequacy of a mere substitute. The image latent in the dream world has been of something never heard, the sounds of children concealed in the leaves. Eliot's source was probably Kipling's 'They,' the story of ghostly children frolicking about the house of a blind woman.[25] In 'Marina' the dream child comes with almost a religious epiphany, and it is hardly accidental that the phrase 'Given or lent?' echoes Alice Meynell's line 'Given, not lent' in her poem 'Unto us a Son is given,' referring to Isaiah, chapter 9.[26]

Marina is not the Child from 'Journey of the Magi,' but she is invested, for purposes of the poem, with the characteristics of flesh clothing a divine emanation. Thus at the instant of Pericles' recognition, although (and because) it is not clear to him whether the child really is 'given,' the images he associates with her are 'stars' and 'the eye.' These are the same already adopted by Eliot in 'The Hollow Men'; again, they are symbols, as are the leaves and the thrush, of the values inherent in the Grail of the romances. Marina is the focal center here, corresponding in a purer form to the hyacinth girl of *The Waste Land*. And for once the communion is not abortive. The meeting brings together, at least on one level of consciousness, a quester and the object of his quest, and there is no division or disappointment.

Such beatitude is far from typical of Eliot's usual symbolic scheme. But the happy nature of the experience in 'Marina' does not violate the principle enunciated in his *After Strange Gods* (1934) that 'ideals' are not the concern of poetry [27]—which can mean that poetry should not show unreal attainments as if they were true. Pericles' happiness occurs where the literal event is not actual and is not supposed to be actual, except as dream. The connection between the actuality of dream and that of waking is simply emotional; the experience has emotional authenticity. Eliot's use of the impersonal situation involved only a partial masking. The status of this poem among his other work is as if he had dispensed with the impersonal and had written about a dream of his own—actual in occurrence, ideal in content. If, instead, he had treated of the actual meeting of Pericles with Marina, he would have had to present as actually joyous the sort of experience which his work always showed as eclipsed and thwarted. His instinct not to rely on the impersonal, that is, rather to make a tension between the actual and the ideal internal to the poem, may well give evidence of an intimate personal symbolism in 'Marina.' As a personal symbol the poem could not have totally reported the mixed private emotion by abstracting merely the constituent of ideal feeling. As it is, in all but the contrivance of situation, it is most likely as personal as 'Animula.' The ground of this opinion would be firmer, of course, if biographical evidence were accessible. But three points are noteworthy: the identification of the speaker with Pericles depends almost wholly on the title; the emergence of the speaker from his dream state, in contrast with the awakening enjoyed by Shakespeare's Pericles, is incomplete; and, finally, in view of the epigraph, it is possible that the speaker is grievously mistaken. The underlying parallel to the Hercules recognition serves to qualify for the reader the flash of pure delight felt by Pericles. There is an irony superior to the poem, and even if inadequately transferred from the epigraph into the monologue, it works an effect.

In the last two strophes Pericles is associated with the decaying ship in which he now moves through the fog. What, 'unknowing, half conscious,' he has made his own is his life itself; it is a life paradoxically identifiable with 'This form, this face, this life / Living to live in a world of time beyond me,' that is, with Marina, and it becomes 'The awakened, lips parted, the hope, the new ships.' The semi-ambiguous, semi-visionary blending of the old with the new harmonizes with the dream world of the event. The vision, with the strange regularity of dream, embraces once more, without impairment of logic, the symbolism of the shores and the woodthrush, so that with the closing words, 'My Daughter,' Marina has been merged into the obscure promise of the serene haven and the song of the bird. The thrush, not quite the same as in *The Waste Land,* connotes exultant life rather than the 'deception' spoken of in 'Burnt Norton.' The setting has a New England look, and Eliot's boyhood memories of the Massachusetts coast (of which he spoke feelingly in a preface written in 1928) were laid under contribution for this poem. But the specific place he had in mind, and indeed mentioned in his original draft, was Rogue Island, lying at the mouth of the New Meadows River, Casco Bay, Maine.

Despite the differences between 'Marina' and the other 'Ariel Poems,' it shares with them a quality looking back to the conclusion of *The Waste Land* as well as to the spiritual struggle in *Ash Wednesday*. The poem communicates its intuition that the obsolete desires and ambitions must be sloughed off before the soul can find its higher mode, its unequivocal unity with the vision. Thus 'Marina' is more Dantean and Platonic than its predecessors. It aspires to transcend the agony of the soul entangled in its past, voiced in earlier poems; it aspires also to transcend the frustration of the soul striving, as in *Ash Wednesday,* to be reconciled; and it reveals, without dwelling on the process of rebirth through suffering, the emotional state which rewards devotion, a state conferring tranquillity and love. That this state is merely foreshadowed is plain from the fact not only that 'Marina' unfolds as a dream landscape but also that Pericles articulates something like a prayer:

> . . . let me
> Resign my life for this life, my speech for that unspoken.

Since the poem has no past or future, one has perhaps no right to speculate on any for Pericles. But if one should imagine a future for him, it would have to be one in which he resigned the withered life for that heralded in his illuminative dream. Had Eliot not altered 'word' to 'speech' after his first draft, one might say something more about the creative and religious overtones of this line. What is crucial here is the possibility of putting the old life behind and moving upward, of 'faring forward,' transhumanized, to 'the Garden / Where all love ends.'

NOTES

1. *Selected Essays,* pp. 172–3.
2. Since this comment was written, Eliot has issued 'The Three Voices of Poetry,' *Atlantic Monthly,* CXCIII, No. 4 (April, 1954), 38–44, in which he recognizes the problems referred to here.
3. *Poetry by T. S. Eliot* ('University of Chicago Round Table,' No. 659, broadcast November 12, 1950), p. 9.
4. 'The Cultivation of Christmas Trees' is dissimilar in mood to the early 'Ariel Poems' and, because of the slackness of its verse, it has less appeal than those. Its relation to 'Animula' is a corrective one. It envisions that the child's wonder and gladness in the presence of 'the first-remembered Christmas tree' can be treasured up untarnished and be increased by repetitions, so that in his old age 'accumulated memories of annual emotion / May be concentrated into a great joy / Which shall also be a great fear.' It thus implies, recalling 'The Dry Salvages,' that by 'approach to the meaning' his vitalizing experiences may assume new form. In this, 'a great joy' would be expected, 'a great fear' perhaps not; yet, as Eliot suggests by alluding to the second chapter of Acts (in which 'fear came upon every soul'), such experience is a type not only of the Epiphany, or 'first coming,' but of Pentecost, prefiguring a 'second coming.' And, in the eyes of an old man nearing death, the affirmative symbol of Birth and Crucifixion offers a reminder of how close he stands to the Power that numbers his days.

   The poem does not explain by what means wonder can survive 'the bored habituation, the fatigue, the tedium, / The awareness of death, the consciousness of failure.' Prayerfully, it only adopts a posture of hope that the child may keep his freshness: 'Let him continue in the spirit of wonder. . . .' It substitutes for the pessimism of 'Animula' the possibility of emotional health. This, for the poet himself, seems to be correlated with still another symbol. Mentioning the oblivion of 'reverence and gaiety' under 'the piety of the convert / Which may be tainted with a self-conceit,' Eliot adds:

   > (And here I remember also with gratitude
   > St. Lucy, her carol, and her crown of fire).

   The naïve story of the early martyr, whom the executioner's fire would not burn and whose feet the Roman troops could not stir, seeks an audience possessing a sincerity equal to its own. But the innocence of St. Lucy's carol of faith and praise can evoke an aesthetic emotion approximating such sincerity. And an understanding of the story's meaning, combined with the reiterated aesthetic emotion, can yield the joy and fear of which Eliot has written.

For the legend of St. Lucy see Sigebert of Gembloux, *Passio Sanctae Luciae Virginis,* ed. Ernest Dümmler, in 'Abhandlungen der Königlichen Akademie der Wissenschaften zu Berlin (philosophische und historische)' (Berlin, 1893), I, 23–43. In Sweden, St. Lucy is a children's Christmas saint.

5. Eliot, *For Lancelot Andrewes* (London, 1928), p. ix.
6. *Selected Essays,* p. 402. In making his choice, Eliot is said to have reacted specifically against Bertrand Russell's *A Free Man's Worship* (*Time,* LV, No. 10 [March 6, 1950], 24).
7. See Drew, pp. 118–19.
8. Andrewes, *Works,* I, 257; *Selected Essays,* p. 297.
9. St.-J. Perse, *Anabasis: A Poem,* trans. T. S. Eliot (London, 1930), pp. 42–7.
10. Eliot, *The Use of Poetry,* p. 148; cited by Louis MacNeice, *The Poetry of W. B. Yeats* (London, New York, and Toronto, 1941), p. 138.
11. Cf. *Othello,* Act V, scene 2, line 351: 'Set you down this.' See *Selected Essays,* p. 111.
12. Eph. 3:2. This occurs in the Book of Common Prayer, Epistle for the Epiphany.
13. Isa. 53:3.
14. Cf. Conrad, 'Heart of Darkness,' in *Youth,* p. 48: '. . . the foreign shores, the foreign faces'; cf. also Swinburne, 'Itylus.'
15. Matt. 8:20.
16. Mark 13:14.
17. Eliot perhaps picked up the name 'Boudin' from the Eumaeus episode of Joyce's *Ulysses,* p. 610, where it is appropriate as a sly allusion to Mr. Bloom's appetite (as a common noun it generally means black pudding). Eliot overlooked this connotation.
18. Cited by Drew, p. 124.
19. Possible sources for the theme of 'Animula' include Baudelaire, 'Le Voyage' (cited in *Selected Essays,* p. 249); Tennyson, *In Memoriam,* xlv; Cardinal Newman, *The Idea of a University* (New York and London, 1927), pp. 331–2 (Preface to 'Elementary Studies'); and *The Education of Henry Adams,* p. 460. The last has been noticed by Robert A. Hume, *Runaway Star: An Appreciation of Henry Adams* (Ithaca, N.Y., 1951), p. 37.
20. E. M. Stephenson, *T. S. Eliot and the Lay Reader* (London, 1946), p. 49.
21. *Ibid.*
22. See Drew, p. 127.
23. Cf. *Pericles,* Act V, scene 1, lines 154–6:

But are you flesh and blood?
Have you a working pulse, and are no fairy?
Motion?

24. Cf. Sidney Lanier, 'The Marshes of Glynn,' lines 101–3:

. . . who will reveal to our waking ken
The forms that swim and the shapes that creep
Under the waters of sleep?

25. Cited with reference to 'Burnt Norton' by Helen L. Gardner, *Four Quartets:* A Commentary, Rajan, p. 62.
26. Cited by Frank Wilson, *Six Essays on the Development of T. S. Eliot,* p. 39.
27. Eliot, *After Strange Gods,* p. 28.

FRANK KERMODE

'Dissociation of Sensibility'
Modern Symbolist Readings of Literary History

(1957)

The primary pigment of poetry is the IMAGE. BLAST

The poetic myths are dead; and the poetic image, which is the myth of the individual, reigns in their stead. C. DAY LEWIS

When the accounts come to be rendered, it may well appear to future historians that the greatest service done by early twentieth-century criticism to contemporary poetry has been this: it has shown poets a specially appropriate way of nourishing themselves from the past. It has shown them that their isolation, and their necessary preoccupation with the Image, do not cut them off from all their predecessors, and that there are ways of looking at the past which provide valuable insights into essentially modern possibilities and predispositions. The need was to bring literary history—and this involved other kinds of history too—to the support of the Image; to rewrite the history of poetry in Symbolist terms. The whole effort crystallised, in 1921, in Mr. Eliot's famous announcement of the doctrine of the dissociation of sensibility, and although this was by no means so original an idea as it has been called, it will necessarily be at the centre of what I have to say about this extremely important phase of my subject.

The doctrine has lately been wilting under well-directed criticism, though there is no doubt that it will continue, whether under the same name or not, whether fallacious or not, to exert a powerful influence for a long time yet. My business here is merely to establish that it has a strong connexion with the development, in the present century, of the theory of the Image, and to ask why it has had such success. What I say about its value as a key to literary history is really incidental to this.

Mr. Eliot first used the expression 'dissociation of sensibility' in an essay on 'The Metaphysical Poets' (1921), and his last recorded comment upon the theory is in his British Academy lecture on Milton (1947). The first passage, as printed in *Selected Essays,* runs like this: Mr. Eliot has been saying that the dramatic verse of the late Elizabethans and early Jacobeans 'expresses a degree of development of sensibility which is not found in any of the prose. . . In Chapman especially there is a direct sensuous apprehension of thought, or a recreation of thought into feeling, which is exactly what we find in Donne. .' He then compares a passage of Chapman's and one by Lord Herbert of Cherbury with bits of Tennyson and Browning, and comments:

> The difference is not a simple difference of degree between poets. It is something which had happened to the mind of England between the time of Donne or Lord Herbert of Cherbury and the time of Tennyson and Browning; it is the difference between the intellectual poet and the reflective poet. Tennyson and Browning are poets, and they think; but they do not feel their thought as immediately as the odour of a rose. A thought to Donne was an experience; it modified his sensibility. When a poet's mind is perfectly equipped for its work, it is constantly amalgamating disparate experience; the ordinary man's experience is chaotic, irregular, fragmentary. The latter falls in love, or reads Spinoza, and these two experiences have nothing to do with each other, or with the noise of the typewriter or the smell of cooking; in the mind of the poet these experiences are always forming new wholes.
>
> We may express the difference by the following theory: The poets of the seventeenth century, the successors of the dramatists of the sixteenth, possessed a mechanism of sensibility which could devour any kind of experience. They are simple, artificial, difficult, or fantastic, as their predecessors were; no less nor more than Dante, Guido Cavalcanti, Guinicelli, or Cino. In the seventeenth century a dissociation of sensibility

> set in, from which we have never recovered; and this dissociation, as is natural, was aggravated by the influence of the most powerful poets of the century, Milton and Dryden.

Observe that there are certain qualifications for poetry described as operative *now,* though possessed by the poets of the seventeenth century and none since (until now?). There are other places in Mr. Eliot's earlier criticism which amplify this statement, but we will content ourselves with his last pronouncement on the subject:

> I believe that the general affirmation represented by the phrase 'dissociation of sensibility' . . . retains some validity; but . . . to lay the burden on the shoulders of Milton and Dryden was a mistake. If such a dissociation did take place, I suspect that the causes are too complex and profound to justify our accounting for the change in terms of literary criticism. All we can say is, that something like this did happen; that it had something to do with the Civil War; that it would be unwise to say it was caused by the Civil War, but that it is a consequence of the same cause which brought about the Civil War; that we must seek the causes in Europe, not in England alone; and for what these causes were, we may dig and dig until we get to a depth at which words and concepts fail us.

In this passage Mr. Eliot seems to be recommending, as a desideratum, what had in fact already been done; for by 1947 supplementary enquiries into the dissociation had long ceased to be conducted entirely in terms of literary criticism. Almost every conceivable aspect of seventeenth-century life had been examined by scholars anxious to validate the concept, though it is true that the investigators were usually historians of literature by profession. In very general terms it might be said that the notion of a pregnant historical crisis, of great importance in every sphere of human activity, was attractive because it gave design and simplicity to history; and because it explained in a subtly agreeable way the torment and division of modern life. Feeling and thinking by turns, aware of the modern preference for intellect over imagination, a double-minded period measured itself by a serenely single-minded one. Poets tried again to be concrete, to charge their thinking with passion, to restore to poetry a truth independent of the presumptuous intellect. They looked admiringly to those early years of the seventeenth century when this was normal, and the scholars attended them with explanations of why it was so, and why it ceased to be so. There was, I think, an implicit parallel with the Fall. Man's soul, since about 1650, had been divided against itself, and it would never be the same again—though correct education could achieve something.

It is a measure of Mr. Eliot's extraordinary persuasiveness that thinkers in this tradition have for so long accepted the seventeenth century as the time of the disaster. As we see from his second pronouncement, he has himself stuck to this position, although he advises us to look back into earlier history for fuller explanations. Nor is his attitude difficult to understand; it is animated by a rich nostalgia for the great period of Anglican divinity, the period when the Church of England, beset on all sides by determined recusancy, confidently proposed itself as truly Catholic and apostolic—looking back, itself, to a vague past when the folly and arrogance of intellect had not yet begun the process of dissociating Christianity. This period ended with the Civil War, and the end of the first Anglo-Catholicism coincided with the end of an admired poetry and a great drama, both affected, to some extent, by ecclesiastically-determined attitudes, the drama remembering (but how faintly?) its devout origins, 'metaphysical poetry' the *concetto predicabile*. What happens is that the Civil War becomes a kind of allegory, with the Puritans as Pride of Intellect, and the King as Spiritual Unity.

The truth is that, if we look to Europe and not to England alone, we see that there was never much chance that the Church of England would be universally recognised as Catholic, and that 'something' had presumably 'happened' long before to predispose people against such recognition. And this is a characteristic situation. It is not merely a matter of wrong dates; however far back one goes one seems to find the symptoms of dissociation. This suggests that there is little historical propriety in treating it as a seventeenth-century event, even when the historian is serious and respectable enough not to assume that it really was an occurrence like, say, Pride's Purge, after which feeling disappeared from certain mental transactions, leaving a Rump of intellect with which we are still conducting our business. With more thoughtful chroniclers there is usually much emphasis on the dissociative force of science, and on the un-dissociated condition of pre-Baconian and pre-Cartesian philosophy and theology. But it is easy enough to show that scientists were already under Elizabeth incurring odium and the suspicion of atheism for a variety of reasons, all coming in the end to the charge that they were setting nature against God. Bacon's position with respect to religious laws that were apparently contrary to reason is very similar to that of many philosophers, especially those affected by Averroes and the great Aristotelian tradition of Padua, from the thirteenth century onward, to Pomponazzi in the early sixteenth and to Cremonini, an influential teacher who was, incidentally, a friend of that very Lord Herbert of Cherbury who was used as an example of the un-dissociated poet. Obviously the rediscovery of Aristotle involved in some sense a dissociation of Christian thought, tending ultimately to some such escape-device as the 'double-truth' of Averroism, first condemned, by a Church anxious to save rational theology, in the 1270s. And if we were to pursue the dissociation back into the past, we should find ourselves in Athens. Elizabethan 'atheism' was far more than a scientific issue; there was genuine anxiety, a real 'naturalist' movement widely affecting ethical and political conduct. Similarly, the condemnations of the 1270s referred not only to Averroism but to the book on love by Andreas Capellanus, and M. Gilson has spoken of 'a sort of polymorphic naturalism stressing the rights of pagan nature' as characteristic of the period as a whole. It would be quite as reasonable to locate the great dissociation in the sixteenth or the thirteenth century as in the seventeenth; nor would it be difficult to construct arguments for other periods. The truth may be that we shall never find a state of culture worth bothering about (from the literary point of view, that is) in which language is so primitive as to admit no thinking that is not numinous; in which there is no possibility of a naturalist assault on the society's beliefs. The Christian 'West' has never wanted to be as primitive even as the Song of Solomon, and its whole immense allegorical tradition is the result of applying intellectual instruments to the dissection of writings in which thought and feeling are, if they are anywhere, inseparable.

But it seems to me much less important that there was not, in the sense in which Mr. Eliot's supporters have thought, a particular and far-reaching catastrophe in the seventeenth century, than that there was, in the twentieth, an urgent need to establish the historicity of such a disaster. And the attempt to answer the question why there should have been takes us back to the Image. The theory of the dissociation of sensibility is, in fact, the most successful version of a Symbolist attempt to explain why the modern world resists works of art that testify to the poet's special, anti-intellectual way of knowing truth. And this attempt obviously involves the hypothesis of an age which was different, an age in which the Image was more readily accessible and acceptable.

When, in fact, the poets and aestheticians of the Image turn their attention to history, it is in search of some golden age when the prevalent mode of knowing was not positivist, and anti-imaginative; when the Image, the intuited, creative reality, was habitually respected; when art was not permanently on the defensive against mechanical and systematic modes of enquiry. Since the order of reality postulated as the proper study of the poet tends, in one way or another, to be granted supernatural attributes, the ideal epoch is usually a religious one. Hence the medievalism of Byzantinism of Hulme and the Decadents, of Yeats and Henry Adams. Hulme, in particular—as we have seen—exposes the whole process; he has to go back, using Worringer as a guide, to a moment of crisis (using one that already existed for historians, but using it in a new way) and achieve the required antithesis between his two age (undissociated and dissociated) by treating all thought between the Renaissance and his own time as of a piece. It was partly because this obviously would not do that the date of the crisis was moved on to 1650. But everybody in the tradition was agreed that there must have been such a crisis; it was necessary to their aesthetic, and the only point of dispute was its date.

There is a passage, to which I have already referred, in Pound's *Make It New,* that illuminates this aspect of the problem.

> When the late T. S. Hulme was trying to be a philosopher . . and fussing about Sorel and Bergson. . . I spoke to him one day of the difference between Guido's precise interpretative metaphor, and the Petrarchian fustion and ornament, pointing out that Guido thought in accurate terms; that the phrases correspond to definite sensations undergone . . . Hulme took some time over it in silence, and then finally said: 'That is more interesting than anything anyone ever said to me. It is more interesting than anything I ever read in a book.'

The only aspects of this odd interchange that I want to discuss are those which are relevant to what I am trying to say about the historiography of modern Symbolist aesthetics. One is that Pound is describing Cavalcanti as a poet of the integral image, and contrasting him with Petrarch, a poet of the ornamental image, the image appended to discourse, the flower stuck in sand. In the one there is 'a unification of thought and feeling'; in the other, a dissociation of them. Another is Hulme's reaction to what Pound said. The general idea could not have been unfamiliar to him; after all, it was the reason why he was fussing about Bergson. But a man is never more impressed by an argument than when it provides unexpected support for opinions he already holds, and Hulme could not have been less than charmed to discover that Petrarch, of all people—the First Man of that Renaissance he blamed so strenuously—already exhibited the symptoms of error that characterised the period, whereas Cavalcanti, an older contemporary of Dante, habituated to the hallowed concept of discontinuity, brought up on Original Sin, had precisely those Imagist qualities, that reluctance to glide away into abstraction, which for Hulme was the index of true poetry. Somewhere between Cavalcanti and Petrarch a dissociation of sensibility, it would seem, had set in; and from it, Hulme was willing to add, we have never recovered.

But we have now to remind ourselves that Mr. Eliot claimed for the poets of the seventeenth century the very qualities of Dante, Cavalcanti, and Cino, and believed that the dissociation came after these later poets. It is not in the nature of the concept of dissasiation that it should occur at random intervals, any more than it is of the Fall; only on some such theory as Yeats's can it occur more than once. What are we to conclude from this confusion?

The fact is that Mr. Eliot's argument for a general dissociation that can be detected in art is meant to satisfy much the same need as Hulme's, and Yeats's. For Hulme, as we have seen, the Renaissance is the critical moment; men began to ignore the human limitations suggested by the doctrine of Original Sin, and nothing has been right since. Romanticism is just the new disease at the stage of mania. For Yeats the great moment in the present historical phase is 1550; for about a century before that there was a tense perfection, celebrated in some of his most splendid prose; but after that everything changed, art faced in the wrong direction, the artist became more and more an exile. In fact Yeats's history is written in terms of this doctrine, written in a world that offended him socially and imaginatively, a world of 'shopkeeping logicians', the very existence of which he had to explain by exhaustive glosses on every conceivable aspect of the idea of dissociation. My own belief is that Yeats's expression of the whole aesthetic-historical complex is by far the most satisfactory and, in terms of poetry, the most fruitful. But the immediate point is that all these writers search history for this critical moment, and because they share much the same poetic heritage, they are all looking for much the same kinds of rightness and wrongness in historical periods. They seek, in short, a historical period possessing the qualities they postulate for the Image: unity, indissociability; qualities which, though passionately desired, are, they say, uniquely hard to come by in the modern world. That poets and critics so diverse in personality as Pound, Hulme, Yeats and Eliot, should all have made such similar incursions into Symbolist historiography is testimony to the great pressure the idea of the Image has exerted in the formative phase of modern poetic. Mr. Eliot's attempt, distinguished from the others by the accident of his personal concerns in theology, is not essentially different from them. It has only been more successful, partly because of his prestige and persuasive force, partly perhaps because of the growing scholarly tendency to medievalise the Renaissance, so that a later date for the split became more acceptable.

The fact remains that Mr. Eliot's is the version that has had wide currency. Like the others, it is, as I have been trying to show, quite useless historically. It will not do to say that it is partly true, or true in a way, as some people now claim. A once-for-all event cannot happen every few years; there cannot be, if the term is to retain the significance it has acquired, dissociations between the archaic Greeks and Phidias, between Catullus and Virgil, between Guido and Petrarch, between Donne and Milton. As a way of speaking about *periods* the expression is much less useful than even 'baroque.' At its worst, it is merely a way of saying which poets one likes, and draping history over them. At its best it is an interesting primitivism, looking for an unmodern virtue, not as the noble savage was sought in the impossibly remote past or in Tahiti, but in Christian Europe right up to some moment in, or shortly after, what is vaguely called the Renaissance. The most deplorable consequence of the doctrine is that the periods and poets chosen to illustrate it are bound to receive perverse treatment; you must misrepresent them if you propose to make them justify a false theory. If the theory helps to produce good poetry (as it did) this is not worth complaining about, provided that it does when this work is accomplished. But this theory shows every sign of surviving, and it is therefore a matter of importance to show how it has distorted Donne and Milton, the two poets most affected by it. Once again, the astonishing degree of distortion imposed here is a measure of the power generated by the Image in modern poetic.

Milton and Donne have been involved in an unhappy relationship (existing only in the fantasies of historians) which has seemed to mean that one of them has to be occulted to enable the other to be lit. Milton was to be put out—though it may be noted that Mr. Eliot's change of opinion about Donne was followed by an upward revision of his estimate of Milton. At the time when Donne was being admired for thinking passionately, Milton was being despised for writing monuments to dead ideas in a dead language. Milton, self-conscious postlapsarian that he was, obstinately thought and discoursed *about* feeling, divorcing the body and soul, the form and matter, of the image. Donne, writing before the same Fall, had his intellect at the tip of his senses.

Superficially this argument was attractive because it gave major status to an obscure poet whose diction was inartificial, even colloquial, and who lived in times supposed to be very like modern times, in that the established order was already being threatened by those 'naturalist' forces which eventually dissociated sensibility. There is, of course, a contradiction here: Donne is admired because he was deeply troubled by the new philosophy, and also because he was lucky enough to live just before it became really troublesome. There is also an error of fact: Donne alludes frequently enough to the 'new philosophy,' but nobody who has examined these allusions in their context can seriously believe he was much put out by it, and considering his religious views it would indeed be surprising if he had been. It might have been useful to the dissociationist argument if somebody had been prepared to capitalise this point, by way of emphasising Donne's pre-dissociation status; but there seems to have been a heavy commitment to the view that Donne was important to modern poets because of the ways in which his world resembled theirs, as well as because it was completely different from theirs. As usual, the history is feeble. But pure criticism has had very similar difficulties: Miss Tuve's now famous demonstration that Donne's images have a logical, or at any rate a pseudo-logical function, was a direct affront to the basis of the theory he was a poet of the modern Image; but it can scarcely have surprised anybody who had read Donne open-eyed and seen how much he depends on dialectical conjuring of various kinds, arriving at the point of wit by subtle syllogistic misdirections, inviting admiration by slight but totally destructive perversities of analogue, which re-route every argument to paradox. Some of this Mr. Eliot perhaps felt when he prematurely prophesied the demise of Donne during the tercentenary celebrations of 1931, and showed how far he had gone towards excluding Donne from the category of unified sensibility, saying outright that in him 'there is a manifest fissure of thought and sensibility.' Donne is, to say the least, of doubtful value to the Symbolist theory—less use than the poetic and critical experiments of some of his European contemporaries might have been. At first glance, one might be excused for wondering how Donne ever got mixed up with the theory of dissociation; the explanation of course lies in nineteenth-century thought.

Mr. F. W. Bateson, in a very important critique of the theory, has noticed in passing how little separates Mr. Eliot's formula from the conventional nineteenth-century view, which he exemplifies by Stopford Brooke's opinion that the Restoration saw the end 'of a poetry in which emotion always accompanied thought.' And something like this view can in fact be found in Coleridge. But after Grosart's edition of 1872 some people were already noticing that Donne wrote poems in which the note of passion, the true voice of feeling, was audible despite the fact that they were love poems unpromisingly couched in terms of alchemy, astronomy and law. It was this discovery of the true voice of feeling in such surroundings that led to what was in effect a late Romantic glorification of Donne. This was contemporary with the Blake revival, the teaching of Pater, and finally with the assimilation of the parallel but more important phenomenon of French Symbolism—in short, with the emergence of the modern Image as it was understood by Symons (a great champion of Donne and the Jacobean drama), and those who came under his influence: Yeats, and later Pound and Eliot. One can watch the older thought-and-feeling formula developing from a Romantic into a characteristically Symbolist hypothesis. George Eliot, who knew Donne by the time she wrote *Middlemarch,* assumes like her master Wordsworth that the true voice comes from artists of higher organic sensibility than other men, but can write in that novel—doubtless unconscious of her role as critical pioneer—that the poet is 'quick to discern,' but also 'quick to feel' because he possesses 'a soul in which knowledge passes instantaneously into feeling, and feeling flashes back as a new organ of knowledge.'

This period of transition is greatly illuminated in a paper recently published by Mr. J. E. Duncan in the *Journal of English and Germanic Philology*. Anyone who has used the Victorian editions upon which much of our reading in seventeenth-century poetry still depends must have occasionally felt that there was some hallucinatory resemblance between certain observations made by the enthusiastic clerical editors and those of Mr. Eliot. Mr. Duncan has collected a great deal of evidence to show, not only that Donne was well and truly revived long before Eliot's essays, and indeed Grierson's edition, but that even 70 years ago people were talking about the poet in what we recognise as the modern way. By 1911, Courthope, in his *History,* was already complaining that it had probably gone too far. Grierson's great edition of the following year was accepted as merely setting the seal on Donne's reputation. But what is more interesting than this mere setting back of the starting post is the terminology in which the Victorian critics, pleased with their rediscovery of the conceit and of hard-thinking poetry, devised in order to praise the Metaphysical poets. They speak of its intellectual cunning *and* its power of 'sensibility' and then, quite early, we find ourselves approaching, with a sort of unconscious inevitability, the modern formula which combines these two qualities as two sides of a coin. Grosart says that Crashaw's thinking 'was so emotional as almost always to tremble into feeling'; Cowley's thought is 'made to pulsate with feeling.' Symons finds that Donne's 'senses speak with unparallelled directness'; Schelling that Donne's contribution to the English lyric was 'intellectualised emotion.' Poets began to find Donne-like qualities in their own work; in so doing, Francis Thompson spoke of his own 'sensoriness instinct with mind,' and the parallel was supported by Symons and by Mrs. Meynell. The familiar comparison between the seventeenth and twentieth centuries began as early as 1900; after that it was easy to play the game of parallel poets, and both Brooke and Bridges were credited with resemblances to Donne. Gosse and Grierson alike saw the similarity between Donne and Baudelaire, and briefly hinted at the parallel between English-Jacobean and French-Symbolist which was later to prove so fertile. Arthur Symons in fact developed the parallel to a considerable extent; he is the link between nineteenth- and twentieth-century orthodoxies of the Image, and of Donne and the seventeenth century.

Long before the great edition of Grierson, which made Donne relatively easy to read, and long before Mr. Eliot's phrase had its remarkable success in the world, powerful aesthetic interests were being satisfied by the conversion of a little-known poet into an English Laforgue; and the same interests demanded a catastrophic start to the modern world shortly after the death of Donne, and before *Paradise Lost,* that great dissociated poem which you must, said Mr. Eliot, read once for the meaning and once for the verse, and which is therefore of no use either to that illiterate audience he desiderates for his unified Symbolist poetry, or for the next best thing, a highly cultivated audience that also likes its art undissociated. The strangest irony in all this—and it is all I have to say about the second of these perverted poets—is that Milton, rather exceptionally, actually believed in and argued for the unity of the soul (a continuum of mind and sense), allowed his insistence on the inseparability of form and matter to lead him into heresy; and believed that poetry took precedence over other activities of the soul because it was simple (undissociated by intellect) sensuous and passionate. But this did not matter; there were overriding reasons why Milton had to be bent or broken. He was the main sufferer in the great experiment of projecting on to an historical scale a developed Romantic-Symbolist theory of the Image. And although, as Mr. Bateson has shown, Mr. Eliot borrowed the phrase 'dissociation of sensibility' from Gourmont's peculiar account of the processes of poetry in the mind of an individual (specifically Laforgue) and applied it to the history of a nation's poetry, it is obvious that behind the theory there is the whole pressure of the tradition I have been discussing. The historical effort of Symbolism has been to identify a period happily ignorant of the war between Image and discourse, an un-dissociated age. In the end, it is not of high importance that any age selected for this role is likely to be found wanting, except of course for the tendency to exclude particular poets and periods from the canon. Hulme could never have justified his selection; Pound was driven to Chinese, and a dubious theory of ideograms; Yeats believed his own theory only in a specially qualified way, admitting that its importance lay in the present and not in the past. This is true of Mr. Eliot also. The essays in which he proposed his theory represent a most fruitful and effective refinement of the Symbolist doctrine, yielding far more than Symons's, for instance, similar though they are in essentials. To attack his position has usually seemed to mean an assault on what most people are content to regard as the main tradition of modern verse.

One such attack, that of Mr. Yvor Winters, seems to me both extremely intelligent and extremely revealing; and it carries me on to the last phase of this essay, a cursory glance at the contemporary relation between Image and discourse. Mr. Winters looks for inconsistencies in Mr. Eliot's criticism, so that he can defend his own position, which is notoriously not a fashionable one. He insists that art is a statement of an understood experience, which it morally evaluates; and that poetry has, in consequence, the same *kind* of meaning as cruder statements of the same sort, so that one would expect it to be paraphrasable. This position is, of course, frankly opposed to a cherished Symbolist doctrine, and Mr. Winters is therefore very hostile to some of Eliot's opinions. For example, the famous sigh for an illiterate audience (analogous, by the way, to Yeats's desire for illiterate actors, and really a hopeless wish for an audience incapable of discourse and so cut off from intellection's universe of death) simply fans Winters' indignation, as does the cognate doctrine that meaning is only the burglar's bait for the housedog of intellect. So, when Eliot writes, in the beautiful essay on Dante, that 'clear visual images are given much more intensity by having a meaning—we do not need to know what the meaning is, but in our awareness of the image we must be aware that the meaning is there too,' and when Mr. Winters bullies him about this, we have a clear picture of the fundamental opposition between a Romantic-Symbolist criticism and a criticism conscientiously in reaction against it. Mr. Eliot says that a poem can be understood before its 'meaning' is taken, though the 'meaning' is not without importance. Winters replies: 'If the meaning is important in the creation of the poem, at any rate, it is foolish to suppose that one can dispense with it in the reading of the poem or that the poet did not take his meaning seriously. Only the frailest barrier exists between the idea of this passage and Poe's theory that the poet should lay claim to a meaning when he is aware of none.'

It is no use saying that Mr. Winters has simply misunderstood; he knows very well what Eliot means, as he shows when he traces Eliot's theory of necessary disorder in modern art to Romantic doctrines of organic form, and speaks of *The Waste Land* and *The Cantos* as belonging to the art of revery. He understands the roots of these poems, and even goes so far as to call Pound 'a sensibility without a mind,' which is, if nothing else, a very just punishment upon abusers of the word 'sensibility.' Mr. Winters, as we should expect, is eccentric in his choice of major modern poets, but he is nevertheless the only critic of any fame who can take for granted the history of the kind of poetry and criticism he is opposed to. In the essay on Eliot he bases a very important argument upon a revealing sentence which is hidden away in the introduction to the *Anabasis* of St. Jean Perse: 'There is a logic of the imagination as well as a logic of concepts.' (We, I hope, understand what this means, and can see how sharply such a belief separates the modern from the 'Metaphysical' poet.) It is hard to resist Winters's argument that here 'the word *logic* is used figuratively,' that it indicates nothing but 'qualitative progression,' 'graduated progression of feeling.' Yet for all that the argument is false. It indicates no *progression* of any sort. Time and space are exorcised; the emblem of this 'logic' is the Dancer. This misunderstanding, slight as it seems, shows that the difference between these two critics is extremely wide. If you want to mean something, says Mr. Winters, you must mean it in the usual way; in other words, form is not significant. But to Mr. Eliot, and to many others, this is an admission that the speaker has no real notion at all of what art is. 'People who do not appreciate poetry,' says Mr. Eliot, 'always find it difficult to distinguish between order and chaos in the arrangement of images.' But Mr. Winters does appreciate poetry. The truth is that he is an anti-Symbolist critic, and this necessarily puts him in opposition to most of his contemporaries. For him, poetry is the impassioned expression on the countenance of *all* science and, as George Eliot called it, an aesthetic teacher. Since he does not believe that it deals in a different order of truth he has not the same difficulties about language, communication and paraphrase as the critics who oppose him.

I draw attention in this sketchy way to Mr. Winters, because he leads us to an understanding of what is one of the main issues of modern poetic. This is the unformulated quarrel between the orthodoxy of Symbolism and the surviving elements of an empirical-utilitarian tradition which, we are assured, is characteristically English. Yeats had a foot in both camps, the one stubbornly holding to the commonalty of the means of discourse and seeking to define those differences of degree which distinguish poetry, the other talking about images (sometimes indeed forgetting about words and their temporal behaviour altogether, or treating them as physical things like bits of string) and taking poetry to be a different kind of thing, a different mode of cognition, involving, at least as a working hypothesis, a different order of reality from any available to ordinary intellection. The difficulty of the first party is to find some way of talking about poetry and its propositions that does not disqualify it from the serious attention of *honnêtes gens;* for example, Richard's 'pseudo-statement' is asking for trouble, Wellek's theory of genre is too technical. On the other side, nobody can any longer (in the present state of semantics) be so offhand about the linguistic problems of the Image as the French Symbolists were. Indeed a good deal of the best modern criticism is interesting as evidence of the oscillations and tensions in the minds of critics between the claims of the Image and the claims of ordinary discourse.

These tensions are visible also in poetry, and it is possible that in the controlling of them the immediate future of our poetry lies, as well as our criticism and ways of looking at the past. At the moment, perhaps, the movement of the 'thirties away from aesthetic monism, the new insistence on the right to discourse, even to say such things as 'We must love one another or die' (as Auden does in an exquisite poem) has ceased. There are good poets who cultivate a quasi-philosophical tone of meditation, but they are careful to have no design upon us, to place their meditation within the confines of reverie; there are others who prefer the ironies of stringently mechanical forms; but no Auden, nobody who wants, apparently, to go that way; and this is a pity. Recently Wallace Stevens has come to be more widely read in this country, and he is a poet who provides a unique, perhaps un-repeatable, solution to the image-and-discourse problem, by making the problem itself the subject of poems:

> Is the poem both peculiar and general?
> There's a meditation there, in which there seems
> To be an evasion, a thing not apprehended or
> Not apprehended well. Does the poet
> Evade us, as in a senseless element?
>
> Evade us, this hot, dependent orator,
> The spokesman at our bluntest barriers,
> Exponent by a form of speech, the speaker
>
> Of a speech only a little of the tongue?

One thing Stevens insists upon, and no poet is now likely to forget it: it is a lesson that Romantic aesthetic has taught once and for all. The poem is

> Part of the *res* and not itself about it.
> The poet speaks the poem as it is,
> Not as it was.

Only by knowing this can the poet be 'the necessary angel of the earth.' The sentiment is Blake's, but it has become everybody's; yet Stevens's answer to the problem—it is the problem of dissociation—though very complete, and achieving in the late poem called 'The Rock' a most moving comprehensiveness, is not available to all poets, and they must seek their own.

Stevens's problems are the problems also of modern criticism (in its way and of necessity almost as obscure as the poetry). The unique power of the poet, however one describes it, is to make images or symbols, however one understands these,—as somehow visual, or, in the tradition of the new semantics, as the neologisms created by shifting contexts. How are these products related to discourse? Is there any way to talk of poetry without breaking up the monad and speaking of thought and image?

The one thing nearly everybody seems to be agreed upon is that the work of art has to be considered as a whole, and that considerations of 'thought' must be subordinated to a critical effort to see the whole as one image; the total work is not *about* anything / 'a poem should not mean but *be*'—which is simply a vernacular way of saying what modern critics mean when they speak of it as 'autotelic' (they even speculate as to whether criticism is not also autotelic—the critic as artist once more). But as simply as this, the position is not much changed since Mallarmé: 'nul vestige d'une philosophie, l'éthique on la métaphysique, ne transparaîtra; j'ajoute qu'il faut incluse et latente. . . le chant jaillit de source innée, antérieure à un concept.' And many of the practical difficulties encountered by the holism of French Symbolism recur in modern critics. Take, for example, the problem which must sometimes arise, of what is the whole work of art. Is it the 'Voyage à Cythère' or is it the whole of *Les Fleurs du Mal?* Is it 'They that have power to hurt' or the whole collection of Shakespeare's Sonnets? Professor Lehmann considers the first of these problems in his *Symbolist Aesthetic,* and seems to decide that the proper course is to take one poem at a time, since we know that *Les Fleurs du Mal* is not 'really a poem with a decisive organization overall' but 'poems loosely strung on a string of predominating attitude.' But how, it might be asked, can we be sure of this without trying the experiment of reading the whole book as a poem? Where do we get this important bit of information, which determines the whole question in advance? Certainly, on the purist view, from some illicit source—a knowledge of Baudelaire's intention. This may seem very extreme; but on the contrary it turns up with the regularity of an orthodoxy. We are told to read the whole of Shakespeare as one work. Mr. Wilson Knight reads all the Sonnets as one poem; he won his spurs by pioneering the Symbolist criticism of the plays, and is the most thoroughgoing of the holist Symbolist critics, unless we dare to say that Mr. Eliot, in his most famous essay, invites us to treat the whole of literature as one work.

There is a problem here, inherent in the Symbolist approach to poetry, which deserves more serious treatment than it gets, since it concerns the definition of what critics are talking about. In practice, of course, they cut the knot in silence, and assume the discontinuity of the poem they happen to be talking about, and even, for the purposes of exposition, talk about parts of poems as if they were wholes (just as they slyly paraphrase). Occasionally they even justify this practice. Mr. W. K. Wimsatt has several good things to say about the problem in his book *The Verbal Icon,* for instance this:

> Extreme holism is obviously contrary to our experience of literature. (We do not wait until the end of the play or novel to know whether the first scene or chapter is brilliant or dull —no long work in fact would ever be witnessed or read if this were so.) A poem, said Coleridge, the father of holism in English criticism, is a composition which proposes 'to itself such delight from the *whole,* as is compatible with a distinct gratification from each component part.' The value of a whole poem, while undoubtedly reflecting something back to the parts, has to grow out of parts which are themselves valuable. *The Rape of the Lock* would not come off were not the couplets witty. We may add that good poems may have dull parts; bad poems, bright parts. How minutely this principle could be urged without arriving at a theory of Longinian 'sudden flashes,' of 'cathartically charged images,' of Arnoldian touchstones, of poetic diction, or of irrelevant local texture, I do not know. Nor what the minimal dimension of wit or local brilliance of structure may be; nor to what extent a loosely constructed whole may be redeemed by the energy of individual chapters or scenes. Yet the validity of partial value as a general principle in tension with holism seems obvious.

Something might be said against this defence of *littérature,* for the 'spatial' view of works of art, and it is worth considering that there are modern works (*Ulysses* is an obvious example) which are deliberately, and for long stretches, extremely tedious, and without any brilliance of local texture. Yet what Mr. Wimsatt says is satisfactory to common sense, and in fact modern holist criticism is closely related, so far as poetry is concerned, to that other Symbolist article which sets up the lyric poem as the norm, so that for the most part only short poems get the full treatment.

Even so, the question of how to treat partial aspects continues to rise and trouble practical critics, and occasionally provides new insights. Mr. Empson, for example, has developed a habit of referring regularly to the whole work in the discussions of its parts; Mr. Ransom has raised a whole theory upon the assertion that the value of 'texture' resides precisely in its irrelevance to the structural concern of the poem, and he is further heretical in allowing no poem to be without some embodied 'prose discourse,' providing the logical relevance denied to the 'texture.' Mr. Winters is right, I think, when he calls this an embarrassing doctrine, holding that Ransom 'does not know what to do with the rational content, how to account for it or evaluate it.' (Mr. Winters of course does know this.) To put the matter so baldly is, of course, to do wrong to Mr. Ransom's intense though urbane efforts to solve an important problem; but my object here is merely to insist that the problem arises quite naturally out of the attempt (which must be made in any modern poetic) to find a place for discourse in a Symbolist poetry. Ransom accepts most of the Symbolist position,—he calls the poetry of the Image 'physical' and the poetry of discourse 'Platonic'—right down to the psychological theory of the artist as isolated or inhibited from action (the check on action he calls 'sensibility') and without a radical reorientation there is simply no room for discourse in the work of art so conceived. The problem comes up again in the associated criticism of Allen Tate. He also believes that art 'has no useful relation to ordinary forms of action,' and accepts a distinction similar to that of Ransom, finding the virtue of poetry in the *tension* between idea and image, or between abstraction and concretion, or between discourse and the symbol which can have no logical relation to it.

Such formulations, however fruitful they may be in the exegesis which stems from them (and it is arguable that they are not fruitful in this way at all) have the disadvantages, as well as the benefits, of their Romantic-Symbolist heritage. Mr. R. W. Stallman, in his useful account of these critics, asks us to distinguish between their 'formalism' and 'the aestheticism of the nineties'; but the differences are by no means as decisive as he suggests, and if one were able to construct a normal modern poetic it would be unlikely to contain much, apart from its semantic content, to surprise Arthur Symons. It is true that a new school of critics, the Chicago 'neo-Aristotelians,' are directing us back to the *Poetics* and away from that preoccupation with metaphor (the rhetorical vehicle of the Image) which is an essential component of modern poetic, but one can truly say, without comment on the quality of this criticism, that, from the standpoint of modern orthodoxy, it is clearly tainted with heresy, the heresy of abstraction. What still prevails is the Symbolist conception of the work of art as aesthetic monad, as the product of a mode of cognition superior to, and different from, that of the sciences. Any alternative is likely to be treated as heretical—dubbed, for instance, 'ornamentalist,' as degrading the status of the Image, and leading to another 'dissociation,' another over-valuation of ideas in poetry similar to that effected by Hobbes. One result of this orthodoxy is that the practical business of criticism becomes enormously strenuous, despite the technical facilities provided by Richards and Empson; and that there is a good deal of what must be called cheating, for example in the matter of paraphrase. Good modern criticism is much more eclectic in method than most theoretical pronouncements suggest; it must not seem to believe in paraphrase (or, sometimes, in any form of historical approach to the work in question) yet these and similar forbidden techniques are in fact frequently employed. It may be said that the strenuousness, as well as the obscurity, of such modern criticism, is a direct consequence of its Symbolist inheritance.

The effects of this inheritance may be traced also, so far as I know them, in the philosopher-aestheticians whom critics tend to take notice of (it would not be easy to say why they take notice of some and not of others). There are naturally many variations; but, to take two recent books, the 'concrete universal' as proposed by Mr. Wimsatt is the same thing as the Symbol of Mrs. Langer under a slightly different aspect. Mrs. Langer's is comfortably traditional in design, if not in execution. It starts from music, where the definition of symbol as 'articulate but non-discursive form' does not raise the same problems of 'content' and 'ideas' as it does in literature; so far she shares the 'aestheticism' of the 'nineties.' (It is interesting, by the way, to find her quoting with approval a passage from Arthur Michel about the dance which would have pleased Mallarmé and Symons and Yeats—the dancer is conceived as oscillating 'between two external poles of tension, thus transplanting the dancing body from the sensually existing atmosphere of materialism and real space into the symbolic supersphere of tension space'; and he speaks of 'the dissolution of the dancer into swaying tension.') When she arrives at the problem of the discursive content of poems, Mrs. Langer's answer is that 'the poet uses discourse to create an illusion, a pure appearance, which is a non-discursive symbolic form.' She distinguishes between this position and that of 'pure poetry' as formulated by Moore and Bremond, accurately calling the latter's a magical solution; it is magical in so far as it is Symbolist, and so, perhaps, in its different way, is hers. But hers is distinguished further by arduous and delightful discriminations. She gives modified approval to Mr. Pottle's view that 'Poetry should be no purer than the purpose demands,' but calls it a philosophical makeshift; exposes the mass of unphilosophical thinking that vitiates most attempts to distinguish between poetry and non-poetry; and argues that to maintain its interest in life poetry has to traffic with 'serious thought.' But 'the framework of subject-matter' becomes part of the symbolic whole; something has to be *done* to it, it must, in the Croce-Collingwood sense, be 'expressed,' and it will then be part of the work of art which is 'a single indivisible symbol, although a highly articulated one.'

Mrs. Langer has undoubtedly found a place for 'discourse' in her 'symbol'—so necessary, when the art is one which uses words—and the success of her books is probably an advance towards the dissociation of Romantic-Symbolist aesthetic from the anti-intellectualism with which it has been so persistently and inevitably associated from the beginning, and so potently since Rimbaud. An age of criticism, for so we tend to think of our epoch, is comforted by the assurance that reason can somehow get at poems, and that criticism itself should not be the autotelic act that Wilde as well as some later critics argued it must be (and as it indeed must, if art is the symbol by definition inexplicable). 'The situation,' says Mr. Wimsatt, 'is something like this: In each poem there is something (an individual intuition—or a concept) which can never be expressed in other terms. It is like the square root of two or like pi, which cannot be expressed by rational numbers, but only as their *limit*. Criticism of poetry is like 1.414 . . . or 3.1416 . . . , not all it would be, yet all that can be had and very useful.'

And this is all the critic can expect. He cannot give up the autonomy of the symbolic work of art, a concept of form which has been near the heart of criticism since Coleridge. And so he cannot expect ever to achieve finality in his own work; he is doomed to be limited, even if he remembers the symbolic origin of the discourse he is extracting for discussion. Not that a good critic would wish it otherwise; he is so accustomed to *defending* poetry on these very grounds, his way of thinking about poetry is, in fact, inclined to be defensive, and even when he is asserting poetry's unique powers there is likely to be a cautious anti-positivism in his tone. Reviewing Mr. Philip Wheelwright's recent book *The Burning Fountain,* Mr. M. H. Abrams points out that this excellent writer is 'a prisoner of the theory he opposes' because he accepts the opposition between scientific and expressive language. And Mr. Abrams goes on to suggest, in a most sympathetic way, that we ought now to go over to the offensive. 'An adequate theory of poetry must be constructed, not by a strategy of defense and limited counter-attack on grounds chosen by a different discipline, but by a positive strategy specifically adapted to disclose the special ends and structures and values, not only of poetry as such, but of the rich diversity of individual poems. What is needed is not merely a "metagrammar" and a "paralogic." What is needed, and what the present yeasty ferment in criticism may well portend, is simply, a poetic.'

If such a poetic emerges it will still, of course, be Symbolist; but it will have a different place for discourse from any found for it during the nineteenth-century struggle with the positivists. It will owe much to modern semantics, but it will not call the discourse of poetry 'pseudo-statement.' Nor will its differences from scientific statement be reduced to differences of degree; it will not become statement transfigured by impassioned expression. The new poetic would be remote from the radicalism of Blake, have little to do with the forlorn hopes of Mallarmé, and less with the disastrous *derèglement* of Rimbaud. We have perhaps learnt to respect order, and felt on our bodies the effect of irrationalism, at any rate when the sphere of action is invaded by certain elements of the Romantic *rêve*. It will be a waking poetic, respecting order. 'Shape' has no chance of interfering with 'form,' to use Coleridge's distinction; but among good poets it never had. But 'reason' will return to poetics, and perhaps Mrs. Langer has shown how to find it a *modus vivendi* with the symbol. One notes also that Mr. Wimsatt, as his title suggests, is willing to allow both meanings of 'symbol' to the words of poetry, I mean those of the semasiologist and of the Romantic critic.

But in the end, of course, these matters are solved by poets and not by critics. That is why, I think, Yeats is so important in what I have been saying. He had a matured poet's concern for the relation of symbol to discourse. He understood that one pole of Symbolist theory is sacramentalism, whether Catholic or theurgic:

> Did God in portioning wine and bread
> Give man His thought, or his mere body?

and was willing to see in the discourse, whether of language or gesture, of the dedicated, symbolic values. He, as we have seen, most fully worked out the problems of the Image and of the nature of the poet's isolation; he understood the importance of magic to Symbolist aesthetic; and he also found his solution to that most urgent problem of discourse, assuming that such a statement as 'The best lack all conviction,' in contact with the vast image out of *Spiritus Mundi,* puts on the knowledge with the power of that image. So the slaves of time, the non-poets, will find a validity in his symbolic poems that is, for them, absent from the pure poetry of the dream. They share with the poet not only the Great Memory, but also the ordinary syntax of the daily life of action.

Yeats's sun may be full of angels hymning Jehovah, but it is also a disc shaped somewhat like a guinea. This is not the dissociation of image that is complained of; it is an admission that art was always made *for* men who habitually move in space and time, whose language is propelled onward by verbs, who cannot always be asked to respect the new enclosure laws of poetry, or such forbidding notices as 'No road through to action.' Somehow, and probably soon, the age of dissociation—which is to say, the age that invented and developed the concept of dissociation—must end.

LOUIS L. MARTZ

The Unicorn in Paterson: William Carlos Williams

(1960)

> This is the first part of a long poem in four parts—that a man in himself is a city beginning, seeking, achieving and concluding his life in ways which the various aspects of a city may embody—if imaginatively conceived—any city, all the details of which may be made to voice his most intimate convictions. Part One introduces the elemental character of the place. The Second Part will comprise the modern replicas. Three will seek a language to make them vocal, and Four, the river below the falls, will be reminiscent of episodes—all that any one man may achieve in a lifetime.

So, in 1946, in his sixty-third year, Dr. Williams introduced the first part of his long poem *Paterson,* 'a gathering up' of a lifetime's devotion to the poetical aim set for himself forty years before, when in his early poem, *The Wanderer,* he dedicated his muse to 'The Passaic, that filthy river.'

> Then the river began to enter my heart,
> Eddying back cool and limpid
> Into the crystal beginning of its days.
> But with the rebound it leaped forward:
> Muddy, then black and shrunken

From *Thought* XXXV (1960). The essay appears as Chapter VIII in *The Poem of the Mind,* published by Oxford University Press.

Till I felt the utter depth of its rottenness . . .
And dropped down knowing this was me now.
But she lifted me and the water took a new tide
Again into the older experiences.
And so, backward and forward,
It tortured itself within me
Until time had been washed finally under,
And the river had found its level
And its last motion had ceased
And I knew all—it became me.

Steadily, tenaciously, amid the multifold demands of a medical career, the books of *Paterson* appeared: and in 1951 the promised four books stood complete, fulfilling the wanderer's goal, and carrying out exactly the four-part design announced in Book I.

No wonder then, that some admirers of *Paterson* were struck with consternation and dismay, a few years later, at the news that a *fifth* book of *Paterson* was in progress! That four-part design, so carefully announced and explained by the poet on several occasions—was it to be discarded now? To say the least, the whole procedure was inconsiderate of those critics who had published careful explanations of the poem's symmetry—and encouraging to those other critics who had felt that Book IV did not fulfill the poem's brilliant beginning. But, as usual, Williams knew exactly what he was doing. When, in 1958, the threatened Book V at last appeared, it proved to be an epilogue or coda, considerably shorter than the other books, and written in a reminiscent mode that served to recapitulate and bind together all the foregoing poem. As Williams himself wrote on the dust jacket of Book V: 'I had to take the world of Paterson into a new dimension if I wanted to give it imaginative validity. Yet I wanted to keep it whole, as it is to me.'

The chief agent and symbol of that wholeness is one that may at first seem incongruous with Williams' lifetime dedication to the local, his persistent refusal to adopt or approve the learned, foreign allusions of Ezra Pound or T. S. Eliot: in Book V the organizing symbol is the series of matchless tapestries in 'The Cloisters' representing 'The Hunt of the Unicorn.' True, Williams had dealt briefly with these tapestries in the third book of *Paterson:*

A tapestry hound
with his thread teeth drawing crimson from
the throat of the unicorn

But there the allusion to the world of traditional art seemed ironically overwhelmed by the surrounding scenes of basement ugliness and the fighting between 'the guys from Paterson' and 'the guys from Newark.' Literally, it is only a short drive from Paterson to 'The Cloisters'—but the gap of nearly five hundred years, the distance from France to the Passaic—these are dimensions strange to Williams, however familiar they may be to Pound or Eliot. But an afternoon spent with the great tapestries will show once more the canniness and subtlety of Williams' poetical strategies in *Paterson.*

Williams is defending and explaining his own technique by suggesting an analogy with the mode of the tapestries; and however unlikely any similarity may at first appear, the essential kinship is truly there. For these tapestries, like *Paterson,* achieve their success through a peculiar combination of the local and the mythical. We have the one hundred and one trees, shrubs, herbs, and flowers so realistically woven that eighty-five of them have been identified by botanists and praised for the exactitude of their reproduction; the 'millefleurs background' is not composed of merely symbolical designs, but the colors burst forth from the actual, recognizable violet, cornflower, daisy, calendula, or dandelion. Yet all this actuality serves to border and center the mythical beast of oriental legend, serves to enfold and surround the human figures, the dogs, birds, and wild beasts, the castles and streams, the spears and hunting horns that crowd the scenes with a happy disregard of perspective—even to the point where the sixth tapestry superimposes the wounding of the unicorn upon an upper corner of the larger scene where the mythical beast is presented dead before the King and Queen. Meanwhile, amid the brilliant distortions of art and the splendor of color in flowers and costume, we find the brutal faces of certain varlets, the dog gutted by the unicorn's horn, the dog biting the unicorn's back, the vicious spears stabbing the milk-white beast, the slanting, provocative, betraying eyes of the female attendant upon the virgin.

. cyclamen, columbine, if the art
with which these flowers have been
put down is to be trusted—and
again oak leaves and twigs
that brush the deer's antlers . .
        the brutish eyes of the deer
        not to be confused

with the eyes of the Queen
are glazed with death .
. a rabbit's rump escaping
through the thicket .

. . .

a tapestry
silk and wool shot with silver threads
a milk white one horned beast
I, Paterson, the King-self
saw the lady
through the rough woods
outside the palace walls
among the stench of sweating horses
and gored hounds
yelping with pain
the heavy breathing pack
to see the dead beast
brought in at last
across the saddle bow
among the oak trees.

The placing of that line, 'I, Paterson, the King-self,' implies a parallel between 'Paterson,' the poet, man, self, and city of the poem, and the Unicorn. The mythical beast is the spirit of the imagination, the immortal presence of art:

The Unicorn
has no match
or mate . the artist
has no peer .

. . .

So through art alone, male and female, a field of
flowers, a tapestry, spring flowers unequaled
in loveliness.
through this hole
at the bottom of the cavern
of death, the imagination
escapes intact
. he bears a collar round his neck
hid in the bristling hair.

Thus in the last of the series, the most famous of the tapestries, the Unicorn appears in peaceful resurrection. So 'Paterson' now writes 'In old age'—the opening line of Book V—and knows the threat of mortality as well as the reassurance promised by everything that the Unicorn represents—as we learn from the long closing passage dominated by the tapestries:

—the aging body
with the deformed great-toe nail
makes itself known
coming
to search me out—with a
rare smile
among the thronging flowers of that field
where the Unicorn
is penned by a low
wooden fence
in April–

. . .

the cranky violet
like a knight in chess,
the cinque-foil,
yellow faced—
this is a French
or Flemish tapestry—
the sweetsmelling primrose
growing close to the ground, that poets
have made famous in England,
I cannot tell it all:
slippered flowers
crimson and white,
balanced to hang
on slender bracts, cups evenly arranged upon a stem,
fox glove, the eglantine
or wild rose,
pink as a lady's ear lobe when it shows
beneath the hair,
campanella, blue and purple tufts
small as forget-me-not among the leaves.

Yellow centers, crimson petals
and the reverse,
dandelion, love-in-a-mist,
corn flowers,
thistle and others
the names and perfumes I do not know.
The woods are filled with holly
(I have told you, this
is a fiction, pay attention),
the yellow flag of the French fields is here
and a congeries of other flowers
as well: daffodils
and gentian, the daisy, columbine
petals
myrtle, dark and light
and calendulas .

Anyone who reads the excellent pamphlet on the flora of the tapestries provided by the museum will see at once that most of the flowers here included by Williams are clearly recognizable and listed under these names; but the poet is not presenting a catalogue: he is recreating the act of personal, immediate, imaginative apprehension. Thus at times the poet gives his own familiar names, draws his own conclusions, imagines likenesses. The 'myrtle, dark and light,' for instance, must be the 'periwinkle (*Vinca*)' which 'appears only in the two normal colors of white and blue.' And the 'cinque-foil,/yellow faced' is not mentioned in the museum's account, but it is not hard to find it suggested by certain flowers. Most important, the familiar, intimate quality of the poet's account reminds us that many of these flowers have appeared in the dozens of flower-poems and the hundreds of flower-images scattered throughout the poetry of William Carlos Williams, from his early tributes to the daisy, the primrose, and the 'yellow cinquefoil,' down through the great tribute to Demuth, 'The Crimson Cyclamen,' and on into the recent long flower-tribute to his wife: 'Asphodel, That Greeny Flower,' where the poet recalls his boyhood collection of 'pressed flowers.' Williams is one of the great poets of flowers and foliage, which he observes and represents with a loving and a scientific accuracy akin to that of the Unicorn tapestries. Indeed, in a passage typical of *Paterson*'s mode of organization, this fifth book itself reminds us from the outset of the poet's personal love of flowers by including on its fourth page a personal letter to 'Dear Bill':

> I wish you and F. could have come. It was a grand day and we missed you two, one and all missed you. Forgetmenot, wild columbine, white and purple violets, white narcissus, wild anemonies and yards and yards of delicate wild windflowers along the brook showed up at their best. . . .
>
> How lovely to read your memories of the place; a place is made of them as well as the world around it. Most of the flowers were put in many years ago and thrive each spring, the wild ones in some new spot that is exciting to see. Hepaticas and bloodroot are now all over the place, and the trees that were infants are now tall creatures filled this season with orioles, some rare warbler like the Myrtle and magnolia warblers and a wren has the best nest in the garage. . . .[1]

So the new Book V suggests that we might regard *Paterson* as a kind of tapestry, woven out of memories and observations, composed by one man's imagination, but written in part by his friends, his patients, and all the milling populace of Paterson, past and present; letters from Williams' friends are scattered amply throughout the poem: Book V devotes a whole page to transcribing a letter from Ezra Pound.

The whole, as Williams insists, is a 'fiction' ('pay attention'), but it is at the same time a personal testament to the poet's vehement belief 'that there is a source *in America* for everything we think or do.' Why, then, he asks, 'Why should I move from this place/where I was born?' —Rutherford, New Jersey, next door to Paterson.[2]

II

To find the source, to discover the place—in America—has been his lifelong aim. Thus we have heard now for about forty years Williams' warm, friendly, admiring, generous disagreement with the poetical directions of his lifelong friend Ezra Pound ('The best enemy United States verse has,' he once declared).[3] And so too, in quite a different tone, we have heard Williams' rasping antagonism toward the achievement of T. S. Eliot. The publication of *The Waste Land,* he declares in his *Autobiography,* was 'the great catastrophe to our letters':

> There was heat in us, a core and a drive that was gathering headway upon the theme of a rediscovery of a primary im-

> petus, the elementary principle of all art, in the local conditions. Our work staggered to a halt for a moment under the blast of Eliot's genius which gave the poem back to the academics. We did not know how to answer him.
>
> Critically Eliot returned us to the classroom just at the moment when I felt that we were on the point of an escape to matters much closer to the essence of a new art form itself—rooted in the locality which should give it fruit. . . .
>
> If with his skill he could have been kept here to be employed by our slowly shaping drive, what strides might we not have taken! . . . By his walking out on us we were stopped, for the moment, cold. It was a bad moment. Only now, as I predicted, have we begun to catch hold again . . . (pp. 146, 174).

In those words, published in the same year as the fourth book of *Paterson,* we have a clue to one aspect of that poem's whole design. The more we read and reread *Paterson,* the more it emerges as a subtly devised protest against the cosmopolitan, the learned, the foreign aspects of such poems as *The Waste Land, Four Quartets,* and *The Cantos*. This is made especially plain near the end of the first book of *Paterson,* where Williams writes:

> Moveless
> he envies the men that ran
> and could run off
> toward the peripheries—
> to other centers, direct—
> for clarity (if
> they found it)
>   loveliness and
> authority in the world—
>
> a sort of springtime
> toward which their minds aspired
> but which he saw,
> within himself—ice bound
>
> and leaped, 'the body, not until
> the following spring, frozen in
> an ice cake' (p. 48).

It is a leap from the Falls: one of the major symbols of the poem; and whether or not the poet, like old Sam Patch, the daring diver, perishes at the river's bottom, the descent must be made:

> Caught (in mind)
> beside the water he looks down, listens!
> But discovers, still, no syllable in the confused
> uproar: missing the sense (though he tries)
> untaught but listening, shakes with the intensity
> of his listening (p. 100).

It is a descent, through memory, to the sources of the self, as Williams makes clear in a passage from the second book of *Paterson* (p. 96)—a passage that later appeared as the opening poem of his collection, *The Desert Music* (1954):

> The descent beckons
> as the ascent beckoned.
> Memory is a kind
> of accomplishment,
> a sort of renewal
> even
> an initiation, since the spaces it opens are new places
> inhabited by hordes
> heretofore unrealized,
> of new kinds—
> since their movements
> are towards new objectives
> (even though formerly they were abandoned)

Thus *Paterson* becomes the full realization of the moral vision, the literary theory, the aesthetic manifesto, set forth in the best of his earlier works, *In the American Grain* (1925). We must not mistake this book for an interpretation of history, although it deals with Montezuma, de Soto, Raleigh, Daniel Boone, and George Washington, and although it contains excerpts from the journals of Columbus and from the writings of Cotton Mather, Ben Franklin, and John Paul Jones. The point is not history but rather a search in the memory of America to discover, to invent, symbols of the ideals from which Williams' life and writings have developed.

In the American Grain works with American figures, but the basic issues of the book are universal. It seeks a way of moving from an old world into a new; it seeks a way of leaving the finished forms of culture and dealing with the roar, the chaos, of the still-to-be-achieved. The book discerns two modes of treating the problem. One is found in Williams' version of the Puritan, who represents here, not a single religious creed, but the way of all men who lack 'the animate touch' (p. 177), and who therefore set up within themselves a 'resistance to the wilderness' which is the new life all about them (pp. 115–16).

In contrast to this view, with 'its rigid clarity, its *inhuman* clarity, its steel-like thrust from the heart of each isolate man straight into the tabernacle of Jehovah' (p. 111), Williams presents another vision, dramatized by a group of great explorers, sensitive to the wonder of the life all about them in the new world. There is Columbus, who on the twelfth of October found a world that was filled with things 'wonderful,' 'handsome,' 'marvelous,' 'beautiful.' 'During that time I walked among the trees which was the most beautiful thing which I had ever seen . . .' (pp. 25–6). They are the very words which twenty-five years later Williams recalls in the fourth book of *Paterson* (p. 209), thus picking up the phrase 'beautiful thing' which has formed the theme of his poem's third book. And we have Cortez, Ponce de Leon, de Soto, Raleigh, and Champlain, 'like no one else about him, watching, keeping the thing whole within him with almost a woman's tenderness —but such an energy for detail—a love of the exact detail—' (pp. 69–70).

In these explorers Williams finds a quality of wonder utterly different from what is found in Cotton Mather's 'Wonders of the Invisible World,' his defense of the Salem witchcraft trials, from which Williams here provides long extracts. In Cotton Mather's own words, the Puritans 'embraced a voluntary Exile in a squallid, horrid American Desart'; they felt themselves 'a People of God settled in those, which were once the *Devil's* Territories' (pp. 82–83). *In the American Grain* then turns from these accounts of witchcraft to a chapter entitled 'Père Sebastian Rasles,' but sixteen pages pass before we meet this missionary to the Indians of Maine. Instead we are moved abruptly from Cotton Mather to the Parisian world of the 1920's, where we find Williams surrounded by Picasso, Gertrude Stein, the Prince of Dahomi, James and Norah Joyce, Bryher, H. D., 'dear Ezra,' and other expatriates. Williams is discussing with Valéry Larbaud the situation of the American writer. 'What we are,' he argues, 'has its origin in what *the nation* in the past has been . . . unless everything that is, proclaim a ground on which it stand, it has no worth . . . what has been morally, aesthetically worth while in America has rested upon peculiar and discoverable ground' (p. 109). And in that ground, he declares, we find 'two flaming doctrines' (p. 127). One is Williams' version of the Puritan, and the other is that represented by Rasles, who here becomes a symbol of a way of life maintained by the animate touch. For thirty-four years, says Williams, this French Jesuit lived among his Indians, '*touching* them every day.' In Rasles Williams discovers 'a spirit, rich, blossoming, generous, able to give and to receive, full of taste, a nose, a tongue, a laugh, enduring, self-forgetful in beneficence—a new spirit in the New World.' His vision of life as imagined by Williams is one the poet can share: 'Nothing shall be ignored. All shall be included. The world is parcel of the Church so that every leaf, every vein in every leaf, the throbbing of the temples is of that mysterious flower. Here is richness, here is color, here is form.' 'Reading his letters, it is a river that brings sweet water to us. *This* is a moral source not reckoned with, peculiarly sensitive and daring in its close embrace of native things' (pp. 120–21).

What does it all mean set thus in Paris, amid exiles gathered from England, Africa, Spain, Ireland, and especially America? These exiles, it seems, must be a modern version of the Puritans. They are those who have felt themselves living in a 'squallid, horrid American Desart'; they have refused, like Cotton Mather, to embrace the wilderness. Williams turns instead to those like Daniel Boone, who, says Williams, 'lived to enjoy ecstasy through his single devotion to the wilderness with which he was surrounded'; like Rasles, Boone sought 'to explore always more deeply, to see, to feel, to touch . . .' (p. 136). For Williams, the trouble with modern American culture is that the meaning of life has been obscured 'by a field of unrelated culture stuccoed upon it,' obscured by what he calls 'the aesthetic adhesions of the present day' (p. 212). He seeks instead the 'impact of the bare soul upon the very twist of the fact which is our world about us' (p. 178). For in this impact, the poet (in us all) discovers or invents the beautiful thing. True, the new world no longer holds 'the orchidean beauty' that Cortez, 'overcome with wonder,' saw in Montezuma's Mexico: 'Streets, public squares, markets, temples, palaces, the city spread its dark life upon the earth of a new world, rooted there, sensitive to its richest beauty, but so completely removed from those foreign contacts which harden and protect, that at the very breath of conquest it vanished' (pp. 27, 30, 31–2). True, we have instead the city—Paterson—that has resulted from the schemes of Alexander Hamilton: 'Paterson he wished to make capital of the country because there was waterpower there which to his time and mind seemed colossal. And so he organized a company to hold the land thereabouts, with dams and sluices, the origin today of the vilest swillhole in christendom, the Passaic River . . .' (p. 195). For all this, Williams argues, we must still, like Boone and Houston, make 'a descent to the ground' of our desire (p. 136). 'However hopeless it may seem, we have no other choice: we must go back to the beginning . . .' (p. 215).[4]

III

From this bare ground Williams then begins his *Paterson;* an answer to those 'who know all the Latin and some of the Sanskrit names' (*Grain,* p. 214). Williams prepares his answer in a way subtly suggested by a passage in the second book of *Paterson,* where he seems to echo wryly one of the most famous passages of Pound, Canto 45, on usury, where Pound adopts the manner of a medieval or a renaissance preacher:

With usura hath no man a house of good stone
each block cut smooth and well fitting
that design might cover their face,
with usura
hath no man a painted paradise on his church wall
harpes et luthes . . .

with usura the line grows thick
with usura is no clear demarcation
and no man can find site for his dwelling.
Stone cutter is kept from his stone
weaver is kept from his loom . . .

Came not by usura Angelico; came not Ambrogio Praedis,
Came no church of cut stone signed: *Adamo me fecit* . . .

Usura rusteth the chisel
It rusteth the craft and the craftsman
It gnaweth the thread in the loom
None learneth to weave gold in her pattern . . .

And now this from *Paterson:*

Without invention nothing is well spaced,
unless the mind change, unless

the stars are new measured, according
to their relative positions, the
line will not change . . .
                    without invention
nothing lies under the witch-hazel
bush, the alder does not grow from among
the hummocks margining the all
but spent channel of the old swale,
the small foot-prints
of the mice under the overhanging
tufts of the bunch-grass will not
appear: without invention the line
will never again take on its ancient
divisions when the word, a supple word,
lived in it, crumbled now to chalk (p. 65).

What does this contrast say of these two poets at their best? Williams' own critical acuteness gives us the answer in one of his letters of 1932:

> So far I believe that Pound's line in his *Cantos*—there is something *like* what we shall achieve. Pound in his mould, a medieval inspiration, patterned on a substitution of medieval simulacra for a possible, not yet extant modern and living material, has made a pre-composition for us. Something which when later (perhaps) packed and realized in living, breathing stuff will (in its changed form) be the thing.[5]

It is a summary of Williams' achievement in *Paterson:* the mold is Pound's, combining verse and prose; the line is Pound's, with its flexible cadences, breaking the pentameter; but everything is altered through Williams' invention, his conviction that bold exploration of the local will result in the discovery of a new world blossoming all about him. Pound's mind lives at its best among the splendors of ancient human artifacts, and when these splendors seem threatened, Pound seeks a social answer. He seeks to make art possible by reforming the economic basis of society. It is a difference between the two friends that Pound has acutely described in his essay on Williams (1928), as he contrasts their two temperaments: 'If he wants to "do" anything about what he sees, this desire for action does not rise until he has meditated in full and at leisure. Where I see scoundrels and vandals, he sees a spectacle or an ineluctable process of nature. Where I want to kill at once, he ruminates.' [6]

At the same time, in his ruminative way, Williams gradually implies some degree of sympathy with Pound's economic views. Among the prose passages of the second book of *Paterson,* we find attacks on the Federal Reserve System; we find, too, implied attacks on Alexander Hamilton's plans for federal financing and for creating a great 'National Manufactory' powered by the Passaic falls. These prose excerpts on financial matters are interwoven with the poetical sermon of the evangelist who, in the second book of *Paterson,* delivers his sermon against money to the birds and trees of the park. But this financial theme, thus introduced, is tightly contained within this section: it lies there dormant, recessive, exerting a tacit pressure on the landscape, until, in the center of Book IV, it bursts out again in a highly Poundian diatribe beginning 'Money: Joke.' Here is a section composed in something like Pound's broken multi-cultural style, with expressions in Hebrew, Spanish, and German, along with very crude American slang; and including too some allusions to the Parthenon, Phidias, and Pallas Athene—all this ending with an overt echo of Pound's unmistakable epistolary style:

IN
venshun.
O.KAY
In venshun

(It sounds like Pound nodding his head to the passage on invention that I have just quoted.)

and seeinz az how yu hv/started. Will you consider
a remedy of a lot:
i.e. LOCAL control of local purchasing
power .
? ?
Difference between squalor of spreading slums
and splendor of renaissance cities (p. 218).

It is a tribute to Pound, yes; but it is not for Williams to conclude his own poem in this foreign vein, it is not for Williams to excoriate the present and celebrate the 'splendor of renaissance cities.' This is an invitation that Williams has already refused to accept in the third book of *Paterson,* entitled 'The Library,' where we find the poet attempting to discover a 'sanctuary to our fears' amid the 'cool of books':

> A cool of books
> will sometimes lead the mind to libraries
> of a hot afternoon, if books can be found
> cool to the sense to lead the mind away (p. 118).

He is attempting to escape from the roar of that Falls which provides the central symbol of this poem, for the roar of the Falls in his mind, 'pouring down,' has left him exhausted.

> . . . a falls unseen
> tumbles and rights itself
> and refalls—and does not cease, falling
> and refalling with a roar, a reverberation
> not of the falls but of its rumor
> unabated (p. 119).

Here, the mysterious evocative symbol of the great Falls of the Passaic comes as close to clarity as we shall ever find it. It seems to represent the roar of human speech, the roar of human thought in the mind; it is the roar of the language coming down from the past, mingling with the present, and now bursting downward over the brain of 'Paterson,' who seeks to find somehow in that fall of speech, the beautiful thing that is the ground of his desire. 'What do I do? I listen, to the water falling. . . . This is my entire occupation' (p. 60). But now he is

> Spent from wandering the useless
> streets these months, faces folded against
> him like clover at nightfall,

and he feels that somehow

> Books will give rest sometimes against
> the uproar of water falling
> and righting itself to refall filling
> the mind with its reverberation (pp. 118–19).

But it is not so. As he sits there reading 'old newspaper files,' old annals of Paterson—things like those prose passages of which his poem is in part compounded—as he reads, he finds the roar there, too: stories of fire, cyclone and flood that now beset the poet until his mind 'reels, starts back amazed from the reading' (p. 120)—until the very poem threatens to break apart upon the page (see p. 164). Where to turn? What to do? In ironical answer, Williams brings in certain excerpts from a letter headed 'S. Liz,' that is, from St. Elizabeth's Hospital:

> re read *all* the Gk tragedies in
> Loeb.—plus Frobenius, plus Gesell.
> plus Brooks Adams
> ef you ain't read him all.—
> Then Golding's Ovid is in
> Everyman's lib.
>
> & nif you want a readin
> list ask papa—but don't
> go rushin to *read* a book
> just cause it is mentioned
> eng passang—is fraugs (p. 165).

Williams' answer to Pound is sly. On the next page, he prints an excerpt from some record evidently found in the Paterson Library concerning the drillings taken at the artesian well of the Passaic Rolling Mill, Paterson, and as the results of this local rock-drill run down the page, the excerpt concludes with this significant suggestion: 'The fact that the rock salt of England, and of some of the other salt mines of Europe, is found in rocks of the same age as this, raises the question whether it may not also be found here.'

'Whether it may not also be found here.' For Williams, it may, it can, it will be found here, as he proves by giving in the final section of Book IV a recovery of the source: the pastoral Paterson of early days at peace with the Falls.

> In a deep-set valley between hills, almost hid
> by dense foliage lay the little village.
> Dominated by the Falls the surrounding country
> was a beautiful wilderness where mountain pink
> and wood violet throve: a place inhabited only
> by straggling trappers and wandering Indians.
>
> . . .
>
> Just off Gun Mill yard, on the gully
> was a long rustic winding stairs leading
> to a cliff on the opposite side of the river.

At the top was Fyfield's tavern—watching
the birds flutter and bathe in the little
pools in the rocks formed by the falling
mist—of the Falls . . .

Here is our home, says the poet, inland by the Falls and not in the outgoing sea, as Williams concludes in the rousing finale of Book IV:

I warn you, the sea is *not* our home.
                    the sea is not our home

Here the sea appears to symbolize something more than simple death, national or personal annihilation. For this is also a sea where 'float words, snaring the seeds':

            the nostalgic sea
sopped with our cries
        Thalassa! Thalassa!
calling us home .
I say to you, Put wax rather in your
ears against the hungry sea
                it is not our home!

. draws us in to drown, of losses
and regrets .

The sea appears to represent the pull of longing toward a lost culture, a pull outward from the source, as he goes on to indicate by an overwrought cry that seems to parody the longing of a Pound or an Eliot:

Oh that the rocks of the Areopagus had
kept their sounds, the voices of the law!
Or that the great theatre of Dionysius
could be aroused by some modern magic

. . .

Thalassa! Thalassa!
        Drink of it, be drunk!
                Thalassa
immaculata: our home, our nostalgic
mother in whom the dead, enwombed again
cry out to us to return .

'. . . not our home!' cries the poet again in violent protest, 'It is NOT our home.' And suddenly at the very close of this fourth book, the scene shifts, the tone shifts, to a common seashore with a man bathing in the sea, and his dog waiting for him on the beach.

> When he came out, lifting his knees
> through the waves she went to him frisking
> her rump awkwardly .
> Wiping his face with his hand he turned
> to look back to the waves, then
> knocking at his ears, walked up
> to stretch out flat on his back in
> the hot sand .

And finally after a brief nap and a quick dressing, the man

> turned again
> to the water's steady roar, as of a distant
> waterfall . Climbing the
> bank, after a few tries, he picked
> some beach plums from a low bush and
> sampled one of them, spitting the seed out,
> then headed inland, followed by the dog

'Headed inland'—here at the very close, Williams echoes once again his prose preparation for this poem, *In the American Grain,* for in the closing pages of that earlier book, he had used the same phrasing to describe the achievement of Edgar Allan Poe. 'His greatness,' Williams there declared, 'is in that he turned his back' upon everything represented by a Longfellow and 'faced inland, to originality, with the identical gesture of a Boone' (p. 226). And indeed Williams' account here of Poe's method in his tales is perhaps the best account of *Paterson* that we have yet received:

> the significance and the secret is: authentic particles, a thousand of which spring to the mind for quotation, taken apart and reknit with a view to emphasize, enforce and make evident, the *method*. Their quality of skill in observation, their heat, local verity, being *overshadowed* only by the detached, the abstract, the cold philosophy of their joining together; a method springing so freshly from the local conditions which determine it, by their emphasis of firm crudity and lack of

> coordinated structure, as to be worthy of most painstaking study—(pp. 230–31).

So the two major works of William Carlos Williams reinforce each other, while the tapestry of *Paterson* recalls the whole body of Williams' poetry, as now six pages from the end of Book V we hear:

> 'the river has returned to its beginnings'
> and backward
> (and forward)
> it tortures itself within me
> until time has been washed finally under:
> and 'I knew all (or enough)
> it became me . '

NOTES

1. This letter (signed 'Josie') seems to allude to Williams' memories of the farm owned by Josephine Herbst and her husband, John Herrmann: see his account of the place in *The Autobiography of William Carlos Williams* (New York: Random House, 1951), pp. 269–71.
2. *In the American Grain* (New Directions Paperbook), p. 109; *Paterson,* Books I–IV (New Directions, New Classics Series), p. 93. Subsequent page-references to these works allude to these editions. In the first editions the pages of *Paterson* are not numbered, perhaps in order to stress the plastic and non-logical organization of the poem.
3. In the Prologue to *Kora in Hell* (1920); reprinted in Williams' *Selected Essays* (New York: Random House, 1954); see p. 24.
4. The foregoing discussion of *In the American Grain* echoes a few paragraphs in my earlier article on Williams, *Poetry New York,* No. 4, 1951, pp. 18–32.
5. *The Selected Letters of William Carlos Williams,* ed. John C. Thirlwall (New York: McDowell, Obolensky, 1957), p. 135.
6. *Literary Essays of Ezra Pound,* ed. T. S. Eliot (London: Faber and Faber, 1954), p. 392.

MONROE K. SPEARS

Auden's Longer Poems

(1963)

FOR THE TIME BEING

Auden's mother, who was devout and to whom he had been very close,[1] died in 1941. *For the Time Being,* dedicated to her memory, was written in 1941–2 [2] The subtitle is 'A Christmas Oratorio'; it is of course too long to be set in its entirety, but an abridgement of it was set by the American composer, Melvin Levy, and performed in New York a few years ago. It follows the oratorio form faithfully, except that musical setting is not essential: i.e. it is an oratorio to be spoken or read. In many respects, the oratorio form enables Auden to achieve effects he sought in the plays: there is no dramatic illusion, no identification, and no dramatic characterization. There is, so to speak, a built-in alienation effect, since in the oratorio singers use only their voices to represent their roles, without acting, and the audience is aware continuously of the singers as singers as well as participants in the drama; hence the characters move in two dimensions, as, simultaneously, the unique historical characters and the moderns who are representing them. The oratorio differs from the plays in presenting a story both historical and thoroughly familiar, so that the traditional Christmas pageant or tableau can be suggested, as well as the miracle play, and the lighter elements of popular song and contemporary language can more effectively surprise the reader who expects a wholly solemn, elevated work. The verse is an equivalent for the kind of distancing produced by musical setting, and in variety of forms and meters it succeeds in producing many of the effects of music. The chorus expresses collective feelings and attitudes in a formal, often exalted manner, while the narrator, voluble, articulate, and thoroughly modern, expresses the other side of the contemporary consciousness. Together, they mediate between the audience and the action more effectively than any of Auden's previous choruses or announcers.

From the religious point of view, the form of the Christmas oratorio immediately suggests three kinds of meaning: (1) the unique Incarnation; (2) by association with Christmas and with other Christmas oratorios, plays, pageants, and the like, the annual attempt in Christendom to apprehend and experience the event as the center of the Christian year; (3) the constant attempt of Christians to understand, make viable, and in some sense repeat the Incarnation in their daily lives. *For the Time Being* generally succeeds in keeping the reader simultaneously aware of all three of these meanings. The piece is the fullest and most balanced expression of Auden's religious attitudes; the ideas and dominant images that have been seen partially and transitionally in other poems here may be seen in their final place as part of an ordered whole. Much could be said of the religious background of the piece (the respective influences of Kirkegaard, Niebuhr, Williams, Cochrane, and Eliot) and of the relation of the ideas in it to those Auden had been expounding both in prose and verse; but I shall forego this kind of discussion in favor of what will, I hope, be more immediately useful—an interpretative commentary keeping close to the work itself.

The first section, 'Advent,' represents in the historical sense the exhaustion and despair of the ancient world on the eve of Christ's birth. (As we have seen, Auden had been much concerned in his prose writings with defining the philosophical impasse of the classical world and the parallel with the present.) But two other levels are constantly present: the perennial situation of man without Christ, and, as the title indicates, the annual Church season of preparation for Christmas—the Incarnation, that is, is presented as a recurring as well as a unique event. The opening chorus is trimeter, iambic but with one anapaest to the line; it is probably modeled (as earlier critics have suggested) on the final chorus of Dryden's 'Secular Masque,' but has a very different effect, suggesting plodding weariness and monotony. The semi-chorus interrupts twice, in very irregular trimeter, to describe the loss of hope of a secular savior; great Hercules is not only unable to reinvigorate the empire but is, himself, utterly lost. The chorus plods on in the original meter: 'Darkness and snow descend,' and 'The evil and armed draw near.' Into their lamentations breaks the rational, mundane voice of the narrator. He complains that an outrageous novelty has been introduced, so that 'nothing / We learnt before It was there is now of the slightest use'; as if the room had 'changed places / With the room behind the mirror over the fireplace.' What has happened, he says, is that the locus of reality has shifted: 'the world of space where events reoccur is still there, / Only now it's no longer real; the real one is nowhere / Where time never moves and nothing can ever happen.' (This central theme of the relation of Time to Reality, of the entry of the Eternal into the world of Time as the center of history, and of the resentment and resistance with which the 'outrageous novelty' is greeted by human beings is inevitably rendered sometimes in tones and images recalling its great modern master, Eliot.) In this first speech the narrator continues to explain the consequences to man's sense of identity and relation to the self: 'although there's a person we know all about / Still bearing our name and loving himself as before, / That person has become a fiction. . . .' The chorus chants in despair, 'Alone, alone, about a dreadful wood / Of conscious evil runs a lost mankind' [3] and concludes, 'We who must die demand a miracle,' since 'Nothing can save us that is possible.' The section ends with a recitative and chorus; the former explores the paradoxical nature of religious truth in long, six-stress lines that are precise and restrained in diction ('The Real is what will strike you as really absurd') and introducing the garden and desert symbols ('For the garden is the only place there is, but you will not find it/Until you have looked for it everywhere and found nowhere that is not a desert'); the Chorus, written in elegiacs (alternating dactylic hexameter and pentameter) and elevated in diction, and hence reminiscent of Greek poetry, describes man's condition and his peculiar temptations and difficulties as compared to the other creatures.

  Alas, his genius is wholly for envy; alas,
The vegetative sadness of lakes, the locomotive beauty
  Of choleric beasts of prey, are nearer than he
To the dreams that deprive him of sleep, the powers that compel him
    to idle,
  To his amorous nymphs and his sanguine athletic gods.

How can his knowledge protect his desire for truth from illusion?
  How can he wait without idols to worship . . .

The second section, 'The Annunciation,' begins with the four faculties—intuition, feeling, sensation, thought—that were once one but were dissociated by the Fall. They identify themselves in the manner of abstractions (e.g. the Seven Deadly Sins) in medieval drama, and the dimeter quatrain they employ at first recalls Goethe's *Faust;* their second speeches are in dramatic blank verse. They are the 'Ambiguous causes / Of all temptation' and 'lure men either / To death or salvation'; their function here is to report what happens in the Garden. The Annunciation proper is expressed in a series of beautiful metaphysical lyrics, majestic and complex for Gabriel and exalted and intense for Mary. Gabriel makes explicit the parallel with Eve in her earlier Garden: she, 'in love with her own will / Denied the will of Love and fell'; but 'What her negation wounded, may / Your affirmation heal today';

> Love's will requires your own, that in
> The flesh whose love you do not know,
> Love's knowledge into flesh may grow.

Mary rejoices that God, as a pledge of his love for the world, 'Should ask to wear me, / From now to their wedding day, / For an engagement ring.' The conceit is brilliant and precise, but the tone of the last image seems to me incongruous and anticlimactic. This fault, if real, is no more than the result of the risk inherent in this metaphysical style. More unfortunate is the refrain in the final part of the section, in which the chorus rejoices because *'There's a Way. There's a Voice.'* For American readers at least, this suggests both the Glory Road of the revivalist and the American, or democratic, Way of Life of the propagandist. Auden may have been misled by the musical analogy here. As a sung choral refrain, the line would probably be unobjectionable, but italicized on the page, it stands out, and the contractions with their suggestion of informality are incongruous with the capitalized abstractions.

The third section, 'The Temptation of St. Joseph,' begins audaciously in the vein of the music hall or popular song. Joseph is made very much the average man trying to have faith in spite of appearances; he asks for one reason for believing in divine justice, 'one / Important and elegant proof / That what my Love had done / Was really at your will / And that your will is Love.' But Gabriel answers only, 'No, you must believe; / Be silent, and sit still' [4]—thus defining the nature of faith. The narrator comments amusingly on the relations between the sexes, concluding by observing that Joseph and Mary must be man and wife as if nothing had occurred; for faith abolishes the distinction between the usual and the exceptional: 'To choose what is difficult all one's days / As if it were easy, that is faith. Joseph, praise.' The section closes with a brilliant semi-chorus in which Joseph and Mary are invoked to pray for various types of sinners: first, the romantic lovers 'Misled by moonlight and the rose' who hope to regain innocence through knowledge of the flesh, believe 'Simultaneous passions make/ One eternal chastity'; then the 'independent embryos' (i.e., presumably, children in the womb) who exhibit the original sin in 'every definite decision / To improve'—even in the 'germ-cell's primary division';[5] finally, the bourgeoisie, the 'proper and conventional,' with their 'indolent fidelity' and their habit-forming 'Domestic hatred,' their willed disease. Auden still describes this type with special acerbity:

O pray for our salvation
Who take the prudent way,
Believing we shall be exempted
From the general condemnation
Because our self-respect is tempted
To incest not adultery . . .

Finally, as types of the 'common ungifted' human being and of marriage, Joseph and Mary are invoked to 'Redeem for the dull the / Average Way.'

Section four, 'The Summons,' forms the dramatic climax, in which mere human wisdom is contrasted with the Christian revelation. Historically, the Magi reveal the inadequacy of classical speculative philosophy, while the Fugal-Chorus in ironic praise of Caesar reveals the inadequacy of ancient statecraft or political philosophy; but the parallel between the years one and 1941 is explicit, and the terms more modern than ancient. In this section Auden has the special problem of avoiding both the powerful influence of Eliot's 'Journey of the Magi' and the clichés of Christmas pageants. He manages this by divesting the Magi of their customary solemn impressiveness and transferring it to the Star, which begins by pronouncing the 'doom of orthodox sophrosyne,' of the classical wisdom of moderation; the faith which replaces it offers no security, but is like the fairy-tale 'Glassy Mountain where are no / Footholds for logic' or a 'Bridge of Dread / Where knowledge but increases vertigo.'[6] The Wise Men speak in stanzas characterized by internal rhyme and a rollicking anapaestic beat, but breaking down into formless prose in the latter part of the stanza to represent frustration and confusion. The first one is a natural scientist: 'With rack and screw

I put Nature through / A thorough inquisition'; but her reaction to the investigator (or torturer) made her unreliable; so he follows the Star 'to discover how to be truthful now.' The second Wise Man has put his faith in the constant flow of Time, but has discovered that the Present disappears under analysis: 'With envy, terror, rage, regret, / We anticipate or remember but never are.' He follows the star 'to discover how to be living *now*' (my italics). The third has been a kind of social scientist, hoping to make passion philanthropic by introducing the concept 'Ought';[7] but calculating the greatest good for the greatest number 'left no time for affection,' and he follows the star 'to discover how to be loving now.' The three of them together sing that after their journey 'At least we know for certain that we are three old sinners' and together they seek 'To discover how to be human now.' The star tells them they must endure terror and tribulation, but if they keep faith all will be well.

In strong contrast comes the voice of the secular state, Caesar's proclamation, followed by a Fugal-Chorus in ironic praise of him. The state is more our own than that of Augustus, and the Seven Kingdoms Caesar has conquered are the boasted achievements of our civilization: Abstract Idea includes everything from language to philosophy, and is the basis of the rest; Natural Cause is obviously the natural sciences (considered as a substitute religion); Infinite Number is mathematics; Credit Exchange is the monetary system and finance capitalism; Inorganic Giants are clearly machines; Organic Dwarfs seem to be drugs, which can not only control disease, pain, and worry but stimulate emotions; the last, Popular Soul, is of course propaganda and the techniques of mass psychology. In style, the repetition of formulas and patterns does produce a fugal effect, and the musical analogy is amusing. This is followed by the narrator's news broadcast, fusing modern and ancient, and concluding once more with the secular boast, 'Our great Empire shall be secure for a thousand years.' But this is followed immediately by the confession that 'no one is taken in, at least not all of the time':

> In our bath, or the subway, or the middle of the night,
> We know very well we are not unlucky but evil,
> That the dream of a Perfect State or No State at all,
> To which we fly for refuge, is a part of our punishment.

And he points out, in orthodox fashion, that societies and epochs are transient details, important only as transmitting 'an everlasting opportunity / That the Kingdom of Heaven may come, not in our present / And not in our future, but in the Fullness of Time.' The section ends with a prayer in chorale form, recalling in meter and diction the traditional hymn (and providing an interesting contrast with the parody hymn 'Not, Father, further . . .' in *The Orators*).

'The Vision of the Shepherds,' the next section, interprets the shepherds in traditional fashion as the poor, though they are modern massmen rather than pastoral types; they keep the mechanism going. This section alone would be enough to confute those who say Auden lacks understanding of or sympathy with the common man; it is shrewd, amusing, and without condescension. The shepherds observe that those who sentimentalize poverty and ignorance have 'done pretty well for themselves,' while those who insist that the poor are important and should stand up for their rights also insist that the individual doesn't matter. But, they say, what is real about us all 'is that each of us is waiting' for the Goods News. The Chorus of Angels then announces to them the 'ingression of Love' and the consequent Gospel: the old 'Authoritarian / Constraint is replaced / By his Covenant, / And a city based / On love and consent / Suggested to men. . . .' The chorus adds that 'after today / The children of men / May be certain that / The Father Abyss / Is affectionate / To all Its creatures, / All, all, all of them. . . .'

'At the Manger' presents the traditional tableau with Wise Men and Shepherds. Mary sings a tender lullaby in modified sepphics (five instead of three eleven-syllable lines, followed by a short line of four instead of the customary five syllables), reflecting that her human flesh and maternal care can only bring the Child anxiety, tears, sorrow, and death. The Wise Men and Shepherds characterize their former selves constrastingly, the death-wish ('arrogant longing to attain the tomb') versus regression ('sullen wish to go back to the womb'), 'Exceptional conceit' with 'average fear,' as they bring, instead of the traditional gifts, their bodies and minds to the Child. The Wise Men have discovered that 'Love is more serious than Philosophy / Who sees no humour in her observation / That Truth is knowing that we know we lie.' Repeating (in a virtuosic display) the same rhymes eight times, they explain why human identity and personality is valuable: 'Love's possibilities of realisation / Require an Otherness that can say *I*' and what the true reality of space and time is: 'Space is the Whom our loves are needed by, / Time is our choice of How to love and Why.'

'The Meditation of Simeon,' in contrast to the stress on Love in the preceding section, emphasizes the philosophical meaning of the Incarnation. Since Simeon is the type of the convert, this is appropriate. As has aften been observed, it is probably the best brief exposition of Auden's religious position, or at least of its intellectual aspect. It is in prose—the first time prose has been used in the oratorio—interspersed with one-line alliterative comments by the chorus, which render emotionally what Simeon has been saying in prose. Simeon's style is eloquent, without any particular mask or characterization; his language is that of the modern intellectual. (There is no resemblance whatever to Eliot's 'Song for Simeon.') He explains first that before the Incarnation could take place, it was necessary that the nature and effects of the Fall become clear, that man understand his original sin and the failure of remedy or escape: 'The Word could not be made Flesh until men had reached a state of absolute contradiction between clarity and despair in which they would have no choice but either to accept absolutely or to reject absolutely. . . .' But now 'that which hitherto we could only passively fear as the incomprehensible I AM, henceforth we may actively love with comprehension that THOU ART.' Simeon then proceeds to spell out the intellectual consequences. First, since 'He is in no sense a symbol,' this existence gives value to all others. The distinction between sin and temptation is clarified, 'for in Him we become fully conscious of Necessity as our freedom to be tempted, and of Freedom as our necessity to have faith.' The meaning of Time is illuminated, for 'the course of History is predictable in the degree to which all men love themselves, and spontaneous in the degree to which each man loves God and through Him his neighbour. (This passage has been cited earlier in the discussion of Love in the shorter poems of this period, as has the one about the elimination of the distinction between the Average and the Exceptional, the Common Man and the Hero: 'disaster is not the impact of a curse upon a few great families, but issues continually from the hubris of every tainted will. Every invalid is Roland . . . , every stenographer Brunnhilde. . . .') A further aesthetic consequence is that the Ridiculous is no longer confined to the Ugly; since 'of themselves all men are without merit, all are ironically assisted to their comic bewilderment by the Grace of God'; hence the logic of fairy tales represents spiritual truth: 'Every Cabinet Minister is the woodcutter's simple-minded son to whom the fishes and the crows are always whispering the whereabouts of the Dancing Water. . . .' Similarly, every situation is now essentially as interesting as any other: 'Every tea-table is a battlefield littered with old catastrophes . . . every martyrdom an occasion for flip cracks and sententious oratory.' Finally, in a passage we have already quoted (above, p. 193),* Simeon explains the metaphysical value of the Trinity: since the Word is united to the Flesh, the One and the Many are simultaneously revealed as real, so that neither can be denied. Truth is One, but 'the possibilities of real knowledge are as many as are the creatures in the very real and most exciting universe that God creates with and for His Love. . . .' Simeon concludes by praying that 'we may depart from our anxiety into His peace.'

As Simeon is the type of the Christian convert and intellectual, Herod, in the next section, 'The Massacre of the Innocents,' is the type of the liberal intellectual, the Manager and Apollonian we have seen in the shorter poems, dedicated to service, progress, and the advancement of reason, now confronted with the Irrational. His speech, which counterbalances Simeon's as the only other one in prose, is a deft fusion of ancient and modern: Herod is both the historical character and the liberal of the late 1930s, trying to cope with the threats of war and fascism.[8] His speech is witty, amusing, and highly persuasive on its own premises: his long struggle to establish law and order and push back superstition is doomed by this irruption of the Irrational. In terms sometimes recalling Yeats's play, 'The Resurrection,' and sometimes recalling Nietzsche, he gloomily predicts the consequences—Reason will be replaced by Revelation, Idealism by Materialism, Justice by Pity. 'Naturally this cannot be allowed to happen,' and he concludes reluctantly that he must send for the military to prevent it. Petulantly, he complains, 'Why can't people be sensible? I don't want to be horrid. Why can't they see that the notion of a finite God is absurd?' It is unreasonable that a decision as to the existence of God should be up to Herod: 'How dare He allow me to decide?' (In other words, he refuses to go beyond the secular and rejects the existentialist Choice.) He concludes uneasily and self-pityingly, 'I've tried to be good. I brush my teeth every night. I haven't had sex for a month. I object. I'm a liberal. I want everyone to be happy. I wish I had never been born.'

The Soldiers speak next, their callous brutality and cynical humor embodying the perennial cruelty and evil of human nature; their speech comes after Herod's with massive irony, reminding us that the end in practice of Herod's plausible speech has been the decision to massacre the Innocents. The fantasy and exaggeration of the Soldiers' speech

* Reference is to work in which this essay was originally published. All such cross references have been retained.—Ed.

and its ironic tall-story 'good fellowship' prevents any effect of striving for pathos, which is merely indicated by the presentation at the end of the section of Rachel weeping for her children in a speech of great power and restraint.

The last section, 'The Flight into Egypt,' presents Joseph and Mary being tempted by Voices of the Desert as they pursue their journey through the looking-glass, i.e., the journey of faith. These Voices seem to represent the temptations of the 'normal' and particularly modern world; [9] they tempt with nonsense songs that sound like advertising commercials gone mad. (*The Age of Anxiety* employs this style extensively.) Joseph and Mary observe that insecurity is the condition natural to humanity: 'Safe in Egypt we shall sigh / For lost insecurity. . . .' Then follows a fine recitative interpreting the Flight as a redemption of the past: 'Fly, Holy Family, from our immediate rage, / That our future may be freed from our past. . . .' [10] The narrator's long speech modulating back to the present of Christmas trees and everyday life is both amusing and profound. The atmosphere of Christmas as it is for most of us is evoked with great precision, and contrasted with its religious meaning: 'Once again / As in previous years we have seen the actual Vision and failed / To do more than entertain it as an agreeable /Possibility, once again we have sent Him away. . . .' We think of the future, of the coming of Lent and Good Friday; 'But, for the time being, here we all are, / Back in the moderate Aristotelian city,' the everyday world. And to deal properly with this world and the present time is most difficult: 'To those who have seen / The Child, however dimly, however incredulously, / The Time Being is, in a sense, the most trying time of all.' To escape our guilt and inhibit our self-reflection, we are tempted to pray for temptation and suffering. They will come,[11] but 'In the meantime / There are bills to be paid, machines to keep in repair, / Irregular verbs to learn, the Time Being to redeem / From insignificance.' In a metaphor developed later in 'Nones' and in the rest of 'Horae Canonicae,' Auden says, 'The happy morning is over, / The night of agony still to come; the time is noon . . .'; and the soul knows that 'God will cheat no one, not even the world of its triumph.' [12] This magnificent conclusion is followed by a rather weak and anticlimactic chorus, perhaps necessary to carry out the musical analogy, but seeming flat on the page.

For the Time Being has enjoyed a good deal of popularity: as we have seen, an abridged version of it was set to music by Melvin Levy and performed in New York in 1959, and it is reprinted entire in *Mod-*

ern Poetry, edited by Maynard Mack, Leonard Dean, and William Frost (New York, 1950)—a widely used textbook—and in *Religious Drama 1,* edited by M. Halverson (New York, 1957); it is performed rather frequently by religious groups. Probably the fact that Eliot's *Four Quartets,* which embody many of the same themes (though in a very different way), happened to appear shortly before it has had much to do with the failure of the oratorio to impress the critics profoundly; comparison with Eliot's towering achievement is inevitable and the result is a foregone conclusion. The oratorio has also suffered from the equally inevitable comparison with the other work that originally appeared in the same volume with it, *The Sea and the Mirror,* which has seemed to most critics more brilliant, novel, and provocative, and therefore has the lion's share of their attention. Considered on its own terms, and at this distance in time, the work may be seen as a unique and remarkable success both formally and as a whole. The traditional forms of the Christmas pageant and oratorio are transformed and deepened to embody the apprehension by the modern consciousness of the central event in history, understood psychologically, emotionally, and intellectually, by constant parallels with contemporary life; the various characters represent various types and also aspects of each of us, and the different episodes represent different aspects of the religious life of the individual, as well as the historical events. There is thus a great range and variety implicit in the scope of the piece, shown most obviously in the formal variety of verse and prose. Throughout, there is a triple consciousness at three levels: first, the unique historical event of the Incarnation; second, the collective, seasonal aspect of Christmas in its place in the Christian year, with its annual attempt to make it possible for Christ to be re-born, so to speak; and finally, the moment-to-moment effort of the individual to redeem everyday life from insignificance, to manifest the Incarnation in himself, to be a Christian. There are, as always in Auden, flaws and unevenness; but the central problem of rendering these three kinds of consciousness simultaneously is solved with brilliant success, and provides an adequate unifying principle for the enormous scope and variety of the piece. The oratorio does not seem dated or topical, nor does the religious attitude expressed seem in any way eccentric or extravagant. Auden placed the oratorio last both in *For the Time Being,* 1944, and in *Collected Poetry,* 1945, presumably because he felt, with justice, that it provided a very suitable conclusion for a volume.

THE SEA AND THE MIRROR

The Sea and the Mirror was written after *For the Time Being,* between 1942 and 1944.[13] Obviously, the religious commitment with its basic shift in perspective would require a new aesthetic formulation; and that is essentially what *The Sea and the Mirror* is: a definition and exploration of the relations between the Mirror of Art and the Sea of Life, or Reality. Appropriately, the piece is a virtuoso display of Auden's technical accomplishment: each character speaks in a different form, and many of them are very complicated indeed—ballade, villanelle, sestina, sapphics, elegiacs, terza rima, syllabic verse, and the prose style of the later James. But there is also a great variety of songs in Auden's best vein.

The Sea and the Mirror has no such definite form to follow as *For the Time Being,* its subtitle being 'A Commentary on Shakespeare's *The Tempest.*' There is the implicit setting of a theater, after a performance of *The Tempest;* the Stage Manager addresses the Critics in the Preface, and the Prompter echoes the last speech. In the first scene, Prospero, packing up to leave the Island, bids farewell to Ariel; in the second, the rest of the cast, on a ship taking them back to Italy from the Island, speak *sotto voce* to each other and to the audience. They are all still in the world of the play, but at the same time are sufficiently detached from it to comment on its meaning and on their future lives; in some sense they are leaving the Enchanted Island of the art work and emerging into 'real' life. The last of them, Caliban, addresses the audience directly and develops explicitly the speculations about the relation between Art and Life suggested both by the play and by the dual roles the other characters have just been playing. It is all done with mirrors: an exercise in illusion, in *trompe-l'oeil* reversals in which mirrors turn out to be paintings and paintings are revealed as windows. In this theme, and in the whole notion of a closet drama which is also a philosophical commentary on itself and on the nature of art, there is some resemblance to Goethe's *Faust.* There is, however, nothing to control the form, no musical analogy and no dramatic action. This becomes clearest in Caliban's address to the audience, which, though very brilliant indeed, is inordinately long (about half the total length) and inordinately subtle for any dramatic analogy, and proliferates into a baroque profusion of distinctions and elaborations. The imagination boggles at the thought of actually staging it. This is not necessarily a defect; it is clearly intended as closet drama, and full advantage is taken of its impracticability for the stage. (The divisions that I have called scenes are called 'chapters' in the first printing.) Just as there is one verse form not even Auden would be audacious enough to attempt here—Shakespearian blank verse—so he must make it very clear that he is not attempting drama in Shakespearian terms, that he is not writing a sequel to *The Tempest*.

In the Preface the Stage Manager discourses to the Critics on the limits of art and its difference from life. Beginning with audience psychology, he argues that it is the predictability, the lack of surprise, that make it enjoyable. Art moves us, but does not affect the will; it does not help us to satisfy 'Between Shall-I and I-Will, / The lion's mouth whose hunger / No metaphors can fill.' (This is parallel to Auden's formulations in prose—see below, pp. 335–6—of the ultimate frivolity of art.) Finally, he suggests that the 'real' world, the other side of the footlights, is also illusory, and concludes in a beautiful pastiche of Shakespeare:

All the rest is silence
On the other side of the wall;
And the silence ripeness,
And the ripeness all.

The meter is the same as that of the opening chorus of *For the Time Being,* but its effect in this witty and elegantly colloquial lyric is quite different. The first scene (or chapter) introduces Prospero saying farewell to Ariel as he packs to leave the island; appropriately, he speaks in elegiacs. The symbolism is basically traditional: Prospero is the writer giving up his art, setting free Ariel (imagination), and leaving the enchanted island (the world of art) to return to the real world. In Kierkegaardian terms, he is renouncing the aesthetic for the religious; or in more general terms he is discovering that art is not a substitute for religion even for the artist, whose art gives him no special privileges from the religious standpoint. Prospero comments that he is glad he has freed Ariel, under whose influence death is inconceivable, for now he can 'really believe I shall die.' He recalls his motives for first resorting to magic in childhood as escape and compensation, and defines magic as 'the power to enchant / That comes from disillusion.' Once we have learned 'to sit still and give no orders' Ariel offers his echo and mirror; 'We have only to believe you, then you dare not lie.' As Prospero bids him farewell, he reflects that Ariel has corrupted him through his own weaknesses and hence he has broken 'Both of the promises I made as an apprentice;— / To hate nothing and to ask nothing for its love'— the first by tempting Antonio into treason, the second in wishing for Caliban's absolute devotion. He describes the other characters; all have been soundly hunted / By their own devils into their human selves' and are pardoned. As he thinks of the probable difficulties of Ferdinand and Miranda, he reflects that he is glad to be through with youth and all its problems—and the longings of youth are embodied ironically in the fine song 'Sing first that green remote Cockagne,' which, like the other two songs in this chapter, Prospero sings to Ariel. Finally, he says, now that the partnership with Ariel is dissolved, that is, now that he has abandoned art and is a man like any other, it is as if he had dreamed all his life about an imaginary journey, 'And now, in my old age, I wake, and this journey really exists, / And I have actually to take it, inch by inch. . . .' His journey, or quest, is the religious one in which he will no longer be interesting, but will appear perfectly ordinary, yet will be (in Kierkegaard's phrase) 'Sailing alone, out over seventy thousand fathoms'; he will not be able to speak, but must 'learn to suffer / Without saying something ironic or funny / On suffering. If he is lucky, he may learn before he dies 'The difference between moonshine and daylight.' The final song contrasts Ariel's unconcern with the human condition: he is an 'unfeeling god,' 'unanxious one' who can therefore sing brilliantly, lightly 'Of separation, / Of bodies and death. . . .'

The second scene presents the supporting cast on the ship going home, as they look back to the island and reflect on their experiences. (They have all been introduced and characterized in Prospero's speech.) Antonio, villain of the play, the wicked usurping brother, is the only character who is unchanged, and he dominates the section. In his terza rima speech he takes an ironic view of the other characters, the metamorphoses and the happy ending: it is all an illusion, a product of Prospero's art—'What a lot a little music can do.' But Antonio makes it impossible for him to renounce his magic by refusing to submit to it: 'as long as I choose / To wear my fashion, whatever you wear / Is a magic robe; while I stand outside / Your circle, the will to charm is still there.' And this is his revenge, to prevent Prospero's return to innocence. After his own speech, and after each of the other characters speaks, Antonio sings a song addressed ironically to Prospero, comparing himself to the character in question. This reiterated opposition gives a certain dramatic tension to the section.

Ferdinand, in a sonnet (with dodecasyllabic lines) addressed to

Miranda, celebrates their love and the mystery of their union in reverent terms. Stephano, the drunken butler, in contrast sings a love song to his belly: it is a ballade, and pathetic rather than humorous, with its refrain, 'A lost thing looks for a lost name.'

Gonzalo, the good old man, defines (in trochaic tetrameter with catalexis) what has happened as they leave the 'island where / All our loves were altered.' He has explained too much, been too fond of his own eloquence, he says; instead he should have 'trusted the Absurd' and reproduced the song (the reference is to Ariel's warning in *Tempest* II, i); but through 'Doubt and insufficient love' he has frozen 'Vision into an idea' and 'made the song / Sound ridiculous and wrong.' Now, however, he can be 'a bell' ready to express the divine will. Adrian and Francisco, the lightweight courtiers, have an amusing couplet suggesting that they have learned that fashionable chit-chat cannot cover up the ultimate issues: 'it's madly ungay when the goldfish die.' [14]

Alonso then makes a long speech, the most substantial and profound as well as the richest poetically in the whole scene. The verse is syllabic (lines of nine syllables) [15] and the stanzas consist of twelve lines in a complex pattern: first two couplets, then a modified envelope quatrain, then a modified alternate quatrain (aabbcddefefc). Alonso begins by advising Ferdinand on the familiar Renaissance theme of the proper behavior for a prince. The two symbols in the first stanza come naturally from *The Tempest,* in which the sea and sea-changes, and yellow sands, have been prominent. At first they are used merely for a contrast between the human and the non-human: the sea and the desert and their creatures regard sceptres, crowns, and kings themselves as no more than physical objects. In the first two stanzas this powerful but essentially simple contract is used as a warning against pride, a reminder of mortality and of human limitations. But then in the next two stanzas the symbols are developed further as the two extremes between which the 'Way of Justice is a tightrope.' [16] The fears they represent are described as, respectively, sinking in the sea 'entangled in rich robes' or standing undressed in the desert exposed to ridicule. The corresponding temptations are, from the sea, 'a night / Where all flesh had peace' and from the desert, 'a brilliant void / Where his mind could be perfectly clear / And all his limitations destroyed.' But to succumb to either of these extremes means 'To join all the unjust kings.' Alonso goes on to warn Ferdinand of the difficulty of holding to the way of justice, avoiding both the 'watery vagueness' and the 'triviality of the sand,' steering between 'lose craving' and 'sharp aversion,' 'aimless jelly' and 'paralysed bone,' remembering 'that the fire and the ice / Are never more than one step away / From the temperate city.' The dying Alonso concludes by advising Ferdinand that if, like him, he should lose his kingdom, he should 'praise the scorching rocks / For their desiccation of your lust' and 'Thank the bitter treatment of the tide / For its dissolution of your pride' so that the 'whirlwind may arrange your will / And the deluge release it.' He may then find the 'spring in the desert, the fruitful / Island in the sea, where flesh and mind / Are delivered from mistrust.'

These are subtle and rich symbols, not to be violated by crude paraphrase; but we may suggest that the sea is associated with the flesh, the senses, potentiality, and subjectivity; the desert with mind, abstraction, the temptation to ignore the limitations of the human creature. Only through balancing one against the other, and allowing each to purge the characteristic vice of the other—the desert drying up lust, the sea dissolving pride—can the two be reconciled and the oasis in the desert or island in the sea be found. (There is a general resemblance to Kierkegaard's Aesthetic/Ethical categories, though the meaning of the symbols is ultimately very different.) [17]

The song of the master and boatswain, 'At Dirty Dick's and Sloppy Joe's' (based on Stephano's song in *The Tempest,* II, ii), makes a fine contrast to the exalted seriousness of Alonso, who has concluded by expressing his readiness 'to welcome / Death, but rejoicing in a new love, / A new peace, having heard the solemn / Music strike and seen the statue move / To forgive our illusion.' [18] Their song is remarkable in combining pathos with the convivial song so that, while the tone remains earthly and humorous, the sailors' loneliness and hopelessness appear movingly underneath. Sebastian, the wicked brother who had tried to kill Alonso, but been prevented by Ariel, next makes his confession and rejoices in his defeat and exposure ('my proof / Of mercy that I wake without a crown'); the form is that of the sestina. Trinculo, the jester, then sings a sad song about his isolation, and Miranda concludes the section with a very beautiful villanelle. Appropriately, it draws its imagery from the world of childhood (fairy tales, nursery rhymes, and the like). Some critics have complained that the first line ('My Dear One is mine as mirrors are lonely') lacks precise meaning; but this seems to me to ignore the context. Miranda is saying that her love is as true and unquestionable as three natural and unquestionable truths—unquestionable, of course, only to an innocent, sheltered, and trusting nature. Mirrors are, to such a nature, lonely of course because there is nobody there; they want somebody to reflect.[19] This is her mode of understanding reality—limited, vulnerable, and probably highly temporary; she still believes fairy-tale happy endings and her understanding of politics is limited to the conviction that good kings are always concerned for the poor. We are meant to keep in mind Prospero's earlier forebodings about the course of her and Ferdinand's love when they are married and out in the everyday world. All this adds overtones of pathos to her villanelle, which expresses a unique innocence and purity as she emerges from childhood into happy love.

Finally, the third scene, almost half of the whole, consists of 'Caliban to the Audience.' [20] Caliban explains that he is appearing instead of Shakespeare to take the curtain call because he is himself 'the begged question you would speak to him *about*.' Speaking in a mild and sympathetic parody of the style of the later James, Caliban in rapid succession puts on three different masks, each time addressing a different group upon a different topic. In the first section, Caliban, speaking for the audience, addresses Shakespeare about the nature of art and its difference from life. The Jamesian tone is highly appropriate, since the English Muse is represented as a society matron whom Shakespeare has offended by the *faux pas* of introducing Caliban (Life, Reality, Nature). The audience wishes to preserve the distinction between Art and Life and Caliban, in a tone of injured complaint, points out to Shakespeare his offense against decorum. The world of Art, the salon of the Muse, is one of freedom without anxiety, of 'the perfectly tidiable case of disorder, the beautiful and serious problem exquisitely set without a single superfluous datum and insoluble with less'; to introduce the symbol of Reality into this world is unforgivable. The audience feels an intentional insult:

> Are we not bound to conclude then, that, whatever snub to the poetic you may have intended incidentally to administer, your profounder motive in so introducing Him to them among whom, because He doesn't belong, He couldn't appear as anything but His distorted parody, a deformed and savage slave, was to deal a mortal face-slapping insult to us among whom he does . . . ?

In life Caliban and Sycorax appear as Cupid and Venus: 'the nude august elated archer of our heaven, the darling single son of Her who, in her right milieu, is certainly no witch but the most sensible of all the gods . . . our great white Queen of Love herself.' This confusion of the realms may lead, the spectators think, to worse consequences:

> Is it possible that, not content with inveigling Caliban into Ariel's kingdom, you have also let loose Ariel in Caliban's? . . . For if the intrusion of the real has disconcerted and incommoded the poetic, that is a mere bagatelle compared to the damage which the poetic would inflict if it ever succeeded in intruding upon the real. We want no Ariel here, breaking down our picket fences in the name of fraternity, seducing our wives in the name of romance, and robbing us of our sacred pecuniary deposits in the name of justice.

After a brief transition, Caliban speaks for Shakespeare: he delivers 'a special message from our late author' to prospective poets ('any gay apprentice in the magical art') on the topic of the poet as citizen, the effect of poetry upon the poet. The partnership with Ariel, magician and familiar, is at first a brilliant success; but when, tiring, the artist wishes to dismiss him, Ariel becomes a 'gibbering fist-clenched creature' —Caliban, 'not a dream amenable to magic but the all too solid flesh you must acknowledge as your own.' Ignoring the ethical, the artist neglects his quotidian self, and when his charms crack, he is left alone with the dark thing he could never abide to be with. The outlook for the future, Caliban comments, is not bright: 'the only chance . . . of my getting a tolerably new master and you a tolerably new man, lies in our both learning . . . to forgive and forget the past, and to keep our respective hopes for the future within moderate, very moderate limits.'

Caliban's final transition is to the religious level, where he speaks for himself and Ariel to the audience on the nature of reality. Life is a journey made up of long waits between the 'three or four decisive instants of transportation'; everyday life is the 'Grandly Average Place from which at odd hours the expresses leave seriously and sombrely for Somewhere':

> But once you leave, no matter in which direction, your next stop will be far outside this land of habit that so democratically stands up for your right to stagestruck hope, and well inside one of those, all equally foreign, uncomfortable and despotic, certainties of failure or success. Here at least I, and Ariel too, are free to warn you not, should we meet again there, to speak to either of us, not to engage either of us as your guide, but there we shall no longer be able to refuse you . . . Here . . .

> I can at least warn you what will happen if at our next meeting you should insist . . . on putting one of us in charge.

The consequences of putting either Caliban or Ariel in charge are vividly portrayed in symbolic fantasies that are fascinating, infinitely suggestive, and impossible to paraphrase. There is an obvious but elusive relation to the sea and desert symbols we have discussed as they appear in 'Alonso to Ferdinand'; in general, Caliban's realm is that of the sea (pure deed, sensation, etc.) while Ariel's corresponds to the desert (pure word, abstraction, etc.); but the correspondence is not exact.[21] Those who take Caliban as guide do so in the hope of recovering the lost Eden of childhood, of which alternative versions are brilliantly evoked:

> Carry me back, Master, to the cathedral town where the canons run through the water meadows with butterfly nets and the old women keep sweet-shops in the cobbled side streets, . . . Pity me, Captain, . . . let me see that harbour once again just as it was before I learned the bad words. Patriarchs wiser than Abraham mended their nets on the modest wharf; white and wonderful beings undressed on the sand-dunes; sunset glittered on the plateglass windows of the Marine Biological Station . . . Look, Uncle, look. They have broken my glasses and I have lost my silver whistle. Pick me up, Uncle, let little Johnny ride away on your massive shoulders to recover his green kingdom . . . O Cupid, Cupid, howls the whole dim chorus, take us home. We have never felt really well in this climate of distinct ideas . . .

(We remember that Caliban appears as Cupid in the 'real' world.) But, says Caliban, he cannot transport them to any such Eden 'which your memory necessarily but falsely conceives of as the ultimately liberal condition,' but only to that state as it really is, a desolate and indifferent scene 'where Liberty stands with her hands behind her back, not caring, not minding *anything*.' Here, he concludes in terms that parody those of atheistic existentialism, 'your existence is indeed free at last to choose its own meaning, that is, to plunge headlong into despair and fall through silence fathomless and dry, all fact your single drop, all value your pure alas.'

The fate of those who put 'my more spiritual colleague,' Ariel, in charge is no happier. These are idealists, Managers, responsible and respectable people (whereas the followers of Caliban have been Hermetics, common, all-too-human men); they surrender to Ariel in the hope of escaping the mess of life:

> Deliver us, dear Spirit, from the tantrums of our telephones and the whispers of our secretaries conspiring against Man; deliver us from these helpless agglomerations of dishevelled creatures with their bed-wetting, vomiting, weeping bodies, their giggling, fugitive, disappointing hearts, and scrawling, blotted, misspelt minds, to whom we have so foolishly tried to bring the light they did not want; deliver us from all the litter of *billets-doux,* empty beer bottles, laundry lists, directives, promissory notes and broken toys, the terrible mess that this particularised life, which we have so futilely attempted to tidy, sullenly insists on leaving behind it; translate us, bright Angel, from this hell of inert and ailing matter . . .

Ariel leads them into a 'nightmare which has all the wealth of exciting action and all the emotional poverty of an adventure story for boys' to fulfill their desire for unconditional freedom. In this realm there is a 'state of perpetual emergency and everlasting improvisation'; all voluntary movements are possible, but 'any sense of direction, any knowledge of where on earth one has come from or where on earth one is going to is completely absent.' Other selves exist, but no one knows who are his friends or enemies, what is going on, what his own role is:

> Everything, in short, suggests Mind but, surrounded by an infinite extension of the adolescent difficulty, a rising of the subjective and subjunctive to ever steeper, stormier heights, the panting frozen expressive gift has collapsed . . .

From this 'nightmare of public solitude' there is no escape; the inevitable end is 'a serious despair, the love nothing, the fear all.' These, Caliban concludes, are 'the alternative routes, the facile glad-handed highway or the virtuous averted track, by which the human effort to make its own fortune arrives all eager at its abruptly dreadful end.'

In the final section Caliban returns to the plight of the artist, discussing it now in ultimate terms, and concerned not with art versus life but with both versus the Divine. The artist is in a 'serio-comic embarrassment' since he cannot represent both divine truth and the human condition of estrangement from the truth: the more truthfully he paints the condition, the less clearly can he indicate the truth from which it is estranged, the brighter his revelation of the truth in its order, its justice, its joy, the fainter shows his picture of your actual condition in all its drabness and sham. . . .' His ultimate aim must be to 'make you unforgettably conscious of the ungarnished offended gap between what you so unquestionably are and what you are commanded without any question to become. . . .' Yet the final danger is that the more he succeeds in doing this 'the more he must strengthen your delusion that an awareness of the gap is in itself a bridge, your interest in your imprisonment a release'; instead of leading to contrition and surrender, 'the regarding of your defects in his mirror' becomes a game, the most interesting of all games. Hence the artist, caught in these dilemmas, must hope 'that some unforeseen mishap will intervene to ruin his effect'; that his art will fail. The final image is the venerable one of the world as stage, but rendered as mock-heroic: life as 'the greatest grand opera rendered by a very provincial touring company indeed.' All of us, as actors, hope for, not applause, but the 'real Word which is our only *raison d'être.*' The mirror and proscenium represent the gulf which separates all life from that 'Wholly Other Life,' yet we can rejoice in the perfected Work which is not ours.

I have tried to indicate only the main outlines of this extremely complex speech, which is full of amusing and fascinating detail. Within the light framework the argument is, of course, intensely serious; but Auden needs the complicated system of masks, the double irony, to enable him to speak seriously.[22] His innovation consists in preparing the reader for ironic argument by creating a faintly ridiculous style and fantastic masks, and then making the argument *not* ironic; the technique is what William Empson might term 'the Fool speaks truth.'

The 'Postscript' is a song addressed to Caliban by Ariel, with echo by the Prompter. It would be rash indeed after Caliban's speech to say in a word what Ariel and Caliban represent here, but the primary meaning would seem to be the traditional one: Ariel is Art with its inhuman perfection and Caliban is Life with all its imperfection. Ariel is a 'shadow cast / By your lameness' partly because art is compensation for the artist's defects (as Freud argued), and partly because art arises from and deals with human imperfection and suffering (this is the theme of Yeats's 'Vacillation': 'Homer is my example and his unchristened heart'). Hence Ariel is 'Helplessly in love with you, / Elegance, art, fascination, / Fascinated by / Drab mortality.' They must forever remain separate but complementary.

What can one say, finally, of *The Sea and the Mirror* as a whole? It is brilliant, infinitely suggestive, and often obscure. It is baroque in the proliferation and complication of its form: full of double and triple ironies as it deals with the relation of Art and Life in the guise of an art work commenting on another art work, shifting back and forth over imaginary footlights with sleight-of-hand rapidity. It is more uneven and less coherent than *For the Time Being,* but perhaps more audacious and varied; and it contains some of Auden's finest poetry. In terms of Auden's career, it is a definitive renunciation of art as magic, a clear distinction between the roles of man and poet, and an extensive definition of the boundaries between life and art.

THE AGE OF ANXIETY

A substantial part of *The Age of Anxiety: A Barogue Eclogue* was written by 1944, and at least half by 1945; [23] the whole was published in October 1947. The subtitle suggests the extravagance of form through which Auden attains distance and indirection. The trappings of the eclogue are there: the slight dramatic form, with dialogue; the singing contest; an elegy; love-songs and laments, with courtship of a shepherdess; a dirge; formal, 'artificial' diction and meter. But this idyll takes place in a Third Avenue bar, and the pastoral imagery is either symbolic or ironic. The Nordic mask is used for the first time since the early 1930s, but with very different effect. Old English meter, with its four heavy stresses and constant alliteration, is imitated rather than, as in the early verse, merely suggested. The style is now a rhetoric consciously assumed, deliberately incongruous with what is said; its effect is therefore mock-heroic or distancing, rather than intensifying and heightening as in, for example, 'Doom is dark. . . .' 'Baroque' indicates the packed, extravagant quality of the piece, full of violent contrasts and incongruities, reflecting the stresses of a baroque age.

The poem may be described as a sympathetic satire on the attempts of human beings to escape, through their own efforts, the anxiety of our age. The anxiety with which the poem deals is, in Auden's view, essentially a religious phenomenon (see above, pp. 178–9, 214), man's 'guilt the insoluble / Final fact, infusing his private / Nexus of needs, his noted aims with / Incomprehensible comprehensive dread / At not being what he knows that before / This world was he was willed to become' (p. 24). Though felt by all men in all times, anxiety is intensified in our civilization with its failure of tradition and belief, its atomism which leaves the individual isolated, without aid or support in his terrifying responsibility for his own ultimate destiny. This condition is further heightened in wartime, when 'everybody is reduced to the anxious status of a shady character or a displaced person, when even the most prudent become worshippers of chance' (p. 4). The scene is a bar, which offers 'an unprejudiced space in which nothing particular ever happens, and a choice of physiological aids to the imagination whereby each may appropriate it for his or her private world of repentant felicitous forms, heavy expensive objects or avenging flames and floods. . . .' The time is All Hallows Eve, and the characters are, metaphorically, souls in purgatory, each dreaming in his own way of escape, but aware (except for Malin) of no recourse beyond the human level. The poem deals with the imaginary worlds they create and through which they reveal themselves. The tone of the poem is mock-heroic: this space in which time is unreal is a parody of the religious 'moment out of time,' as their alcoholically-induced visions are parodies of religious visions. The genre is the Quest, in which everyman seeks spiritual knowledge. There is a generalized parallel with Dante's *Purgatorio* in the sevenfold division of ages and stages and in the vision of innocence as goal, of which the archetype is the Eden regained in Dante's twenty-eighth canto. This, however, is 'negative knowledge' (p. 136); the piece is a mock-pastoral because it is a quest for innocence, but the anxiety from which the characters imagine escape through a variously attained innocence can be overcome only by faith. Their myth is of regaining the lost Eden of childhood, the happy prelapsarian place where Eros is unconfined because Logos is unknown; but only the Christian Agape can make Eros and Logos one, can make, that is, Love become Law; only faith can enable man to take 'short views' and 'redeem the time.'

The four characters are sharply distinguished; each bears a different relation to the main symbolic patterns of the poem and each moves through his own private world of symbols. The parallels and contrasts among them are contrapuntal in abundance and intricacy. Malin, the Canadian airman and Medical Intelligence officer, is the most intelligent and perceptive of them, and functions as guide and commentator; he disclaims having faith (pp. 135–6), but his viewpoint is distinctively Christian, and he is certainly aware of the true problem—as the others are not. Rosetta, the Jewish department-store buyer, has achieved material success, but her race makes her a special case of homelessness and spiritual insecurity; she moves through a dream-world dominated by the Innocent Landscape of the detective story,[24] upon which reality intrudes in images of isolation and persecution. Since she is the only one who changes, discarding her illusory and accepting her real childhood with all its implications, she is, in a sense, the protagonist. Quant, the aging Irish widower, is outwardly a failure, his intelligence much superior to his position as clerk; he denies, humorously or bitterly, any meaning in life, and his typical imagery is that of classical mythology. Perhaps he represents Kierkegaard's 'despair of weakness.' Emble, the handsome young American sailor, is insecure youth seeking a vocation and success; his images are of the Quest, the sea (potentiality, belief), mountains (difficult action, choice). Physically he is exceptional, the potential Aesthetic Hero, but unable to find a Quest; in contrast, Quant is no hero, Malin perhaps the potential Ethical Hero, that is, possessing superior knowledge, but not absolutely committed as is the Religious Hero.

At the beginning of the poem, the characters are introduced in their private reveries, each a variation on the central theme of guilt and innocence. A newscast recalls them to the present, and the War symbolism becomes dominant. The effect of the Nordic mask is to take away the specificity of World War II by merging it with all wars, to extend the situation from the topical and contemporary to the universal. Unable to agree on the significance of the war (their interpretations reveal their philosophies),[25] the characters agree to discuss, not the past or the future, but the 'incessant Now of / The traveller through time.' Malin states the subject: man's perennial attempt to become reconciled to himself, to escape guilt, anxiety, and dread.

Part II, 'The Seven Ages,' puts Shakespeare's seven ages into psychological terms. Every infant repeats the Fall: 'that ban tempts him; / He jumps and is judged: he joins mankind, / The fallen families, freedom lost, / Love becomes Law.' Eros and Logos henceforth conflict; the will is corrupt. In the Second Age, realizing he 'has laid his life-bet with a lying self / Who wins or welches,' the child becomes self-conscious and divided, lives isolated in dreams and self-pitying fantasies. In the Third Age, 'learning to love, at length he is taught / To know he does not'; sexual love, being still narcissism, ends in disillusion: Quant's surrealist description of the sightseeing voyage to Venus Island puts this vividly. The Fourth Age presents Everyman emerging from the domination of Eros (abandoning his fantasies of being exceptional, loved for himself alone) into the real world of 'theology and horses.' Rosetta, persisting in her regression, protests, 'Too soon we embrace that / Impermanent appetitive flux . . . which adults fear / Is real and right'; Emble remarks that this 'real' world is full of perversions of Eros: 'a dean sits / Making bedroom eyes at a beef steak / As wholly oral as the avid creatures / Of the celibate sea,' financiers lust for money, while average married people, losing interest in sex, long for change, the Absolute Instant. Quant replies that the Unexpected is always present, any stability illusory: 'We are mocked by unmeaning.' In the Fifth Age, Malin goes on, he obtains worldly approval and success. Emble describes the youthful fear of never attaining this:

> . . . To be young means
> To be all on edge, to be held waiting in
> A packed lounge for a Personal Call
> From Long Distance, for the low voice that
> Defines one's future . . . It is getting late.
> Shall we ever be asked for? Are we simply
> Not wanted at all?

Quant describes failure to obtain success; Rosetta argues that it is meaningless in our time, and Quant replies that all times are the same, history has no meaning. The Sixth Age shows Everyman aging, unhappy, longing for the innocence of childhood. Again, each character interprets in his own terms: Quant portrays the aging failure, who has abandoned the Quest after one glimpse of the 'glaciers guarding the Good Place,' and who returns with a consciousness of his own evil; Rosetta describes the innocent dolls running down, the paternal landscape fading, the illusion lost; Emble remembers the garden to which he has lost the key; the desert is now his home. In the Seventh Age, Everyman's 'last illusions have lost patience / With the human enterprise,' and at death he is 'modest at last.' Ironically, each character then returns to his illusions, unaffected by the analysis: Rosetta thinks of the deaths of lovable eccentrics in her Innocent Landscape; Emble compares himself with the Average ('Must I end like that?'); Quant, describing odd deaths, takes refuge in humor and cynicism.

Part III, 'The Seven Stages,' is based on the pattern of the Quest. This journey homeward to the center of time, the Quiet Kingdom, follows the 'Regressive road to Grandmother's House': i.e., it is a parody-Quest for an unrecoverable Innocence consisting in being non-human like a doll, or ignorant of the Logos like a child. Rosetta, appropriately, serves as guide; but the members of the group have achieved an alcoholic rapport which allows them to 'function as a single organism.'

Since they seek 'that state of prehistoric happiness which, by human beings, can only be imagined in terms of a landscape bearing a symbolic resemblance to the human body,' the landscape is all moralized (cf. the earlier discussion of this technique, pp. 141ff.). Because the complex symbolism of each stage is interpreted differently, in an intricate counterpointing, by each character, an adequate commentary on this section would run to inordinate length; I can therefore give only the briefest of outlines. Isolated at the beginning, each character finds enough water (belief, hope) to motivate his Quest. Climbing the mountains (action, choice) they arrive at a watershed in the 'high heartland' (in terms of the body, the heart as seat of the will and emotions). Thence they proceed in the second stage to the maritime plains, where each reacts characteristically: Rosetta sees the ports as disorderly, Emble in military terms; Malin sees in the ocean a metaphysical and religious 'border,' and Quant is overwhelmed by its immensity: the desperate spirit is 'a speck drowning / In whose wanton mansions where the whales take / Their huge fruitions.' The third stage takes them inland to the Metropolis (civilization; in terms of the body, the brain), on which they comment in the fourth stage. The City is a 'facetious culture,' outwardly planned and orderly, but ignoring ultimate questions; the planners have taken care of everything but the anxiety and evil of individuals. In the Big House, the fifth stage, Rosetta finds only her imaginary childhood environment turned sour, its innocence corrupted, 'mating and malice of men and beasts.' As they race away, each makes a typical comment; Malin fears that failure will indicate sin; Quant believes the average is safest; Emble rejoices in his superiority but tries to look modest; Rosetta says, 'I can't hope to be first / So let me be last.' The Graveyard at the end of this stage represents the end of secular planning for the individual, the fact that it omits. The sixth stage takes them to the Hermetic Gardens (in the symbolic body, the genitals); on the journey each feels sexual attraction. The implication is that sexual love is narcissistic, the object self-created: Malin's impulse is really towards a son created in his own image, Quant's toward a daughter-wife. The beauty of the gardens, recalling their sins of love, afflicts them with psychosomatic disease, and the seventh stage takes them alone into the forest, despairing of love. At the edge they encounter the Desert, 'lands beyond love,' i.e. the place of trial; confronted by this, all feel self-doubt. Thus they refuse to attempt the only true Quest, to become aware of the religious Choice; and 'their fears are confirmed, their hopes denied. For the world from which their journey has been one long flight rises up before them now. . . .' All feel guilt and see visions of terror; then they return to themselves and the present.

Part IV, 'The Dirge,' is dominated by the City symbol. Discouraged by the apparent meaninglessness of nature and the hopeless situation of man, the characters think of some 'semi-divine stranger with superhuman powers, some Gilgamesh or Napoleon, some Solon or Sherlock Holmes' who promises to rescue man and nature, but who always dies or disappears. This is, of course, the False Messiah, the Secular Savior to whom, without Christianity, mankind will always look for relief from anxiety and guilt. This dirge is therefore a parody: the Lawgiver they ironically lament is the Hero of all Quests, the Lucky Son, the Grail Knight, Caesar and any dictator—the universal Exceptional Man in whom the Average, to escape responsibility, put their faith. In psychological terms, he is the Father-image, 'Our lost dad, / Our colossal father.' The characters cannot, however, take this solution seriously.

Part V, 'The Masque,' resumes the Quest pattern: the theme now is sexual love, the Erotic Quest of Emble and Rosetta, perennial Prince and Princess. Auden comments that in wartime 'even the crudest kind of positive affection between persons seems extraordinarily beautiful, a noble symbol of the peace and forgiveness of which the whole world stands so desperately in need.' So Malin invokes 'Heavenly Venus' as a quasi-Platonic symbol of universal love, in contrast to Quant's previous bitter picture of Venus Island. Emble woos in his characteristic Quest images; Rosetta replies in her Innocent Landscape. Though aware that sexual love is regressive and narcissistic, Malin and Quant tolerantly urge them to cherish their illusions. The Vision of Innocence they all participate in is the crowning illusion, the climax of the whole poem as a parody Dream Quest: each describes in his own terms the triumph of Eros and Innocence (the false goal they pursue throughout the poem). But all the illusions fail, Emble passes out, and Rosetta renounces her dream of 'the Innocent Place where / His law can't look,' of 'a home like theirs.' Abandoning her Innocent Landscape, she accepts her real childhood ('the semi-detached / Brick villa in Laburnum Crescent, / The poky parlor . . .'), her 'poor fat father,' and the fact of her race which he symbolizes: 'Time is our trade, to be tense our gift / Whose woe is our weight; for we are His Chosen.' For her there is no escape from evil, insecurity, the hard fate of her race; accepting these realities, she concludes by reciting the Jewish Creed in Hebrew.

Part VI, 'Epilogue,' consists of Malin's meditations on the nature of love and time (the first time in the poem that the Christian concepts of Agape and Logos have been introduced other than by negative implication), counterpointed by Quant's meditations on the Heraclitan flux of time and the meaningless cycles of history: there is always a war and a peace-treaty, bringing hopes for a better world which are always doomed to disappointment. Malin reflects that we do not learn from the past, that the future looks bleak:

> Yet the noble despair of the poets
> Is nothing of the sort; it is silly
> To refuse the tasks of time
> And, overlooking our lives,
> Cry—'Miserable wicked me,
> How interesting I am.'
> We would rather be ruined than changed,
> We would rather die in our dread
> Than climb the cross of the moment
> And let our illusions die.

But after this passage—which, if any, is the 'message' of the poem—he returns to his negative knowledge: we cannot understand the relation between time and eternity, the 'clock we are bound to obey / And the miracle we must not despair of'; we cannot conceive of Agape, of how the 'raging lion is to lime / With the yearning unicorn.' Neither reason nor imagination can enable us to comprehend these matters; the meaning is 'reserved / For the eyes of faith to find,' and our own efforts, without Grace, cannot achieve faith. Eros is corrupt; our passions pray to 'primitive totems'; science or no science, our dreams are of 'Bacchus or the Great Boyg or Baal-Peor, / Fortune's Ferris-wheel or the physical sound / Of our own names'; our worship is mostly 'so much galimatias to get out of / Knowing our neighbor.' Thus 'in choosing how many / And how much they will love, our minds insist on / Their own disorder as their own punishment.' Yet 'His love observes / His appalling promise,' and Divine Grace, Agape, is vouchsafed us, 'His Good ingressant on our gross occasions,' in our 'mad unbelief' as we 'wait unawares for His World to come.'

The Age of Anxiety was received rather coolly by the critics, most of whom thought it too artificial and rhetorical, lacking in dramatic quality—all the characters aspects of Auden, saying the same thing—

and, as a war poem or a tract for the times, unrealistic and superficial. As usual, the most damning comment was made by Randall Jarrell:

> *The Age of Anxiety* is the worst thing Auden has written since 'The Dance of Death'; it is the equivalent of Wordsworth's 'Ecclesiastical Sonnets.' The man who, during the thirties, was one of the five or six best poets in the world has gradually turned into a rhetoric mill grinding away at the bottom of Limbo, into an automation that keeps making little jokes, little plays on words, little rhetorical engines, as compulsively and unendingly and uneasily as a neurotic washes his hands.
>
> (*The Nation,* Oct. 18, 1947)

On the other hand, Leonard Bernstein was inspired by the poem, which he called 'fascinating and hair-raising,' to write 'The Age of Anxiety (Symphony No. 2 for Piano and Orchestra) (After W. H. Auden),' completed in 1949, which is interesting as an attempt to produce a musical equivalent, rather than a setting of any part of the work. Bernstein divides the poem into two parts, following it section by section but without pause between the three sections of each part. The prologue consists of a 'lonely improvisation' by two clarinets and echotone, and is followed by 'a long descending scale which acts as a bridge into the realm of the unconscious, where most of the poem takes place.' [26] The Seven Ages and Seven Stages are both variation movements. Part II begins with The Dirge, which employs a twelve-tone row; The Masque 'is a kind of scherzo for piano and percussion alone . . . in which a kind of fantastic piano-jazz is employed'; to represent the anticlimactic end 'the piano protagonist is traumatized by the intervention of the orchestra for four bars of hectic jazz. When the orchestra stops, . . . a *pianino* in the orchestra is continuing the Masque, repetitiously and with waning energy, as the Epilogue begins.' The piano-protagonist does not take part in the Epilogue, but observes it; the orchestra is a mirror in which he sees himself. But he does toward the end contribute to the orchestra's declaration of faith 'one eager chord of confirmation.'

John Bayley, in *The Romantic Survival* (1957), goes so far as to call *Age* Auden's 'greatest achievement to date, and the one which best shows the true nature of his scope and talent' (p. 185). He likes the modesty and sympathy of tone, the effects of tenderness and pathos—'the poetry of Rosetta is perhaps the most moving he has written'—and most of all the fact that here Auden can give free rein to his characteristic 'exuberance of particularity,' which Bayley considers to link Auden both to the Romantics and to the novel, especially Dickens. I have expressed my admiration for, and debt to, Mr. Bayley's book, which seems to me to contain the most perceptive criticism of Auden that has appeared in recent years. I am dubious, however, about Mr. Bayley's thesis as a whole (see above, p. 65), and I suspect that he over-rates the *Age* because of the neatness with which it fits his argument. The mere presence of the 'exuberance of particularity' or the 'trivia of the consciousness' does not necessarily make *Age,* or any other poem, good; one must point out, with pedagogical obviousness, that what matters is how they are used, what kind of coherence and unity they form.

My own view is that *Age* is almost as far from being Auden's best as it is from being his worst poem. It is full of provocative and fascinating ideas, many of which do not quite come off—like the Seven Ages and the landscape-body analogy in the Seven Stages. It is, like all the other long poems, uneven; but it contains more flats than the others perhaps because of the use of the single meter for most of the poem, and because some of the ideas seem to be carried on too long. The Seven Stages is the best part, because (for one thing) it contains more variety in form—all the lyrics published separately (except the Dirge) and those preserved in *Selected Poetry* are from this section. It is not as rich nor varied nor profound as either 'For the Time Being' or 'The Sea and the Mirror,' as I see it. But it is a brilliant and moving and impressive performance, and one we would not willingly be without.

The three long works we have considered in this section complement each other in certain interesting respects, and together they constitute a unity. The beliefs and attitudes that are basic to all of Auden's writing after 1940 are defined in them in a manner that seems, retrospectively, almost programmatic: religious in *For the Time Being,* aesthetic in *The Sea and the Mirror* (in which the central ideas of *The Dyer's Hand,* 1962, are already implicit), and social-psychological in *The Age of Anxiety*. In technique, *For the Time Being* is external and objective, *The Age of Anxiety* internal and subjective, with *The Sea and the Mirror* intermediate. Auden has written no long poems since, and certainly one reason is that the three works together make a kind of triptych, a completed achievement.

Aesthetically, perhaps the central weakness of *Age* is that the Quest is largely internal: the social-psychological diagnosis of contemporary anxiety, isolation, and anonymous solitude is represented in subjective terms, with all the action psychic and no real interaction among the characters. In terms of the pendulum-swing that I have tried to avoid suggesting as a metaphor, this is a swing in the direction of fantasy, in contrast to the diagnosis-swing described at the end of the last section. But the longer works to be considered in the next section—opera libretti and sequences of companion poems—exhibit a kind of compensating countermovement. Operas, through dream-literature, have a dramatic objectivity; they are embodied in music, and performed; and the companion poems have an external framework, of canonical hours or moralized landscape. In the later poems the Island of fantasy, which has figured in the earlier poetry as amorous escape or selfish isolation, in *The Sea and the Mirror* as Art, and in *The Age of Anxiety* as one form of the false alcoholic Eden sought by all the characters, is located definitively outside the realm of Clio and identified either with Eden (timeless and supernatural) or with the dominion of Dame Kind.

NOTES

1. *Letters from Iceland,* p. 239: 'The Church of Saint Aidan at Smallheath to my mother / Where she may pray for this poor world and me'; p. 204, 'We imitate our loves: well, neighbours say / I grow more like my mother every day.' In 'A Literary Transference' (1940) Auden says that Hardy 'looked like my father: that broad unpampered moustache, bald forehead and deeply lined sympathetic face belonged to the other world of feeling and sensation (for I, like my mother, was a thinking-intuitive).'
2. It was 'begun in Ann Arbor and finished before I came to Swathmore' (letter to M.K.S., March 21, 1962). Several portions were published in periodicals: 'At the Manger' in *Commonweal,* Dec. 25, 1942; 'Herod Considers the Massacre of the Innocents' in *Harpers,* Dec. 1943; 'After Christmas' (the Narrator's final speech) in *Harpers,* Jan. 1944.
3. There is an obvious allusion to the beginning of the *Divine Comedy.*
4. Cf. Psalm 46:10 and the 'Prayer for Quiet Confidence' in the *Book of Common Prayer.*
5. See above, pp. 189–90, for Auden's definition of Eros as the basic will to self-actualization without which no creature can exist; but in a note to 'New Year Letter' (*Double Man,* p. 107) Auden distinguishes between doing evil and sinning: 'To do evil is to act contrary to self-interest. It is possible for all living creatures to do this because their knowledge of their self-interest is false or inadequate. Thus the animals

whose evolution is complete, whose knowledge of their relations to the rest of creation is fixed, can do evil, but they cannot sin.'

6. Cf. Auden's volume of selections from Kierkegaard, p. 30: 'Christianity is certainly not melancholy, it is, on the contrary, glad tidings—for the melancholy; to the frivolous it is certainly not glad tidings, for it wishes first of all to make them serious. That is the road we all have to take—over the Bridge of Sighs into eternity.'
7. The image is a brilliant one that perhaps needs paraphrase: observing that the Venus of the Soma (i.e., the biological Eros of note 5, above) is myopic, he hopes that his moral imperative will rectify the optical errors (lens-flare and lens-coma) that mislead the sensual eye.
8. Randall Jarrell, in his brilliant but inimical essay, 'Freud to Paul: The Stages of Auden's Ideology,' *Partisan Review,* Fall 1945, complains that Auden chose Herod rather than Pilate to represent the typical Liberal: 'We are so *used* to rejecting Herod as a particularly bogey-ish Churchill that Auden can count on our going right on rejecting him when he is presented as Sir Stafford Cripps' (p. 442). One wonders whether Jarrell can actually have thought Auden was free to replace Herod by Pilate, as if they were both fictional characters.
9. Auden explains the symbolism of the Desert in *The Enchafèd Flood* (1950): it is the abode of those who reject or are rejected by the City, with the modern connotations of spiritual drouth, triviality, mechanization, and level uniformity. In 'The Shield of Achilles' and 'Plains' the Desert is the symbol of modern life at its worst.
10. The manuscript of this is in the Lockwood Memorial Library at the University of Buffalo, in the *Sea and the Mirror* notebook.
11. Cf. the epigraph: 'Shall we continue in sin, that grace may abound? God forbid.'
12. In his review of translations of Kafka, *The New Republic,* 1941, Auden quotes Kafka's aphorism, 'One must cheat no one, not even the world of its triumph.' (It is included in the *Viking Book of Aphorisms,* p. 92.)
13. Letter from Auden referred to in note 2, above. Only two portions appeared in periodicals: 'Preface' in *The Atlantic Monthly* for Aug. 1944 and 'Alonzo to Ferdinand' in *Partisan Review,* Oct. 1943.

    The piece is dedicated to James and Tania Stern, who collaborated with Auden in translating Brecht's *Caucasion Chalk Circle* (see note 18 to the preceding section) and translated *Grimm's Fairy Tales* (New York, 1944; Auden reviewed the translation) and Kafka's *Letters to Milena* (London and New York, 1953).

The Lockwood Memorial Library at the University of Buffalo has the notebook Auden used in writing 'The Sea and the Mirror,' consisting of more than 100 pages containing everything from first tentative lists of characters and verse forms to much of the finished work. This manuscript would provide rich material for a study of the process of composition; it effectively gives the lie to any notion that Auden is a careless writer who never blots a line, for it shows him both revising painstakingly and minutely and often completely rewriting passages in a different form or style. Perhaps I should note that I deliberately refrained from consulting the manuscript until after I had written my interpretation of 'The Sea and the Mirror,' because I did not want to risk confusing what Auden intended (as revealed by the manuscript) with what is actually in the finished work; obviously, the two are not necessarily the same, particularly in a long work written over a considerable period of time. I then used it as a negative check, to make sure I had not gone astray or missed any major significance. A diagram Auden gives toward the end is worth reproducing as an indication of the polarities in terms of which he was thinking (manuscript p. 105):

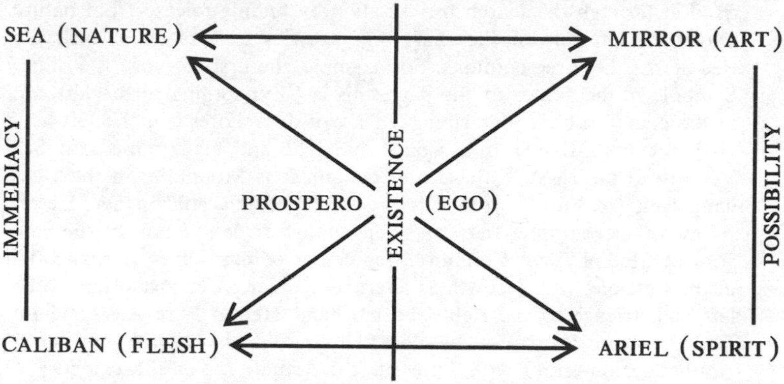

14. 'Gay' is New York slang for homosexual, and very likely this connotation is relevant.
15. According to G. S. Fraser (*The Modern Writer and his World,* London, 1953, p. 245) this is Auden's first use of syllabic meter, and it probably owes something to Marianne Moore's example. Fraser seems to me right on both counts. (It is worth noting that Auden reviewed a volume of Miss Moore's verse in 1944.) Hoggart (pp. 106–10) analyzes part of the speech. The Buffalo manuscript indicates that Auden took more pains with this than with any other speech; there are at least six or eight different versions of it, occupying manuscript pp. 44–70, in different meters and styles.
16. Cf. 'Many Happy Returns' (*Collected Poetry,* p. 71): 'Tao is a tightrope . . .' This poem is in many respects a lighter parallel to *The Sea and the Mirror.*
17. While he was writing *The Sea and the Mirror* Auden was teaching at

Swarthmore a course called 'Romanticism from Rousseau to Hitler,' and he used in it a diagram which is interesting because it shows the polarities in terms of which his mind was working and the associations various symbols had for him. Since it casts some light upon Caliban's description of his and Ariel's kingdoms, as well as upon the passage now in question, a brief description of it may be worthwhile.

Beginning with the Fall from Paradise (Eden) into This World (or from Essential into Existential Being), the chart tabulates in the center column the characteristics of Dualism of Experience or Knowledge of Good and Evil in This World. An arrow to the left-hand column indicates the search for salvation by finding refuge in nature, leading to the Hell of the Pure Deed, of Power without Purpose; and the left-hand column tabulates the characteristics of this state. The right-hand column describes the Hell of the Pure Word, of Knowledge without Power, arrived at through the search for salvation by finding release from nature. Down the left side of the chart runs a series of categories, each carried across the three columns. For example, the first category is Primary Symbol: in the center of the page, this is City; verging to the left, still in the center column describing This World, is Forest; in the left-hand Hell (of Pure Deed) it is Common Night and at extreme left, Sea. Verging to the right in the center column it is Mountain; in the right-hand Hell (of Pure Word) it is Private Light and, still farther, Desert. A few other examples may be given, though in less detail. In the category of Metaphysical Condition, the center column gives Actualization of the Possible, with Growth as alternative description; Art verges to the left and Science to the right; the left-hand Hell is Pure Aesthetic Immediacy with Pure Ethical Potentiality, and the right-hand one is Aesthetic Non-entity with Pure Ethical Actuality. For the category of Order the center is Differentiated Unity or Civilization, with Rivers and Country verging left to the Hell of Monist Unity (water) and Barbaric Vagueness, while Roads and Towns verge right to the Hell of Dissociated Multiplicity and Decadent Triviality. In the category, Sin, the central condition is Anxiety with Criminals and Bohemians verging left to the Hell of Sensuality, while Police and Bourgeois Pharisees verge right to the Hell of Pride. Finally, the last category, The Quest, indicates the alternative methods of attaining Forgiveness (Purgatory) through, on the left, 'The voluntary journey of the corrupt mind through the sea. Purgation of pride by Dissolution' and, on the right, 'The voluntary passing of the corrupt body through the desert. Purgation of lust by Desiccation.' (Arrows indicate that each condition must pass through the other to achieve the goal.) On the left of the center column the descriptions are Fertilizing the Waste Land and The Island; on the right, Draining the Swamp and The Oasis.

Kenneth Lewars, a member of Auden's seminar in Romanticism at

Swarthmore, preserved the original of this chart and reproduced it in his M.A. thesis, 'The Quest in Auden's Poems and Plays' (Columbia, 1947). I am indebted to Samuel Hynes for calling the chart to my attention and giving me a copy of it, and to Mr. Lewars as well as Mr. Auden for allowing me to quote from it. Mr. Lewars intends to publish shortly a thorough study of the chart (which is a lengthy document covering three typescript pages) together with a complete reproduction; this should be an article of unusual interest. Many of the ideas tabulated in the chart—especially those dealing with archetypal symbols—were worked out by Auden in *The Enchafèd Flood,* 1950.

18. As Hoggart points out, the reference is to the end of *The Winter's Tale.* There is also a possible allusion by contrast to the end of *Don Giovanni,* this statue not punishing but forgiving.
19. In relation to the basic symbolism of the whole piece, there is a further ironic meaning: the mirror of art is indeed always lonely.
20. In the Buffalo MS., there are several drafts of the beginning of Caliban's speech. The first is in verse (MS., p. 97): 'Ladies and gentlemen, please keep your seats. / An unidentified plane is reported / Approaching the city. Probably only a false alarm / But naturally, we cannot afford / To take any chances. So all our lights are out / And we must sit in the dark. I can guess / What you are thinking: How odd this feels: to be sitting / In a theatre when the final curtain has fallen / On a dream that ended agreeably with wedding bells / Substantial rewards for the good, and for the bad / Nothing worse than a ducking. . . .' This is revised (still in verse), and then a prose version begun on p. 103, but with no trace of the Henry James style of the final version.
21. There is also a relation to the Logos-Kairos symbolism discussed above, and to Kierkegaard's Aesthetic/Ethical categories (pp. 181–2 above). The philosophy of A. N. Whitehead is definitely in the background here and elsewhere in the poem, most explicitly in the triviality/vagueness antithesis (cf. *Process and Reality,* New York 1929, pp. 170–72). Auden quotes *Process and Reality* in the notes to 'New Year Letter' (*The Double Man,* p. 153) and shows Whitehead's influence in other poems 1939–44; Whitehead appears frequently in the *Viking Book of Aphorisms* (1962), and the analysis of various types of 'societies' in *The Dyer's Hand* owes something to him.
22. Like other ironists, Auden has paid the penalty of being taken literally. He has been accused of snobbery (by Bayley, p. 145) because Caliban refers to 'collarless herds who eat blancmange and have never said anything witty' (p. 379); but Caliban here is parodying the naive snobbery of the audience (in the snobbish accents of James). Similarly, Auden has been accused (by Harry Levin, in an otherwise very brilliant review of *For the Time Being* in *The New Republic,* Sept. 18, 1944) of remoteness from common life because Caliban says 'there is probably no

one whose real name is Brown' (p. 398); but Caliban is here parodying adolescent romanticism, 'an infinite extension of the adolescent difficulty, a rising of the subjective and subjunctive to ever steeper, stormier heights' (p. 398). Both passages are about as far from statements by Auden in his own person as they could possibly be.

23. Letter W.H.A. to M.K.S., March 21, 1962. Reviews of *For the Time Being* in Sept. 1944 reported *The Age of Anxiety* as in progress. Two excerpts were published in American magazines: 'Spinster's Song' (*Age,* p. 80) in *The New Yorker,* Sept. 28, 1946, and 'Metropolis' (*Age,* p. 75) in *Commonweal,* Dec. 20, 1946. In England 'Lament for a Lawgiver' (*Age,* p. 104) was published in *Horizon,* March 1948.

    The poem was dedicated to John Betjeman, for whose volume *Slick but not Streamlined* Auden wrote an introduction in the same year.

24. See 'The Guilty Vicarage: Notes on the Detective Story by an Addict,' 1948; included in *The Dyer's Hand* (1962). This analysis of the detective story as a form of magic, not art, whose function is to indulge the fantasy of escape from guilt, casts much light upon the central theme of *Age* as well as upon Rosetta's fantasy-world.

25. Emble justifies the war in simple and popular terms: Rome fell through softness, 'Better this than barbarian misrule'; Malin replies that the new barbarian was born here, inside the City, and we share the blame ('A crime has occurred, accusing all'); Quant sees no meaning beyond a temporary 'defense of friends against foes' hate'; Rosetta thinks the war will change nothing and its end will see a return to the 'lies and lethargies' of peace.

26. From Bernstein's own description on the jacket of Col. ML 4325.

RICHARD ELLMANN

Yeats Without Analogue

(1964)

When we think of Yeats's mind in concentration, brooding upon silence, as he said, 'like a long-legged fly upon a stream,' we may well hesitate to clatter in armed with our newfangled muskets—our readers' guides and commentaries, our iconographies and identities—and to aim them at that noble quarry. The danger was brought home to me the other day when the editor of a continental encyclopedia invited me to write an article about Yeats. Being understandably fearful of American caprices, he supplied me with detailed instructions on how to proceed. I should be sure to show Yeats as a late Pre-Raphaelite, as a member of the Rhymers' Club and of the Savoy group, as a symbolist in the school of Mallarmé, as a leader in the revival of William Blake, as a participant in the Celtic Renaissance. I should make clear that he was a friend of Oscar Wilde, of Madame Blavatsky, of Lady Gregory, of the magician Macgregor Mathers, of Ezra Pound. I should demonstrate the effect upon Yeats of other arts. The prescription was intimidating, and as I tried to follow it my misgivings increased. Was Yeats really a jack-of-all-movements? Did he putter about in the past? Was he an other-people's-friend? And, while the encyclopedist was German, I have an uneasy feeling that I have not been blameless in helping to establish the kind of criticism of Yeats which made this detailed assignment a logical outcome. But I will not incriminate only myself. Yeats is in some present peril everywhere of being swallowed up by the great whale of literary history. We must do what we can to help him out of that indiscriminate belly.

From *Kenyon Review* XXVI (1964). Reprinted by permission of the author and Kenyon Review.

To be told that what looks new is really old, that every step forward is a step backward, is hard on trail blazers, and Yeats was impatient enough with those of us who edit and annotate lines young men tossing in their beds rhymed out in love's despair. We need not, however, repudiate editing or annotating; Yeats comforts us elsewhere when he says that 'truth flourishes where the student's lamp has shone.' But to read the literature on Yeats is to come to feel that the search for his sources and analogues has become disproportioned, and that a tendency is growing to turn all that marvelously innovative poetry into a resumé of what other people have written. An inspired resumé, of course, but still a resumé. Sometimes the resumé includes what other people have painted or carved, too. A few years ago, for example, my friend G.D.P. Allt suggested that Yeats's poem 'Leda and the Swan' grew out of a painting of this subject by Michelangelo and possibly also out of a drawing of Jupiter and Ganymede by the same artist. Later Giorgio Melchiori, developing these hints in an important book, reproduced three copies of Michelangelo's lost picture, the drawing too, a picture of Leda and the swan by a follower of Leonardo and one by Gustave Moreau, and then a Hellenistic statue of the same subject. Seven in all. But the conclusion to which a study of these works of art brings one is that Yeats has done something different from any: not only are his graphic details at variance (none of them shows the bird's beak holding the nape of Leda's neck), but the whole intellectual weight is distinct.

In Michelangelo what is expressed is the suave perfection of the union of human and divine. Under the pressure of Christian doctrine, there is no irony recognized in this union. Yeats has a different object, as he makes clear at once:

> A sudden blow, the great wings beating still
> Above the staggering girl . . .

For Yeats the significance of this mating is that it is not tender or easy; the bird, filled with divine power and knowledge, is still the brute blood of the air. The incongruities are glossed over by Michelangelo; in Yeats they are heightened. The sense of disproportion, of shock, of rape, is captured in those phrases which describe the blow, the flapping of huge wings, the strange dark webs, the catching of the helpless Leda. She is dazed and overcome, not cajoled, and the god, once the sexual crisis is past, lets her drop from his indifferent beak. I do not mean that Yeats is a naturalist as Michelangelo is an idealist; both of these positions are too easy. Rather, what Yeats does is to let both views of the subject coalesce, to see them with double sight, and this is why his poem is modern as Michelangelo's painting is not. Mr. Melchiori shows intelligently how fond Yeats was of the personality of Michelangelo, but, whether fond or not, Yeats belongs to a different persuasion from the Renaissance.

The issue of a pictorial source for 'Leda and the Swan' was drawn more sharply two summers ago, when Charles Madge published in the *Times Literary Supplement* a reproduction of a Greek bas-relief which Yeats probably saw in the British Museum. This carving is much more convincing than Allt's or Mr. Melchiori's examples; in it the details are in fact the same as in the first part of the poem. The resemblance is too close for coincidence. The only question is, what does it prove? Mr. Melchiori wrote a letter to the editor conceding that this illustration was more apt than his own, but declaring that it confirmed his theory that visual imagery had priority for Yeats. But does it? Priority has become an offensive word, and it is not an easy thing to determine. Presumably Yeats knew from his reading who Leda was before he saw the bas-relief at the British Museum. Is it not hopeless to attempt to determine through which sense a poet is most deeply affected? For example, if we were to grant that the bas-relief helped Yeats to frame the octave of the sonnet, what inspired the next three lines?

> A shudder in the loins engenders there
> The broken wall, the burning roof and tower,
> And Agamemnon dead.

There is nothing in the bas-relief to suggest these aftereffects of the coupling. Is it useful to speculate on how Yeats conceived of the image of burning? Did he see a fire, hear the crackling of flames, smell burn, scorch his hand, taste something that was too hot? Or did he remember Marlowe's description of 'flaming Jupiter' when he appeared not to Leda but 'to hapless Semele'? Or Rossetti's refrain about 'Troy-town's on fire.' Even if we determined beyond doubt that he had seen a picture of a fire, or a bas-relief of it, or read a poem, we could still not explain the telescoping of historical events in those lines. Or the stages of the sexual violation which are probably implied in the series of images—the broken wall, the burning roof and tower, and Agamemnon dead. It is conceivable that he found these out by personal experience, and that the suggested relation of sexual stages to historical events came as an ironic echo of the octave from his own mind, not someone else's. And if we admit this possibility, we can ask more peremptorily what is the use of trying to isolate creative motivation. The only effect is to minimize the role of the poet in shaping his impressions.

We can go farther and say that, given this bas-relief, Yeats's poem does not necessarily emerge from it. He uses its details insofar as they are convenient, but his emphasis is not the Greek artist's, either. For the Greek, the rape of Leda by the swan was apparently a magnificent variety of sexual assault; he was interested in its minute physical oddities; the god and the woman receive his equal attention. In Yeats, however, the interest is centered on the mortal woman, on the psychological implications for her and, by extension, for us. We watch Leda's reactions, not the god's. And Yeats goes beyond the strangely assorted pair to meditate on the destructiveness of sexual passion, on its power to upheave the world. In the end of the poem, he exclaims in bewilderment at the disparity between gods and men, between the minds as well as the bodies of Zeus and Leda. The generating theme of the poem is a feeling he had from childhood of the tantalizing imperfection of human life; his own experience told him that power and knowledge could never exist together, that to acquire one was to lose the other. All Yeats's poetry embodies this theme. Leda and the swan are only one of many embodiments of it in his verse. When we study that verse we put source after source behind us until we are in the poet's mind, not in the British Museum.

If painters and sculptors have not provided us with enough analogues, we have all been unable to resist comparing Yeats with William Blake. Two books have been written to elicit these similarities. Certainly Yeats had a passion for Blake, and certainly he spent three years from 1889 to 1892 strenuously editing and commenting on the Prophetic Books. It is tempting to relate Blake's Four Zoas to Yeats's Four Faculties, and I have done so elsewhere. Even if connections can be made, however, is it not time to emphasize the disconnections instead? When we think of Blake, we think of a mind of almost unprecedented assertiveness. When we think of Yeats, we think of a force of almost unprecedented modulation. Blake, as Yeats himself tells us, 'beat upon the wall / Till truth obeyed his call.' Yeats is rather a great cat in his dealings with truth than a beater upon walls. Blake condemns the world of the five senses, Yeats gives it substantial acceptance. Blake is determined that England should become heaven, Yeats is not sure that even Ireland will achieve this goal. Blake impresses us by his initial and unswerving conviction, Yeats by his serpentine struggle toward bold declaration. Blake commits himself to his own system and spends most of his creative years elaborating it in special terms. Yeats remains ambiguous about his symbology, lodges it in prose, and never uses its special terms in his verse unless they have accepted as well as eccentrically personal meanings. Finally, Yeats wrote an explanation of Blake, a favor that Blake, who hated explanations, would never have done for Yeats.

Since Yeats is not Blake, perhaps he is Mallarmé. Graham Hough, a critic I respect too much not to wish to disagree with, contends in a recent book that the early Yeats as least belongs to the French symbolists. 'Symbolism,' Mr. Hough points out, 'moves in the direction of an impassable gulf. . . . For the symbolist poet there is no question of describing an experience; the moment of illumination only occurs in its embodiment in some particular artistic form. There is no question of relating it to the experience of a lifetime, for it is unique, it exists in the poem alone.' And he finds in the early Yeats the symbolist doctrine full-blown, though contaminated a little by a non-literary occultism. The fact that it is contaminated at all should warn us. I cannot concede to Mr. Hough that even in the early Yeats there is any desire for an autonomous art, separated from life and experience by an impassable gulf. We have been taught so often that we live in a degenerate age, that the audience has become obtuse and sterile, that writers have detached themselves from it perforce, that we are almost embarrassed when we bethink ourselves of the sizable number of our best writers who are not alienated, not isolated, not even inaccessible. Yeats's early dream was not to live in an ivory tower, but on an Irish island, not in unnature, but in nature, not in a place he had never seen, but in a place he had grown up. If there was anything that he shied away from it was the separation of his art from his life, of his work from his audience. Consider all those interrelations he set up between himself and his public by founding Irish literary societies in London and Dublin, by attaching his affections to a woman who was an Irish nationalist, by writing poems which should be Irish, local, amorous. All these poems confirm an intention to stay on earth, however much he may hint at the existence of another world.

When Yeats seriously contemplates leaving the observable world, he customarily points out what a mistake it would be. For example, in one of his earliest poems, 'The Seeker,' the hero is so enraptured by the pursuit of an otherworldly ideal that he cannot fight in battle, and men say his heart has been stolen by the spirits. At last, after a lifetime of unheroic behavior and tenacious searching, he reaches the visionary figure he has sought. But she is no image of transcendent beauty, instead she is a 'bearded witch,' and when asked her name replies, 'Men call me infamy.' Yeats suppressed this object-lesson for symbolists about the danger of isolating experience from an ideal, but its theme is common to many poems he retained.

In 'Fergus and the Druid,' Fergus begs the gift of other-worldly wisdom; receiving it, he is appalled and laments,

> But now I have grown nothing, knowing all.
> Ah! Druid, Druid, how great webs of sorrow
> Lay hidden in the small slate-coloured thing!

So far from yielding to another world of the spirit, Yeats in his verse is always demonstrating that we had better cling to this one. In the poem which he put at the beginning of his second volume of verse, 'To the Rose upon the Rood of Time,' he acknowledges his fear that he may do what Mallarmé perhaps wished to, and 'learn to chaunt a tongue men do not know.' Yeats testifies to his determination to keep in touch with common things, with the weak worm, the field mouse, with 'heavy mortal hopes that toil and pass.' He acknowledges the call of isolation, but affirms that he will resist it. His next volume, *The Wind among the Reeds,* also begins with an appeal from the other world, this time from the Sidhe who call, 'Away, come away.' We listen to their musical voices without obeying. Occasionally someone is taken away, like the child the fairies steal in *The Land of Heart's Desire,* but the fairies are baleful and predatory here. In Yeats's later poetry the same struggle is portrayed: it becomes the theme of such poems as 'Vacillation' and 'A Dialogue of Self and Soul,' but, while the poet tries to play fair, the dialogue, and his vacillation, have always the same resolution. To follow the soul into another world is to give up one's heart and self, and, worst of all for a poet, to give up one's tongue, for in the presence of that unblemished world our tongue's a stone, in the simplicity of fire we are struck dumb. The poet is committed to this world by his profession as well as by his temperament.

How different all this sounds from Mallarmé, for whom the artist treats experience as gingerly and probingly as a detective looking for the incomprehensible crime which appearances cover up. Mallarmé constitutes the poet a specialist in reality, a detective writing for detectives. What can be said in the open is not worth saying. Mallarmé's acknowledged image of the poet is the awesome magus who evokes by words an intangible reality. But this is a French magus more than an Irish one. Yeats, who knew magic at first hand as Mallarmé did not, took a homelier view of it. One thinks of his experiments in putting certain substances under his pillow to see what effect his dreams might have upon them, or they upon his dreams. And for Yeats the incantatory word is not something achieved by exclusion of much of the mind; it is achieved by a spiritual struggle of the whole being, of which the poetic imagination forms a part, and it is inside, not outside, the stress of experience. Unassumingly, too, Yeats does not talk of the magician as a manufacturer but as an importer; his images are not created new but come from the Great Memory, a kind of collective imagination. In Mallarmé, the attempt is to separate the poem from all that is not poem, to abolish the poet, to free an object originally palpable so that it becomes impalpable. All real bouquets render up their fragrance to form an essence they do not themselves possess.

In Yeats, the emphasis is on the tangibility of the images which the artist cleans and perfects, and on the struggle to clean and perfect them. The poet is not ostracized from his poem, he is its all-important inhabitant. The act of creation itself is curiously democratic for Yeats, comparable to other forms of intense endeavor, so that the poet can represent his work as human, too. He must write with such airs that one believes he has a sword upstairs. The desire to see Mallarmé in Yeats has encouraged a misconception of some of his best poems. His pursuit of images is taken as an escape from experience, when the images are rather focuses of experience. In 'The Circus Animals' Desertion,' Yeats at first seems to take another view, as when he says,

> Players and painted stage took all my love,
> And not those things that they were emblems of,

but even here the word 'emblems' recalls to us the dependent character of the images. And his conclusion recognizes firmly the dependence of art upon life:

> Those masterful images because complete
> Grew in pure mind, but out of what began?
> A mound of refuse or the sweepings of a street,
> Old kettles, old bottles, and a broken can,
> Old iron, old bones, old rags, that raving slut
> Who keeps the till. Now that my ladder's gone,

I must lie down where all the ladders start
In the foul rag-and-boneshop of the heart.

An excellent critic interprets these lines to mean that Yeats is in despair at the idea of lying down in his heart, at being 'left to live merely, when living is most difficult, life having been used up in another cause.' But this is reading Yeats's words without considering their intonation. While the poet is disgusted for the moment with his own heart, he is well aware that this heart has engendered all his images. He pleads necessity for what he does by desire; he *wants,* in short, to lie down in the foul rag-and-boneshop of the heart. For, as he says in 'Two Songs from a Play,'

Whatever flames upon the night
Man's own resinous heart has fed,

and in 'Vacillation,'

From man's blood-sodden heart are sprung
Those branches of the night and day
Where the gaudy moon is hung.

At the end of the poem 'Byzantium,' Yeats, having described the miraculous creations which are produced in art, suddenly recalls the flood of time from which they come, and sees the time-world as made up of passionate images too:

Those images that yet
Fresh images beget,
That dolphin-torn, that gong-tormented sea.

We have been asked to believe that these lines express Yeats's revulsion from the welter of experience, when clearly they imply that even from the vantage point of Byzantium that welter is fascinating.

So I do not think we can describe Yeats as alienated or even as aloof, either from his own experience or from other people's. From childhood on he is delighted with the life of peasants, with Irish life. Mallarmé, always straining to avoid space and time, would find Irish nationalism an absurdity, as perhaps it is, though Yeats did not think so. Yeats even wrote his poem, 'To Ireland in the Coming Times,' to establish his rightful place once and for all as Ireland, his claim to be counted one with the Irish poets Davis, Mangan, Ferguson. And at the end of his life he wrote a poem to make sure that his body after death should be Irish, too:

Under bare Ben Bulben's head
In Drumcliff churchyard Yeats is laid.

Yet, I do not find it very helpful either to consider Yeats, as sometimes is done, one of a group of Irish poets who freshened up Celtic legends. Yeats could be and wanted to be provincial, but he could also be cosmopolitan. When he wrote *A Vision,* he forgot he was an Irishman. And, while he calls the fairies by their Irish name of the Sidhe, I suspect that they too are internationalists. His later versions of preternatural beings are, except in the play *The Dreaming of the Bones,* indifferent to race although they retain their interest in families and in individuals. Irishness is an essential quality, but a secondary one.

Perhaps then we should pursue another direction by seeing Yeats as a follower of the occult tradition or, as it has been renamed by one critic, the Platonic tradition. But here too his allegiance is doubtful. If we try to think of him as a Platonist we have to remember he wrote a poem to say, 'Those Platonists are a curse . . . God's fire upon the wane,' and another in which he said, 'I cry in Plato's teeth.' If we mean by Platonism the later followers of Plato, we have to remember that Yeats also wrote, 'I mock Plotinus' thought,' and that he buffeted Plotinus as well as Plato about in several poems. At moments his theories seem to coincide with Plato's, as in that heroic defense of a woman's primping, 'Before the World Was Made.' In a way she agrees that this world is a copy of a more perfect Platonic one, but the real theme is her deliberate energy in attempting to override human imperfection. Plato's philosophy is used only to the extent that it can be made Yeatsian, the extent to which the bodiless can be bodied.

If we ally Yeats with the occultists who followed in secret a metaphysical tradition, we will find him asserting his independence of them, too. There is danger in connecting him too closely with either Macgregor Mathers or Madame Blavatsky, for he quarrelled and broke with both of them. Insofar as occultism is cloistered and moralistic—and most magicians are tediously moralistic or immoralistic—Yeats stands apart from them. Insofar as they hope to alter the phenomenal world, Yeats is very skeptical. The phenomenal world is not so easily dismissed, or at least not for long. Insofar as they hold converse with spirits and win from them preternatural powers, Yeats is only sporadically credulous and then for his own reasons. Fundamentally he is like Queen Edain in 'The Two Kings,' who rejects the advances of an immortal lover so as to stay with her mortal one. We long for immortal essences, but when they accost us we resist. The poet, firm among the five senses, imagines their perfection, not their abandonment. He tolerates the ideal only when it is covered with what he calls 'casual flesh.'

In seeking to emphasize the degree to which Yeats is unlike Michelangelo or Plato or Blavatsky or Mallarmé or Blake, I have the ulterior motive of offering another view. What is the mental atmosphere that makes Yeats's poems so individualistic? We might try to establish first the outer borders of his mind, with the initial admission that, as Yeats said, these are constantly shifting; and then its inner qualities. The intimation that seems to have been with him from the earliest days is that life as we generally experience it is incomplete, but that at times it appears to transcend itself and yield moments of completeness or near-completeness, moments when, as he says half-humorously in the poem 'There,' 'all the barrel-hoops are knit . . . all the serpent-tails are bit.' In his early work, Yeats conceives of the boundary line between the worlds of completeness and incompleteness as twilit; in his later work it is lit by lightning. Whether the light is blurred or stark, there are strange crossings-over.

The trespassers come from both directions, from this world to that, from that world to this. The fairies or Sidhe would like to translate us, to possess us, to catch us in nets of dreams, to tempt us, to remind us of what we lack and they have, and sometimes they succeed. More often they only manage to make us miserable. Something about the world of generation saddens them, as if the separation of worlds were difficult for them, too, to bear, and caused them suffering. In middle life, Yeats discards the fairies (as he already had given up the Rose), and begins to call the denizens of the other world antiselves or simply ghosts; in his later work they are usually spirits in his verse, daimons in his prose. Under their changed names, they continue to busy themselves about us.

Some readers of Yeats are put off by this metaphysical population, and by his related interest in all sorts of extrasensory perception. Could Yeats really have believed in these things? they ask. But to ask this question is to show that one is several generations in time behind Yeats, who asked with more point whether the word *belief* belonged to our age at all. He used many locutions to avoid the term, and it can be said that nothing is farther from his mind than simple credence. The word *God* he generally skirted with the same dexterity. It is puzzling to read a recent interpretation of the poem, 'Mohini Chatterjee,' where there is the line, 'I asked if I should pray.' The critic says that Yeats asks if he should pray to God; but Yeats doesn't mention God, and it is not at all certain that he is addressing himself to that early authority. He may be invoking his deeper self, or some daimon or group of daimons, or some indeterminate object, or he may be meditating with an even vaguer audience, praying to no one and to nothing, just praying. Occasionally Yeats does make use in his verse of supernatural machinery or of preternatural machinery, but always without precise or credal commitment.

He needs this machinery because of his conviction, as I have indicated, that there is a conceivable life which is better than human life in that it is complete, undiminished, unimpairable. Let us call this the daimonic world. In relation to the daimons we are mere abstracts. Yeats astonishes us by the bluntness with which he makes clear the defects of our own world. But having made clear its limitations, he suddenly enters upon its defense. It has pain, it has struggle, it has tragedy, elements denied to the daimons. Seen from their point of view, life always fails. Yet it does not fail utterly, for man can imagine their state even if he cannot participate in it. And the capacity to imagine is redemptive; man, in a frenzy at being limited, overthrows much of that limitation. He defiantly asserts his imagined self against futility, and to imagine heroism is to become a hero.

And now we are led from a comparison of worlds to one of people. Man, according to Yeats's view, is a being who is always endeavoring to construct by fiction what he lacks in fact. Born incomplete, he conceives of completeness and to that extent attains it. We outfling ourselves upon the universe, people the desert with our fertile images. The hero does this unconsciously, the artist consciously, but all men do it in their degree. The dead bone upon the shore in 'Three Things' sings still of human love. Space and time are unreal, Yeats sometimes concedes to the philosophers, but he says they are marvelously unreal; they, and life and death, heaven and hell, day and night, are human images imposed like form upon the void. Yeats looks at two withered old women, Eva Gore-Booth and Constance Markiewicz, and writes of them,

> The light of evening, Lissadell,
> Great windows open to the south,
> Two girls in silk kimonos, both
> Beautiful, one a gazelle.

The girls in the gazebo of the country-house are summoned up by the poet as more real than the decrepit women; if the great gazebo of the world is false, it must be true as well. It is true when it conforms, as at moments it does, to our image of perfection.

But the mind has another glory besides its power to create: it can also destroy. Man lowers his plumb line into the darkness and establishes measurement, form, number, intellect. But he has hardly established all these before he casts the line away, as if every imaginative construct could only momentarily satisfy his creative need and must then be demolished. 'What's the meaning of all song?' Yeats asks in 'Vacillation,' and replies, 'Let all things pass away.' His most powerful statement of this kind is in the poem called 'Meru,' where the hermits on the Indian mountain sum up in themselves this dissatisfaction with every human fabrication. They are Asiatic hermits, but Yeats recognizes that every mind has an Asiatic aspect which would destroy the shows of this world—shows which he associates with Europe. We live in 'manifold illusion'; and, as Yeats puts it in another poem, 'mirror on mirror mirrored is all the show.' Having put on our finery, we take it off again. We strip the masks we have created for ourselves. We descend into our own abyss; if we cannot burn up the gazebo, we scornfully aspire to do so. The urge to destruction, like the urge to creation, is a defiance of limits; we transcend ourselves by refusing to accept completely anything that is human, and then indomitably we begin fabricating again. As Yeats says in 'Lapis Lazuli,'

> All things fall and are built again.
> And those that build them again are gay.

If we try now to relate Yeats's poems more narrowly to the contrast between daimons and men on the one hand, and between man and his limitations on the other, I think we will see that each such contrast gains its force from a confrontation of passive acceptance with energetic defiance. It would be so easy to grant, as any objective witness would, that the poet's daughter should not associate with a man who has the worst of all bad names. When he admonishes her, however, she replies unanswerably, 'But his hair is beautiful, / Cold as the March wind his eyes.' In a greater poem, it would be so easy to concede that Maud Gonne had behaved badly toward Yeats; but the sense of 'No Second Troy' is that this aspect of her life is of no consequence, and the important thing is that she has tried to live by the high laws of imagination. The poet is always faced with a common-sense solution, as by a sort of minimum wage, and always chooses to take nothing rather than take that. If Maud Gonne's energies were destructive, that was because she lived in a world of outworn images and had to destroy them. The pacific soul, which Yeats contrasts in his later verse with the military self, always offers a conventional way to heaven, and the self always rejects it, preferring the turmoil of this world, with its desperate search for words and images, to an easy and dumbstriking heaven. Every poem establishes alternatives to indicate only one choice is worth making, and that the agonized, unremunerative, heroic one.

These are not Yeats's ideas or beliefs; they are the mental atmosphere in which he lived, or, if that term sounds too climatic, they are the seethings, the agitations of his mind which he learned to control and direct. His symbolism has to be understood not as a borrowing from Mallarmé but as the only way in which he could express himself. 'I have no speech but symbol,' he wrote. His symbols are condensations of his theme that all struggle is futile except the struggle with futility, his recognition of the problem of the empty cornucopia, the crowded void. Each symbol is a kind of revolving disc, like Yeats's wheel or moon with their dark and light phases in *A Vision*. We can compare the tower in the poem of that name with the one in 'The Black Tower'; in the first it is intellectual aspiration, in the second it is the insubstantiality of that aspiration. The image of the tree also has its two sides, not only in the poem, 'The Two Trees,' but when it emerges as an epitome of unity in 'Among School Children' and then as an image of decay in 'the old thorn tree' of 'A Man Young and Old.' The dance is frantic, purposeless destruction in 'Nineteen Hundred and Nineteen,' while in 'Among School Children' it is composed perfection. 'The Peacock' is a symbol of the lavishing imagination, but in 'Nineteen Hundred and Nineteen,' when the blind Robert Artisson brings the mad Lady Kyteller peacock feathers, it seems some image of beauty gone hollow.

Not only are the symbols double-natured in different poems; they usually take on shifting implications within the same poem, as if they were being slowly revolved. The ancestral houses described in 'Meditations in Time of Civil War' summon up glory only to remind us of its transience. In 'Two Songs from a Play,' the staring virgin brings her divine child to begin a new cycle of time, as if it were the only cycle, yet the muses know that there are many cycles, that this has all been done before and will be done again. The pomp of the new god is contrasted with images of darkness and nullity; as Yeats says in one of his finest images of the doubling involved in all identity, 'The painter's brush consumes his dreams.' 'Only an aching heart,' he declares ('Meditations in Time of Civil War') 'conceives a changeless work of art.' 'The Tower' that dominates the countryside has ruin in its history; on the other hand, 'The Black Tower,' so ruined as to be indefensible, finds defenders. The great-rooted blossomer is the tree in its springtime only, the perfection of dancing is achieved only momentarily before the turmoil of the greenroom begins again. Yeats is fond of showing how ambiguous the word *dream* itself is, since it is at once something brilliantly imagined and something delusive, real and unreal, 'flowers' ('I pray that I ever be weaving') and 'cold snows' ('Meditations'). But all his key words share in this property; youth is strength and folly, old age is wisdom and debility. Images of substance are always on the verge of nothingness, narrowly balanced: 'The boughs have withered because I have told them my dreams.' 'Through all the lying days of my youth / I swayed my leaves and flowers in the sun; / Now I may wither into the truth.' Even art participates in this double-nature. For though all-powerful in its own realm, that realm is balanced uneasily between this world and the daimonic one. If it became daimonic it would be ethereal, insubstantial; if it became human, it would be helpless. Yeats summarizes this condition of art in 'Byzantium,' where he writes of those artistic fires of Byzantine forges that they are

> Dying into a dance,
> An agony of trance,
> An agony of flame that cannot singe a sleeve.

In art the fires are all-powerful, but in life they have no effect at all. The same mediation is evident in 'Sailing to Byzantium,' where the bird is at once more than human in its golden perfection and less than human in its toylike character; out of generation, it yet must sing of generation, of what is past, passing, or to come, irrevocably dependent upon the nature which it affects to spurn.

Not only do the symbols turn like wheels, but the intellectual or thematic content of each poem balances two meanings contingent upon each other. The poem 'Friends,' for example, begins with two orthodox examples of friendship, Lady Gregory and Mrs. Shakespear, and then takes up Maud Gonne, who is totally unfriendly. The secret of the poem is that she has unconsciously given him more than the others gave consciously, that she did so because she represented a more fundamental energy. In 'The Magi' Yeats plays upon the standard picture of the magi dazzled by Christ's miraculous birth, and perplexes them with his human death. In 'The Second Coming' he accepts the title from Christianity but represents the new god as destructive rather than benign, a monster rather than a lamb. In 'The Cold Heaven' a hideous afterlife, where injustice prevails, confronts the naked soul in search of paradise. Or, to take a lighter example, there is his short poem with the long title, 'On Hearing That the Students of Our New University Have Joined the Agitation against Immoral Literature,'

> Where, where but here have Pride and Truth
> That long to give themselves for wage,
> To shake their wicked sides at youth
> Restraining reckless middle-age?

The poem's subtlety derives from its conceiving of Pride and Truth not as draped Grecian caryatids but as middle-aged prostitutes. Yet the denigration is mocking, as if he would remind us how lofty a wage pride and truth really demand.

I sometimes think that we could try to codify the laws that govern the complexities of Yeats's poetry. Every poem offers alternative positions. While the choice between them may surprise us, we can be sure it will be based upon a preference for what is imprudent, reckless, contrary to fact, but that in so choosing the poet does not act out of folly but out of understandable passion. The alternative is never completely overwhelmed, but remains like the other side of the moon, or, to use another of Yeats's images, like some imprisoned animal, ready to burst out again with its message of common sense or of renunciation of the world. The basic choice of the poem is reflected in the symbols, which either contain the same alternatives or at any rate imply them, as day implies night. The poem ends not in a considered conclusion but in a kind of breathlessness, a break-through from the domain of caution and calculation to that of imprudence and imagination; the poem gathers its strength from putting down one view with another, from saying, against the utmost opposition, what must be said.

Usually, the poems take one of two directions: either they are visionary, concerned with matters of prophecy, of the relations of the time-world and daimonic timelessness, or they are concerned with human enterprise, the relations of people with each other or with their own secret hopes and ambitions. In the visionary poems such as 'Leda and the Swan' or 'The Second Coming,' Yeats is concerned to intermesh the divine world with the animal, to show the world of time as centaurlike, beautiful, and monstrous, aspiring and deformed. In the poems which deal with artists or with heroes or with other men, he wishes also to show how brute fact may be transmogrified, how we can sacrifice ourselves, in the only form of religious practice he sanctions, to our imagined selves which offer far higher standards than anything offered by social convention. If we must suffer, it is better to create the world in which we suffer, and this is what heroes do spontaneously, artists do consciously, and all men do in their degree.

To represent his themes Yeats originally tried to dislodge conventional attitudes by a slow rhythm which would attenuate sense and draw it onward, as it were, into new possibilities. Sense would make way like some equerry before the sovereign spirit. Gradually he substituted for this rhythm of longing and fascination a rhythm of conquest. Like Jupiter, the daimons penetrate our world by shock, and we in turn surprise them by sudden incursions, as when, in an ordinary shop, our bodies of a sudden blaze. We do not hope to intermingle but to encroach upon each other. The language of this struggle needs to be vigorous, for it must bring us beyond statement to the central agitation of the mind, where mission and futility brother each other, where, as in the sun, destruction and creation go on at once. The mind is a rage, not a warehouse. And while Michelangelo and Blake and Mallarmé and the rest may be tutelary spirits on the perimeter of this consciousness, at its center we see only and supremely Yeats.

THOMAS R. WHITAKER

Poet of Anglo-Ireland

(1964)

Preserve what is living and help the two Irelands, Gaelic Ireland and Anglo Ireland so to unite that neither shall shed its pride.

Pages from a Diary . . .[1]

I prefer that the defeated cause should be more vividly described than that which has the advertisement of victory. No battle has been finally won or lost. *Wheels and Butterflies*[2]

I

When, in the late nineties, Yeats placed himself in a personal relation to Ireland, he not only moved toward a more autobiographical poetry and a dramatic relation to history but also took an important step toward a specific historical allegiance that would deeply affect his poetry. His early attachment to Sligo, his family heritage, his fruitful reliance upon Coole Park—all pointed toward the Anglo-Irish tradition. But the nationalism that had conflicted with his early provincial attachment yet more decidedly conflicted with any attachment to Anglo-Ireland.

As Yeats recalled in 1930, the question was complicated by his early romanticism. Anglo-Ireland was part of the eighteenth century and, though such nationalists as John O'Leary and J. F. Taylor praised that century and 'seemed of it,' Yeats himself had first 'ignored it' because he wanted 'romantic furniture' and then 'hated it' because political op-

From *Swan and Shadow* by Thomas R. Whitaker. Reprinted by permission of the publisher, The University of North Carolina Press.

ponents 'used it to cry down Irish literature that sought audience or theme in Ireland.' [3] He turned away from Goldsmith and Burke because he considered them 'a part of the English system,' and he turned away from Swift because he acknowledged no verse between Cowley and Smart, no prose between Sir Thomas Browne and Landor.[4] There were yet further complications. His early sympathy for the peasantry was not only nationalistic and romantic, but also religious and economic. At seventeen, 'bored by an Irish Protestant point of view that suggested by its blank abstraction chloride of lime,' he had sought out the peasant's pagan and Catholic lore.[5] For him as for his father, Protestantism brought to mind the stereotype of the Belfast man, epitome of puritanical commercialism.[6] Moreover, Yeats was then one who could praise the noble tradition which had made 'neither for great wealth nor great poverty' and condemn the 'new and ignoblc' tradition of the vulgar rich, 'perfected and in part discovered by the English-speaking people,' which had made the arts all but impossible.[7] He could also attack the wealthy as decayed gentry. In 1889, for example, he had criticized Robert Louis Stevenson's Chevalier Burke, in *The Master of Ballantrae*, as a false portrayal of the typical Irishman:

> He is really a broken-down Norman gentleman, a type found only among the gentry who make up what is called 'the English Garrison.' He is from the same source as the Hell Fire Club and all the reckless braggadocio of the eighteenth century in Ireland; one of that class who, feeling the uncertainty of their tenures, as Froude explains it, lived the most devil-may-care existence. . . . They are bad, but none of our making; English settlers bore them, English laws moulded them. No one who knows the serious, reserved and suspicious Irish peasant ever held them in any way representative of the national type.[8]

By 1891, after much study of the eighteenth century in preparation for a historical essay never published,[9] Yeats was only a little less antagonistic to the Anglo-Irish gentry. It is a class, he said, 'that held its acres once at the sword's point, and a little later were pleased by the tinsel villany [sic] of the Hell Fire Club.' Its existence had been 'a pleasant thing enough for the world. It introduced a new wit—a humor whose essence was dare-devilry and good-comradeship, half real, half assumed.' But for Ireland it had been 'almost entirely an evil.' Not the least of its sins had been 'the creation in the narrow circle of its dependents of the pattern used later on for . . . "the stage Irishman." ' The quality of the humor aside, Yeats agreed with William Carleton that the peasant 'is not appeased because the foot that passes over him is shod with laughter.' [10] In the novels of Croker, Lover, and Lever, Yeats saw the image of this gentry, usually with 'a hospitable, genial, good soldier-like disposition,' but with 'no more sense of responsibility, as a class, than have the *dullahans, thivishes, bowas,* and *water sheries* of the spirit-ridden peasantry.' That lack of responsibility explained why the Anglo-Irish had never had a poet: 'Poetry needs a God, a cause, or a country.' Maria Edgeworth was consequently the only novelist of the gentry to receive Yeats's full praise:

> She constantly satirized their recklessness, their love of all things English, their oppression of and contempt for their own country. . . . Her novels give, indeed, systematically the mean and vulgar side of all that gay life celebrated by Lever.[11]

It is no wonder that Yeats's *Representative Irish Tales,* which contains these comments, was reviewed by one periodical, as Yeats said later, 'under the idea that it was written by a barbarous super-republican American.' [12]

But after the turn of the century, when Yeats began to formulate his own conservative synthesis, his view of the aristocracy changed markedly. He was both pursuing his anti-self and discovering his own heritage. By 1904 he treated with respect and admiration not only the ancient Irish and Norman-Irish aristocracy but also the Anglo-Irish of the eighteenth century. The stories retold in Lady Gregory's *Gods and Fighting Men,* he said,

> helped to sing the old Irish and Norman-Irish aristocracy to their end. They heard the hereditary poets and story-tellers, and they took to horse and died fighting against Elizabeth or against Cromwell; and when an English-speaking aristocracy had their place, it listened to no poetry indeed, but it felt about it in the popular mind an exacting and ancient tribunal, and began a play that had for spectators men and women that loved the high wasteful virtues.

He no longer saw foreign exploiters wearing the mask of harsh comedy. The English were at least trying to learn an ancient role from their conquered spectators.

> I do not think that their own mixed blood or the habit of their time need take all, or nearly all, credit or discredit for the impulse that made our modern gentlemen fight duels over pocket-handkerchiefs, and set out to play ball against the gates of Jerusalem for a wager, and scatter money before the public eye; and at last, after an epoch of such eloquence the world has hardly seen its like, lose their public spirit and their high heart and grow querulous and selfish as men do who have played life out not heartily but with noise and tumult. Had they understood the people and the game a little better, they might have created an aristocracy in an age that has lost the meaning of the word.

Yeats now criticized the Anglo-Irish primarily not for cruelty and irresponsibility but for lack of depth and complexity in their passion. In order to 'create a great community,' he would now re-create the old aristocratic foundations of life—but 'not as they existed in that splendid misunderstanding of the eighteenth century.'[13]

As he clarified his aristocratic ideal, he distinguished it from its debased versions. Though he was pursuing an anti-self, that anti-self was no character portrayed by Lever or Lover. Even in 1904 he saw the nineteenth-century querulousness and selfishness as twice removed from the ancient ideal. And when, during the 1920's, he finally accepted the Anglo-Irish tradition as his own, he could define it all the more firmly. No longer was Chevalier Burke typical of the gentry as a whole—broken-down Norman gentlemen, eighteenth-century braggadocios, and nineteenth-century English Garrison. A gulf had opened between the age of Swift and the gay and vulgar life chronicled in the novels Yeats read in his youth. After the French Revolution, he said, the 'Protestant Ascendancy with its sense of responsibility' gave place to the 'Garrison, a political party of Protestant and Catholic landowners, merchants and officials.' These 'loved the soil of Ireland'—'the merchant loved with an ardour, I have not met elsewhere, some sea-board town where he had made his money, or spent his youth'—but

> they could give to a people they thought unfit for self-government, nothing but a condescending affection. They preferred frieze-coated humourists, dare-devils upon horseback, to ordinary men and women; created in Ireland and elsewhere an audience that welcomed the vivid imaginations of Lever, Lover, Somerville and Ross.[14]

For the moment Yeats could dissociate even his immediate parental stock from the Protestant Ascendancy with which he poetically identified himself.

Paradoxically, his complete allegiance to Anglo-Ireland was made possible by the establishment in 1922 of the Irish Free State. Nine years later Yeats described its effect with his usual vivid oversimplification. The 'mere existence' of the new Irish state, he said, had delivered artists from 'obsession.' No longer distracted by political nationalism, they could now give full attention to their work.

> Freedom from obsession brought me a transformation akin to religious conversion. I had thought much of my fellow-workers—Synge, Lady Gregory, Lane—but had seen nothing in Protestant Ireland as a whole but its faults, had carried through my projects in face of its opposition or indifference, had fed my imagination upon the legends of the Catholic villages or upon medieval poetry; but now my affection turned to my own people, to my own ancestors, to the books they had read.[15]

Though the transformation had really been long in developing, his memory stressed this essential truth: with Protestant Ireland now but a component of a free Irish state, he could change his allegiance without seeming, to himself or others, to desert the nationalist cause.

But political reasons had not disappeared from his mind. The Anglo-Irish, he thought, had much to teach a young state seeking political stability. Momentarily forgetting the praise O'Leary and Taylor had given the eighteenth century, he said, 'Now that Ireland was substituting traditions of government for the rhetoric of agitation, our eighteenth century had regained its importance.' And religion was still of political significance to him, though the 'obsession' was different:

> It seemed that we the Protestants had a part to play at last that might find us allies everywhere, for we alone had not to assume in public discussion of all great issues that we could find in St. Mark or St. Matthew a shorthand report of the words of Christ attested before a magistrate. We sought religious conviction by a more difficult research . . .[16]

He was perhaps remembering that in 1925, after his speech on divorce in the Irish Senate, a passionate and ironic plea for tolerance, one senator had angrily retorted that the Gospel according to St. Matthew was historically accurate and, furthermore, should be the law of the land.[17] Catholic censorship had of course plagued Yeats ever since the controversy over *The Countess Cathleen.* But before Irish Independence he had argued (with some reason) that such confusion of art with homiletics derived from English bourgeois puritanism and was therefore grotesquely out of place in Ireland under the apparent protection of the Roman Church.[18] Now, as Protestantism came to mean the heroism of Parnell rather than the calculation of the Belfast man, and as Catholicism came to mean a crude intellectual tyranny in modern Ireland rather than a rich medieval culture, Yeats's historical analysis and his strategy changed. If, as he came to believe, in his country the Church *was* Babbitt,[19] co-operation was impossible.

It is clear that Yeats had changed not his passion but its object. With rebellious pride the growing boy had defended the Catholic peasantry against the Anglo-Irish gentry; with that same pride the ageing man defended the heirs of those Anglo-Irish against the new Catholic rulers of the Irish Free State. The boy had learned, with his Fenianism, the righteous indignation and aristocratic integrity of John O'Leary; the man saw O'Leary's spiritual ancestry in the people of Jonathan Swift. In 1925, concluding his senate speech on the divorce question, Yeats said:

> I think it is tragic that within three years of this country gaining its independence we should be discussing a measure which a minority of this nation considers to be grossly oppressive. I am proud to consider myself a typical man of that minority. We against whom you have done this thing, are no petty people. We are one of the great stocks of Europe. We are the people of Burke; we are the people of Grattan; we are the people of Swift, the people of Parnell. We have created the most of the modern literature of this country. We have created the best of its political intelligence. Yet I do not altogether regret what has happened. I shall be able to find out, if not I, my children will be able to find out whether we have lost our stamina or not. You have defined our position and given us a popular following. If we have not lost our stamina then your victory will be brief, and your defeat final, and when it comes this nation may be transformed.[20]

Nearly three decades before, Yeats had written to George Russell: 'Absorb Ireland and her tragedy and you will be the poet of a people, perhaps the poet of a new insurrection.' [21] That counsel he had really directed to himself—and now, political circumstances reversed, directed to himself again. For one who continually sought emblems of adversity, who rejoiced in the fallen world from which he tried to escape, the repetition of the tragedy was not altogether matter for regret.

II

Such, in brief, was Yeats's revaluation of the Anglo-Irish heritage that he was to explore during the rest of his life. Establishing a possessive relation to that strand of history, he had in 1917 acquired the Norman tower at Ballylee, 'a permanent symbol of my work plainly visible to the passerby.' His theories of art, he said, depended upon just such 'rooting of mythology in the earth.' [22] Partly because its main theme is not the Anglo-Irish heritage itself, 'The Tower' (1925) illustrates how, uniting the pride of the two Irelands, Yeats had gradually rooted his own mythology in that soil of the past.

'What shall I do with this absurdity . . . ?' After the vigorous complaint against old age, posing the problem of the 'Excited, passionate, fantastical / Imagination' that is 'derided by / A sort of battered kettle at the heel,' the speaker of 'The Tower' enters upon a tortuous and elliptical reverie. Far from bidding the Muse 'go pack,' he invokes images and memories from the spiritualized soil, 'For I would ask a question of them all.' But he does not ask the question in this dialogue with history until ten stanzas later. Meanwhile we follow, with fascination and some perplexity, what seems but brilliant improvisation, a Yeatsian preponderance of means over ends like that apparent (but merely apparent) in 'All Souls Night.'

The personages invoked, however, all testify to the richly varied past that is now the speaker's possession. Mrs. French is a figure from that cruel eighteenth-century comedy which Yeats once, with Carleton, utterly rejected. The ballad-poet Raftery had composed in the eighteenth-century tradition a tribute to one Mary Hynes, the remaining foundation of whose house the speaker has just stared upon. In *The Celtic Twilight* Yeats had re-created their story and its setting with quiet sympathy.[23] There too he had mentioned the man 'drowned in the great bog of Cloone' because of Raftery's song. Red Hanrahan is even more completely a possession: Yeats created him as Raftery had created the moonlit image of Mary Hynes, and 'drove him drunk or sober' across the countryside as Raftery had driven the men bewitched by his song. But Hanrahan too came from the eighteenth century: the original name Yeats gave to that poet and hedge-schoolmaster, O'Sullivan Rua, suggests his prototype, the Irish peasant poet, Eoghan Ruadh Ó. Suileabháin.[24] Finally, the 'ancient bankrupt master of this house' is (like the first founder in 'Meditations in Time of Civil War') parallel to the speaker himself, save that he had 'finished his dog's day.'

These and some lesser figures now inhabit a common limbo. Accessible to the speaker's call, they are his present re-creations, who stand ready to instruct him. Both creatures and masters, they are possessed by the speaker and they possess him. That is so because they variouly embody the power and the predicament of the excited, passionate, fantastical imagination: an outrageous power, maiming, blinding, maddening, murdering—the 'horrible splendour of desire.' If the farmer was Mrs. French's victim, so the drowned man was Raftery's, so Hanrahan was Yeats's; and perhaps the ancient bankrupt master of the Norman tower was, like Raftery, Yeats, Hanrahan, and all imaginative men, victim not only of circumstance but also of that very imagination which now has made him 'fabulous.' Down the centuries we see 'Rough men-at-arms,' images of that same 'horrible splendour of desire,' who

> Come with loud cry and panting breast
> To break upon a sleeper's rest
> While their great wooden dice beat on the board.

It is precisely that splendor which the speaker himself now defiantly elects, in full knowledge of its destructive power, as his highly traditional goal:

> the tragedy began
> With homer that was a blind man,
> And Helen has all living hearts betrayed.
> O may the moon and sunlight seem
> One inextricable beam,
> For if I triumph I must make men mad.

Only such triumph now seems possible to the ageing poet under 'the day's declining beam,' deserted as the blind man is by all things belonging to 'the prosaic light of day,' condemned to the moonlit realm of the imagination. Here, yet more violently than in 'Meditations in Time of Civil War,' the predicament reverses that of Wordsworth's 'Ode on the Intimations of Immortality,' where the speaker is troubled by the fading of the visionary light 'into the light of common day.'

If, when Yeats's speaker finally asks his question—

Did all old men and women, rich and poor,
Who trod upon these rocks or passed this door,
Whether in public or in secret rage
As I do now against old age?

—it now seems anticlimactic, that is because already the undeniable fact of age pales before the splendor of the fantastical imagination that remains. The embodied spirits stand before him, mute witnesses to his predicament, yet witnesses now far more to the continuing power that resides within him. And the calculated anticlimax is surmounted by a strange turn of events:

Go therefore; but leave Hanrahan,
For I need all his mighty memories.

The speaker retains out of that company the one who is most completely his creature and his master. His own mighty memories are not enough; he needs a memory's memory. Yet that paradoxical declaration of dependence leads not to a genuine question but to a final taunt:

Old lecher with a love on every wind,
Bring up out of that deep considering mind
All that you have discovered in the grave,
For it is certain that you have
Reckoned up every unforeknown, unseeing
Plunge, lured by a softening eye,
Or by a touch or a sigh,
Into the labyrinth of another's being;

Does the imagination dwell the most
Upon a woman won or a woman lost?
If on the lost, admit you turned aside
From a great labyrinth out of pride,
Cowardice, some silly over-subtle thought
Or anything called conscience once;
And that if memory recur, the sun's
Under eclipse and the day blotted out.

As he evokes longingly the 'great labyrinth' unexplored, he establishes a precarious victory over the transcendent image of Hanrahan which he has created. He tortures Hanrahan now as long ago with his own horrible splendor of desire. Even for Hanrahan experience must have been limited; he—like Homer, Raftery, and the speaker himself—is sentenced to the world of the blind.

However, a strange though characteristic irony enters here. The speaker is forcing upon Hanrahan, who has reckoned up or measured his experience, a more disturbing self-measurement. Hanrahan's explorations and hence his being have been limited by his own ego—directly through 'pride' or 'cowardice,' or indirectly through the masks of intellect or conscience. He has been limited by the 'fear or moral ambition' which always threaten creative activity, for desire—as this taunt obliquely recognizes—also demands surrender of self. We must, of course, see in the speaker's taunt to Hanrahan his own self-knowledge and self-judgment. In other words, his own often wildly egocentric celebration of desire here moves to a yet further recognition of its pitfalls: the limitation of fulfilment inherent in the ego's anxious possession of that world which it has created and known. Appropriately, therefore, his phrasing approaches Blake's description of how 'Los could enter into Enitharmon's bosom & explore / Its intricate Labyrinths' only when 'the Obdurate heart was broken.' [25] The bearing of this recognition upon his own problem of clinging to life and thus inhibiting the exploration of death will emerge implicitly in the rest of the poem.

Grasping the implications of this long review of images and memories, and moving on to the concluding testament, declaration of faith, and plan for the future, we may be struck by a similarity to another great dramatic monologue, by a poet whom the early Yeats admired. Despite many differences, Tennyson's 'Ulysses' contains the same initially perplexing fusion of complaint, elegy, and defiant assertion—a fusion that renders, in heroic opposition to the finitude of human life, the infinitude of the creative and exploring mind. In both poems the selection of an ageing speaker heightens that contrast; the firm possession of a labyrinthine past makes more poignant the precarious tenure of the present and the vastness of all that is yet unexplored. Against all odds both protagonists try to project the achievements of the past into the present and on into an open future. But the speaker of 'The Tower,' himself a bitterly realistic poet for all his fantastic assertions, is explicitly concerned with the problem that Ulysses merely exemplifies—the problem that Yeats, in his long preparation for the poem, had once defined: 'It may be,' he had said in *The Celtic Twilight,* 'that in a few years Fable, who changes mortalities to immortalities in her caulron,' will have changed blind Raftery to a perfect symbol of 'the magnificence and penury of dreams.' [26]

In the second part of 'The Tower' the speaker has evoked those aspects of his Anglo-Irish heritage which best symbolize the horrible splendor of the imagination wrought to its highest pitch. In his realism he dryly accepts, in his defiance he ironically exalts, Mrs. French, 'Gifted with so fine an ear,' as well as 'beauty's blind rambling celebrant.' Having dramatically vindicated the imagination in the face of all that is temporal, having seen also that anxious possession of the world created and known is a bar to further creation and exploration, he may now rest in a more serene faith in the independence of the imagination and in a 'pride' that is not the ego's apprehensive desire to possess and dominate but the whole being's exultant sense of creative giving. He may therefore evoke without irony a quite different aspect of the Anglo-Irish heritage—that which Yeats had celebrated in his Senate speech of the same year:

> It is time that I wrote my will;
> I choose upstanding men
> That climb the streams until
> The fountain leap, and at dawn
> Drop their cast at the side
> Of dripping stone; I declare
> They shall inherit my pride,
> The pride of people that were
> Bound neither to Cause nor to State,
> Neither to slaves that were spat on,
> Nor to the tyrants that spat,
> The people of Burke and of Grattan
> That gave, though free to refuse—

If Houses of Lords and Houses of Commons are something other than human life, certain individuals who are politically active may yet be, as they are here, 'what Blake called "naked beauty displayed." . . . The great men of the eighteenth century were that beauty; Parnell had something of it, O'Leary something . . .' [27] Fisherman, fountain, dawn, with their connotations of natural richness and vitality, of Irish landscape and ceremony of innocence, help to define the beneficent pride of Anglo-Ireland, which is now (in an act consonant with its own nature) bequeathed at a moment of exultant self-giving to that new age for which Yeats had always hoped—an age 'that will understand with Blake that the Holy Spirit is "an intellectual fountain," and that the kinds and degrees of beauty are the images of its authority.' [28]

That 'beauty' implies no mere aestheticism but rather what Yeats in 1902 had called 'the pure joy that only comes out of things that have never been indentured to any cause' and that is a prerequisite for the 'impartial meditation about character and destiny we call the artistic life.' [29]

As this phrase in 'The Tower' moves toward its final sustained cadence, it introduces further images of the authority of that fountain which is the possession of no person; 'pride' becomes yet more clearly impersonal—the pride of a natural largesse (of morn, horn, showers, hour) which works through individuals:

> Pride, like that of the morn,
> When the headlong light is loose,

—antithetical to that moment in 'The Second Coming' which the line echoes 'The blood-dimmed tide is loosed'—

> Or that of the fabulous horn,
> Or that of the sudden shower
> When all streams are dry,
> Or that of the hour
> When the swan must fix his eye
> Upon a fading gleam,
> Float out upon a long
> Last reach of glittering stream
> And there sing his last song.

As the shower modulates into the song of the swan (which, like Tennyson's dying Merlin, follows the gleam [30]), we recall that this very testament is such a shower or song in the arid landscape of decrepit age. Then penury of the imagination, almost eclipsed by its magnificence, now appears only in such implications, or in the momentary defiance which the thought of the swan and his fading world brings:

> And I declare my faith:
> I mock Plotinus' thought
> And cry in Plato's teeth,
> Death and life were not
> Till man made up the whole,
> Made lock, stock and barrel
> Out of his bitter soul,
> Aye, sun and moon and star, all.
> And further add to that

That, being dead, we rise,
Dream and so create
Translunar Paradise.

As the word 'bitter' recognizes, these consciously defiant articles of faith are what in 1930 Yeats called 'all that heroic casuistry, all that assertion of the eternity of what nature declares ephemeral.' [31] Yet in the poem they are truths of the imagination: 'For if I triumph I must make men mad.' The speaker is earning his right (declared in 'To a Young Beauty') to attend that late but select dinner of which Landor once spoke, with Landor himself and with Donne, who also had proudly declared, 'Death be not proud.'

Turning to the future, he demonstrates through yet further shifts of tone, the imaginative validity of his argument. When Tennyson's Ulysses cast his thoughts beyond the sunset, he strangely merged death, a newer world, and a reliving of the past. But even more than for Ulysses, for this speaker penury and magnificence now meet and are reconciled in serene ambiguity:

I have prepared my peace
With learned Italian things
And the proud stones of Greece,
Poet's imaginings
And memories of love,
Memories of the words of women,
All those things whereof
Man makes a superhuman
Mirror-resembling dream.

He has prepared his peace in the mirroring world of the imagination; but though he had referred to a future translunar Paradise, this peace is a present reality. The lines also state that he has made his peace with the things of the world which he must abandon. The slackening verse movement indicates that the speaker is beginning to rest after his orgy of creation, as Eternal Man rested on the seventh day, the mirroring imagination sufficient unto the moment.[32] The simile that follows re-creates this moment, but with a difference. It moves from daws who 'chatter and scream, / And drop twigs layer upon layer'—the life process of 'preparing'—to the mother bird who

will rest
On their hollow top,
And so warm her wild nest.

The simile further devalues preparatory life and the materials it accumulates, as opposed to the culminating moment; and it presents that peaceful and extended moment as one of brooding yet 'wild' creativity.

A new vista of contemplative activity has opened. The speaker now must—and can—'leave both faith and pride' to others. It is, as he says, both a bequeathing and also now a quiet abandonment by one whose metal has been broken. From one point of view, we may say that, magnificence having been created, penury can be accepted. But penury has also been seen as a creative state itself. The obdurate heart broken, another labyrinth can be entered and explored. Hence there is little trace, in the final phrase of this testamentary song, of the proud credo uttered a moment before. The phrase begins by asserting the creative force inherent in any act of the imagination:

> Now shall I make my soul,
> Compelling it to study
> In a learned school . . .

But it modulates to something quite different from the last song of the defiant swan:

> Till the wreck of body,
> Slow decay of blood,
> Testy delirium
> Or dull decrepitude,
> Or what worse evil come—
> The death of friends, or death
> Of every brilliant eye
> That made a catch in the breath—
> Seem but the clouds of the sky
> When the horizon fades;
> Or a bird's sleepy cry
> Among the deepening shades.

The speaker approaches Keats's view that the world is the vale of Soul-making, a 'School' in which each soul learns its 'Identity.' [33] But he leaves carefully unspecified the content of school and soul. He presents only, in all realism, the prospect of a fading world. More strictly, evil and loss no longer seem important; but as the metaphors suggest, with them fades all that is temporal. The lines render, in a quiet mode, that 'tragic joy' which, Yeats had said in 1904, reaches its climax 'when the world itself has slipped away in death.' A similar thought had come to Yeats on the occasion of Synge's death: 'He had no need of our sympathies. It was as though we and the things about us died away from him and not he from us.' [34] But in 'The Tower' that darkening of the world of mirroring realities, that fading of the gleam on which the swan fixes its eye, is the final act of the eternal imagination. The poem has moved to the acceptance of death, and to the creation of death in that acceptance. The horrible splendor of desire—the creative and destructive, illuminating and blinding power of the imagination—here attains its final ethereal harmony: 'a bird's sleepy cry / Among the deepening shades.'

III

In re-creating history the speaker of 'The Tower' moves beyond history. Following him, we have seen some ways in which Yeats was now grounding his concepts and symbols in the soil of Anglo-Ireland. But he wished to discover yet further relations between the people of Burke and the defiant swan, the Italian things, and the stones of Greece. In 1930 he wrote in his diary:

> How much of my reading is to discover the English and Irish originals of my thought, its first language, and where no such originals exist, its relation to what original did. I seek more than idioms, for thoughts become more vivid when I find they were thought out in historical circumstances which affect those in which I live, or, which is perhaps the same thing, were thought first by men my ancestors may have known.[35]

He was delighted to find Anglo-Irish prototypes for his own theory of history and his own conservatism. Swift's *Discourse of the Contests and Dissensions between the Nobles and Commons in Athens and Rome,* he thought, led up to Edmund Burke 'so clearly that one may claim that Anglo-Ireland recreated conservative thought in one as in the other. Indeed the *Discourse* with its law of history might be for us what Vico is to the Italians, had we a thinking nation.' [36] In a moment of excitement he took a yet more extreme position. The *Discourse,* he said,

> is more important to modern thought than Vico and certainly foreshadowed Flinders Petrie, Frobenius, Henry Adams, Spengler, and very exactly and closely Gerald Heard. It needs interpretation, for it had to take the form of a pamphlet in-

> telligible to the Whig nobility. He saw civilisation 'exploding' —to use Heard's term—just before the final state, and that final state as a tyranny, and he took from a Latin writer the conviction that every civilisation carries with it from the first what shall bring it to an end.[37]

Burke borrowed or rediscovered Swift's insight into historical process, Yeats concluded, while Coleridge borrowed 'all but that inevitable end.' [38]

Discovering such English and Irish originals—studying 'the rebirth of European spirituality in the mind of Berkeley, the restoration of European order in the mind of Burke' [39]—Yeats found thoughts becoming more vivid not merely because he had established a historical relation to those thinkers but also because he was not studying 'thought' alone. He would agree in part with the description of such study given by R. G. Collingwood, who also learned from Vico and Croce:

> I plunge beneath the surface of my mind and there live a life in which I not merely think about Nelson but am Nelson, and thus in thinking about Nelson think about myself. . . . If what the historian knows is past thoughts, and if he knows them by re-thinking them himself, it follows that the knowledge he achieves by historical enquiry is not knowledge of his situation as opposed to knowledge of himself. . . . He must be, in fact, a microcosm of all the history he can know.[40]

But Yeats would go yet further. It is characteristic that, attributing a similar Vichian theory of historical knowledge to Swift, he introduced a characteristically passionate complication: it is to Vanessa that Swift says, in *The Words upon the Window-Pane,* 'When I rebuilt Rome in your mind it was as though I walked its streets.' [41] He was studying whole men—and learning, in that study, about a microcosmic whole man in the present.

That is why he could say, 'I have before me an ideal expression in which all that I have, clay and spirit alike, assist; it is as though I most approximate towards that expression when I carry with me the greatest amount of hereditary thought and feeling, even national and family hatred and pride.' [42] He elaborated that goal when revising these diary notations for publication in *Wheels and Butterflies:*

> Swift haunts me; he is always just around the next corner. Sometimes it is a thought of my great-great-grandmother, a

> friend of that Archbishop King who sent him to England about the 'First Fruits,' sometimes it is S. Patrick's, where I have gone to wander and meditate, that brings him to mind, sometimes I remember something hard or harsh in O'Leary or in Taylor, or in the public speech of our statesmen, that reminds me by its style of his verse or prose. Did he not speak, perhaps, with just such an intonation? This instinct for what is near and yet hidden is in reality a return to the sources of our power, and therefore a claim made upon the future. Thought seems more true, emotion more deep, spoken by someone who touches my pride, who seems to claim me of his kindred, who seems to make me a part of some national mythology, nor is mythology mere ostentation, mere vanity if it draws me onward to the unknown; another turn of the gyre and myth is wisdom, pride, discipline.[43]

These eighteenth-century men—and especially Berkeley and Swift—were therefore complex masks with whom Yeats might converse and from whom he might learn of 'what is near and yet hidden.' Each stood before him as both reflection and shadow: projection of his own consciously held position and also of potentialities within himself that he had not yet fully discerned. Each stood also as 'cosmic' reflection and shadow: intimation of an ideal passion and ideal unity, and embodiment of the tensions of the fallen world. Early in the century, before his complete allegiance to Anglo-Ireland, Yeats had suggested the use to which he would put these figures: 'There is scarcely a man who has led the Irish people, at any time, who may not give some day to a great writer precisely that symbol he may require for the expression of himself.'[44] But he had more fully suggested their meaning even earlier, in 1896, when Swift alone had seemed to him to transcend a fallen century. He had said then of Swift:

> He did not become . . . a great light of his time because of the utility of his projects or of any high standard of honest thinking—for some of his most famous projects were expressions of a paradoxical anger, while others he defended with arguments which even he could not have believed—but because he revealed in his writings and in his life a more intense nature, a more living temperament, than any of his contemporaries. He was as near a supreme man as that fallen age could produce, and that he did not labour, as Blake says the supreme

> man should, 'to bring again the golden age' by revealing it in his work and his life, but fought, as with battered and smoke-blackened armour in the mouth of the pit, is to the discredit of 'the century of philosophers': a century which had set chop-logic in the place of the mysterious power, obscure as a touch from behind a curtain, that had governed 'the century of poets.'

But even that fighting in the mouth of the pit—which Yeats was increasingly to see as a substantial part of his own vocation—was, he had said in 1896, a way of revealing 'a more powerful and passionate, a more divine world than ours.' For Swift had 'given the world an unforgettable parable by building an overpowering genius upon the wreckage of the merely human faculties.' [45] The parable was of central importance to an admirer of *King Lear* who would later write 'Sailing to Byzantium' and 'The Tower' and would dramatize in *The Words upon the Window-Pane* the ageing Swift's dread of madness as a *hysterica passio* of historical dimensions.

That play itself is more than a spiritualist tour de force or an ingenious device for bringing historical drama into a modern setting. Like 'The Tower,' it renders the sense of a dramatic interpenetration of past and present. Indeed, the Swift who haunted Yeats, who was always just round the next corner, was audible to him also: 'I can hear Swift's voice in his letters speaking the sentences at whatever pace makes their sound and idiom expressive. He speaks and we listen at leisure.' [46] Mediumship was an apt vehicle for what Yeats himself experienced as a psychological reality, a source of power 'near yet hidden.' Hence the scenario of the Anglo-Irish past, like that of *A Vision* or that of the early romances, might lend to the moods a voice. The dramatic perspective of *The Words upon the Window-Pane* recalls that of *On Baile's Strand:* the madness and death of the heroic are seen from the vantage-point of the unheroic and utilitarian milieu which mirrors ourselves and which has helped to drive the hero over the edge of sanity. But what once appeared in the context of Irish myth has now been discerned in the experienced drama of history.

Like Swift, Berkeley was for Yeats a complex mirror of ideal and reality. The great enemy of the abstract, he wished to 'create a philosophy so concrete that the common people could understand it.' 'Descartes, Locke and Newton took away the world and gave us its excrement instead,' said Yeats. 'Berkeley restored the world'—'the world that only exists because it shines and sounds.'[47] In so describing a reparation of the fall presented in 'Fragments,' Yeats was not applauding Berkeley's idealism as it is usually conceived:

> Sometimes when I think of him what flitted before his eyes flits before mine also, I half perceive a world like that of the Zen priest in Japan or China, but am hurried back into abstraction after but an instant.[48]

Similarly in *A Vision,* turning in reaction against his own abstract system toward 'a reality which is concrete, sensuous, bodily,' Yeats recalled passages 'written by Japanese monks on attaining Nirvana.'[49] For Zen, Nirvana is no escape from the wheel except as it is an immediate and concrete apprehension of that harmony which the wheel merely symbolizes. It is no release from individual consciousness except as it is a moment of enlightenment in which the error of abstraction which posits cut-off individuals disappears. It is thus cognate with the goal of spiritual alchemy and is an 'affirmation' that transcends the opposites, a 'word' that cannot be refuted. Zen shares with Yeats the view that 'You can refute Hegel but not the Saint or the Song of Sixpence.'[50]

'You ask me what is my religion and I hit you across the mouth.'[51] That Zen retort might well have been uttered by the young Berkeley whom Yeats envisioned, 'solitary, talkative, ecstatic, destructive.' Such a temperament, Yeats thought, Berkeley also showed in later years 'though but in glimpses or as something divined or inferred' behind the complacent mask of the mature bishop, which he wore because, in a time 'terrified of religious scepticism and political anarchy,' it 'hid from himself and others his own anarchy and scepticism.'[52] Yeats was here glimpsing a tension within his own conservative 'pose,' though he had more complex dramatic and psychological techniques for realizing and so transcending it. Thinking of Berkeley's isolation, Yeats also thought of his own father 'and of others born into the Anglo-Irish solitude.'[53] Such men he saw as isolated from Ireland ('scattered men in an ignorant country'[54]), isolated by their genius in a time of imaginative ebb tide (for Berkeley the 'first great imaginative wave had sunk, the second had not risen'[55] and isolated both physically and spiritually from England. Considering this last fact, Yeats saw in them the best elements of an Irish culture in which 'solitaries flourish,' a culture which has the 'sense for what is permanent.'

> Born in such community Berkeley with his belief in perception, that abstract ideas are mere words, Swift with his love of

> perfect nature, of the Houyhnhnms, his disbelief in Newton's system and in every sort of machine, Goldsmith and his delight in the particulars of common life that shocked his contemporaries, Burke with his conviction that all states not grown slowly like a forest tree are tyrannies, found in England an opposite that stung their own thought into expression and made it lucid.[56]

Like Yeats himself, they were caught between contraries, goaded into passionate thought and action, and enabled to play a triumphantly liberating role—that of 'hardship borne and chosen out of pride and joy.' [57] Their soil too had been spiritualized by tragedy. 'The historical dialectic,' Yeats said, 'trampled upon their minds in that brutal Ireland, product of two generations of civil war . . . ; they were the trodden grapes and became wine.' [58]

As a quasi-ideal culture, eighteenth-century Ireland suggested the Renaissance and Periclean Athens. Yeats saw 'in Bolingbroke the last pose and in Swift the last passion of the Renaissance.' [59] Professionalism was not yet a curse. 'Unity of being was still possible though somewhat over-rationalised and abstract, more diagram than body': the fall described in 'Statistics' was just beginning. But when 'Swift sank into imbecility or madness his epoch had finished in the British Isles.' [60] Thus far, Yeats's description suggests his Phase 18, from 1550 to 1650 (the picture of Europe after 1650 is much less favorable in 'Dove or Swan' [61]; but Swift's epoch was also a delayed and imperfect Phase 15:

> I seek an image of the modern mind's discovery of itself, of its own permanent form, in that one Irish century that escaped from darkness and confusion. I would that our fifteenth, sixteenth, or even our seventeenth century had been the clear mirror, but fate decided against us.[62]

Hence a submerged analogy with Phase 15, that time when the shadow of history becomes a clear mirror, runs through Yeats's vision of the Enlightenment. Corbet, in *The Words upon the Window-Pane,* gives the conventional interpretation: 'That arrogant intellect free at last from superstition.' But Yeats calls that 'the young man's overstatement full of the unexamined suppositions of common speech,' and he adds:

> I saw Asia in the carved stones of Blenheim, not in the pride of great abstract masses, but in that humility of flower-like intricacy—the particular blades of the grass; nor can chance

> have thrown into contiguous generations Spinoza and Swift, an absorption of the whole intellect in God, a fakir-like contempt for all human desire . . . ; the elaboration and spread of Masonic symbolism, its God made in the image of a Christopher Wren; Berkeley's declaration, modified later, that physical pleasure is the *Summum Bonum,* Heaven's sole reality, his counter-truth to that of Spinoza. . . . Spinoza and the Masons, Berkeley and Swift, speculative and practical intellect, stood there free at last from all prepossessions and touched the extremes of thought . . .[63]

That is the 'horizontal dance' of opposites, *primary* and *antithetical,* Asiatic and European, which Yeats noticed in 'Dove or Swan' only as Phase 15 approaches and recedes.[64] It is the clear mirror, the mind's discovery of 'its own permanent form'—a repetition of that self-discovery which, according to Hegel, took place in fifth-century Greece. For Yeats, Berkeley fought the 'Irish Salamis,' which resulted in the 'birth of the national intellect.'[65]

Though the fusion of extremes was incomplcte, though there was no real full moon when 'all abounds and flows,' it was a near miss. The Anglo-Irish would seem

> the Gymnosophists of Strabo close at hand, could they but ignore what was harsh and logical in themselves, or the China of the Dutch cabinet-makers, of the *Citizen of the World:* the long-settled rule of powerful men, no great dogmatic structure, few great crowded streets, scattered unprogressive communities, much handiwork, wisdom wound into the roots of the grass.[66]

And the epoch passed, like that of Greece, with a sinking into the *primary*. The 'mechanicians mocked by Gulliver' prevailed; the 'moment of freedom could not last':

> Did not Rousseau within five years of the death of Swift publish his *Discourse upon Arts and Sciences* and discover instinctive harmony not in heroic effort, not in Cato and Brutus, not among impossible animals . . . but among savages, and thereby beget the sans-culottes of Marat? After the arrogance of power the humility of a servant.[67]

Anglo-Ireland seemed thus to combine transcendental ideal and fallen reality. Yeats cast two crosslights upon it, revealing the virtues of

Phidian Athens and the Renaissance as well as the tragic conflicts of modern Ireland. If, in his prose, the vision lacks complete coherence, it nevertheless testifies to his continual attempt to hold in a single thought reality and justice. The poetry itself brings that double vision into a single paradoxical focus.

IV

In the two poems celebrating Swift, Goldsmith, Berkeley, and Burke, that double vision is evident as a living tradition is viewed from the dramatic perspective. 'The Seven Sages' begins with a trivial boasting, a parody of Yeats's own celebration of his family memories:

> *The First.* My great-grandfather spoke to Edmund Burke
> In Grattan's house.
> *The Second.* My great-grandfather shared
> A pot-house bench with Oliver Goldsmith once.
> *The Third.* My great-grandfather's father talked of music,
> Drank tar-water with the Bishop of Cloyne.
> *The Fourth.* But mine saw Stella once.

Yet what is trivial? Tar water? Berkeley's *Siris,* as Coleridge said, 'beginning with Tar ends with the Trinity, the omne scibile forming the interspace.' Yeats himself said: 'And the tar water, and the cures it worked, what a subject for a discourse! Could he not lead his reader—especially if that reader drank tar water every morning—from tar to light?' [68] For these Anglo-Irish, logic is one with passion, and the loftiest intellectual achievement is rooted in the humblest biographical facts. The question of the fifth stage may then not arise from the inconsequence of senility:

> *The Fifth.* Whence came our thought?
> *The Sixth.* From four great minds that hated Whiggery.
> *The Fifth.* Burke was a Whig.
> *The Sixth.* Whether they knew or not,
> Goldsmith and Burke, Swift and the Bishop of Cloyne
> All hated Whiggery; but what is Whiggery?
> A levelling, rancorous, rational sort of mind
> That never looked out of the eye of a saint
> Or out of a drunkard's eye.
> *The Seventh.* All's Whiggery now,
> But we old men are massed against the world.

Quite aware of the liberties he takes with history, the sixth sage praises both an intensely subjective vision and the objective ability to share the unusual vision of another. And though the seventh applies his redefined epithet much as the old soldier in Tate's 'To the Lacedemonians' applies another such—

> All are born Yankees of the race of men
> And this, too, now the country of the damned

—the sages embody a somewhat more dryly comic heroism. As the poem proceeds, however, their 'massed' opposition gains in dignity and richness. They carry on the magnanimity of dissent in 'Burke's great melody,' the love for the common life in what 'Oliver Goldsmith sang,' the savage indignation chiseled on the 'tomb of Swift,' and the persuasive utterance of Berkeley, leading 'from tar to light':

> a voice
> Soft as the rustle of a reed from Cloyne
> That gathers volume; now a thunder-clap.

Once more an apparently inconsequent remark leads us back to origins:

> *The Sixth*. What schooling had these four?
> *The Seventh*. They walked the roads
> Mimicking what they heard, as children mimic;
> They understood that wisdom comes of beggary.

Though the poem returns to the apparently trivial, the last word has the resonance of a tradition maintained in spite of, and because of, adversity. It has the resonance, too, of the understanding in 'The Tower' that magnificence arises from penury, and the understanding in 'Meditations in Time of Civil War' that the honeybees may 'build in the crevices / Of loosening masonry.' 'Beggary' is the state of 'fruitful void,' known by the wise fool or by the visionary poet who has become again 'unaccommodated by minds magnanimous in victory, heroic in defeat, firm in apparent eccentricity, yet humble before the simplest facts of experience.'

In 'Blood and the Moon,' because the speaker is no simple sage but the owner of the tower, the double vision is more complex, and a more painful wisdom comes of a more extreme beggary.

> Blessed be this place,
> More blessed still this tower;
> A bloody, arrogant power

Rose out of the race
Uttering, mastering it,
Rose like these walls from these
Storm-beaten cottages—
In mockery I have set
A powerful emblem up
And sing it rhyme upon rhyme
In mockery of a time
Half dead at the top.

In Vichian manner he re-erects the tower that rose out of the race, paradoxically both expression and master of Ireland. As he blesses that tower, his emblem joins spirit and blood in a fruitful if precarious marriage that mocks his own less vital, more incoherent time.

Then, after recalling towers that variously combined wisdom and directing power, he sings his own symbol of the compelling harmonies of life:

I declare this tower is my symbol; I declare
This winding, gyring, spiring treadmill of a stair is my ancestral stair;
That Goldsmith and the Dean, Berkeley and Burke have travelled there.

That firm pronouncement, with its relish for the bitter and salt of effort and repetition on the winding path of nature, gives body to the nostalgia of the narrator of 'Rosa Alchemica,' who had boasted of his 'wide staircase, where Swift had passed joking and railing, and Curran telling stories and quoting Greek.' [69] In various ways the following triplets balance wisdom and power, spirit and clay:

Swift beating on his breast in sibylline frenzy blind
Because the heart in his blood-sodden breast had dragged him down into mankind,
Goldsmith deliberately sipping at the honey-pot of his mind,

—prophetic illumination because of enforced suffering and compassion, balanced by judicious mental delectation—

And haughtier-headed Burke that proved the State a tree,
That this unconquerable labyrinth of the birds, century after century,
Cast but dead leaves to mathematical equality;

—proud logic supporting the organic richness and force of a body politics that transcends the dead level of rationalist structures—

And God-appointed Berkeley that proved all things a dream,
That this pragmatical, preposterous pig of a world, its farrow
that so solid seem,
Must vanish on the instant if the mind but change its theme;

—a magical, whimsical power of the mind to annihilate the gross solidity of flesh. From sibylline frenzy to subjective mind's ascendancy, it is a rich chord: Anglo-Ireland 'free at last from all prepossession' and touching the 'extremes of thought.' The precarious harmony is that of the 'winding, gyring, spiring treadmill' of life itself, with its continual shifts and counterstresses:

Saeva Indignatio and the labourer's hire,
The strength that gives our blood and state magnanimity of
its own desire;
Everything that is not God consumed with intellectual fire.

Far more precarious, however, than the unity of that blessed and bloody tower is the speaker's possession of it. Hence, indeed, the note of forced rhetoric in his mocking and his celebration; for, despite his declaration, he is of the time which he mocks. His emblem is at most a passionate mental re-enactment of that eighteenth-century power. It is proper, therefore, that his series was climaxed not by Swift but by Berkeley, whose consuming intellectual fire leads toward the more extreme perception of the speaker himself. Stepping now outside his mentally possessed tradition, he returns to his own time. The opposites so variously unified begin to fall apart in his mind.

The purity of the unclouded moon
Has flung its arrowy shaft upon the floor.
Seven centuries have passed and it is pure,
The blood of innocence has left no stain,
There, on blood-saturated ground, have stood
Soldier, assassin, executioner,
Whether for daily pittance or in blind fear
Or out of abstract hatred, and shed blood,
But could not cast a single jet thereon.
Odour of blood on the ancestral stair!
And we that have shed none must gather here
And clamour in drunken frenzy for the moon.

Spirit and blood no longer meet and interpenetrate in the miracle of various life. The lunar shaft is inviolable; on the ancestral stair is blood shed for base motives. The speaker, now barred from the realm of physical power, can but clamor in drunken frenzy for that of spirit. His stair is no longer the gyre of life but a deathly limbo between blood and the moon. It is as though the sequence hoped for in 'The Magi' were reversed.

As the speaker now turns his gaze upward from the bestial floor toward the sky, the opposites fall further apart. A Blake engraving captioned 'I Want! I Want!' depicts a ladder leaning against the moon, a small figure at the base beginning its climb; Yeats's 'John Sherman' mentions a brooch in the form of 'a ladder leaning against the moon and a butterfly climbing up it.' [70] Symbols of the soul's impossible ascent, they may have led Yeats to use here the dying butterflies in the waste room atop Thoor Ballylee, as the speaker's clamor for the moon leads to a half-mocking perception of beauty in death:

> Upon the dusty, glittering windows cling,
> And seem to cling upon the moonlit skies,
> Tortoiseshell butterflies, peacock butterflies,
> A couple of night-moths are on the wing.
> Is every modern nation like the tower,
> Half dead at the top?

He then turns upon his argument and denies the wisdom of Swift's heart, of Goldsmith's honeypot, of Burke's haughty head, even of Berkeley's mind, which fully controlled a living world:

> No matter what I said,
> For wisdom is the property of the dead,
> A something incompatible with life; and power,
> Like everything that has the stain of blood,
> A property of the living; but no stain
> Can come upon the visage of the moon
> When it has looked in glory from a cloud.

That abrupt and arrogant reversal is tinged, he knows, with 'drunken frenzy' and bitter mockery. It is as though he would justify both the separation of the opposites which he must endure and his own deathly yearnings. He is still caught, like his modern tower, in a realm that is neither blood nor moon. But is his frenzy utterly different from that which emerged from Swift's middle state? As the victim of his historical moment, he has at least the wisdom appropriate to his condition:

half-dead, barred from full life or death, he knows himself. And in knowing himself, in holding reality and justice in a single thought, he does in fact take another step on the winding stair of life.

The strength of this poem, like that of 'Meditations in Time of Civil War,' could not exist without the speaker's vigorous honesty. Despite a rather common critical assumption based upon our usual blindnesses, self-dramatization does not preclude self-knowledge. Hence, though the detailed conflicts of 'Blood and the Moon' derive from a historical predicament, its final meaning is of the Dantesque order that Yeats saw in all art worthy the name: 'the disengaging of a soul from place and history, its suspension in a beautiful or terrible light to await the Judgment, though it must be, seeing that all its days were a Last Day, judged already.' [71]

V

Beginning with a direct personal relation to Ireland, moving in widening circles through the re-experienced drama of the past, Yeats could reach a universal history—the Renaissance, Phidian Athens, all the antinomies of *primary* and *antithetical* or of blood and the moon. Fleetingly in personal meditation, enduringly in the poems, he merged dramatic experience and panoramic vision in a full-bodied yet comprehensive reality.

> Now that I am old and live in the past I often think of those ancestors of whom I have some detailed information. Such and such a diner-out and a charming man never did anything; such and such lost the never very great family fortune in some wild-cat scheme; such and such, perhaps deliberately for he was a strange, deep man, married into a family known for harsh dominating strength of character. Then, as my mood deepens, I discover all these men in my single mind, think that I myself have gone through them all at this very moment, and wonder if the balance has come right; then I go beyond those minds and my single mind and discover that I have been describing everybody's struggle, and the gyres turn in my thought.[72]

The experienced and re-experienced drama leads toward the panoramic vision. That statement of 1938 alludes to a richness of content that results from years of meditation, and it conforms to Yeats's understanding of Vico's theory of historical knowledge. But the basic technique of the meditation itself, like so many of his 'truths,' had been with Yeats since his twenties. He had presented it in his Blake study as the means of redeeming fallen man, of creating the apocalypse through the power of imagination:

> The mood of the seer, no longer bound in by the particular experiences of his body, spreads out and enters into the particular experiences of an ever-widening circle of other lives and beings, for it will more and more grow one with that portion of the mood essence which is common to all that lives. The circle of the individuality will widen out until other individualities are contained within it, and their thoughts, and the persistent thought-symbols which are their spiritual or mental bodies, will grow visible to it. He who has thus passed into the impersonal portion of his own mind perceives that it is not a mind but all minds. Hence Blake's statement that 'Albion,' or man, once contained all 'the starry heavens,' and his description of their flight from him as he materialized. When once a man has re-entered into this, his ancient state, he perceives all things as with the eyes of God.[73]

But that 'truth' possessed so early was now tested by passion and reinforced by the experience of others. Whether or not Yeats had noted Emerson's remark that 'Dante's praise is that he dared to write his autobiography in colossal cipher, or into universality,' he himself saw others do much the same thing:

> Swift seemed to shape his narrative of history upon some clairvoyant vision of his own life, for he saw civilisation pass from comparative happiness and youthful vigour to an old age of violence and self-contempt, whereas Vico saw it begin in penury like himself and end as he himself would end in a long inactive peace.[74]

Hegel and Balzac, he thought, also 'saw history as a personal experience.' He knew, of course, that each personal vision must, to some degree, be unique: 'When I allow my meditation to expand until the mind of my family merges into everybody's mind, I discover there, not only what Vico and Balzac found, but my own particular amusements and interests.'[75] History as vision is limited by one's own mental breadth and depth; history as dramatic experience is limited by the extent to which one has, in one's own life, gone over the whole ground. But to seek history in any other way, Yeats believed, is to compile anatomies of last year's leaves and not to see or create a living forest.

That understanding of history informs most of Yeats's major poems. But one, 'Coole Park and Ballylee, 1931,' shows with unusual clarity the meditative process widening out from immediate personal experience toward the panoramic vision. Its rapid yet oblique movement depends upon Yeats's gradually developed 'universalism' or 'seeing of unity everywhere,' attained through the 'glove' of intimately possessed particulars. The emblems of the poem are not postulated so much as discovered, for the speaker meditates upon a concrete world that presses in upon him, demanding significant articulation.

> Under my window-ledge the waters race,
> Otters below and moor-hens on the top,
> Run for a mile undimmed in Heaven's face
> Then darkening through 'dark' Raftery's 'cellar' drop,
> Run underground, rise in a rocky place
> In Coole demesne, and there to finish up
> Spread to a lake and drop into a hole.
> What's water but the generated soul?

Though recalling Porphyry on the cave of the nymphs, or Yeats on the streams of Shelley's Alastor and the Witch of Atlas,[76] the stanza does not flatly apply some neo-Platonic system. The final question expresses the sudden illumination toward which the specific meditation has moved. The abstract equivalence is but the simplest and most certain part of that illumination—enough to focus tentatively its matrix of particulars. ('I prefer to include in my definition of water a little duckweed or a few fish. I have never met that poor naked creature H_2O.' [77]) We go over the course again in retrospect: the soul's pristine vigor, the strange doubleness of its psychic life (moor hen and otter), its swift youthful accomplishment; then adversity or seeming death (the darkness of Raftery's 'cellar' [78] suggesting that of the 'dark man' himself), forcing the soul downward into the realm of otters but not preventing its eventual creative victory as it rises 'in a rocky place' (which recalls, among other things, the 'place of stone' in 'To a Friend Whose Work Has Come to Nothing'); there, finally, its serene fulfilment and death. But to spell out must not be to limit this 'clairvoyant vision'—to deny, for example, a longer temporal course depicted, which prepares for the poem's later widening of focus: the stream which moves past the Norman tower, past the 'strong cellar' of the ballad-poet Raftery, to Coole demesne, the residence of Lady Gregory. Though the subject of the meditation will not achieve final definition until the end of the poem, its area is already clear: the accomplishment and the transience of a soul and of a tradition.

The complex stream has led the speaker from his post of observation, his window ledge, to Coole demesne and its suggestions of imminent death. He turns from that thought, but cannot turn from either the mood or the site, both of which seem engendered by the thought.

> Upon the border of that lake's a wood
> Now all dry sticks under a wintry sun,
> And in a copse of beeches there I stood,
> For Nature's pulled her tragic buskin on
> And all the rant's a mirror of my mood:
> At sudden thunder of the mounting swan
> I turned about and looked where branches break
> The glittering reaches of the flooded lake.

The 'dry sticks' suggest the end of a life and of an era, the arriving of the 'wintry sun' of solar *primary*. The immediate Yeatsian response, where such 'branches *break*/ The glittering reaches,' is tragic 'rant': the soul's defiant effort to 'rise in a rocky place,' to transmute a final hole to a temporary cellar. As in 'Nineteen Hundred and Nineteen,' the 'thunder of the mounting swan' echoes that response. Yet even that image must in turn be altered by the overwhelming sense of transience:

> Another emblem there! That stormy white
> But seems a concentration of the sky;
> And, like the soul, it sails into the sight
> And in the morning's gone, no man knows why;
> And is so lovely that it sets to right
> What knowledge or its lack had set awry,
> So arrogantly pure, a child might think
> It can be murdered with a spot of ink.

An emblem of what? Yeats, in an often-cited letter, said, 'a symbol of inspiration, I think.' [79] But we should not ignore his own uncertainty: here as elsewhere the poem refuses to be caught in the net of any simple abstract equivalent. Stormy, even divine power and beauty, arrogant purity—yet seemingly more transient than the soul itself: whether it is that soul, comes to the soul, mirrors the soul, or is created by the soul, it suggests the momentary fulfilment of spirit that redeems the imperfect temporal world.

Twice in this stanza the stream of thought carries the speaker toward the idea of death; once he pulls back, with a third 'And,' to start his celebration anew—but again, irresistibly, a quality suggests its negation. The oblique rendering of the transience of poetic power, human life, and historical tradition can no longer be maintained. The unstated cause of the 'mood,' evaded repeatedly, demands utterance. The fact to be confronted is not 'sudden thunder' but 'dry sticks':

> Sound of a stick upon the floor, a sound
> From somebody that toils from chair to chair . . .

The theme of personal mortality finds its specific focus, crucially unnamed, and the earlier implications of the end of an era, the end of a period of artistic accomplishment, begin to unfold:

> Beloved books that famous hands have bound,
> Old marble heads, old pictures everywhere;
> Great rooms where travelled men and children found
> Content or joy; a last inheritor
> Where none has reigned that lacked a name and fame
> Or out of folly into folly came.

After describing further that spot where persons as well as trees and gardens were rooted, that placid lake filled by the turbulent stream of time, the speaker turns to the rootless and superficial present, and his mood deepens. This is a more complex adversity—'all that great glory spent.' The 'glittering reaches of the flooded lake' of history too are dimming. The only glory now possible would be that song celebrated in 'The Tower,' when the swan fixes his eye upon a fading gleam; but the swan can no longer sing:

> We were the last romantics—chose for theme
> Traditional sanctity and loveliness;
> Whatever's written in what poets name
> The book of the people; whatever most can bless
> The mind of man or elevate a rhyme;
> But all is changed, that high horse riderless,
> Though mounted in that saddle Homer rode
> Where the swan drifts upon a darkened flood.

As the 'Last Arcadian' once mourned the death of the 'woods of Arcady,' one who *was* a last romantic now mourns 'dry sticks' on Coole estate. But the gain in richness and depth is considerable. The growing boy knew that the intimately possessed particulars of life might lead toward the universal; but John Sherman, standing by the riverside of his youth, saw little more than 'familiar sights—boys riding in the stream to the saddle-girths . . . , a swan asleep.' [80] The ageing man, standing in imagination by the final lake, looks through such sights, transmuted, upon the landscape of the past. That 'darkening flood'—which so marvelously widens and deepens the water imagery—is not the lesser adversity, the 'darkening' drop into Raftery's cellar which helped to create 'dark' Raftery's 'book of the people' [81]—or helped 'dark' Milton 'build the lofty rhyme.' No stream rises; no swan mounts. Pegasus is riderless, and we see no wings. The stream of generation has moved from that double image of youthful vitality, 'Otters below and moor-hens on the top,' to a double image of its dying fall, drifting swan upon shadow.

The speaker, ostensibly surviving his own significant life, looks back from a 'last inheritor' at Coole Park into an indefinite past, from himself and others who were the last romantics to Raftery, Milton, and Homer. It seems a vision not of the cycles of history but of a radical fall. Yet winter does lead to spring, a riderless horse may be ridden, a drifting swan may mount. Even in despair the emblems cannot deny the force of life that produces a continual dialogue between Yeats and the temporal world. Indeed, in this final stanza the mediation itself rises to great lyricism as it claims its impossibility. No more than Lycidas does this swan of a past era float upon his watery bier unwept. Song mourning the lack of song belies itself. Yeats, who knew that no battle has even been finally lost, knew also that tradition may live in the lament for its passing.

NOTES

1. *1930D,* pp. 54–55.
2. *Wheels and Butterflies* (New York, 1935), p. 98.
3. *1930D,* p. 10.
4. *Wheels and Butterflies,* p. 7.
5. *E&I,* p. 428 (1932).
6. *Further Letters of John Butler Yeats,* selected by Lennox Robinson (Dundrum, 1930), pp. 57 ff.
7. *Ideals in Ireland,* ed. Augusta Gregory (London, 1901), pp. 105, 106.

8. *Letters to the New Island,* ed. Horace Reynolds (Cambridge, Mass., 1934), pp. 90–91.
9. See *The Letters of W. B. Yeats,* ed. Allan Wade (New York, 1955), pp. 154*n.,* 156.
10. *Representative Irish Tales* (London, 1891), I, 2–3, 11.
11. *Ibid.,* I, 5–6, 7.
12. Inscribed in Quinn's copy of the collection, quoted by Allan Wade, *A Bibliography of the Writings of W. B. Yeats* (London, 1951), p. 214.
13. Gregory, *Gods and Fighting Men,* intro. by Yeats (London, 1904), pp. xxii–xxiii.
14. *The King of the Great Clock Tower* (New York, 1935), p. 27.
15. 'Ireland 1921–1931,' *Spectator,* CXLVIII (Jan. 1932), 137.
16. *Idem.*
17. Seanad Eirann, *Parliamentary Debates,* V, 434–43, contains Yeats's speech, and V, 443–80, the angry debate that followed.
18. *P&C,* pp. 192–93.
19. See Ezra Pound, *Guide to Kulchur* (London, 1938), p. 155.
20. Seanad Eirann, *Parliamentary Debates,* V, 443.
21. Wade, *Letters,* p. 295.
22. *W. B. Yeats and T. Sturge Moore: Their Correspondence 1901–1937,* ed. Ursula Bridge (London, 1953), p. 114.
23. *CW,* V, 27 ff.
24. See Wade, *A Bibliography of Yeats,* pp. 38–39, for some original titles. John V. Kelleher called my attention to the prototype.
25. *The Complete Writings of William Blake,* ed. Geoffrey Keynes (London, 1957), p. 342.
26. *CW,* V, 37–38.
27. *1930D,* p. 54.
28. *E&I,* p. 78 (1900).
29. *P&C,* p. 41.
30. Alfred Tennyson, 'Merlin and the Gleam.'
31. *1930D,* p. 8.
32. Cf. an early draft of 'The Tower': 'Why could no Rabbi say / That Eternal Man / Rested the seventh day' (Richard Ellmann, *The Identity of Yeats* [New York, 1954], p. 225*n.*).
33. *The Letters of John Keats,* ed. Maurice B. Forman (London, 1952; 4th ed.), pp. 334–35. The tone with which Yeats evokes the symbolic paradise in the last part of 'The Tower' also suggests Keats (*Letters,* p. 102): '. . . almost any Man may like the spider spin from his own inwards his own airy Citadel—the points of leaves and twigs on which the spider begins his work are few, and she fills the air with a beautiful circuiting. Man should be content with as few points to tip with the fine Web of his Soul, and weave a tapestry empyrean full of symbols for his spiritual eye, of softness for his spiritual touch, of space for his wan-

dering, of distinctness for his luxury.' Cf. Yeats's use of the spider to describe subjective men, *Au,* p. 116.

34. *P&C,* p. 123; *Au,* p. 311.
35. *1930D,* pp. 5–6.
36. *1930D,* p. 4.
37. *1930D,* p. 28. Though here distorting Swift's thought to bring it closer to his own, he qualified these views for publication (see *Wheels and Butterflies,* pp. 16–20); and he was at least correct in finding in Swift, who partly followed Polybius, a strong suspicion that the irony of history might require the rise and fall of successive civilizations. See Jonathan Swift, *A Tale of a Tub, with Other Early Works,* ed. Herbert Davis (Oxford, 1939), pp. 217, 228 ff.
38. *1930D,* p. 28.
39. *1930D,* p. 55.
40. Collingwood, *An Autobiography* (London, 1939), pp. 113, 114, 115. Cf. Benedetto Croce, *History as the Story of Liberty,* tr. Sylvia Sprigge (New York, 1941), pp. 1920: 'the present state of my mind constitutes the material, and consequently the documentation for an historical judgment. . . . Man is a microcosm, not in the natural sense, but in the historical sense . . .' But Yeats would reject Croce's sharp distinction between the historical imagination and the 'poetic fancy' (*ibid.,* p. 127).
41. *CPlays,* p. 383.
42. *1930D,* p. 6.
43. *Wheels and Butterflies,* pp. 7–8.
44. *P&C,* p. 95.
45. 'The New Irish Library,' *Bookman,* X (June, 1896), 83.
46. *1930D,* p. 6.
47. *1930D,* pp. 17, 41, 42.
48. *1930D,* pp. 17–18.
49. *V–B,* pp. 214–15. The passages occur in what Yeats called 'an admirable and exciting book,' D. T. Suzuki, *Essays in Zen Buddhism, First Series* (London, 1927), pp. 234, 241*n.*
50. Wade, *Letters,* p. 922. See Suzuki, *Essays in Zen Buddhism,* pp. 47, 51, 216, 260–61.
51. *V–B,* p. 215.
52. *E&I,* pp. 397, 398 (1931).
53. *1930D,* p. 41.
54. Oliver St. John Gogarty, *Wild Apples,* intro. by Yeats (Dublin, 1930), sig. A-7.
55. *E&I,* p. 399.
56. *E&I,* pp. 401, 402.
57. Gogarty, *Wild Apples,* sig. A-6–A-6v.
58. *The King of the Great Clock Tower,* p. 26.
59. Wade, *Letters,* p. 773.

60. *Wheels and Butterflies,* pp. 21–22.
61. *V–B,* pp. 145 ff., 293 ff.
62. *Wheels and Butterflies,* p. 7.
63. *Wheels and Butterflies,* pp. 22–23.
64. *V–B,* pp. 270, 281, 291. With the Asiatic 'flower-like intricacy' compare the Persian decorations (V–B, p. 281) which are *primary,* and which Yeats found in Strzygowski.
65. *1930D,* pp. 51, 54. Cf. *Wheels and Butterflies,* p. 11.
66. *Wheels and Butterflies,* p. 23.
67. *Ibid.,* p. 27.
68. Samuel Taylor Coleridge, *Biographia Literaria,* ed. John Shawcross (Oxford, 1907), I, 201; *1930D,* p. 40.
69. 'Rosa Alchemica,' *Savoy,* No. 2 (Apr., 1896), p. 59.
70. Blake, *Complete Writings,* p. 766; *John Sherman and Dhoya* (London, 1891), p. 141.
71. *E&I,* p. 339.
72. *On the Boiler,* p. 22.
73. *E&Y,* I, 244.
74. *The Complete Works of Ralph Waldo Emerson,* ed. E. W. Emerson (Boston and New York, 1903–4), III, 37; *Wheels and Butterflies,* pp. 16–17.
75. *On the Boiler,* p. 22.
76. *E&I,* pp. 80 ff. (1900), contains a lengthy discussion of such symbolism. Alastor, for example, 'passed in his boat along a river in a cave; and when for the last time he felt the presence of the spirit he loved and followed, it was when he watched his image in a silent well; and when he died it was where a river fell into "an abysmal chasm" . . .' (p. 80). Alastor's apostrophe to the stream (lines 502 ff.) makes explicit the kind of symbolism Yeats's first stanza leaves implicit:

> 'O stream!
> Whose source is inaccessibly profound,
> Whither do thy mysterious waters tend
> Thou imagest my life. Thy darksome stillness,
> Thy dazzling waves, thy loud and hollow gulfs,
> Thy searchless fountain, and invisible course
> Have each their type in me . . .'

77. *Yeats and Moore: Their Correspondence,* p. 69 (1926).
78. *The Celtic Twilight* (CW, V, 28) foreshadows this passage. Yeats talked to an old man about Mary Hynes, and 'about a poem in Irish, Raftery . . . made about her, and how it said, "there is a strong cellar in Ballylee." He said the strong cellar was the great hole where the river sank underground, and he brought me to a deep pool, where an otter hurried away under a grey boulder, and told me that many fish came up out

of the dark water at early morning "to taste the fresh water coming down from the hills." '

79. Quoted by Joseph Hone, *W. B. Yeats, 1865–1939* (London, 1942), p. 455.
80. *John Sherman and Dhoya,* p. 65.
81. For Raftery's phrase, see *P&C,* p. 180.

DONALD DAVIE

The Rock-Drill Cantos

(1964)

I have said that one may read quite a long way into the *Cantos* in the spirit of 'Lordly men are to earth o'er given' ('The Seafarer') or of 'We seem to have lost the radiant world' (as in the essay on Cavalcanti). This is the point indeed at which Pound is most clearly a man of his generation; T. S. Eliot's extraordinarily influential notion of 'the dissociation of sensibility' is only one version of the belief in a calamitous Fall, an expulsion from some historical Eden, that seems to have been an imaginative necessity as well for Yeats and Pound, for T. E. Hulme, and for Henry Adams before any of them.[1] For Pound as a young man the Fall came between Cavalcanti and Petrarch, and he seems to have persuaded Hulme to agree with him; for Yeats it came about 1550; for Eliot, some time between 1590 and 1650. Pound's position as he later developed it, however, was closer to Yeats's than to Eliot's, for he and Yeats embraced a cyclical view of historical change that permitted them to conceive of such calamities as having happened more than once, at corresponding stages in other cultural cycles than that of recorded history in Western Europe. Whereas Yeats interested himself in the cyclical theories of Spengler, Pound from about 1925 onwards pledged himself to Spengler's master, the neglected German thinker and explorer Leo Frobenius, who is accordingly drawn upon in later cantos.[2] Pound differs from all his old associates, characteristically, by choosing for his hero not a theorist but a scientist, whose conclusions are arrived at inductively from observations 'in the field'; and, in fact, since Frobenius like Louis Agassiz can be regarded as the pupil of Friedrich Heinrich Alexander, Baron von Humboldt (1769–1859), he takes his place (along with Ernest Fenollosa) in the line of succession, as Pound sees it, of the heroes of modern science. This gives to Pound's historical nostalgia an altogether sturdier and more substantial, though also a more cluttered, appearance than the nostalgias of Eliot and Yeats.

All the same, in the case of all these men, those of their writings that rely most heavily on this pseudo-history are already tiresome. In Eliot's case little damage is done, for he mostly reserved this kind of thinking for his essays, which, having served their vast polemical purpose, are already 'dated' and outdated, as the poems are not. And in Yeats's work there are only a few poems, like 'The Statues,' that seem irretrievably damaged. Unfortunately, whole tracts of the *Cantos* are laid waste in this way, because they rest, if they are to be persuasive, on an encyclopaedic knowledge of recorded history such as we know that Pound neither possesses nor could possess. The failure of the American History and Chinese History cantos can be explained in other ways; but they would have been barren in the long run, even if they had been written according to a less perverse poetic method, and by a man more in control of himself than Pound was in the 1930's. For, although they derive in one way from a genuinely scientific humility, and seek to inculcate such humility in the reader, the whole plan of them is absurdly, even insanely, presumptuous; there is simply too much recorded history available for any one to offer to speak of it with such confidence as Pound does.

It is the arrogance that is damaging, not the nostalgia, for time and again in the *Cantos* the nostalgia for a vanished Europe is controlled and personal enough to rise to the level of elegy, as it did in 'Provincia Deserta,' and as it does in a recent interview, when Pound endorses the description of himself as 'the last American living the tragedy of Europe.' [3] Nothing is so mean-minded nor so wide of the mark as the common British sneer at Eliot and Pound alike that, being Americans, the Europe they speak of is a never-never land. The spectator sees most of the play, and if these Americans can see European civilization as a whole in a way no European can, that is their advantage, and something their European readers can profit from. It is abundantly possible and profitable to read the *Cantos* for the sake of the recurrent passages of elegiac lament; the landscape in Canto 20, for example, can be enjoyed in the same way as 'Provincia Deserta,' whether the landscape is taken as that of Freiburg or Provence. This elegiac feeling pervades the Pisan cantos.

On the other hand, the Pisan sequence is so refreshing after the score or more of cantos that precede it largely because the poet is here content to let his mind play mournfully over the past without pretending to understand it or pass judgment on it. It is, therefore, all the more discouraging that the next several cantos to appear (85 to 89) thrust us back into Chinese and American history in a way that seems to be sadly familiar. However, it is not so familiar as it seems. The mere look of Canto 85 on the page, especially in the very beautiful Italian printing of *Rock-Drill,*[4] announces it as 'unreadable': bold black Chinese characters, in various sizes, are ranged up and down and across, interspersed with sparse print which includes Roman and Arabic numerals, Greek, Latin, French, and phonetic transcriptions of Chinese, as well as English. This is at least an advance on the Chinese History and American History cantos, which looked readable but were not. All the same, what are we to do with it? Most readers will understandably decide that life is too short, and will close the book—though reluctantly, because of the beauty in the look of it. For others, the way out is in a note at the end to the effect that 'the numerical references are to Couvreur's Chou King.' For, whereas the Chinese History cantos become no more readable if they are taken page by page along with their source in Mailla's *Histoire générale,* nor do the Adams cantos become readable along with John Adams's Diaries, Canto 85, which is unreadable in isolation, becomes, if not in the normal sense readable, at any rate fascinating and instructive when set beside Couvreur. What we experience then is certainly not in any normal sense a poem in the English language. On the other hand, William Blake's marginalia to Reynolds's *Discourses* are more interesting than all but the best of Blake's poems; and they require, to be appreciated fully, that we have a volume of Reynolds open before us, beside a volume of Blake. In the same way Pound's marginalia to Couvreur are more interesting than all but the best of the other cantos. The analogy breaks down, however, in that the interest of Blake's marginalia is in Blake's ideas, whereas the ideas of the *Chou King* become interesting only by virtue of the language that first Couvreur and then Pound have discovered for them. It is this that makes Canto 85 nearer to poetry as normally conceived than Blake's marginalia are.

Couvreur offers both a French and a Latin translation of his Chinese text, and his versions in both languages are very distinguished, as Pound acknowledges by reproducing so much of both. The marginal translations that Pound offers in English—'Our dynasty came in because of a great sensibility,' 'We flop if we cannot maintain the awareness,' 'Awareness restful and fake is fatiguing'—emerge all the more salient and memorable from this polyglot context. But the most important of them are carefully embedded in this context so that to take the force of them we have to reconstruct, with Couvreur's volume before us, the whole linguistic situation from which they derive. For instance, between the phrase, 'not water, ôu iu chouèi,' and the phrase, 'There be thy mirrour in men,' there come, in column down the middle of the page, three Chinese characters, with to the right of them phonetic transcriptions of two of them and a numerical reference. We have to follow the reference to the page of Couvreur in order to unearth the ancient adage, 'Take not for glass the water's crystal, but other men'—a very important prefiguring of what will be the governing metaphor of Canto 90. Any one is at liberty to decide that he cannot afford to take this trouble. But at least Canto 85 is the logical conclusion of ways of writing that in earlier cantos were adopted sporadically and inconsistently. In particular, it represents a recognition by Pound that for him a poem could be almost as much a composition in the space of the printed page as a shape emerging out of the time it takes in the reading; and it shows him also settling with himself, as he had not settled when he wrote the Adams cantos, how far a poem made up of marginalia upon a source can stand independent of that source. Canto 85 has to be read along with its source; there is no other way to read it. Of course the ideal reader whom Pound envisages will no longer be blank in front of Chinese characters; he will have learned from *The Unwobbling Pivot* to recognize such old acquaintances as the characters for 'the total light-process' and for 'tensile light.'

However, it is in Cantos 86 to 89 that our lack of confidence in Pound as a historian does most damage. The plan and the intention are understandable enough: Canto 85 has established, being a digest of the history classic, the *Chou King,* a standard for moral judgments of historical eras; and so in the next few cantos we plunge into the time of recorded history, just as we had to do before and after the Usura canto (45). But inevitably our hearts sink as we face yet more pages of historical anecdotes capsulated and mangled, obiter dicta of past statesmen torn from their historical context, and roll-calls of names from the past. In particular, we may be mutinous when we discover that Cantos 88 and 89 draw on yet another source-book in American history, Thomas Hart Benton's *Thirty Years' View*. There are things of value and interest in for instance Canto 87, but to most readers, even devoted ones, these appear only when they glance back over these pages from the vantage point of the later cantos in the *Rock-Drill* sequence.

We seem to move, from Canto 90 onwards, into a blessedly different world from that in which Polk and Tyler and Randolf of Roanoke play their imperfectly apprehended roles on the stage of nineteenth-century America. Clark Emery defines this world by contrast with the Pisan Cantos:

> In Canto 90 (and those following) of the Rock-Drill group, the myth becomes of extreme importance. We seem to be witnessing the gradual but inevitable victory of the paradisal—a victory taking place in the heart and mind of Pound himself. Throughout these cantos, Castalia appears to be the objective correlative of the place in which Pound, through prayer, humility, agony, comes to union with the process. The union—or the approach to the union—is imagized by the return of the altar to the grove, the 'substantiation' of Tyro and Alcmene, the ascension of a procession, and the upward climb of a new mythic component, the Princess Ra-Set. Where, in Canto 82, Pound was drawn by Gea Terra, and in 83 found no basis under Taishan (a holy mountain whose summit is to be achieved, as the city of Dioce is to be built) but the brightness of Hudor, in the *Rock-Drill* cantos he has moved into air, into light, and beyond. And where, in Canto 80, the raft broke and the waters went over the Odysseus-Pound, in 95 Leucothoe has pity and rescues him.[5]

What Emery calls 'the myth' might as well be called, quite simply, 'myth.' With Canto 90 we ascend from the world of history to the world of myth. It was this world to which we were introduced in the first two cantos of all, and we have never been allowed to lose sight of it altogether. Canto 47, for instance, which took us, nothing loath, from history into pre-history, by that token took us into myth—from the labor of trying to understand history into the relief of transcending it. In cantos like Canto 90, which are based on myth, the ethics that the poet commends are underpinned by metaphysical or religious intuitions, rather than by historical evidence; and yet it is the basic assumption of the *Cantos* that we have no right to our religious apprehensions unless we have taken the historical evidence into consideration.

Indeed, the myths that are useful to us, the only myths we apprehend and enter into with all seriousness, are those that raise as it were to a new power, or into a new dimension, perceptions we have already arrived at by other means. Canto 90, for example, presents as myth perceptions about the use of hewn stone by sculptor and architect, perceptions with which we are already familiar from the memoir of Gaudier-Brzeska, Canto 17, and many other passages. Hugh Kenner, it is true, in what is the most valuable account yet given of the *Rock-Drill* cantos,[6] declares that in them, 'the precision of natural renewal has replaced the cut stone of the early cantos.' But in Canto 90 marble plays very much the same role as in Canto 17:

> 'From the colour the nature
> & by the nature the sign!'
> Beatific spirits welding together
> as in one ash-tree in Ygdrasail.
> Baucis, Philemon.
> Castalia is the name of that fount in the hill's fold,
> the sea below,
> narrow beach,
> Templum aedificans, not yet marble,
> 'Amphion!'

Amphion, thus invoked, stands inevitably for music and the power of music, especially as defined in *Guide to Kulchur* (p. 283):

> The magic of music is in its effect on volition.
> A sudden clearing of the mind of rubbish and the re-establishment of a sense of proportion.

For the Canto proceeds a few lines later to precisely that 'sense of proportion':

> Builders had kept the proportion,
> did Jacques de Molay
> know these proportions?

And the masonic associations of Jacques de Molay (accompanied by a reference we have met before, to a shadowless room in Poitiers [7]) look forward to the achieved act, on the way to which music's cleansing was only a necessary first stage. For the achieved act is a stone or marble artifact:

> The architect from the painter,
> the stone under elm
> Taking form now,
> the rilievi,
> the curled stone at the marge

From 'not yet marble' to 'the curled stone at the marge' graphs the movement toward perfection.

What the architect makes, however, is in the first place an altar, as Clark Emery points out. For in between 'not yet marble' and 'the curled stone' has come, along with material familiar from earlier cantos (for instance the Adonis ritual at the mouth of the river):

> Grove hath its altar
> under elms, in that temple, in silence
> a lone nymph by the pool.
> Wei and Han rushing together
> two rivers together
> bright fish and flotsam
> torn bough in the flood
> and the waters clear with the flowing

Thus, the act is less an artistic achievement than a religious one; or rather it is a particularly solemn and worthy act of art in that it is a religious act also. For Pound's dislike of the Judaic element in Christianity stems specifically from the prohibition of graven images, since whenever religious apprehensions are not fixed in the images that an artist makes of them they are handed over instead to those who will codify them in prohibitions, and so betray them:

> To replace the marble goddess on her pedestal at Terracina is worth more than a metaphysical argument.[8]

And it is for this reason that Pound always wishes the Hellenic element in Christianity to outweigh the Hebraic:

> Tradition inheres . . . in the images of the gods and gets lost in dogmatic definitions. History is recorded in monuments, and *that* is why they get destroyed.[9]

It is not an uncommon attitude, but Pound's expression of it is uncommon. For instance, in an earlier passage that we encounter as we move from the music of Amphion to the architecture of the altar, the distinction between Hellenic and Hebraic is carried in two words, 'Sibylla' and 'Isis':

> Castalia like the moonlight
>   and the waves rise and fall,
> Evita, beer-halls, semina motuum,
>   to parched grass, now is rain
> not arrogant from habit,
>   but furious from perception,
>   Sibylla,
> from under the rubble heap
>   m'elevasti
> from the dulled edge beyond pain,
>   m'elevasti
> out of Erebus, the deep-lying
>   from the wind under the earth,
>   m'elevasti
> from the dulled air and the dust
>   m'elevasti
> by the great flight,
>   m'elevasti,
>   Isis Kuanon
>   from the cusp of the moon,
>   m'elevasti
> the viper stirs in the dust,
>   the blue serpent
> glides from the rock pool
>   And they take lights now down to the water . . .

'Sibylla' and also 'Isis' seem to come in here out of Thaddeus Zielinski's *La Sibylle,* which argues that the Christianity of the Roman Church 'was psychologically prepared for by the cult of Eleusis, the cult of the Great Goddesses, the cult of Apollo, and the cult of Isis' (Emery, p. 9). And it follows, as Emery says, 'that when Christian theologians turned from pagan teaching to Judaic, from Ovid and Hesiod to Moses and David, they falsified the true faith.'

Of course, there is much more to the passage just quoted than this cryptic allusion. And all of it—the beer-halls no less than Isis Kuanon—can be glossed without much difficulty. What needs to be noticed, however, is that, as we lend ourselves to the liturgical sway of the powerful rhythms, we do not ask for glosses because after a while we are letting the rhythm carry us over details half-understood or not understood at all. However little we like the snapped-off, jerking rhythms of the cantos that try to comprehend history, we need them to offset these rhythms of the myth that surpasses history; we need the one to validate the other, and, although Pound may have got the proportions between them wrong, some proportion there has to be.

Thus, it is not too soon to look back at one of the unattractive cantos preceding Canto 90. We may permit 'semina motuum' in the passage just quoted to call up 'causa motuum' from Canto 87:

> in pochi,
> causa motuum,
> pine seed splitting cliff's edge.
> Only sequoias are slow enough.
> BinBin 'is beauty.'
> 'Slowness is beauty.':

'BinBin' conceals, maddeningly enough, the identity of Laurence Binyon, whose 'Slowness is beauty' was applauded as a partial but moving truth in *Guide to Kulchur*. But more than beauty is being spoken of, for elsewhere in this canto we have heard (echoing *Guide to Kulchur* again):

> But an economic idea will not (Mencken auctor) go into them in less than a geological epoch.

Thus the few who are 'causa motuum,' by processes as gradual as those by which a pine splits the edge of a cliff or by which the sequoia grows, are men who originate ideas as well as men who create art. But immediately after this, there comes in Canto 87 precisely the same sequence of references as those we have traced, following Hugh Kenner, in Canto 90. After Binyon here, as after 'Amphion!' there, come the characters for the San Ku, the Chinese council of three which in the Tcheou dynasty had the function, according to Couvreur, 'à faire briller l'action du ciel et de la terre.' And then, precisely as in Canto 90, we get the unshadowed room at Poitiers, Jacques de Molay and 'the proportion':

to Poictiers.
The tower wherein, at one point, is no shadow,
and Jacques de Molay, is where?
and the 'Section,' the proportions,
lending, perhaps, not at interest, but resisting.
Then false fronts, barocco.
'We have,' said Mencius, 'but phenomena'
monumenta. In nature are signatures
needing no verbal tradition,
oak leaf never plane leaf. John Heydon.
Σελλοί sleep there on the ground
And old Jarge held there was a tradition,
that was not mere epistemology.

The identical sequence of references which, in Canto 90, takes place in the personal time of an artist proceeding to his artifact or the man of affairs to significant action, in Canto 87 takes place on the time-scale of historical epochs. The right ideas about economic morality, and with them the right ideas about artistic (architectural) practice, rise for a few years, are submerged for centuries, then show up again. This is in keeping with Canto 87 as a whole, which deals with peaks and subsequent declines in cultural traditions: the American 'paideuma' of John Adams fading through the nineteenth century; the Chinese culture transmitted to Japan; high points of Roman culture represented by Antoninus and Salmasius; of Greek by Ocellus and Justinian; of mediaeval by Erigena, Richard of Saint Victor, and Dante. Thus, the relation between 'monumenta' and 'In nature are signatures' is a wry one. The allegedly hollow monumentality of Baroque building is indeed 'a monument' to wrong thinking and wrong morality; it reveals, symptomatically, as surely as do vegetable forms, a truth, but an unpalatable one. And the phrase 'in nature' is to be understood as sardonically opposed to 'in history,' which is unstated: in nature the leaf shapes, as Σελλοί (the original inhabitants of Dodona guarding the oracles of Zeus), are oracular, they signify a truth; but a phenomenon such as the Baroque style signifies the truth only by being symptomatic of its perversion.

The objections to Pound the historian remain. One may still refuse to believe that the connection between right ideas about economics and right practice in architecture can be plotted down the centuries, as Pound would have us believe. But at least we perceive that the poet is once again in command of his material, not only keeping a calculated proportion between history-material and myth-material but balancing one against the other artistically, by contriving parallels between them.

As for the altar that is raised in Canto 90, it remains to ask what god it is dedicated to. And the last page of the canto reassuringly reveals, in imagery that has been familiar ever since Canto 2, that the God is Dionysus, patron of the creatures of earth and under-earth. Thus, though Clark Emery is right to say that as we move from the Pisan cantos to *Rock-Drill,* we tend to move from the elements of earth and water into those of air and fire, yet earth and the earthy are not left behind. This is very important, and Canto 91 will explain it.

The myth of Canto 90 is not created *ad hoc* like the mythologies of William Blake. Many another before Pound had envisaged stone prodigiously shaping itself and falling into place at the behest of music. Walter Pater was one, in his 'Apollo in Picardy':

> Almost suddenly tie-beam and rafter knit themselves together into the stone, and the dark, dry, roomy place was closed in securely to this day. Mere audible music, certainly, had counted for something in the operations of an art, held at its best (as we know) to be a sort of music made visible. That idle singer, one might fancy, by an art beyond art, had attracted beams and stones into their fit places.

And in 'Apollo in Picardy' Pater does what in his essay on 'Aesthetic Poetry' he had asked modern literature to do and what he had seen William Morris as doing already—that is to say, he makes play with deliberate anachronism, making the figure of Apollo out of ancient Greece reappear disguised in mediaeval France. Pater's idea that archetypal figures and archetypal situations recur in different historical epochs (a perception that in his late essay on Raphael he found embodied by that master in paint) is one that, as has been seen, governs much of Pound's writing in the Cantos, though it has been suggested that he got the idea of it from Laforgue's *Moralités légendaires.* There seems no reason why Pound should not have found it rather in these earlier experiments by Pater, for it is likely that Yeats would have pressed Pater upon his attention.

At any rate, the element of cyclical recurrence and renewal, which governs so many of Pound's ideas about history, governs also his choice of myth and his treatment of myth, in *Rock-Drill* as earlier. It informs also his understanding of science:

> The clover enduring,
> basalt crumbled with time.
> Are they the same leaves?
> that was an intelligent question.

Kenner comments very aptly on these lines from Canto 94:

> For one of the purposes of the poem, they are the same leaves; since the form persists, a mode of intelligence informing, as Agassiz would have said, the vegetable order. The visible is a signature of the invisible. . . .

And undoubtedly John Heydon's doctrine of signatures is one of the guide lines through these cantos; it explains, for instance, the birds and beasts reading *virtù* (the 'virtue' of the herbalists) out of the signatures of vegetable forms, at the beginning of Canto 92:

> so will the weasel eat rue,
> and the swallows nip celandine

And this is one example out of many. Yet if we see only the *paradisal* element in these cantos, if we see their structure of values as wholly Platonic (the idea of the leaf persisting behind the metamorphoses of all leafy phenomena), there is the danger that we shall murmur, 'All passion spent,' and see Pound coming to rest in a well-earned quietism. And this is far from the truth; Pound is as ever, in these late cantos, strenuous, urgent, and (his own word) 'unstill.'

The reconciliation is in the idea of 'metamorphosis,' for this is the idea that combines similitude in difference with an absorbed interest in the differences. And accordingly, in Canto 90 as in Canto 2, the pagan authority whom Pound wants to substitute for the tables of the Old Testament law is Ovid:

> He will . . . substitute for the Moses of the Old Testament the Ovid of the *Metamorphoses*, with his recognition of the vivifying personal immediacy of supernatural forces and the constant penetration of the supernatural into the natural, producing change; his good sense in maintaining a separateness of the empirically knowable from the experienced unknowable and in accepting the fact of the unknowable instead of

> speculating upon, generalizing from, and dogmatizing in terms of it; and his polytheistic tolerance so sharply to be discriminated from the dictatorial nay-saying which Pound finds characteristic of the Jewish scripture. (Emery, p. 9.)

Hence, in the fifth line of Canto 90, 'Baucis, Philemon.' As Ovid's case of ideally harmonious human marriage they are an instance of perfect 'welding together' ('Beatific spirits welding together'), but also, as some have thought, their story represents the still point in Ovid's poem, the harmony achieved out of its flux of metamorphosis.

Canto 91 is good enough to raise again questions about the assumptions that underlie the procedures of the *Cantos* as a whole, for here many of these procedures are inventive, resourceful, and controlled as at few other places in the whole enormous work. Yvor Winters has challenged the basic assumptions of Pound's method perhaps more justly and searchingly than any other:

> There are a few loosely related themes running through the work, or at least there sometimes appear to be. The structure appears to be that of more or less free association, or progression through reverie. Sensory perception replaces idea. Pound, early in his career, adopted the inversion derived from Locke by the associationists: since all ideas arise from sensory impressions, all ideas can be expressed in terms of sensory impressions. But of course they cannot be: When we attempt this method, what we get is sensory impressions alone, and we have no way of knowing whether we have had any ideas or not.[10]

This is admirably succinct. And it comes as a timely warning against supposing that when we have set Canto 90 against Pound's recorded idcas about the Hellenic and Hebraic components in Christianity, we have as it were broken the code of the poem, which we can now throw aside like so much packaging. Moreover—what is more important—the state, in Winters's words, of not knowing 'whether we have had any ideas or not' is an accurate description of the state of mind we find ourselves in when we have been reading the *Cantos*.

One may still turn the force of Winters's objection. For this state, of not knowing whether we have had ideas or not, may be precisely the state of mind that Pound aimed to produce—and for good reasons. Perhaps by his arrangements of sensory impressions (that is to say, of images) Pound aimed to express, not 'ideas,' some of which admittedly cannot be expressed in this way, but rather a state of mind in which ideas as it were tremble on the edge of expression. Indeed, this is what we found him doing in Canto 17, when he re-created the fantasy about the nature of Istrian marble which, arguably, inspired the builders of Venice. 'Fantasy,' as used by Adrian Stokes in that connection, seemed to mean precisely the state of mind in which ideas tremble on the edge of expression. What we get in Canto 17 is not quite the idea of Venice held in the mind of the Venetian builder before he began to build; rather we have expressed the state of mind in the builder immediately before the idea crystallizes. In fact, the idea crystallizes only in the process of building, and the achieved building is the only crystallization possible.

Something very like this has been claimed for another poem of our time, 'Thirteen Ways of Looking at a Blackbird,' by Wallace Stevens. This poem, according to Albert William Levi, re-creates 'that moment when the resemblances of sense and of feeling are themselves fused in such a way as to point to the resemblances between ideas.' [11] And Levi quotes from Stevens himself:

> The truth seems to be that we live in concepts of the imagination before the reason has established them. If this is true, then reason is simply the methodizer of the imagination. It may be that the imagination is a miracle of logic and that its exquisite divinations are calculations beyond analysis, as the conclusions of the reason are calculations wholly within analysis.

This is hardly acceptable as it stands: to call the imagination 'a miracle of logic' is to play fast and loose with the word 'logic,' just as speaking of 'concepts of the imagination' is to loosen unmanageably the meaning of concept. Yet Stevens in a blurred and extravagant way is expressing what is reasonable enough: we live (at least some of the time) in arrangements of images which, as mental experiences, have a clear connection with those experiences that the reason is subsequently to establish as concepts. And thus it seems possible that Canto 17 and Canto 91 alike illustrate, as does Stevens's poem according to Levi, 'the moment at which the ideas of sensation merge (in most un-Lockian fashion) into the ideas of reflection.'

At least twice Pound has tried to re-create such moments in his prose. In his essay on mediaevalism, which was reprinted in *Make It New,* he wrote:

> We appear to have lost the radiant world where one thought cuts through another with clean edge, a world of moving energies *'mezzo oscuro rade,' 'risplende in se perpetuale effecto,'* magnetisms that take form, that are seen, or that border the visible, the matter of Dante's *Paradiso,* the glass under water, the form that seems a form seen in a mirror. . . .

And the reference to magnetism connects this with a passage from *Guide to Kulchur* (p. 152):

> 'I made it out of a mouthful of air,' wrote Bill Yeats in his heyday. The *forma,* the immortal *concetto,* the concept, the dynamic form which is like the rose pattern driven into the dead iron-filings by the magnet, not by material contact with the magnet itself, but separate from the magnet. Cut off by the layer of glass, the dust and filings rise and spring into order. Thus the *forma,* the concept rises from death. . . .

Here too 'concept' is used loosely. For it is plain that, speaking at all strictly, the *forma* and the concept are distinct. In the first passage, for instance, the *forma* evoked is something common to any number of mediaeval concepts; the one form can be, as it were, separated out into several distinct concepts, some belonging to physics, some to metaphysics, some to psychology, and so on. The one pattern informs all these different manifestations. And the point to be made is that Pound in the *Cantos* characteristically aims at re-creating not the concept, any or all of them, but rather the *forma,* the thing behind them and common to them all. By arranging sensory impressions he aims to state, not ideas, but the form behind and in ideas, the moment before that 'fine thing held in the mind' has precipitated out now this idea, now that.

The image of immaculate conceptions ('I made it out of a mouthful of air'—and the pun on conception is central to Pound's poetry) relates the passage from *Guide to Kulchur* to one from Canto 91, on virgin birth:

> Merlin's fader may no man know
> Merlin's moder is made a nun.

Lord, thaet scop the dayes lihte,
    all that she knew was a spirit bright,
A movement that moved in cloth of gold
    into her chamber.

But the images of these passages from the prose—especially those of glass and water, and of glass under water—pervade the whole canto. It begins with two lines of music in archaic notation set to words in Provençal; and continues:

that the body of light come forth
    from the body of fire
And that your eyes come to the surface
    from the deep wherein they were sunken,
Reina—for 300 years,
    and now sunken
That your eyes come forth from their caves
    & light then
        as the holly-leaf
    qui laborat, orat
Thus Undine came to the rock,
            by Circeo
and the stone eyes again looking seaward.

The lines of music make the important if obvious point that at the level of the *forma,* the artists of a period are at one with the conceptual thinkers; the *forma* is behind and in the music of the thirteenth century just as it is behind and in Grosseteste's work on the physics of light. And indeed, when Pound in *Guide to Kulchur* wants to illustrate how 'the *forma,* the concept rises from death,' his example is from art, from the history of European song. In Canto 91 the example is the same; and even a casual reader of Pound will recognize it as the stock example. The mediaeval *forma* that Pound particularly values is re-created whenever the tradition of song (originating, Pound thinks, in Provence) is momentarily recovered, for instance by Henry Lawes in England in the seventeenth century. It is for this reason that Pound's version of the 'Donna mi prega' is dedicated 'to Thomas Campion his ghost, and to the ghost of Henry Lawes, as prayer for the revival of music.' The whole of Canto 91 is, from one point of view, just that prayer repeated. The 'queen,' the *forma,* has been lost 'for 300 years'

—three hundred years since the heyday of Henry Lawes, the cryptic reference thus taking up the archaic music at the head of the page.

But it is important to realize that what is lost, according to Pound, is not just one technique of musical composition nor even one attitude toward such composition; what has gone is not a knack nor an expertise, but a *forma*. It is important to grasp this, because this determines what we mean by saying that it (the *forma*, the tradition) is 'lost.' Pound has protested indignantly at people who credit him with re-creating a lost sensibility.[12] It is lost in one sense, but in another it never can be lost. In the poem Pound says that it is 'sunken,' and this is no mere poeticism, it is more precise than 'lost' would be. This is proved by the prose passages we glanced at. The *forma* when it is manifest to thinkers and artists, informing their activities, is like 'glass under water'; when we say that it is 'lost,' we do not mean that it is mislaid (in which case strenuous search would recover it) nor that it is gone for good, but that the glass has sunk back under the water so far that it can no longer be seen. The metaphor is more precise than any formulation in prose. The prayer, accordingly, is for the *forma* to rise through the waves again, not right to the surface but to just under the surface—'Thus Undine came to the rock.' At the same time the thinkers and artists must be looking for it; eyes must again look seaward. They are stone eyes because the waiting upon the *forma* must be a ritual ceremonious act, the invocation of a spirit or a god; and the waiting must also be an act of art, because this is the only ceremony that can be trusted—the stone eyes are, for instance, those of the marble goddess replaced on her pedestal at Terracina. The eyes are of stone because they are the eyes of stone statues raised, as by the Greeks, to express man's ceremonious waiting upon the elemental energies of air and water. It may be objected that we are given here not glass under water, but eyes under water; but eyes have most of the properties of glass (a man may for instance see himself mirrored in the pupils of another's eyes), together with an active *virtu* in themselves. The *forma* is an active and activating principle; and eyes under water is therefore a more precise ikon than the glass under water that Pound offered earlier in his prose.

The matters remaining to be explained from these lines are those which most clearly relate Canto 91 to other cantos. Thus, the lines 'that the body of light come forth/from the body of fire' take up the imagery of the previous canto; here it is sufficient to note the obvious analogy between light, lambent air, coming clear out of fire, and the eyes coming clear as they rise through the water. More important are the lines 'as the holly leaf / qui laborat, orat.' Obviously the distinction between the eternal *forma* and its manifestations temporarily in act, concept, and artifact is in many ways like the Platonic distinction between the unchanging Idea of a table and its temporal manifestations in this table and that one. Hence the relevance here of a matter much canvassed in other cantos of this sequence, always in images of foliage; the neo-Platonic doctrine of 'signatures,' by which every particular holly leaf vouches for an identical *forma* reduplicated endlessly as every holly leaf in its generation grows and withers. The holly leaf, simply by being itself, celebrates a spiritual order, just as, by an old compassionate doctrine, the simple man simply fulfilling his proper vocation makes thereby an act of piety—'qui laborat, orat.'

There follow several lines making up one of Pound's characteristic rolls of honor, naming those who seem to him to have stood for this truth or for aspects of it: Apollonius of Tyana, Pythagoras, Ocellus the Pythagorean philosopher, and Justinian the law-giver. An odd name out is that of 'Helen of Tyre.' The locution links Helen of Troy with that of Eleanor of Castile and other Eleanors of crusading and Provençal times; [13] and we know from the earliest cantos of all that Pound has used the recurrence of this name, and of feminine beauty going along with it, as a witty or fanciful analogy to the great theme of an idea (in the Platonic sense), or a *forma,* fitfully manifested at moments in history. Hence the point of renewed reference to the Platonic signatures, 'from brown leaf and twig.'

The poem continues:

The GREAT CRYSTAL
                                        doubling the pine, and to cloud.
                        pensar di lieis m'es ripaus
Miss Tudor moved them with galleons
from deep eye, versus armada
from the green deep
                                        he saw it,
in the green deep of an eye:
        Crystal waves weaving together toward the gt/healing

Light *compenetrans* of the spirits
The Princess Ra-Set has climbed
            to the great knees of stone,

She enters protection,
        the great cloud is about her,
She has entered the protection of crystal
                                        convien che si mova
                                        la mente, amando
                                                XXVI, 34
Light & the flowing crystal
        never gin in cut glass had such clarity
That Drake saw the splendour and wreckage
        in that clarity
Gods moving in crystal

This writing, unlike the opening passage, is uneven in quality. As against the incomparable compression of 'doubling the pine, and to cloud,' there is, in 'green deep of an eye,' an apparently unintended echo of a line from Yeats quoted facetiously in the Pisan sequence, and the remembered facetiousness does harm. However, the meaning continues to be reasonably clear. Water (doubling the pine by reflecting it, and transformed to cloud by evaporation) is now invoked as 'the Great Crystal,' and the Elizabethan seaman Drake, no less than the queen 'Miss Tudor' who protected him, is conceived as entertaining, in his seafaring, some fantasy of his kind, of sea water as the signature of transcendent clarity. Since a cloud is nothing but sea water moving in the sky, the Princess Ra-Set who climbs into cloud (her hieroglyph is over the page—a barge or gondola on water) is rapt into the clarity just as Drake is when he puts to sea. These illustrations, Drake and Ra-Set, are chosen from a multitude of other possibilities; we should attend, not to seeing how they fit in, but to seeing what they fit into, the re-creation in terms of constellated images of the fantasy held in the mind by any man who wants to act or to speak or to think with clarity. The poet is restoring to life the dead metaphor in the cliché 'crystal clear.' Working with the three elements of water, air, and fire, he builds up, in each of them and compounded out of all of them, the image of the crystal-clear as the ultimate, or nearly ultimate, good. Pound wants to restore to the expression, 'crystal clear,' and to the fantasy behind it, the imaginative urgency and power that will inspire men to realize the fantasy in act and artifact.

After a brief snatch of roll-call (Apollonius, Ocellus, John Heydon), comes a passage about 'the golden sun-boat.' This seems to be a description of Ra-Set's hieroglyph, from which we gather that she was herself a goddess, or more appropriately a priestess, of the sun; the phrase loops over intervening lines to hook on to 'Ra-Set over crystal' and her hieroglyph. This sets the key for what is the main business of these lines, the movement from sea water to sun, or rather the extenson of the fantasy of the one to unite with the fantasy of the other; if we were to lift the experience from the level of fantasy to the level of concept (a lifting which, as we have seen, it is essential for Pound *not* to make), we could say that the idea of crystal clarity is being brought into harmony with the sun-derived ideas of vigor, fecundity, and ardor. If it is remembered how often Platonic thought has lent itself to strenuous asceticism, and to a crude opposition of supposedly pure spirit to allegedly impure flesh, we shall realize how necessary it is to guard against such misunderstanding by bringing in ideas of fertility and vigor. It is for just this reason that Pound, as in Canto 90, makes the presiding divinity in these matters not Minerva (say) but Zagreus-Dionysus-Bacchus. And this explains why the missing element, earth, had to join in the dance of the other elements at the end of Canto 90.

None of this is at all new. The concluding passage of Canto 90, evoking 'the great cats approaching,' the leopards attending Dionysus answering the ritual call, is only the latest of many passages in the *Cantos* making the point that any invocation of the spirits of air, of perceptions more than usually delicate and subtle, must also be an invocation of the chthonic powers, the spirits of earth and under-earth. Thus it is that at this stage in Canto 91, when the new context has been prepared for them, we encounter themes long familiar from points earlier in the poem. This continual taking up of certain thematic references, each time seen differently because each time in a new context, is one of the peculiar glories of the *Cantos,* and of the poetic method they exemplify. So here:

> 'Tamuz! Tamuz!'
> They set lights now in the sea
> and the sea's claw gathers them outward.
> The peasant wives hide cocoons now
> under their aprons
> for Tamuz

The cult of Tamuz, especially the local cult that centers upon the ochreous stain appearing at a certain season on a river of the Middle East (the stain on the waters being taken by the worshipper for the blood of Tamuz yearly slain afresh) has been drawn upon repeatedly at earlier stages of the poem, and in words ('the sea's claw gathers them outward') hardly different from the words used here. The watching of the estuary for the fearful sign is plainly related to that watching of the waters already evoked in connection with Undine and with Drake; but since Tamuz is a fertility god, and his cult a fertility cult focussed on the equinox, the one reference makes the necessary bridge from sea to sun, from clarity to fecundity. The cocoons hidden under the aprons to help Tamuz by sympathetic magic have also appeared before, and have been manipulated in several ways. To take one instance, in Canto 77 and elsewhere this has been played off against a sort of parody-ritual in a society based on money values rather than on natural fecundity:

> 'Trade, trade, trade . . .' sang Lanier
> and they say the gold her grandmother carried under
> her skirts for Jeff Davis
> drowned her when she slipped from the landing boat.

(Whether these lines in isolation are poetry or prose is a pedantic question; the relationship between these lines and others from elsewhere is a poetic relationship.)

At this point in Canto 91, between 'hsien' on one side and 'tensile' on the other, appears a Chinese character. With these clues to guide us it does not matter if we do not recognize the character; we can realize that Pound is appealing to Confucian authority. And again, whether the appeal can be sustained (we are told that Pound's translations of Chinese are idiosyncratic) does not concern us. We can take Confucius provisionally on Pound's terms, for the sake of Pound's poem; and if we do so, we perceive the same bridge being built from the other end—the sun standing in Confucian sensibility for fertility indeed but also for the clarity of tensile light. Pound would maintain—and this is his justification for printing Chinese characters—that the Chinese ideogram can override unnecessary distinctions in a way our writing cannot. Here, for instance, it is not a case of fertility *but also* clarity; it is on the contrary a matter of fertility and clarity together as two aspects of one thing, which is precisely the notion that Pound wants to establish.

Drake now reappears ('That Drake saw the armada'), and after Ra-Set with her hieroglyph, we continue:

in the Queen's eye the reflection
& sea-wrack—
green deep of the sea-cave
ne quaesaris.
He asked not
nor wavered, seeing, nor had fear of the wood-queen, Artemis
that is Diana
nor had killed save by the hunting rite,
sanctus.
Thus sang it:
Leafdi Diana, leove Diana
Heye Diana, help me to neode
Witte me thurh crafte
whuder ich maei lidhan
to wonsom londe.

The Queen of the first line is the 'Reina' who was besought to return at the start of the canto. She stands for the *forma* that is sunken. But she is also Drake's queen, Miss Tudor, and it seems that Drake was reintroduced to make this plain. Elizabeth, of course, was celebrated by innumerable poets as Diana. But in any case Diana, at once the moon goddess of the skies and the sylvan goddess of the chase, is yet another bridge—as Tamuz was, and the Chinese character—between the clarity of light ('the Great Crystal') and 'the furry assemblage,' the woodland beasts of the powers of earth. The elements of fire and water, air and earth have by this stage been drawn together into 'the Great Crystal'; and this means (if once again we raise to conceptual level what Pound so resolutely keeps below it) that to attain the ideal clarity in act, thought, or artifact, makes demands on all men's faculties, the earthiest as well as the most refined. The archaic language of the renewed invocation to the lost Queen—this time in her capacity as a goddess of earth, of woods, and of the chase—looks forward to the only slightly less archaic language of the lines about the birth of Merlin, which follow almost immediately. But it has the more important function of presenting, not as an idea but manifested concretely in words, that mediaeval sensibility in which the *forma* was present and operative as in the modern sensibility it is not.[14]

It follows that such exegesis as has just been attempted is necessarily wide of the mark and wrong-headed, for, since it proceeds by raising to the explicitness of ideas matters that the poet goes to great lengths not to make thus explicit, the reading that exegesis offers is necessarily a travesty of what the poetry means and is. Perhaps this is true of all poetry whatever, but it is true to such a degree of the *Cantos* that Pound seems to have had before him, as one main objective, the baffling and defeating of commentators and evegetes. If so, he has succeeded, for the *Cantos* defeat exegesis merely by inviting it so inexhaustibly. The self-defeating exercise nevertheless may be undertaken to make a point of polemic—in the present case to rebut a case made by Yvor Winters. Winters maintains that Pound's procedure is based on the fallacy that, since all concepts arise from sense impressions, all concepts can be expressed in terms of images. Pound may hold this view, or he may have held it once. But since, in the *Cantos,* he seeks to create or re-create not concepts but the *forma* behind and in concepts (or, in Adrian Stokes's terms, fantasies that precede conceptualizing as they precede artistic endeavor), it follows that the erroneous post-Lockian view, if he holds it or has ever held it, does not damage or invalidate his poem.

When 'ideas' do come into this poetry, the poetry immediately goes to pieces around them. This happens in Canto 91 in a passage printed in abusive slang, which is as despicable in diction and style as the despicable ideas it promulgates—'and, in this, their kikery functioned.' After this disastrous lurch of tone comes a long passage in which the structure of the images comes close to what Winters describes as 'more or less free association, or progression through reverie.' It should be clear that the structure of the lines so far considered does not answer to this description. That much of the *Cantos* does answer to it is undeniable. But this looseness of organization over long stretches is deliberate. For only if we are presented with references thus disorganized can we appreciate the drama of their gradual drawing together toward the high points of the poem, where what began as random associations are seen to organize themselves into constellations ever more taut and brilliant, and ultimately into the *forma.* This gradual clarifying and drawing together (which has an analogue in social organizations—see Canto 93, 'Swedenborg said "of societies" / by attraction') can be seen taking place not just inside a canto but over a sequence of many cantos.

The weight of Winters's objection falls elsewhere, however; and, surprisingly, Pound appears to have foreseen it and guarded against it. In one of his latest pieces of criticism, an introduction to reproductions of paintings by Ceri Martinelli, Pound has censured what he sees as a new orthodoxy derived from misunderstanding of a painter, Percy Wyndham Lewis, whom Pound had championed many years before:

> Lewis said something about art not having any insides, not meaning what several misinterpreters have assumed. I had a word in the early preface to some studies of Cavalcanti. Frate Egidio had already written against those who mistake the eye for the mind.

Mistaking the eye for the mind is precisely what Winters accuses Pound of doing. The early preface to Cavalcanti is presumably the essay on mediaevalism, containing a passage that is indeed, as we have seen and as Pound implies, sufficient of itself to disprove Winters's contention. 'Frate Egidio' appears in the notes to Pound's version of 'Donna mi prega'; he is Egidio Colonna, an orthodox commentator suspicious of the heterodox Cavalcanti. And he appears also in Canto 94, which starts with several references to John Adams and what followed him in American thought about civics. It continues:

> Beyond civic order:
>   l'AMOR.
> Was it Frate Egidio—'per la mente'
>   looking down and reproving
> 'who shd/mistake the eye for the mind.'
> Above, prana, the light,
>   past light, the crystal.
> Above crystal, the jade!

A hierarchy is established among kinds of creditable activity. The setting up and maintaining of civic order, exemplified by John Adams, is one sort of praiseworthy activity. Beyond this comes activity under the aegis of love. Beyond that comes 'the light,' beyond that 'the crystal,' beyond that 'the jade.' What is meant by 'the crystal' we have seen from Canto 91; it is the wooing into awareness, and the holding in awareness, of the *forma*. What lies beyond or even above this is 'the jade.' And a clue to what this may be is provided perhaps by an essay on Brancusi, which dates from as far back as 1921:

> But the contemplation of form or of formal-beauty leading into the infinite must be dissociated from the dazzle of crystal; there is a sort of relation, but there is the more important di-

> vergence; with the crystal it is a hypnosis, or a contemplative fixation of thought, or an excitement of the 'subconscious' or unconscious (whatever the devil they may be), and with the ideal form in marble it is an approach to the infinite *by form,* by precisely the highest possible degree of consciousness of formal perfection; as free of accident as any of the philosophical demands of a 'Paradiso' can make it.[15]

If this indeed is the right gloss on 'the jade,' it seems that last as first Pound is taking his bearings from the art of sculpture. But it is from sculpture seen in its aspect of carving, as making manifest what is extant. In the Brancusi essay Pound is insistent—what Brancusi gives is 'not "his" world of form, but as much as he has found of "the" world of form.' In the last analysis the art that comes of a marriage between the artist and nature is still, for Pound, superior to the art that comes by immaculate conception, self-generated—'I made it out of a mouthful of air.'

NOTES

1. See Frank Kermode, *Romantic Image* (London, 1957), ch. VIII.
2. See Guy Davenport, 'Pound and Frobenius,' in *Motive and Method in the Cantos of Ezra Pound* (New York, 1954).
3. 'The Art of Poetry, V,' *The Paris Review,* 28 (Summer-Fall, 1962), 51.
4. *Section: Rock-Drill, 85–95 de los cantares* (Milan, 1955).
5. Clark Emery, *Ideas into Action: A Study of Pound's Cantos* (Coral Gables, Fla., 1958), p. 109.
6. 'Under the Larches of Paradise,' in *Gnomon* (New York, 1958).
7. See *Guide to Kulchur,* p. 109.
8. *Carta Da Visita* (Rome, 1942); translated by J. Drummond as *A Visiting Card* (London, 1952). Cf. *Guide to Kulchur,* Ch. 30.
9. *A Visiting Card.*
10. *The Function of Criticism* (Denver, 1957), p. 47.
11. 'A Note on Wallace Stevens and the Poem of Perspective,' *Perspective,* VII, 3 (Autumn 1954), 137–46.
12. Introduction to *La Martinelli* (Milan, 1956).
13. George Dekker, *Sailing After Knowledge* (London, 1963), pp. 200–201, points out that the Provençal line set to archaic music at the head of this Canto 'appears to be Pound's own pastiche of lines taken from Bernart de Ventadorn & Guillem de Poitou'; and that it was Eleanor of Aquitaine 'to whom Bernart's song was directed across the English Channel.'

14. Noel Stock, in *Poet in Exile: Ezra Pound* (Manchester, 1964) points out (pp. 25–26) that for Pound religious rites originate with the hunting tribes, worshipping Diana as goddess of the chase, whereas primitive shepherd cultures, fattening for the kill, do not rise to religious perceptions of any fineness.
15. *Literary Essays of Ezra Pound,* ed. T. S. Eliot (London, 1954), p. 444.

HELEN VENDLER

Stevens' *Like Decorations in a Nigger Cemetery* (1966)

The title is an ellipsis: it should be read [My Poems Are] *Like Decorations in a Nigger Cemetery*. This is Stevens' flagrant borrowed simile for a wilderness of poems, fifty of them, an experiment in poetry as epigram, or poetry as fossil bones: 'Piece the world together, boys, but not with your hands' (192).[1] The poem, a token of things to come, is, like many foretastes, perversely experimental. Though the poetry of disconnection is Stevens' most adequate form, and though the gaps from canto to canto in the long poems will always challenge the best efforts of critical articulation, still the discontinuity will never again be so arrogant as in this example. There are no bridges here for the magnifico; he must migrate from one 'floral tribute' to another, some visionary, some cynical, some bitter, some prophetic, some comic. Each is a 'nigger fragment, a *mystique* / For the spirit left helpless by the intelligence' (265). They are fragments of vision seen in the mirror of the mind refusing to reconstruct itself, refusing the attempt to make a whole from the ruses that were shattered by the large. *Harmonium* was by no means a harmony: all of Stevens is in it, and not in embryo either; but although its tonal spectrum is as diverse as the one we find in *Decorations,* it is less shocking because the tones are presented in separate units, not heaped together ruthlessly in one poem. In *Decorations,* the work seems to be left to the reader, since he must do the ordering of impressions; these are haiku as potentially articulable, like the *Adagia*. Whether *Decorations* is any more than fifty short pieces pretending to be one poem is debatable, but if we believe in Stevens' good faith we must assume he thought it a viable whole. His wholes were always melting into each other, of course; he once wanted to call *Harmonium* 'The Grand Poem: Preliminary Minutiae,' [2] and he thought, as Samuel French Morse remarks in *Opus Posthumous,* of calling his *Collected Poems* 'The Whole of Harmonium'—it was all one poem to him, clearly, but yet he did divide it into parts.

The sense of death and fatal chill is the 'subject' of *Decorations,*[3] as it will be the subject of *The Auroras of Autumn,* but to read only physical death into Stevens' lines is to limit his range. To be dead is also not to live in a physical world, to 'live a skeleton's life, / As a disbeliever in reality, / A countryman of all the bones in the world' (*OP,* 117), and Stevens is afraid, in his fifty-sixth year, that he is already shrivelling into that dwarf-form. His depletion is his specter, and his wrestlings with it make up *Decorations*. The resources of man facing death compose the metaphorical range of the poem; from legacies left to heirs to the desire for heaven, from stoicism to cynicism, from hedonism to nostalgia, from self-delusion to a willed belief that life is as real as death. Stevens chooses to express no preference among these responses, except by the implicit preference accorded by convention to the beginning and end.

The mythologizing of Whitman-as-sun into a prophetic figure begins the poem boldly, in a partially tempered version of Stevens' boisterous tone. Instead of the ring of men chanting in orgy on a summer morn, we have the Whitman-sun chanting on the ruddy shore of an autumn day. He is a Jovian figure, moving with large-mannered motions, 'A giant, on the horizon, glistening' (442), 'rugged and luminous' (479), one of Stevens' many chanting figures:

> Nothing is final, he chants. No man shall see the end.
> His beard is of fire and his staff is a leaping flame.

Like the 'new resemblance of the sun' in *An Ordinary Evening in New Haven,* this sun is 'a mythological form, a festival sphere / A great bosom, beard and being, alive with age' (466), with all the equivocal sentimentality still attached to our images of Jehovah. From this rather self-indulgent flame, the poem proceeds to its ending in snow, and the immortality of the chanting sun gives way, finally, to the stoic's revenge—lopping off his feet, as Blake said, so as not to want shoes.

Human solidarity (advocated in the penultimate stanza) is no defense against decay, since there is no strength that can withstand process; only wisdom, by its slyness, anticipates destruction, slipping from the grip of winter by anticipating its clasp. What can winter do to one who has already forsaken casinos for igloos?

> . . . Can all men, together, avenge
> One of the leaves that have fallen in autumn?
> But the wise man avenges by building his city in snow. (1)

Neither sand nor rock, as in the Bible, but snow; and not a house but a city; and not 'on,' but 'in,' with its diffuseness of reference. This preventive avenging is stated as a proverb, and the suggested vengeance is reaffirmed by the telling dactyls of the last line. It is a remark, however, not an accomplishment; what it means to build a city in snow is to use this rhetoric of cunning, to put to bold use intimations of despair, to counter the erosions of process by one's own ice palace, not to regret autumn; to be the snow man, in short, and to decorate the cemetery. To write of nothing that is not there is almost impossible to Stevens with his gift for nostalgic reminiscence, for the poetry of the vanished, but to write of the nothing that *is* there is more possible to him, and accounts for some of his most brilliant poems ('The Snow Man,' 'No Possum, No Sop, No Taters,' 'The Plain Sense of Things,' 'The Course of a Particular'). The full rhetoric of nostalgia and the taut rhetoric of the minimal are at war in him, profitably; sadness and stoicism contend, and forth the particulars of poetry come. There is a curiosity in Stevens' stoicism that redeems it from indifference or listlessness. As the joyless becomes the norm, the inveterate aesthetician's eye remarks the change:

> It was when the trees were leafless first in November
> And their blackness became apparent, that one first
> Knew the eccentric to be the base of design. (iii)

We scarcely have a name for a tone of this sort, verging, as it does, as close to irony as extreme dryness can bring it, grafting schoolmaster's language and impersonal detachment onto a sinister paradox of disorder, all to express a tragic intimation. It is the tone of the doctor investigating his own mortal disease and writing his report, embodying an intrinsic pathos as the clinician records his own decline. Stevens is remarkable in his evasions of the first person singular, and the options of avoidance are many—'one' and 'he' and 'we' are Stevens' favorites, as well as the 'I' of dramatic monologue. 'We' is perhaps tarnished for us by its long use in 'high sentence': it belongs to the rhetoric of sermons, of political oratory, and of moral verse. Though Stevens is fond of its oracular potentialities ('We live in an old chaos of the sun') he uses it chiefly as a signal of an experience not peculiar to the poet, reserving for that special case the particularized 'he.' In the long poems, Stevens is uncomfortable with any pronoun after a while, and prefers (abandoning his practice in the *Comedian*) to change from first-person to third-person to second-person at will. In this respect again, *Decorations* is the most eccentric of the long poems, as the speaker metamorphoses from detached aesthetician and scholar 'one') to one of us ('we') to a man alone ('Shall I grapple with my destroyers?') to a man having a dialogue with a servant (xxvi) to a commentator on someone else ('It needed the heavy nights of drenching weather / To make him return to people'). The extreme variation of speakers makes us, in defense, assume a single sensibility 'behind' the scene, a puppet-master of whom we can say only that he is a man revolving thoughts on middle age, death, and the compensations of creation. This temptation to impose order by a thematic statement explains the natural tendency to reduce Stevens to his subject matter, to look for consistency of some kind in such a welter of styles, even at the cost of making the manner disappear entirely.

The speaker of *Decorations* has a horror of dying 'a parish death' (in which the cost of burial of a pauper is borne by the parish), because the irony is too great: Death the priest in his opulent purple and white vestments set against the pine coffin and maimed rites of the pauper.[4] How to cheat death of that triumph, how to redeem our own ignominy, is the question of the poem, and the answer of course is both pitiful (we decorate the cemetery with grotesque poem-bouquets) and stern (we build our city in snow). The third 'answer'—that the sun is eternal and so our death is fictitious—begins the poem, but never assumes any real importance in it, except in canto xlvii, where the sun's indifference to the world, its self-sustenance ('It must create its colors out of itself'), is insisted upon. The cantos explicitly about poetry[5] both attempt to exalt it by Stevens' religious intonations (vii, xv, xxxvi, xlviii) and yet reduce it by its carnality and its ineffectual 'comedy of hollow sounds' (xiii, xxii). In the most ironic passage of all, Stevens visualizes his fifty stanzas as so many sausage links, presided over by the 'god of the sausages' or possibly an even more insignificant Muse, a mere patron saint sanctifying himself by a complacent self-regard (xlii).[6]

The oddest characteristic of *Decorations* is its abjuring of verbs. In at least a fifth of the poem the stanzas are syntactically incomplete, and verbs have been dispensed with. Partly, this yields a quality of epigram ('Out of sight, out of mind') which helps to give the poem its extraordinary aridity, and partly it strengthens the sense that these are jottings, adagia, epitaphs, the daily *pensées* of the inspector of gravestones. Usually, the verbs can be easily supplied, since Stevens is not interested in mystification for its own sake, but the absence of an opening clause impersonalizes the topic further:

What we confront in death is What I want to write about is What we truly experience is	Not the ocean of the virtuosi But the ugly alien, the mask that speaks Things unintelligible, yet understood. (xxxix)

The stanza could imply any of the previous beginnings, but its strength lies in not needing them. The formula used in this stanza (Not X but Y) is one of Stevens' commonest, and is frequently preceded elsewhere by 'he wanted' or 'he saw.' The absence here of such a verb creates the phrase as an immediate object of perception to the reader, with no intervening subject, as Stevens achieves the poetry of no perceiver, the landscape poetry of the mind, so to speak.[7] The personal voice, with its clamor of selfhood, is too desperately intrusive, and yet invented personae carry the immediate flavor of irony. One solution, adopted here, is to drop the subject voice entirely.

Another is to reproduce the interior musing of the mind, as the mind has no subject-relation to itself, needs no explanations to itself of its own hurdles, and can speak in ellipses:

> The album of Corot is premature.
> A little later when the sky is black.
> Mist that is golden is not wholly mist. (xxxviii)

If we supply the missing links, the verse might read:

> [Do not offer me] the album [of reproductions of paintings of summer] of Corot. [That] is premature [—to solace myself with art in the absence of the reality it reproduces, since some-

> thing of summer is still left. Give me the album] a little later when the sky is black. [It is true that the mists of autumn are around me, but they are tinged with the gold of summer still, and] mist that is golden is not wholly mist.

Or, as Stevens put it briefly to Hi Simons, 'Do not show me Corot while it is still summer; do not show me pictures of summer while it is still summer; even the mist is golden; wait until a little later' (*L*, 349). My amplification of the original lines, and Stevens' paraphrase of them, both lose the dryness of the poem, where Stevens' truncated dismissal of art is flavored with epigram in the punning near-chiasmus of sound—mist, golden, wholly, mist—and where something like malice supervenes on the foreboding of the second line.

One of the continuing pleasures in reading Stevens is to feel his rapidity of change as he is flicked by various feelings. Despair overlaid by wry cynicism—'There is no such thing as innocence in autumn'—is succeeded immediately by a pallor of hope—'Yet, it may be, innocence is never lost' (xliv). The autonomy of the stanzas of *Decorations* suggests that all its exertions exist simultaneously rather than successively.[8] Though Stevens can order his poems temporally, as his nostalgias, farewells, and prophecies attest, here, as in other long poems, the unity is radial, not linear. Stevens' true subject in *Decorations* becomes the complexity of mental response as he gives intimations, in these fifty stanzas, of almost all possible reactions to the decay that is its topic. If this is a poetry of meditation, it does not have the sustained progressive development that we know in other meditative poets: it is the staccato meditation of intimation and dismissal, of fits and starts, revulsions and shrugs, lightenings and sloughs, the play of the mind and sensibility over a topic.

Except for two sections (i and iv), the stanzas are of three or four lines, and depend almost entirely on very simple rhetorical figures for their form—antithesis, for instance, in the dominating contrasts of summer and winter, rich and poor, the mechanical and the human, the social and the private:

> A bridge above the bright and blue of water
> And the same bridge when the river is frozen.
> Rich Tweedle-dum, poor Tweedle-dee. (xxiv)

Such antitheses stress the indistinguishability of the basic forms underlying the qualitative apparel. The decorations are a mediation between the living and the dead, and the not-yet-dead-but no-longer-quite-alive speaker stands between the systems of antitheses,

> Between farewell and the absence of farewell,
> The final mercy and the final loss,
> The wind and the sudden falling of the wind. (x)

Sometimes the rhetorical figure will come from magic, as in the deliberately trivial arithmetic by which one ascertains the density of life by dividing the number of legs one sees by two (xliii), or in the more enigmatic series of instances leading to an induction of canto xxiii:

> The fish are in the fishman's window,
> The grain is in the baker's shop,
> The hunter shouts as the pheasant falls.
> Consider the odd morphology of regret.

Decorations is a poem of regret; placing decorations on graves is a gesture of regret; and yet these actions are reserved by the human world for its own members alone. No regret is expended on the deaths of the fish, the wheat, the pheasant, but rather we buy, sell, and deal in death of all sorts without regret every day. But the compression of the verse forces us to leap from the three instances to the antithesis of the final ironic line without the explicit connectives of conventional logic.

The internal echoes in *Decorations* are casual, with certain spheres of metaphorical reference in the ascendant (sun and frost, wealth and poverty, vanished religion set against the new hymns sung by the various birds) but again, there is no particular consistency. There are, for instance, six poems about birds [9] (I omit the pheasant, who does not sing, but only falls) and they vary in symbolic meaning. The birds 'singing in the yellow patios, / Pecking at more lascivious rinds than ours, / From sheer Gemütlichkeit' (xiii), are both satirized and envied in their sensual and sentimental ease. To equate lasciviousness with bourgeois *Gemütlichkeit* is to dismiss it aesthetically rather than morally. The absence of possible lasciviousness is the deprivation of the next bird, the unmated leaden pigeon who, Stevens conjectures, must miss the symmetry of a female leaden mate. Imagining her, he makes her better than she would have been in reality, makes her not a leaden mortal pigeon but a silver ideal dove, and creates a transcendent ethereal bird who, like other Stevensian ideal figures, lives in a place of perpetual undulation:

The leaden pigeon on the entrance gate
Must miss the symmetry of a leaden mate,
Must see her fans of silver undulate. (xiv)

Oriole and crow, the extremes of music in the natural world, form a simple opposition (xxv), and comment on the tendency of this declining decorator of cemeteries to distrust the beautiful and opulent. The sterile androgynous fowls of canto xxx, one a day creature and one a night creature, are perhaps allied to the sun and moon, those two elements between which Crispin voyages. Singly, they are impotent, because creation requires the separations of gender:

The hen-cock crows at midnight and lays no egg,
The cock-hen crows all day. But cockerel shrieks,
Hen shudders: the copious egg is made and laid.

The final fertility, Stevens might say in a less outrageous way, is in the journey back and forth between the antithetical states, not in any imagined confluence of opposites. Only with the interpenetration, but no identification, of the antithetical elements can the shrill vocalism of crowing become the copious egg, an exhibit scrutinized here at arm's length.

As for the rare and royal purple bird (xxxiii), he finds his rarity not exalting but boring; like the poet of abnormal sensibility, he has no company, and must sing to himself, if only to provide some fictitious company. Though purple is the color of royalty, it is also, in Stevens, the color of middle age, of the malady of the quotidian, leading 'through all its purples to the final slate' (96) of some unimaginable bleakness. Finally, Stevens leaves us with an image of the impotence of poetry—though it may live radiantly beyond much lustier blurs, it lives uncertainly and not for long (xxxii). Time, not the song of the cuckoo (even though cuckoos, if any bird, might appeal to the mad clockmaker of this universe), is the regulative principle of this clanking mechanism, the world:

Everything ticks like a clock. The cabinet
Of a man gone mad, after all, for time, in spite
Of the cuckoos, a man with a mania for clocks. (xlvi)

All that Stevens expects of his reader, then, is a hazy notion, certainly traditional enough, that birds are a figure for poetry, but it is understood that as the context differs, so will the bird. In a context of clock-time, he will be a cuckoo; in a context of lonely regal rarity, he will be a purple bird; in a context of fertility and shrillness, cock and hen; in a context of the real and ideal, a pigeon-dove; in the context of beauty of song, oriole versus crow; and in the context of reality, in the yellow patios, an anonymous figure, a 'meaningless natural effigy' (xx), trite and uninteresting until given a 'revealing abberation' by the observant eye. This flexibility of reference is necessary in invoking other image clusters in the poem—the theatre, the weather, and so on. Stevens' metaphors are extremely provisional in their species, but quite permanent in their genus, and the vegetation still abounds in forms, as the *Collected Poems* declare.

The alternative to varying the species of bird is of course to vary the environment of the bird, as Stevens had done in *Thirteen Ways of Looking at a Blackbird,*[10] an early poem that in its epigrammatic and elliptic form anticipates *Decorations* (just as its variational scheme resembles 'Sea Surface Full of Clouds' or 'Variations on a Summer Day' and as its theme is allied to 'Domination of Black'). The Ananke or Necessity of *Decorations* appears in the *Blackbird* as the black principle, the eccentric which is the base of design, the strict, the final, the intrinsic, the limiting, the temporal. The blackbird is the only element in nature which is aesthetically compatible with bleak light and bare limbs: he is, we may say, a certain kind of language, opposed to euphony, to those 'noble accents and lucid inescapable rhythms' which Stevens used so memorably elsewhere in *Harmonium*. To choose the blackbird over the pigeon is a possible aesthetic for Stevens, and it is different from the aesthetic of Crispin who chose arrant stinks, the antiaesthetic. There are thirteen ways of looking at a blackbird because thirteen is the eccentric number; Stevens is almost medieval in his relish for external form. This poetry will be one of inflection and innuendo; the inflections are the heard melodies [11] (the whistling of the blackbird) and the innuendoes are what is left out (the silence just after the whistling):

> I do not know which to prefer,
> The beauty of inflections
> Or the beauty of innuendoes,
> The blackbird whistling
> Or just after. (v)

As a description of both *Blackbird* and *Decorations* this could hardly be bettered. Stevens himself called *Blackbird* a collection of sensations, rather than of epigrams or of ideas (*L,* 251), but the later remarks on it to Henry Church are intellectual ones: that the last section was intended to convey despair, that section xii existed to convey the 'compulsion frequently back of the things that we do' (*L,* 240). We are not falsifying the poem entirely, then, if we ask how, by varying the blackbird's surroundings, Stevens conveys to us both the sensations and the ideas which exist with them.

The blackbird, symbol for the condition of being, has perhaps something in common with Eliot's 'shadow' that falls between potency and act, desire and consummation. But Stevens would deny that it is a remediable or accidental intrusion between two things that without it would be better off. It is, rather, of one substance with the things it relates:

> A man and a woman
> Are one.
> A man and a woman and a blackbird
> Are one. (iv)

Between the man and the woman is the blackbird, one with them; between the man's mood and his environment is the blackbird, the indecipherable cause of the mood which is man's response to nature (vi); between the man of Haddam and their imagined golden birds is the blackbird, the real on which they construct their 'artifice of eternity' (vii); between the haunted man and his protective glass coach is the terror of the blackbird (xi); it lies at the base even of our powerful verbal defenses, those beautiful glass coaches of euphony and lucidity. It is, finally, the principle of our final relation to the universe, our compulsions, first of all:

> The river is moving
> The blackbird must be flying. (xii)

and lastly, our despair at death:

> It was evening all afternoon.
> It was snowing
> And it was going to snow.
> The blackbird sat
> In the cedar-limbs. (xiii)

But neurosis and death are only instances of a pervasive relational eccentricity. Our extent in space (as well as in time) goes only as far as the blackbird goes—the blackbird *is* our 'line of vision' (ix), as it is our line of thought: when we are of two minds (or, as Stevens presses it, 'of three minds'), it is not as if we had a blackbird, an oriole, and a pigeon in view, but only 'a tree / In which there are three blackbirds' (ii). The blackbird is by no means all—it is surrounded by the vastness of twenty mountains, the autumn winds, the snow—but though only a small part, it is the determining focus of relation.

Blackbird is undoubtedly a more finished poem than *Decorations,* its fineness of structure making for remarkable strength, as Stevens pursues his single image for a single theme through several aspects. Its subject, the 'new aesthetic' of the spare and the eccentric as it arises from flaw and mortality, prohibits the use of the oratorical mode of *Sunday Morning,* a mode which becomes a blemish in certain stanzas (notably viii and xlviii) of the usually tight-reined *Decorations*. *Blackbird* depends wholly on contraction, on the simple declarative sentence reduced almost to the infantile. Just as the declarative sentence is the simplest grammatical figure, so tautology is the simplest rhetorical form, and Stevens deliberately approaches it:

> A man and a woman
> Are one.
> A man and a woman and a blackbird
> Are one. (iv)
>
> It was snowing
> And it was going to snow. (xiii)
>
> I know. . . . accents. . . .
> But I know
> That the blackbird is involved
> In what I know. (viii)

Like Stevens' *exotisme voulu,* this is simplicity *voulu,* calling flamboyant attention to itself in a way that the unobtrusive simplicity of colloquial language does not. As an instrument, it is brilliant but limited, and clearly will not do for much more than thirteen stanzas. The increased expanse of *Decorations* comes at the cost of high finish, but promises perfections still far away, in the greater long poems to come. Meanwhile, these two poems together represent Stevens' most remarkable compression of his naturally voluminous self, a new asperity of language over a long span, a daringly varied meditative form, and a willingness, in the case of the later poem, to sacrifice finish for experiment's sake.

NOTES

1. The poem was first published in *Poetry,* XLV (February, 1935), 239–49. Republished in *Ideas of Order* (Alcestis Press, 1935, Knopf, 1936). For the title, cf. *L,* 272: 'The title refers to the litter that one usually finds in a nigger cemetery and is a phrase used by Judge Powell last winter in Key West.' Numbers in parentheses refer to pages in Wallace Stevens, *Collected Poems* (N.Y., 1955). Numbers preceded by *L* refer to pages in Wallace Stevens, *Letters,* ed. Holly Stevens (N.Y., 1966). Those preceded by *OP* refer to pages in Wallace Stevens, *Opus Posthumous,* ed. Samuel French Morse (N.Y., 1957).
2. Noted in *Wallace Stevens Checklist, ed. S. F. Morse* (Denver, 1963), 10.
3. The poem was apparently written in November, 1934. See letters to Zabel (*L,* 271, 272). Autumn, as Stevens wrote to Latimer (*L,* 349), is a metaphor.
4. Stevens seems too modest in saying that this section 'consists of the statement of two unrelated ideas: the first is that we do not die simply; we are attended by a figure. It might be easier for us to turn away from that figure. The second is that we should not die like a poor parishioner; a man should meet death for what it is' (*L,* 349). The ideas may be unrelated, but the imagery is not; the ecclesiastical 'parish' calls up the sacerdotal Death.
5. vii, viii, xv, xxii, xxv, xxix, xxx, xxxii, xxxiii, xxxvi, xlvii, xlviii, in my reading.
6. Stevens' own explanation of this section is generalized, as usual: 'An anthropomorphic god is simply a projection of itself by a race of egoists, which it is natural for them to treat as sacred' (*L,* 349). He leaves unexplained the image of egoists as sausage-makers, but as I say above, it seems an ironic self-reference, given this linked poem.
7. Cf. *Notes,* I, vi, constructed on this principle.
8. The stanzas, Stevens said, were composed on the way to and from the office, discontinuously (*L,* 272).
9. xiii, xiv, xxv, xxx, xxxiii, xlvi.
10. First published in *Others,* ed. Alfred Kreymborg (Knopf, 1917); republished in *Harmonium* (Knopf, 1923).
11. Karl Stern remarks on the debt to Keats in his *Wallace Stevens* (Ann Arbor, 1966), 131.

JOHN F. LYNEN

The Poet's Meaning and the Poem's World

(1966)

In the preface to his recent book on Frost, Radcliffe Squires explains that since poetry expresses the ineffable, he will leave that task to the poet and limit his discussion of Frost's work to 'its legality of language, its relevance to life, and above all its truth and honor of concept—the philosophic muse that speaks in the center of his poetry, giving, in the final analysis, intensity and endurance.' There is no need to quarrel with Squires's very thoughtful study which in fact transcends the limits its author sets, but the sentence is an apt illustration of the prevailing attitude towards Frost—in the colleges, if not generally. Readers seem unwilling to discriminate between the poems, preferring to consider them together as parts of some one great poem which constitutes a sort of life record. It would be an overstatement to say that Frost the culture hero is more in demand than Frost the poet. But there is a strong tendency to value Frost's poems as phases in the story of the poet's triumph in making sense of his own experience, rather than to suppose that in a life one cannot ever have the skill or the information to judge, Frost wrote a number of poems each of which, when read by itself, can make sense of reality for *us*. One wishes very much to believe in what Carlyle termed 'the hero as poet,' for since in our time the battle to make sense is normally lost, there is greater need to believe that someone did win it than that particular poems succeed. The approach I am describing need not seem biographical; it can stake all on the poet's successful life while scarcely mentioning it, simply by pro-

From *The Southern Review* III new series (1966). Reprinted by permission of the author and The Southern Review.

ceeding as the quotation from Squires' preface would seem to recommend—by studying the truthfulness of the poems. For when the poems are discussed in this way, they are implicitly treated as records of the historical Robert Frost's encounters with a world familiar to all of us.

In a sense, of course, the poems are such records—though not only that—yet since the world is not simply 'out there' as something everyone knows and sees in the same way, determining a poem's truthfulness is obviously not just a process of holding it up to the universe, as the customs will compare a passport photo with the original. How are we to get at 'relevance to life'? That is the question; and if because the art of a poem cannot be fully explained one had better leave it alone and concentrate on its tenor, merely; even so our uncertainties are not disposed of, for the question then arises as to how one decides what the poem 'says' unless one attends to its way of saying. That is why Squires, though mainly interested in Frost's themes, finds it natural to acknowledge the opposite approach—that of the critics who prefer to begin with language rather than idea. When such premises are in force as those which seem to be implied by Squires' preface, concept and style tend to be polarized, so that one is faced with the choice of proceeding as if Frost's language were but the means of setting forth an idea, or as if an idea, by running to elaborate implication, supplies the plot for a drama of expression. 'Legality of language' beautifully suggests the latter approach. One discusses the subtle and richly orchestrated effects of Frost's language without much considering the world whose laws this language obeys. 'Legality' by what standard? That of the 'real world,' it turns out once more, except that now it is a world composed simply of words rather than just of 'things,' that is, objects of thought.

One does not object to the premise of a real world, which seems indispensable, but to the treating of it as more than a premise. The real world is the question to be answered, and instead of bringing a knowledge of nearly everything to the poem—as if that were the primary enigma—one reads the poem in order to see more clearly what the real world is like. The reverence which holds art a subject too sacred to discuss seems rather less meritorious when one realizes how much knowledge it assumes one can have without being indebted to the imagination. What has been ruled out of bounds as 'the ineffable' in order that we will not be distracted from the study of the poet's ideas and stylistic techniques is the visionary world within which the ideas are true and the style a meaningful way of speaking.

We all are doomed to broken-off careers,
And so's the nation, so's the total race.
The earth itself is liable to the fate
Of meaninglessly being broken off.

It would be an easy matter to prove that this is patently false as a statement about the real world. One could object that the end of the world cannot be meaningless, because the terms contain a judgment; a meaningless end is extremely meaningful. And one could point out that there can be no such thing as a 'broken-off' career, since anything that could be called a career has an end, by definition. In sum, one could argue that Frost is supposing a situation that cannot pertain; one in which there is a world where meaningless things happen, though minds exist, or one in which at some future epoch there will be meaninglessness but no one present to be aware of meanings which are absent. These are absurd complaints, of course, as absurd as it would be to argue that someone has falsely declared the weather to be 'boiling hot,' because the temperature is below 212°. My point is that what appears to be a discussion of the truth of Frost's statements and his use of words can involve a subtle form of reading out of context—the practice of placing his context within our world. In criticizing his use of 'meaningless' and 'career' I have really been insisting on the commonplace philosophic doctrine that all things have a mental side, are known to consciousness. But ought one not rather to see where Frost's words lead, the assumed world they indicate by the rules they obey? In that world our metaphysics may prove false.

The lines I have quoted come just before the end of 'The Lesson for Today,' and to make out the linguistic laws of this poem in detail, one would have to attend to such shifts of tone as that which follows:

The earth itself is liable to the fate
Of meaninglessly being broken off.
(And hence so many literary tears
At which my inclination is to scoff.)
I may have wept that any should have died
Or missed their chance, or not have been their best,
Or seen their riches, fame, or love denied.

There is in the last three lines a certain heightening of feeling which comes from the echoing, or more properly, the reaffirming of a traditional poetic style:

The lyf so short, the craft so long to lerne,
Th' assay so hard, so sharp the conquerynge,
The dredful joye, alwey that slit so yerne . . . .

Frost is not alluding to these particular lines or even recollecting Chaucer. The manner is one he could have acquired from Robinson or Housman, but it goes back to Chaucer and Frost's use of it here symbolizes his ability to bring his world into relation to those of earlier poets—to speak as if he were describing the same landscape which Chaucer had in view, though from a different position.

Such shifts in Frost's manner of speaking occur throughout the poem and manifest the principle of its development. Frost is talking to Alcuin, and if the sometimes awful humor ('You were not Charles' nor anybody's fool') seems meant only to show that eighth-century scholars were just folks too, that is one way of posing the main question. Just how *can* one talk to Alcuin? or, in other words, bring a remote epoch into relation with the present? Alcuin, of course, is a test case; unless one can talk to him there is no such thing as history, what passes for it being merely a myth assembled from the prejudices of today. If one cannot talk to Alcuin there is no way of knowing the experience of earlier times. The *terms* of life in the eighth century are lost. The *words* no longer exist. And this signifies the absence of a common ground. But the requisite common ground can be no less than a world, for what else is the context of any sentence? We cannot understand the eighth century because our world is not the same as Alcuin's. Not at all the same? No, entirely different.

Frost disagrees, and I have pushed this argument against history to its incredible conclusion merely to indicate the way his echoing of earlier styles proves relevant to his theme. Alcuin's lesson to Charlemagne's young noblemen in the palace school was 'how to be unhappy yet polite'; while the idea Frost proposes as the 'lesson for today' is that 'One age is like another for the soul.' But are these lessons really so different? Apparently not. By emphasizing the sameness of the human situation, Frost undertakes to recast Alcuin's lesson in contemporary terms. For the world is the same old world, a world where 'There's always something to be sorry for,' a world which can't be changed, 'a hard place to save the soul,' but whose wickedness and difficulty are the conditions of human virtue. Take away the evil of the world, and 'Its separateness from Heaven could be waived; / It might as well at once be kingdom-come.' Frost is concerned to discredit the 'liberal' premises of progress, amelioration, and human perfectibility. As in *The Sun Also Rises,* the same old world, the same ancient ills confront every generation, and for Frost, as for Hemingway, the problem a man faces is always and essentially a problem of *style*.

If Alcuin's 'how to be unhappy yet polite' seems terribly simple, that is so because we have forgotten the old senses of key terms in this formula. Read 'unfortunate' for 'unhappy,' 'gentle' or 'chivalrous' for 'polite,' and the old lesson is restored. By the same token modern certainties need not separate us from other epochs if we recognize that they are just instances of our style, 'polite' usage according to the decorum of scientific thought. What is the advantage of being belittled by comparison with the space of modern astronomy rather than by the God of Alcuin's faith? Are not both comparisons the means of expressing the same thing? Are not both ways of defining man's limitations? At the least, there is an area of shared meaning, and hence a world which Alcuin's and Frost's worlds are versions of. This more inclusive world is a world of language also, as we see when modern 'disgrace' is turned inside out to reveal a theological lining. It is not a question of whether Frost's 'disgrace' or Alcuin's 'need of grace' is the 'right' term. Alcuin's term appeals, because 'Art and religion love the somber chord,' but Frost prefers the carnival fun of tearing the masks of fact from the faces of metaphors, and the brash reductiveness of 'disgrace' is one of his examples of the way the assuming of a new style, in this case a style of plucky understatement, gives man the power to be himself. The morally right acts, the acts which in a positive way define the actor and make a person of him are not deeds which change the human situation but ways of acting within it. One acts according to the way one takes the world, and the way one takes the world is a style which one's way of speaking not only reflects but helps to create. A style is an ethic, as such poems as 'The Code' fictionally demonstrate. And in 'The Lesson for Today' echoing earlier styles is a means of showing that the poet shares values these styles assume: 'There's always something to be sorry for, / A sordid peace or an outrageous war.' Here Frost's manner briefly merges with Dryden's, not only by the handling of the couplet, with its smart rhyme, antithesis, and centered caesura, but by registering a certain casualness of attitude which implies that the big subjects are somewhat comic if one speaks of them as a gentleman ought, without excessive excitement. To say that wars are 'outrageous' is not to belittle them, but to suggest that it would be soft to expect anything else: wars are *outrageous*, just as the mortal wound of a duellist is the deuce, the very devil.

By such modulations Frost would gradually enlarge the landscape of consciousness until it appears that all epochs have the same world in view. Since a style is the manifestation of an ethic it defines a perspective and presents an interpretation of the world.Thus the ways of speaking which prevail during an epoch reveal that period. By modulating his manner through a number of earlier styles, Frost would show us how many other modes of experience can be accommodated to his own. In this, however, his success is narrowly limited, less because of the difficulty of relating modern American speech to Old English and Medieval Latin (though a specimen of the latter is effectively worked in) than because the dramatic situation is weakly conceived. One recollects Proust's ridicule of the lycée assignment to write a letter from Sophocles to Racine. In addressing Alcuin, Frost exploits the same absurdity. How fantastic to imagine speaking to a poet of the eighth century! And yet somehow it works! A connection is established. Alcuin would know what Frost is saying. That is the effect Frost has tried for. But the links between Alcuin and Frost must be more than rhetorical. Frost must place himself and Alcuin in a fully realized setting; if the languages really fit together they should blend into a unified situation. Theoretically the place in which I am located is a world which contains Madras and Copenhagen, but to know this in more than a notional way would require enlarging my panorama in Whitman's manner, until it takes in the intervening space. And similarly with respect to time, the millennium separating Frost from Alcuin can only be overpassed if the two epochs can be visualized as coexisting within an entire world. Perhaps this could have been done by the poet Frost describes having seen in the graveyard with a watering pot 'resuscitating flowers / (Make no mistake about its being bones'). At least in *The Waste Land* the chaotic coexistence of styles, and therefore of modes of experience, which do not form a world, is somehow rendered as a situation. 'The Lesson for Today' is not so successful, because the poet has failed to find a common ground of belief with Alcuin's age. Frost would end beautifully with:

> I hold your doctrine of Memento Mori.
> And were an epitaph to be my story
> I'd have a short one ready for my own.

I would have written of me on my stone:
I had a lover's quarrel with the world.

Taken by itself this is superb, but it is too good as an ending, for the poem does not support it. Frost would conclude with a way of speaking which is distinctly of himself and his own time, yet acknowledges Alcuin's point of view as a valid and understandable one. This is effected on the level of idea. Frost asserts that for a man in any age the evils he suffers are a function of the life he loves. It is hardship that brings out man's merits, evil that makes virtue possible, death that makes life precious. In short, Frost concludes with a modern version of Alcuin's 'doctrine of Memento Mori.' But the meeting of minds is merely theoretical, for Frost has not created for his poetic self or speaker a situation either distinct or inclusive enough to make Alcuin's variety of belief relevant, much less credible.

It may be argued that I am taking the whole poem the wrong way, since the situation it depicts is not really one in which we see Frost and Alcuin conversing. That is just comic supposing, as the first paragraph explains. The real situation is one in which Frost imagines himself appearing before a live audience. One can easily picture him delivering the poem as a lecture to an assemblage of students, teachers, and 'townees.' By way of amusedly recognizing the ritualistic quality of his performances in college 'chapels,' he announces 'The Lesson for Today' and is off on the track of his thesis. The audience has forced him into a priestly role, a role he finds he rather likes, and he will square this with his conscience. He will show that he is a modern Alcuin because what he is now saying is the lesson the priest once taught, but put in modern terms.

No one will object that Frost has not indicated this actual situation visibly any more than that in a love poem there is no balcony or summerhouse. The fault is rather that Frost's treatment of this situation is rhetorical, not poetic. The orator responds to a situation, the poet creates it. Instead of making his words merely conform to certain givens, or even, perhaps, influence them, he must *express* these givens —and without seeming to. He must indicate a world of unmentioned facts, so that the reader has the sense of things glimpsed from the corner of the eye, or located behind him or just below the horizon. This is not accomplished either by naturalistic accumulations of detail or by drawing lines of reference between things named. Not the statements, the ideas, nor the images of the poem, but its assumptions must be harmonized. The assumptions are 'fields,' and it is a question whether there is ground connecting them, or whether they are adrift, like islands of cloud.

It is the discontinuity of assumptions that makes 'The Lesson for Today' dissatisfying. Frost cannot very well argue that medieval Christianity was a way of putting things different from ours but just as valid, if he is going to venture such witticisms as the remark that:

> The cloister and the observatory saint
> Take comfort in about the same complaint.

If so important a word in the medieval vocabulary as 'saint' turns out to be silly, the linguistic argument breaks down. And if the world, the flesh, and the devil add up to a 'complaint' Frost's 'lover's quarrel with the world' cannot be taken seriously either. We cannot require that the poem's world should contain very unpleasant facts, any more than that it should have mermaids or nuclear reactors, since that would be asking for conformity to the world as we see it. The only proper requirement is that it *be* a world. Such false notes as 'complaint' illustrate the emotional shallowness one finds in Frost's poems when the dramatic situation is not fully enough conceived.

Frost's achievement in poetry is obscured, even subtly disparaged, when quotations from poems such as 'The Lesson for Today' are employed to support interpretations of his work as if they were as meaningful as passages in better poems. Take, for example, the line, 'There's nothing but injustice to be had.' Most readers will acknowledge the irony of this; they will see that it disparages self-pity and yet deftly grants that when one talks about the world man confronts, one has to begin by conceding some terrible facts. Yet even granting this agreement among readers, the line could be interpreted as a complacent dismissal of injustice as something trivial in a large-minded view of experience, or it could be read as a courageously tight-lipped acceptance of a bitter reality, and these alternatives can only be reconciled by narrowing consciousness to 'like it or lump it.' This is not the fault of the line but of the entire context. The poem is so vague that one cannot imagine the sort of particular fact the speaker has in mind when he utters this line.

One cannot then separate the question of meaning from the question of value. The study of Frost's ideas and the analysis of his style meet in language; both work from assumptions about what Frost's words mean. But what *do* they mean? It would seem questionable linguistics to attempt to answer without considering the situation within which Frost's words are uttered. In his best work nearly everything depends upon the dramatic situation. Not because the subject is dramatic, though it often is. Not because we see something happen—the dawning of an insight, a change of attitude, or simply an outward event. Such happenings are in the center of attention and serve as Frost's primary symbols. But the true action—that which the poem, rather than the character, enacts—is the turning of a situation into a world.

The quality of profound wisdom one encounters in 'Neither Out Far Nor In Deep,' the quality which leads one to imagine a 'philosophic muse,' is probably the result of the poem's being more knowing than the poet:

> They cannot look out far.
> They cannot look in deep.
> But when was that ever a bar
> To any watch they keep?

One is impressed by Frost's ability to produce complications on the level of idea. The people staring out to sea are absurd, because they are just counting two-funnelled excursion boats, or simply have to look somewhere, and there is the humor of a heroic pose struck by accident; but then, if the watch they keep is a judgment upon them, we must hypothesize some duty they neglect, so that their failure to keep a proper watch bears witness indirectly to a faith they lack. Yet even men's most earnest efforts to keep watch parody some better attitude, and to think of humanity is to see it as both condemned and exalted by its duties, since so impossibly much is asked. For example, the people on the shore instinctively keep watch against some unimaginable evil the sea seems to conceal, a Jamesian beast in the jungle that is the more deadly in that nature's plangent surfaces prevent us from seeing what sort of beast it will be. But then one's common sense asks, aren't these merely ordinary people on the beach after all, whose seaward watch is the most casual thing in the world? And of course, that is just the point. Any human gesture, trivial and unthinking as it may be, is impossible to extricate from the context of ultimate purposes. If the people on the beach are people at all they are much more than just people on the beach.

Though 'Neither Out Far Nor In Deep' is demonstrably complex and subtle in thought, this does not explain its success. The implications I have traced out, and which could be elaborated in various other ways, are rather prosaic in themselves—fitting subjects for the essayist or philosopher. We must still consider why Frost's speculations matter. Surely it is not that they lead to an answer we can accept, as if the poet had put the truth in a nut shell. The truth is not an idea, but a situation. The ending, so ambiguous as a statement of idea, is conclusive by virtue of its power to assemble and harmonize all the situation's aspects. Ultimately this situation is the speaker's. When we say, well, perhaps the people on the shore are not looking at anything at all, we see how deeply implicated the speaker is in the scene he describes, for he cannot rest satisfied with such common sense, but must make more of the odd fact that everyone seems to be gazing out to sea. This insistence of his that there be a higher cause is inseparable from his vision of the landscape. Though in fact Frost's idea was probably borrowed from the first chapter of *Moby-Dick,* he has managed to make it appear to spring from immediate sensation:

As long as it takes to pass
A ship keeps raising its hull;
The wetter ground like glass
Reflects a standing gull.

This is the ground of the moral, psychological, and philosophic mysteries, a physical world whose strangeness transcends all explanations. How a ship both stands and moves, how the slick sand duplicates the gull—these are things one might or might not see. The point is that they are there, whether noticed or not, things in themselves, having contour, substance, design, and therefore meaning. One does not know what they mean, but they are not meaningless. Their distinctness as particulars having certain definite qualities gives them some meaning, at the least, that they are meaningful objects. And for the speaker the people on the shore are objects too. He cannot tell what they are thinking. He is challenged by one more opaque surface. And yet he is sure they are thinking of something; he is certain that these objects are human beings, and to know that is to find some meaning. Here the mystery of the gull's reflection is duplicated; as the reflection has a meaning though one can only see the least part of it, its meaningfulness, so the human world is absolutely meaningful and is composed of true meanings, though all one sees are human beings looking out upon the world, and the world that confronts them, as the sea the shore, by virtue of being *not* human.

'What do the people see out there?' 'Do they notice anything at all?' 'What sort of watch do they keep? Should they keep?' Instead of supposing that these are ultimate questions, one ought to conclude that they are the questions this landscape poses. It is the seashore scene where the vast empty expanses of sand and water give the few objects here and there a preternatural distinctness and the sun creates surrealistically precise shadows that makes these questions seem the ultimate ones. You could say that they are for Frost merely means of describing the scenery. But this landscape, in turn, belongs within a larger one, the whole world. Beyond the visible setting there are innumerable other places, where the crucial questions are different.

This world beyond is out of sight, for the speaker. It is not what *he* is talking about. And the same was probably true for the historical Robert Frost, who in writing the poem focused upon the landscape in his mind's eye and had merely a 'feel' for everything outside the perimeter of this scene. But it is from the world beyond, which the poet instinctively assumes, that the poem derives its merit. The persona talks as if the people on the shore were representative of all humanity; and he takes their watch upon the sea as a symbol of man's relation to the universe. But in that he doubts, wonders, laughs, is subtly frightened, we are reminded of his human nature, and realize that we are not getting the truth pure and simple, but as it appears from his point of view. Note, for instance, his somewhat paranoid use of 'they'; in making an exception of himself, he stands off from the scene, which encourages the reader to stand off, in turn, from him. One cannot avoid wondering about the reasons behind his questions. If a person were to ask where all the people in an airport lobby are going, how could the question be answered? Even if one could name all the other places in the world, this would not do as an answer, because the travelers' destinations are purposes as well as cities—they are headed, let us say, towards certain life-situations. It is just as peculiar to ask why all the people along the shore are looking out towards the sea; to answer one would have to say everything not only about human nature but the entire universe. Yet just as the gull's reflection has the minimal meaning of being meaningful, so the speaker's question suggests an answer of sorts. We may not see the real situation—the world as it actually is—but something of it is revealed by the speaker's motives, something of isolation, of fear, of the way the self builds the world around it from the substance of its own nature, something of the failure of such construction, since every new perception, by its very certainty—like the categorically present or not present hull on the horizon—poses a new question.

Thus behind the world the speaker has in view, the world he is making statements about and which is the subject of the opinions the critics can quote by way of formulating Frost's thought, there is this assumed situation, the other, larger, and more mysterious world, scarcely 'known,' but none the less real for that, since its existence is proved by the harmony of the speaker's diverse feelings.

It is in terms of this world that the poem's statements should be interpreted, and when so considered they have quite a different look. The mere facts turn out to be perceptions; for instance, that all the people on the shore are looking at the sea is the speaker's impression, true, perhaps, but psychologically, as a subjectively stylized picture. And though we may agree with the speaker's ideas, they are not, for us, identical with the poem's total meaning, but merely ways of expressing this. For instance, we may accept his belief that all humanity keeps watch on an alien and implicitly dangerous universe, but we do not accept it in the same way or for the same reasons. The way the speaker's mind works, the way his opinions grow out of his perceptions is the ground of our belief, while he is drawing inferences from the things he sees. It is his need to make something of the ambiguous landscape—the necessity he manifests to keep watch—that persuades us all humanity watches. And our belief is much less categorical. While the speaker thinks he faintly discerns some universal formula, the reader tends to feel only that the real world is such that if one were looking at this landscape, one might very well have such thoughts. Or someone might.

My point is not the familiar one that a poem's statements should be read in context; I would go further than that and say that the context is the main thing, Frost's stated or implied opinions and his style being but the means of expressing this. No one would take Iago's statements for Shakespeare's, but readers tend to accept those of Frost's fictional speakers as his own, not only because the persona is commonly a fictional version of the poet himself, but also because philosophizing is often the essential action the Frost poem portrays. The event we attend to is a more or less explanatory monologue on many occasions—sometimes even a debate; or it is a narrative which pretends to express some covert lesson. And the style is often speculative, even didactic, runs to humorous allegory, is full of intimations of larger issues. Thus the reader is conditioned to think in terms of what Frost is 'driving at.' Why should the wall be mended? what does sleep mean? why is Frost 'out for stars'? what besides ocean water will be broken? The more the reader attends to the 'thought' of the poem, the more Frost's art will seem to dwindle to a merely craftsmanly style of expressiveness. To be sure, idea is all if you define idea broadly enough to mean imaginative vision, and style is all in the sense that everything else in the poem depends upon the poet's way with words. But Frost's emphasis upon the need to catch 'the sound of speech' in poetry should suffice to remind us how dependent, in his own, both matter and manner are upon dramatic situation. The merits of Frost's style are the result of his ability to make language function as the utterance of someone speaking. And the merits of his ideas are the result of their being true. But it is Frost's power to conceive a whole world of circumstances that counts most, for only there are the words speech and the statements meaningful enough to be true.

It is the sense of the surrounding world that makes a poem like 'Design' far more valuable than such poems as 'For Once, Then Something.' The latter deals with important matters—the way in which the searcher's assumptions determine the things he is able to find (the supposedly right way of looking down wells is that which would enable one to find an axehead), and thus the question whether there can not be a 'that' that is not a 'what,' a 'something' so objective that it lies beyond self and has not been conceptualized by the percipient's mind. But these problems are disingenuously 'set up' by a fable of the most unconvincing kind. That 'Others taunt me with having knelt at well-curbs / Always wrong to the light' is hardly to be believed, and it represents well the poem's narrow emotional range. What feelings does the speaker have but pride and contempt, perhaps complicated by a bit of curiosity? 'Others' simply serve to supply a background of folly for his not too modestly understated wisdom. The trouble is that the issues do not engage the speaker enough to bring him out; their interest is strictly theoretical. There is no situation in terms of which they might matter. In Frost's best poems, the dramatic circumstances are intimated by tone, but here, though there are beautiful contrasts of style—compare '*Once,* when trying with chin against a well-curb' with 'Water came to rebuke the too clear water'—the speech gestures lack significance, for they refer to no significant shifts of attitude or feeling.

'Design' has just the background of circumstance and subliminally felt tensions the lack of which makes the other poem a minor affair.

Though here also there is elaborate theorizing from a slight example and a sort of comic allegory, the speaker's light assays seem to indicate by vaguely disturbing certain areas of mind which are approached, but never intruded upon. One senses the presence of beliefs which are not engaged, fears the speaker has decided he will not worry about, memories he could bring to mind if he would. For Frost's rhetoric keeps turning into characterization; the control needed to state things accurately hints at all the aspects of thought and feeling the speaker has to fence out or suppress. Instead of arguing that a trivial experience can be made important in theory, as he does in 'For Once, Then, Something,' the speaker asks why an incident he knows is trivial keeps turning into something important and strangely representative, keeps provoking the mind to make more of it, keeps throwing out hints we cannot ignore of doubts too vast to entertain, terrors too overwhelming to be credited. It is the speaker's turning away from the strange conclusions fancy and logic jointly sponsor that best indicates the world beyond the situation he considers. In saying, oh, well, perhaps my premises were wrong, for there may be things too trivial to be significant, he acknowledges a context more real than the world of reason and imagination, and feelings more important than his current emotion.

There is in Frost a strange discrepancy between intellectual daring and rockbound conviction. He may speak of the kind of poem he writes as 'a momentary stay against confusion,' he may stress the need to meet each moment freshly, the touch-and-go nature of reason, the necessity to stake all on a metaphor; but Frost's rashness is balanced by a conservatism which remains loyal to its prejudices forever. James M. Cox has made the brilliantly pertinent observation that it is an essential feature of Frost's poetry that the poet seems always to have been exactly the same. This underlines the significance of the way the first poem in Frost's first book ends: 'They would not find me changed from him they knew— / Only more sure of all I thought was true.' However venturesome Frost's speculations may be, they exist within a set of beliefs he never questions, and, indeed, often delights in proclaiming beyond question. If a few decades ago these sacred premises were thought to present a merely political riddle, now they are ignored altogether in favor of Frost's seemingly free play of mind. And, to be sure, as opinions these beliefs are mere prejudices; but they are much more than that, or evidences of much more. They manifest the assumed world within which Frost's theories are examined and his experiences occur; and this world must remain absolutely unquestioned if Frost's ideas or objects are to be seen at all. In the weaker poems, the assumed world is so vague that the poet's adventures, like some of Tom Sawyer's, risk too little to matter. In the best of Frost's poems, however, this world is the source of all feeling, the ground of all belief.

T. S. Eliot remarks, in discussing Bradley, 'We never know, in any assertion, just what, or how much, we are asserting.' Since every statement intends to be true, to realize its total meaning one would have to envision the whole world that it implies. Experience does not start from scratch; the exploration of things now presenting themselves to consciousness (whether as present or recollected or foreseen) is also a process of discovering where one's assumptions lead. In a letter of 1924 in which he describes a course he has just finished teaching, Frost explains:

> I was determined to have it out with my youngers and betters as to what thinking really was. We reached an agreement that most of what they had regarded as thinking, their own and other people's, was nothing but voting—taking sides on an issue they had nothing to do with laying down. But not on that account did we despair. We went bravely to work to discover, not only if we couldn't have ideas, but if we hadn't had them, a few of them, at least, without knowing it. Many were ready to give up beaten and own themselves no thinkers in my sense of the word. They never set up to be original. They never pretended to put this and that together for themselves, never had a metaphor, never made an analogy. But they had, I knew. So I put them on the operating table and proceeded to take ideas they didn't know they had out of them as a prestidigitator takes rabbits and pigeons you have declared yourself innocent of out of your pockets, trouserlegs and even mouth. Only a few resented being thus shown up and caught with the goods on them.*

Frost's final poems *seem* to develop in the same way, as discoveries of the world he has known all along. As he explains in 'The Figure a Poem Makes':

* Letter from Robert Frost to Louis Untermeyer, dated August 12, 1924, in *Selected Letters of Robert Frost*, edited by Lawrance Thompson (New York, 1964), pp. 302–3.

> For me the initial delight is in the surprise of remembering something I didn't know I knew. I am in a place, in a situation, as if I had materialized from cloud or risen out of the ground. There is a glad recognition of the long lost and the rest follows.

This is a fiction which the poet's belief has made so credible that the simple truthfulness of his statements or their eloquence often seem the only mysteries of his art.

HAROLD BLOOM

Yeats and the Romantics

(1968)

Yeats remarks in his *Autobiographies* that we are never satisfied with the maturity of those whom we have admired in boyhood, and that insight is the ironic undersong of this essay. I commence though with another kind of irony. There is a bad paradox in the relationship between the poetry of our time and what was the most influential of our critical schools, the rhetorical or formalistic New Criticism. The best of our modern poets, in Britain and America alike, were Romantics, akin in creative procedure and in theme to a main tradition in English poetry, the line that runs from aspects of Spenser and of Milton, through Blake and Wordsworth, Coleridge, Shelley and Keats on to Tennyson, Browning, Swinburne and William Morris. Yeats and D. H. Lawrence in Great Britain, Wallace Stevens and Hart Crane in this country, are the legitimate inheritors of this Spenserian or Romantic line of poets, whose theme is the saving transformation that attends some form of humanism, and whose creative mode is the heterocosm, or the poem as an alternative world to that of nature. These opening remarks are polemical, and yet are intended as mere description. That they should be polemical is the consequence of a considerable body of critical misrepresentation that has been applied to Yeats and to Lawrence, to Stevens and to Crane. The rhetorical critics who have admired these poets have justified such admiration, where they could, by distorting the nature of the work they read. R. P. Blackmur gave us Wallace Stevens, that most Wordsworthian of poets, as another Alexander Pope, elegantly troping a Late Augustan idea of order into

This essay is just published in this volume.

the essential gaudiness of what we were asked to believe was a deliberately minor poetry. Allen Tate, with the pugnacity of strong-minded mis-information, assured us that Yeats's Romanticism would be invented by his critics. With Lawrence and Hart Crane, the New Criticism sought safer grounds, and judged those fierce Romantics as splendid failures, as men who did not know enough, and who ostentatiously lacked the inner check, the saving Eliotic balance of the only true tradition.

One hopes to seek only the pure purposes of the pure critic—plainly to propound a poet—and yet so many extra-critical cultural preferences have become critical principle among the followers of Eliot, and their students, and now *their* students' students, that one is compelled to affirm again the continuity of the best modern poetry with nineteenth-century poetic tradition. With Yeats, one begins with mere external fact. He edited Spenser and Blake, Blake on a very large scale, and edited very badly indeed. He wrote extensive commentaries on Blake, again very bad indeed, as well as the best critical essay yet written on Shelley's poetry, balanced later in life by one of the worst. He called William Morris his 'chief of men,' and said of Morris's romances that they were the only works he read very slowly, unable to bear the notion of ever being finished. He began, as he said, in all things Pre-Raphaelite, and passed to the companionship of the Tragic Generation, the Rhymers' Club of the Nineties, two of whom, Ernest Dowson and Lionel Johnson, haunted him to the end of his own life.

All these are only antecedents. They do not refute the barren but still prevalent critical commonplace that Yeats's greatness is in the utter contrast between his earlier manner, pejoratively called Romantic, and his late style, so curiously called 'Metaphysical' by many of the New Critics. Against this false commonplace I urge the contrary statement: Yeats began as a mock or decadent Romantic, and matured into a true one, a genuine inheritor of the fulfilled renown of Blake and of Shelley, the apocalyptic myth-makers among the Romantics. To chronicle the attitudes of Yeats towards Blake and Shelley, and towards Shelley in particular, is to chronicle also the stages by which Yeats found at last his true self as a poet.

No poet, I suppose, has ever assumed as many deliberate masks as Yeats did, or been so adept at self-dramatization. At such necromancy of the self perhaps Byron was Yeats's peer, but Byron was all that Yeats merely hoped to be, a nobleman, an adventurer and a genuinely tormented quester, who could seek to become that single one in his own age whose search after his own self might prove to be authentic. The mask-seeking quests of Yeats were searches for a voice or voices, rather than a self or selves. Yeats lusted after communal voices, that the authority of many might strengthen the speech of his own tongue. His search took him first to the voice of the folk, next to spirit voices, and at last to the voices of the dead. In the dank morasses of occult and arcane traditions, he sought a tone rather than a language, a stance rather than a doctrine.

When a poet, or I suppose any man, wishes to speak with the voice of many men, and yet despises the multitude of mankind, as Yeats most assuredly did, he risks an error that manifests itself as flatulence in the world of the imagination, and Fascism in the world of events. This error Yeats did not avoid, and a certain silliness throughout his work is the sad consequence. The Yeats who wrote eccentric essays about eugenics, who composed marching songs for an Irish Fascist brigade, and who loved to go about his house brandishing a Japanese ceremonial sword—this Yeats can safely be ignored, for he scarcely is to be encountered in the important poems and plays. It is the occult Yeats who is not so easily ignored, though he was only a little less absurd. This is the Yeats who was an intimate of MacGregor Mathers and of Madame Blavatsky; the Yeats whose chief emotion at the outbreak of World War I was annoyance that he was thus prevented from pursuing a particularly promising poltergeist in Transylvania; the Yeats, who on learning that his true daimon or dark opposite was the dead sage, Leo Africanus, proceeded not only to write letters to that great personage, but judiciously composed the replies also. Of this Yeats we have heard rather too much and are likely to hear rather too much more in the future, for a school of Yeatsian occult enthusiasts has risen among us, in this country and in Britain, as eager to drown the poems and plays in a mass of arcane commentary, as their friends have already all but drowned the poetry of Spenser, Blake and Shelley. We are now given a neoplatonized and cabbalized Yeats, whom to understand we must first master an august company that ranges from Cornelius Agrippa to Madame Blavatsky, from the astral wanderings of Swedenborg to the secret speculations of the Rosicrucians.

With Yeats—as opposed to Blake and Shelley—the scholarly and pseudo-scholarly researchers into esoterica appear at first to be on safe ground, for the subject of their investigations really did share their preternatural interests. But Yeats the poet was much wiser than Yeats the man, and the occultizers are welcome to the man. The vulgar error of the occultizers of Yeats's verse is only a local instance of a widespread malady in modern scholarly criticism, one whose final cause is the influence of the history-of-ideas, that most pernicious of anti-poetic disciplines. From this source has come the confused notion that the sources of a poet's thought, and the meaning of his verbal figures, are to be found in philosophy or in other discursive modes of organized knowledge, such as history, theology and psychology. But the argument of poetry is not a philosophical one, or frequently a discursive argument of any sort. Poems, as Milton said, really are more passionate and more sensuous than philosophic ideas are, but if they are simpler, as Milton added, it is a simplicity that opposes itself to complication, rather than to complexity. There is, as Blake theorized, a contrary logic of the imagination, in which the possibility of coherence counts for more than the iron law of non-contradiction. What matters to a poet, or perhaps one ought to say to the poet in a poet, is only that element in any notion that can help him to write his poem, and that element is already a form of poetry, for only poetry can be made into poems, as Wallace Stevens wittily surmised. That is why poets, in their poems, are more likely to be influenced by other poets than by discursive writers of any kind whatsoever. In speaking of poetic influences, we stumble now-a-days upon another confusion that inhibits our apprehension of poetry, for even when we speak of one poet influencing another, we so rarely know just what we mean, or else perversely we seek a verbal echoing as the full substance of what such influencing can mean. To study the relation of Yeats's poetry to Blake's or to Shelley's might teach us not only something of value about Yeats, but might clarify the whole problem of how and why one poem helps to form another.

I begin however, with the more conventional gestures of chronology, with the young Yeats first learning his craft. Yeats says that he had a relatively late sexual awakening, when nearly seventeen, and that his first sexual reveries took their images from Shelley's poems *Alastor* and *Prince Athanase,* and from Byron's *Manfred*—all to be expected from a boy who was seventeen in 1882. Yeats's first poetry was an attempt at a Spenserian epic on the story of Roland, which was abandoned for the Spenserian and Shelleyan blend that was to develop into Yeats's first published poetry, not to be found in his *Collected Poems,* but printed in the *Dublin University Review* when Yeats was twenty, and now available in the appendices to the Variorum Edition of his poetry.

The longest and most ambitious of these works is an allegorical verse-drama, *The Island of Statues,* subtitled by Yeats *An Arcadian Faery Tale*—in *Two Acts,* which I shall briefly summarize. Two Arcadian shepherds, timid but clamorous creatures, love a proud shepherdess who scorns them for their lack of courage. A hunter, to win her love, goes forth on a quest to the enchanted Island of Statues, seeking a mysterious Flower, which is guarded by a dread enchantress. The choice of the wrong flower on this Island has turned many a quester into stone, and the hunter suffers a similar fate. He is then sought in turn by his shepherdess, who pauses long enough in her wanderings to provoke her two timid pastoral suitors into a mutually destructive duel for the favors she does not intend to grant. Reaching the enchanted Island of Statues in the disguise of a boy, she entices the enchantress into falling in love with her, and so gains the enchanted flower, with which she restores the statues into breathing flesh, and thus destroys the poor enchantress, as earlier she had destroyed her shepherd-suitors. This frightening little Arcadian drama ends with the shepherdess, her hunter-lover and the other restored statues resolving to remain forever on the Island. The closing touch, befitting the play's theme, is that the rising moon casts the shadows of the hunter and the other restored creatures far across the grass, but the destructively successful quester, the shepherdess, stands shadowless in the moonlight, symbolizing the loss of her soul. Yeats, in later life, writing about Shelley, said that a man's mind at twenty contains everything of importance it will ever possess. Whatever we think of this as a general principle, it does seem relevant to Yeats himself. *The Island of Statues* takes its Circe-like enchantress from Spenser, and most of its verse-texture from Shelley, yet its decadent and savage theme is curiously Yeats's own, holding in embryo much that is to come. The shepherdess's desire to convert her Arcadian lovers into murderous men-of-action; the equivocal Enchantress longing for the embrace of ordinary flesh; the frozen sculpture that ensues from a defeated naturalistic quest; the mocking and embittering moonlight that exposes an occult victory as a human defeat—all these, despite their Pre-Raphaelite colorings, are emblems that Yeats was never to abandon. But the verse-drama, and most of its companion-pieces written up through 1885, he certainly did abandon. One of these pieces, a dramatic poem called *The Seeker,* introduces an Old Knight who has devoted sixty years to a dream-led wandering in search of his beloved enchantress. Her vision had made him a coward on the field of battle;

now at last he has found her and craves a single glance at her face before he dies. A sudden light bursts over her, and he sees her as what she is—a bearded witch, called Infamy by men. The witch raises a mirror, in which the Knight sees his own shadowed face and form, and he dies. This grim fantasy is rather clearly blended out of Shelley's *Alastor* and Spenser's Fradubio discovering that his beloved is the Whore of Infamy, Duessa; but Yeats's allegory is characteristically more savage and more destructively self-directed. The quest that reduces a man-of-action to a coward is truly only a lust after infamy, and ends with a mirrored image of the faded self. Though Yeats rejected *The Seeker* as he had *The Island of Statues,* he chose long afterwards to open his *Collected Poems* with a Song originally printed as an Epilogue to both *The Island of Statues* and *The Seeker.* A satyr enters, carrying a sea-shell, emblem of poetic prophecy in Wordsworth and in Shelley. He chants:

> The woods of Arcady are dead,
> And over is their antique joy,
> Of old the world on dreaming fed—
> Grey truth is now her painted toy—
> But O, sick children of the world,
> Of all the many changing things
> In dreary dancing past us whirled,
> To the old cracked tune that Chronos sings,
> Words alone are certain good.

The chant goes on to offer the hypothesis that our world may be only a sudden flaming word, soon to be silenced. The reader is therefore urged not to seek action or truth, but only whatever story a murmuring sea-shell will give to him, after which the satyr closes by insisting on the value of mere dreaming as its own end. As an epilogue to works that have given us a vision of the dream as self-destruction, this is very curious, and even the young poet's faith in a verbal universe is rather disconcertingly allied to the Shelleyan image of a self-consuming flame. What Yeats had attained to in 1885 was precisely that dead-end of vision that Shelley had come to in *Alastor* some seventy years before, and moreover at about the same age at which Shelley also had come to the crossways of life and art. That this parallel between the two poets was altogether deliberate on Yeats's part, one has not the slightest doubt. His Arcadian plays were followed in 1886 by the dramatic poem *Mosada* and the much more powerful *The Two*

Titans, both of them overwhelmingly Shelleyan poems. In *Mosada* a Moorish maiden is martyred by the Inquisition because she practises magic in order to recover a vision of her lost Christian lover, who by a characteristic Yeatsian touch enters the poem as his own anti-self, no less than the Grand Inquisitor. *The Two Titans* is rather mis-leadingly subtitled *A Political Poem* and therefore has been read subtly but reductively by Richard Ellmann as an allegory of Ireland's bondage to England. Yet here, though with a rhetoric so Shelleyan as to be scarcely his own at all, Yeats wrote the most imaginatively impressive poem of his youth before *The Wonderings of Usheen,* though it perhaps has its preposterous aspects if it is read as political allegory alone. Gerard Manley Hopkins, resident in Dublin during 1886, read *The Two Titans,* called its allegory 'strained and unworkable' yet found the poem to contain fine lines and vivid imagery. *The Two Titans* is a mixture of the archetypal situations presented by Shelley in two very different poems, the baffled quest-romance *Alastor,* and the darkly triumphant lyrical drama, *Prometheus Unbound*. One of Yeats's Titans is 'a grey-haired youth' like the doomed poet in Shelley's *Alastor;* like Prometheus he is imprisoned on a rock, but this is a wave-beaten promontory, where he is chained to a fiercely dreaming Sibyl of a Titaness. The poem is thus either an anticipation of Blake's influence on Yeats, as it reproduces the situation most powerfully set forth by Blake at the opening of his ballad, *The Mental Traveller,* or more likely, it is the first of the many times that the influences of Blake and Shelley will mingle in Yeats's poetry, until their confluence will help produce such masterpieces as *The Second Coming* and the Byzantium poems. All that happens in Yeats's *The Two Titans* is that the enchained poet makes yet another heroic attempt to get free of the Titaness and fails, receiving as his reward a sadistic kiss from his tyrannical captor, who is yet as bound as he is. On the Shelleyan and Blakean analogues, the poem has a clear and impressive meaning—the poet, if he relies on a naturalistic Muse, participates in the bondage of nature, and is devoured by his own Muse, destroyed by the cyclic rhythms of a running-down natural world. With *The Two Titans* we come to the end of Yeats's first poetic period—he now is twenty-one years old; a considerable poet rather desperately struggling with an overwhelming influence, Shelley's, that he must somehow modify if he is to achieve his own individuality, and just beginning to undergo the kindred influence of Blake—more liberating for being free of the very personal elements in Yeats's early Shelley-obsession.

Some poets, as we know, never recover from the immortal wound of the poetry they first come to love, though they learn to mask their relationship to their own earlier selves. In 1914, when he was nearly fifty, Yeats wrote the very beautiful section of his *Autobiographies* entitled *Reveries Over Childhood and Youth.* He was past the mid-point of his poetic career, and already well into that middle style in which he is furthest from Romantic tradition, the style of the volumes *The Green Helmet* and *Responsibilities,* a bitter, restrained style, relying on the themes of self-correction, disillusionment, a new control. His poetic models for a time will be Landor and Donne and what he has to say in 1914 of his own earlier feelings for Shelley is therefore not likely to be colored by a strong positive emotion, and is all the more valuable for our present purpose, which is to trace how a poetic influence can apparently be repudiated, and yet go underground, like Coleridge's Sacred River, until it emerges finally with a turbulence of creation and destruction, in a form more powerful than before.

The seventeen-year-old Yeats, experiencing the awakening of sexuality, slept out among the rocks in the wilds around Howth Castle, where later he would walk with Maud Gonne in that most desperately unsuccessful and yet poetically fruitful of courtships. 'As I climbed along the narrow ledge,' he reminisced, 'I was now Manfred on his glacier, and now Prince Athanase with his solitary lamp, but I soon chose Alastor for my chief of men and longed to share his melancholy, and maybe at last to disappear from everybody's sight as he disappeared, drifting in a boat along some slow-moving river between great trees. When I thought of women they were modelled on those in my favorite poets and loved in brief tragedy, or like the girl in *The Revolt of Islam,* accompanied their lovers through all manner of wild places, lawless women without homes and without children.'

The avenging daimon or Alastor in Shelley's poem is the dark double of the melancholy poet, the spirit of solitude that will haunt him and drive him on to destruction. As such he is probably Yeats's first literary encounter with the notion of an anti-self, to be so richly developed later in Yeats's writing. Prince Athanase, the young magus in his lonely tower, we will meet many times again in Yeats's work, while the lawless heroine, Cyntha, of Shelley's *Revolt of Islam,* will inform Yeats's heroic conception of Maud Gonne as a rebel against all established order.

The antithetical solitude of the young Shelley, with his gentleness and humanitarian character, who yet creates as the heroes of his early poetry the isolated figures of sage, magician, violent revolutionary, and proudly solitary noble and poet, is very clearly the ultimate origin of Yeats's later theories of the mask and the antithetical self. The young Yeats elaborated a not very convincing autobiographical parallel between himself and the young Shelley—since Shelley was persecuted at Eton as 'Shelley the atheist' so Yeats was made miserable at school in London as 'the Mad Irishman.' John Butler Yeats, the poet's father, occupies the role of Shelley's Dr. Lind, nursing the imagination of the young poet. Yeats noted also the adolescent Shelley's interest in the occult, though he either ignored or condemned the mature Shelley's dismissal of such interests.

Later in the *Reveries Over Childhood and Youth* Yeats tells us that he made Shelley's *Prometheus Unbound* the first of his sacred books or poetic scriptures. In *Four Years,* the next of his *Autobiographies,* the influence of Shelley is cited as having given him his two prime images. 'In later years,' he writes, 'my mind gave itself to gregarious Shelley's dream of a young man, his hair blanched with sorrow, studying philosophy in some lonely tower, or of his old man, master of all human knowledge, hidden from human sight in some shell-strewn cavern on the Mediterranean shore.' The young man is Prince Athanase:

> His soul had wedded Wisdom, and her dower
> Is love and justice, clothed in which he sate
> Apart from men, as in a lonely tower,
>
> Pitying the tumult of their dark estate.

The image of the old man was to haunt Yeats's poetry even more decisively. In *Four Years* he calls it the passage of poetry that 'above all ran perpetually in my ears.' It is the dialogue from *Hellas* concerning the sage Ahasuerus, the Wandering Jew who will become the Old Rocky Face of *The Gyres,* that daimonic intelligence we must urge to look out at our world from his secret home, 'where he dwells in a sea-cavern / 'Mid the Demonesi,' less accessible than the Sultan or God:

> Some feign that he is Enoch; others dream
> He was pre-Adamite, and has survived
> Cycles of generation and of ruin.

These two images are the *personae* of Yeats in the first and in the final phases of his career as a poet—the prematurely old young man seeking the secret wisdom, and the ageless old magus who has conquered age by long possessing such wisdom. Between is the bitter phase of the middle-Yeats, anti-Romantic against his own grain, lamenting that traditional sanctity and loveliness have vanished, and that Romantic Ireland is dead and gone.

Both these images, as Yeats himself said, are always opposite to the natural self or the natural world, an insight as to the poetic role arrived at by Shelley and by Blake alike. We can see Yeats demonstrating an astonishing critical power as he ascertains this truth in the magnificent essay on Shelley written in 1900, and curiously mis-entitled *The Philosophy of Shelley's Poetry,* for it is a study of Shelley's imagery, and even more of the emotional dialetic of Shelley's poetry, and finally one of the earliest studies of poetry as myth-making that we have. For Yeats it was more than just an essay on Shelley—the erstwhile disciple was now thirty-five, at the mid-point of his life, and consciously determined to throw off the embroidered coat of his earlier poetry—to demonstrate, for a while, that there's more enterprise in walking naked. In that coat there were prominently displayed what Yeats called the reds and yellows that Shelley had gathered in Italy. The poet of *The Rose* and *The Wind Among the Reeds* now sought what his father had called 'unity of being'—to write in perfect tune with the tension of his own lyre. At least one aim of Yeats's essay on Shelley is to demonstrate that the poet of *Prometheus Unbound* lacked this Unity of Being, and so could not realize his full gifts as a poet.

The clue to Yeats's dissatisfaction with Shelley is given by Yeats throughout this otherwise model essay. Shelley—we know—was the most heroic of agnostics, humanistically convinced that 'the deep truth is imageless,' as Demogorgon puts it in *Prometheus Unbound.* But Yeats, who hungered after belief, could not accept this. He in effect blames Shelley for not being Yeats—for not seeking the support of a popular mythology, or of magic and occult tradition—indeed he closes his essay by denouncing Shelley for having been 'content merely to write verses,' when he possessed and should have realized the religion-making faculty. He cannot then forgive Shelley for not having founded a new faith, and he contrasts Shelley to Blake, for he believes that this is precisely what Blake attempted to do. Critically speaking, this is both fascinatingly perverse and yet of the utmost importance. Yeats has read Shelley with great accuracy and insight, but will not abide in that reading, for if Shelley's way as a poet is right, then indeed Yeats's developing way is wrong. In compensation, Yeats has read Blake with great inaccuracy and deliberately befuddled insight, so as to produce an antithetical poetic father to take Shelley's place.

Before moving on to Blake and Yeats, a closer inspection of Yeats's first essay on Shelley should serve to test these generalizations. Yeats begins by stating his early belief about the relation between poetry and philosophy. 'I thought,' he writes, 'that whatever of philosophy has been made poetry is alone permanent, and that one should begin to arrange it in some regular order, rejecting nothing as the make-believe of the poets.' From this early principle he goes on to state his mature belief at thirty-five—'I am now certain' he affirms, 'that the imagination has some way of lighting on the truth that the reason has not,' and he offers as evidence for his certainty that he has just re-read *Prometheus Unbound,* and it seems to him to have an even more certain place than he had thought among the sacred books of the world. He then proceeds to show that Shelley's *Prometheus* is an apocalyptic work, and he brilliantly parallels Shelley and Blake by way of Shelley's most Blakean poem, *The Witch of Atlas.* It is the calculating faculty or reason that creates ugliness, and the freed faculty of imagination that alone creates the exuberance that is beauty, and so becomes the supreme agency of what a poet can consider as moral good. In the poet's infinite desire to break through natural barriers and so uncover an altogether human universe Yeats magnificently locates the common ground held by Blake and by Shelley. As Yeats quotes and describes passage after passage from Shelley to support his characterization of that great Promethean as the poet of infinite desire, he reveals also to the student of his own later poetry just those passages that will be transformed into crucial moments in such poems as *Leda and the Swan, Nineteen Hundred and Nineteen, The Second Coming, Sailing to Byzantium,* and *Byzantium, Two Songs from a Play, The Gyres* and the death-poem, *Under Ben Bulben.* All these poems have quite direct verbal echoes of or allusions to the Shelleyan passages that Yeats quotes. Yet this is of only secondary importance in a consideration of Yeats's Romanticism, or even in seeking to understand the complexity of Shelley's abiding influence on Yeats's poetry. More vital is the argument that Yeats proceeds to conduct with Shelley, once he has demonstrated the religious intensity of Shelley's unappeasable and apocalyptic desires, those infinite aspirations towards a world where subject and object, thought and passion, lover and beloved, shall be joined in perfect wholeness.

Inevitably Yeats concentrates on Shelley's speculations upon death and survival, for the single great theme uniting all of Yeats's poetry from the very start, as he himself proclaimed, is a passion against old age, and the insistence that man has somehow invented death. Shelley died at twenty-nine and Blake was too great a humanist to regard the fear of death as more than a failure of the imagination, but Yeats lived into his seventy-fourth year, and surrendered his imaginative humanism to a rage for survival in some form, however desperately unimaginative. The seeds of this surrender can be found in the most astonishing moment in Yeats's first Shelley essay, when he suddenly passes from quoting the nobly agnostic quatrains that conclude *The Sensitive Plant* to the incredible deduction that those quatrains show Shelley's belief in the *Anima Mundi* or Great Memory in which all our smaller selves survive. It is an intellectual comedy of dismal intensity to first read Shelley's last quatrain and then Yeats's comment upon it. Here is Shelley:

> For love, and beauty, and delight
> There is no death nor change; their might
> Exceeds our organs, which endure
> No light, being themselves obscure.

What these lines clearly say is that our senses are inadequate to the full humanity of our desire; Blake says precisely the same in *The Marriage of Heaven and Hell* when he proclaims that 'if the doors of perception were cleansed everything would appear to man as it is, infinite. For man has closed himself up, till he sees all things thro' narrow chinks of his cavern.' But in Yeats's reading Shelley's lines are a reference to a palpable spirit-world, a universe of squeaking phantasms that can be invoked by a Soho medium or a self-induced trance. Having so mis-read, Yeats goes on to condemn Shelley for having no roots in Irish folklore, Hindu theosophy, and cabbalistic magic. It is Shelley's freedom from this witch's cauldron, we are asked to believe, that gives some of his poetry that air of rootless fantasy the anti-Shelleyans breathe and condemn. Shelley, Yeats goes on to say, had reawakened in himself the age of faith, but failed to understand that the content of such faith now rested in peasant superstitions and the arcane doctrines of the Rosicrucians. Shelley, we know, was an urbane and gracious man, and a visionary with profound though limited respect for human reason. In his spirit, we can shrug off Yeats at his silliest, and marvel at a great poet's wilfulness. We will return to Yeats on Shelley but only after considering Yeats on Blake, an interpretative mare's nest whose perversities are not to be shrugged off quite so easily.

Of the three volumes of the Yeats-Ellis edition of Blake, the Text, the System, the Meaning—it is a little difficult to decide just which now appears the most outrageous. The text is the preposterous consequence of the editorial tradition of re-writing Blake that the Rossettis and Swinburne had so grandly begun. The System is not Blake's at all, but a lovely mixture of Blavatsky and bluster, and the Meaning, as Northrop Frye rightly remarked, is considerably more difficult to grasp than Blake's own. Yeats is much more enlightening, both on Blake and his own relation to Blake, in the two essays first published with 'The Philosophy of Shelley's Poetry' in the critical volume, *Ideas of Good and Evil*. These essays—the brief 'William Blake and the Imagination' and the more ambitious 'Blake and his Illustrations to the Divine Comedy'—were written four years after the Yeats-Ellis edition of Blake appeared and three years before the Shelley essay was written, and clearly prepare the way in Yeats's attempt to substitute Blake for Shelley as his archetype of the poet. Already, in the Yeats-Ellis edition, a personal identification had been suggested by Yeats's happy and altogether original discovery that William Blake had really been an Irishman, whose true name was O'Neill. Though Yeats, after a bombardment by Swinburne, gave up this startling notion, he did become more and more convinced that he was a new incarnation of the earlier William.

We understand today that Blake was an epic poet consciously in the Protestant tradition of Spenser and Milton, and not any sort of a mystic, a word he never uses. Blake's divine vision is of a more human man, and not of God at all, and the mystic's way of union with a supernatural reality that exists outside of himself is the negation of everything Blake believed. We have also progressed to a point where we see that Blake had a genial contempt for all occultists; that he repudiated Swedenborg, and sought the mental companionship of the poets, and not the theosophists. But Yeats simply did not want to know this, and his writings on Blake had a good deal to do with the misconceptions of Blake-as-mystic and Blake-as-arcane-speculator that somehow manage to drift on in the popular and even the learnèd consciousness. Yeats took from Swedenborg and from occult tradition in general, the doctrine of correspondence, the belief that everything visible has an invisible counterpart in the spiritual world. The ultimate origin of this doctrine is the brief Hermetic text called the Smaragdine

Tablet, mentioned approvingly by Yeats both in his prose and poetry. But Blake, in a crucial moment in his major poem, the epic *Jerusalem,* condemns the Smaragdine Tablet and all theosophy with it, calling it an attempt on the part of the Spectre, or abstract intellect, to destroy imagination by drawing Los, the Poetic Genius of man, down into the Indefinite, where no one can believe without demonstration, and where the living form of poetry is darkened by the mathematic form of abstract speculation. Coming to this passage in his commentary in the Yeats-Ellis edition, Yeats chose to ignore Blake's emphatic rejection of this central occult text. When one is done blinking at such high-handedness, one accepts it as another moment of involuntary revelation on Yeats's part. He needed magic, he had to have the occult support of mystery, yet he needed also the authority of Romantic poetic tradition, and he was perfectly willing to distort that tradition to satisfy what he considered his imaginative need. With this as background, we can now consider Yeats's essays on Blake, where he tries to assert the essential affinity between Blake and himself, while indicating his own advantages over Blake in having a national mythology still to be exploited.

The brief essay on 'Blake and the Imagination' begins by praising Blake as having been the first to announce the religion of art. It is not clear that Yeats is not confounding Blake with Oscar Wilde, until he goes on to say that Blake believed the imaginative arts to be the greatest of Divine revelations, which is true. But soon we see where Yeats is taking us: Blake, we are told, was a symbolist who had to invent his symbols, a man crying out for a mythology, and trying to make one because he could not find one to his hands. This is sublimely to misunderstand Blake, who would have made his own mythology in any case, for he believed that this is the function of poets, to speak an individual Word so clearly and coherently that it would necessarily be the Word of God, that is, the Imagination in man. Yeats closes his essay with the wish that Blake had taken his myths from Ancient Norway or Ancient Wales or, best of all, Ancient Ireland, for then he would have been less arbitrary and less obscure. Yeats is of course rationalizing his own use of Irish mythology, and so did not mind contradicting his own description of Blake's belief in art as the only source of divine revelation.

In the long essay on 'Blake's Illustrations to Dante' Yeats is refreshingly improved as a critic; he understands the apocalyptic aim of Blake as a correcter-by-illustrations of other mens' visions, and he seems warier of chiding Blake for not having had the good fortune to have read Lady Gregory on the Irish mythological cycles. He sets forth expertly Blake's quarrel with Dante, based on Blake's insistence that 'God took always a human shape,' and on Blake's conviction that Dante mixed with his genuinely imaginative visions those symbols that were enemies to the imagination because drawn from an idolatry of nature or, at the other extreme, from the abstract diagramming of the theologians. As though he forsees his own writing of *A Vision* decades later, Yeats is nervous about this disagreement, and refuses to commit himself as between Blake and Dante.

Yeats's own poetry during the painful years of his transition, let us say, from the turn of the century through the Easter Rebellion in 1916, has little to do with the myth-making of either Blake or Shelley, little to do that is with either a complex attempt at creating a new mythology, like Blake's, or with the affirmation of the possibilities of mythical relationship, like Shelley's. For Yeats, the turning-point as poet and man came in October 1917, at the age of fifty-two, with his marriage, and with the revelation made to him by the spirits (as he asks us to believe) through the mediumship of his wife. The origins of Yeats's systematic mythology, as set forth in *A Vision,* are in this curious moment of elemental breakthrough, though it took Yeats twenty years of revision before the dictation of spirits had properly flowered into what Ellmann calls esoteric Yeatsianism.

The complications of *A Vision* do not concern the subject I am discussing, except to note that the book is more thoroughly quarried out of Blake than either Yeats or his critics have realized, though I would add that the result is a parody of Blake rather than a work in his tradition. What does concern the present subject is the character-analysis carried out upon Blake and Shelley by Yeats in the exposition of the Great Wheel, or human incarnations founded upon the phases of the moon. Blake, we are told, is a man of phase 16—his will is the Positive Man, his true Mask illusion, his true creative mind dominated by vehemence. He is classified with the apocalyptic satirist Rabelais, with the brutally comic Aretino, and even with that witty cosmic charlatan, Paracelsus. For all these, Yeats says, 'discover symbolism to express the overflowing and bursting of the mind.' In them Yeats finds 'always an element of frenzy, and almost always a delight in certain glowing or shining images of concentrated force: in the smith's forge; in the heart; in the human form in its most vigorous development.' Yet, according to Yeats, this is a phase haunted by the false Mask of delusion, and the false creative mind of opinionated will, and doomed finally to the deterministic body of fate Yeats calls Enforced Illusion, for this is the last phase of those who suffer rather than do violence. It is just short of the ideal phase for a poet, for it is followed by phase 17, named for its will as 'The Daimonic Man' and here we find Dante, Shelley of course and Landor, and though he does not explicitly say so in *A Vision,* Yeats himself, as he made clear to his family and friends, and in his unpublished work. The man of phase 17, Yeats says, 'is called the *Daimonic* man because Unity of Being, and consequent expression of *Daimonic* thought, is now more easy than at any other phase.' What Yeats for a while believed Shelley to lack, Shelley now seems to possess in abundance. The reason for this reversal is simply that Yeats is beginning to recognize again what he was ruefully to admit in a late essay on *Prometheus Unbound,* written in 1932, that Shelley had shaped his imaginative career to a greater extent than any other poet. The Daimonic Man has a true mask of simplification through Intensity and a creative mind which reaches creative imagination through *antithetical emotion.* His false mask is dispersal, and his false creative mind manifests itself through what Yeats eloquently called 'enforced self-realization.' The tragic Body of Fate of the Daimonic Man has the terrible loneliness about it that Yeats expresses in a single word: 'Loss.' Though he strains to fit Dante into this characterization and briefly mentions Landor, it is perfectly clear that all of Yeats's description of this—his own phase—is founded on a deeply passionate and indeed emotionally self-contradictory account of Shelley. This is—Yeats says—the phase where all mental images flow, change, flutter, cry out, or mix into something else, but without, as at phase 16, Blake's phase, breaking and bruising one another, for the phase of Shelley and Yeats is without frenzy. The Will is falling asunder, but without explosion and noise, and the poet's intellect finds, Yeats says, not the impassioned myth that Blake found, but a mask of simplicity that is also intensity, the mask of Prince Athanase in his lonely tower, or ageless Ahasuerus in his caverns measureless to man. Every object of desire selected by the intellect for a representation of the mask as Image, usually a Woman, is always snatched away by the Body of Fate. So Yeats assimilates Maud Gonne to that pathetically intense sequence of Shelleyan epipsyches—Harriet, Mary Godwin, Claire Clairmont, Emilia Viviani, Jane Williams; those morning stars who always faded in the experiential dawn. The result is nightmare, a phantasm world in which every object becomes an emblem of loss, of the world's separation from the self. As a reading of the central dialectic of Shelley's poetry I do not think that this is likely ever to be bettered. But Yeats, alas, does not stop there—he must go further, must break from the prison of his own earlier self. Shelley, he goes on to say, 'lacked the Vision of Evil, could not conceive of the world as a continual conflict, so, though great poet he certainly was, he was not of the greatest kind.' Because he lacked this Yeatsian Vision of Evil, Shelley fell into an *automatonism,* as Yeats calls it, evading hatred by giving himself up to fantastic, constricted images. It is from this Shelleyan fate that Yeats believes he has saved himself, for to the daimonic intensity of a Shelley he has added Blake's conception of the contraries, a vision of evil in which all things are seen as living one another's death, dying one another's life, progressing always through the continual conflict of creative strife.

That Yeats knew better about Shelley we know from his earlier essay on that poet, where he correctly understands the great myth of Demogorgon in *Prometheus Unbound* as the principle of continual conflict that turns over the cycle in the universe from Jupiter to Prometheus, and that threatens destruction again in a world that cannot by its nature be finally redeemed. But Yeats *needed* his myth of Shelley as an embryonic Yeats who had fallen short of the Vision of Evil. Hence the late essay on *Prometheus* of 1932, in which Demogorgon is re-interpreted as being uninterpretable, as making the whole poem incoherent, for now Yeats must see him as the most monstrous of all Shelley's nightmare images of the negation of desire. Yet even here, in an essay clearly intended as a critical palinode, as an anti-Shelleyan document, the full force of Shelley's power upon Yeats breaks through. He has attacked Shelley for not being a mystic, unlike Yeats himself and Blake. The attack is weak—none of the three poets was in fact anything of a mystic—but Yeats throws the strength of his considerable rhetoric into the attack: Shelley's 'system of thought'—he says—'was constructed by his logical faculty to satisfy desire, not a symbolical revelation received after the suspension of all desire.' In the zeal of his rejecting passion Yeats makes his strongest indictment of Shelley, asserting: 'He was the tyrant of his own being.' After all that, one would expect a declaration of Yeatsian freedom from this mistaken being, but what follows is one of those moments of total self-revelation in which the paradoxical greatness of the mask-seeking Yeats consists. I quote it in full, so as to preserve its weight and complexity:

> When I was in my early twenties Shelley was much talked about. London had its important 'Shelley Society,' *The Cenci* had been performed and forbidden, provincial sketching clubs displayed pictures by young women of the burning of Shelley's body. The orthodox religion, as our mothers had taught it, was no longer credible; those who could not substitute connoisseurship, or some humanitarian or scientific pursuit, found a substitute in Shelley. He had shared our curiosities, our political problems, our conviction that, despite all experience to the contrary, love is enough; and unlike Blake, isolated by an arbitrary symbolism, he seemed to sum up all that was metaphysical in English poetry. When in middle life I looked back I found that he and not Blake, whom I had studied more and with more approval, had shaped my life, and when I thought of the tumultuous and often tragic lives of friends or acquaintance, I attributed to his direct or indirect influence their Jacobin frenzies, their brown demons.

Rather than analyze this confession of influence, I want only to note it, and to pass on to characterize Yeats's later poems by way of a rather large generalization about *all* English poetry since the very early nineteenth century. Modern poetry in English begins with the difficult greatness of Blake and of Wordsworth, and the different modes each invented have been the only significant kinds of poetry written during the past hundred and fifty years. Blake restored myth-making to poetry; Wordsworth inaugurated that heroic nakedness of direct confrontation between the self and nature in which so many poets since Shelley and Keats have followed him, down to Stevens and Lawrence in our own time. However much Yeats tried to be like Blake, he did not succeed; *A Vision* remains one of the curiosities of literature, and the poems written out of it usually succeed through their powerful independence of its not always very imaginative categories. Yeats, despite himself, became a great poet of the Wordsworthian kind, a poet of autobiographical self-recognition, whose theme had less and less to do with the content of the poetic vision, and more and more to do with the relationship of the poet to his own vision. Yet Yeats never learned to like or understand Wordsworth, and so he took the central model for his typical lyric of confrontation from those almost involuntary Wordsworthian disciples, Shelley and Keats, and more clearly from Shelley, even in the Byzantium poems, which have so clear a relationship to Keats's *Urn* and *Nightingale* odes.

At the beginning of this essay I spoke of how little we understand the process by which one poet influences another, and I want to return to that mysterious process now as I close. In old-fashioned terms one can demonstrate that more lines of Yeats allude to or repeat more lines of Shelley than of any other poet, but all this would show us is that the memory does not easily lose the stores it has gathered up by a poet's twentieth year. Stylistically, late Yeats and Shelley have a great deal in common, though that must sound odd in the ears of anyone who is still much under the influence of recent aberrations in the history of taste. I cannot read the final stanzas of *The Witch of Atlas* without thinking of the *Byzantium* poems, and this is more than my own eccentricity. Yet the deepest influence of Shelley on Yeats is not in style but in something far more fundamental—Shelley's most characteristic poetry has the same relation to the lyrics of *The Tower* and *The Winding Stair* that the Japanese Noh drama has to Yeats's plays—the very idea of the act that is the Yeatsian poem is Shelley's. In Shelley when he is most himself—in the *Ode to the West Wind, Adonais, The Triumph of Life*—one feels the entire weight of a poet's vocation and life veering on the destiny of the relational event that is the poem. When the poem breaks, as in Shelley it so frequently does out of sheer agnostic honesty, as in Yeats it sometimes does out of an extraordinary mixture of self-dramatization and heroic desperation—then the very concept of a poet breaks with it, in a fitting imaginative gesture for a daimonic man, that man whose role it is to hold himself open to unity of being. The Yeats of poems like *A Dialogue of Self and Soul, Vacillation* and the haunting *The Man and the Echo* is a very human, very Romantic and very Shelleyan Yeats, existing in the perilous dialectic that witnesses every object of desire disappearing into another experiential loss, that dares the true Romantic agony in which dialogue collapses towards monologue, and the confrontation of love expires into the crippling loneliness of enforced self-realization. Yeats strove mightily to overcome the Shelleyan identity of his own youth, but I think it fortunate that he failed in that striving. We would have lost the poet who finally cast his own mythologies aside, to cry aloud in the perfect moment of agnostic confrontation in the poetry of our time, the very humanistic and Shelleyan cry of almost his last poem:

> O Rocky Voice
> Shall we in that great night rejoice?
> What do we know but that we face
> One another in this place?